D1503498

SHAKESPEARE
AND
THE MUSICAL STAGE
a guide to sources, studies,

and first performances

SHAKESPEARE
AND
THE MUSICAL STAGE

a guide to sources, studies,

and first performances

EDWARD R. HOTALING

G.K. Hall & Co.
70 Lincoln Street, Boston, Mass.

"Shakespeare and the Musical Stage: A Guide to Sources, Studies,
and First Performances."

First published 1990
by G.K. Hall & Co.
70 Lincoln Street
Boston, Massachusetts 02111

10 9 8 7 6 5 4 3 2 1

Library of Congress Cataloging-in-Publication Data

Hotaling, Edward.
    Shakespeare and the musical stage : a guide to sources, studies,
and first performances / by Edward R. Hotaling.
      p. cm.
    Includes bibliographical references.
    ISBN 0-8161-9070-4
    1. Shakespeare, William, 1564-1616 – Musical settings – Bibliography.
    2. Operas – Themes, motives, Literary – Bibliography. I. Title.
ML 128.04H68 1990
782.1 – dc20   89-26776
                                                    CIP
                                                     MN

MANUFACTURED IN THE UNITED STATES OF AMERICA

for

DORIS, MICHAEL, and JOHN

Contents

PREFACE

This book took its first form as a list of operas based on plays by Shakespeare, which was to serve as a source of information for a number of kinds of comparative studies I hoped to make. Similar lists had been published in the past, but I had found them to be incomplete and often unreliable.

My work began as an attempt to verify and update the list by Winton Dean of operas based on Shakespeare found in *Shakespeare in Music* edited by Phyllis Hartnoll, the most extensive one of which I was aware. Verification and updating were necessary both because the date of publication was 1964 and because the author did not vouch for the list's accuracy.

Because primary sources were not readily available to me, I began with the standard reference works, the *Union Catalog*, and Stieger's *Opernlexicon*, etc. These were both tremendously helpful—they provided a wealth of detail and lead to new possibilities— and constantly frustrating—they were frequently contradictory, even self-contradictory.

1. Sources did not always agree about the relationship of the work to Shakespeare's plays.
2. The date and place of the premiere performance was often disputed.
3. The type of composition was variously described. In particular, there was often confusion as to whether a composition was incidental music to a play or a work for the musical stage.
4. Librettists were given as composers.

I also became aware that the data I was finding was raising some questions that went beyond my resolving conflicting evidence. Two of the most vexing were these:

1. What is an opera? This matter presented itself most forcefully in the case of "English opera," where there is considerable disagreement as to whether a work such as Purcell's *Fairy Queen* is an opera or a type of incidental music. Other issues involved the inclusion of pantomimes and parodies.

ix

2.   What does "based on Shakespeare" mean? Works which were commonly accepted as being based on Shakespeare ranged from those which followed Shakespeare's text closely to those which contained not an important phrase or character from any of his plays [i.e., *Georget et Georgette* by Alexandre and *Westside Story* by Leonard Bernstein].

After considering these questions, I took the position that my list should be inclusive rather than exclusive. I, therefore, determined to include any composition which anyone had proposed as being based on Shakespeare and any work whose title suggested that it might be based on Shakespeare. A few works were included, too, which never progressed past the idea stage. These guidelines governed my searches, but for practical reasons I eventually decided to exclude from this book the more than two hundred operas I discovered whose titles mentioned Cleopatra, Julius Caesar, and Pyramus and Thisbe unless I had some clear indication that they had in fact derived from Shakespeare.

The weight of evidence indicated clearly that if I was to attempt to resolve these questions, I must find the primary sources of information— librettos and scores. I was aided in this task by grants from the University of Central Florida and the Southern Regional Education Board and by a sabbatical leave during the spring of 1988 which made possible my visiting a number of collections in Europe.

It is important to note that the results of my research were kept in an computer database, because this has shaped both the way in which information was gathered and how it is presented in this book. When possible, I attempted to secure photocopies of the title pages, lists of characters, etc., of the works on my list and then later to enter this information into the database. This method was the most satisfactory because I could later re-examine these photocopies to check for errors and omissions. At other times I took my computer into libraries and entered information directly from sources. In the case of my European research, I printed out my data before I traveled, entered new data by hand in my printout as I found it, and added this new data to the database when I returned. [I was seldom able to make photocopies.] This latter method has had the potential for the most errors.

I should also like to point out that because my list continued to grow, I may have missed finding primary sources in some of the libraries I visited because at the time I was there I was not yet looking specifically for them. However, I hope such omissions will be minimal in this case, because the final collections I visited were those of the British Library and the Library of Congress, where the majority of material on this subject is to be found.

My ideas about what to include also changed with time. I had hoped at the beginning to make a judgement upon which others could rely as to whether each work I listed was based on Shakespeare. I soon found that I was often unable to do that for two principal reasons: (1) my judgement would be based on opinion; (2) I could find no primary sources to support my opinion or that of others. I therefore determined to give my suggestion about a work's relationship to Shakespeare, but to also include an indication of what kind of evidence supported my view.

Because a list of a work's characters was often an important element in any decision which might be made about a compositions relation to Shakespeare, I added any information I could find which concerned the cast, characters, voice parts, etc. Relatively late, I decided to include my sources of information for the date and place of the premiere, an area about which there was often much disagreement.

I hope that my information has evolved into a form and content which will add to the knowledge of this subject and not one that provides unnecessary confusion. My hope has caused me to refrain from making some simple deductions about such matters as the nationality of composers and the language in which a work was premiered. My reasoning was that others could do that as easily as I, if they determined that a "likely answer" was sufficient for their purposes. When I give this information, I base it upon my primary sources or secondary sources which seem to me to be trustworthy and undisputed.

Inevitably, however, some information such as that which reports composers' and librettists' dates—though potentially of critical importance—I could not verify.

The knowledge which is assembled here has been limited by time and resources and cannot be considered definitive. In fact, it's chief value may well be to aid and stimulate further research. In its present form, this book represents a compromise between what information may exist and the costs in time and money to find it. Hopefully, this compromise will not prevent it from becoming a useful handbook to this subject.

I take pleasure in acknowledging the assistance of many friends and colleagues. The staffs at the Library of Congress and the British Library were more than kind and helpful in providing the hundreds of scores and librettos upon which the core of this research was based. Frau Dr. Gertraud Haberkamp at the Bayerische Staatsbibliothek was particularly cooperative in allowing me access to the data collected by the West German RISM Libretto Project. At my own university, the interlibrary loan division headed by Cheryl Mahan and later Cheryl Ruppert provided essential services. Professors Anthony Cervone, Anna Farina, Karl Heinz Barsch, and Elmar Fetscher assisted with translations and the deciphering of many eighteenth and nineteenth century librettos. Professor Fetscher was particularly helpful in assisting me with reading several sources in Gothic script and Mr. Schatz's handwriting. Finally, I thank my colleague Professor Bruce Whisler who provided resources and encouragement when they were most needed. The shortcoming that remain are my own. In the explanations which follow, I hope that I have acknowledged the most serious of them. In spite of them all, I hope that this handbook will be useful.

EXPLANATION OF DATA HEADINGS

Composer

The name of the composer is given along with dates when they could be found. While it might seem that this category should be free from error, it is possible that this is not the case. A number of compositions were originally found in references with only a composer's last name and without an exact title. In a few of these cases—when I could find no other reference which exactly fit my information—I furnished that which was most probable.

Title

I have attempted to give the titles of works in the language in which the work was first performed/ and or written as well as any alternate titles. If the original language was French, Italian, or German, I do not give an English translation. With other languages I usually offer an English version if it might be helpful. In a few instances I have been unable to determine the title in the original language. I those cases I have used titles in translation.

I have chosen to italicize the whole of the title line although in some instances some words in the line such as "or" connecting two different was of referring to a work (i.e. *Shylock or The Venus of Venice*) might not always properly be considered part of the title.

Status

The abbreviation indicates my best judgement as to whether the work is for the musical stage and based on Shakespeare. The judgement is always founded on what evidence I have. That evidence, of course, may possibly be untrustworthy. If it is the only evidence I have, however, I generally accept it. Because I normally, identify the sources of my evidence, the reader can make up his own mind about the quality of the evidence and the acceptability of my decision. Abbreviations used:

Y	Positive primary or secondary evidence
N	Negative primary or secondary evidence
NO	Not a work for the musical stage
I	Evidence is inconclusive or conflicting
?	No significant evidence
AP	Shakespeare is a character

Evidence

I considered evidence to be primary only if it came from a score or libretto for that work. Any other evidence I considered secondary. This is, of course, a simplistic classification system that does not attempt to consider the nature of the secondary evidence and treats the information in Stieger's *Opernlexicon* as being more or less equal to references found in a book by a composer's son. In point of fact, for a number of reasons I rarely consulted biographies or other references to composers' works. Sometimes this was for lack of time, but mostly it was because this material was not readily available to me or did not exist at all. In any case, there are a number of examples where the libretto and score do not state the obvious. For example, no score or libretto that I have seen for *Westside Story* by Bernstein mentions Shakespeare although the literature which concerns this musical takes its relationship to *Romeo and Juliet* for granted as will almost anyone who sees the work staged. In other words, some of the secondary evidence should be convincing enough for anyone to accept.

It is particularly important to use this information to help estimate the accuracy of the other data. In the vast majority of cases, if the evidence noted is not primary or no characters are listed, the data came from secondary sources.

Abbreviations used:

P   Primary source: score or libretto
S   Secondary source [any other source]

Text

The author of the text of the composition is given with date when they are known. If the composer is also the author of the text, then the heading reads composer. Otherwise, the heading reads"unknown."

Type

I have taken the description from a libretto or score when I could find them. It should be noted, however, that a composition is not always described in the same terms even at a single performance. When primary information was not available, the description comes from secondary sources, which may also disagree concerning the type. This kind of disagreement is most marked in the area of "English operas."

Acts

The number of acts as well as information about prologues, scenes, etc., is given when known.

Language

I have indicated the language sung at the premiere when it seemed obvious from the score or libretto or when I found it stated in a secondary source I believed trustworthy. Otherwise, I have left the heading blank, even though in most cases the language could be correctly inferred from other evidence.

Premiere

As much information about the city, date and theater is supplied as I could find. I have not attempted to bring consistency to the names of the theaters referenced. The date is written in the format: year (4 digits), month (2 digits), day (2 digits). This permits sorting the dates as numbers (a capability of any database) rather than as a date (a database function which is often limited to certain years or missing entirely).

Source of Premiere Information

I decided near the end of my research to add this category principally to indicate when this information came from primary sources. Alternately, I have often listed a secondary source if I did not have primary evidence and when I was certain from where these facts came. (I did not systematically record my sources until relatively late.)

Publisher

In most cases I have given information about the earliest published vocal score that I could personally examine. Certainly, I have not attempted to furnish a list of printed editions. Perhaps, the most important fact here is whether the work was published at all. I listed piano vocal scores in preference to full scores because they are more likely to include information about the cast, characters, and premiere.

Abbreviations used:

s	Score
vs	Vocal score
l	Libretto

Yes

Sources which support both a composition's being a work for the musical stage and it's being based on Shakespeare's plays. Please note that while I have routinely consulted one or more editions of Groves, MGG, Stieger, Mellen, etc., I did not attempt to find every secondary source that might have mentioned the work even among the standard references, particularly when the secondary sources which mentioned it agreed. Therefore, the omission of the name of a source may not be a reliable indication that a work was not mentioned there.

No

Sources which either deny that the composition is meant for the musical stage or that it is based on Shakespeare's plays.

Comments

A wide range of information is given under this heading. Often, an abbreviation will be given followed by a colon and some information. Only that which follows the colon and precedes the statement's period belong to the source or sources indicated. If no source is given, the remarks should in almost all cases be understood as coming from the author.

Cast

As much information about the characters, voice ranges, and cast of the premiere is given as I could find, whether I believed the work to be based on Shakespeare or not. Characters are in upper case. Descriptive phrases are in upper and lower case. Voice parts are in parentheses. Cast names are in brackets. Normally these facts are taken from a score or libretto. When this is not the case, the source is mentioned in the Comment section.

SORTINGS OF THE INFORMATION

Because the information in this handbook is in a computer database, it is easy to organize it in a number of ways which some may find helpful. I have therefore included alphabetical or chronological arrangements of the following categories:

> Title
> City
> Date of Premiere
> Text
> Play
> Status

All of the information in these categories is usually as complete as that in the main listing. Accompanying categories, particularly those containing data about the title and composer may at times omit some information such as variant names or titles or composers' dates in order to save space.

The method of alphabetizing these lists is not always standard due to the idiosyncrasies of the computer software used to create it. I hope that the sorted listings will helpful none the less.

Finally, I have furnished two lists of sources found in the Library of Congress and the British Library. In the case of sources in the British Library, I have divided the heading into two parts. The call number before the slash is that of a score; the one following is that of a libretto.

The call numbering for the Library of Congress is not so consistent. In most cases there is only one call number and it is that of a score. If there is a slash, the call number following is usually that of a libretto that is not in the Schatz libretto collection. That collection, which is on microfilm, has its own heading which tells the number of the libretto in the collection and the reel of microfilm on which it is found.

In the large majority of cases, the references are to the only ones available in the library. In the case of scores, they are a choice between a full score and a vocal score or between the libretto if the premiere and that of other performances. In some cases—such a that of the Verdi operas—they represent only a token of the material available.

I hasten to point out that now and then the call numbers are for items that I was never able to see because they were incorrectly shelved or otherwise unavailable when I requested them. One or two items in the Schatz Libretto Collection are for unexplained reasons not on microfilm at all even though they are listed in the catalog.

Please understand that an "N" abbreviation in this heading should be taken as an admission on my part that I was unable to find any reference to the work described. It is not a categorical denial that no reference exists there. A blank heading indicates that I did not attempt to find the composition, undoubtedly because I had not become aware of it up to the time when I last did my research at that institution.

ABBREVIATIONS

LIBRARIES

Symbol	Name and Location
A:Wgm	Gesellschaft der Musikfreunde in Wien: Vienna, Austria
A:Wn	Österreichische Nationalbibliothek [K. K. Hofbibliothek], Musiksammlung: Vienna, Austria.
A:Wst	Stadtbibliothek, Musiksammlung: Vienna, Austria.
B:Ba	Bibliothèque Royale Albert 1er: Brussels, Belgium.*
B:Ba	Conservatorie Royal de Musique, Bibliothèque: Brussels, Belgium.*
D-brd:Mbs	Bayerische Staatsbibliothek [Königliche, Hof- und Staatsbibliothek], Musiksammlung: Munich, Germany.*
F:Pn	Bibliothèque nationale: Paris, France.*
F:Po	Bibliothèque, Musée del'Opéra: Paris, France.*
GB:Lbm	British Library: London, England.*
I:Nc	Biblioteca del Conservatorio di Musica S. Pietro a Maiella: Naples, Italy.
I:Vgc	Biblioteca e Istituto di Lettere, Musica e Teatro della Fondazione Giorgio Cini (S. Giorgio Maggiore): Venice, Italy.*
US:Bp	Boston Public Library, Music Department: Boston (Massachusetts), U.S.A.

Symbol	Name and Location
US:NYp	New York Public Library at Lincoln Center: New York (New York), U.S.A.
US:CHua	University of Virginia, Music Library: Charlottesville (Virginia), U.S.A.*
US:G	University of Florida, Music Library: Gainesville (Florida), U.S.A.*
US:Wc	Library of Congress, Music Division: Washington (District of Columbia), U.S.A.*

*   Indicates research was performed at the institution.

SOURCES OF INFORMATION

Abbreviation   Source

AMCL
: Richmond, Eero ed. *Catalog of The American Music Center Library, Vol 4: Opera and Music Theater Works.* New York: American Music Center.

Baker's
: Baker, Theodore. *Baker's Biographical Dictionary of Musicians.* [Edition depends upon entry]

Bauman
: Bauman, Thomas. German Opera, 1770 -1800, Vols 7 and 20. New York: Garland Publishing, Inc, 1986.

Blom
: Blom, Eric. *Everyman's Dictionary of Music.* London: J. M. Dent and Sons, 1954.

Bloom
: Bloom, Ken. *American Song,* Vols. I and II. New York: Facts on File Publications, 1985.

Bordman
: Bordman, Gerald. *American Musical Theatre: A Chronicle.* New York: Oxford University Press, 1978.

BCM
: British Catalogue of Music

Clément
: Clément, Félix, and Pierre Larousse. *Dictionnaire des opéras* . . . . Rev. ed. Arthur Pougin. Paris: Larousse, 1905. [Reprinted--New York: Da Capo, 1969.]

CPM
: British Library. *The Catalogue of Printed Music in the British Library to 1980.* New York: K. G. Saur, 1981-88.

Culshaw
: Culshaw, John. *Wagner: the Man and his Music.* New York: E. P. Dutton.

Dent
: Dent, Edward J. *Opera.* London: Penguin Books, 1953.

Deutsch
: Deutsch, Otto Erich. *Handel: A Documentary Bibliography.* New York: W. W. Norton, Inc., 1954.

Abbreviation	Source
Eitner	Eitner, Robert. *Biographisch-bibliographisches Quellen-Lexickon der Musiker und Musikgelehrten der christlichen Zeitrechnung bis zur Mitte des 19. Jahrhunderts.* 10 vols., 1899-1904.
Ewen	Ewen, David. *The New Encyclopedia of the Opera.* New York: Hill and Wang, 1971.
Fétis	Fétis, François Joseph. *Biographie universelle des musiciens et bibliogrophie générale de la musique.* 2nd ed. 1860-66.
Fiske	Fiske, Roger. English Theater Music in the Eighteenth Century, 2nd ed. Oxford: Oxford University Press, 1986.
Friedlaender	Friedlaender, Max. "Shakespeares Werke in der Musik," *Jahrbuch der Deutchen Shakespeare-Gesellschaft.* XXXVII (1901), 85-122.
Garlington	Garlington, Aubrey S. Jr. Sources for the Study of Nineteenth Century Italian Opera in the Syracuse University Libraries: An Annotated Libretto List. Syracuse, N.Y.: Syarcuse University Libraries, 1976.
Gänzl	Gänzl, Kurt. *British Musical Theatre: Volume 1: 1865-1914; Volume 2: 1915-1984.* New York: Oxford University Press, 1987.
Green	Green, Stanley. Encyclopaedia of the Musical Theatre. New York: Dodd, Mead & Company, 1976.
Gruber	Gruber, Clemens M. *Opern-Uraufführengen. Ein internationales Verzeichnes von der Renaissance bis zur Gegenwart.* Wein: Gesellschaft für Musiktheater, 1978.
Hartnoll	Hartnoll, Phyllis ed. *Shakespeare in Music.* London: Macmillan & Co. Ltd., 1964. [Reprint--New York: Da Capo Press].

Abbreviation	Source
Hauger	Hauger, George. "English Musical Theatre 1830-1900" in *Theatre Notebook*, vol XXXVI, Nos. 2, 3. London, The Society for Theatre Research, 1982.
Loewenberg	Loewenberg, Alfred. *Annals of Opera 1597-1940.* 3nd ed., revised and corrected. New York: Rowman and Littlefield, 1978.
Manferrari	Manferrari, Umberto. *Dizionario universale delle opere melodrammatiche.* 3 Vols. Firenze: Sansoni Antiquariato, 1954-55.
Mellen	Parsons, Charles. *The Mellen Opera Reference Index, Vols. 1-6.* Lewiston, New York: The Edwin Mellen Press, 1986- .
MGG	*Die Musik in Geschicte und Gegenwart; allgemine Enzyklopädie der Musik .... Ed. Friedrich Blume. Kassel: Bärenrieter, 1949-* .
Moore	*Moore, Frank Ledlie. Crowell's Handbook of World Opera.* Westpoint, Conn.: Greenwood Press, 1974 [reprint].
Neef	Neef, Sigrid. *Handbuch der russichen und sowjetichen Oper.* Berlin: Henschelverlag Kunst und Gesellschaft, 1985.
Nicoll	Nicoll, Allardyce. *A History of English Drama 1660-1900,* 2nd Ed. London: Cambridge University Press, 1955.
Northouse	Northouse, Cameron. *Twentieth Century Opera in England and the United States.* Boston: G. K. Hall & Co., 1976.
NUC	*National Union Catalog Pre-1956 Imprints.* London: Mansell, 1968- .

Abbreviation	Source
NYP	New York (City) Public Library. The Research Libraries. *Second Edition of the Dictionary Catalog of the Music Collection.* Boston: G. K. Hall, 1982.
New Grove	*The New Grove Dictionary of Music and Musicians.* Ed. Stanley Sadie. London: Macmillan, 1980.
Osborne	Osborne, Charles. *The Complete Operas of Verdi.* New York: Alfred A. Knopf, 1970.
Oxford	Rosenthal, Harold D. and John Hamilton Warrack. *The Concise Oxford Dictionary of the Opera.* 2nd ed London: Oxford University Press, 1979.
Pitou	Pitou, Spire. *The Paris Opéra: Rococo and Romantic, 1715-1815* [Vol. II]. Westport, Connecticut: Greenwood Press, 1985.
Riemann	Riemann, Hugo. *Opern-Handbuch.* Leipzig: C. A. Koch, 1887.
Sartori	Sartori, Claudio. *Tentativo di Catalogo Unio dei Libretti Italiani a stampa Fino All'anno. 1800.*
Schatz MS	Albert Schatz Manuscript Collection. Washington, D.C.: Library of Congress.
Simas	Simas, Rick. *The Musicals No One Came to See.* New York: Garland Publishing, Inc., 1987.
Slonimsky	Slonimsky, Nicolas. *Music Since 1900.* [Edition depends upon date of entry.]
Sonneck	*Catalogue of Opera Librettos Printed before 1800* prepared by O. G. T. Sonneck. Washington, D. C.: Government Printing Office, 1914. [Reprints—New York: Burt Franklin, 1967; New York: Johnson Reprint, 1970.]

Abbreviation	Source
Squire	Squire, W. B. "Shakespearean Operas," *A Book of Homage to Shakespeare*. Ed. Israel Gollancz. England: Oxford University Press, 1916.
Steiger	Steiger, Franz. *Opernlexikon*. Tutzing: Schneider, 1975 - 1983.
Towers	Towers, John. *Dictionary-Catalogue of Operas and Operettas Which Have Been Performed on the Public Stage*. 2 vols. [Reprint--New York: Da Capo Press, 1967.]
Tumbusch	Tumbusch, Tom. *Guide to Broadway Musical Theater*. New York, N.Y.: Richards Rosen Press, Inc., 1972.
UC	*Catalog of the Opera Collections in the Music Libraries: University of California, Berkeley; University of California, Los Angeles*. Boston: G. K. Hall, 1983.
White	White, Eric Walter. *A Register of First Performances of English Operas and Semi-Operas from the 16th Century to 1980*. London: The Society for Theatre Research, 1983.
Wilson	Wilson, Christopher. *Shakespeare and Music*. London: "The Stage" Office, 1922. [Reprint--New York: Da Capo Press, 1977.]
WWV	Deathridge, John; Martin Geck and Egon Voss. *Wagner Werk-Verzeichnis*. Mainz: B. Schott's Söhne, 1986.

SHAKESPEARE
AND
THE MUSICAL STAGE

Jean Van den Acker (1828-   )

Romeo en Marielle [Tout pour l'amour]

Status: ?
Text: Unknown
Type: Opera-comique   **Acts:** 1   **Language:** Flemish
Premiere: Antwerp, Belgium: National Tooneel • 1859 10 26
Play: *Romeo and Juliet*

Adolphe-Charles Adam (1803-1856)

Falstaff

Status: Y   **Evidence:** S
Text: Vernoy de Saint-Georges, Jules (1801-1876), and
          Adolphe de Leuven (1803-1884)
Type: Opéra-Comique   **Acts:** 1   **Language:** French
Premiere: Paris, France: Théâtre Lyrique, Salle du Théâtre-
          Ristorique • 1856 01 18
Source of Premiere Information: Score
Play: *Merry Wives of Windsor*
Publisher: Paris: Chez S. Richault, c.1856. [vs]
Yes: Blom, Friedlaender, Groves V, Hartnoll, Mellen, New Groves,
          NUC, Oxford, Squire, Wilson

Cast: SIR JOHN FALSTAFF (B.) [M. Hermann-Léon] • SIMPSON
(T.) [M. Legrand] • PISTOLET (T.) [M. Allais] • LE SCHÉRIF (B.) [M.
Leroy] • BRAS D'ACIER (B.) [Mr. H. Adam] • POLLY (S.) [Mlle.
Bourgeois] • MARGARETT (S.) [Mlle. Garnier] • MISTRESS MARTINN
(S.) [Mlle. Vadé]

Richard Adler (1921-   )

Music Is

Status: Y   **Evidence:** S
Text: Abbott, George (book) and Will Holt (lyrics)
Type: Broadway Show   **Language:** English
Premiere: New York, U.S.A.: St. James Theatre • 1976 12 20

3

Source of Premiere Information: Simas
Play: *Twelfth Night*
Yes: Simas

Cast: SEBASTIAN [Joel Higgins] • OLIVIA [Sherry Mathis] • MALVOLIO [Christopher Hewitt]

Charles Guillaume Alexandre (1734-1770)

Georget et Georgette

Status: Y   **Evidence:** S
Text: Guerville, Harny de
Type: Operá comique   **Acts:** 1   **Language:** French
Premiere: Paris, France: Théâtre de l'Opéra comique a la foire
        St. Laurent • 1761 07 28
Source of Premiere Information: Libretto
Play: *Tempest*
Publisher: Paris: Chez Mr. Le Duc, etc. c.1775 [s]
Yes: LIBRETTO, Dent

Comments: Dent: Based on Shadwell's adaptation of the Dryden-Davenant version of *The Tempest*. The scenes utilized do not occur in Shakespeare at all. F-Po: Opéra comique en 1 acte . . . [par Harny de Guerville] Opéra comique de la foire S. Laurent, [28 juillet 1761] dans Théâtre de la Foire, 1765. Tome V.

Cast: URSINUS [M. La Ruette] • MOROSINE [Mlle. Deschamps] • GEORGET [Mlle. Arnout] • GEORGETTE [Mlle. Luzi] • LUCAS [M. Odinot] • NICOLE [Mlle. Louison] • LE SEIGNEUR [M. Clerval] • UN PAYSAN [M. S. Aubert] •—• **Chorus:** PAYSANS ET PAYSANNES

Franco Alfano (1876-1954)

Miranda

Status: ?
Text: Fogazzaro, Antonio
Type: Seria   **Acts:** 2   **Language:** Italian
Premiere: Leipzig, Germany: Stadttheater • 1896 00 00

Source of Premiere Information: Stieger
Play: *Tempest*

Comments: Mellen: composed in1886. New Grove: unperformed,
unpublished.

Alexander Aliabiev (1787-1851)

The Storm

Status: NO   **Evidence:** P
Language: NA
Premiere: 1835 00 00 c.
Play: *Tempest*
Yes: Oxford
No: SCORE

Comments: The Storm, is a symphonic picture from the opera *A
Mermaid and a Fisherman.*

Volshebnaya noch

Status: Y   **Evidence:** S
Text: Unknown
Premiere: 1839 00 00
Play: *Midsummer Night's Dream*
Yes: Oxford

Comments: Groves V: he supplied incidental music for
Shakespeare's *Merry Wives of Windsor* and *Midsummer Night's
Dream.* Date is when composed.

Giuseppe Allegra

Il Sogno di una Notte

Status: ?
Text: Novelli, Auguste (1867-1927)
Type: Com.   **Acts:** 3   **Language:** Italian

5

Premiere: Florence, Italy: Teatro Alfieri • 1931 03 00
Source of Premiere Information: Mellen
Play: *Midsummer Night's Dream*

Florent Alpaerts (1876-1954)

Shylock

Status: Y   **Evidence:** S
Text: Mélis, Hubert
Type: Opera   **Acts:** 3   **Language:** Flemish
Premiere: Antwerp, Belgium: Royal Flemish Opera • 1913 11 22
Source of Premiere Information: Mellen
Play: *Merchant of Venice*
Yes: Baker's, Groves V, Hartnoll, Loewenberg, Mellen, New Groves,
    Oxford, Stieger

Comments: Loewenberg: only opera by the composer.

David Amram (1930-   )

Twelfth Night

Status: Y   **Evidence:** P
Text: Papp, Joseph (1921-   ) and Composer
Type: Opera   **Acts:** 2/ 5 Scenes   **Language:** English
Premiere: Glens Falls, NY, U.S.A.: Lake George Opera Company
    • 1968 00 00
Source of Premiere Information: AMCL
Play: *Twelfth Night*
Publisher: New York: C. F. Peters Corp., 1972 [vs]
Yes: SCORE, AMCL

Comments: Mellen: 3 acts.

Cast: FESTE (Tenor) • ORSINO, Duke of Illyria (Bass-Baritone) •
VIOLA (Mezzo-Soprano) • SIR TOBY BELCH (Bass) • MARIA
(Soprano) • SIR ANDREW AGUECHEEK (Tenor) • THE COUNTESS
OLIVIA (Soprano) • MALVOLIO (Bass-Baritone) • ANTONIO
(Baritone) • 1ST OFFICER (Tenor) • 2ND OFFICER (Baritone) •

SEBASTIAN (Tenor) • A PRIEST (Baritone) •—•
Chorus: ATTENDANTS TO OLIVIA

Johann André (1741-1799)

König Lear

Status: Y   **Evidence:** S
Text: Unknown
Type: Singspiel   **Acts:** 5   **Language:** German
Premiere: Berlin, Germany: Döbbelins Oper Theater
  • 1780 00 00 ?
Source of Premiere Information: Mellen
Play: *Lear*
Yes: Clément, Mellen

Comments: It is likely that this is incidental music to the play.

Macbeth

Status: NO   **Evidence:** S
Premiere: Berlin, Germany: Döbbelins Oper Theater • 1780 10 03
Source of Premiere Information: Stieger
Play: *Macbeth*
No: Stieger

Comments: Stieger: it is incidental music.

Gaetano Andreozzi [Jommellino] (1755-1826)

Amleto

Status: Y   **Evidence:** P
Text: Foppa, Giuseppe Maria (1760-1845)
Type: Dramma per musica   **Acts:** 2   **Language:** Italian
Premiere: Padua, Italy: Teatro Nuovo • 1792 06 13
Source of Premiere Information: Mellen
Play: *Hamlet*

7

Yes: LIBRETTO, Friedlaender, Mellen, Oxford, Stieger

Comments: Libretto: based on the tragedy *Amleto* by Ducis. [Ducis is a translator of Shakespeare.] Friedlaender: Genua, 1793. Date: fiera del santo.
Cast: AMLETO [Sig. Girolamo Crescentini] • GELTRUDE [Sig. Carolina Goletti] • CLAUDIO [Sig. Adamo Bianchi] • AMELIA [Sig. Margherita Bianchi] • NORCESTO, Confidente di Amleto [Sig. Pietro Bonini] •——• **Chorus:** CORO

John Charles Bond-Andrews (1857-1899)

Herne's Oak, or The Rose of Windsor [also Herne the Hunter]

Status: Y **Evidence:** S
Text: Parke, Walter
Type: Comic Opera **Language:** English
Premiere: Liverpool, England: Prince of Wales Theatre
• 1887 10 24
Source of Premiere Information: Gänzl
Play: *Merry Wives of Windsor*
Yes: Mellen

Comments: Gänzl: it concerns Henry VIII. Gänzl does not mention Shakespeare. Characters and cast from Gänzl.

Cast: HENRY VIII [Michael Dwyer] • WILL SOMERS [Clarence Hunt] • HUBERT SHEENE [Victor de Lore] • MARTIN BASSETT [J. S. R. Page] • CAPTAIN [Chas. Prescott] • MARJORIE BASSETT [Kate Lynn] • ROGER [Miss Ackworth] • HERNE THE HUNTER [F. F. Clive (Charles Prescott)] • EARL OF WESTBOURNE [James Leverett] • CONSTABLE [Joseph Burgess] • SAILOR [David Class] • LADY JOAN MANDEVILLE [Amy F. Martin] • JUDITH BASSETT [Madge Inglis] • RALPH [Miss Telford] • GENTLEMAN USHER [Mr. Jarman]

Pasquale Anfossi (1727-1797)

Cajo Mario

Status: ?
Text: Roccaforte, Gaetano
Type: Dramma per musica   **Acts:** 3   **Language:** Italian
Premiere: Venice, Italy: Teatro di San Benedetto • 1770 11 00
Source of Premiere Information: Schatz MS
Play: *Coriolanus*

Arturo de Angelis [De Angeles] (1879-   )

La Tempesta

Status: Y   **Evidence:** S
Text: Sodini, Angelo
Type: Opera seria   **Acts:** 3   **Language:** Italian
Premiere: Perugia, Italy: Teatro Morlacchi • 1905 05 07
Source of Premiere Information: Mellen
Play: *Tempest*
Yes: Mellen, Oxford, Stieger

Comments: Manferrari: dr. lir. 2 p. e interm. 7 maggio 1905.

Lázló Angyal

The Tempest

Status: Y   **Evidence:** S
Text: Unknown
Premiere: 1900 00 00 c.
Play: *Tempest*
Yes: Oxford

Comments: Composer's first name may be Armand.

John Ansell (1874-   )

The King's Bride [Violette]

Status: ?
Text: Slee, Norman D.
Type: Comic Opera   **Acts:** 2   **Language:** English
Premiere: London, England: Lyric Theater • 1918 05 11
Source of Premiere Information: Stieger
Play: *Twelfth Night*
Publisher: London: Ascherberg, Hopwood & Crew, 1918 [vs].

Comments: Stieger: gives titles as being different operas; H. D. Slee. Score and libretto do not mention Shakespeare.
Cast: KONRAD • FREDA • KATHIE • FRANZ • MYNETTE • AVIS • RUDOLPH • PEPSTEIN • PRINCESS • KING • BLUMENKOHL • BACKER • DOLCH •—• **Chorus:** CHORUS

Ferdinand d'Antoine (1750-   )

Ende gut, alles gut oder Der Fürst und sein Volk

Status: ?
Text: Unknown
Type: Singspiel   **Acts:** 2   **Language:** German
Premiere: Bonn, Germany: Hoftheater • 1792 05 09
Source of Premiere Information: Mellen
Play: *All's Well That Ends Well*

Comments: Friedlaender: Cologne, 1794 00 00.

Leon Ardin

Antony and Cleopatra

Status: Y   **Evidence:** P
Text: Composer
Type: Opera   **Acts:** 4   **Language:** Italian

Premiere: 1919 00 00
Play: *Anthony and Cleopatra*
Publisher: New York: Composer, 1919 [s].
Yes: SCORE, Mellen, Oxford

Comments: Mellen: language is English; date is when composed.

Cast: MARCO ANTONIO (Tenore) • CLEOPATRA (Soprano) •
CARMIANA (Mezzo) • ERO (Baritono) • ENOBARBO (Basso) •
MARDIANO (Baritono Buffo) • UN INDOVINO (Basso) •——•
Chorus: OFFICIERS, SOLDIERS, ATTENDANTS, ETC.

Adolf Arensen (1855-   )

Viola

Status: Y   **Evidence:** P
Text: Genée, Franz Friedrich Richard (1823-1895)
Type: Kom. opera   **Acts:** 3   **Language:** German
Premiere: Hamburg, Germany: Stadttheater • 1893 03 16
Source of Premiere Information: Mellen
Play: *Twelfth Night*
Yes: LIBRETTO, Stieger

Cast: ORSINO, Herzog von Illyria • OLIVIA, eine reiche Gräfin •
JUNKER TOBIAS v. RÜLP, ihr Oheim • JUNKER CHRISTOPH v.
BLEICHENWANG • MALVOLIO, Olivas Haushofmeister •
SEBASTIAN, ein junger Edelmann • VIOLA, dessen
Zwillingsschwester • ANTONIO, ein Schiffshauptmann • ERSTER
SEEMANN • ZWEITER SEEMANN • MARIA, Olivias
Kammermädchen • VALENTIN, Page des Herzogs • CURIO, Page
des Herzogs •——• **Chorus:** HERREN VOM HOFE, DAMEN,
GEFOLGE, MATROSEN, GERICHTSDIENER, MUSIKANTEN

Dominick Argento (1927-   )

Christopher Sly

Status: Y   **Evidence:** P
Text: Manlove, John
Type: Comic opera   **Acts:** 1/2 Scenes and an Interlude
           Language: English
Premiere: Minneapolis, U.S.A.: University of Minnesota
    • 1963 05 31
Source of Premiere Information: Mellen
Play: *Taming of the Shrew*
Publisher: New York: Boosey and Hawks, 1968 [vs]
Yes: SCORE, AMCL, Baker's, Mellen, Oxford, Slonimsky

Comments: Score: based on the induction [sic] to Shakespeare's
The Taming of the Shrew. Mellen: 1967 05 31.

Cast: PETER TURPH, a tailor (Tenor) • HENRY PIMPERNELL, a
smith (Bass-Baritone) • CHRISTOPHER SLY, a tinker (Bass-Baritone)
• MARION HACKET, hostess of the ale-house (Mezzo-Soprano) •
THREE HUNTSMEN later THREE SERVANTS • 1ST (Baritone) •
2ND (Tenor) • 3RD (Bass) • A LORD (Tenor) • TWO LADIES (Lyric
Sopranos) • 1ST (Lyric Soprano) • 2ND (Lyric Soprano) • A PAGE
(Soprano) • AN OFFICER OF THE LAW, MUSICIANS (Non-Singing
Roles)

Attilio Ariosti (1666-c.1740)

Il Coriolano

Status: N   **Evidence:** S
Text: Haym, Nicola Francesco [after Pietro Pariati] (1679-1729)
Type: Operette   **Acts:** 3   **Language:** Italian
Premiere: London, England: King's Theater in the Haymarket
    • 1723 02 19
Source of Premiere Information: Stieger
Play: *Coriolanus*
Publisher: London: Richard Meares.
No: Friedlaender

Cast: [Sig.r Berenstatt] • [Sig.a Cuzzoni] • [Sig.r Senesini] • [Mrs. Robinson] • [Sig.a Durastanti] • [Sig.r Boschi]

Michael Arne and C. Dibdin, J. Battishill, C. Burney, Hook, J. C. Smith

Fairy Tale

Status: Y   **Evidence:** P
Text: Colman (Sr.), George (1733-1794)
Type: Burletta   **Acts:** 2   **Language:** English
Premiere: London, England: Drury Lane Theatre • 1763 11 26
Source of Premiere Information: Sonneck
Play: *Midsummer Night's Dream*
Publisher: London: Charles and Samuel Thompson, n.d.
      [selections]
Yes: LIBRETTO, Fiske, Groves V, Mellen, Sonneck, Stieger, White

Comments: Title: The favorite new Songs of Duet in the Fairy Tale, Sung by Miss Wright and Master Rawworth bound with selections from other works by Michael Arne. Text is an abridgement of Garrick's alteration of *Midsummer Night's Dream* variously ascribed to Garrick and George Coleman. Stieger: 3 acts; 1764. Mellen: 1763 11 27.

Cast: QUINCE, a Carpenter • BOTTOM, the Weaver • SNUG, the Joiner • FLUTE, the Bellows-mender • SNOUT, the Tinker • STARVELING, the Taylor • OBERON, King of the Fairies • TITANIA, Queen of the Fairies • PUCK • FIRST FAIRY • SECOND FAIRY • Cast included: Mr. Vernon, Miss Wright, and Mrs. Scot •—•
Chorus: FAIRIES ATTENDING THE KING AND QUEEN

Thomas Augustine Arne (1710-1778)

The Fairy Prince

Status: Y   **Evidence:** P
Text: Colman (Sr.), George (1733-1794)
Type: Masque   **Acts:** 3   **Language:** English
Premiere: London, England: Covent Garden • 1771 11 12
Source of Premiere Information: Stieger

Play: *Midsummer Night's Dream*
Publisher: London: Welcker, 1771 [s].
Yes: LIBRETTO, Groves V
No: Fiske, Mellen, White

Comments: Fiske: Colman rewrote Ben Johnson's masque, *Oberon, the Fairy Prince*; Sylvan sung by Robert Owenson; Second Fairy by Miss Brown. Ben Johnson's masque, *Oberon*, has passages from Shakespeare and Dryden. Mellen: 2 acts.

Cast: SILENUS [Mr. Reinhold] • FIRST SATYR [Mr. Matlocks] • SECOND SATYR AND ECHO [Mr. Bellamy] • THIRD SATYR [Mr. Phillips] • FOURTH SATYR [Mr. Baker] • FIFTH SATYR [Mr. Fox] • SYLVAN [Mr. Owenson] • PRINCIPAL FAIRIES [Two Children, being their first appearance on any stage]WOOD NYMPH [Mrs. Baker] • NYMPHS [Mrs. Baker and a Gentlewoman] • DANCE OF NYMPHS AND SATYRS [Messrs. Fishar, Aldridge, Mad. Manesiere, etc., etc.] • OTHERS IN CAST (Named in Score): Mrs. Woodman, Master Wood, Miss Brown •—• **Chorus:** DANCERS: SATYRS, SYLVANS, WOOD NYMPHS, FAIRIES

The Tempest

Status: NO   **Evidence:** P
Type: English Opera   **Language:** English
Premiere: London, England: Drury Lane • 1746 00 00
Source of Premiere Information: Stieger
Play: *Tempest*
No: SCORE, Groves V, Stieger

Comments: Groves V, Stieger: incidental music. Title: Vocal Music to . . . *The Tempest.*

Thomas Augustine Arne (1710-1778), Samuel Arnold (1740-1802) and others

The Sheep-Shearing or Florizel and Perdita

Status: Y   **Evidence:** P
Text: Morgan, Mac Namara
Type: A Dramatic Pastoral   **Acts:** Prologue/2/Epilogue
        Language: English
Premiere: London, England: Covent Garden • 1754 03 25
Source of Premiere Information: Stieger
Play: *Winter's Tale*
Yes: LIBRETTO, Groves V, Mellen, Sonneck, Stieger, White

Comments: An alteration founded on the fourth and fifth acts of *Winter's Tale*.

Cast: POLLIXENES, King of Bithynia • FLORIZEL, the Prince, his son • CAMILLO, a Sicilian Lord, in banishment • ANTIGONUS, a Sicilian Lord, disguised as an old Shepherd under the Name of Alcon • AUTOLICUS, an arch Pedler • CLOWN • PAN • PRIEST • PERDITA, supposed Daughter to Alcon • DORCUS • MOPSA •—• **Chorus:** SHEPHERDS, SHEPHERDESSES, SINGERS, AND DANCERS

Dennis Drew Arundell (1898-   )

A Midsummer Night's Dream

Status: Y   **Evidence:** S
Text: Unknown
Type: Opera   **Language:** English
Premiere: 1930 00 00
Play: *Midsummer Night's Dream*
Yes: Groves V, Hartnoll, Mellen, Oxford

Comments: Oxford: 1930.

Mario Aspa (1799-1868)

La Gioventù di Enrico V

Status: ?
Text: Unknown
Type: Opera
Premiere: Reggio Calabria, Italy: Teatro Borbonio • 1822 00 00
Source of Premiere Information: Stieger
Play: *Henry IV*

Comments: Stieger: libretto is by Romani; during Carnival.

Franz Asplmayr [Aspelmayr] (1728-1786)

Leben und Tod des Königs Macbeth

Status: I   **Evidence:** S
Text: Moll, [Franz?]
Type: Pantomime   **Language:** German
Premiere: Vienna, Austria • 1777 00 00
Source of Premiere Information: Mellen
Play: *Macbeth*
Yes: Blom, Groves V, Hartnoll, Mellen, Oxford
No: Baker's

Comments: Baker's: music for Shakespeare's *Macbeth*. New Groves: 1771. Blom: it is a pantomime. Mellen: it is a singspiel; the date is when composed; it is based on Shakespeare.

Der Sturm

Status: I   **Evidence:** S
Text: Schink, Johann Friedrich (1755-1835)
Type: Opera   **Acts:** 1   **Language:** German
Premiere: Vienna, Austria • 1781 00 00
Source of Premiere Information: Stieger
Play: *Tempest*
Yes: Friedlaender, Hartnoll, Manferrari, Mellen, Oxford, Squire,
     Stieger

No: Baker's, Groves V

Comments: Baker's: music for Shakespeare's *The Tempest*. Groves V: incidental music; 1779-80. MGG: 1782. Manferrari: melodramma in 1 act, Vienna, Nationaltheater, primavera 1782. Schatz MS: 1790 09 00. Mellen: singspiel in 3 acts, Vienna 1782. Friedlaender: 1786; not published.

Percy Lee Atherton (1871-   ) and Ernest Hamlin Abbott

Hamlet, Prince of Denmark or The Sport, the Spook and the Spinster

Status: Y   **Evidence:** S
Text: Blake, G. B., J. A. Wilder, and Samuel Francis Batchelder
Type: Musical Burlesque   **Acts:** 3   **Language:** English
Premiere: New York, Boston, and Cambridge, U.S.A. • 1893 04 00
Source of Premiere Information: Score
Play: *Hamlet*
Publisher: Boston: Miles and Thompson, c1893.
Yes: Characters

Comments: Presented by the Hasty Pudding Club of Harvard University.

Cast: HAMLET, Prince of Denmark [James A. Wilder] • HORATIO [F. H. J. Gade] • BOLOGNIUS [Clarence R. Falk] • LAERTES [George D. Wells] • GHOST [Henry A. Frothingham] • ROSENCRANTZ [Gordon K. Bell] • GUILDENSTERN [Robert Emmet] • MESSENGER [Charles B. Earle] • BIRD OF DAWNING [Charles B. Earle] • OSRIC [Walter Cary] • A GENTLEMAN [Shelden E. Marvin] • GERTRUDE, Queen of Denmark [J. Harleston Parker] • OPHELIA [Archibald R. Tisdale] • JULIET [Bulkeley Wells] •—•
Chorus: COURTIERS, LADIES, DANCERS, AND GUARDS

Kurt Atterberg (1887-1974)

Stormen, Op. 49

Status: Y   **Evidence:** S
Text: Composer
Type: Opera   **Acts:** 3   **Language:** Swedish
Premiere: Stockholm, Sweden: Royal Theater • 1948 09 19
Source of Premiere Information: Mellen
Play: *Tempest*
Yes: Baker's, Groves V, Hartnoll, Mellen, MGG, Oxford

Comments: MGG: this and *Ein Vintersaga* on Shakespeare are
incidental music. New Grove: Op. 18 and *Ein Vintersaga* are
incidental music; Op. 49 is an opera. Groves V: 1948 09 09; awarded
prize offered by Royal Opera for its 50 year Jubilee.

Thomas Attwood (1765-1838)

Hermione, or Valour's Triumph

Status: ?
Text: Dibdin, Thomas John (1771-1841)
Type: Musical Interlude   **Language:** English
Premiere: London, England: Covent Garden • 1800 04 05
Play: *Winter's Tale*

Comments: Nicoll: *The Hermione, or Retaliation.* Mellen:
        1800 03 31.

Edmond Audran (1840-1901)

Gillette de Narbonne [Gillette, or Count and Countess; Gilda di Guascogna]

Status: Y   **Evidence:** S
Text: Chivot, Henri Charles (1830-1897) and Henri Alfred Duru
        (1829-1889)
Type: Opéra comique   **Acts:** 3   **Language:** French

Premiere: Paris, France: Bouffes-Parisiens • 1882 11 11
Source of Premiere Information: Libretto
Play: *All's Well That Ends Well*
Publisher: Paris: Choudens Pére et Fils, 1883 [vs]
Yes: Friedlaender, Groves V, Hartnoll, Loewenberg, Mellen, Oxford

Comments: Groves V: based on *Much Ado about Nothing*. Score does not mention Shakespeare. Mellen: it is also based on Boccaccio's *Decameron*.

Cast: LE COMTE ROGER DE LIGNOLLE (Baryton) [Mr. Morlet] • OLIVER, fils du Roi René (Tenor) [Mr. Lamy] • GRIFFARDIN, précepteur d'Oliver (Buffo) [Mr. Mauge] • LE ROI RÉNÉ [Mr. Riga] • LE SÉNÉCHAL (Baryton) • BARIGOUL, Ambergiste • RICHARD, amie de Roger • LANDRY, amie de Roger • GILLETTE (Soprano) [Mme Grisier-Montbazon] • ROSITA (Mezzo Soprano) [Mme Gélabert] • CHATEAUNEUF [Mme Rivero] • BOISLAURIER [Mme D'Arly] •—•
Chorus: PAGES ET NAPOLITAINS, DEMOISELLES D'HONNEUR, SEIGNEURS ET DAMES, PAYSANS, PAYSANNES, SOLDATS

Theodore Aylward (1731-1801)

A Midsummer Night's Dream

Status: NO   **Evidence:** S
Type: Play with song
Premiere: London, England • 179? 00 00
Play: *Midsummer Night's Dream*
No: Friedlaender, Stieger

Comments: Stieger: it is incidental music. Friedlaender: Six Songs in . . . . *Cymbeline* and *Midsummer Night's Dream*; Partitur gedruckt in London.

August Louis Baeyens (1895-1966)

Coriolanus

Status: Y   **Evidence:** S
Text: Burgerdijk, A. T.

Type: Opera   **Acts:** 10 Scenes   **Language:** Flemish
Premiere: Antwerp, Belgium: Royal Flemish Opera • 1941 11 27
Source of Premiere Information: Mellen
Play: *Coriolanus*
Yes: Baker's, Groves V, Hartnoll, New Grove, Oxford

Comments: Baker's: 1941; a radio opera. Mellen: date is for a concert performance.

John Balamos

As You Like It

Status: Y   **Evidence:** S
Text: Seitz, Dran and Tani [book and lyrics]
Type: Broadway Show   **Language:** English
Premiere: New York, U.S.A.: Theater de Lys • 1964 10 27
Source of Premiere Information: Simas
Play: *As You Like It*
Yes: Simas

Michael William Balfe (1808-1870)

Enrico IV al passo della Marna

Status: ?
Text: Unknown
Type: Melodramma   **Acts:** 1   **Language:** Italian
Premiere: Milan, Italy: Teatro Carcano • 1833 02 19
Source of Premiere Information: Stieger
Play: *Henry IV*

Comments: White: the author of the Italian libretto is unknown.

Cast: ENRICO IV, detto il Bearnese (Tenore) [Signor Lorenzo Bonfigli] • DU-CHAMP, Capitano della lega [Signor Carlo Crosa] • COSTANTINO, Postalano (Basse) [Signor Guglielmo Balfe] • GERVASIO, suo fratello, Mugnajo e marito di [Signor Carlo Cambiaggio] • CRISTINA [Signora Lina Roser-Balfe] •—•
Chorus: CONTADINI E DI SOLDATI DELLA LEGA

Falstaff

Status: Y   **Evidence:** P
Text: Maggioni, S. Manfredo
Type: Comic opera   **Acts:** 2   **Language:** Italian
Premiere: London, England: Her Majesty's Theatre in the
       Haymarket • 1838 07 19
Source of Premiere Information: Libretto gives month and
       year. Day from Schatz Catalog.
Play: *Merry Wives of Windsor*
Publisher: London: Cramer, Beale and Co., 1845?
Yes: LIBRETTO, Blom, Friedlaender, Groves V, Hartnoll,
       Loewenberg, Oxford, Stieger, Wilson

Comments: Baker's: in Italian in London; only Italian opera Balfe
wrote for London. Stieger: text by I.M. Maggioni. Loewenberg lists
under Shakespeare in index but says nothing about Shakespeare in
main entry. Score does not mention Shakespeare. Friedlaender:
Covent Garden.

Cast: SIR JOHN FALSTAFF [Sig. Lablache] • CHARLES FENTON
[Sig. Rubini] • MR. FORD [Sig. Tamburini] • MR. PAGE [Sig. Morelli] •
GEORGE, Servant to Falstaff [Sig. Galli] • ROBIN, Servant at the Inn
[M. Salabert] • MRS. FORD [Made Grisi] • MRS. PAGE [Madlle
Caremoli] • MISS ANNETTE PAGE [Made Albertazzi] • MRS.
QUICKLY, Servant to Mr. Ford [Made Castelli] •—•
Chorus: SERVANTS, FORESTERS, PEASANTS, &c.

John Banister [Bannister] (c.1625-1679); Giovanni Battista Draghi; Matthew Locke (c. 1621-1677); Pelham Humfrey [Humphrey] (1647-1674); and Pietro Reggio

The Tempest [The Enchanted Island]

Status: Y   **Evidence:** P
Text: Shadwell, Thomas after the 1667 adaptation by John Dryden
       (1631-1701) and William Davenant (1605-1668)
Type: Dramatic opera   **Acts:** 5   **Language:** English
Premiere: London, England: Duke of York's Theater in Dorset
       Gardens • 1674 04 30

21

Source of Premiere Information: White, who is not certain of
   the day.
Play: *Tempest*
Yes: LIBRETTO, Clément, Oxford, Squire, Stieger, White

Comments: Stieger: 1665. New Grove: 1667. Schatz MS: 1670
01 00. Fiske: Locke wrote the instrumental movements, Humfrey the
masques, Banister most of the single songs.

Cast: ALONZO, Duke of Savoy, and Usurper of the Dukedom of
Mantua • FERDINAND, his son • PROSPERO, right Duke of Millain •
ANTONIO, his Brother, Usurper of the Dukedom • GONZALO, a
Nobleman of Savoy • HIPPOLYTO, one that never saw Woman, right
Heir of the Dukedom of Mantua • STEPHANO, Master of the Ship •
MUSTACHO, his Mate • TRINCALO, Boatswain • VENTOSO, a
Marriner • SEVERAL MARRINERS • A CABIN BOY • MIRANDA,
Daughter to Prospero that never saw man • DORINDA, Daughter to
Prospero that never saw man • ARIEL, an Aiery Spirit, attendant on
Prospero • CALABAN, Monster of the Isle • SYCORAX, his sister •—•
Chorus: SEVERAL SPIRITS, GUARDS TO PROSPERO

Samuel Barber (1910-1981)

Antony and Cleopatra, Op. 40

Status: Y   **Evidence:** P
Text: Zeffirelli, Franco (1923-   )
Type: Opera   **Acts:** 3/16 scenes   **Language:** English
Premiere: New York, U.S.A.: Metropolitan Opera • 1966 09 16
Source of Premiere Information: Score
Play: *Antony and Cleopatra*
Publisher: New York: G. Schirmer, 1966 [vs]
Yes: SCORE, LIBRETTO, New Grove, Oxford

Comments: Commissioned for opening of new Metropolitan Opera
House in Lincoln Center, NYC. Cast from Opera News 9/17/1966.

Cast: CLEOPATRA, Queen of Egypt (Soprano) [Leontyne Price] •
OCTAVIA, Caesar's sister (Lyric Soprano) [Mary Ellen Pracht] •
CHARMIAN, Attendant on Cleopatra (Mezzo-Soprano) [Rosalind
Elias] • IRAS, Attendant on Cleopatra (Contralto) [Belen Amparan] •
ANTONY, a Roman General (High Bass) [Justino Diaz] • CAESAR
(Octavius), ruler of Rome (Tenor) [Jess Thomas] • AGRIPPA, Senator

(Bass) [John Macurdy] • LEPIDUS, Senator (Tenore Buffo) [Robert
Nagy] • MAECENAS, Senator (Baritone) [Russell Christopher] •
ENOBARBUS, Friend to Antony (Bass) [Ezio Flagello] • EROS,
Shield-bearer to Antony (Young Man's voice [Tenor or High Baritone)
[Bruce Scott (debut)] • DOLABELLA, an officer of Antony (Baritone)
[Gene Boucher] • THIDIAS, Ambassador from Caesar (Tenor or High
Baritone) [Robert Goodloe] • CANIDIUS, Officer to Antony (Baritone)
[Lloyd Strang] • DEMETRIUS, Officer to Antony (Low Tenor) [Norman
Giffin] • SCARUS, Officer to Antony (Bass) [Ron Bottcher (debut)] •
DECREATAS, Officer to Antony (Bass) [Louis Sgarro] • MARDIAN, a
Eunuch (High Tenor) [Andrea Velis] • A RUSTIC (Baritone or Bass) []
• MESSENGER (Tenor) [Paul Franke] • SOOTHSAYER (Bass)
[Lorenzo Alvary] • ALEXAS, Attendant on Cleopatra (Bass)
[Raymond Michalski] • A SOLDIER OF ANTONY (Tenor) [] • A
CAPTAIN OF ANTONY (Tenor) [Dan Marek] • A SOLDIER OF
ANTONY (Bass) [John Trehy] • FIRST GUARD IN ANTONY'S CAMP
(Tenor) [Robert Schmorr] • SECOND GUARD IN ANTONY'S CAMP
(Bass) [Edward Ghazal] • THIRD GUARD IN ANTONY'S CAMP (Bass)
[Norman Scott] • FIRST WATCHMAN (Bass) [Paul De Paola] •
SECOND WATCHMAN (Bass) [Luis Forero] • A SOLDIER OF
CAESAR (Tenor) [Gabor Carelli] • A SENTINEL (Bass) [Peter Sliker] •
A CLOWN (Baritone) [Clifford Harvuot] •—•
Chorus: PEOPLE OF THE EMPIRE, ATTENDANTS ON
CLEOPATRA, SENATORS, GUARDS, WATCHMEN, SOLDIERS

Carlo Emanuele di Barbieri (1822-1867)

Perdita oder Ein Wintermärchen

Status: Y   **Evidence:** P
Text: Gross, Karl
Type: Romantische Oper   **Acts:** 4   **Language:** German
Premiere: Prague, Czechoslovakia: Deutsches Landestheater
    • 1865 01 11
Source of Premiere Information: Schatz Catalog
Play: *Winter's Tale*
Publisher: Vienna: Franz Kretz, 1865.
Yes: LIBRETTO, Friedlaender, Hartnoll, Loewenberg, New Grove,
    Oxford, Stieger

Comments: New Grove: it is his one important opera. Mellen:
Leipzig, Opernhaus. Based on Frans von Dingelstedt's version of
Shakespeare's *Winter's Tale*.

23

Cast: LEONTES, König von Sizilien • HERMONIE, dessen Gemahlin • MAMILIUS, ihr Sohn • PAULINA, Vertraute Hermionens • BASSIANUS, Leontes Vertrauter • LEANDER, König von Arkadien • FLORIEZEL, dessen Sohn • TYTIRUS, ein Schäfer in Arkadien • PERDITA • EIN DIENER HERMIONES • CLEOMENES, Sicilianischer Hofherr • RIKETAS, Leander's Bertrauter • EIN SPRECHER APOLLOS•—• **Chorus:** SICILIANISCHE EDLE, HERREN UND DAMEN, ARKADISCHE EDLE, PRIESTER APOLLO'S IN DELPHI. WOLF. ARKADISCHE SCHÄFER UND SCHÄFERINNEN, MÄHER u. u.

John Edmond Barkworth (1858-1929)

Romeo and Juliet

Status: Y   **Evidence:** P
Text: Composer
Type: Opera   **Acts:** 4   **Language:** English
Premiere: Middlesborough, England: Harrison-Frewin Company • 1916 01 07
Source of Premiere Information: Loewenberg
Play: *Romeo and Juliet*
Publisher: London: Mac Donaugh, Capdeville & Co., Ltd., 1926 [vs]
Yes: SCORE, Blom, Groves V, Hartnoll, Loewenberg, New Grove, Northouse, White

Comments: Hartnoll: sets Shakespeare's text almost unaltered; it is his principal work.

Cast: JULIET, Daughter to Capulet (Soprano) • LADY CAPULET (Mezzo-Soprano) • NURSE TO JULIET (Contralto) • ROMEO, son to Montague (Tenor) • MERCUTIO (Baritone) • CAPULET (Baritone) • MONTAGUE (Baritone) • ESCALUS, Prince of Verona (Bass) • PARIS (Tenor) • BENVOLIO (Baritone) • TYBALT (Bass) • FRIAR LAWRENCE, a Franciscan (Baritone) • BALTHASAR, servant to Romeo (Baritone) • SAMPSON, servant to Capulet (Baritone) • GREGORY, servant to Capulet • PETER, servant to Juliet's Nurse (Baritone) • AN APOTHECARY (Baritone) • ABRAM, servant to Montague (Tenor) • FIRST and SECOND CAVALIERS (Tenors) • POTPAN, PAGE (Mute), ROSALINE (Mute) •—•
Chorus: CITIZENS, GUESTS, POPULACE, BRIDESMAIDS, GUARDS, TRUMPETERS.

H. C. Barry

Shylock or The Venus of Venice

Status: Y   **Evidence:** S
Text: Turner, Montague
Type: Operatic Burlesque   **Acts:** 3   **Language:** English
Premiere: Lincoln, England: Theatre Royal • 1892 08 01
Source of Premiere Information: Gänzl
Play: *Merchant of Venice*
Yes: Gänzl

Comments: Characters and cast from Gänzl.

Cast: SHYLOCK [John E. Coyle] • MR ANTONIO SR [George Wallace] • INTERROGATER [Bruce Bertini] • TOKIO CHUCKEO [Walter Wood] • BASSANIO [Grace Serata] • SALERINO [Polly Elcho] • MENETA [Lillie Dagmar] • PORTIA [Florence Carlile] • JESSICA [Ernest Autherley] • THE McTUBAL [Jesmond Johnstone] • THE DOGE [Montague Turner] • HYPNOTISER [George Gibbens] • GRATIANO [Daisy Dalton] • LORENZO [Constance Conway] • DONATO [Vivenne d'Arcy] • SALANIO [Doris Melville] • NERISSA [Florence Engelmann]

Curt Beck (1910 -   )

König Lear

Status: ?
Text: Unknown
Play: *Lear*

Comments: Not performed.

Herbert Bedford (1867-1945)

Love Scene from Shakespeare's "Romeo and Juliet" for Contralto and Baritone

Status: NO   **Evidence:** P
Type: Love scene   **Acts:** NA   **Language:** English
Premiere: Norwich, England: Festival • 1902 00 00
Play: *Romeo and Juliet*
 No: Title

Adrian Wells Beecham (1904-   )

Love's Labour's Lost [Peines d'Amour Perdues]

Status: Y   **Evidence:** P
Text: Composer after Shakespeare
Type: Comic Opera   **Acts:** 2   **Language:** English
Premiere: 1936 00 00
Play: *Love's Labour's Lost*
Publisher: Stratford-on Avon: Composer, c.1936 [vs]
Yes: SCORE, Hartnoll, Mellen, Oxford

Comments: SCORE: text by Shakespeare; French transcription by Jean Chantavoine. Mellen: date is when composed. White: was never produced.

Cast: LE ROI • BIRON • DUMAINE • LONGAVILLE • LA PRINCESSE • BOYET • MARIA • KATHERINE • ROSALINE • COSTARD • HOLOFERNE • JACQUENETTE • DULLET • NATHANIEL • MOTH. [only abbreviation given] •—•
Chorus: CHORUS

The Merchant of Venice

Status: Y   **Evidence:** P
Text: Composer after Shakespeare
Type: Opera   **Acts:** 3   **Language:** English
Premiere: London, England: Duke of York's Theatre • 1920 11 20
Source of Premiere Information: Mellen
Play: *Merchant of Venice*

Publisher: London: Schott and Co., 1922 [vs]
Yes: SCORE, Hartnoll, Mellen, Oxford

Comments: Mellen: 1922 11 20. White: 4 acts, Brighton, Grand Theatre, 1922 09 18.

Cast: PORTIA [Ena Riess] • JESSICA [Desiree Ellinger] • NERISSA [Ella Milne] • ANTONIO [Webster Millar] • LORENZO [Frank Webster] • SALARIO [Dewey Gibson] • GRATIANO [Howard Fry] • BASSANIO [Gregory Stroud] • PRINCE OF MOROCO [Norman Williams] • PRINCE OF ARRAGON [Andrew Leith] • LAUNCELOT [Andrew Leith] • SALANIO [John Van Zyl] • DUKE OF VENICE [John Van Zyl] • STEPHANO [Leslie May] • TUBAL [A. Halstead] • SHYLOCK [Augustus Milner] •—• **Chorus:** CHORUS

Anton Beer-Walbrunn [Anton Beer] (1864-1929)

Der Sturm

Status: Y   **Evidence:** S
Text: Unknown
Type: Dramma
Premiere: Munich, Germany • 1914 07 00
Source of Premiere Information: Stieger
Play: *Tempest*
Yes: Baker's, Stieger

Comments: May not have been performed.

Vincenzo Bellini (1801-1835)

I Capuleti e i Montecchi

Status: Y   **Evidence:** S
Text: Romani, Felice (1788-1865)
Type: Tragedia lirica   **Acts:** 3   **Language:** Italian
Premiere: Venice, Italy: Gran Teatro La Fenice • 1830 03 11
Source of Premiere Information: Loewenberg
Play: *Romeo and Juliet*
Publisher: Milan: Presso Giovani Ricordi, 1830 [vs]

27

Yes: Blom, Friedlaender, Groves V, Hartnoll, Loewenberg, Mellen, Oxford, Squire, Stieger, Wilson

Comments: Last act is usually added from Vaccai's opera.

Cast: CAPELLIO, principale fra i Capuleti, e padre di [Sig. Antoldi] • GIULIETTA, amante di [Sig.a Carradori Allan] • ROMEO, Capo dei Montecchi [Sig.a Grisi] • TEBALDO, partigiano dei Capuleti, destinato sposo a Giulietta [Sig. Bonfigli] • LORENZO, medico e famigliare di Capellio [Sig. Cavalieri]

George Anton [Jirí Antonín] Benda (1722-1795)

Romeo und Julie

Status: Y   **Evidence:** P
Text: Gotter, Friedrich Wilhelm (1746-1797)
Type: Ernsthaftes Singspiel   **Acts:** 3   **Language:** German
Premiere: Gotha, Germany: Herzogl. Hoftheater • 1776 09 25
Source of Premiere Information: Loewenberg
Play: *Romeo and Juliet*
Publisher: Leipzig: Verlage der Dykischen Buchhandlung, 1778 [vs]
Yes: LIBRETTO, Blom, Friedlaender, Groves V, Hartnoll, Loewenberg, Mellen, New Grove, Oxford, Squire, Stieger, Wilson

Comments: Friedlaender: 1778 00 00.   Facsimile of the score is published by Garland.

Cast: CAPELLET, Edler von Verona (Tenor) • JULIE, seine Tochter (Sopran) • LORENZO, sein Hauskapellan (Spoken) • LAURA, Juliens Freundin (Sopran) • ROMEO MONTECCHI (Tenor) • FRANCESCO, dessen Diener (Spoken) • EIN LEIDTRAGENDER (Tenor) •——•
Chorus: LEIDTRAGENDE, MÄDCHEN, TRAUERGEFOLGE (Spoken)

Pascal Bentoiu (1927-   )

Hamlet, Op. 18

Status: Y   **Evidence:** P
Text: Composer
Type: Opera   **Acts:** 1   **Language:** Rumanian
Premiere: Bucharest, Rumania • 1971 11 19
Play: Hamlet
Publisher: Milan: Edisioni Suvini Zerboni, 1972 [vs]
Yes: SCORE, Mellen, Oxford

Cast: AMLETO (Tenore) • LO SPETTRO (La voce del cantante che interpreta al parte di Amleto, registrata su nastra magnetico. • IL RE CLAUDIO (Basso) • POLONIO (Tenore) • OFELIA (Soprano) • LA REGINA GERTRUDE (Mezzosoprano) • LA REGINA DELLO SPETTACOLO (Soprano) • IL RE DELLO SPETTACOLO (Tenore) • LUCIANO (Mimo-ballerino) • OSRICK (Baritono) • LAERTE (Baritono)
Chorus: Coro misto: Signori, Signore, Guardie, La folla.

Tommaso Benvenuti (1838-1906)

Guglielmo Shakespeare

Status: AP   **Evidence:** P
Text: Piave, Francesco Maria (1810-1876)
Type: Melodramma   **Acts:** 3   **Language:** Italian
Premiere: Parma, Italy: Regio Teatro • 1861 02 14
Source of Premiere Information: Mellen
Play: Shakespeare Appears
Yes: LIBRETTO

Cast: GUGLIELMO SHAKSPEARE [Sechspir] (1.° Baritono) [sig. Lodovico Batti] • ELIZABETTA, regina d'Inghilterra (Contralto) [sig.a Gaglielmina Flori] • ILCONTE ROBERTO ESSEX, suo favorito (1.° Tenore) [sig. Pietro Bignardi] • OLIVIA, attrice (1.° Soprano) [sig.a Eufrisina Poinsot] • ALICE, sua cameriera (2.° Soprano) [sig.a Rosina Rainieri] • IL MARCJESE DI WINCESTRA, 1.° Ministro (Basso profondo) [sig. Marco Ghini] • LORD EGLAMOUR (2.° Basso) [sig. Giacomo Vercellini]] • LORD BRIGHT (2.° Basso) [sig. Giuseppe Romanelli] • TOM HATWAY, cognato di Sechspir (2.° Tenor) [sig. Ercole Braglia] • FELTON, capo comico (2.° Tenor) [sig. Gaetano

Benfali] • IL CONSTABILE della Torre di Londra (Basso comprimario) [sig. N. N.] •— **Chorus:** LORDI, LEDI, ANCELLE, POPOLO, ATTORI

Johann Hermann Berens (1826-1880)

Riccardo

Status: ?
Text: Arlberg, Fritz (1830-1896)
Type: Comic Opera   **Acts:** 3   **Language:** Swedish
Premiere: Stockholm, Sweden • 1869 03 00
Source of Premiere Information: Mellen
Play: *Richard III*

Comments: Stieger: 1869 02 00; it is after Scribe.

En Sommarnattsdröm

Status: AP   **Evidence:** S
Text: Stjernström, J. (n.d. Französ)
Type: Operette   **Acts:** 2   **Language:** Swedish
Premiere: Stockholm, Sweden: Mindre Theater • 1856 10 27
Play: *Midsummer Night's Dream*
Yes: Stieger
No: Friedlaender, Groves V

Comments: Groves V: incidental music. Schatz MS: original libretto by Joseph Bernard Rosier and Adolph de Leuven. Friedlaender: the libretto is a Swedish translation of the libretto used for Thomas' opera, *Le songe d'une nuit d'été*.

Violetta

Status: N   **Evidence:** S
Text: Granberg, J. L.
Type: Rom. Opera   **Acts:** 3   **Language:** Swedish
Premiere: Stockholm, Sweden: Kgl.Th. • 1855 02 00
Play: *Twelfth Night*
No: Groves V

Comments: Groves V: incidental music. Stieger: 1855 01 00.
Mellen: 2 acts.

Henri Berény (1871-1932)

Das Wintermärchen

Status: Y   **Evidence:** S
Text: Prasch
Type: Oper
Premiere: 1898 00 00
Play: *Winter's Tale*
Yes: Hartnoll, Oxford

Comments: Date is when composed.

Hector Berlioz (1803-1869)

Béatrice et Bénédict

Status: Y   **Evidence:** P
Text: Composer
Type: Opéra comique   **Acts:** 2   **Language:** French
Premiere: Baden-Baden, Germany: Nouveau théâtre • 1862 08 09
Source of Premiere Information: Score
Play: *Much Ado About Nothing*
Publisher: Paris: G. Brandus and S. Dufour, 1862 [vs]; pub. now by
        Bärenreiter and Kalmus
Yes: SCORE, Baker's, Blom, Friedlaender, Groves V, Hartnoll,
        Loewenberg, Mellen, MGG, New Grove, Oxford, Squire,
        Stieger, Wilson

Comments: First performance was in a German translation.

Cast: BÉATRICE (Mezzo Soprano) [Mme Charton-Demeur] • HÉRO
(Soprano) [Mlle Monrose] • URSULE (Contralto) [Mme Geoffroy] •
BÉNÉDICT (Tenor) [M. Montaubry] • CLAUDIO (Baryton) [M. Lefort] •
DON PEDRO (Basse) [M. Balanqué] • SOMARONE (Basse) [M.
Prilleux]] • LEONATO [M. Guerrin] • UN TABELLION • UN

MESSAGER • DEUX DOMESTIQUES •—•
Chorus: CHŒUR DE PEUPLE

Hamlet

Status: Y   **Evidence:** S
Text: Unknown
Type: Idea for opera
Play: *Hamlet*
Yes: Groves V

Giuseppe Antonio Bernabei (1649-1732)

Érmione

Status: N   **Evidence:** P
Text: Terzago, Ventura
Type: Dramma per musica   **Acts:** 3   **Language:** Italian
Premiere: Munich, Germany: Teatro di Corte • 1680 07 11
Source of Premiere Information: Libretto
Play: *Winter's Tale*
No: LIBRETTO, Riemann (see composer Gianettini)

Comments: Sonneck: the composer of the music is not mentioned. [He is incorrect.] Most of his scores are preserved at Munich and Vienna. Mellen: Munich, Hoftheater.

Cast: MENELAO, Rè di Sparta in abito di privata Soldato col nome di Delmite • ELENA, sua moglie • ERMIONE, sua figlivola • ORESTE, amante d'Ermione in figura di schiavo seguace di • PILLADE, suo amico • PIRRO, figlivolo d'Achille innamorato d'Ermione • ANDROMACHE, sposa di Pirro vestita da maschio col nome d'Ormindo • ADRASPE, Luogotenente del Regno • ERGASTO, nobile Spartano confidente della Regina • ALFEA, Nodrice d'Ermione • BIROLLO servo d'Oreste • 4 STALLARI • GIOVE, che scende sull'aquila, La quale porta negli artigli Ganimede •—•
Chorus: PAGGI E DONZETTE CON ELENA, PAGGI E DONZETTE CON ERMIONE, PAGGI E CAVALIERI CON PIRRO, GUARDIE CON ADRASPE, SCUDIERE CON ERGASTO, STALLARI NELLE REGIE STALLE, PAGGI E GUARDIE IN FINE CON IL RE

Vincenzo Bernabei (c.1666-1690)

Gli Equivoci d'Amore

Status: ?
Text: Teofilo, Giovanni
Type: Melodr.
Premiere: Vienna, Austria: Hoftheater • 1689 00 00
Play: *Midsummer Night's Dream*

Comments: This may be the work Stieger lists as *Gli accidenti (equivoci) d'amore* by Giuseppe Antonio Bernabei premiered perhaps in Rome in 1960. Date: winter.

Leonard Bernstein (1918-　　　)

West Side Story

Status: Y　　**Evidence:** S
Text: Sondheim, Stephen and Arthur Laurents
Type: Musical Play　　**Acts:** 2　　**Language:** English
Premiere: New York, U.S.A.: Winter Garden • 1957 09 26
Source of Premiere Information: Libretto
Play: *Romeo and Juliet*
Publisher: New York: G. Schirmer 1959 [vs]
Yes: Bordman, Green

Comments: Conception by Jerome Robbins.

Cast: THE JETS: • RIFF, The Leader [Mickey Calin] • TONY, His Friend [Larry Kert] • ACTION [Eddie Roll] • A-RAB [Tony Mordente] • BABY JOHN [David Winters] • SNOWBOY [Grover Dale] • BIG DEAL [Martin Charnin] • DIESEL [Hank Brunjes] • GEE-TAR [Tommy Abbott] • MOUTHPIECE [Frank Green] • TIGER [Lowell Harris] • THEIR GIRLS: • GRAZIELLA [Wilma Curley] • VELMA [Carole D'Andrea] • MINNIE [Nanette Rosen] • CLARICE [Marilyn D'Honau] • PAULINE [Julie Oser] • ANYBODY'S [Lee Becker] • THE SHARKS: • BERNARDO, The Leader [Ken Le Roy] • MARIA, His Sister [Carol Lawrence] • ANITA, His Girl [Chita Rivera] • CHINO, His Friend [Jamie Ssnchez] • PEPE [George Marcy] • INDIO [Noel Schwartz] • LUIS [Al De Sio] • ANXIOUS [Gene Gavin] • NIBBLES [Ronnie Lee] • JUANO [Jay Norman] • TORO [Erne Castaldo] • MOOSE [Jack Murray] •

THEIR GIRLS: • ROSALIA [Marilyn Cooper] • CONSUELO [Reri Grist]
• TERESITA [Carmen Guiterrez] • FRANCISCA [Elizabeth Taylor] •
ESTRELLA [Lynn Ross] • MARGARITA [Liane Plane] • THE
ADULTS: • DOC [Art Smith] • SCHRANK [Arch Johnson] • KRUPKE
[William Bramley] • GLAD HAND [John Harkins]

Henri-Montan Berton (1767-1844)

Montano et Stéphanie

Status: N   **Evidence:** S
Text: Dejaure, [Jean-Claude Bédéno known as] (1761-1799)
Type: Opéra comique   **Acts:** 3   **Language:** French
Premiere: Paris, France: Opéra Comique • 1799 04 15
Source of Premiere Information: Score
Play: *Much Ado About Nothing*
Publisher: Paris: Chez Des Lauriers, [1799]. [s]
Yes: Friedlaender
No: Loewenberg, Mellen

Comments: Loewenberg: based on an episode in Aristo's *Orlando
furioso.*

Cast: STÉPHANIE (Sop.) • MONTANO (Alto) • LEONATI (Bass) •
ALTAMONT (Ten.) • FABRICE (Speaking) • SALVATOR (Ten.) •—•
Chorus: CHEUR DE PAYSANS, PLUSIEURS FEMMES

Ferdinando Giuseppe Bertoni (1725-1813)

Cajo Mario

Status: ?
Text: Roccaforte, Gaetano
Type: Dramma per musica   **Acts:** 3   **Language:** Italian
Premiere: Venice, Italy: Teatro di La Benedetto • 1781 05 04
Source of Premiere Information: Mellen
Play: *Coriolanus*

Rick Besoyan

Babes in the Wood, or Who Killed Cock Robin

Status: Y   **Evidence:** S
Text: Besoyan, Rick (book and lyrics)
Type: Broadway Show   **Language:** English
Premiere: New York, U.S.A.: Orpheum Theatre • 1964 12 28
Source of Premiere Information: Simas
Play: *Midsummer Night's Dream*
Yes: Green, Simas

Comments: Bordman: 1964 12 24.

Francesco Bianchi (1752-1810)

Cajo Mario

Status: ?
Text: Roccaforte, Gaetano
Type: Dramma per musica   **Acts:** 3   **Language:** Italian
Premiere: Naples, Italy: Real Teatro di San Carlo • 1784 05 30
Source of Premiere Information: Schatz MS
Play: *Coriolanus*

Sir Henry Rowley Bishop (1786-1855)

Antony and Cleopatra

Status: NO   **Evidence:** S
Language: English
Premiere: , England • 1813 00 00
Play: *Antony and Cleopatra*
Yes: Groves V

As You Like It

Status: NO   **Evidence:** P
Type: Pasticcio opera   **Acts:** 5   **Language:** English
Premiere: London, England: Covent Garden • 1816 00 00
Play: *As You Like It*
Publisher: London: 1824.
No: SCORE, Blom, Groves V

Comments: Blom, Groves V: incidental music. Title: The Whole of the music in *As You Like It*, to which are added the three songs composed for the above play by Dr. Arne, the poetry selected from the Plays, etc. of Shakespeare.

The Comedy of Errors

Status: NO   **Evidence:** P
Text: Reynolds, Frederic
Type: Pasticcio opera   **Acts:** 5   **Language:** English
Premiere: London, England: Covent Garden • 1819 12 11
Source of Premiere Information: Stieger
Play: *Comedy of Errors*
Publisher: London: Goulding, D'Amaine Potter & Co. 1819? [vs]
Yes: Oxford, White
No: SCORE, LIBRETTO, Groves V, Stieger

Comments: Title: The Overture, Songs, Two Duetts and Glees in Shakespeare's *Comedy of Errors*. Performed at the Theatre Royal, Covent Garden. Words Selected entirely from Shakespeare. The Music Composed and the whole adapted and compressed from the Score for the Voice and Piano Forte by Henry R. Bishop . . . .

Cast: LUCIANA [Miss Tree] • ANTIPHOLIS OF EPHESUS [Mr. Durusett] • ADRIANA [Miss Stephens] • CERIMON [Mr. Payne] • [also Mr. Taylor, Mr. Comer, Mr. I. Isaccs]

Henri Quatre [Paris in the Olden Times]

Status: N   **Evidence:** P
Text: Morton, Thomas (1764-1838)
Type: Musical romance   **Acts:** 3   **Language:** English
Premiere: London, England: Covent Garden • 1820 04 22
Source of Premiere Information: Mellen

36

Play: *Henry IV*
Yes: Friedlaender
No: LIBRETTO

Comments: Plot concerns Henri Quatre of France. Libretto: The Spectator is requested not to compare, too rigidly, the Incidents presented in this Piece, with the History of Henri Quatre. . . .

Cast: HENRI [Mr. Macready] • SULLY [Mr. Egerton] • CRILLON [Mr. Hunt] • GENERAL D'AUMONT, Uncle to Frederic and Florence [Mr. Fawcett] • EUGENE DE BIRON, Officer in the same regiment [Mr. C. Kemble] • FREDERIC ST. LEON, Officer in the same regiment [Mr. Abbott] • O'DONNEL, an Irish Officer in the Frenchg Service [Mr. John Johnstone] • MOUSTACHE, an old Soldier [Mr. Emery] • JOCRISSE, Nephew to Gervais and Garçon of the Inn [Mr. Liston] • GERVAIS, an Innkeeper [Mr. Duruset] • PINCEAU, a Sign Painter [Mr. Blanchard] • GERMAIN [Mr. Comer] • AID DE CAMP [Mr. Mears] • OFFICER [Mr. Jefferies] • PAGE [Master Longhurst] • ENGLISH GENERAL • FLORENCE ST. LEON, beloved by Eugene [Miss Stephens] • CLOTILDE DE BIRON, beloved by Frederic [Miss Brunton] • LUISON, married to Jocrisse [Miss M. Tree] •—•
Chorus: OFFICERS, SOLDIERS, DOMESTICS, PEASANTS, ETC.

The Merry Wives of Windsor

Status: I   **Evidence:** S
Text: Reynolds, F.
Language: English
Premiere: London, England: Drury Lane Theatre • 1824 02 20
Play: *Merry Wives of Windsor*
Yes: White
No: Groves V

A Midsummer Night's Dream

Status: I   **Evidence:** S
Text: Garrick, David (1717-1779) and new lyrics by Frederic Reynolds
Type: Opéra anglais   **Acts:** 3   **Language:** English
Premiere: London, England: Covent Garden • 1816 01 17
Source of Premiere Information: Stieger
Play: *Midsummer Night's Dream*
Publisher: London:Goulding, D'Almaine, Potter & Co. 1916.

Yes: Manferrari, White, Wilson
No: Friedlaender, Groves V, Schatz MS, Stieger

Comments: Title: The Overture, Songs, Duetts, Trios, Quartetts, Choruses, Marches & Melodramatic Music in Shakespeare's *Midsummer Night's Dream* . . . the whole of the music, with the exception of five pieces, altered from Arne, Smith, Battishill, Cooke & Handel, entirely new & composed, adapted and arranged, by H. R. Bishop.

Cast: HERMIA [Miss Stephens] • QUINCE [Mr. Emery] • SNOUT [Mr. Blanchard] • STARVELING • SNUG • BOTTOM [Mr. Liston] • FIRST FAIRY [Miss Matthews] • DEMETRIUS [Mr. Sinclair] • OBERON [Mr. Durusett] • SECOND FAIRY [Mrs. Liston] • THIRD FAIRY [Miss McAllpine] • FOURTH FAIRY [Miss Burrel]

The Tempest

Status: I   **Evidence:** S
Text: Reynolds, Frederic
Language: English
Premiere: London, England: Covent Garden • 1821 05 15
Play: *Tempest*
Yes: White
No: Groves V

Twelfth Night

Status: NO   **Evidence:** P
Text: Reynolds, F.
Type: Pasticcio opera   **Language:** English
Premiere: London, England: Drury Lane Theatre • 1820 11 08
Source of Premiere Information: Date from White
Play: *Twelfth Night*
Publisher: London: Goulding, D'Almaine, Potter, & Co. [vs]
Yes: White
No: SCORE, Groves V, Stieger, Wilson

Comments: Title: The Songs, Duetts and Glees, in Shakespeare's play of *Twelfth Night*, performed at the Theatre Royal, Covent Garden. The Words Selected entirely from Shakespeare's Plays, Poems and Sonnets. Composed Selected and Arranged by Henry R. Bishop. White: Covent Garden. Stieger: Covent Garden.

Cast: VIOLA [Miss M. Tree] • CURIO [Mr. Payne] • VALENTINE [Mr. Taylor] • SALANIO [Mr. Comer] • BENVOLIO [Mr. Tinney] • OLIVIA [Miss Greene] • FABIAN [Mr. Durusett] • PAGE [Master Longhurst] • CLOWN [Mr. Fancett]

The Two Gentlemen of Verona

Status: NO   **Evidence:** S
Type: Pasticcio opera   **Language:** English
Premiere: London, England: Covent Garden • 1821 11 29
Source of Premiere Information: Stieger
Play: *Two Gentlemen of Verona*
Publisher: London: Goulding, D'Almaine Potter and Co. [vs]
Yes: Squire
No: Groves V, Stieger, Wilson

Comments: Title: The Overture, Songs, Duetts,Glees and Choruses in Shakespeare's play of the *Two Gentlemen of Verona*, as performed at the Theatre Royal, Covent Garden. The Words Selected entirely from Shakespeare's Plays, Poems and Sonnets. The Music Composed (with the exception of Two Melodies) and the whole adapted and compressed from the score for the Voice and Piano Forte by Henry R. Bishop. The score gives no indication of the number of acts.

Cast: PHILIPPO [Master Longhurst] • JULIA [Miss Tree] • SYLVIA [Miss Hallande] • RODOLPHO • CARLOS • LICENZIO • UBALDO • LUIGI • [Also: Mr. Pyne, Mr. Taylor, Mr. Isaccs, Mr. Tinney]

Georges Bizet (1838-1875)

Hamlet

Status: Y   **Evidence:** S
Text: Unknown
Type: Opera project
Play: *Hamlet*
Yes: Groves V

Macbeth

Status: ?
Text: Unknown
Type: Opera Project
Play: *Macbeth*
Yes: Groves V

Boris Blacher (1903-1975)

Romeo und Julia

Status: Y   **Evidence:** P
Text: Composer
Type: Kammeroper   **Acts:** 3 pts.   **Language:** German
Premiere: Berlin, Germany: Radio • 1947 00 00
Play: *Romeo and Juliet*
Publisher: Vienna: Universal-Edition, 1950 [vs]
Yes: SCORE, LIBRETTO, Baker's, Hartnoll, Mellen, MGG, New
       Grove, Oxford

Comments: MGG: Kammer-Oratorium. New Grove: Berlin-
Zehlendorf,1947. Blom, Groves V: this is a scenic oratorio. Mellen:
opera, 1 act, Salzburg, 1950 08 09.

Cast: ROMEO (Tenor) • JULIA (Sopran) • LADY CAPULET (Alt) •
DIE AMME (Alt) • CAPULET (Bass) • TYBALT (Tenor) • BENVOLIO
(Bass) • PETER (Sopran oder Tenor) • 1. MUSIKANT (Sprechrolle) •
2. MUSIKANT (Sprechrolle) • 3. MUSIKANT (Sprechrolle) •—•
Chorus: CHOR

Ernest Bloch (1880-1959)

Macbeth

Status: Y   **Evidence:** P
Text: Fleg, Edmond [Edmond Flegenheimer] (1874-   )
Type: Lyric Drama   **Acts:** P/3 (7 scenes)
        Language: French
Premiere: Paris, France: Opéra Comique • 1910 11 30
Source of Premiere Information: Mellen
Play: *Macbeth*
Publisher: Paris: G. Astruc & Cie 1910 [vs]

Yes: SCORE, LIBRETTO, Baker's, Blom, Groves V, Hartnoll, Loewenberg, Mellen, MGG, Oxford, Squire, Stieger, Wilson

Comments: His only opera.

Cast: MACBETH (Baryton) [M. H. Albers] • MACDUFF (Basse chantante) [M. Vieuille] • BANQUO (Ténor Grave) [M. Jean Laure] • DUNCAN (Ténor) [M. Féodoroff] • MALCOLM (Ténor) [M. Mario] • LENNOX (Ténor grave) [M. Vaurs] • LE PORTIER (Baryton) [M. Delvoye] • UN VIEILLARD (Basse) [M. Payan] • UN SERVITEUR (Ténor) [M. Pasquier] • UN MURTRIER (Basse) [M. Azema] • PREMIERE APPARITION (Basse) [M. Guillamat] • LADY MACBETH (Soprano) [Mme. L. Breval] • LADY MACDUFF (Soprano) [Mme. L. Vauthrin] • PREMIERE SORCIERE (Soprano) [Mme. Duvernay] • DEUXIEME SORCIERE (Mezzo soprano) [Mme. Brohly] • TROISIEME SORCIERE (Contralto) [Mme. Charbonnel] • LE FILS DE MACDUFF (Mezzo) [Mme. Carrière] • TROISIEME APPARITION (Contralto) [Mme. Raveau] • FLÉANCE (Rôle muet) [Mme. Fayolle] • L'ENFANT DE MACDUFF [La Petite Privat] •——•
Chorus: SEIGNEURS, DAMES DE LA COUR, SOLDATS, PAYSANS, SPECTRES

Emmanuel de Bondeville (1898-   )

Antonine et Cléopatre

Status: Y   **Evidence:** P
Text: Composer
Type: Opera   **Acts:** 3   **Language:** French
Premiere: Rouen, France: Théâtre des Arts • 1974 03 08
Source of Premiere Information: Score
Play: *Antony and Cleopatra*
Publisher: Paris: Éditions Choudens, 1975 [vs]
Yes: SCORE, Mellen, Oxford

Comments: Mellen: text by F.V. Hugo. François Victor Hugo translated the text into French. Slonimsky: 1974 03 10.

Cast: CLÉOPATRE [Viorica Cortez] • OCTAVIE [Hélène Garetti] • MARC-ANTOINE [Maurice Maiewsky] • OCTAVE [Jean-Pierre Laffage] • ENOBARBUS [Jacques Mars] • CHARMION [Annick Bougant] • THYRÉUS [Bernard Malet] • DÉMÉTRIUS-SCARUS [Alain Mazzola] • DERCÉTAS, un messager [Francis Costa] • PROCULÉUS

[Michel Mamel] • MÉNAS-MARDIAN [Jacques Sazy] • DIOMEDE [Philippe Desert]

Hans von Borodcicz

König Lear

Status: ?
Text: Composer
Premiere: Brunn: Stadtheater
Source of Premiere Information: Schatz MS
Play: Lear

Renzo Bossi (1883-1965)

Volpino il Calderaio, Op. 32

Status: Y   **Evidence:** S
Text: Orsini, Luigi
Type: Commedia lirica   **Acts:** 1   **Language:** Italian
Premiere: Milan, Italy: Teatro Carcano • 1925 11 13
Source of Premiere Information: Loewenberg
Play: *Taming of the Shrew*
Publisher: Bologna: F. Bongiovanni, ca.1926 [vs]
Yes: Blom, Groves V, Hartnoll, Loewenberg, Mellen, New Grove, Oxford

Comments: The score does not mention Shakespeare.

Cast: MESSER ORLANDO (Baritono) • MONNA LIDIA (Soprano) • VOLPINO (Tenore) • 1° OSPITE (Baritono) • 2° OSPITE (Baritono) • 3° OSPITE • 1° SERVO (Tenore comico) • 2° SERVO (Baritono) • 3° SERVO (Baritono) • 4° SERVO (Basso) • 5° SERVO (Comparsa)

Pietro Bottacio

La Bisbetica Domata

Status: ?
Text: Spiritini, Massimo
Type: Opera buffa   **Acts:** 2   **Language:** Italian
Premiere: Verona , Italy: Teatre Filharmonica • 1928 03 00
Source of Premiere Information: Mellen
Play: *Taming of the Shrew*

Rutland Boughton (1878- 1960)

Againcourt

Status: NO   **Evidence:** P
Text: Composer
Type: Dramatic Scene   **Acts:** NA   **Language:** English
Premiere: Gastonbury, England: Festival • 1924 08 26
Source of Premiere Information: Score
Play: *Henry V*
Publisher: London: Joseph Williams Limited, 1926 [vs]
Yes: Blom, Groves V, Mellen, Oxford
No: SCORE

Comments: Score: *Agincourt*. A Dramatic Scene for Male Voices/Solo and Chorus/Being an adaption from/ Shakespeare/ With the addition of an/ Early English Hymn. Work performed with costumes and Stage-decoration.

Cast: KING HENRY V [Frank Mullins] • ERPINGHAM [Frederick Woodhouse] • BATES [Charles Hedges] • WILLIAMS [Leyland White] • PISTOL [Harry Carter] • GLOUSTER [Frank Phillips]

William Boyce (1710-1779)

Florizel and Perdita

Status: NO   **Evidence:** S

43

Text: Garrick, David (1717-1779)
Type: Comedy   **Language:** English
Premiere: London, England: Drury Lane? • 1756 01 21
Play: *Winter's Tale*
Yes: Groves V
No: New Grove

Comments: New Grove: music for animating the statue and 3-part song. Stieger: incidental music. Garrick's adaptation of the text.

Hermann Brandauer (1887-1962)

Caesario

Status: ?
Text: Unknown
Play: *Twelfth Night*

Comments: Never performed.

Geoffrey Brawn

At the Sign of the Angel or A Little Touch of Harry in the Night

Status: Y   **Evidence:** S
Text: Stevens, Dudley
Type: Musical   **Acts:** 2   **Language:** English
Premiere: London, England: Players' Theatre • 1975 09 24
Source of Premiere Information: Gänzl
Play: *Henry IV Parts I and II*
Yes: Gänzl

Comments: Gänzl: play-within-a-play. Characters and cast from Gänzl.

Cast: PRINCE HAL [Clifton Todd] • FALSTAFF [Robin Hunter] • NED POINS [Deryk Parkin] • BARDOLPH [Larry Drew] • PETO [Norman Warwick] • CUTHBERT CUTTER [Christopher Wren] • KING HENRY IV [John Bailey] • HOSTESS [Anthony Bateman] • FRANCIS

[Peter Landon] • PRINCE JOHN [Michael Sadler] • LORD CHIEF
JUSTICE/WORCESTER [Edward Lyon] • HOTSPUR/PISTOL [Martin
Wimbush] • DOLL/ANCIENT [Alan Reebeck] • PAGE/ANCIENT [Mike
Fields] • YORK/TRAVELLER [Richard Pescud] •
FANG/DOUGLAS/SHERRIFF [Michael Boothe] •
SNARE/TRAVELLER/ANCIENT [Warwick Evans] •
MESSENGER/SHERRIFF'S MAN [John Denton] •
CHOIRBOY/DERRICK [Adrian Barnes]

Lord Edward Benjamin Britten (1913-1976)

A Midsummer Night's Dream, Op. 64

Status: Y   **Evidence:** P
Text: Composer and Peter Pears (1910-)
Type: Opera   **Acts:** 3   **Language:** English
Premiere: Aldeburgh, England: Jubilee Hall • 1960 06 11
Source of Premiere Information: Mellen
Play: *Midsummer Night's Dream*
Publisher: London: Hawks & Son, 1960 [vs, l]
Yes: SCORE, LIBRETTO, Baker's, Hartnoll, Mellen, New Grove,
      Oxford

Comments: White: presented by the English Opera Group.

Cast: OBERON, King of the Fairies (Counter-tenor [or Contralto]) •
TYTANIA, Queen of the Fairies (Coloratura Soprano) • PUCK
(Acrobat, speaking role) • THESEUS, Duke of Athens (Bass) •
HIPPOLYTA, Queen of the Amazons, betrothed to Theseus
(Contralto) • LYSANDER, in love with Hermia (Tenor) • DEMETRIUS,
in love with Hermia (Baritone) • HERMIA, in love with Lysander
(Mezzo-soprano) • HELLENA, in love with Demetrius (Soprano) •
BOTTOM, a weaver (Bass-baritone) • QUINCE, a carpenter (Bass) •
FLUTE, a bellows-mender (Tenor) • SNUG, a joiner (Bass) • SNOUT,
a tinker (Tenor) • STARVELING, a tailor (Baritone) • COBWEB,
(Treble) • PEASEBLOSSOM, (Treble) • MUSTARDSEED, (Treble) •
MOTH, (Treble) •—• **Chorus:** FAIRIES (Trebles or Sopranos)

Neely Bruce

Pyramus and Thisbe

Status: ?
Text: Unknown
Type: Opera   **Language:** English
Premiere: University, Alabama, U.S.A.: University of Alabama
• 1967 11 14
Source of Premiere Information: Mellen
Play: *Midsummer Night's Dream*

Max Bruce (1838-1920)

Hermione, Op. 40

Status: Y   **Evidence:** P
Text: Hopffer, Karl Emil Heinrich (1838-1877)
Type: Grosse oper   **Acts:** 4   **Language:** German
Premiere: Berlin, Germany: Staatsoper • 1872 03 21
Source of Premiere Information: Loewenberg
Play: *Winter's Tale*
Publisher: Berlin: N. Simrock, 1872 [s]
Yes: SCORE, LIBRETTO, Baker's, Blom, Friedlaender, Groves V,
Hartnoll, Loewenberg, Mellen, MGG, New Grove, Oxford,
Squire, Stieger, Wilson

Cast: LEONTES, König von Sizilien (Bariton) • HERMIONE, seine
Gemahlin (Sopran) • MAMILIUS, Kind • PERDITA, Kind • PERDITA
(Sopran) • POLYXENES, König von Arkadien (Tenor) • FLORIZEL,
sein Sohn (Tenor) • IRENE, Witwe eines vertriebenen Königs, am
Hofe des Leontes weiland (Alt) • CAMILLO, ein elder Sizilianer (Bass)
• TITYRUS, ein arkadischer Schäfer (Bass) • DER OBERPRIESTER
Apollos (Bass) • FRAUEN der Hermione • EIN KERKERMEISTER
Chorus: HOFLEUTE, PRIESTER, RICHTER, WACHEN,
SCHÄFER, LANDLEUTE, VOLK, DIENER

Fernand Brumagne (1887-1939)

Le Marchand de Venise

Status: Y   **Evidence:** S
Text: Spaak, Paul
Type: Opera   **Acts:** 4   **Language:** French
Premiere: Brussels, Belgium: Théâtre Royal de la Monnaie
  • 1933 01 30
Source of Premiere Information: Mellen
Play: *Merchant of Venice*
Yes: Groves V, Hartnoll, Mellen, Oxford

Thomas Busby (1755-1838)

Fair Fugitives

Status: N   **Evidence:** S
Text: Porter, Anna Maria
Type: Musical Entertainment   **Acts:** 2   **Language:** English
Premiere: London, England: Covent Garden • 1803 05 12
Source of Premiere Information: Schatz MS
Play: *Midsummer Night's Dream*
No: Squire

Comments: Nicoll: Librettist is James Byrne. Librettist from Schatz
  MS.

Antonio Buzzolla (1815-1871)

Amleto

Status: Y   **Evidence:** P
Text: Peruzzini, Giovanni (1815-1869)
Type: Tragedia lirica   **Acts:** 4   **Language:** Italian
Premiere: Venice, Italy: Teatro La Fenice • 1848 02 24
Source of Premiere Information: Schatz MS
Play: *Hamlet*
Publisher: Milan: Ricordi, 1848 [vs]
Yes: LIBRETTO, Friedlaender, Hartnoll, Mellen, Oxford, Stieger

Comments: Hartnoll: 1847. Mellen: 1847 02 24. Score: carnevale 1847-48.

Cast: CLAUDIO, pretendente al trono di Danimarca (Baritono) [Signor Varesi] • GERTRUDE, vedova del defunto Re (Primo Soprano) [Signora De La Grange] • AMLETO, di lui figlio (Primo Tenore) [Signor Conti] • OFELIA, felia di Claudio (Seconda Donna) [Signora N.N.] • NORCESTO, Cortigiano ed amico d'Amleto (Secondo Basso) [Signor N.N.] • POLONIO, confidente di Claudio, altro Cortigiano (Secondo Tenore) [Signor N.N.] • LO SPECTRO del defunto re [N. N.] •—• **Chorus:** GRANDI DEL REGNO, CORTIGIANI, DAME, POPOLO, SEUDIERI

Antonio Cagnoni (1828-1896)

Il Re Lear

Status: Y   **Evidence:** P
Text: Ghislanzoni, Antonio (1824-1893)
Type: Tragedia lirica   **Acts:** 4/7   **Language:** Italian
Premiere: 1893 00 00
Source of Premiere Information: Stieger
Play: *Lear*
Publisher: Milan: Stabilimento Musicale, 1900 [vs]
Yes: SCORE, Groves V, Hartnoll, Oxford, Stieger

Comments: Mellen: 1890 00 00; very doubtful. Date is when composed; work not performed

Cast: LEAR, Re di Brettagna (Baritono) • Cordelia (Soprano) • REGANA (Mezzo-Soprano) • IL MATTO (Soprano) • EDGARO, figlio di Gloster (1.° Tenore) • IL CONTE DI GLOSTER (1.° Basso) • GONERILLA (Comprimaria) • IL DUCA DI CORNOVAGLIA (2.° Tenore) • IL CONTE DI KENT (2.° Basso) • EDMONDO (3.° Basso) • IL DUCA DI BORGOGNA (N. N.) • IL DUCA DI ALBANIA (N. N.) •—• **Chorus:** CAVALIERI, MESSI, UFFICIALI, DAMIGELLE, POPOLO

Antonio Caldara (1670-1736)

Cajo Marzio Coriolano

Status: N   **Evidence:** S
Text: Pariati, Pietro (1665-1733)
Type: Opera   **Language:** Italian
Premiere: Vienna, Austria: Theater der Favorita • 1717 08 28
Source of Premiere Information: Stieger
Play: *Coriolanus*
No: Friedlaender

Comments: Mellen: Hoftheater.

François van Campenhout (1779-1848)

Gillette de Narbonne

Status: ?
Text: Unknown
Type: Opera   **Acts:** 3
Play: *All's Well That Ends Well*

Comments: Manferrari: composer's dates (1780-1845). Stieger: not performed.

Conrado del Campo y Zabaleta
[Conrado del Campo] (1879-1953)

Los Amantes de Verona

Status: Y   **Evidence:** S
Text: Unknown
Type: Opera   **Acts:** 4   **Language:** Spanish
Premiere: Madrid?, Spain • 1909 00 00
Play: *Romeo and Juliet*
Publisher: New Grove gives some information.
Yes: Baker's, Blom, Groves V, Hartnoll, Mellen, Oxford, Stieger

Comments: Baker's, Stieger: title is *Romeo y Julieta*. Stieger: 1916 00 00. Mellen: date is when composed.

Luigi Canepá (1849-1919)

Riccardo III

Status: N   **Evidence:** P
Text: Fulgonio, Fulvio (1832-1904)
Type: Dramma lirico   **Acts:** 4   **Language:** Italian
Premiere: Milan, Italy: Teatro Carcano • 1879 11 10
Source of Premiere Information: Year and place from libretto. Day from Stieger.
Play: *Richard III*
Yes: Friedlaender, Hartnoll, Oxford, Stieger, Wilson
No: LIBRETTO, Garlington, Mellen

Comments: Introductory material by the librettist claims that he has not modeled his libretto on the famous play of Shakespeare, as some journalists had asserted, but on a drama by Victor Séjour. Friedlaender: not published.

Cast: RICARDO, Re [sig. Ludovico Buti] • RISMONDO, Principe [Sig. Franco De-Angelis] • SCROOP, Raul di Fulckes [Sig. Davide Majocchi] • RUTLANDO, Conf. di Riccardo [Sig. Giuseppe Ceresa] • ELISABETTA, Regina madre [Sig. Emilia Maggiu Trapani] • ELISABETTA, di lei Figlia [Sig. Francesca Prevost] •—•
Chorus: CAVALIERE, MARINAI, SOLDATI, DAME, POPOLANE ED ANCELLE

Pietro Canonica (1869-   )

Miranda

Status: Y   **Evidence:** P
Text: Bernardi, Carlo
Type: Visione lirico   **Acts:** 3   **Language:** Italian
Premiere: San Remo, Italy: Teatro Casino Municipale • 1937 03 05
Source of Premiere Information: Mellen
Play: *Tempest*

Publisher: Milan: Carisch S. A., 1937 [vs]
Yes: SCORE, LIBRETTO, Oxford

Comments: Stieger: title is *The Tempest.* Mellen: title is *Mirando.*

Cast: PROSPERO, Legittimo e spodestato Duca di Milano
(Baritono) • MIRANDA, Sua figlia (Soprano) • ANTONIO, Fratello di
Prospero, Usurpatore del Ducato di Milano (Baritono) • ALONSO, Re
di Napoli (Basso) • SEBASTIANO, Suo fratello (Baritono) •
FERDINANDO, Figlió del Re di Napoli (Basso) • GONZALO, Vecchio
consigliere del Re di Napoli (Basso) • STEFANO, Dispensiere della
nave naufragata (Tenore) • CALIBANO, Essere mostruoso (Tenore) •
ARIELE, Spirito aereo (Soprano) •—• **Chorus:** NAUFRAGHI, SILFI

Giovanni Maria Capelli [Capello] (1648-1726)

Rosalinda [Erginia Mascherata]

Status: N   **Evidence:** S
Text: Marchi, Antonio
Type: Opéra italien   **Acts:** 3   **Language:** Italian
Premiere: Venice, Italy: Teatro di San Angelo • 1692 00 00
Source of Premiere Information: Mellen
Play: *As You Like It*
No: Squire

Comments: Squire: 1693 00 00. Clément: Cet opéra fut joué à
Rovigo sous le titre de *Ergina Mascherata*, in 1717.

Michele Enrico Carafa di Colobrano [Michel Carafa] (1787-1872) and Aimé Ambroise Simon Leborne (1797-1866)

La Violette, ou Gérard de Nevers

Status: N   **Evidence:** P
Text: Planard, François Antoine Eugène de (178?-1853)
Type: Opéra-comique   **Acts:** 3   **Language:** French
Premiere: Paris, France: Opéra Comique • 1828 10 07

Source of Premiere Information: Libretto
Play: *Twelfth Night*
Publisher: Paris: Me. Ve. Leduc,1829? [s]
No: SCORE, LIBRETTO, Clément, Schatz MS

Comments: It is based on Tressan's novel, *Gérard de Nevers*.
Mellen: text by Planard with Leborne.

Cast: GÉRARD, jeune et riche chevalier [M. Chollet] • EURIANT,
jeune orpheline, sa cousine [Mille Prévost] • LE COMTE DE
FORETZ, amoureux d'Euriant [M. Huet] • LE CONNÉTABLE DE
FRANCE, vieux guerrier [M. Boullard] • RICHARDET, jardinier du
château de Gérard [M. Féréol] • MARGUERITE, jeune fille [Mme
Gigaut] •—• **Chorus:** BARONS, CHEVALIERS, ÉCUYERS, PAGES
ET DAMES DE LA COUR, VALETS, VILLAGEOIS ET
VILLAGEOISES

Giuseppe Carcani (1703-1779)

Ambleto

Status: N   **Evidence:** P
Text: Zeno, Apostolo (1668-1750) and Pietro Pariati (1665-1733)
Type: Dramma per musica   **Acts:** 3   **Language:** Italian
Premiere: Venice, Italy: Theatro di Sant' Angelo • 1741 12 26
Source of Premiere Information: Year and place from libretto.
         Day from Stieger.
Play: *Hamlet*
Yes: Friedlaender
No: LIBRETTO

Comments: Taken from Saxo Grammaticus. LIBRETTO: carnovale
dell anno MDCCXLII. Mellen: composer is Carcano; Venice
(t. Sant'Angelo) 1742 12 26.

Cast: FENGONE, Tiranno di Dannimarca [Il Sig. Felice Novelli] •
GERILDA, Moglie di Fengone, e Madre di Amleto [La Sig. Margherita
Chimenti] • AMBLETO, Erede legittimo del Regno, amante di
Veremonda [Il Sig. Giuseppe Bracceschi] • VEREMONDA,
Principessa di Allanda, amante di Ambleto [La Sig. Giacinta Forcellini]
• VALDEMARO, Generale del Regno [Il Sig. Stefano Leonardi] •

SIFFRIDO, Confidente di Fengone, e Capitano delle guardie Reali
[La Sig. Rosalba Buini]

M. Carl [pseud. Carlo]

Julius Caesar

Status: Y   **Evidence:** S
Text: Unknown
Premiere: 1870 00 00 c.
Play: *Julius Caesar*
Yes: Friedlaender

Comments: Friedlaender: In den 70er Jahren des 19.
Jahrhunderts hat der Gothaer Hofmusikus M. Carl (pseudonym:
Carlo) einen *Julius Cäsar*, Oper nach Shakespeare komponiert. Das
Werk ist nicht zur Aufführung gelangt, indessen sind die Ouverture
und einzelne Nummern der Oper in einem Arrangement für
Militärmusik im Drucke erschienen.

Luigi Carlini

La Gioventù di Enrico V

Status: ?
Text: Romani, Felice (1788-1865)
Type: Dramma per musica   **Acts:** 2   **Language:** Italian
Premiere: Naples, Italy: Teatro Nuovo • 1819 00 00
Source of Premiere Information: Libretto
Play: *Henry IV*

Comments: Librettist from Riemann. Stieger: the libretto is "nach
Duval [a translator of Shakespeare]." Manferrari: librettist is Tarducci
"dr. sem. 2 a., Napoli, Tr. Nuovo, primavera 1819. No librettist is
mentioned in libretto. This libretto and that of Mercandante's *Enrico*,
which was written by Romani, are not the same. Schatz MS:
spring 1819.

Cast: IL PRINCIPE ENRICO [Signor Giacomo Guglieli] • IL CONTE
ROCESTER [Signor Antonio Tamburrini] • EDUARDO [Signor Luigi

de Rosa] • CAPITANO COOP [Signor Gennaro Luzio il giovane] •
BETTINA [Signora Corolina Brizzi] • MILADY CLARA [Signora Luigia
Romitz] • WILLIAM, Cameriere del Principe •——•
Chorus: CORTIGIANI, GARZONI DI TAVERNA

Charles Frederick Carlson (1875-1937)

Merchant of Venice

Status: Y   **Evidence:** S
Text: Composer
Language: English
Premiere: 1920 00 00
Play: *Merchant of Venice*
Yes: Mellen, Oxford

Frank Osmond Carr (1858-   )

In Town

Status: Y   **Evidence:** S
Text: Ross, Adrian and James Leader
Type: Musical comedy   **Acts:** 2   **Language:** English
Premiere: London, England: Prince of Wales Theatre • 1892 10 15
Source of Premiere Information: Gänzl
Play: *Romeo and Juliet*
Publisher: London: Joseph Williams, 1892 [vs].
Yes: Gänzl

Comments: Gänzl: the show-within-a-show is a burlesque of
Romeo and Juliet. Score does not mention Shakespeare.
Characters and cast from Gänzl.

Cast: CAPTAIN ARTHUR CODDINGTON [Arthur Roberts/W. Louis
Bradfield] • THE DUKE OF DUFFSHIRE [Eric Lewis] • LORD
CLANSIDE [Phyllis Broughton/Millie Hylton] • LORD ALEXANDER
KINCADDIE [Douglas Patrick] • REV. SAMUEL HOPKINS [Ernest
Bantock/Frederick Vaughan] • BENOLI [Harry Grattan/Henry N.
Wenman/Ernest Cosham/George Minshull] • HOFFMAN [Fritz
Rimma] • FRITZ [Edgar Frazer/c. Wingrove] • MR. DRIVER [F. Lovell] •

SHRIMP, a call-boy [Jenny Rogers/Florence Thropp/Edmund Payne]
• BLOGGINS [Frederick Vaughan/Fred Farleigh/Sidney Watson] •
LADY GWENDOLINE [Belle Harcourt/Cate Cutler/Louie Pounds] •
LADY EVANGELINE [Daisy Gilpin] • FLO FANSHAWE [Sylvia
Grey/Nellie Simmonds] • BOB [Maud Hobson/Carrie Benton] • BILLIE
[Blanche Massey] • LOTTIE[Hetty Hamer/Florence Henderson] •
LILLIE [Nellie Simmons] • CLARA [Kate Cannon] • THE DUCHESS
OF DUFFSHIRE [Maria Davis] • KITTY HETHERTON Florence St
John/Kate Cutler (Louie Pounds)] • FANNY [Florence Lloyd] •
MOLLY [Florence Henderson/Ethel Earle] • MARIE [Louie
Pounds/Maud Wilmot] • EVA [Topsy Sinden • LETTY [Rose
Batchelor] • NELLIE [Violet Dene] • PAS DE QUATRE GIRLS [Topsy
Sinden, Adelaide Astor, Bob Robina, Violet Dene]

Lodovico Luigi Caruso (1754-1822)

Amleto

Status: Y   **Evidence:** S
Text: Foppa, Giuseppe Maria (1760-1845)
Type: Dramma per musica   **Acts:** 2   **Language:** Italian
Premiere: Florence, Italy: Teatro degl' Immobili in via della Pergola
    • 1789 12 27
Source of Premiere Information: Mellen
Play: *Hamlet*
Yes: Friedlaender, Garlington, Groves V, Hartnoll, Mellen, Oxford,
    Stieger

Comments: Mellen: text by F. Dosseno; same librettist as
Andreozzi's *Amleto* [Mellen gives G. M. Foppa as the librettist for
Andreozzi's *Amleto*]. Manferrari: librettist is F. Dorseno Aborigine
Biturgiense, P. A.; Garlington: Pietro Dorseno (not cited), and
introductory material gives Shakespeare's play equal billing with a
play of the same title by Ducis. [Dulcis is a translator of Shakespeare.]

Cast: AMLETO [Vincent Bortolini] • AMALIA [Teresa Saporiti] •
GELTRUDA [Rosa Catenacci] • CLAUDIO [Gio. Giustiniani] •
NORCETE [Antonio Balelli] • VOLTEMARO [Giuseppe Giovi]

La Tempesta

Status: Y   **Evidence:** S
Text: Unknown
Type: Comedia   **Acts:** 2   **Language:** Italian
Premiere: Naples, Italy: Teatro Nuovo • 1799 00 00
Source of Premiere Information: Stieger
Play: *Tempest*
Yes: Hartnoll, Oxford, Squire, Stieger

Comments: Date: spring.

Mario Castelnuovo-Tedesco (1895-1968)

Il Mercante di Venezia, Op. 181

Status: Y   **Evidence:** S
Text: Composer
Type: Opera   **Acts:** 3   **Language:** Italian
Premiere: Florence, Italy: Maggio Musicale • 1961 05 25
Play: *Merchant of Venice*
Publisher: Milan: G. Ricordi, 1961 [vs, l]
Yes: SCORE, LIBRETTO, Baker's, Hartnoll, Mellen, New Grove,
    Oxford

Comments: Won 1st prize at the International Competition at La
Scala. Mellen: composed 1933, t. Pergola.

Cast: ANTONIO, un mercante di Venezia (Baritono) • BASSANIO,
amico suo, innamorato di Porzia (Baritono) • GRAZIANO, amico di
Antonio e di Bassanio (Baritono) • LORENZO, innamorato di Gessica
(Tenore) • SHYLOCK, un ricco Ebreo (Basso) • IL DOGE DI VENEZIA
(Basso) • BALDASSARRE, un servo di Porzia (Tenore) • TUBAL, un
Ebreo, amico di Shylock (Tenore) • PORZIA, una ricca ereditiera
(Mezzo-Soprano) • NERISSA, la sua damigella (Soprano-leggero) •
GESSICA, figlia di Shylock (Soprano lirico) • IL PRINCIPE DEL
MAROCCO (Mimo) • IL PRINCIPE DI ARAGONA (Mimo) •——•
Chorus: I VICINI DI SHYLOCK, SIGNORI DI VENEZIA, MAGISTRATI
DELLA CORTE DI GIUSTIZIA, SERVITORI DI PORZIA ECC.

Tutto e bène quello che finisce bène, Op. 182

Status: Y   **Evidence:** S
Text: Composer
Language: Italian
Premiere: 1958 00 00
Play: *All's Well That Ends Well*
Yes: Baker's, Hartnoll, Mellen, New Groves, Oxford

Comments: 1958 is the date composed. Baker's:1959.
Unperformed.

Lorenzo Cattani (c.1620-c.1695)

Cajo Marzio Coriolano

Status: N   **Evidence:** S
Text: Moniglia, Giovanni Andrea
Type: Opera   **Acts:** 3   **Language:** Italian
Premiere: Florence, Italy: Accademia di Casino • 1686 00 00
Source of Premiere Information: Stieger
Play: *Coriolanus*
No: Friedlaender

Comments: Friedlaender: Pisa, 1700. Mellen: summer 1685.

Pietro Francesco Cavalli [Pier Francesco Calletti-Bruni] (1602-1676)

Coriolano

Status: N   **Evidence:** S
Text: Ivanovich, Christoforo
Type: Drama   **Acts:** 3   **Language:** Italian
Premiere: Piacenza, Italy: Teatro Ducale • 1669 00 00
Source of Premiere Information: Stieger
Play: *Coriolanus*
No: Friedlaender

Comments: Friedlaender: Parma, 1660. Characters and cast from Sartori.

Cast: CORIOLANO [Gio. Batt. Pizzala] • SILENIO [D. Giorgio Martinelli] • TITURIO [Sebastiano Cioni] • SESTO FURIO [Antonio Formenti] • APPIO CLAUDIO [Carlo Andrea Clerici] • VITELLIO [Carlo Antonio Riccardi] • EMILIO [Alesandro Bifolchi] • MARTIA [Antonia Coresi] • VOLUNNIA [Anna Caterina Bertini] • EMILIA [Caterrina Forti di 10 anni] • VETTURIA [Filippo Bombaglia, detto il Monello] • MOMERCO [D. Tommaso Bovio]

Ruperto Chapí y Lorente (1851-1909)

La Tempestad

Status: N   **Evidence:** P
Text: Ramos Carrión, Miguel (1845-1915)
Type: Melodrama fantástico [zarzuela]   **Acts:** 3
        Language: Spanish
Premiere: Madrid, Spain: Teatro de la Jovellanos • 1882 03 11
Source of Premiere Information: Loewenberg
Play: *Tempest*
Publisher: Madrid: Unión Musical española, 1931 [vs]
No: LIBRETTO, Loewenberg, Mellen, New Grove, Squire

Comments: New Grove, Mellen, Loewenberg: founded on Erckmann-Chatrian's *Le Juif Polonais [El Judío Polaco]*. Stieger: t. Zarzuela. Mellen: t. Tivoli.

Cast: ANGELA [Sra. Cortése de Pedral] • ROBERTO [Sra. Franco de Salas] • MARGARITA [Sra. Rivas] • UNA ALDEANA [Srta. González (D.a Elisa)] • SIMON [Sr. Ferrer] • BELTRAN [Sr. Berges] • MATEO [Sr. Orejón] • EL JUEZ [Sr. Subirá] • EL PROCURADOR [Sr. Belloc] • UN PESCADOR [Sr. Jiménez] • MARINERO 1.° [Sr. Barragán] • IDEM 2.° [Sr. Vidal]

Tom Chatburn

The Gay Venetians

Status: Y   **Evidence:** S
Text: Composer
Type: Musical comedy   **Language:** English
Premiere: Derby, England: Hippodrome • 1955 04 04
Source of Premiere Information: Gänzl
Play: *Merchant of Venice*
Yes: Gänzl

Comments: Characters and cast from Gänzl.

Cast: LORENZO [Richard Morgan] • GOBBO [Bruce Gordon] •
ANTONIO [Gerald Deacon] • BASSANIO [William Dickie] • GRATIANO
[Frank Lawless] • PRINCE OF MOROCCO [Dale Williams] • PRINCE
OF ARAGON [Douglas Thomson] • DUKE OF VENICE [C. Denier
Warren] • NERISSA [Sara Gregory] • PORTIA [Linda Gray] •
SHYLOCK [Meier Tzelniker] • PORTIA'S MAID [Jane Martin] •
JESSICA [Helen Hurst] • SALANIO [Roy Desmond] • LISA [Mary
Dean] • SALARINO [Graham Jones] • LUCRETIA [Phoebe Lewis] •
LEONARDO [Graham Ross] • MESSENGER [James Culliford] • GINA
[Joyce Wording] • FIAMETTA [Elspeth Ross] • DUCAL COURT
USHER [Don Carson] • STEPHANO [Lawrence Richardson]

Hippolyte-André-Jean-Baptiste Chélard (1789-1861)

Macbeth

Status: Y   **Evidence:** P
Text: Rougêt de Lisle, Claude Joseph (1760-1836) and
        Augustin Hix
Type: Tragédie lyrique   **Acts:** 3   **Language:** French
Premiere: Paris, France: Théâtre de l'Academie royale de musique,
        Salle provisoire de la rue Le Peletier • 1827 06 29
Source of Premiere Information: Loewenberg
Play: *Macbeth*
Publisher: Munich: Theodor Lachner, 1828 [vs]
Yes: SCORE, Blom, Friedlaender, Groves V, Hartnoll, Loewenberg,
        Mellen, Oxford, Squire, Stieger, Wilson

Comments: Hix not mentioned in the libretto. Loewenberg lists under Shakespeare in index but says nothing about Shakespeare in main entry. Libretto does not mention Shakespeare.

Cast: DUNCAN (Basse) [M. Dabadie] • MACBETH (Basse) [M. Dérivis] • DOUGLAS, jeune lord destiné a la main de Moïna (Ténor) [M. Adolphe Nourrit] • LENOX [M. Bonel] • SEYTON, (Ténor) officier ecossais [M. Trevaax] • TROIS BARDES [MM. Massol, Ferd. Prévôt, Bouvenne] • LE CONNÉTABLE, du château d'Inverness [M. Pouilley] • NORMANN, soldat [M. Pouilley] • LUDOVIC, agent de lady Macbeth [M. Ferd. Prévôt] • MOINA, fille de Duncan (Soprano) [Mme. Cinti] • LADY MACBETH (Soprano) [Mme. Dabadie] • LADY NORFOLK [Mme. Sévres] • ELSIE, sorcieres (Soprano) [Mme. Javurek] • NONA, sorcieres (Soprano) [Mme. Quiney] • GROEME, sorcieres (Soprano) [Mme. Le Brun] •—• **Chorus:** LORDS, JEUNES FILLES, SUITE DE DOUGLAS, SUITES DE MOINA ET DE LADY MACBETH, OFFICIERS, PAGES DE MACBETH, ETC.

Robert Chignell

Romeo and Juliet

Status: Y   **Evidence:** S
Text: Unknown
Type: Opera
Premiere: 191? 00 00
Play: *Romeo and Juliet*
Yes: Stieger, Northouse

Antony Choudens (1849-1902)

Cymbeline

Status: ?
Text: Meilhac, Henri
Type: Comedia   **Acts:** 2
Premiere: Paris, France: Théâtre Lyrique • 1884 00 00
Play: *Cymbeline*

Comments: Friedlaender: 1879 00 00 (composed); not performed.
Date: spring.

Ján Cikker (1911-   )

Coriolanus

Status: Y   **Evidence:** P
Text: Composer
Type: Opera   **Acts:** 3   **Language:** Czech
Premiere: Prague, Czechoslovakia: Narodni Divádlo • 1974 03 21
Play: *Coriolanus*
Publisher: Bratislava: Slovensky Hudobny Fond, 1973 [vs]
Yes: SCORE, Baker's, Mellen, Oxford

Comments: Mellen: 1974 05 21.

Cast: ROMANS: • CAIUS MARCIUS, afterward CORIOLANUS
(Baritone) • MENENIUS AGRIPPA, friend to Coriolanus (Bass) •
COMINIUS, general against the Volscians (Tenor) • EDIL, messenger
of the Senate (Spoken role) • SICINIUS, tribune of the people
(Tenor) • BRUTUS, tribune of the people (Baritone) • VOLUMNIA,
mother to Coriolanus (Alto) • VIRGILIA, wife to Coriolanus (Soprano) •
YOUNG MARCIUS, son to Coriolanus (No role) • FIRST CITIZEN,
Plebeian (Tenor) • SECOND CITIZEN, Plebeian (Baritone) • THIRD
CITIZEN, Plebeian (Bass) • FOURTH CITIZEN, Plebeian (Bass) •
FIFTH CITIZEN, Plebeian (Tenor) • VOLSCIANS: • TULLUS
AUFIDIUS, general of the Volscians (Tenor) • SENATOR (Baritone) •
YOUNG WOMAN (Soprano) • FIRST SERVING WOMAN to Aufidius
(Soprano) • SECOND SERVING WOMAN to Aufidius (Mezzo-
Soprano) • MAN-SERVANT (Tenor) •—• **Chorus:** ROMANS AND
VOLSCIANS, PATRICIANS AND PLEBEIANS, SENATORS,
AEDILES, SOLDIERS, WOMEN AND GIRLS, PRIESTS

Domenico Nicola Cimarosa [Cimmarosa] (1749-1801)

Cajo Mario

Status: ?
Text: Roccaforte, Gaetano
Type: Dramma per musica   **Acts:** 3   **Language:** Italian
Premiere: Rome, Italy: Teatro Dame • 1780 01 00
Source of Premiere Information: Mellen
Play: *Coriolanus*

Comments: Schatz MS: carnevale 1780.

Philip Greeley Clapp (1888-1954)

The Taming of the Shrew

Status: Y   **Evidence:** S
Text: Unknown
Language: English
Premiere: 1948 00 00
Play: *Taming of the Shrew*
Yes: Groves V, Hartnoll, New Groves, Oxford

Comments: Date is when composed. Never performed.

James Siree Hamilton Clarke (1840-1912)

Merchant of Venice

Status: NO   **Evidence:** P
Language: English
Premiere: London, England: Lyceum Theatre • 1879 11 01
Source of Premiere Information: Score
Play: *Merchant of Venice*
Publisher: London: J. B. Cramer & Co., 1879
No: SCORE, Groves V, Stieger

Comments: Groves V: wrote music to Hamlet (1878), *The Merchant of Venice* (1879), *King Lear* (1892), and *Cymbeline* (1896) which it lists as incidental music. Stieger: incidental music. Score: Music to the *Merchant of Venice*.

Jeremiah Clarke (1669?-1707)

Titus Andronicus

Status: I   **Evidence:** S
Text: Ravenscroft, E.
Premiere: 1687 00 00
Source of Premiere Information: Stieger
Play: *Titus Andronicus*
Yes: New Groves
No: Groves V, Stieger

Comments: Groves V, Stieger: music for a play.

Jean Claudric [pseu. of Jean Bacri] (1930-   )

Othello Story

Status: ?
Text: Vidalin, Maurice
Type: Comédie Musicale   **Language:** French
Premiere: 1972 00 00
Play: *Othello*
Publisher: Paris: Sté. des Nouvelles Editions EDDIE BARCLAY
        [1972]

Comments: Found one song from work at US:Wc: "La Bouteille. " Librettist may only be for this selection.

Lawrance Arthur Collingwood (1887-1982)

Macbeth

Status: Y   **Evidence:** S
Text: Composer
Type: Opera   **Acts:** 3   **Language:** English
Premiere: London, England: Sadler's Wells Theatre • 1934 04 12
Source of Premiere Information: Loewenberg
Play: *Macbeth*
Yes: Blom, Groves V, Hartnoll, Loewenberg, Mellen, Oxford,
    Stieger, Northouse, White

Comments: New Grove: 1937. Stieger: 1925. Mellen: 1927 11
10, in concert London (Queen's Hall). Dent: 1937. Northouse:
1927 11 12.

Paolo Conte (1890-   )

Shakespeare, the Playmaker

Status: A P
Text: Unknown
Type: s.   **Acts:** 1
Premiere: New York, U.S.A.: Tr. d. Opera • 1916 06 00
Play: Other

Comments: Manferrari: pel centenario di Shakespeare.

Nicolò Conti

Cajo Marzio Coriolano [Marzio Coriolano]

Status: ?
Text: Pariati, Pietro (1665-1733)
Type: Opera   **Language:** Italian
Premiere: Napels, Italy: Teatro s. Bartolomeo • 1734 00 00
Source of Premiere Information: Stieger
Play: *Coriolanus*

Comments: Schatz MS, Stieger: Carnevale.

Thomas Simpson Cooke [Tom Cooke] (1782-1848)

Malvina

Status: ?
Text: Macfarren, George, Sr.
Type: National ballad opera   **Acts:** 3   **Language:** English
Premiere: London, England: Drury Lane Theatre • 1826 01 28
Source of Premiere Information: Mellen
Play: *All's Well That Ends Well*
Publisher: London: Goulding and D'Almaine1826? [vs].

Comments: Title: Overture, songs, duets, glees, marches and ballet in the national ballad opera of *Malvina*. The poetry by G. MacFarren . . . . Score and libretto do not mention Shakespeare. Stieger: 1826 02 04.

Cast: FINGAL, King of Scotland [Mr. Powell] • OSCAR, his Son [Mr. Sinclair] • TOSCAR, Father of Malvina [Mr. Pope] • STARNO, his Warder [Mr. Bedford] • RURO, Oscar's Attendant [Mr. Fitzwilliam] • SHILRIC, a Pedlar [Mr. Harley] • HUGIN, Page to the King [Mr. Honnor] • TRAVELLERS [Mr. Yarnold, Mr. Plumstead] • BARDS AND MINSTRELS [Messrs. G. Smith, Nicoll, Eames, Gibbon, Goodson, Nelson, Povey, Read, Randall, Sheriff, Vaughan, &c.] • CATHLIN, her Attendant [Miss Povey] • FEMALE BARDS [Mesdms. Tennant, Southwell, Gould, Gaskill, C. Carr, G. Carr, Munro, &c.] • PRINCIPAL DANCERS [Mr. and Mrs. Noble] • CATHULLIN, Lord of Ulster [Mr. Horn] • MORVEN, Irish Chieftain [Mr. Archer] • CONLATH, Irish Chieftain [Mr. Wallack] • MORNA [Miss Kelly] •—
Chorus: LEADERS OF THE SCOTTISH ARMY, STANDARD BEARERS, VASSALS, PEASANTS, IRISH CHIEFS, ENSIGNS, SOLDIERS, ETC.

Oberon, or The Charmed Horn

Status: ?
Text: Unknown
Type: Burletta   **Language:** English
Premiere: London, England: Drury Lane Theatre • 1826 00 00

Source of Premiere Information: Stieger
Play: *Midsummer Night's Dream*

Thomas Simpson Cooke [Tom Cooke] (1782-1848) and John Braham [Abraham] (1774-1856) and Others

The Taming of the Shrew

Status: I   **Evidence:** S
Text: Unknown
Type: Operatic Farce   **Language:** English
Premiere: London, England: Drury Lane Theatre • 1828 05 14
Play: *Taming of the Shrew*
Yes: Hartnoll, Oxford, Wilson, White
No: Groves V

Comments: New Grove: his theatrical music, composed as it was for operas which were essentially plays intersperced with songs. Stieger: Lyceum Theater. White: this pasticcio score including borrowings from Rossini, Mercadante, and Sir John Stevenson. Stieger: 1828, Lyceum.

Michael Andrew Angus Costa (1808-1884)

Malvina

Status: ?
Text: Schmidt, Giovanni
Type: Dramma per musica   **Acts:** 2   **Language:** Italian
Premiere: Naples, Italy: Teatro di San Carlo • 1829 02 07
Source of Premiere Information: Schatz MS
Play: *All's Well That Ends Well*

Comments: Mellen: composer's nom de plume is Michele Andrea Agniello.

Giulio Cottrau (1831-1916)

Cordelia [Re Lear]

Status: Y   **Evidence:** P
Text: Composer
Type: Opera seria   **Acts:** 2   **Language:** Italian
Premiere: Padua, Italy: Teatro del Corso • 1913 08 24
Play: *Lear*
Publisher: Rome: Presso l'autore, 1913? [vs]
Yes: SCORE, Hartnoll, Mellen, Oxford, Stieger

Comments: Manferrari, Mellen, Stieger: 1913 08 26.

Cast: LEAR • CORDELIA • GONERILLA • REGANA • IL RE DEI FRANCHI E KENT

Pericle re di Tiro

Status: Y   **Evidence:** P
Text: Composer
Type: Dramma   **Acts:** 1 (Porlogue and 4 scenes)
   Language: Italian
Premiere: 1915 00 00
Play: *Pericles, Prince of Tyre*
Publisher: Rome: Stamp. mus. C. Carocci, c.1915 [vs]
Yes: SCORE, Hartnoll, Mellen, Oxford
Comments: Composed for London c. 1915 but not performed.
Manferrari: performed at Covent Garden in 1916. Date is when composed.

Cast: PERICLE • ELICANO • SIMONIDE • TAISA • MARINA •
LASIMACO • CERIMONE • LICORIDA • DIANA • ESCANO •—•
Chorus: CHORUS

Girolamo Crescentini (1762-1846)?

Roméo et Juliette

Status: ?
Text: Unknown
Play: *Romeo and Juliet*

Comments: New Grove: he composed the aria "Ombra adorata aspetta" which he inserted into Zingarelli's *Giulietta e Romeo*. Composer may be Antonio Crescenti.

Donna Cribari

Pop

Status: Y   **Evidence:** S
Text: Schiff, Larry and Chuck Knull (book and lyrics)
Type: Broadway Show   **Language:** English
Premiere: New York, U.S.A.: Players Theater • 1974 04 03
Source of Premiere Information: Simas
Play: *Lear*
Yes: Green, Simas

Hugo Daffner (1882-1936)

Macbeth

Status: Y   **Evidence:** S
Text: Unknown
Type: Opera   **Language:** German
Premiere: 1930 00 00
Source of Premiere Information: Mellen
Play: *Macbeth*
Yes: Mellen, Oxford

Comments: Mellen: date is when composed. Not performed.

Nicolas Dalayrac (1753-1809)

Tout pour l'amour ou Roméo et Juliette

Status: Y   **Evidence:** S
Text: Boutet de Monvel, Jaques Marie (1749-1812)
Type: Opéra comique   **Acts:** 4   **Language:** French
Premiere: Paris, France: Opéra Comique, rue Favart • 1792 07 06
Source of Preniere Information: Stieger
Play: *Romeo and Juliet*
Yes: Blom, Dent, Friedlaender, Groves V, Hartnoll, Mellen, Oxford,
        Squire, Stieger

Comments: Groves V: Opera has a happy ending. Riemann: 1762
07 06. Stieger: theater is Comédie Ital. Manferrari gives info. as
above. Schatz MS: opera in 3 acts. Mellen: 1792 07 07.
Friedlaender: vocal score published in Paris in 1793.

Leopold Damrosch (1832-1885)

Romeo und Julia

Status: Y   **Evidence:** S
Text: Unknown
Type: Oper   **Acts:** 4   **Language:** German
Premiere: Wroclaw [Breslau], Poland • 1862 00 00
Play: *Romeo and Juliet*
Yes: Friedlaender

Comments: Friedlaender: not published. Walter Damrosch reports
in *My Musical Life* (p. 36) that his father had composed an opera on
Shakespeare's *Romeo and Juliet* in the old Weimar days which he
had subsequently destroyed because he was dissatisfied with it.

Franz Danzi

Malvina [Die Wolfsjagd]

Status: ?
Text: Römer
Type: Singspiel   **Language:** German
Premiere: Karlsruhe, Germany: Hoftheater • 1814 12 26
Source of Premiere Information: Schatz MS
Play: *All's Well That Ends Well*

Comments: Mellen: Malwine, 1814 12 20.

Adolphe Isaac David (1842-1897)

L' Orage

Status: ?
Text: Millanvoye, Bertrand Casimir (-1913) and
          Paul Eudel (1837-   )
Type: Monomime   **Acts:** 1
Premiere: Paris, France: Bodinière • 1893 11 29
Source of Premiere Information: Stieger
Play: *Tempest*
Publisher: Paris: Henri Tellier [1894]

Félicien César David (1810-1876)

Le Saphir or Tout est bien, qui finit bien

Status: Y   **Evidence:** S
Text: Leuven, Adolphe de (1803-1884), Michel Florentin Carré
          (1819-1872), and T. Hadot
Type: Opéra-comique   **Acts:** 3   **Language:** French
Premiere: Paris, France: Théâtre de l'Opéra Comique • 1865 03 08
Source of Premiere Information: Score
Play: *All's Well That Ends Well*
Publisher: Paris: E. et A. Girod [vs]
Yes: Mellen, Oxford, Schatz MS

Comments: Neither the score or the libretto mention Shakespeare.

Cast: GASTON (1er Tenor) [M. Montaubry] • PAROLE (1re Basse chantante ou Baryton) [M. Gourdin] • HERMINE (Soprano 1re chanteuse) [Mme. Cico] • FIAMMETTA (Dugazon) [Mme. Girard] • LA REINE (Soprano) [Mme. Baretti] • OLIVER (Soprano 2me chanteuse [Mme. Tual] • LUCREZIA (Duègne) [Mme. Revilly]

Auguste de Boeck [De Boeck] (1865-1937)

Een Winternachtsdroom

Status: Y   **Evidence:** S
Text: Du Catillon, Léonce
Type: Zangspel   **Acts:** Voorspel/2   **Language:** Flemish
Premiere: Antwerp, Belgium: Nederlandsch Lyrisch Tooneel
    • 1902 12 20
Source of Premiere Information: Mellen
Play: *Midsummer Night's Dream*
Publisher: Bruxelles: Breitkoph & Härtel
Yes: Oxford

Comments: Manferrari: com. 1 a., Anversa, Tr. dell' Opera Fiamminga, gennaio 1903. Baker's: *Winternachtsdroom (Le Songe d'une nuit d'hiver;* 1903*)*

Cast: PRINSES ZONNESTRALL (Sop) [Mej. Van Elsacker] • HEKS KALLERKAAI (Mezzo) [Mej. Furth] • FREJA (Sop) [Mej. Van Canter] • KONING DAGERAAD (Tenor) [Mr. K. Berkmans] • VRIEZEMAN (Bariton) [Mr. Wauquier]

Amadeo De Filippi (1900-   )

Malvolio

Status: Y   **Evidence:** S
Text: Unknown
Type: Opera   **Acts:** 2
Premiere: 1937 00 00
Play: *Twelfth Night*

Yes: Blom, Groves V, Hartnoll, Oxford

Comments: May have been composed in 1937.

Claude Debussy (1862-1918)

As You Like It

Status: Y   **Evidence:** S
Text: Unknown
Type: Projected Opera
Play: *As You Like It*
Yes: Groves V

Louis Pierre Deffès (1819-1900)

Jessica

Status: Y   **Evidence:** S
Text: Adenis, Jules (1823-1900) and Henri Boisseaux (1821-1863)
Type: Opera   **Acts:** 4   **Language:** French
Premiere: Toulouse, France: Théâtre du Capitole • 1898 03 25
Source of Premiere Information: Loewenberg
Play: *Merchant of Venice*
Yes: Hartnoll, Loewenberg, Mellen, Oxford, Stieger, Wilson

Comments: Stieger, Manferrari: 5 acts. Loewenberg: it was his best work.

Eugène Déjazet (1825-1880)

Rhum et eau en juillet

Status: Y   **Evidence:** S
Text: Jallais, Amedée de (1829-   )
Type: Parodie   **Acts:** 6 Tableaux   **Language:** French
Premiere: Paris, France: Théâtre Déjazet • 1867 07 00
Source of Premiere Information: Mellen

Play: *Romeo and Juliet*
Yes: Friedlaender, Mellen, Riemann, Stieger, Schatz MS

Comments: Friedlaender, Mellen, Riemann, Stieger, Schatz MS:
it is a parody of Gounod's *Roméo et Juliette.*

Raffaele Del Fante

La Tempesta

Status: Y   **Evidence:** S
Text: Fleres, Ugo
Type: Opéra sérieux   **Acts:** 3   **Language:** Italian
Premiere: Livorno, Italy: Teatro Politeama • 1900 08 14
Source of Premiere Information: Mellen
Play: *Tempest*
Yes: Mellen, Oxford, Stieger

Marcel Delannoy (1898-1962)

Puck

Status: Y   **Evidence:** P
Text: Boll, André (1896-   )
Type: Opéra-féerique   **Acts:** 3   **Language:** French
Premiere: Strasbourg, France: Théâtre Municipal • 1949 01 29
Source of Premiere Information: Score
Play: *Midsummer Night's Dream*
Publisher: Verlag der Autoren, 1951 [vs]
Yes: SCORE, Baker's, Groves V, Hartnoll, Mellen, MGG, New Grove,
    Oxford

Cast: LE ROYAUME DES FEES • PUCK (Danseur) [M. Roland April]
• TITANIA (Soprano-colorature) [Mme Monda-Million] • OBERON
(Basse chantante) [M. Georges Jongejans] • UNE FEE (Soprano
lyrique) [Mme Nany-Arnaud] • LE MONDE DES HUMAINS • THESSE
(Ténor demi-caractère [M. Roger Barnier] • DEMETRIUS (Ténor
léger) [M. Paul Derenne] • HELENE (Mezzo-soprano) [Mme Marika-
Stephanides] • LYSANDRE (Baryton Martin) [M. Georges Verguet] •
HERMIA (Soprano lyrique léger [Mme Jacqueline Drozin] • QUINCE

[HÉLANDRE] (Ténorino bouffe) [M. N. Kedroff] • BOTTOM
[LYSENE] (Ténor bouffe) [M. Rene Herent] • SNUG [HERMIUS]
(Baryton bouffe) [M. B. Akiaroff] • FLUTE [DÉMÉTRIA] (Basse
bouffe) [M. B. Borissoff] • EGEE (Comédien) [M. Paul Parmentier] •
HIPPOLYTE (Rôle muet) [Mme Eveline Mischke]

Frederick Delius (1862-1934)

Romeo und Juliet auf dem Dorfe [A Village Romeo and Juliet]

Status: N   **Evidence:** P
Text: Delius, Jelka
Type: Music drama   **Acts:** 6 Scenes   **Language:** English
(first performance in German translation)
Premiere: Berlin, Germany: Komische Oper • 1907 02 21
Source of Premiere Information: Mellen
Play: *Romeo and Juliet*
Publisher: Berlin: Verlag Harmonie, 1910 [vs, s]
No: SCORE, Mellen

Comments: On Gottfried Keller's novel, *Romeo und Juliet auf dem Dorfe;* has nothing to do with Shakespeare's play. White: text by composer.

Cast: MANZ, reicher bauer (Bariton) • MARTI, reicher bauer (Bariton) • SALI, Manzens Sohn (Tenor) • VRENCHEN, Martis Tochter (Sopran) • DER SCHWARZE GEIGER, rechtmäßiger Erbe des Brachlands (Bariton) • ERSTER BAUER (Bariton) • ZWEITER BAUER (Bariton) • ERSTE BAÜERIN (Sopran) • ZWEITE BAÜERIN (Sopran) • DRITTE BAÜERIN (Alt) • PFEFFERKUCHENFRAU (Sopran) • GLÜCKSRADFRAU (Sopran) • SCHMUCKWARENFRAU (Alt) • POSSENREISSER (Tenor) • KARUSSELLMANN (Bariton) • SCHIESSBUDENMANN (Baß) • DAS SCHLANKE MÄDCHEN (Sopran) • DAS WILDE MÄDCHEN (Alt) • DER ARME HORNIST (Tenor) • DER BUCKLIGE BASSGEIGER (Baß) • ERSTER SCHIFFER (Bariton) • ZWEITER SCHIFFER (Bariton) • DRITTER Schiffer (Tenor) •—•
Chorus: VAGABUNDEN, BAUERN, SCHIFFER

Otto Didam (1890-1966)

Julia und Romeo

Status: ?
Text: Unknown
Play: *Romeo and Juliet*

Comments: Gruber: never performed.

Carl Ditters von Dittersdorf (1739-1799)

Die lustigen Weiber von Windsor und der dicke Hans

Status: Y   **Evidence:** S
Text: Römer, Georg Christian (1766-1829) [altered]
Type: Singspiel   **Acts:** 2   **Language:** German
Premiere: Brunswick [Oels], Germany: Braunschweig-Oelsische
    Hoftheater • 1796 06 25
Source of Premiere Information: Place and year from score.
    Day from Mellen.
Play: *Merry Wives of Windsor*
Yes: Blom, Clément, Friedlaender, Groves V, Hartnoll, Mellen, New
    Groves, Oxford, Schatz MS, Squire, Stieger

Comments: MGG, Friedlaender, Mellen: text by Herklots.

Cast: RITTER HANNS FALLSTAFF [Herr Alexi sen.] • HERR
WALLAUF [Herr Katzor] • MADAM WALLAUF [Dem.elle Cariline
Alexi] • HERR RUTHAL [Herr Alexi jun.] • MADAM RUTHAL [Mad.me
Wotruba] • LUISE [Dem.elle Wotruba] • WARNEK [Herr Rösner] •
FRAU KLAPPER [Mad.me Golisch] • ERSTER GLÄUBIGER [Herr
Ernst] • ZWEITER GLÄUBIGER [Herr Golisch] • DRITTER
GLÄUBIGER [Herr Müller] •—• **Chorus:** GERICHTSDIENER,
KNECHTE, VERKLEIDETE FEEN

Arpád [Adolph] Doppler (1857-1927)

Viel Lärm um Lichts

Status: Y   **Evidence:** P
Text: Harlacher, August
Type: Oper   **Acts:** 3   **Language:** German
Premiere: Leipzig, Germany: Neues Stadttheater auf d.
   Augustusplatz • 1896 03 13
Source of Premiere Information: Mellen
Play: *Much Ado About Nothing*
Yes: LIBRETTO, Groves V, Hartnoll, Mellen, New Grove, Oxford,
   Stieger

Comments: Manferrari, Mellen: composer's dates are Graz, Stiria
1850-1906.

Cast: DON PEDRO, Prinz von Arragon • LEONATO, Gouverneur
von Messina • DON JUAN, Pedros Halbbruder • CLAUDIO, ein
florentinischer Graf • BENEDIKT, ein Edelmann aus Padua • HERO,
Leonatos Tochter • BEATRICE, Leonatos Richte • MARGARETE,
Heros Kammermädchen • BORACHIO, Don Juans Begleiter •
HOLZAPFEL, Greichtsdiener •—• **Chorus:** GEFOLGE DON
PEDROS, DIENER UND PAGEN LEONATOS, GÄSTE, WACHEN

Jaroslav Doubrava (1909-1960)

Sen noci svatojanske

Status: Y   **Evidence:** S
Text: Composer and Rudolf Vonásek
Type: Opera   **Acts:** 3   **Language:** Czech
Premiere: Opava, Czechoslovakia • 1969 12 21
Source of Premiere Information: Mellen
Play: *Midsummer Night's Dream*
Yes: Baker's, Hartnoll, Mellen, New Groves, Oxford

Comments: Translation of title: *A Midsummer Night's Dream;* first
performance was posthumous. Oxford: composed in 1948.
Completed by Jiri Jaroch.

Hugh A. Douglas

Romeo and Juliet Up to Larks

Status: Y   **Evidence:** S
Text: Cane, Claude and M. B. Lucas
Type: Burlesque   **Acts:** 2   **Language:** English
Premiere: London, England • 1890 00 00 ?
Source of Premiere Information: Stieger
Play: *Romeo and Juliet*
Publisher: London: Marriot & Williams,c.1890 [vs]
Yes: Plot

Comments: Romeo marries Juliet and Tybalt marries Rosaline.

Cast: ROSALINE • ROMEO • JULIET • PRINCE • CAPULET • TYBALT •—• **Chorus:** CHORUS, DANCERS

Antonio Draghi (1635-1700)

Timone misantropo

Status: ?
Text: Minato, Niccolò
Type: Drama per musica   **Language:** Italian
Premiere: Vienna, Austria: Hoftheater • 1696 00 00
Source of Premiere Information: Mellen
Play: *Timon of Athens*

Comments: Mellen: one aria by Emperor Leopold I; Carnival. Libretto printed in Vienna. Libretist unknown.

Jef Van Durme (1907-1965)

Anthony and Cleopatra

Status: Y   **Evidence:** S
Text: Unknown
Type: Opera

Premiere: 1959 00 00 c.
Play: *Anthony and Cleopatra*
Yes: Baker's

King Lear

Status: Y   **Evidence:** S
Text: Unknown
Type: Opera
Premiere: 1957 00 00 c.
Play: *Lear*
Yes: Baker's, Oxford

Richard III

Status: Y   **Evidence:** S
Text: Unknown
Type: Opera
Premiere: 1961 00 00 c.
Play: *Richard III*
Yes: Baker's

Victor-Alphonse Duvernoy (1842-1907)

La Tempête

Status: NO   **Evidence:** P
Text: Silvestre, Paul Armand (1837-1901) and Pierre Berton
Type: Drame lyrique   **Acts:** 3 parts   **Language:** French
Premiere: Paris, France: Théâtre du Châtelet • 1880 11 18
Source of Premiere Information: Libretto
Play: *Tempest*
Publisher: Paris: E. et A. Girod, 1880 [vs]
Yes: Friedlaender, Mellen, Oxford, Stieger, Wilson
No: SCORE, LIBRETTO, Baker's

Comments: Score: Poéme symphonic en trois parties pour soli, choeurs et orchestra. Paroles de A. Silvestre et P. Berton d'après Shakespeare. Clément describes the work. Friedlaender: 1880 11 24.

Cast: PROSPERO [M. Faure] • FERDINAND [M. Vergnet] • CALIBAN [M. Gailhard] • MIRANDA [Mme. G. Kraus] • ARIEL [Mme. Franck-Duvernoy] •——•
Chorus: ESPRITS, MATELOTS, NAUFRAGÉS, ETC.

Florimond Van Duyse [Duyze] (1843-1910)

Rosalinde

Status: ?
Text: Rosseels, E.
Type: Opéra   **Acts:** 3   **Language:** Flemish
Premiere: Antwerp, Belgium: National Tooneel • 1864 01 17
Source of Premiere Information: Mellen
Play: *As You Like It*

Thomas Hugh [Tom] Eastwood (1922-   )

Christopher Sly

Status: Y   **Evidence:** S
Text: Duncan, Ronald Frederic Henry (1914-   )
Type: Chamber Opera   **Acts:** Prologue/3/Epilogue
         Language: English
Premiere: London, England: Royal Court Theatre • 1960 01 24
Source of Premiere Information: Mellen
Play: *Taming of the Shrew*
Yes: Groves, Mellen, Oxford, White

Comments: Oxford: gives incorrect title. The best known of Eastwood's works. White: presented by the English Opera Group.

Johann Ernst Eberlin [Eberle] (1702-1762)

Ricardus Impius, Angliae Rex, ab Henrico Richmondæ Comite vita simul et regno excitus

Status: NO   **Evidence:** S
Text: Unknown
Type: Drama with Music
Premiere: Salzburg, Austria: Benedictine Convent • 1750 09 04
Source of Premiere Information: Stieger
Play: *Richard III*
Yes: Wilson

Comments: Rieman: it was first produced by students; it is a Latin drama with music.

Max Carl Eberwein (1786-1868)

Romeo und Julie

Status: ?
Text: Kokmüller, Aug
Acts: 2
Premiere: 1858 00 00 ?
Play: *Romeo and Juliet*

Arne Eggen (1881-1955)

Cymbelyn

Status: Y   **Evidence:** S
Text: Rytter, Henrik
Type: Opera   **Language:** Norwegian
Premiere: Oslo, Norway • 1951 12 07
Source of Premiere Information: Mellen
Play: *Cymbeline*

Yes: Baker's, Groves V, Hartnoll, Mellen, MGG, New Groves, Oxford
Comments: New Grove: 1948.

Charles P. Emery

Romeo, the Radical or Obstruction and Effect

Status: Y   **Evidence:** S
Text: Composer
Type: Comic opera   **Acts:** 1   **Language:** English
Premiere: Walsall, England: Alexandra Theatre • 1882 08 14
Source of Premiere Information: Gänzl
Play: *Romeo and Juliet*
Yes: Gänzl

Comments: Characters and cast from Gänzl.

Cast: TYBALT TORIO [Charles P. Emery] • ROMEO IRVINGO [E. Allen] • PETER THE PERT [Little Rosey May] • CAPULET [W. R. Glenney] • JULIET TEMO [Beatrice Thompson] • NURSE MARGERY [Rose Emery]

Adam Joseph Emmert (1765-1812)

Der Sturm

Status: Y   **Evidence:** S
Text: Unknown
Type: Singspiel   **Language:** German
Premiere: Salzburg, Austria: Hoftheater • 1806 00 00
Source of Premiere Information: Mellen
Play: *Tempest*
Yes: Friedlaender, Hartnoll, Mellen, New Grove, Oxford, Squire, Stieger

Comments: New Grove: city is Ansbach.

Hans Ulrich Engelmann (1921-)

Ophelia, Op. 36

Status: Y **Evidence:** S
Text: Goldschmidt, Miriam
Type: Opera **Acts:** 1 **Language:** German
Premiere: Hannover, Germany: Radio • 1969 02 01
Source of Premiere Information: Mellen
Play: *Hamlet*
Yes: Mellen, Oxford

Comments: Oxford: based on Shakespeare but distantly related.
Baker's: music for action theater. Mellen: revised, West Berlin
(Opernhaus) 1970 05 15.

Ludwig Engländer (1851-1914)

The Belle of Bohemia

Status: Y **Evidence:** S
Text: Smith, Harry Bache
Type: Musical farce **Acts:** 2 **Language:** English
Premiere: New York, U.S.A.: Casino Theatre • 1900 09 24
Source of Premiere Information: Mellen
Play: *Comedy of Errors*
Publisher: New York: Edward Schuberth and Co. 1900 [selections]
Yes: Gänzl

Comments: Gänzl: based on the *Comedy of Errors'* two Dromios
idea.

Heimo Erbse (1924-)

Julietta, Op. 15

Status: N **Evidence:** P
Text: Composer
Type: Opera semiseria **Acts:** 4 **Language:** German
Premiere: Salzburg, Austria: Salzburger Festspiele • 1959 08 17

Source of Premiere Information: Mellen
Play: *Romeo and Juliet*
Publisher: Frankfurt: C. F. Peters 1959 [vs].
No: SCORE

Comments: Score: nach Heinrich von Kleist's Novelle *Die Marquise von O.* Mellen: 3 acts.

Cast: JULIETTA, verwitwete Marquise von O . . . (Sopran) •
KOMMANDANT, Juliettas Vater (Bass) • MUTTER, Juliettas Mutter
(Mezzosopran) • FORSTMEISTER, Juliettas Bruder (Tenor) •
GRAFFREIHERR VON FALKENBERG, Obristlieutnant einer
feindlichen Streitmacht (Bariton) • ARZT (Bass) • BABETT, Juliettas
Amme und Faktotum im Hause des Kommandanten (Alt) •
LEOPARDO, Diener im Hause des Kommandanten (Tenor) •
ALFONSO, Diener im Hause des Kommandanten (Bass) •
PERSONEN DER PANTOMIMISCHEN SZENEN: • JULIETTA •
GRAF • KOMMANDANT •—•
Chorus: SIPPE, DIENER, LANDLEUTE UND KIRCHENSÄNGER,
SECHS AMMEN, BALLETT DER DIENER, LANDLEUTE,
ZEITUNGSVERKÄUFER, AMOR UND PSYCHE.
PANTOMIMISCHEN SZENEN: SOLDATEN DES GRAFEN UND
KOMMANDANTEN, FRAUEN, HOCHZEITSGÄSTE, KINDER

Vincenzo Fabrizi (1765-after 1812?)

La Tempestà ossia Da un disordine ne nasce un ordine

Status: Y   **Evidence:** S
Text: Mallio, Michele
Type: Farsa a cinque voci   **Acts:** 2   **Language:** Italian
Premiere: Rome, Italy: Teatro Capranica • 1788 01 00
Source of Premiere Information: Mellen
Play: *Tempest*
Yes: Hartnoll, Oxford, Squire

Comments: Manferrari: 3 acts, gennaio 1788. Mellen: Intermezzo,
2 scenes; Carnival. Schatz MS has 1788 changed to 1787.

Cast: CONTE ARMIDORO [Carlo Rovedini] • SANDRA [Andrea
Martini] • LENINA [Paolo Belli] • CECCO [Francesco Antonucci] • D.
TESTONE [Gioachino Caribaldi]

Franco Faccio (1840-1891)

Amleto

Status: Y   **Evidence:** S
Text: Boito, Arrigo (1842-1918)
Type: Tragedia lirica   **Acts:** 4   **Language:** Italian
Premiere: Genoa, Italy: Teatro Carlo Felice • 1865 05 30
Source of Premiere Information: Loewenberg
Play: *Hamlet*
Publisher: Milan: Ricordi, 1865? [vs]
Yes: Baker's, Blom, Friedlaender, Groves V, Hartnoll, Loewenberg,
       Mellen, Schatz MS, Stieger, Wilson

Comments: Score [selections] and libretto do not mention
Shakespeare.

Cast: AMLETO, Principe di Danimarca (Tenore) [Sigr. Mario Tiberini]
• CLAUDIO, Re di Danimarca (Baritone) [Sigr. Cotogni] • POLONIO,
Lord ciamberlano • ORAZIO, amico di Amleto • MARCELLO, uffiziale
• LAERTE, figlio di Polonio • OFELIA, figlia di Polonio (Soprano)
[Signora Tiberini] • GELTRUDE, Regina di Danimarca, madre di
Amleto (Soprano) [Siga. Corani] • LO SPETTRO (Basso) [Sigr.
Bagagiolo] • UN SACERDOTE • TRE CANTORI • PRIMO BECCHINO
• SECONDO BECCHINO •—• **Chorus:** CORTIGIANI, PAGGI, DAME,
UFFIZIALI, SOLDATI, POPOLO

Richard Falk (1878-1949)

Was ihr Wollt

Status: ?
Text: Unknown
Play: *Twelfth Night*

Comments: Gruber: not performed.

Guido Farina (1903-   )

La Dodisesima Notte

Status: Y   **Evidence:** S
Text: Possenti, A.
Type: Opera buffa   **Acts:** 3   **Language:** Italian
Premiere: Milan, Italy: Teatro Filodrammatici • 1929 05 11
Source of Premiere Information: Mellen
Play: *Twelfth Night*
Yes: Groves V, Hartnoll, Mellen, Oxford

Alexander Faris

R Loves J

Status: Y   **Evidence:** S
Text: Ustinov, Peter [Lyrics by Julian More]
Type: Musical   **Acts:** 2   **Language:** English
Premiere: Chichester, England: Chichester Festival • 1973 07 11
Source of Premiere Information: Gänzl
Play: *Romeo and Juliet*
Yes: Gänzl

Comments: Gänzl: Julian More helped supply the music.
Characters and cast from Gänzl.

Cast: THE GENERAL [Topol] • JULIET MOULSWORTH [Rosemary Williams] • HOOPER MOULSWORTH [Richard Owens] • BEULAH MOULSWORTH [Pip Hinton] • FREDDIE VANDERSTUYT [Robert Colman] • IGOR ROMANOFF [David Watson] • VADIM ROMANOFF [Alan Dudley] • EVDOKIA ROMANOFF [Mercia Glossop] • MARFA ZLOTOCHIENKO [Anna Dawson] • THE SPY [Dudley Stevens] • RAFI [Richard Denning] • JAN [Andy Mulligan] • ARCHBISHOP [Brian Hayes] • FOREIGN MINISTER [Anthony Brown] • ROSA [Cristina Avery] • RAOUL [Derek Beard] • JEMIMA [Adrienne Burgess] • ROLF [Michael Burgess] • JASMIN [Gemma Craven] • JACQUETTA [Lucinda Gane] • JONAH [David Hartley] • RAQUELA [Kim Hartman] • JAZEBEL [Eirian James] • RUDI [Reginald Jessup] • RITA [Patricia Kerry] • ROBERTO [Ian Milton] • RIMA [Cynthia Morey] • BROTHER REG [Barry McGinn] • JOSIE [Nelda Quilliam] • BROTHER JIM [Robert Selbie]

Arthur George Farwell (1872-1952)

Caliban by the Yellow Sands, Opus 47

Status: Y   **Evidence:** S
Text: Mackaye, Percy Wallace (1875-1956)
Type: Masque   **Language:** English
Premiere: New York, U.S.A. • 1916 05 00
Play: *Tempest*
Publisher: New York: G. Schirmer, 1916
Yes: Blom, Groves V, Hartnoll, Oxford

Comments: Baker's: Music for pageants, including Percy
MacKaye's *Caliban by the Yellow Sands*; written for the Shakespeare
tercentenary. New Grove: choruses and incidental music. Groves V:
Shakespeare Tercentenary Masque. Several choruses are on texts
by Shakespeare.

R. Feigerl

Der Stein der Weisen

Status: ?
Text: Unknown
Type: Operetta   **Acts:** 3   **Language:** German
Premiere: Bautzen, Germany: Stadttheater • 1922 01 00
Source of Premiere Information: Stieger
Play: *Tempest*

Alfonso Ferraboso II (1575-1628) and Robert Johnson (1583-1633)

Oberon, the Fairy Prince

Status: ?
Text: Jonson, Ben (1573-1637)
Type: Masque   **Acts:** 1   **Language:** English
Premiere: London, England: Whitehall, Banqueting House
    • 1611 01 01
Source of Premiere Information: White

Play: *Midsummer Night's Dream*

Comments: White: some of the music has survived; the saytrs' dance was incorporated into Shakespeare's *The Winter's Tale*.

Vencenzo Emidio Carmine Ferroni (1858-1934)

Romeo and Juliet

Status: Y   **Evidence:** S
Text: Unknown
Premiere: 1900 00 00 c.
Play: *Romeo and Juliet*
Yes: Oxford

Zdenko Fibich (1850-1900)

Boure, Opus 40 [Der Sturm]

Status: Y   **Evidence:** P
Text: Vrchlicky, Jaroslav [pseud. of Emil Bohus Frida] (1853-1912)
Type: Opera   **Acts:** 3   **Language:** Czech
Premiere: Prague, Czechoslovakia: Narodni Divádlo • 1895 03 01
Source of Premiere Information: Loewenberg
Play: *Tempest*
Publisher: Prag: Fr. A. Urbánek, 1895 [vs]
Yes: SCORE, Blom, Friedlaender, Groves V, Hartnoll, Loewenberg, Mellen, New Grove, Oxford, Squire, Wilson

Cast: ALONSO, král Neapolsky • SEBASTIANO, jeho bratr • FERNANDO, syn krále Neapolského • ANTONIO, bratr Prosperuv nepravy vévoda Milánsky • GONZALO, ADRIANO, dvorané • PROSPERO, kouzelník byvaly vévoda Milánsky • MIRANDA, jeho dcera • KALIBAN • TRINKULO, STEFANO, dobrodruzi • ARIEL • SBOR DUCHU, SBOR DRUZINY

Graham Field

Dick Deterred

Status: Y   **Evidence:** S
Text: Edgar, David
Type: Musical   **Acts:** 2   **Language:** English
Premiere: London, England: Bush Theatre • 1974 02 25
Source of Premiere Information: Gänzl
Play: *Richard III*
Yes: Gänzl

Comments: Gänzl: guying the Watergate affair. Characters and cast from Gänzl.

Cast: EDWARD IV PART 2/BOB, Duke of Buckingham/VIRGILIO DIGHTON [Philip Jackson] • EDWARD IV PART 3/SIR JOHN BRACKENBURY/BISHOP OF ELY/RIOT COP [Harry Ditson] • RICHARD, Duke of Gloucester [Gregory Floy] • DUKE OF CLARENCE/CITIZEN OF FLORIDA/TYRRELL/SIR RON CATESBY [John Grillo] • LORD HASTINGS/MURDERER/SIR JAMES FOREST/EARL OF RICHMOND [Robert Bridges] • ANNE/MARGARET PLANTAGANET/FIRST MONK/GHOST [Deborah Grant] • ELIZABETH/PRINCE OF WALES/MARTHA/SECOND MONK/GHOST [Sharon Adair]

Valentino Fioravanti (1764-1837)

La Capricciosa pentita

Status: ?
Text: Romanelli, Luigi (1751-1839)
Type: Melodramma Giocoso   **Acts:** 2   **Language:** Italian
Premiere: Milan, Italy: Teatro alla Scala • 1802 10 02
Source of Premiere Information: Mellen
Play: *Taming of the Shrew*

Comments: Mellen gives several other titles used at subsequent performances.

Cast: LINDORA, Romana, destinata Sposa al • BARON CASTAGNA, di Velletri • GUILIA, di lui Nipote • SIMONE, Frattore die

Campagna al servizio del medesimo • VALERIO, Uffiziale, Servente di Lindora, e suo compagno de viaggio • NESPOLA, Maggiordomo del Barone • BERNARDO, Locandiere • GIANNINA, di lui Sorella

Enrico IV al passo della Marna

Status: ?
Text: Torelli, Serafino
Type: Farsa   **Acts:** 1   **Language:** Italian
Premiere: Rome, Italy: Teatro della Valle • 1818 09 09
Source of Premiere Information: Mellen
Play: *Henry IV*

Comments: Schatz MS: Juli 1818.

Jan F. Fischer (1921-   )

Romeo, Julie a tma [Romeo, Juliet and Darkness]

Status: N   **Evidence:** P
Text: Composer
Type: Opera   **Acts:** 2   **Language:** Czech
Premiere: Brno [Brünn], Czechoslovakia: Státní Divádlo • 1962 09 14
Source of Premiere Information: Mellen
Play: *Romeo and Juliet*
Publisher: Prag-Bratislava: Panton, 1964 [vs]
Yes: Mellen, Oxford
No: SCORE

Comments: Score: based on the novel of the same name by Jan Otcenasek. Mellen: based on both the story by Otcenasek and Shakespeare.

John Abraham Fisher (1744-1806)

Macbeth

Status: NO **Evidence:** S
Type: Music for the opening. **Language:** NA
Premiere: London, England • 1777 00 00 ?
Source of Premiere Information: Stieger
Play: *Macbeth*
No: Groves V, Stieger

Comments: Groves V: music for the opening scene. Stieger: incidental music.

Friedrich Fleischmann (1766-1798)

Die Geisterinsel

Status: Y **Evidence:** S
Text: Gotter, Johann Friedrich Wilhelm (1746-1797) and Friedrich Hildebrand von Einsiedel (1750-1828)
Type: Oper **Acts:** 3 **Language:** German
Premiere: Weimar, Germany • 1798 05 19
Source of Premiere Information: Loewenberg
Play: *Tempest*
Yes: Friedlaender, Groves V, Hartnoll, Loewenberg, Mellen, MGG, Oxford, Squire, Stieger

Comments: Loewenberg reference found in col 542. Stieger: Frankfurt a.M. 1792. Manferrari: com. 2 a., Ratisbona, (Baviera), Stadttheater, anno 1796. Friedlaender: Regensburg, 1798; not published. Mellen: Ratisbon, Hoftheater 1796. There is little agreement among sources about the date and place of the premiere of this opera and the one by Haack on the same text. What is particularly curious is that Bauman' preface to vol. 7 of German Opera, 1770-1800 states "in 1797 Gotter died with *Die Geisterinsel* yet unset and unsung." His introductory notes to Vol. 20 give the premiere of this work as 1792, Frankfurt A/M, National Theater and that of Haack's as 1794, Settin.

Cast: The characters should be the same as those given for Reichardt's *Die Geisterinsel.*

Friedrich von Flotow (1813-1883)

Ein Wintermärchen

Status: I **Evidence:** S
Text: Unknown
Language: German
Premiere: Weimar, Germany: Hoftheater • 1859 10 23
Play: *Winter's Tale*
Yes: Manferrari, Mellen
No: Groves V, Stieger

Comments: Groves V: Incidental music to the play *A Winter's Tale*
produced in Weimar, Court Theatre, 23 Oct. 1859. Stieger:
incidental music; German by Dingelstedt; 1859 11 00. Manferrari: F.
von Dingelstedt; op a a., Weimar Tr. di Corte, novembre 1859.
Mellen: *Un Conte d'hiver*, opera, Weimar, Hoftheater, 1859 11 00,
Dingelstedt, French. The call number of the score at the Library of
Congress indicates that it is incidental music.

Joseph Brohuslav Foerster (1859-1951)

Jessika, Opus 60

Status: Y **Evidence:** P
Text: Vrchlicky, Jaroslav [pseud. of Emil Bohus Frida] (1853-1912)
Type: Komische opera **Acts:** 3 **Language:** Czech
Premiere: Prague, Czechoslovakia: Czech National Theater
    • 1905 04 16
Source of Premiere Information: Loewenberg
Play: *Merchant of Venice*
Publisher: Vienna: Universal Edition, 1909 [vs]
Yes: SCORE, Blom, Groves V, Hartnoll, Loewenberg, Mellen, New
    Grove, Oxford, Stieger

Comments: Manferrari: s. 2 a., Praga, Tr. Nazionale Ceco,
primavera 1905.

Cast: DOGE VON VENEDIG (Bariton oder Baß) • ANTONIO, ein
Kaufmann (Bariton II) • BASSANIO, sein Freund (Bariton I) •
LORENZO, sein Freund (Tenor lyr.) • GRAZIANO, sein Freund (Baß
buffo) • SHYLOK, Jude (Baß I) • TUBAL, sein Freund (Baß II) •

LANZELOT GOBBO, Shyloks Diener (Tenor buffo) • JESSIKA, Shyloks Tochter (Sopran, jug. dram.) • PORZIA, eine reiche Erbin (Sopran, hochdram.) • GERICHTSHEROLD (Bariton oder Baß) • GONDOLIER (Tenor) • PORZIAS HEROLD (Sprechrolle) •—• **Chorus:** SENATOREN VON VENEDIG, BEAMTE DES GERICHTSHOFES, MASKEN, BEDIENTE DER PORZIA, PAGEN UND ANDERES GEFOLGE, VOLK.

Jacques Foignet (1755-1836)

L' Orage

Status: ?
Text: Monnet
Type: Opéra villageois   **Acts:** 1   **Language:** French
Premiere: Paris, France: Théâtre des Variétés [Montansier]
• 1798 06 09
Source of Premiere Information: Mellen
Play: *Tempest*

Comments: Riemann: 1798 07 09. Stieger: 1798 06 10. Manferrari: 9 giugno 1798.

Cast: MARCEL, La boureur [Amiel] • MARTHE, femme de Marcel [C.nne Barroyer] • CÉCILE, leur fille ainée [C.nne Dumas] • BABET, sœur de Cécile [C.nne Carolinne] • JULIEN, amoureus de Cécile [Xavier] • THOMAS, Menuier, père de Julien [Bonioli] • TROIS PETITS GARÇONS, fils de Marcel

Zdenek Folprecht (1900-1961)

Lásky hra osudná [The Fateful Game of Love], Opus 3

Status: Y   **Evidence:** S
Text: Capek, Josef (1887-) and Karel Capek (1890-1938)
Type: Opera   **Acts:** 1   **Language:** Czech
Premiere: Bratislava, Czechoslovakia • 1926 11 13
Source of Premiere Information: Mellen

Play: *Love's Labour's Lost*
Yes: Hartnoll, Mellen, Oxford

Hippolyte Honoré Joseph Court de Fontmichel (1799-?)

Amleto

Status: Y   **Evidence:** S
Text: Unknown
Type: Opera   **Acts:** 5
Premiere: 1837 00 00 ?
Play: *Hamlet*
Yes: Stieger

Comments: Stieger: not performed.

Jean Kurt Forest (1909-1975)

Hamlet

Status: N   **Evidence:** S
Text: Composer
Type: Opera   **Acts:** 5 Bildern   **Language:** German
Premiere: Berlin, Germany: Berlin/DDR (concert) • 1973 10 15
Play: *Hamlet*
No: Gruber

Comments: Gruber: nach S. Grammaticus und F. de Belleforest.

A. Francastel

Henry IV

Status: ?
Text: Saint-Hilaire V. de and Michel Delaporte
Type: Drame historique   **Acts:** 3/7 tableaux
          Language: French

Premiere: Paris, France: Théâtre National du Cirque-Olympiade
• 1846 10 17
Play: *Henry IV*

Ernst Frank (1847-1889)

Der Sturm

Status: Y   **Evidence:** S
Text: Wildmann, Joseph Victor
Type: Musical Fairy Tale   **Acts:** 3   **Language:** German
Premiere: Hannover, Germany: Stadttheatre • 1887 10 15
Source of Premiere Information: Date is from Schatz MS
Play: *Tempest*
Yes: Baker's, Blom, Friedlaender, Groves V, Hartnoll, Mellen, New
Groves, Oxford, Schatz MS, Squire, Stieger

Comments: Manferrari: 2 acts. Mellen: 1887 10 14.

Johann Wolfgang Frank (1644-?1710)

Timon

Status: Y   **Evidence:** S
Text: Unknown
Type: Masque
Play: *Timon of Athens*
Yes: Blom

Vito Frazzi (1888-1975)

Re Lear

Status: Y   **Evidence:** P
Text: Papini, Giovanni
Type: Music dramma   **Acts:** 3   **Language:** Italian
Premiere: Florence, Italy: Teatro Comunale • 1939 04 29

Play: *Lear*
Publisher: Florence: G. and P. Mignani, 1936 [vs]
Yes: SCORE, Baker's, Groves V, Hartnoll, Mellen, MGG, New Grove, Oxford

Comments: Manferrari: Teatro Vitt. Emanuele. Work was copyrighted by the composer in 1936. Mellen: t. Victorio Emanuele; 1939 04 28. Mellen: Giuseppe Papini.

Cast: RE LEAR, Re di Bretagna (Baritono) • GONERILLA, Sua filia (Mezzo Soprano) • REGANA, Sua filia (Soprano) • LA VOCE DI CORDELIA (Soprano) • IL MATTO (Tenore) • IL CONTE DI KENT (Baritono) • IL DUCA DI CORNOVAGLIA (Tenore) • IL DUCA D'ALBANIA (Basso) • IL CONTE DI GLOSTER (Basso) • EDGARDO, suo figlio (Tenore) • EDMONDO, bastardo di Gloster (Tenore) • OSVALDO, Maggiordomo di Gonerilla (Tenore) • UN ARALDO (Basso) • UN VECCHIO •—• **Chorus:** LA FOLLA (Coro di voci miste), CAVALIERI DEL SEGUITO DI RE LEAR, UFFICIALI, PERSONE DEL SEGUITO DI GONERILLA E DI REGANA

Francisco de Freitas Gazul (1869-   )

As Violetas

Status: ?
Text: Unknown
Type: Operetta **Acts:** 1 **Language:** Portuguese
Premiere: Lisbon, Portugal: Théâtre Trinidade • 1892 00 00
Source of Premiere Information: Mellen
Play: *Twelfth Night*

Giovanni Domenico Freschi (1640-1690)

Rosalinda

Status: ?
Text: Folchi, Fr.
Type: Opera **Acts:** 3 **Language:** Italian
Premiere: Venice, Italy: Teatro di Piazza o delle Grazie • 1694 00 00

Source of Premiere Information: Mellen
Play: *As You Like It*

Comments: Groves V: the opera has been attributed to him without sufficient evidence. Manferrari, Mellen: text by A. Marchi. Date: carnival.

Wilhelm Freudenberg (1838-1928)

Kleopatra

Status: Y   **Evidence:** S
Text: Pasqué, Ernst Heinrich Anton (1821-1892)
Type: Oper   **Acts:** 4   **Language:** German
Premiere: Magdeburg, Germany: Stadttheater • 1882 01 12
Source of Premiere Information: Mellen
Play: *Antony and Cleopatra*
Yes: Friedlaender, Mellen, Schatz MS

Comments: Manferrari: 3 acts, dicembre 1881. The libretto, published by E. Göhmann in Hannover, is dated 1880. Friedlaender: score not published.

Cast: KLEOPATRA, Königin von Aegypten (Mezzo-Sopran) • MARC ANTONIUS, Triumvirn (Bariton) • CÄSAR OCTAVIANUS, Triumvirn (Tiefer Tenor) • OCTAVIA, Cäsars Schwester (Jugendliche Sängerin) • HARO, ein Fischer aus Alexandria (Hoher [lyr.] Tenor) • AGRIPPA, Cäsars Feldherr (Baß) • DER PONTIFEX MAXIMUS (Baß) • ABENOBARBUS, Feldherr Marc Antonius (Zweite Tenorpartie) • LYDIA, VertraUte der Kleopatra (Sopran) •—• **Chorus:** CHOR

Kresimir Fribec (1908-   )

Romeo and Juliet

Status: Y   **Evidence:** S
Text: Unknown
Type: Opera   **Language:** Yugoslavian
Premiere: Zagreb, Yugoslavia • 1955 06 21
Source of Premiere Information: Mellen

Play: *Romeo and Juliet*
Yes: Mellen, Oxford

Wenzel Robert Count von Gallenberg (1783-1839)

Amleto

Status: I   **Evidence:** S
Text: Henry, L.
Type: Pantomime tragique   **Acts:** 5
Premiere: Paris, France • 1816 00 00
Source of Premiere Information: Squire
Play: *Hamlet*
Yes: Friedlaender, Squire

Comments: Friedlaender: it is a ballet; Milan, 1817. Stieger: Milan; carnival, 1817 Scala.

Baldassarre Galuppi [called Buranello] (1706-1785)

Cajo Mario

Status: ?
Text: Roccaforte, Gaetano
Type: Dramma per musica   **Acts:** 3   **Language:** Italian
Premiere: Venice, Italy: Teatro San Giovanni Grisostomo • 1764 05 31
Source of Premiere Information: Mellen
Play: *Coriolanus*

Comments: Schatz MS: Teatro Grimani.

Enrico

Status: N   **Evidence:** P
Text: Vanneschi, Francesco
Type: Dramma per musica   **Acts:** 3   **Language:** Italian

Premiere: London, England: King's Theater in the Haymarket
• 1743 01 01
Source of Premiere Information: Fiske
Play: *Henry IV*
Publisher: London: I. Walsh, 1744 [vs]
No: LIBRETTO

Comments: Sartori: Florence (Teatro di Via del Cocomero) nel carnevale del-l'anno 1732. Date of libretto is 1742. Shakespeare is not mentioned in it.

Cast: HENRICUS, King of Sicily [Signor Monticelli] • ELVIDA, Daughter of Sifred [Signora Visconti] • SIFRED, Great Chancellor of the Kingdom and Governor of Henricus [Signor Amorevoli] • CONSTANTIA, Daughter of Rogero, in live with D. Fernando [Signora Frasi] • DON FERNANDO, Brother to Henricus [Signora Galli] • ROBERTO, in love with Elvida [Signora Contini]

Manuel Vincente del Popolo Garcia (1775-1832)

La Gioventù di Enrico V

Status: Y   **Evidence:** S
Text: Romani, Felice? (1788-1865)
Type: Opera   **Acts:** 2   **Language:** Italian
Premiere: New York, U.S.A.: Park Theater • 1827 00 00
Source of Premiere Information: Mellen
Play: *Henry IV*
Yes: Manferrari

Comments: Stieger: libretto by Romani. Manferrari: (da Shakespeare) 2 a. New York Park-Theatre, estate 1827.

Giulietta e Romeo

Status: Y   **Evidence:** S
Text: Unknown
Type: Opera   **Language:** Italian
Premiere: New York, U.S.A.: Park Theater • 1826 00 00
Source of Premiere Information: Mellen

Play: *Romeo and Juliet*
Yes: Friedlaender, Stieger

Comments: Stieger: 1825 00 00. Manferrari: *Giulietta e Romeo* (ignoto) com....., New York, Park-Theater, settembre 1826. Mellen: title is *Romeo*.

Carlo Francesco Gasperini [Gasparini] (1668-1727)

Ambleto

Status: N   **Evidence:** S
Text: Zeno, Apostolo (1668-1750) and Pietro Pariati (1665-1733)
Type: Drama per musica   **Acts:** 3   **Language:** Italian
Premiere: Venice, Italy: Teatro Tron di San Cassano • 1705 12 26
Source of Premiere Information: Date from Stieger
Play: *Hamlet*
Publisher: New Grove: D-Bds, Songs published in London, 1712.
Yes: Blom, Friedlaender, Wilson
No: Librettist

Comments: Taken from Saxo Grammaticus. Stieger: Carnival.

Cast: AMBLETO, Erede legittimo del Regno, amante de Veremonda [Il Sig. Niccola Grimaldi] • VEREMONDA, Principessa di Allanda, amante di Ambleto [La Sig. Maria Domenica Pini] • FENGONE, Tiranno di Danimarca [Il Sig. Lorenzo Santorini] • GERILDA, moglie di Fengone, e Madre di Ambleto [La Sig. Maria Maddalena Bonavia] • ILDEGARDE, Principessa Danese [La Sig. Vittoria Costa] • VALDEMARO, Generale del Regno [Il Sig. Pasqualino Betti] • SIFFRIDO, Confidente di Fengone, e Capitano delle guardie Reali [Il Sig. Domenico Fontani]

GI' Equivoci d'amore e d'innocenza

Status: ?
Text: Salvi, Antonio
Type: Dramma per Musica   **Acts:** 3   **Language:** Italian
Premiere: Venice, Italy: Teatro Grimani San Giovanni Grisostomo
        • 1723 11 23

Source of Premiere Information: Year and place from libretto.
Date from Mellen.
Play: *Midsummer Night's Dream*

Cast: LEONORA, Regina d'Aragona [La Sig. Faustina Bordoni] • D.
CARLO SANCIO, Generale dell'Armi [Il Signor Antonio Bernachi] •
RAIMONDO, Padre di D. Carlo [Il Sig. Gio. Battista] • ELVIDA,
Contessa di Barcellona [La Sig. Maria Teresa Cotti] • RAMIRO, Duca
di Villa Reale [Il Sig. Bortolameo Bartoli] • ERNESTO, Fratello d'Elvida
[Il Sig. Antonio Baldi]

Nicholas Comyn Gatty (1874-1946)

Macbeth

Status: Y   **Evidence:** S
Text: Unknown
Type: Opera   **Acts:** 4   **Language:** English
Premiere: London, England: Surrey Theatre • 1920 00 00 c.
Source of Premiere Information: Mellen
Play: *Macbeth*
Publisher: M.S.
Yes: Blom, Groves V, Hartnoll, Mellen, Oxford, Stieger

Comments: Groves V: has remained unperformed. Mellen: date is
when composed.

The Tempest

Status: Y   **Evidence:** P
Text: Gatty, Reginald M.
Type: Opera   **Acts:** 3   **Language:** English
Premiere: London, England: Surrey Theatre • 1920 04 17
Source of Premiere Information: Score
Play: *Tempest*
Publisher: London: Stainer & Bell, 1933 [vs]
Yes: SCORE, Blom, Groves V, Hartnoll, Loewenberg, Mellen,
Northouse, Oxford, Stieger, White

Cast: ALONZO, King of Naples (Baritone) • SEBASTIAN, his
brother (Bass) • PROSPERO, the rightful duke of Milan (Bass
Baritone) • ANTONIO, his brother, the usurping duke (Bass) •

FERDINAND, son of Alonzo (Tenor) • GONZALO, an honest old counsellor (Baritone) • CALIBAN, a savage and deformed slave (Baritone) • TRINCULO, a Jester (Tenor) • STEPHANO, a drunken butler (Bass) • BOATSWAIN (Baritone) • MIRANDA, daughter of Prospero (Soprano) • ARIEL, an airy Spirit (Soprano) • IRIS, spirit (Soprano) • CERES, spirit (Soprano) • JUNO, spirit (Soprano) •——•
Chorus: SAILORS (Tenors and Basses); SPIRITS (Sopranos only); BALLET OF REAPERS AND NYMPHS

Edmond Germain Gaujac (1895-1962)

Les Amantes de Vérone

Status: Y   **Evidence:** S
Text: Unknown
Language: French
Premiere: Toulouse, France • 1950 00 00
Play: *Romeo and Juliet*
Yes: Hartnoll, Oxford

Comments: Oxford: 1955.

Joaquin Romualdo Gaztambide y Garbayo (1822-1870)

El sueño de una noche de verano

Status: ?
Text: Escosura, Patricio de la (1807-1878)
Type: Zarzuela   **Acts:** 3   **Language:** Spanish
Premiere: Madrid, Spain: Teatro del Circo • 1852 02 21
Source of Premiere Information: Mellen
Play: *Midsummer Night's Dream*

Comments: Stieger: 2 acts. Schatz MS: based on de Leuven and Rosiers libretto [see Thomas, Berens, Lillo].

Giuseppe Gazzaniga (1743-1818)

Gli Equivoci

Status: ?
Text: Unknown
Play: *Comedy of Errors*

Stanley Jay Gelber

Love and Let Love

Status: Y   **Evidence:** P
Text: Lollos, John (book); John Lollos and Don Christopher (lyrics)
Type: Broadway Show   **Acts:** 2   **Language:** English
Premiere: New York, U.S.A.: Sheridan Square Playhouse
     • 1968 01 03
Source of Premiere Information: Simas
Play: *Twelfth Night*
Publisher: New York: Sam Fox Publishing Co., 1969 [vs]
Yes: SCORE, Simas, Green

Comments: Simas: subsequently titled *Twelfth Night.*

Franz Friedrich Richard Genée (1823-1895) and Louis Roth

Zwillinge

Status: ?
Text: Zell, F. [Camillo Walzel] and Composer
Type: Operette   **Acts:** 3   **Language:** German
Premiere: Vienna, Austria: Theater an d. Wien • 1885 02 14
Source of Premiere Information: Mellen
Play: *Comedy of Errors*

Comments: Libretto does not mention Shakespeare.

Cast: GEORGINE VON CALLAC • CLAPOTTE, ihre Zofe •
DUPRAT, Armeelieferant • ABRILLON • FARIGOUL • CAPTAIN

VICTOR BLONDEAU • DANBERVAL • GEORGE, dessen
Pflegesohn • MADELAINE • POMPONNE • ROSE-MARIE,
Marketenderin • BRUTUS, Wirth • CHARMETTE, seine Schwester •
BEN-SELLIM, ein Mameluck, Diener Victors • THEMISTOCLES •
SCÄVOLA • AGRIPPINA • EIN CORPORAL • EIN KELLNER •——•
Chorus: MUSCADIN'S UND MITGLIEDER DES CLUB: JEUNESSE
DORÉE, WOLF, SOLDATEN, REKRUTEN, MUSIKER, KELLNER,
GÄSTE

Pietro Mercandetti Generali (1783?-1832)

Rodrigo di Valencia

Status: Y   **Evidence:** S
Text: Romani, Felice (1788-1865)
Type: Melodramma Serio   **Acts:** 2   **Language:** Italian
Premiere: Milan, Italy: Teatro alla Scala • 1817 03 08
Source of Premiere Information: Mellen
Play: *Lear*
Yes: Stieger

Cast: RODRIGO, Duca di Valenza [Sig. Filippo Galli] • ALVARO,
Conte di Candia, padre di [Sig. Ranieri Remorini] • RAMIRO, Amante
di [Signora Carolina Bassi] • ELMONDA, ultima figlia di Rodrigo
[Signora Francesca Maffei Festa] • OSUALDO, Conte di Bariana,
marito di [Sig. Domenico Donzelli] • ELVIRA, seconda figlia di
Rodrigo [Signora Elena Badoera] • ULRICO, Conte di Murcia, marito
di Rodoguna, prima filia di Rodrigo [Sig. Giovanni Antonio Biscottini]
Chorus: CORI E COMPARSE

René Gerber (1908-   )

Roméo et Juliette

Status: ?
Text: Unknown
Play: *Romeo and Juliet*

Comments: Not performed.

Thaddäus Gerl (1766-1844); Henneberg and Benedikt Schack (1758-1826)

Der Stein der Weisen oder Die Zauberinsel

Status: ?
Text: Schikaneder, Emanuel [originally Johann Schikeneder] (1751-1812)
Type: Singspiel   **Acts:** 2   **Language:** German
Premiere: Vienna, Austria: Theater auf der Weiden • 1790 09 11
Source of Premiere Information: Mellen
Play: *Tempest*

Comments: Mellen: Brno 1797.

Franz Xaver Gevel

Rinaldo und Camilla oder Die Zauberinsel

Status: ?
Text: Hille
Type: Comic Opera   **Acts:** 3   **Language:** German
Premiere: Vienna, Austria: Theater in der Leopoldstadt • 1812 01 22
Play: *Tempest*

Alberto Ghislanzoni (1897-   )

Re Lear

Status: Y   **Evidence:** S
Text: Composer
Type: Opera   **Acts:** 3   **Language:** Italian
Premiere: Rome, Italy: Teatro Reale dell'Opera • 1937 04 24
Source of Premiere Information: Year and place from score. Date from Loewenberg.
Play: *Lear*
Publisher: Rome: Theo-Muccy [1937] [vs]
Yes: Blom, Hartnoll, Loewenberg, Mellen, Oxford

Comments: Mellen: Roma t.dell'Opera; 1937 04 28. Score does not mention Shakespeare.

Cast: RE LEAR (Baritono) • GONERILLA, Sue figlia (Contralto) • REGANA, Sue figlia (Mezzosoprano) • CORDELIA, Sue figlia (Soprano) • IL CONTE DI KENT (Baritono) • IL CONTE DI GLOSTER (Basso) • EDGARDO, figlio di Gloster (Tenore) • EDMONDO, figlio bastardo di Gloster (Basso) • IL MATTO DEL RE (Tenore) • IL DUCA D'ALBANIA (Tenore) • IL DUCA DI CORNOVAGLIA (Basso) • IL RE DI FRANCIA • UN UFFICIALE DI FRANCIA (Basso) •—•
Chorus: NOBILI, CAVALIERI, PAGGI, UFFICIALI, ARALDI, SOLDATI D'INGHILTERRA E DI FRANCIA, SERVI

Vittorio Giannini (1903-1966)

The Taming of the Shrew

Status: Y   **Evidence:** P
Text: Composer and Dorothy Fee
Type: Opera   **Acts:** 3/4 scenes   **Language:** English
Premiere: Cincinnati, U.S.A.: Music Hall [in concert form]
    • 1953 01 31
Source of Premiere Information: Mellen
Play: *Taming of the Shrew*
Publisher: New York: Ricordi, 1945, 1953, 1954 [vs, l]
Yes: SCORE, Hartnoll, Oxford

Comments: Baker's: his most appreciated opera; the libretto is an adaptation of the play with additional text from sonnets and *Romeo and Juliet*. Mellen: produced as the first color television broadcast of an opera N.Y.C. (NBC 1954 03 13); librettist is Dorothea Fee. Score: D. Fee.

Cast: BAPTISTA, a wealthy gentleman of Padua (Bass) • KATHARINA, his elder daughter (Dramatic Soprano) • BIANCA, his younger daughter (Lyric Soprano) • PETRUCHIO, suitor to Katharina (Baritone) • HORTENSIO (LICIO), suitor to Bianca (Baritone) • LUCENTIO (CAMBIO), suitor to Bianca (Tenor) • GREMIO, suitor to Bianca (Tenor) • VINCENTIO, father of Lucentio (Bass) • TRANIO (LUCENTIO), servant to Lucentio (Bass) • BIONDELLO, servant to Lucentio (Baritone) • GRUMIO, servant to Petruchio (Tenor) • CURTIS, servant to Petruchio (BASS) • A PEDANT (Tenor) • A

TAILOR (Tenor) •——•
Chorus: SERVANTS OF BAPTISTA, MAIDS OF KATHARINA

Cecil Armstrong Gibbs (1889-1960)

Twelfth Night, Opus 115

Status: Y　**Evidence:** S
Text: Currie
Type: Opera　　**Acts:** 3　　**Language:** English
Premiere: 1947 00 00
Source of Premiere Information: Mellen
Play: *Twelfth Night*
Yes: Groves V, Hartnoll, Mellen, Moore, New Grove, Oxford

Comments: Year is when composed. Groves V: article on Gibbs lists opera; article on Shakespeare does not.

James Gilbert

Good Time Johnny

Status: Y　**Evidence:** S
Text: More, Julian [Lyrics by Julian More and James Gilbert]
Type: Musical　　**Language:** English
Premiere: Birmingham, England: Repertory Theatre • 1971 12 16
Source of Premiere Information: Gänzl
Play: *Merry Wives of Windsor*
Yes: Gänzl

Comments: Characters and cast from Gänzl.

Cast: VERA FORBES [Colette Gleeson] • FORBES [John Baddeley] • ROSA PAGET [Felicity Harrison] • PAGET [Paul Chapman] • BARNETT [Eric Flynn] • NIMMO [Adrian Lawson] • GUNN [Malcolm Rennie] • QUEENIE [Joan Sims] • SIR JOHN [Ronnie Barker/John Baddeley • DOLLY [Valerie Griffiths] • OLD WAITER [John Gill] • PONGO [Adrian James]

Mikhail Ivanovitch Glinka (1804-1857)

Hamlet

Status: Y   **Evidence:** S
Text: Unknown
Type: Opera sketch
Premiere: , U.S.S.R. • 1843 00 00
Play: *Hamlet*
Yes: Neef

Comments: Neef: not performed.

Stefano Gobatti (1852-1913)

Cordelia

Status: Y   **Evidence:** S
Text: Ormeville, Carlo d' (1840-1924)
Type: Dramma lirico   **Acts:** 5   **Language:** Italian
Premiere: Bologna, Italy: Teatro Comunale • 1881 12 06
Source of Premiere Information: Mellen
Play: *Lear*
Publisher: New Grove: I-Bc
Yes: Friedlaender, Hartnoll, Mellen, Oxford

Comments: Stieger: 3 acts. Schatz MS: 1881 12 05. Only the year is given in the libretto.

Cast: CORDELIA SARACINI, giovane patrizia Senese (Soprano drammatico) • ERCOLE, suo fratello, capo del partito Ghibellino (Baritono) • GUALDO, ricco popolano, capo del partito Guelfo (Tenore) • AZZOLINO, vescovo di Siena (Primo Basso) • UBERTA, nutrice di Cordelia (Mezzo Soprano) • GINO, suo figlio, scadiere di Ercole Saracini (Soprano leggiero) • UGO, amico e seguace di Gualdo (Secondo Tenore) • TOLOMEI, Uficiale Ghibellino e seguace del Saracini (Secondo Basso) •— **Chorus:** SOLDATI ED UFFICIALI GUELFI E GHIBELLINI, POPOLANI E POPOLANE, ARTIGIANI, PORTA INSEGNE DELLE SOCIETA, PORTA INSEGNE GUELFI E GHIBELLINI, CAPI DELLO STATO, CAPI DEL CONSIGLIO, MAGISTRATI, SIGNORI, RAGAZZI DEL POPOLO, CLERO DELLA CATTEDRALE, CANONIEI, ACCOLITI, CHIERICI

Alexander Goedicke [Aleksandr Fedorovich Gedike] (1877-1957)

Macbeth

Status: Y **Evidence:** S
Text: Composer
Type: Opera
Premiere: 1944 00 00
Play: *Macbeth*
Yes: Oxford

Herman Goetz (1840-1876)

Der Widerspänstigen Zähmung [La Megère apprivoisée; Caterina e Petruccio]

Status: Y **Evidence:** P
Text: Widmann, Joseph Victor (1842-1911)
Type: Komische Oper **Acts:** 4 **Language:** German
Premiere: Mannheim, Germany: Nationaltheater • 1874 10 11
Source of Premiere Information: Loewenberg
Play: *Taming of the Shrew*
Publisher: Leipzig: Fr. Kistner, 1875 [vs]
Yes: SCORE, LIBRETTO, Baker's, Blom, Friedlaender, Groves V, Hartnoll, Loewenberg, Mellen, New Grove, Oxford, Squire, Stieger, Wilson

Comments: Baker's: his most famous work. MGG: His first opera. Stieger: 3 acts. Schatz MS: earliest performance is London, Drury Lane 1878 10 12. Wilson: text by Joseph Victor Erdmann; Götz's only complete opera.

Cast: BAPTISTA, ein reicher Edelmann in Padua (Baß) • KATHARINE, seine Tochter (Sopran) • BIANKA, seine Tochter (Sopran) • HORTENSIO, Biankas Freier (Baß) • LUCENTIO, Bianka Freier (Tenor) • PETRUCHIO, ein Edelmann aus Verona (Bariton) • GRUMIO, sein Diener (Baß) • EIN SCHNEIDER (Tenor) •—• **Chorus:** BAPTISTAS UND PETRUCHIOS DIENERSCHAFT, HOCHZEITSGÄSTE, NACHBARINNEN UND ANDERE NEBENPERSONEN

Edward M. Goldman (1917-)

Macbeth

Status: Y **Evidence:** S
Text: Composer
Type: Opera **Acts:** 3/7 scenes **Language:** English
Premiere: 1961 00 00
Play: *Macbeth*
Publisher: New York: American Music Center [vs]
Yes: AMCL

Comments: Date is when composed.

Chorus: SATB

Carl Goldmark (1830-1915)

Ein Wintermärchen

Status: Y **Evidence:** P
Text: Willner, Alfred Maria (1859-1929)
Type: Opera **Acts:** 3 **Language:** German
Premiere: Vienna, Austria: Opernhaus • 1908 01 02
Source of Premiere Information: Loewenberg
Play: *Winter's Tale*
Publisher: Vienna: W. Karczaga und C. Wallner, 1907 [vs]
Yes: SCORE, Blom, Groves V, Hartnoll, Loewenberg, MGG, Mellen, New Grove, Oxford, Stieger

Comments: Score: frei nach Shakespeare, 3 acts. Loewenberg, Mellen: 4 acts. Manferrari: 2 acts.

Cast: LEONTES, König von Slzilien (Tenor) • HERMIONE, dessen Gemahlin (Sopran) • MAMILLIUS, beider Sohn • PERDITA, beider Tochter (Hoher Sopran) • POLIXENES, König von Böhmem (Bariton) • FLORIZEL, dessen Sohn (Tenor) • CAMILLO, Vertrauter des Leontes (Baß-Bariton) • ANTIGONUS, Befehlshaber der königlichen Wache (Baß-Bariton) • PAULINA, dessen Gattin (Mezzosopran) • CLEOMENES, ein Edle am Hofe des Leontes (Baß) • DION, eineEdle am Hofe des Leontes (Tenor) • VALENTIN, ein alter Schäfer (Baß) • EIN HAUSIERER (Baß) • EINE DIENERIN DES

109

LEONTES •—• **Chorus:** MÄDCHEN UND FRAUEN ALS GEFOLGE DER KÖNIGIN HERMIONE, EDLE ALS GEFOLGE DES LEONTES UND DES POLIXENES, JUNGE UND ALTE SCHAFHIRTEN, JUNGE SCHÄFERINNEN

François Joseph Gossec (1734-1829)

Hylas et Sylvie

Status: I   **Evidence:** S
Text: Rochon de Chabannes, Marc-Antoine-Jacques (1730-1800)
Type: Pastorale   **Acts:** 1   **Language:** French
Premiere: Paris, France: Comédie-Française • 1768 12 10
Source of Premiere Information: Pitou
Play: *Tempest*
Yes: Pitou
No: Groves V

Comments: Pitou: performed at the home of the duchess de Mazarin [Chilly] on 1768 09 07. Groves V classifies it as incidental music: divertissements for Rochon de Chabannes' pastorale . . . . Mellen: Chantilly, 1768 11 07. Stieger: Paris, 1776, Opéra.

Charles François Gounod (1818-1893)

Roméo et Juliette

Status: Y   **Evidence:** P
Text: Barbier, Jules (1825-1901) and Michel Florentin Carré
        (1819-1872)
Type: Opéra   **Acts:** 5   **Language:** French
Premiere: Paris, France: Théâtre Lyrique • 1867 04 27
Source of Premiere Information: Loewenberg
Play: *Romeo and Juliet*
Publisher: Paris: Choudens, 1867 [vs].
Yes: LIBRETTO, Blom, Friedlaender, Groves V, Hartnoll,
        Loewenberg, Mellen, MGG, New Grove, Oxford, Squire,
        Stieger, Wilson

Comments: Score does not mention Shakespeare. German libretto in Schatz Collection (Cologne and Leipzig) mentions Shakespeare.

Cast: JULIETTE (Soprano) [Mme. Marie Miolan-Carvalho] • STÉPHANO (Soprano) [Melle. Daram] • GERTRUDE (Mezzo-Soprano) [Mme. Duclos] • ROMÉO (Ténor) [M. Michot] • TYBALT (Ténor) [M. Puget] • BENVOLIO (Ténor) [M. Laurent] • MERCUTIO (Baryton) [M. Barré] • PARIS (Baryton) [M. Laveissière] • GRÉGORIO (Baryton) [M. Troy jeune] • CAPULET (Basse chantante) [M. Troy] • FRERE LAURENT (Basse) [M. Cazaux] • LE DUC (Basse) [M. Wartel] • FRERE JEAN (Basse) [M. Neveu]

Alfredo Grandi

Amleto

Status: Y   **Evidence:** S
Text: Gargano, Aristide
Type: Comédie musicale   **Acts:** 3   **Language:** Italian
Premiere: Bologna, Italy: Teatro Brunetti • 1898 03 27
Source of Premiere Information: Mellen
Play: *Hamlet*
Yes: Mellen, Oxford

Karl Heinrich Graun (1701-1759)

Coriolano

Status: N   **Evidence:** S
Text: Villati, Leopoldo de
Type: Tragedia per Musica   **Acts:** 3   **Language:** Italian
Premiere: Berlin, Germany: Hoftheater • 1749 12 03
Source of Premiere Information: Schatz Catalog
Play: *Coriolanus*
No: Friedlaender

Comments: Friedlaender: 1750. Mennicke, Stieger: 1749 12 19. Libretto by Villati is based on a prose sketch by Frederick the Great. Score does not mention Shakespeare.

Cast: CORIOLANO • VOLUNNIA, sua moglie • VETTURIA, Madre di Coriolano • SESTO FURIO, Console • SICINIO, altro Console • FLAVIO, figliuolo di Coriolano • AZZIO TULLO, Principe de'Volsci • OLIBRIO, Senatore Romano •—• **Chorus:** SENATORI ROMANI, UFFIZIALI E SOLDATI VOLSCI, VESTALI, DAME ROMANE, SACERDOTI ROMANI, POPOLO ROMANO E LITTORI

Peter Greenwall

The Three Caskets, or Venice Re-served

Status: Y **Evidence:** S
Text: Snell, Gordon
Type: Operetta **Acts:** 1 **Language:** English
Premiere: London, England: Players' Theatre • 1956 11 05
Source of Premiere Information: Gänzl
Play: *Merchant of Venice*
Yes: Gänzl

Comments: Gänzl: based on the casket scene; expanded version was staged in 1961 also at Players'. Characters and cast from Gänzl.

Cast: MISS PORTIA BROWNE [Margaret Burton] • NERINA [Patricia Rowlands] • CLARISSA [Mavis Traill] • PATRICK O'LARRAGON [Denis Martin] • MOROCCO JOE [Robin Hunter] • HON. PERCY BASSANIO [John Gower] • JESSIE KERR [Jeanne Lusby] • LAURENCE [Brian Blades]

Georg Christoph Grosheim (1764-1841)

Titania, oder Liebe durch Zauberei

Status: Y **Evidence:** S
Text: Weber, Oberst von
Type: Singspiel **Acts:** 2 **Language:** German
Premiere: Kassel, Germany: Hof-Operntheater • 1792 00 00
Source of Premiere Information: Year and city from libretto.
Play: *Midsummer Night's Dream*
Yes: Schatz MS

Comments: There is a quote from Shakespeare on title page of libretto. Sonneck: the preface says that the text was composed by Grosheim. Sonneck is in error; it says Grosheim is the composer. Stieger: 1798.

Cast: TITANIA, Königin der Feen • OBERON, König der Elfen • PUCK • GOLDINE • PETER SQUENE, der Cantor aus Stolzenbain • CASPAR SCHNAUZ, der Schreiner • FRANZ FLAUT, der Kesselflicker • MARTIN SCNOCK [SCHOCK?], der Müller • MARX SCHLUCKEN, der Schneider •—• **Chorus:** FEEN, ELFEN

Howard Groth

Petruchio

Status: Y   **Evidence:** S
Text: Composer
Type: Opera   **Acts:** 2   **Language:** English
Premiere: Conway, Arkansas, U.S.A.: Arkansas State College: Ida
    Waldron Memorial Auditorium • 1954 03 29
Source of Premiere Information: Mellen
Play: *Taming of the Shrew*
Yes: Mellen, Oxford

Pietro Alessandro Guglielmi (1728-1804)

Admeto, Re di Tessaglia

Status: N   **Evidence:** S
Text: Palomba, Giuseppe (wrote 1765-1825)
Type: Dramma per musica   **Acts:** 2   **Language:** Italian
Premiere: Naples, Italy: Teatro del Fondo della Separazione dei
    Lucri • 1794 10 05
Source of Premiere Information: Libretto gives place and year.
    Schatz MS gives date.
Play: *Hamlet*
No: Plot, Characters

Cast: ADMETO, Re di Tessaglia [Il Sig. Matteo Babini] • CLOE, figlia di Palemone [La Sig. Elena Cantoni] • APOLLO [Il Sig. Gerolino

Braura] • MOPSA, moglie di Palemone [La Sig. Margherita Delicati] • PALEMONE [Sig. Giuseppe Trabalza] • ERGASTO [La Sig. Guglelmina Tortoni] • LISA, altra Figlia di Palemone [La Sig. Antonia Dascovurt]

Pietro Carlo Guglielmi (1763-1817)

Romeo e Giulietta [I Capuletti ed i Montecchi]

Status: Y   **Evidence:** P
Text: Buonaiuti, Serafino
Type: Opera   **Acts:** 2   **Language:** Italian
Premiere: London, England: King's Theater in the Haymarket
    • 1810 02 20
Source of Premiere Information: Mellen
Play: *Romeo and Juliet*
Publisher: Published; several detached numbers in British Library
Yes: LIBRETTO, Friedlaender, Groves V, Hartnoll, Mellen, Squire, Stieger, Wilson

Comments: Baker's: gives a detailed listing of where his operas are found. Groves V: paying tribute to the local genius. Manferrari: 30 marzo 1810.

Cast: ROMEO MONTAGUE, in love with [Signor Tramezzani] • JULIET CAPULET, betrothed to [Signora Calderini] • PARIS, Count of Lodrone [Signora Collini] • ANTONIO, Juliet's Father [Signor Beaghetti] • BLANCH, Juliet's Governess [Signora Bianchi] • FATHER LORENZO, a Franciscan Friar [Signor Rovedino] • TIBALT, Nephew to Antonio [Signor DeGiovanni] • BALTHASAR, Servant to Romeo [Signor DeGiovanni] • MERCUTIO, a Friend to Romeo [A Chorist] •—• **Chorus:** FRIENDS TO THE MONTAGUES, FRIENDS TO THE CAPULETS, PEOPLE OF VERONA, MUSICIANS, ATTENDANTS AND SERVANTS

Friedrich Gulda (1930-   )

Maß für Maß

Status: ?
Text: Unknown
Play: *Measure for Measure*

Comments: Not performed.

Friedrich Haack (1760-1827)

Die Geisterinsel

Status: Y   **Evidence:** S
Text: Gotter, Johann Friedrich Wilhelm (1746-1797) and Friedrich
    Hildebrand von Einsiedel (1750-1828)
Type: Singspiel   **Acts:** 3   **Language:** German
Premiere: Stettin, Poland: Neues Theater • 1794 00 00
Source of Premiere Information: Stieger
Play: *Tempest*
Yes: Friedlaender, Groves V, Hartnoll, Mellen, New Grove, Oxford,
    Stieger

Comments: Friedlaender: unpublished; composed in 1794 in
Settin. See comments to Fleischmann's *Die Geisterinsel.*

Cast: The characters should be the same as those given for
Reichardt's Die Geisterinsel.

Alois Hába (1893-1973)

Tempest

Status: I   **Evidence:** S
Text: Unknown
Play: *Tempest*
Publisher: Vienna: Universal-Edition, 1919
Yes: Moore

Comments: New Grove lists no opera by Haba on the subject of *The Tempest.* British Library lists Musik zu Shakespeare's *Der Sturm*. . . Op. 65 by Weingartner. Klavierauszug mit Text von A. Hába. Moore is probably incorrect.

Reynaldo Hahn (1874-1947)

Beaucoup de bruit pour rien

Status: Y   **Evidence:** S
Text: Sarment, Jean
Type: Musical Comedy   **Acts:** 4   **Language:** French
Premiere: Paris, France: Théâtre de la Madeleine • 1936 03 00
Play: *Much Ado About Nothing*
Yes: Hartnoll, MGG, New Grove, Oxford

Malvina

Status: ?
Text: Donnay, Maurice and Henri Duvernois [Henri Simon
        Schwabacher] (1875-1937)
Type: Opérette   **Acts:** 3/4 Tableaux   **Language:** French
Premiere: Paris, France: Théâtre Municipal de la Gaité-Lyrique
        • 1935 03 23
Source of Premiere Information: Score
Play: *All's Well That Ends Well*
Publisher: Paris: Heugel, 1935 [vs]

Comments: Score does not mention Shakespeare.

Cast: MALVINA [Mlle Renéé Camia] • ADÉLE, sa seur [Mlle Marguerite Thibault] • MME CHOCARD, leur mére [Mlle Charlotte Clasis] • MME DE RIGLDIER [Mlle Blanche Delimoges] • LÉOCADIE [Mlle Vander] • CAROLINE [Mlle May Muriel] • HÉLOISE [Mlle Ginette Dinot] • BERTHE [Mlle Yvette Darcy] • IRMA [Mlle Maud Siva] • MME DE RIGALDIER [Mlle Clara Dorel] • JULES VALÉRIEN [M. Roger Bourdin] • ARTHUR [M. Robert Allard] • M. CHOCARD [M. Carpentier] • DE BALZAC [M. Descombes] • LE GAMIN [M. Paul Maquaire] • GARDE NATIONEL [M. Geó Lastry] • PERE DE MME DE RIGALDIER [M. Mathieu] • UN HOME [M. Péronne]

Le Marchand de Vénise

Status: Y   **Evidence:** P
Text: Zamaçois, Miguel
Type: Opéra   **Acts:** 3 and 5 tableaux   **Language:** French
Premiere: Paris, France: Théâtre National de l'Opéra • 1935 03 25
Source of Premiere Information: Score
Play: *Merchant of Venice*
Publisher: Paris: Heugel & Cie, 1935 [vs]
Yes: SCORE, LIBRETTO, Baker's, Blom, Groves V, Hartnoll,
     Loewenberg, Mellen, MGG, New Grove, Oxford

Comments: Mellen:1935 03 21.

Cast: PORTIA (Soprano) [Mme Fanny Heldy] • NÉRISSA, suivante
et amie de Portia (Mezzo-Soprano) [Mme Renée Mahé] • JESSICA,
fille de Shylock (Soprano) [Mme Odette Renaudin] • LA
GOUVERNANTE (Soprano) [Mme Andrée Marilliet] • UNE
SERVANTE (Soprano) [Mme Vial] • SHYLOCK, juif usurier de Venise
(Basse) [M. André Pernet] • BASSANIO, ami d'Antonio, amoureux de
Portia (Baryton) [M. Martial Singher] • ANTONIO, riche marchand
vénitien (Basse) [M. Paul Cabanel] • GRATIANO, amoureux de
Nérissa (Ténor) [M. Henri Le Clézio] • LORENZO, amoureux de
Jessica (Ténor) [M. Chastenet] • TUBAL, juif ami de Shylock (Basse)
[M. Louis Morot] • LE PRINCE D'ARAGON (Ténor) [M. Edmond
Rambaud] • LE PRINCE DE MAROC (Basse) [M. Etcheverry] • LE
MASQUE (Ténor) [M. Raoul Gilles] • LE DOGE (Basse) [M. Narçon] •
UNE VOIX (Ténor) [M. Madlen] • L'AUDIENCIER (Basse) [M. Ernst] •
UN GRAND DE VENISE (Baryton) [M. Forest] • PREMIER VÉNITIEN
(Ténor) [M. Gilles] • DEUXIEME VÉNITIEN (Ténor) [M. Gourgues] •
PREMIER JUIF (Basse) [M. Médus] • DEUXIEME JUIF (Basse) [M.
Pactat] • TROISIEME JUIF (Ténor) [M. Madlen] • PREMIER
SERVITEUR (Basse) [M. Ernst] • DEUXIEME SERVITEUR (Baryton)
[M. Forest] • UN SERVITEUR (Ténor) [M. Deleu] • SALARINO (Ténor)
[M. Deleu] • SIX VÉNITIENNES [Mmes Vial, Holnay, Nathan, Cléry,
Lumière, Douls] • SIX VÉNITIENS [MM. De Leu, Madlen, Gourgues,
Anglès, Hontarrède, Demagny] • LE CONFIDENT DU PRINCE DE
MAROC (rôle muet) [M. Castel] •— **Chorus:** SUITE DU PRINCE DE
MAROC ET DU PRINCE D'ARAGON, VÉNITIENS, VÉNITIENNES,
JUIFS, GARDES, ETC. . . . ., PAGES

Roger Haines

Fire Angel

Status: Y   **Evidence:** S
Text: Bentley, Paul
Type: Musical   **Acts:** 2   **Language:** English
Premiere: London, England: Wimbledon Theatre • 1977 02 25
Source of Premiere Information: Gänzl
Play: *Merchant of Venice*
Yes: Gänzl

Comments: Gänzl: completely revised and expanded adaptation of
Shylock by Haines and Bently. Interim production earlier in Belgium.
Characters and cast from Gänzl.

Cast: MAMMA DOC [Gaye Brown] • WAITER/FIRE [Mark Tyme] •
THE DOGE/PHOENIX [Keith Hodiak] • GOLD/LITTLE GIRL [Belinda
Nash] • SILVER/BRIDE [Wanda Rokicki] • LEAD/DEATH [Libby
Rose] • BOUNCER/THIRD HOOD [Colin Fay] • SPIDER GIRL/MOON
[Helen Baker] • HOT PANTS GIRL/SUN [Jeni Evans] • GREEN
GIRL/FISH [Myra Sands] • PURPLE GIRL/STARS [Megg Nicol] •
GEISHA GIRL/FISH [Paulette Hegeny] • DON PIRANHA [Ian Burford]
• LUCY PIRANHA [Helen Chappelle/Paulette Hegney] • ANGELO
SACRAMONA [Anthony Wood] • BOBBY SACRAMONA [Julian
Littman] • BRIDEGROOM/RICCI THE HIT [Ludovico Romano] • JOE
DE ROSA [Derek Smith] • 1ST HOOD/WHORE [David Wheldon-
Williams] • COP/2ND HOOD/OCTOPUS [Joshua Bancel] •
BABY/4TH HOOD [Richard Roman] • 5TH HOOD [Peter Karrie] • 6TH
HOOD [Terence Hillyer] • DIARRHOEA DAVE [Larrington Walker] •
BARACH [Colm Wilkinson/Paul Bentley] • DEBORAH [Linda
Kendrick] • TROUSER GIRL/STATUE OF LIBERTY [Pauline
Crawford]

Shylock [Fire Angel]

Status: Y   **Evidence:** S
Text: Bentley, Paul
Type: Musical   **Acts:** 2   **Language:** English
Premiere: Edinburgh, Scotland: St Columbia-by-the-Castle
• 1974 08 16
Source of Premiere Information: Gänzl
Play: *Merchant of Venice*
Yes: Gänzl

Comments: Gänzl: revised version produced as *Fire Angel* in 1977. Characters and cast from Gänzl.

Cast: DOGE/LORENZO/ENGLISH SUITOR [Andrew Wadsworth] • ANTONIO/SUN PRIEST/SCOTS SUITOR [Anthony O'Driscoll] • BASSANIO/SOLANIO/RUSSIAN SUITOR [Earl Adair] • GRATIANO/TUBAL/GERMAN SUITOR/MOROCCAN SUITOR [Arthur Kohn] • PORTIA [Pamela Obermayer] • NERISSA [Elizabeth Handover] • SHYLOCK [Paul Bentley] • JESSICA [Helen Murphy Glavin]

Alfred Matthew Hale (1875-   )

The Tempest

Status: Y   **Evidence:** S
Text: Composer?
Language: English
Premiere: London, England: Queen's Hall [Only parts performed] • 1912 02 28
Play: *Tempest*
Publisher: Published
Yes: Hartnoll, Oxford, Wilson

Comments: Oxford: published 1917.

Jacques François Fromental Elie Halévy (1799-1862)

Guido et Ginevre ou La Peste de Florence

Status: I   **Evidence:** S
Text: Scribe, Augustin Eugène (1791-1861)
Type: Opera   **Acts:** 5   **Language:** French
Premiere: Paris, France: Théâtre del Académie royale de Musique, Salle provisoire de la rue Le Peletier • 1838 03 05
Source of Premiere Information: Mellen
Play: *Romeo and Juliet*
Publisher: Paris: G. Brandus, 1938 [vs]

Yes: Friedlaender
No: Clément

Comments: New Grove: revised in 4 acts. Clément: Le sujet du livret reproduit un épisode raconté par M. Delécluze dan son histoire de Florence. Plot described briefly in Riemann. Stieger: 4 acts. Manferrari: 3 acts, Paris, Académe R. de Musique, 9 Marzo 1838. Score: 5 acts. Friedlaender: . . . der Text in mehrenen Scenen unmittlelbar an *Romeo und Julia* anknüpft.

Cast: GINEVARA, Fille de Cosme de Médicis (Soprano) • RICCIARDA, Cantatrice (Soprano) • LEONORE, Femme de la suite de Ginevra (Soprano) • ANTONIETTA, Jeune paysanne (Soprano) • GIDO, Jeune Sculpteur (Ténor) • FORTE BRACCIO, Condottiêre (Ténor) • COSME DE MÉDICIS (Basse) • MANFREDI, duc de Ferrare (Basse) • LORENZO, Intendant de Médicis (Basse) • TEOBALDO, Sacristain de la Cathédrale de Florence (Basse) •—•
Chorus: CHŒURS

La Tempesta

Status: Y   **Evidence:** P
Text: Scribe, Augustin Eugène (1791-1861) [Original French]
Type: Opéra italien   **Acts:** Prologue/3   **Language:** Italian
Premiere: London, England: Her Majesty's Theatre in the
          Haymarket • 1850 06 08
Source of Premiere Information: Loewenberg
Play: *Tempest*
Publisher: Paris: G. Brandus et cie., 1850? [vs]
Yes: LIBRETTO, Blom, Friedlaender, Groves V, Hartnoll,
          Loewenberg, Mellen, MGG, Oxford, Schatz MS, Squire,
          Stieger, Wilson

Comments: In Italian in London (translation by Giannone, Pietro); Groves V: book was originally adapted by Scribe from Shakespeare for Mendelssohn; 3 acts. Clément has description of the work. Manferrari:18 giugno 1850. Libretto (French/Italian) at Opèra: 2 acts. Score: 3 acts. Conducted by Balfe.

Cast: ALONZO, re di Napoli (Tenore) [Signor Lorenzo] • PROSPERO, duca di Mllano (Basso) [Signor Coletti] • ANTONIO, fratello di Prospero (Basso) [Signor Lablache] • FERNANDO, principe di Napoli (Tenore) [Signor Baucarde] • TRINCOLO, marinaro (Basso) [Signor Ferrari] • STEFANO, marinaro (Tenore) [Madlle Parodi] •

SICORACE (Soprano) [Madlle Ida Bertrand] • UN SPIRITO DELL'
AERE (Soprano) [Madlle Giuliani] • ARIEL [Madlle Carlotta Grisi] •
CALIBANO, figliuolo di Sicorace (Basso) [Signor Lablache] •
MIRANDA, figilia di Prospero (Soprano) [Madame Sontag] •——•
Chorus: MARINARI, GENII, ARIELE, SILFIDI

Sidney Halpern

Macbeth

Status: Y   **Evidence:** S
Text: Composer
Type: Opera   **Acts:** 1   **Language:** English
Premiere: New York, U.S.A.: Off-Broadway Opera Company
    • 1965 04 04
Source of Premiere Information: Mellen
Play: *Macbeth*
Yes: Mellen, Northouse, Oxford

Comments: There is a holograph score for a *Macbeth* Overture in
the NY Public Library.

Eduard Hamel (1811-   )

Malvina

Status: Y   **Evidence:** S
Text: Steppes, Dr. Adolph (1796-   )
Type: Komisch-Romantische Oper   **Acts:** 3
        Language: German
Premiere: Hamburg, Germany: Stadttheater • 1857 03 16
Source of Premiere Information: Mellen
Play: *All's Well That Ends Well*
Yes: Mellen, Schatz MS, Stieger

Comments: First performance 1855 07 00 was private. Above was
first public performance. Stieger lists works by Schindelmeisser and
Hirlemann [sic] with similar titles but does not say they are based on
Shakespeare.

Cast: DER KÖNIG VON FRANKREICH • RAIMUND, Graf von
Toulouse • TONNEAU, Leibarzt des Königs • GRAF VON BELLE-
MAIN, königlicher Offizier • GRAF VON VILLARD, königlicher Offizier
• MALVINA, eine Waise, von der Mutter Raimunds erzogen •
DORINA, eine junge Wirthin • EIN PAGE • EIN SOLDAT DER
GARNISON ZU RIZZA •—• **Chorus:** KÖNIGLICHE OFFIZIERE,
FRANZÖSISCHE SOLDATEN, SOLDATEN DER GARNISON ZU
RIZZA, HOFHERREN, EHRENDAMEN, PAGEN, PILGERINNEN,
MASKEN, GENSD'ARMEN, ERZBISCHOF, GEISTLICHE,
CHORKNABEN, VOLK u. s. w.

Georg Friederich Händel (1685-1759)

Admeto, Re di Tessaglia

Status: N   **Evidence:** S
Text: Rolli, Paolo Antonio (1687-1765)
Type: Opera   **Acts:** 3   **Language:** Italian
Premiere: London, England: King's Theatre in the Haymarket
    • 1727 01 31
Source of Premiere Information: Mellen
Play: *Hamlet*
Publisher: London: J. Cluer, 1727 [s]
No: Sonneck

Comments: Mellen: libretto is an altered version of Aurelio Aureli's
L'Antigona delusa da Alceste. Loewenberg: 1727 02 11.
Characters and cast from Deutsch.

Cast: ADMETO (Alto) [Signor Senesino] • ALCESTE (Mezzo-
Soprano) [Signora Faustina] • ERCOLE (Bass) [Signor Boschi] •
ORINDO (Contralto) [Signora Dotti] • TRASIMEDE (Counter-Tenor)
[Signor Baldi] • ANTIGONA (Soprano) [Signora Cuzzoni] • MERASPE
(Bass) [Signor Palmerini]

J. F. J. Hanssens

Gillette de Narbonne

Status: ?
Text: Unknown
Type: Opera
Premiere: 1830 00 00 ?
Play: *All's Well That Ends Well*

Comments: No cross-listings in Stieger. J. F.J. seems to be incorrect. May be Charles-Louis (Jr. or Sr.). Not listed in Hanssens Jr.'s Catalog of works in Charles-Louis Hanssens by Louis Bärwolf; Bruxelles: 1894. Most of his operas were first performed at Th. de La Monaie.

John Harbison (1938-   )

The Winter's Tale

Status: Y   **Evidence:** S
Text: Composer
Type: Opera   **Acts:** 2   **Language:** English
Premiere: San Francisco, U.S.A.: Opera • 1979 08 20
Source of Premiere Information: Mellen
Play: *Winter's Tale*
Publisher: New York: Associated Music Publishers [s, vs]
Yes: AMCL, Mellen

Wally Harper

Sensations

Status: Y   **Evidence:** S
Text: Zakrzewski, Paul (book and lyrics)
Type: Broadway Show   **Language:** English
Premiere: New York, U.S.A.: Theatre Four • 1970 10 25
Source of Premiere Information: Simas
Play: *Romeo and Juliet*
Yes: Simas

Fritz Bennicke Hart (1874-1949)

Malvolio, Opus 14

Status: Y   **Evidence:** S
Text: Composer
Type: Opera   **Acts:** 3   **Language:** English
Premiere: Melbourne, Australia: By Conservatory Students
    • 1918 12 05
Play: *Twelfth Night*
Yes: Groves V, Hartnoll, Mellen, New Groves, Oxford, Slonimsky,
    Stieger

Hermann Heinrich (1891-   )

Viel Lärm um Nichts

Status: Y   **Evidence:** S
Text: Composer
Type: Opera   **Acts:** 3   **Language:** German
Premiere: Frankfurt/Oder, Germany • 1956 08 18
Play: *Much Ado About Nothing*
Yes: Gruber, Hartnoll, Mellen, Oxford

Comments: Mellen: Frankfort-am-Main, Kleisttheater.

Johann Daniel Hensel (1757-1839)

Die Geisterinsel

Status: Y   **Evidence:** P
Text: Composer [after Shakespeare, Friedrich Wilhelm Gotter
    (1746-1797) and Johann Wilhelm Döring (1760-   )]
Type: Singspiel   **Acts:** 4   **Language:** German
Premiere: Hirschberg, Germany • 1799 01 00
Source of Premiere Information: Year and place from libretto.
Play: *Tempest*
Yes: LIBRETTO, Hartnoll, Mellen, Oxford, Squire, Stieger

Comments: Mellen: 1800 00 00. A revised version of Gotter's libretto used previously by Fleischmann, Haack, Reichardt, and Zumsteeg.

Cast: PROSPERO, gewesener Herzog von Mailand. Zaubeer • MIRANDA, seine Tochter • FERNANDO, Prinz von Neapel • FABIO, Page des Prinzen (von einer Sängerin gespielt) • TRINKULO, Hofnarr des Prinzen • STEFANO, Küchen u. Kellermeister des Prinzen • ARIEL, ein Sylphe (Von einer Sängerin gespielt) • KALIBAN, ein Gnome. Sohn der Sykorar • MAJA, ein Schatten (von einer sanft tragischen Aktrice gespielt) • SYKORAR, ein Schatten (Von einer heftig tragischen Aktrice [allenfalls von einem Akteur] gespielt) • ANTONIO, Bruder des Prospero, unrechtmäßiger Herzog von Mailand •—• **Chorus:** GEISTER, SYLPHEN UND SYLPHIDEN, SCHIFFSVOLK UND MATROSEN VON ALLERLEI RANGE

Louis Joseph Ferdinand Hérold (1791-1833)

La Gioventù di Enrico V [La Jeunesse d'Henry V]

Status: N   **Evidence:** P
Text: Composer
Type: Opéra-Comique   **Acts:** 2   **Language:** Italian
Premiere: Naples, Italy: Teatro del Fondo • 1815 01 05
Source of Premiere Information: Score
Play: *Henry IV*
Publisher: Paris: Mackar et Noël, 1894 [vs]
Yes: Manferrari
No: SCORE, Groves V, Mellen, Squire

Comments: Groves V: His first opera; libretto by composer, translated by Landriani, based on Alexandre Duval's *La Jeunesse de Henri V.*

Cast: IL PRINCIPE ENRICO (Tenore) [Il signor Garcia] • IL CONTE ROCESTER (Tenore) [Il signor Donzelli] • LADY CLARA (Mezzo-Soprano) [La signira de Bernardis] • EDUARDO (Soprano) [La signora Darcanelli Corradi] • COPP (Basso) [Il signor Lombardi] • BETTINA (Soprano) [La signora Pontiggia] • WILLIAM, che non parla, cameriere del principe • UN SERVO DELLA TAVERNA •—•
Chorus: GARZONI DELLA TAVERNA

Werner Herx

Der Orakelspruch

Status: N   **Evidence:** P
Text: Salice-Contessa, Carl Wilhelm and Christoph Ernest von
        Houwald
Type: Operette (Posse)   **Acts:** 1   **Language:** German
Premiere: Paris, France: Vaudeville Théâtre • 1849 00 00
Play: *Winter's Tale*
No: LIBRETTO

Comments: Mellen: operetta, Antwerpen; 1849, composer,
German. Stieger: Amsterdam 1849. Libretto: nach Comtessa's und
C. von Houwald's Schriften bearbeitet und in Musik gesetzt von
W. Herx.

Cast: FLORINDE, eine Fee • LUCIE, ihre Tochter • MARKO, ihr
Gärtner • SYLVIO, ein Jäger • ROSA, ein Mädchen • MOCK, ein
Bucklicher • EIN GENIUS •——•
Chorus: JUNGER MÄDCHEN, BUCKLICHE

Ludwig Hess (1877-1944)

Was ihr Wollt

Status: Y   **Evidence:** S
Text: Composer
Type: Opera   **Acts:** 5
Premiere: Stettin, Poland • 1941 03 30
Play: *Twelfth Night*
Yes: Gruber

Hal Hester and Danny Apolinar

Your Own Thing

Status: Y   **Evidence:** P
Text: Driver, Donald (book) Hal Hester and Danny Apolinar (lyrics)
Type: Rock Musical   **Language:** English

Premiere: New York, U.S.A.: Off-Broadway • 1968 01 13
Source of Premiere Information: Tumbush
Play: *Twelfth Night*
Publisher: New York: National General Music Publishing Co.
        1968 [vs]
Yes: SCORE, Bordman, Green, Tumbush

Cast: ORSON [Tom Ligon] • OLIVIA [Marcia Rodd] • VIOLA [Leland Palmer] • SEBASTIAN [Rusty Thacker]

Richard Franz Joseph Heuberger (1850-1914)

Viola

Status: ?
Text: Unknown
Play: *Twelfth Night*

Comments: Unfinished.

Leslie Hays Heward (1897-1943)

Hamlet

Status: Y   **Evidence:** S
Text: Unknown
Type: Unfinished opera
Premiere: 1916 00 00
Play: *Hamlet*
Publisher: MGG: all scores have remained in manuscript
Yes: Groves V, Hartnoll, Oxford

Comments: Groves V: Composed 1916, unfinished. New Grove: his 2 operas are unfinished.

Aristide Hignard (1822-1898)

Hamlet

Status: Y   **Evidence:** P
Text: Garal, Pierre de
Type: Tragédie lyrique   **Acts:** 5 and 9 Tableaux
        Language: French
Premiere: Nantes, France: Grand Théâtre • 1888 04 21
Source of Premiere Information: Loewenberg
Play: *Hamlet*
Publisher: Paris: E. Heu, 1868 [vs]
Yes: SCORE, LIBRETTO, Blom, Friedlaender, Hartnoll,
        Loewenberg, Mellen, Oxford, Schatz MS, Stieger, Wilson

Comments: Baker's: his best opera; came out the same year as
Thomas' and suffered therefore. Manferrari: librettist is E. Garnier.
Loewenberg notes that the score was published as early as 1868 but
the opera was not performed until later because of the success of
Thomas' opera on the same subject.

Cast: OPHÉLIE, Fille de Polonius (Soprano) • GERTRUDE, Reine
de Danemark (Mezzo-Soprano) • HAMLET, son fils, Neveu de
Claudius (Ténor) • POLONIUS, Chambellan (Ténor) • MARCELL,
Garde (Ténor) • UN MESSAGER (Ténor) • LAERTE, Fils de Polonius
(Baryton) • HORATIO, Ami d'Hamlet (Baryton) • GUILDENSTERN,
Courtisan (Baryton) • UN INTERPRETE (Baryton) • CLAUDIUS, Roi
de Danemark (Basse) • LE SPECTRE, du père d'Hamlet (Basse) •
ROSENCRANTZ, Courtisan (Basse) • UN FOSSOYEUR (Basse) • UN
PRETRE (Basse) • BERNARD, Garde (Basse) • FORTINBRAS,
Prince de Norvège • OSRIC, Seigneur • DEUS AMBASSADEURS •
UN OFFICIER • UN COMÉDIEN • UNE DANSEUSE • LE ROI DE LA
PIECE • LA REINE DE LA PIECE •—•
Chorus: SEIGNEURS, DAMES, COURTISANS, JEUNES FILLES,
COMÉDIENS, MOINES, PEUPLE ET GENS DE SUITE

J. L. A. Hignett

Hamlet

Status: N   **Evidence:** S
Text: Unknown
Play: *Hamlet*

Comments: This is likely a mistaken reference in Towers to *Hamlet* by Aristide Hignard (1822-1898).

Hermann Hirschbach (1812-1888)

Othello

Status: Y   **Evidence:** S
Text: Unknown
Type: Opera   **Language:** German
Play: *Othello*
Yes: Stieger

Comments: Stieger: posthumous; not performed.

Franz Anton Hoffmeister (1754-1812)

Rosalinde, oder Die Macht der Feen

Status: ?
Text: Schikaneder, Emanuel [originally Johann Schikeneder] (1751-1812)
Type: Komische Oper   **Acts:** 3   **Language:** German
Premiere: Vienna, Austria: Theater auf der Weiden • 1796 04 23
Source of Premiere Information: Mellen
Play: *As You Like It*
Publisher: Braunschweig: Verlage des Musicalischen Magarzins

Comments: Manferrari: libretto is by E. G. Schikaneder in 1 act, Vienna Tr. an der Wein, 24 aprile 1796.

Cast: RUNCKA (Mezzo Sopran) • MERKUR (Tenor) • SIRENA (Sopran) • HUY (Bariton) • ROSALINDE (Mezzo Sopran) • SELIDANO (Tenor)

Der Schiffbruch

Status: Y   **Evidence:** S
Text: Korndorfer, Georg
Type: Singspiel   **Language:** German
Premiere: Vienna, Austria: Theater auf der Landstrasse
        • 1792 07 22
Source of Premiere Information: Mellen
Play: *Tempest*
Yes: Mellen, Oxford

Johann Hofmann [Hoffmann]

Ritter Hans von Dampf

Status: Y   **Evidence:** S
Text: Unknown
Type: Kom. Singspiel   **Language:** German
Premiere: Vienna, Austria: Theater in der Leopoldstadt
        • 1800 11 06
Source of Premiere Information: Mellen
Play: *Merry Wives of Windsor*
Yes: Schatz MS, Stieger

Gustav Hohmann (1850-   )

Hermione, oder Der kleine Vicomte

Status: N   **Evidence:** S
Text: Blum, Carl Ludwig
Type: Operette   **Acts:** 2   **Language:** German
Premiere: Lisbon, Portugal: Stadttheater • 1887 03 27
Play: *Winter's Tale*
No: Schatz MS, Stieger

Comments: Schatz MS, Stieger: nach Bayard's *Le vicomte de Letosières*. Mellen, Stieger: Lisbon, 1887 04 00.

Hans Holenia (1890-1972)

Viola [Was Ihr wollt], Opus 21

Status: Y   **Evidence:** S
Text: Widowitz, Oskar
Type: Opera   **Acts:** Vsp./3   **Language:** German
Premiere: Graz, Austria: Opernhaus • 1934 11 17
Source of Premiere Information: Loewenberg
Play: *Twelfth Night*
Publisher: MGG: Selbsverlag; Ouv., Wien. A-Tempo-Verlag
Yes: Blom, Gruber, Hartnoll, Loewenberg, Mellen, Oxford, Stieger

Comments: US:Wc has the overture to this work. Manferrari: Tr. Municipale.

Jan David Holland (1746-1827)

Pantomime zu Hamlet

Status: NO   **Evidence:** P
Type: Pantomime   **Acts:** 7 Aufzugen   **Language:** German
Premiere: Hamburg, Germany • 1786 00 00
Source of Premiere Information: Libretto
Play: *Hamlet*
Yes: Groves V, Stieger
No: SCORE

Comments: Mellen: composer's dates 1746-1815. The music referred to consists of approximately 160 measures for the klavier inserted at the end of the German text for the play [divided into 6 acts]. Title page indicates music is for a ballet; Holland is not mentioned. That the music is by Holland is the conjecture of CPM. Stieger: Berlin, 1790.

Gustav Holst (1874-1934)

At the Boar's Head, Opus 42

Status: Y   **Evidence:** P
Text: Composer
Type: Musical Interlude   **Acts:** 1   **Language:** English
Premiere: Manchester, England: British National Opera Company
• 1925 04 03
Source of Premiere Information: Loewenberg
Play: *Henry IV, Parts 1 and 2*
Publisher: London: Novello, 1925 [vs]
Yes: SCORE, Blom, Groves V, Hartnoll, Loewenberg, Mellen, New
Grove, Oxford, White

Comments: Score: The Libretto Taken From Shakespeare's
King Henry IV.

Cast: FALSTAFF • PRINCE HAL • POINS • BARDOLPH • PETO •
GADSHILL • PISTOL • PISTOL'S TWO COMPANIONS • HOSTESS
(Dame Quickly) • DOLL TEARSHEET • SOLDIERS (Unseen) • A
DRAWER

Arthur Honegger (1892-1955)

La Tempête

Status: NO   **Evidence:** P
Language: NA
Premiere: 1923 00 00
Source of Premiere Information: Stieger
Play: *Tempest*
Yes: Manferrari
No: SCORE

Comments: Manferrari: an opera. It is incidental music.

Julius Hopp (1819-1885)

Hammlet

Status: Y   **Evidence:** P
Text: Composer
Type: Operelle   **Acts:** 6 Bildern   **Language:** German
Premiere: Vienna, Austria: Strampfer Theater • 1874 01 29
Source of Premiere Information: Stieger
Play: *Hamlet*
Yes: SCORE, LIBRETTO, Oxford

Cast: CLAUDIUS, König von Dänemark • GERTRUD, Witwe des vorigen Königs, seine Braut • HAMLET, ihr Sohn, Neffe des gegenwärtigen Königs • HORATIO, sein Freund • POLONIUS, Oberhofmeister und Gesamtminister • OFELIA, seine Tochter • LAERTES, sein Sohn • MARCELLUS, Offizier • BERNARDO, Offizier • CORNELIUS, Offizier • FRANZISKO, Offizier • DER GEIST VON HAMLET'S VATER • EIN SCHAUSPIELER •—• **Chorus:** HERRN UND DAMEN VOM HOFE, SCHAUSPIELER UND SCHAUSPIELERINNEN, WACHEN, GEISTER, DÄMONEN, DIENER

Karel Horky (1909-   )

Jed z Elsinoru [The Poison from Elsinore]

Status: Y   **Evidence:** P
Text: Renc, Václav
Type: Opera   **Acts:** 2   **Language:** Czech
Premiere: Brno [Brünn], Czechoslovakia: Státní Divádlo • 1969 11 11
Source of Premiere Information: Slonimsky
Play: *Hamlet*
Yes: LIBRETTO, Baker's, Oxford, Slominsky
No: Mellen

Comments: Oxford: distantly related. Mellen: based on a story by M. Rejnus. Libretto is based on the radio play, *Urhamlet*, which grew from the conviction that both President Kennedy and Hamlet's father were murdered because of a power struggle.

Charles Edward Horn (1786-1849), and Samuel Webbe Jr.

Merry Wives of Windsor

Status: I   **Evidence:** S
Text: Unknown
Language: English
Premiere: London, England: Drury Lane Theatre • 1823 00 00
Play: *Merry Wives of Windsor*
Yes: Oxford
No: Stieger, New Grove, NUC

Comments: Stieger: incidental music. New Grove: Comedy, after Shakespeare, DL, 20 Feb 1824; collab. J. Parry, S. Webbe, and others. GB:Lbm has a selection titled: Trip, Trip, away as sung by Miss Povey and the Chorus of Fairies in the Revived Comedy of the *Merry Wives of Windsor* Composed by Charles E. Horn.

Horner

König Lear

Status: ?
Text: Composer
Premiere: Prag
Source of Premiere Information: Schatz MS
Play: Lear

George Hüe (1858-1948)

Titania

Status: I   **Evidence:** S
Text: Gallet, Louis (1835-1898) and André Corneau (1857-   )
Type: Musical drama   **Acts:** 3   **Language:** French
Premiere: Paris, France: Opéra Comique • 1903 01 20
Source of Premiere Information: Mellen
Play: *Midsummer Night's Dream*
Publisher: Paris: Choudens, Editeur, 1903 [vs]

Yes: Blom, Groves V, Mellen, Oxford
No: Clément

Comments: Has no closer link with Shakespeare than a quarrel between Oberon and Titania; Groves V: it is after Shakespeare. Clément discusses the opera and says it is based on the old legend *Huon de Bordeaux* from which Shakespeare also took material.

Cast: MATHIAS • ROBIN • YANN • HERMINE • TITANIA • OBÉRON • PHILIDA (Dancer) •—• **Chorus:** JEUNES FILLES

Gervase Hughes (1905-   )

Scenes from Twelfth Night

Status: Y   **Evidence:** S
Text: Unknown
Type: Opera
Play: *Twelfth Night*
Yes: Groves V (Sup. Vol.)

Comments: Groves V: opera is unfinished. [It is listed in the Supplement, but not in Shakespeare article.]

Th. Hulemann

Malvine I re (Malvine the First)

Status: ?
Text: MacNab and P. Manoury
Type: Opéra comique   **Acts:** 3   **Language:** French
Premiere: Paris, France: Théâtre des Folies Dramatiques
        • 1900 06 23
Source of Premiere Information: Schatz MS
Play: *All's Well That Ends Well*

Paul Xaver Désiré Richard, Marquis d'Ivry [used Richard Yrvid as a nom de plume] (1829-1903)

Les Amantes de Vérone

Status: Y   **Evidence:** P
Text: Composer
Type: Drame Lyríque   **Acts:** 5/6 Tableaux
    Language: French
Premiere: Paris, France: Théâtre Ventadour • 1878 10 12
Source of Premiere Information: Loewenberg
Play: *Romeo and Juliet*
Publisher: Paris: G. Flaxland, 1867 [vs]
Yes: SCORE, LIBRETTO, Baker's, Blom, Friedlaender, Groves V, Hartnoll, Loewenberg, Mellen, Oxford, Squire, Stieger, Wilson

Comments: Performed for the first time in 4 acts at l'École de Mr Gilbert Louis Duprez in Paris, 1867 05 12. Score: 4 acts. Libretto [Paris 1878] in GB:Lbm gives the date/place as 1878 10 10, Théâtre-Lyrique. Characters and cast from Schatz Libretto Collection number 4946.

Cast: CAPULET [M. Dufriche] • ROMÉO MONTAIGU [M. Capoul] • LORENZO, moine franciscain [M. Taskin] • TYBALT, neveu de Capulet [M. Max Christophe] • MERCUTIO, ami de Roméo [M. Fromant] • BENVOLIO, ami de Roméo [M. Labarre] • LE HÉRAULT DUCAL [M. Dardignac] • DEUXIEME CAPULET [M. Barielle] • GENNARO, ami de Roméo et de Mercutio [M. Colomb] • ANDREA, ami de Roméo et de Mercutio [M. Fille] • PETRUCCIO, ami de Roméo et de Mercutio [M. Escala] • LODOVICO, ami de Roméo et de Mercutio [M. Martin] • STENIO, ami de Roméo et de Mercutio [M. Raynal] • ERCOLE, ami de Roméo et de Mercutio [M. Bonjean] • TIBERIO, ami de Roméo et de Mercutio [M. Coste] • UBERTIO, ami de Roméo et de Mercutio [M. Savigny] • PARIS [M. Blanc] • BALTHAZAR, page de Roméo (personnage muet) • LES DEUX PAGES DE PARIS (personnages muets) • JULIETTE [Mme Heilbron] • LA NOURRICE [Mme Lhéritier] •—• **Chorus:** DAMES ET SIGNEURS DE VERONE, BOURGEOIS, JEUNES GENS ET JEUNES FILLES, HOMMES D'ARMES, LA FOULE

Edward Jakobowski [pseud. of Edward Belville] (1858-)

Erminie

Status: N   **Evidence:** S
Text: Bellamy, Claxson and Harry Paulton (1842-1917)
Type: Comic Opera   **Acts:** 2   **Language:** English
Premiere: Birmingham, England: Grand Theatre • 1885 10 26
Source of Premiere Information: Gänzl
Play: *Winter's Tale*
Publisher: London: Joseph Williams, 1887 [vs]
No: Mellen

Comments: Mellen: operetta 2 acts, 1985 11 09, based on a drama by Robert Macaire. Characters and cast from Gänzl.

Cast: MARQUIS DE PONTVERT [Fred Mervin] • EUGENE MARCEL [Henry Bracy] • VICOMTE DE BRISSAC [Horace Bolini] • DELAUNAY [Kate Everleigh/Miss Amalia] • SARGEANT [A. D. Pierrepoint/Herbert George] • DUFOIS, the landlord [George Marler/Ambrose Collini] • SIMON, a waiter [J. W. Bradbury/Frank Seymour/Lytton Grey] • HENRI [Stanley Betjeman] • PIERRE [Lottie Leigh/Nellie Carlton] • CHEVALIER DE BRABAZON [Percy Compton/Frank Barsby/C. A. Randolph] • RAVANNES [Frank Wyatt] • CADEAU [Harry Paulton] • CERISE MARCEL [Violet Melnotte (Marie Huntley)] • JAVOTTE [Kate Munroe] • MARIE [Edith Vane] • CLEMENTINE [Delia Merton/Mary Webb] • PRINCESSE DE GRAMPONEUR [M. A. Victor] • ERMINIE DE PONTVERT [Florence St John/Marie Tempest] • M. ST BRICE [Nellie Gordon] • M. D'AUVIGNE [Kitty Graham] • M. DE NAILLES [Marie Huntley] • M. DE SANGRES [Violet Leigh] • MME ST BRICE [Lillie Teesdale] • MME DE LAGE [Ada Maxwell] • MME BREFCHAMP [Ethel Selwyn] • MME DE CHATEAULIN [Millie Gerard] • ANTOINETTE [Madge Bruce] • CHARLOTTE [Emilie Campbell] • JEANETTE [Anita Marzan] • MIGNON [Florence Dudley/Stella Carr] • ROSALIE [Carrie Solomon] • NINICHE [Helen Gwynne] • NANINE [Mary Webb/J. Dudley] • FANCHETTE [Sylvia Southgate] •—
Chorus: SOLDIERS

David Jenkins (1848-1915)

The Enchanted Isle (Scenes from Shakespeare's 'Tempest')

Status: NO   **Evidence:** P
Text: Islwyn [William Thomas]
Language: English
Premiere: 1880 00 00
Play: *Tempest*
Publisher: Aberystwyth: Composer, 1902 [vs]
Yes: Oxford, Mellen
No: SCORE

Comments: Mellen: *The Enchanted Isle*, opera 1 act (3 scenes), composed c.1880?, text by composer, English, based on Shakespeare's *Tempest*. Score: five scenes from Islwyn's Poem "The Storm."

Ivan Jirko (1926-1978)

The Twelfth Night [Vecer Trikralovy]

Status: Y   **Evidence:** S
Text: Composer
Type: Opera   **Acts:** 3   **Language:** Czech
Premiere: Liberec, Czechoslovakia • 1967 02 25
Source of Premiere Information: Mellen
Play: *Twelfth Night*
Yes: Baker's, Mellen, Oxford

Comments: Oxford: based on *As You Like It*.

Robert Johnson (1583-1633)

The Tempest

Status: NO   **Evidence:** S
Language: English
Premiere: London, England • 1612 00 00

138

Play: *Tempest*
No: Stieger, GB-Lbm

Comments: Stieger: incidental music. CPM: after Johnson's name it says Composer of music to *The Tempest*; lists 2 songs from *The Tempest* set by his [Shakespeare] contemporary Robert Johnson.

Nicolo Jommelli [Jomelli] (1714-1774)

Caio Mario [Cajo Mario]

Status: N   **Evidence:** S
Text: Roccaforte, Gaetano
Type: Drama per musica   **Acts:** 3   **Language:** Italian
Premiere: Rome, Italy: Teatro di Torre Argentina • 1746 02 06
Source of Premiere Information: Score
Play: *Coriolanus*
No: Friedlaender

Cast: CAJO MARIO, Console di Roma • MARZIA CALFURNIA, sua Figlia destinata Sposi di Annio • ANNIO, Patrizio Romano, Amante di Marzia • RODOPE, Principessa di Numida, fotto Nome di Prissa, Amante occulta di Annio • LUCIO, Amante di Rodope, ed inimico occulto di Marzia, ed Annio • AQUILIO, Presetto delle Armi Romane, Amico d'Annio

Cliff Jones

Rockabye Hamlet

Status: Y   **Evidence:** S
Text: Jones, Cliff (book and lyrics)
Type: Broadway Show   **Language:** English
Premiere: New York, U.S.A.: Minskoff Theatre • 1976 02 17
Source of Premiere Information: Simas
Play: *Hamlet*
Yes: Simas, Bordman

Comments: Simas: previously titled *Hamlet, A Contemporary Musical*; previously presented under title Kronborg; subsequently presented under title *Something's Rockin' in Denmark*.

Johann August Just (c.1750-1791?)

Le marchand de Venise [Koopman van Smyrna]

Status: I   **Evidence:** S
Text: Unknown
Type: Opera   **Language:** French
Premiere: Amsterdam, Holland • 1787 00 00
Source of Premiere Information: Stieger
Play: *Merchant of Venice*
Yes: Clément, Oxford
No: Squire

Comments: Squire: this work is the *Koopman van Smyrna* first produced at Bonn in 1782. Mellen: 1773.

Johann Christian Kaffka [Kafka] (1754-1815)

Antonius und Cleopatra

Status: Y   **Evidence:** S
Text: Arien, Bernhard Christian d'
Type: Duodrama mit Gesang   **Acts:** 2   **Language:** German
Premiere: Berlin, Germany: Dobbinschestheater • 1779 11 15
Source of Premiere Information: Mellen
Play: *Antony and Cleopatra*
Publisher: New Grove: D-Bds
Yes: Hartnoll, Mellen, Oxford

Comments: Manferrari: 3 act opera first performed in Breslavia, Tr. Civico, spring 1781. Schatz libretto numbers are from the catalog; items are not on microfilm at place indicated.

Cast: ANTONIUS • CLEOPATRA • BOTE • KRIEGER

Sergius Kagen (1909-1964)

Hamlet

Status: Y   **Evidence:** P
Text: Composer
Type: Opera   **Acts:** 5   **Language:** English
Premiere: Baltimore, U.S.A.: Peabody Conservatory of Music
     • 1962 11 09
Source of Premiere Information: Mellen
Play: *Hamlet*
Publisher: Manuscript copy
Yes: SCORE, Mellen, Hartnoll

Comments: Score: A cut version of Shakespeare's play.
Mellen: 3 acts.

Cast: KING • QUEEN • LAERTES • POLONIUS • HAMLET •
HORATIO • MARCELLUS • BERNARDO • GHOST • OPHELIA

Janis Kalnins (1904-   )

Hamlets

Status: Y   **Evidence:** P
Text: Chekhov, Michael (1891-1955)
Type: Opera   **Acts:** 3   **Language:** Latvian
Premiere: Riga, Soviet Union: Latvijas Nacionata Opera
     • 1936 02 17
Source of Premiere Information: Loewenberg
Play: *Hamlet*
Yes: SCORE, Hartnoll, Loewenberg, Mellen, Oxford

Comments: Mellen: Alfred Kalnins (1879-   ) [father of Janis]; based
on Julijs Rozes' Latvian translation of *Hamlet*.

Cast: POLONIJS (Bass) • LAERTS (Tenor) • OFELIJA (Soprano) •
HAMLETS (Tenor) • KARALIS (Baritone) • KARALIENE (Alto) •
HORACIO (Bass) • MARCELLO (Bass) • BERNARDO (Bass) • GARS
(Bass) • GONZAGO (Bass) • BAPTISTA (Tenor) • LUKIANS (Tenor) •
I. KAPRACIS (Bass) • II. KAPRACIS (Tenor)

Friedrich August Kanne (1778-1833)

Malvina, oder Putzerls Abenteuer

Status: ?
Text: Pfahler, Adalbert
Type: Singspiel   **Acts:** 2   **Language:** German
Premiere: Leipzig, Germany • 1815 00 00
Source of Premiere Information: Mellen
Play: *All's Well That Ends Well*

Comments: Schatz MS, Stieger: Text by Albin Pfaller; Vienna 1823 03 19, Th. a. d. Wien.

Miranda oder Das Schwert der Rache

Status: I   **Evidence:** S
Text: Composer
Type: Heroisch-komische Oper   **Acts:** 3
     Language: German
Premiere: Vienna, Austria: Theater an der Wien • 1811 09 14
Source of Premiere Information: Mellen
Play: *Tempest*
Yes: Oxford

Comments: Oxford: 1808. Schatz: Orig. Ausz. Wien 1811.

Cast: DER KÖNIG • MIRANDA, Tochter des vorigen Königs Riccardo • ALONZO, Prinz vom königl. Hause, verbannt • PEDRILLO, Diener des Königs • DIEGO, Diener des Königs • ELMIRE, Vertraute der Prinzessin • DER SCHATTEN DES KÖNIGS RICCARDO • ERSTER RÄUBER • ZWEYTER RÄUBER • DRITTER RÄUBER • VIERTER RÄUBER • EIN FISCHER • EIN OFFICIER • GROSSE DES REICHS • LEIBWACHEN • WOLF •—•
Chorus: JÄGER, SOLDATEN ALONZOS

Rudolf Karel, (1880-1945)

Zkroceni zlé zeny [The Taming of the Shrew]

Status: Y   **Evidence:** S
Text: Unknown
Type: Opera   **Language:** Czech
Premiere: 1943 00 00
Source of Premiere Information: Mellen
Play: *Taming of the Shrew*
Yes: Groves V, Hartnoll, Mellen, MGG, Mellen

Comments: Groves V, MGG, Mellen: unfinished, not performed.
Date is when composed.

Nikolai Ivanovich Kasanli [Kazanli, Kazanly] (1869-1916)

Miranda (Poliedniaia bor'ba) [Der Letzte Kampf]

Status: I   **Evidence:** S
Text: Polilova, N.
Type: Dramatische Oper   **Acts:** 3   **Language:** Russian
Premiere: St. Petersburg, Soviet Union: Maria Theater
• 1910 03 00
Source of Premiere Information: Mellen
Play: *Tempest*
Publisher: Leipzig: Jul. Heinr. Zimmermann [1907]
Yes: Mellen, Stieger

Comments: Shakespeare is not mentioned in the score.

Cast: MIRANDA (Sopran) • ODONDE TERRY, Großmeister des
Tempelherrn-Ordens (Baß) • PERCEVAL ERAL, Tempelherr (Tenor)
• GUY DE CORVILLE Tempelherr (Tenor) • BERTRAND DELZANE
Tempelherr (Bariton) • EIN WAFFENKNABE (Alt) • GRAF REGINALD
Chorus: RITTER, WAFFENTRÄGER, DIENER, PILGER, FRAUEN
UND KINDER

Vladimir Nikititch Kashperov (1827-1894)

The Storm [Groza]

Status: I   **Evidence:** S
Text: Composer
Type: Opera   **Acts:** 4   **Language:** Russian
Premiere: St. Petersburg, Russia • 1867 11 11
Source of Premiere Information: Stieger
Play: *Tempest*
Yes: Friedlaender, Manferrari, Squire
No: Groves V, Mellen

Comments: Groves V: based on the drama, *Groza*, by Ostrovsky; was an attempt at national opera. Manferrari: *La Tempesta* (da Shakespeare) com. 2 a., Pietroburgo e Mosca, Tr. Imperiale, autunno 1867. Friedlaender: Moskau. Mellen: A. Ostrovsky: Groza; Moscow and St. Petersburg, 1867 11 11.

Hugo Kaun (1863-1932)

Falstaff

Status: I   **Evidence:** S
Text: Unknown
Language: English
Premiere: Saratoga, N.Y., U.S.A. • 1895 00 00
Play: *Merry Wives of Windsor*
Yes: Blom
No: Groves V

Comments: Groves V: it is Sir John Falstaf, a Humoresque for Orchestra. Hugo Kaun was in the US (Milwaukee) from 1884 to 1901. Mellen: Kauen.

Edward H. J. Keurvels (1853-1916)

Hamlet

Status: Y **Evidence:** S
Text: Unknown
Type: Opera **Language:** Flemish
Premiere: Antwerp, Belgium: Royal Flemish Opera • 1891 00 00
Source of Premiere Information: Mellen
Play: *Hamlet*
Yes: Mellen, Oxford

Tikhon Nikolaevich Khrennikov [Chrennikow] (1913-)

Brati [Brothers]

Status: N **Evidence:** S
Text: Fajko, Alexej (1893-) after Nikolai E. Virta
Type: Oper **Acts:** 4/6 Bildern **Language:** Russian
Premiere: Moscow, U.S.S.R.: Musikalisches Theater W. I.
Nemirowitsch-Dantschenko • 1939 05 31
Source of Premiere Information: Mellen
Play: *Tempest*
No: Mellen, Neef, New Grove

Comments: Neef: nach Motiven dem Roman *Einsamkeit* von
Nikolai Wirta. Mellen: Virta: Solitude; produced as *In the Storm*,
Moscow, 1952 10 10; revised Moscow, 1952 10 12 [V burin, Op. 8;
Im Sturm]. Characters from Neef.

Cast: WLADIMIR ILJITSCH LENIN (Sprechrolle) • FROL BAJEW,
Dorfältester (Baß) • NATALJA, seine Tochter (Sopran) • ANDREJ,
alter Bauer (Tenor) • AKSINJA, Bäuerin (Mezzosopran) • IHRE
SÖHNE: LJONKA, LISTRAT (Bariton, Tenor) • STOROSHEW,
Großbauer (Baß) • ANTONOW, konterrevolutionärer Bandenführer
(Tenor) • KOSOWA, seine Geliebte (Mezzosopran) • AFONKA (Baß)
• KARAS (Tenor) • FEDJUSCHA (Bariton) • TSCHIRIKIN (Baß) •
ERSTES UND ZWEITES MÄDCHEN (Sopran, Mezzosopran) • EIN
VERWACHSENER MANN (Tenor) • ERSTER UND ZWEITER
BAUER (Baß, Bariton) • EIN MILITÄR (Bariton oder hoher Baß) •
SEKRETÄR LENINS (Bariton oder hoher Baß) •——•

Chorus: BAUERN, BÄUERINNEN, PARTISANEN, ANTONOWLEUTE (Gemischter Chor und Ballett)

Mnogo shuma iz nichego [Viel Lärm aus Leidenschaft, Much Ado About Hearts]

Status: Y   **Evidence:** S
Text: Unknown
Type: Comic opera   **Acts:** 2   **Language:** Russian
Premiere: Moscow, Soviet Union: Chamber Music Theater
    • 1972 03 29
Source of Premiere Information: Mellen
Play: *Much Ado About Nothing*
Yes: Mellen, Neef

Comments: New Grove: Khrennikov wrote incidental music to *Much Ado* in 1936 and a ballet on *Much Ado* in 1976. New Grove does not mention an opera on that subject.

V buriu [Im Sturm, Into the Storm]

Status: N   **Evidence:** S
Text: Faiko, Alexei and Nicolai Bitry
Type: Opera   **Acts:** 4/6 Scenes   **Language:** Russian
Premiere: Moscow, U.S.S.R.: V. I. Nemirovi • 1939 10 10
Source of Premiere Information: Neef
Play: *Tempest*
Publisher: State Music Publications, 1954
No: Neef

Comments: Neef: nach Motiven des Romans *Einsamkeit* von Nikolai Wirta; libretto von Alexej Fajko und Nikolai Wirta; a revised version was given in Moscow on 1952 10 12. The score dated 1954 gives A. Faiko and N. Bitry as the librettists; the librettists of the revised version may have been different from those of the premiere.

Cast: V. I. LENIN (Speaking) • FROL BAYEV (Bass) • NATALYA, his daughter (Soprano) • ANDREI, an old peasant (Tenor) • AKSINYA, a peasant (Mezzo-Soprano) • LISTRAT, her son (Baritone) • LYONKA, her son (Tenor) • STOROZHEV, important peasant (Bass) • ANTONOV, a counter-revolutionary group leader (Tenor) • KOSOVA (Mezzo-Soprano) • AFONKA (Bass) • KARAS (Tenor) • FEDYUSHA (Baritone) • TCHIRIKIN (Bass) • FIRST GIRL (Soprano) • SECOND

GIRL (Mezzo-Soprano) • HUNCHBACKED SERF (Tenor) • FIRST PEASANT (Bass) • SECOND PEASANT (Baritone) • SOLDIER (Baritone [or High Bass]) • LENIN'S SECRETARY (Baritone [or High Bass]) •—• **Chorus:** PEASANTS, PARTISIANS, PEOPLE FROM ANTONOV, BALLET

Herman Kipper (1826-1910)

Perdita oder Das Rosenfest

Status: ?
Text: Unknown
Type: Optte f. Liedertafel
Play: *Winter's Tale*

Hermann Kirchner (1861-1928)

Viola

Status: Y   **Evidence:** S
Text: Composer
Type: Comic Opera   **Acts:** Vsp./3   **Language:** German
Premiere: Hermannstadt, Germany: Stadttheater • 1904 02 05
Source of Premiere Information: Mellen
Play: *Twelfth Night*
Yes: Gruber, Mellen, Stieger

Giselher Wolfgang Klebe (1925-   )

Die Ermordung Cäsars, Op. 32

Status: Y   **Evidence:** P
Text: Composer
Type: Oper   **Acts:** 1   **Language:** German
Premiere: Essen, Germany: Städtische Bühne • 1959 09 20
Source of Premiere Information: Score
Play: *Julius Caesar*
Publisher: Berlin: Bote & Bock, 1960 [vs]

Yes: SCORE, Baker's, Hartnoll, Mellen, New Grove, Oxford

Comments: Text after a translation by August Wilhelm von Schlegel.

Cast: CÄSAR (Bariton) • MARC ANTON (Bariton) • PUBLIUS, Senator (Tenor [Sprechgesang]) • POPILIUS LENA (Sprechstimme) • BRUTUS (Bariton) • CASSIUS (Tenorbuffo) • CASCA (Baß) • DECIUS (Sprechstimme) • METELLUS CIMBER (Sprechstimme) • EIN WAHRSAGER (Baß) • CINNA, ein Poet (Tenor) •—•
Chorus: VOLK VON ROM

Carl Franz Xaver Kleinheinz (1765-1832)

Hamlet, Prinz vom Tandelmarkt

Status: ?
Text: Perinet, Joachim (1763-1816)
Type: Paradie   **Acts:** 3   **Language:** German
Premiere: Budapest, Hungary: K Stadt Theater • 1826 02 13
Play: Hamlet

Comments: Stieger: *Hamlet, Prinz vom Tandelmarkt*, 2 acts. If Meretzek's opera is based on Shakespeare, this one should be too. NUC: composer's dates (1772-1832). A reference card at A:Wn gives a date for the libretto as 1807. Premiere in Buda before it was joined with Pest to become Budapest.

Herman David Koppel (1908-   )

Macbeth, Op. 79

Status: Y   **Evidence:** S
Text: Unknown
Type: Opera   **Language:** Danish
Premiere: Copenhagen, Denmark: Konglige Theater • 1970 05 22
Yes: Baker's, Mellen, Oxford

Source of Premiere Information: Mellen
Play: Macbeth

Karel Kovarovic (1862-1920)

Perdita

Status: ?
Text: Unknown
Type: Opera   **Acts:** 3
Premiere: Prague, Czechoslovakia: Kgl. bohemian Landes-
    Nationaltheatre
Source of Premiere Information: Schatz MS
Play: *Winter's Tale*

Isa Krejcí (1904-1968)

Pozdvizení v Efesu [The Upheaval in Ephesus]

Status: Y   **Evidence:** P
Text: Bachtík, Josef
Type: Opera   **Acts:** 2   **Language:** Czech
Premiere: Prague, Czechoslovakia: Narodni Divádlo • 1946 09 08
Source of Premiere Information: Mellen
Play: *Comedy of Errors*
Publisher: Praha: Frantisek Novák, 1944 [vs]
Yes: SCORE, Baker's, Blom, Groves V, Hartnoll, Mellen, MGG, New
    Grove, Oxford

Comments: MGG: first performed on the radio1945 02 25 in
Prague. Score: Text podle Shakespearovy Komedie omylu napsal
Josef Bachtík.

Arthur Kreutz (1906-   )

Sourwood Mountain

Status: Y   **Evidence:** S
Text: Kreutz, Zoë Lund Schiller
Type: Opera   **Acts:** 1/5 Scenes   **Language:** English
Premiere: University, Miss., U.S.A.: University of Mississippi Music
    Department • 1959 01 08
Source of Premiere Information: Score

Play: *Romeo and Juliet*
Publisher: New York: Franco Colombo, 1963 [vs]
Yes: AMCL

Comments: The score does not mention Shakespeare. Mellen: Kreutz (1907-).

Cast: THE JUDGE (Baritone) • DANNY LOVELL (Baritone [tenor]) • LUCY PORTER (Soprano) • IDA PORTER (Soprano) • BEN PORTER (Baritone [bass]) • LAVINIA LOVELL (Speaking role) • THREE MEN (Speaking roles) • THREE WOMEN (Speaking roles) •—•
Chorus: CHORUS

Conradin Kreutzer (1780-1849)

Cordelia (Floretta ou La Folle de Glaris) [First named Adele von Budoy]

Status: N   **Evidence:** P
Text: Wolff, Pius Alexander (1782-1828)
Type: Opera   **Acts:** 1   **Language:** German
Premiere: Donaueschingen, Germany: Hoftheater • 1819 00 00
Source of Premiere Information: Stieger
Play: *Lear*
Publisher: Vienna n.d.
Yes: Friedlaender, Mellen, Squire, Wilson
No: LIBRETTO, Groves V

Comments: MGG: komp. während der Donaueschinger Zeit, vermutlich dort auch uraufgef.; 1819, 2/15/23 Wien (Kärntertor-Theater). Groves V: this is a melodrama by Pius Alexander Wolf, *Adele von Budov* (1819) which later on in a revised form became *Cordelia*. Friedlaender: An Sh.'s Drama knüpft dieses Werk nur lose an. The action takes place in the Pyrenees in 1814. Date: autumn.

Cast: CORDELIA • EIN LANDGEISTLICHER • EIN KIND •—•
Chorus: HIRTEN, BAUERN, JÄGER

Rodolphe Kreutzer (1766-1831)

Imogène, ou La Gageure indiscrète

Status: Y **Evidence:** S
Text: Dejaure, [Jean-Claude Bédéno known as] (1761-1799)
Type: Comédie melee d'ariettes# **Acts:** 3
    Language: French
Premiere: Paris, France: Théâtre de l'Opéra Comique National, rue
    Favart • 1796 04 27
Source of Premiere Information: Mellen
Play: *Cymbeline*
Yes: Groves V, Hartnoll, Mellen, Oxford

Comments: Groves V: at one place it says that it is based on
Shakespeare and at another that it is on Boccaccio.

Max Krohn (1886-   )

Was ihr Wollt

Status: ?
Text: Unknown
Play: *Twelfth Night*

Comments: Not performed.

Friedrich Daniel Rudolph Kuhlau (1786-1832)

Musik Til William Shakspeare [sic], *Op. 74*

Status: NO **Evidence:** P
Text: Boye, Caspar Johannes
Type: Romantisk Shauspiel
Premiere: Copenhagen, Denmark: Konglige Theater • 1826 03 28
Play: *Other*
Publisher: Copenhagen: Samfundet Til Udgivelse Af Dansk Musik,
    III, No. 57, 1873 [vs, excerpts]
No: Groves V

Comments: Groves V: incidental music to a play on Shakespeare by Boye. Cast and number of acts not given in score.

[Konrad Max?] Kunz (1812-1875)

The Tempest

Status: Y   **Evidence:** S
Text: Unknown
Premiere: 1847 00 00
Play: *Tempest*

Friedrich Ludwig Æmilius Kunzen [Kuntzen] (1761-1817)

Holger Danske oder Oberon [Holgar the Dane]

Status: N   **Evidence:** P
Text: Baggesen, Jens Emanuel (1764-1826)
Type: Opera   **Acts:** 3   **Language:** Danish
Premiere: Copenhagen, Denmark: Konglige Theater • 1789 03 31
Source of Premiere Information: Mellen
Play: *Midsummer Night's Dream*
Publisher: Copenhagen: S. Sönnichsen, 1790 [vs]
No: SCORE

Comments: Jens Emanuel Baggesen's Danish original was based on Christoph Martin Wieland's *Oberon*. German translation by Carl Friedrich Cramer. Manferrari: 2 acts.

Cast: OBERON, Konig der Elfen • TITANIA, Konigin der Sylphen • HOLGER DANSKE • BUURMAN, Sultan von Babylon oder Bagdad • REZIA, seine Tochter • LANGULAFFER, Prinz von Libanon, Bräutigam der Rezia • BOBUL, Sultan von Tunis • ALMANSARIS, Sultain von Tunis • SACHERASMIN, Schildknapp Holgers • MARYLLI, TINNI, TITY: Drey Sylphiden • DER MUFTI VON BABYLON • EIN HEROLD • SCLAVINNEN DER ALMANSARIS • DAS ECHO
Chorus: ELFEN, SYLPHEN, SYLPHIDEN, TÜRKISCHE SAENGERN, WACHE, TÜRKISCHE HOFBEDIENTE, VERSCHNITTENE, DERWISCHE u.s.w.

Stormen

Status: Y   **Evidence:** P
Text: Sander, Levin Christian (1756-1819)
Type: Syngespil   **Acts:** 3   **Language:** Danish
Premiere: Copenhagen, Denmark • 1818 00 00
Play: *Tempest*
Yes: LIBRETTO, Blom, Hartnoll

Cast: ALONSO, Konge i Neapel • FERNANDO, hans Son •
GONZALO, en Olding; og andre Hofmand i hans Folge • PROSPER
ALBANO, den retmæssige Hertug af Mailand • MIRANDA, hans
Datter • ANTONIO, hans Broder, uretmæssig Besidder af Mailand •
STEPHANO, en fuld Rjeldermester • TRINCULO, en Hofnar •
SKIBSPATRON, Baadsmand, og Søefolk • SETEBOS, en ond
Aand, usynlig • CALIBAN, en vild og styg Slave • ARIEL, en ætherisk
Aand • There is more that needs to be translated. •—•
Chorus: SOLANA, ALVA, OG ANDRE ELVERPIGER, MIRANDAS
LEDSAGERINDER, OG SAALŒNGE BUNDNE TIL DET JORDISKE
LIVS LOVE; SØERØVERE FRA SETBOSØEN

Paul Kurzbach (1902-   )

Romeo and Julia auf dem Lande

Status: ?
Text: Unknown
Play: *Romeo and Juliet*

Comments: Not performed.

Johann Heinrich Küster (c.1780-1842)

Henrik den Fjerde

Status: ?
Text: Ahlgren, Johan Samuel
Type: Lyr. Drama   **Acts:** 3
Premiere: Stockholm, Sweden: Kongl Operalmset • 1810 12 19
Source of Premiere Information: Schatz MS

Play: *Henry IV*

Comments: Schatz MS: based on Barnabé Farmian de Rosoy's *La Bataille d'Ivry.*

Arthur Kusterer (1896-1967)

Was ihr Wollt

Status: Y   **Evidence:** P
Text: Composer
Type: Oper   **Acts:** 3   **Language:** German
Premiere: Dresden, Germany • 1932 12 16
Play: *Twelfth Night*
Yes: LIBRETTO, Gruber, Hartnoll, Manferrari, Oxford

Comments: Manferrari: *Comme il Vois Plaire.* Text arranged after the translation by A. W. Schlegel.

Cast: ORSINO, Herzog von Illyrien (Bariton) • SEBASTIAN, Violas Bruder • ANTONIO, einSchiffshauptmann (Baß) • EIN SCHIFFSHAUPTMANN (Baß) • VALENTIN, Kavalier des Herzogs (Baß) • CURIO, Kavalier des Herzogs (Bariton) • JUNKER TOBIAS VON KÜLP, Olivias Oheim (Baß) • JUNKER ANDREAS VON BLEICHENWANG (Tenor) • NARR, in Olivias Diensten (Tenor) • OLIVIA, eine reiche Gräfin (Sopran) • VIOLA, Sebastians Schwester (Sopran) • MARIA, Olivias Kammermädchen (Sopran)

Arturo La Rosa

Otello

Status: ?
Text: Composer
Type: Parodia   **Acts:** 1   **Language:** Italian
Premiere: Genoa, Italy: Politeania Genovesa • 1897 02 00
Play: *Othello*

John Frederich Lampe (1703?-1751)

Pyramus and Thisbe

Status: Y   **Evidence:** P
Text: Leveridge, Richard (c. 1670-1758)
Type: Mock-opera   **Acts:** 1   **Language:** English
Premiere: London, England: Covent Garden • 1745 01 25
Source of Premiere Information: Place from score. Date from
    Mellen.
Play: *Midsummer Night's Dream*
Publisher: London: I Walsh, 1745 [s]
Yes: SCORE, Blom, Friedlaender, Groves V, Hartnoll, MGG, New
    Grove, Oxford, Squire, Wilson

Comments: Partly based on Leveridge 1716.

Cast: PYRAMUS [Mr. Beard] • THISBE [Mrs. Lampe] • WALL [Mr.
Laguerre] • LION [Mr. Reinhold] • MOON [Mr. Roberts]

Felice Lattuada (1882-1962)

La Tempesta

Status: Y   **Evidence:** P
Text: Rossato, Arturo (1882-1942)
Type: Opera   **Acts:** Prologue/3   **Language:** Italian
Premiere: Milan, Italy: Teatro dal Verme • 1922 11 23
Source of Premiere Information: Loewenberg
Play: *Tempest*
Publisher: Milan: G. Ricordi [vs]
Yes: LIBRETTO, Blom, Groves V, Hartnoll, Loewenberg, New
    Grove, Oxford, Stieger

Comments: Stieger: 1922 12 23.   Manferrari: 1922 11 22, 4 acts.

Cast: IL RE DELL'ISOLA (Baritono) • MIRANDA (Soprano) •
FERNANDO (Tenore) • CALIBANO (Basso) • ARIEL (Soprano
leggero) • L'USURPATORE (Basso) • STEFANO (Baritono) • IL
BUFFONE (Tenore) •—•
Chorus: LA CIURMA—LA CORTE, GLI ELFI—I GNOMI—LE FATE

Adolph L. Lauer [Freiherr von Münchofen] (1796-1874)

Der Orakelspruch

Status: ?
Text: Salice-Contessa, Carl Wilhelm
Type: Oper   **Acts:** 1   **Language:** German
Premiere: Berlin, Germany: Königl. Opernhaus • 1832 01 08
Source of Premiere Information: Mellen
Play: *Winter's Tale*

B. Laufer

Shylock

Status: Y   **Evidence:** S
Text: Unknown
Premiere: 1929 00 00
Play: *Merchant of Venice*
Yes: Hartnoll, Oxford

Comments: Composed in 1929?

Vincenzo Lavina [Lavigna] (1767-1836)

Il Coriolano

Status: N   **Evidence:** S
Text: Romanelli, Luigi (1751-1839)
Type: Opera   **Language:** Italian
Premiere: Torino, Italy: Teatro Regio • 1806 00 00
Source of Premiere Information: Mellen
Play: *Coriolanus*
No: Friedlaender

Comments: Mellen: Carnival.

Wesley LaViolette (1894-1978)

Shylock

Status: Y   **Evidence:** S
Text: Unknown
Type: Opera   **Acts:** 3   **Language:** English
Premiere: 1929 00 00
Source of Premiere Information: Mellen
Play: *Merchant of Venice*
Yes: Mellen, Oxford

Comments: Baker's: composed in 1927; it was awarded the David Bispham Memorial Medal, 1930; excerpts performed in Chicago, Feb. 9, 1930. Date is when composed.

Frédéric Le Rey (1858-   )

La Mégère apprivoisée

Status: Y   **Evidence:** P
Text: Deshays, Émile
Type: Comédie-lyrique   **Acts:** 3/4 Tableaux
          Language: French
Premiere: Rouen, France: Théâtre des Arts • 1895 12 00
Source of Premiere Information: Score
Play: *Taming of the Shrew*
Publisher: Paris: M. Paul Dupont,1895 [vs]
Yes: SCORE, Mellen, Oxford, Stieger

Comments: Mellen: 1896 03 28.

Cast: PETRUCHIO (Baryton) • LUCENTIO (Ténor lèger) • BAPTISTA (Basse chantante) • GRUMIO (Second Ténor) • CURTIS (Trial) • CATHARINA (Mezzo-Sopran ou Falcon) • BIANCA (Chanteuse légère • BIONDELLO (Dugazon Travesti)

157

Charles Alexandre Lecocq (1832-1918)

Marjolaine

Status: Y   **Evidence:** S
Text: Vanloo, Abert and Eugène Leterrier
Type: Opéra-bouffe   **Acts:** 3   **Language:** French
Premiere: Paris, France: Théâtre de La Renaissance • 1877 02 03
Source of Premiere Information: Score, libretto
Play: *Cymbeline*
Publisher: Paris: Brandus & Cie
Yes: Bordman

Comments: Bordman: based losely on *Cymbeline* and Johann Strauss' first operetta *La Reine Indigo.*

Cast: PALAMEDE VAN DER BOOM [M. Berthelier] • ANNIBAL DE L'ESTRAPADE [M. Vauthier] • FRICKEL [M. Puget] • PÉTERSCHOP [M. Caliste] • LE BOURGMESTRE [M. Hervier] • D'ESCOUBLAC [M. Gaussins] • SCHAERBECK [M. Valotte] • UN CRIEUR [M. Cailloux] • DEUX ÉCHEVINS [MM. Robillot et Gisors] • MARJOLAINE [Mme Jeanne Granier] • AVELINE [Mme Théol] • PÉTRUS [Mme Carli] • KARL [Mme Ribes] • CHRISTIAN [Mme Bied] • ROBERT [Mme Dareine] • CHRISTOPHE [Mme Dianie] • FRANZ [FRANTZ] [Mme Andrée] • UNE JEUNE FILLE [Mme Néline] • GUDULE [Mme Davenay] • CHARLOTTE [UNE PAYSANNE] [Mme Dhaucourt] •—• **Chorus:** BOURGEOIS, BOURGEOISES, DOMESTIQUES, HALLEBARDIERS, PAYSANS, PAYSANNES, HOMMES ET FEMMES DU PEUPLE

Isidore Édouard Legouix (1834-1916)

Un Othello

Status: N   **Evidence:** S
Text: Nuitter, Charles [Pseud. for Charles Truinet] (1828-1899) and
         A. de Beaumont
Type: Opérette-bouffe   **Acts:** 1   **Language:** French
Premiere: Paris, France: Théâtre des Champs-Élysées
         • 1863 06 19
Source of Premiere Information: Score
Play: *Othello*

Publisher: Paris: O. Legouix,1863 [vs]
No: Characters, Plot

Cast: MARDOCHÉE [M.r Bourgoin] • BALTAZARD, Artiste [M.r Georges] • JULIE, Femme de Mardochée [M.lle Victoria]

Alan Leichtling

The Tempest

Status: ?
Text: Roepke, Gabriella
Type: Opera   **Acts:** 1
Play: *Tempest*

Ruggiero Leoncavallo (1858-1919)

Un Songe d'une nuit d'été

Status: Y   **Evidence:** S
Text: Unknown
Type: Opera Comique
Premiere: Paris, France: Private performance • 1889 11 00
Source of Premiere Information: Stieger
Play: *Midsummer Night's Dream*
Yes: Stieger

Leopold I, Holy Roman Emperor (1640-1705)

Timòne, Misantropo

Status: Y   **Evidence:** S
Text: Unknown
Type: Italian Opera   **Acts:** 3   **Language:** Latin
Premiere: Vienna, Austria • 1696 00 00
Play: *Timon of Athens*
Publisher: State Library in Vienna
Yes: Friedlaender, Hartnoll, Oxford, Squire, Wilson

Comments: MGG: nur 2 Akt erhalten. Work listed among the manuscripts in A:Wn [16008. Leopoldina.]

Robert Leukauf (1902-1976)

Das Wintermärchen

Status: ?
Text: Unknown
Type: Opera
Play: *Winter's Tale*

Comments: Not performed.

Richard Leverage (c. 1670-1758)

Macbeth

Status: NO   **Evidence:** S
Text: Davenant, Charles
Language: English
Premiere: London, England • 1702 11 21
Play: *Macbeth*
Publisher: New Grove: GB-Cfm, Cke, Lbm, Lcm; US-Bp, NYp, Ws
Yes: New Grove
No: Dent, Groves V, Stieger

Comments: New Grove: The music pubd in 1770 by Boyce as The Original Songs Airs & Choruses . . . in *Macbeth* and attrib. Locke is almost certainly by Leverige. Groves V, Stieger: it is incidental music. In any case Dent states the the words set are not Shakespeare's but are the interpolations from Middleton's play, *The Witch*. [Dent, p.154]. Stieger: 1708.

The Comic Masque of Pyramus and Thisbe

Status: Y   **Evidence:** S
Text: Composer
Type: Comic Masque   **Acts:** 1   **Language:** English

Premiere: London, England: Theatre in Lincoln's Inn Fields
  • 1716 04 11
Source of Premiere Information: White
Play: *Midsummer Night's Dream*
Publisher: New Grove: Libretto London 1716; music lost
Yes: Blom, Fiske, Groves V, Hartnoll, MGG, New Groves, Oxford,
    Schatz MS, Squire

Comments: Mellen: Librettist is L. Theobald. Fiske: London, Drury
Lane; Leverage played Prologue and Bottom.

Carl August Freiherr von Lichtenstein (1767-1845)

Ende gut, alles gut

Status: ?
Text: Huber, Franz Xaver
Type: Singspiel   **Acts:** 1   **Language:** German
Premiere: Dessau, Germany: Hoftheater • 1800 10 26
Source of Premiere Information: Mellen
Play: *All's Well That Ends Well*

Comments: Stieger: text by Huber. Schatz MS:1800 10 16.
Librettist from Schatz MS.

Giuseppe Lillo (1814-1863)

Il Sogno d'una Notte estiva, or La Gioventù di Shakespeare

Status: AP   **Evidence:** P
Text: Giannini, Giuseppe Sesto
Type: Commedia Lirica   **Acts:** 3   **Language:** Italian
Premiere: Naples, Italy: Teatro Nuovo • 1851 12 29
Source of Premiere Information: Year and place from libretto.
    Day from Manferrari
Play: *Shakespeare Appears*
Yes: Oxford
No: LIBRETTO, Friedlaender, Riemann

Comments: Riemann: Shakespeare is the hero in the opera. Friedlaender: the same libretto used by Thomas and Berens.

Cast: GUGLIELMO SHAKESPEARE [signor Mastriani] • SIR GOFFREDO FALSTAFF, intendente del castello e parco del grande sceriffo di Londra [signor Cammarano] • ARTURO MORTON, baronetto [signor Bettiui] • TOM, ostr [signor Grandillo] • LADY ARABELLA, giovine vedova, sorella del grande sceriffo [signora Gianfredi] • EMMA, sua damigella [signora M. Eboli] • NELLY, nipote di Tom [signora G. Eboli] • UN PAGGIO •——•
Chorus: SERVE, CUOCHI E GARZOPI D'OSTERIA, ATTORI E ATTRICI, SIGNORI E DAME, GUARDABOSCHI

Thomas Linley II (1756-1778)

The Tempest or The Enchanted Island

Status: NO   **Evidence:** S
Text: Kemble, John Philip (1757-1822) adaptation from
            Shakespeare-Dryden
Type: Comedy With Songs   **Language:** English
Premiere: London, England: Drury Lane Theatre • 1777 01 04
Source of Premiere Information: Fiske
Play: *Tempest*
Yes: Schatz MS
No: Fiske, Groves V, Stieger

Comments: Stieger: incidental music. Groves V also lists *Macbeth* as Tragedy [probably also incidental music]. Schatz MS: based on Shakespeare; librettist is Richard Brinley Sheridan; 1777 00 00. Fiske: Linley wrote some additional music for a revival of *The Tempest*.

A. Liota

Romeo and Juliet

Status: Y   **Evidence:** S
Text: Unknown
Language: English

Premiere: New York, U.S.A. • 1969 01 07
Play: *Romeo and Juliet*
Yes: Northouse

Henry Charles Litolff (1818-1891)

König Lear

Status: Y   **Evidence:** P
Text: Adenis, Jules (1823-1900) and Eugène Adenis (1823-1900)
Type: Oper   **Acts:** 3
Play: *Lear*
Yes: SCORE

Cast: LEAR • GONERILL • CORDÉLIA • KENT • AGANIPPUS • RÉGANE • LE FOU • ALBANY • COROAILLES • OSWALO

Matthew Locke (c. 1621-1677) and Robert Johnson

Macbeth

Status: NO   **Evidence:** P
Text: Davenant, Sir William (16061668)
Type: Tragedy with songs and dances   **Acts:** 5
        Language: English
Premiere: London, England: Duke of York's Theatre in Dorset Gardens • 1673 02 18
Source of Premiere Information: White, who is not certain of the day.
Play: *Macbeth*
No: SCORE, Groves V, Stieger

Comments: Stieger: it is incidental music; 1672. Score: The Original Songs Airs and Choruses which were introduced in the Tragedy of *Macbeth*. Composed by Matthew Locke, etc. Revised and Corrected by Dr. Boyce. See Leverage: *Macbeth*.

Edward James Loder (1813-1865)

Robin Goodfellow or the Frolics of Puck

Status: ?
Text: Composer
Type: Ballad opera   **Acts:** 1   **Language:** English
Premiere: London, England: Princess's Theater, Oxford Street
 • 1848 12 06
Source of Premiere Information: Mellen
Play: *Midsummer Night's Dream*
Publisher: London: S. G. Fairbrother, 1848

Comments: Manferrari: Drury Lane; 1 act. Libretto does not mention Shakespeare.

Cast: SIR RICHARD MORTON [Mr. Weiss] • SIR HYACINTH LUTESTRING [Mr. Henry] • WALTER BURTON [Mr. Charles Braham] • ROCKTON [Mr. C. Fischer] • GOODBOY [Mr. Paulo] • MAYLAND [Mr. Stacey] • THE LADY ALICE [Miss Emma Stanley] • MABEL [Mrs. Weiss] • RETAINERS, TENANTRY, GUESTS, GUARDS, PURITAN SOLDIERS, AND ROYALISTS • OBERON, King of the Fairies [Miss Kenworthy] • PUCK, commonly called Robin Goodfellow [Miss Poole] • MUSTARD SEED [Miss Wilkinson] • GNATFLY [Miss Weymouth] • TITANIA, Queen of the Fairies [Miss Georgiana Smithson] • MAYDEW {Miss Le Clercq] • ROSEBUD [Miss Barrett] •—•
Chorus: ATTENDANT FAIRIES, etc., etc.

Mihovil Logar (1902-   )

Four Scenes from Shakespeare

Status: I   **Evidence:** S
Text: Unknown
Premiere: 1956 00 00 ?
Play: *Other*
Yes: Groves V, Oxford
No: Baker's

Comments: Baker's: it is incidental music (1954).

Carl Adolf Lorenz (1837-1923)

Die Komödie der Irrungen

Status: Y **Evidence:** S
Text: Composer
Type: Opera **Acts:** 3 **Language:** German
Premiere: Stettin, Poland • 1939 03 11
Source of Premiere Information: Slonimsky
Play: *Comedy of Errors*
Publisher: Berlin: Schlesinger, 188?
Yes: Hartnoll, Gruber, Mellen, Oxford

Comments: Mellen: compossed 1890. Listed in US:Bp catalog.
Friedlaender list opera but does not know if it is based on
Shakespeare. Slonimsky: 2 acts.

Otto Ludwig (1813-1865)

Romeo und Julie

Status: Y **Evidence:** S
Text: Unknown
Type: Opera
Play: *Romeo and Juliet*
Yes: Stieger

Comments: Stieger: not finished.

Florence Pauline [Wickham] Lueder (1882-1962)

As You Like It

Status: Y **Evidence:** P
Text: Cooksey, Curtis
Type: Operetta **Acts:** 3/2 scenes **Language:** English
Play: *As You Like It*

Publisher: n. pl., c1933.
Yes: LIBRETTO

Rosalind

Status: Y   **Evidence:** P
Text: Composer
Type: Light opera   **Acts:** 3
Premiere: Dresden, Germany • 1938 00 00
Play: *As You Like It*
Yes: SCORE, Mellen, Baker's

Comments: Baker's: Rosalynd. Orchestration and arrangements by Erich Mirsch-Riccius; translation by Alexander von Hamm and N. Stiller. Mellen: Carmel, New York, Rockridge Theater, 1938 08 05.

William Meyer Lutz

Merry-Go-Round

Status: AP   **Evidence:** S
Text: Hicks, Seymour
Type: Musical farce [Revue]   **Acts:** 2   **Language:** English
Premiere: London, England: Coronet Theatre • 1899 04 24
Source of Premiere Information: Gänzl
Play: *Other*
Yes: Gänzl

Comments: Gänzl: lyrics by Aubrey Hopwood; additional songs by Robert Martin, Ellaline Terriss, Brandon Thomas, Harry Hunter and Edmund Forman. Characters and cast from Gänzl.

Cast: CHARLIE DALRYMPLE [Lionel Mackinder] • ALGY SCOTT [Joseph Wilson] • TOBY PRESCOTT [Sydney Harcourt] • HORACE DALE [Leslie Holland] • WILLIAM SHAKESPEARE [Martin Adeson] • WINCH [Frank Wheeler] • NORAH [Frances Earle] • LYDIA [Ethel Palliser] • MOLLY [Florence Lloyd] • MARY [Gracie Leigh] • ANNE, the cook [Hetty Chapman] •——• **Chorus:** CHORUS OF 40

Hector Macarig and Alfonso Deperis

Otello Tamburo

Status: ?
Text: Bertossi, A. and Alfonso Deperis
Type: Scherzo Comico   **Acts:** 3   **Language:** Italian
Premiere: Cormons, Italy • 1892 05 00
Source of Premiere Information: Stieger
Play: *Othello*
Yes: Friedlaender

Comments: A:Wn: catalog refers to libretto dated Gorizia 1891.
Friedlaender: Marcarig; parodie.

Galt MacDermot

Cressida

Status: Y   **Evidence:** S
Text: Papp, Joseph
Play: *Troilus and Cressida*
Yes: Northouse

Two Gentlemen of Verona

Status: Y   **Evidence:** P
Text: Guare, John and Mell Shapiro [lyrics by John Guare]
Type: Musical   **Acts:** 2   **Language:** English
Premiere: New York, U.S.A.: St. James Theatre • 1971 12 01
Source of Premiere Information: Score
Play: *Two Gentlemen of Verona*
Publisher: New York: Chappell & Co., Inc. 1973 [vs]
Yes: SCORE, Bordman, Green

Cast: THRURIO [Frank O'Brien] • SPEED [Jose Perez] •
VALENTINE [Clifton Davis] • PROTEUS [Raul Julia] • JULIA [Diana
Davila] • LUCETTA [Alix Elias] • LAUNCE [John Bottoms] • ANTONIO
[Frederic Warriner] • CRAB [Phineas] • DUKE OF MILAN [Norman
Matlock] • SILVIA [Jonelle Allen] • TAVERN HOST [Frederic Warriner]

• EGLAMOUR [Alvin Lum] •—•
Chorus: CITIZENS OF VERONA AND MILAN

George Alexander MacFarren (1813-1887)

Hamlet

Status: ?
Text: Unknown
Type: Seria   **Acts:** 2
Premiere: London, England: Queen's Theatre • 1861 00 00
Play: *Hamlet*

Comments: Date: spring.

Alexei Machavariani (1913-   )

Hamlet

Status: Y   **Evidence:** S
Text: Unknown
Type: Opera   **Language:** Russian
Premiere: Tbilisi, Soviet Union • 1964 00 00
Play: *Hamlet*
Yes: Hartnoll, Mellen

Comments: New Grove: 1965. Mellen: it is an opera; composed 1963. It may be a ballet; see his *Othello*.

Othello

Status: NO   **Evidence:** P
Acts: 4   **Language:** Russian
Premiere: Tbilisi, Soviet Union • 1963 00 00
Play: *Othello*
Yes: Hartnoll, Mellen, Oxford
No: SCORE, New Grove

Comments: Mellen: date is when composed; it is an opera. It is a ballet.

Alick Maclean [Alexander Morvaren] (1872-1936)

Petruccio

Status: I   **Evidence:** S
Text: Ross, Sheridan
Type: Romantic Opera   **Acts:** 1   **Language:** English
Premiere: London, England: Covent Garden • 1895 07 29
Source of Premiere Information: Score
Play: *Taming of the Shrew*
Publisher: London: Willcocks & Co.
Yes: Blom, Groves V, Hartnoll, Loewenberg, Oxford
No: Mellen

Comments: Mellen: Won the 1985 Moody-Manners Opera Company prize for one-act opera by British subject; 1895 09 26; not based on Shakespeare but on an original tragic play. Stieger, Manferrari:1895 05 29. Mellen: Sheridan Ross is the pseudonym of composer's sister. Schatz MS: 1895 06 29. Neither score nor libretto mention Shakespeare. Hauger: 1895 06 29. White: 1895 07 25. Date on cover of score at US:Wc is clearly July 29, 1895.

Cast: THE MOTHER, An Italian, who three years previously had migrated from her own land with her children (Contralto) • ELVIRA, Her daughter, the bride of Petruccio (Soprano) • GIOVANNI, Elvira's elder brother (Baritone) • RUBINO, Formerly betrothed to Elvira (Tenor) • PETRUCCIO, A well-to-do Creole (Bass) • MARIO, Elvira's little Brother

Giovanni (Giuseppe?) Maganini

Enrico IV al passo della Marna

Status: N   **Evidence:** P
Text: Torelli, Serafino
Type: Melodramma semiseria   **Acts:** 2   **Language:** Italian
Premiere: Pisa, Italy: Teatro de' Ravrivati [sp?] • 1825 00 00
Play: *Henry IV*

No: Schatz MS

Comments: Date and place from Schatz MS. Mellen: Magagnini; Florence: Accademia dei Risoluti 1826 07 27. Stieger: Carnival 1826. Libretto: Torelli took the argumento of the libretto from the comedy of Giovanni Battista Viassolo, named *Camillo Federici, Il pericolo di Enrico IV, al passo della Marna.* Cast is taken from Libretto for the 1826 performance in Florence. It may not be that of the first performance.

Cast: ENRICO IV, Re di Francia e Navarra [Sig. Frederigo Samballino] • IL DUCA DI TURNAI, Colonnello nell'armata della Lega [Sig. Giovanni Cappelli] • MENGONE, Barcajolo Fratello di [Sig, Mariano Stefanori] • LANFRANCO, Molinaro Padre di [Sig. Ferdinando Vannelli] • COSTANZA [Signora Adelaide Maldotti] • GHITA, Giovane contadina parente di Costanza [Signora Angiola Corrì] • ROBERTO Garzone di Mengone, che non parla [N. N.] • UN UFFIZIAL MAGGIORE DEL RE [N. N.] •— **Chorus:** CONTADINI, MULINARI, BARCAJOLI, SOLDATI DELLA LEGA, SOLDATI DEL RE

Francesco Maggioni (1720-1782)

Cajo Marzio Coriolano

Status: ?
Text: Pariati, Pietro (1665-1733)
Type: Opera   **Acts:** 3   **Language:** Italian
Premiere: Livorno, Italy: Teatro di San Sebastiano • 1744 00 00
Source of Premiere Information: Schatz MS
Play: *Coriolanus*

Comments: Schatz MS, Mellen: autumn.

Giuseppe Paolo Magni (c.1650-1737)

Admeto, Rè di Tessaglia

Status: ?
Text: Auerara, Abbé Pietro d'
Type: Melodramma   **Acts:** 3   **Language:** Italian

Premiere: Milan, Italy: Regio Ducal Teatro • 1702 00 00
Source of Premiere Information: Year and place from libretto.
Play: *Hamlet*

Comments: Date: Carnival.

Cast: ADMETO, Rè di Tessaglia • DORILLA, Figlia d'Admeto •
ELVIDA, Figlia d'Admeto • ALMIRO, Pastore della stirpe di Fetonte •
LEANDRO, Pastore della stirpe d'Epafo • GILDE, Ninfa riconosciuta
poi per Sorella d'Almiro • FILINDO, Figlio d'Admeto stolido • OLINDA,
Villanella Figlia de Zoila • ZOLIA, Vecchia • MOMO, Dio de'Maldicenti
sotto il nome di Batto Seruo • NETTUNO • TETI • APOLLO

Marsha Malamet

Dreamstuff

Status: Y   **Evidence:** S
Text: Ashman, Howard (book) and Dennis Green (lyrics)
Type: Broadway Show   **Language:** English
Premiere: New York, U.S.A.: WPA Theatre • 1976 04 02
Source of Premiere Information: Simas
Play: *Tempest*
Yes: Simas

Gian Francesco Malipiero (1882-1973)

Antonio e Cleopatra

Status: Y   **Evidence:** P
Text: Composer
Type: Dramma musicale   **Acts:** 3/6 quadri
      Language: Italian
Premiere: Florence, Italy: R. teatro Vitorio Emanuele II • 1938 05 04
Source of Premiere Information: Libretto
Play: *Antony and Cleopatra*
Publisher: Milan: Suvini Zerboni, 1938 [vs]
Yes: SCORE, LIBRETTO, Blom, Hartnoll, Loewenberg, Mellen, New
      Grove, Oxford

Cast: MARCO ANTONIO • CLEOPATRA, Regina d'Egitto • CARMIA, ancella della Regina • IRAS, ancella della Regina • OTTAVIANO CESARE • LEPIDO • SESTO POMPEO • DOMIZIO ENOBARBO, amico di Marco Antonio • EROS, amico di Marco Antonio • SCARO, amico di Marco Antonio • MECENE, amico di Ottaviano Cesare • AGRIPPA, amico di Ottaviano Cesare • DOLABELLA, amico di Ottaviano Cesare • TIREO, Messaggero di Cesare • MENAS, Amico di Pompeo • ALEXA, al servizio di Cleopatra • DIOMEDE, al servizio di Cleopatra • UN INDOVINO • UN CONTADINO • PRIMO SOLDATO • SECONDO SOLDATO • PRIMO MESSAGGERO DI MARC ANTONIO • SECONDO MESSAGGERO DI MARC ANTONIO • MESSAGGERO DI CLEOPATRA • UN SERVO
Chorus: SERVITORI E SOLDATI

Giulio Cesare

Status: Y   **Evidence:** P
Text: Composer
Type: Dramma musicale   **Acts:** 3/7 quadri
        Language: Italian
Premiere: Genoa, Italy: Teatro Carlo Felice • 1936 02 08
Source of Premiere Information: Baker's
Play: *Julius Caesar*
Publisher: Milan: Ricordi, 1935 [vs]
Yes: SCORE, LIBRETTO, Blom, Groves V, Hartnoll, Loewenberg, Mellen, MGG, New Grove, Oxford

Cast: UN TRIBUNO (Baritono) • PRIMO CITTADINO (Baritono) • SECONDO CITTADINO (Baritono) • CESARE (Baritono) • CALPURNIA (Soprano) • MARCO ANTONIO (Tenore) • BRUTO (Baritono) • CASSIO (Baritono) • CASCA (Tenore) • LUCIO, Servo di Bruto (Tenore) • PORZIA, Moglie di Bruto (Soprano) • LIGARIO (Tenore) • UN SERVO DI CESARE (Baritono) • METELLO CIMBER (Baritono) • PRIMO CITTADINO (Baritono) • SECONDO CITTADINO (Baritono) • TERZO CITTADINO (Tenore) • OTTAVIANO (Tenore) • IL MESSAGGERO (Baritono) • PINDARO (Tenore) • VOLUMNIO (Baritono) • STRATONE (Basso) •—•
Chorus: CITTADINI, POPOLO, SOLDATI

Romeo e Guilietta (scene 5 of Monde celesti e infernali)

Status: Y **Evidence:** P
Text: Composer
Type: Opera **Acts:** 3/7 donne **Language:** Italian
Premiere: Venice, Italy: Teatro la Fenice • 1961 02 02
Source of Premiere Information: Libretto
Play: *Romeo and Juliet*
Publisher: Milan: Ricordi, 1950.
Yes: LIBRETTO, Groves V, Hartnoll, Oxford

Comments: Baker's, Mellen: a broadcast concert version was performed on Turin Radio,1950 01 12.

Cast: ROMEO (Tenore) [Angelo Mori] • GIULIETTA (Soprano) [Magda Olivero]

Luigi Mancinelli (1848-1921)

Il Sogno di una notte d'estate

Status: Y **Evidence:** P
Text: Salvatori, Fausto
Type: Fantasia lirica **Acts:** 3 **Language:** Italian
Premiere: Rome, Italy • 1917 00 00
Play: *Midsummer Night's Dream*
Publisher: Bolonia: Pizzi & Ci. 1922 [vs]
Yes: LIBRETTO, Baker's, Blom, Groves V, Hartnoll, Mellen, MGG,
    New Grove, Oxford, Stieger

Comments: Composed in 1917. MGG: Finished 1917; posthum veoff, 1922, aufgef. New Grove: not performed. Baker's: not produced. Stieger: posthumous, 1921. Score: Edizione Postuma curata dal Maestro Leone Rossi; does not mention Shakespeare. Libretto dated 1922, Rome: dal *Midsummer Night's Dream* di William Shakespeare.

Cast: TESEO, Duca d'Atene (Basso comprimario) • LISANDRO, amante di Ermia (Tenore) • DEMETRIO, amante di Ermia (Baritono) • FILOSTRATO, Direttore delle feste di Teseo (Tenore comprimario) • IPPOLITA, Regina delle Amazzoni, fidanzata a Teséo (Soprano

comprimario) • ERMIA, amante di Lisandro • ELENA, amante di
Demetrio • QUINCE, carpentiere (Tenore comprimario) • SNUG,
legnaiuolo (Baritono comprimario) • BOTTOM, tessitore (Baritono
comprimario) • FLUTE, racconciamantici (Tenore comprimario) •
SNOUT, calderaio (Basso comprimario) • STARVELING, sarto (Basso
comprimario) • OBERON • TITANIA • PUCK •—• **Chorus:**
CAVALIERI, POPOLO, DONNE, ATLETI, GUERRIERI D'ATENE

Giuseppe Manusardi (1807?-   )

Un sogno di Primavera [Un rêve de printemps]

Status: Y   **Evidence:** S
Text: Principessa in Campagna, La
Type: Melodramma comico   **Acts:** 2   **Language:** Italian
Premiere: Milan, Italy: Teatro Re in San Salvatore • 1842 12 00
Source of Premiere Information: Year and place from libretto.
    Month from Stieger.
Play: *Midsummer Night's Dream*
Publisher: Milan: G. Canti [1847?]
Yes: Hartnoll, Oxford

Comments: Manferrari: librettist is anonymous. Librettist comes
from Schatz MS. Libretto: Parole del Signor N.N.; does not mention
Shakespeare. Friedlaender: Mamusardi. Date: Carnival.

Cast: LA CONTESSA AURELIA [Marietta Cazzaniga] • ISOLINA,
amica della Con.a [Luigia Perzoli] • ROSETTA, contadina [Adelaide
Morandini] • IL CONTIO D'ALTARIVA [Donati Luigi] • IL CAPITANO
ROLANDO [Carlo De Bellatti] • SIBILONE, contadino [Carlo
Cambiaggio] •—• **Chorus:** SERVI, CONTADINI

Filippo Marchetti (1831-1902)

Romeo e Giulietta

Status: Y   **Evidence:** P
Text: Marcello, Marco Marcelliano (1820-1865)
Type: Dramma lirico   **Acts:** 4   **Language:** Italian
Premiere: Trieste, Italy: Teatro Comunale • 1865 10 24

Source of Premiere Information: Score gives place and year.
　　　Day from Loewenberg.
Play: *Romeo and Juliet*
Publisher: Milan: F. Luca 1865? [vs]
Yes: LIBRETTO, Baker's, Blom, Friedlaender, Groves V, Hartnoll,
　　　Loewenberg, Mellen, New Grove, Oxford, Squire, Stieger

Comments: Schatz catalog, Schatz MS, Stieger and Manferrari:
1865 10 24. Mellen: 1865 10 25.

Cast: CAPPELLIO de'Cappelletti [Sig.r Giovanni Casonato] •
GIULIETTA, sua Figlia [Sig.ra Tiberini Ortolani] • TEBALDO, nipote di
Cappellio [Sig.r Ignazio Cancelli] • PARIDE, congiunto dei Scaligeri
[Sig.r Leone Giraldoni] • ROMEO de'Montecchi [Sig.r Mario Teberini]
• FRATE LORENZO [Sig.r Paolo Medini] • BALDASSARRE,
famigliare di Romeo [Sig.r N. N.] • MARTA, nutrice di Giulietta [Sig.ra
Angelina Zamboni] • UN SERVO DI CASA CAPPELLETTI [Sig.r N.
N.] • UN VECCHIO POPOLANO [Sig.r N. N.] •——•
Chorus: CITTADINI VERONESI E DONNE, CAVALIERI E DAME,
ATTENENTI DI CASA CAPPELLETTI, MASCHERE, FRATI,
SCHERANI, INVITATI, SERVI, DOMESTICI, POPOLO

Luigi Marescalchi (1745-1805)

Giuletta e Romeo

Status: Y　　**Evidence:** S
Text: Foppa, Giuseppe Maria (1760-1845)
Type: Tragedia　　　**Acts:** 3　　　**Language:** Italian
Premiere: Rome, Italy: Teatro di Torre Argentina • 1789 00 00
Source of Premiere Information: Mellen
Play: *Romeo and Juliet*
Yes: Friedlaender, Hartnoll, Mellen, Oxford, Squire, Wilson

Comments: Based on the same libretto as Zingarelli's opera.

Marescotti

Amleto

Status: Y   **Evidence:** S
Text: Unknown
Type: Opera   **Language:** Italian
Premiere: Siena, Italy • 1894 00 00
Source of Premiere Information: Mellen
Play: *Hamlet*
Yes: Mellen, Oxford

Maximilian Maretzek (1821-1897)

Hamlet

Status: Y   **Evidence:** S
Text: Perinet, Joachim (1763-1816)
Type: Opera   **Acts:** 3   **Language:** German
Premiere: Brno, Czechoslovakia: Stadttheater • 1840 11 05
Source of Premiere Information: Schatz MS
Play: *Hamlet*
Yes: Clemént, Hartnoll, Manferrari, Mellen, Oxford, Stieger

Comments: Baker's: 1843. Mellen: 1840 11 14.

George William Louis Marshall-Hall [G. W. Hall] (1862-1915)

Romeo and Juliet

Status: Y   **Evidence:** P
Text: Composer?
Type: Opera   **Acts:** 4   **Language:** English
Premiere: 1914 00 00 ?
Play: *Romeo and Juliet*
Publisher: London: Enoch and Sons, c.1914 [vs]
Yes: SCORE, Mellen

Comments: German version from the famous translation of Johann
Ludwig Tieck (1773-1853) and August Wilhelm von Schlegel (1767-
1845).

Cast: ESCALUS, Prince of Verona (Baritone) • PARIS, a young
nobleman (Tenor) • CAPULET (Bass) • TYBALT, nephew to Capulet
(Bass) • PETER, servant to Capulet (Bass) • ROMEO, son to
Montague (Tenor) • MERCUTIO, friend to Romeo (Baritone) •
BENVOLIO, friend to Romeo (Bass) • FRIAR LAURENCE, Franciscan
(Bass) • LADY CAPULET, Wife of Capulet (Soprano) • JULIET,
Daughter to Capulet (Soprano) • NURSE, to Juliet (Contralto) •
MONTAGUE (Mute) •—•
Chorus: CITIZENS OF VERONA, KINSFOLK TO BOTH HOUSES,
MASKERS, GUARDS, AND ATTENDANTS

Vicente Martín y Soler [Vincenzo Martini, Martini lo Spagnuolo] (1754-1806)

La Capricciosa corretta [So bessert sie sich]

Status: N   **Evidence:** S
Text: Ponte, Lorenzo da
Type: Dramma giocoso per musica   **Acts:** 2
          Language: Italian
Premiere: London, England: Haymarket • 1794 05 17
Source of Premiere Information: Sonneck
Play: *Taming of the Shrew*
No: Squire

Comments: Squire: mentioned in some dictionaries, has an entirely
different plot. Friedlaender: 1785.

Cast: CIPRIGNA • BONARIO • ISABELLA • VALERIO • CILIA •
FIUTA • CONTE LELIO • DON GIGLIO

Frank Martin (1890-1974)

Der Sturm

Status: Y   **Evidence:** P
Text: Composer
Type: Zauber-Lustspiel   **Acts:** 3 (9 scenes)
    Language: German
Premiere: Vienna, Austria: Staatsoper • 1956 06 17
Source of Premiere Information: Gruber
Play: *Tempest*
Publisher: Vienna: Universal Edition, 1955 [vs]
Yes: SCORE, Hartnoll, Mellen, MGG, New Grove, Oxford

Comments: The only opera MGG lists for him. New Grove: 1956 06 18. Gruber: 5 Bildern. German translation of Shakespeare by A.W. von Schlegel.

Cast: ALONSO, König von Neapel (Bass) • SEBASTIAN, sein Bruder (Bass) • PROSPERO, der rechtmäßige Herzog von Mailand (Bass-Bariton) • ANTONIO, sein Bruder, der unrechtmäßige Herzog von Mailand (Tenor) • FERDINAND, Sohn des Königs von Neapel (Tenor) • GONZALO, ein ehrlicher, alter Rat des Königs (Bass-Bariton) • ADRIAN, Herr vom Hofe (Tenor) • CALIBAN, ein wilder und mißgestalter Sklave (Bass) • TRINCULO, ein Spaßmacher (Tenor) • STEPHANO, ein betrunkener Kellner (Bariton) • BOOTSMANN (Hoher Bariton) • MIRANDA, Tochter des Prospero (Sopran) • ARIEL, ein Luftgeist (Tänzer) • EIN SCHIFFSPATRON (Gesprochen) •—•
Chorus: IRIS, CERES, JUNO, NYMPHEN, SCHNITTER (Ballett-Gruppe); MATROSEN

Giovanni Martini [Johann Paul Ægidius Schwartzendorf; Martini il Tedesco; Jean Paul Egide] (1741-1816)

Henri IV, ou La Bataille d'Ivry

Status: N   **Evidence:** S
Text: Rosoi, Barnabé Farmian de [Rosoy, De Rosoy]
Type: Drame Lyrique   **Acts:** 3   **Language:** French
Premiere: Paris, France: Comédiens italiens ordinaires du Roy
    • 1774 11 14

Source of Premiere Information: Libretto
Play: *Henry IV*
Publisher: Paris: Siber, 1875? [vs]
No: Cast, Plot

Comments: New Grove: 1774, Versailles.

Cast: HENRI IV, Roi de France et de Navarre [Le Sr. Clairval] • LE MARÉCHAL DE BRION [Le Sr. Trial] • LE MARÉCHAL D'AUMONT [Le Sr. Narbonne] • LE COMTE DE DURFORT [Le Sr. Roussel] • LE COLONEL SCHOMBERG [Le Sr. Demery] • LE MARQUIS DE LENONCOURT, Amant d'Eugénie [Le Sr. Suin] • LE CHEVALIER DE LENONCOURT, Amant d'Eugénie [Le Sr. Julien] • ROGER, riche Commerçant [Le Sr. Nainville] • EUGÉNIE, Fille de Roger [La Dlle. Trial] • LA MARQUISE DE LENONCOURT [La Dlle. Billioni] • OFICIERS DE LA SUITE DU ROI [Les Srs. Desbrosses, Thomassin, Gaillard, Desormery, Morel, Leclerc] •—•
Chorus: TROUPE DE GUERRIERS

Bernadetta Matuszczak (1933-   )

Julia i Romeo

Status: Y   **Evidence:** P
Text: Iwaszkiewicza, Jaroslav
Type: Chamber Opera   **Acts:** 5 Scenes   **Language:** Polish
Premiere: Warsaw, Poland: Wielki t. • 1970 11 19
Play: *Romeo and Juliet*
Publisher: Kraków: Polsikie Wydawnictwo Muzyczne, 1979 [vs]
Yes: SCORE, New Grove, Oxford

Comments: New Grove: Wiesbaden 1972; composed 1967.

Cast: JULIA (Mezzo Soprano) • ROMEO (Baritono) • FATUM (Pantomimi) •—• **Chorus:** CHORUS

Étienne Nicolas Méhul (1763-1817)

Le Jeune Henri [Gabrielle d'Estrées où les Amours d'Henri IV]

Status: ?
Text: Saint-Just, Claude Godard d'Aucour de
Type: Opéra comique   **Acts:** 2   **Language:** French
Premiere: Paris, France: Opéra Comique, rue Favart • 1797 05 01
Source of Premiere Information: Groves V
Play: *Henry IV*
Publisher: Paris: Meysenberg [vs]

Comments: See note to opera *La Gioventù di Enrico V* by Morlacchi. Groves V: librettist is Jean Nicolas Bouilly [1763-1842]. Manferrari: librettist is J. B. Bouilly. Stieger: *La chasse du jeune Henri* [This is the name given to the overture and to later versions of the opera. Score: Paroles de M. de Saint-Just.

Cast: HENRI IV [M. Elleviou] • D'ESTRÉES, Seigneur de Cœuves [M. Solié] • GABRIELLE, sa Fille [Mme Saint-Aubin] • ÉLOI, Soldat [M. Moreau] • ESTELLE, jeune fille attachée à Gabrielle [Mme Gaveaudan] • CRILLON [M. Gaveaux] •— **Chorus:** SEIGNEURS ET SOLDATS DE L'ARMÉE DE HENRI, LIGUEURS

Giambattista [Giovanni Battista] Meiners (1826-1897)

Riccardo III

Status: Y   **Evidence:** S
Text: Codebò, Andrea (1821-1828)
Type: Melodrama   **Acts:** 3   **Language:** Italian
Premiere: Milan, Italy: Teatro alla Scala • 1859 11 12
Source of Premiere Information: Libretto
Play: *Richard III*
Yes: Clément, Friedlaender, Mellen, Oxford, Stieger
No: Squires

Comments: Libretto does not mention Shakespeare.
Friedlaender: not published.

Cast: RICCARDO III [Sig.r Giovanni Corsi] • ISABELLA [Sig.a
Ortolani-Tiberini] • RICHEMONT [Sig.r Mario Tiberini] • UGO [Sig.r
Giuseppe Echeveria] • RUTLAND [Sig.r Giacomo Redaelli] •
KENNEDY [Sig.a Orsola Bignami] •⸺ **Chorus:** GRANDI DEL
REGNO, SGHERRI, DAME, CAVALIERI, MASCHERE, PARTIGIANI
DELLA CORONA, ANCELLE D'ISABELLA, POPOLO D'AMBO I
SESSI, BALLERINI

Mélésville [Honoré Marie Joseph, Baron Duveyrier] (1787-1865)

Gillette de Narbonne

Status: ?
Text: Composer and Scribe
Type: Vaudeville   **Acts:** 1
Premiere: Paris, France: Theatre Nouveauté • 1829 00 00
Source of Premiere Information: Stieger
Play: *All's Well That Ends Well*

Comments: Mélesville was a librettist and he may have written the
libretto for an opera with this name.

Edmond Membrée (1820-1882)

Roméo et Juliette

Status: ?
Text: Unknown
Type: Opera?
Play: *Romeo and Juliet*

Antonio Mercadal y Pons (1850-1873)

Giulietta e Romeo

Status: Y   **Evidence:** S
Text: Unknown
Type: Dramma per musica   **Acts:** 3   **Language:** Spanish
Premiere: Port-Mahon [Minorca], Spain: Teatro dell'Opera
    • 1873 03 00
Play: *Romeo and Juliet*
Yes: Friedlaender, Hartnoll, Mellen, Oxford, Squire, Stieger

Comments: Stieger: 1873 02 00.

Giuseppe Saverio Raffele Mercadante (1795-1870)

Amleto

Status: Y   **Evidence:** P
Text: Romani, Felice (1788-1865)
Type: Melodramma tragico   **Acts:** 2   **Language:** Italian
Premiere: Milan, Italy: Teatro alla Scala • 1822 12 26
Source of Premiere Information: Year and place from libretto.
    Date from Mellen.
Play: *Hamlet*
Publisher: Autograph I-Mr, copy I-Nc
Yes: LIBRETTO, Friedlaender, Hartnoll, Mellen, New Grove, Oxford,
    Stieger

Comments: Manferrari, Mellen: 3 acts.

Cast: GELTRUDE, Regina di Danimarca [Signora Teresa Belloc] •
CLAUDIO, Principe del sangua [Sig. Luigi Lablache] • AMELIA, sua
figlia, amante di Amleto, e promessa sposa di [Signora Giuseppa
Rovetta] • ALDANO, Principe di Norvegia [Sig. Savino Monelli] •
AMLETO, figlio di Geltrude, erede del Trono di Danimarca [Signora
Isabella Fabbrica] • NORCESTO, Cavaliere, amico d' Amleto [Sig.
Carlo Poggioli] • SIVARDO, Uffiziale, confidente di Claudio [Sig. Carlo
Donà] • ALBINA, Dama di Corte [Signora Angelo Maria Silvestri
Bertozzi] •—• **Chorus:** DAME E CAVALIERI, GUERRIERI DANESI E
NORVEGI, PARTIGIANI DI CLAUDIO

La Gioventù di Enrico V

Status: Y   **Evidence:** S
Text: Romani, Felice (1788-1865)
Type: Melodramma   **Acts:** 4   **Language:** Italian
Premiere: Milan, Italy: Teatro alla Scala • 1834 11 25
Source of Premiere Information: Year and place from libretto.
     Date from Mellen.
Play: *Henry IV, Parts 1 and 2*
Publisher: New Grove: vs excerpts (Milan ?1835)
Yes: Hartnoll, New Grove, Oxford, Squire, Wilson

Comments: New Grove: partly after Shakespeare.

Cast: ENRICO, Principe di Galles [Sig.r Orazio Cartagenova] •
ARTURO DI NORTHUMBERLAND [Sig.r Domenico Reina] • LORD
ARCOURT, compagno di Enrico [Sig.r Ignazio Marini] • SIR JOHN
FALSTAFF, altro compagno di Enrico [Sig.r Vincenzo Galli] • IL
PRINCIPE DI LANCASTRO, fratello di Enrico [Sig.r Domenico
Spiaggi] • IL SERIFFO [Sig.r Napoleone Marconi] • IL RE D'ARMI
[Sig.r Raineri Pochini] • MISS ELISA, sorella d'Arcourt [Sig.a
Almerinda Manzoccri] • MISTRISS MARTINN, Ostessa [Giuseppina
Leva] •— **Chorus:** SIGNORI, COMPAGNI D'ENRICO, DAME,
CAVALIERE, MASCHERE, VETTURALI, SOLDATI, POPOLO

Violetta

Status: ?
Text: Arienzo, Marco d' (1811-1877)
Type: Melodramma   **Acts:** 4   **Language:** Italian
Premiere: Naples, Italy: Teatro Nuovo • 1853 10 01
Source of Premiere Information: Stieger
Play: *Twelfth Night*
Publisher: Milano: F. Lucca [1852] [vs]

Comments: New Grove: 1953 01 10, autograph I:Nc; vocal score
(Milan n.d.). Manferrari: 10 gennaio 1853. Cast is not the same as
those given in libretto (Naples 1852). Schatz MS: 1852 12 00.

Cast: VIOLETTA [Sig.ra Lucia Escott] • ROSALBA [Sig.ra
Enrichetta Cherubini] • GIACOMO [Sig.r Giuseppe Fiovavanti] •
ODINO [Sig.r Luigi Bianchi] • BERARDO [Sig.r Cammarano] • IL

LANDAMANO [Sig.r N.N.] • FIORINA [Sig.ra N.N.] • UN CAPORALE
[Sig.r N.N.] • UN VILLANO [Sig.r N.N.]

Gustave Michaelis (1828-1887)

Die Lustigen Weiber von Berlin

Status: ?
Text: Meyer, Felix
Type: Liederspiel   **Acts:** 1/2 Bildern   **Language:** German
Premiere: Berlin, Germany: Callenbach's Vaudeville Theater
     • 1862 05 00
Source of Premiere Information: Schatz MS
Play: *Merry Wives of Windsor*

Comments: Stieger: 1861, Kallenbach Th.

Cast: HERR GRÜNGELB, ein alter Junggeselle • HERR FRÖHLICH
• MADAME FRÖHLICH • HERR SEELIG • MADAME SEELIG • HERR
SCHMÄCHLICH • MADAME SCHMÄCHLICH • PETER HAHN, Diener
bei Fröhlich • HANNCHEN, Dienerin bei Fröhlich

Gustave Michaelis (1828-1887)

Othello in Kyritz

Status: ?
Text: Linberer, Robert
Type: Komische Opern-Scene
Play: *Othello*

Edmond Jean Louis Missa (1861-1910)

Dinah

Status: Y   **Evidence:** P
Text: Carré, Michel Antoine (1865-1945) and Paul de Choudens
    (-1925)
Type: Comédie lyrique   **Acts:** 4   **Language:** French
Premiere: Paris, France: Théâtre de la Comédie Parisienne
    • 1894 06 25
Source of Premiere Information: Date from score. Place from
    Stieger.
Play: *Cymbeline*
Publisher: Paris: Choudens Fils, 1884 [vs]
Yes: SCORE, Blom, Groves V, Hartnoll, Mellen, MGG, Oxford,
    Wilson

Comments: Stieger: 1894 06 28. Schatz MS, US:NYp: 3 acts,
1894 06 25. Mellen: 1894 06 27.

Cast: METANO (Ténor) [M. Engel] • IACHIMO (Baryton) [M.
Manoury] • PHILARIO (Basse chantante) [M. R. LAFON] • DINAH
(Soprano) [Melle Marcolini] • FLORA (Chanteuse légère [Melle
Lambrecht] • UN OFFICIER [M. Ch. Faber] •—•
Chorus: SEIGNEURS, COURTISANES

Richard Mohaupt (1904-1957)

Double Trouble [Zwillingskomödie]

Status: N   **Evidence:** P
Text: Maren, Roger
Type: Opera   **Acts:** Prologue,1, Epilogue
    Language: English (translation)
Premiere: Louisville, Kentucky, U.S.A.: Kentucky Opera
    Association • 1954 12 04
Source of Premiere Information: Mellen
Play: *Comedy of Errors*
No: SCORE, Groves V, Gruber, Moore

Comments: Score: based on Plautus' *Menaechmi* [the source of
Shakespeare's *Comedy of Errors*].

Cast: HOCUS (Bass-Baritone) • POCUS Hocus' twin brother (Bass-Baritone) • NAGGIA, Hocus' wife (Mezzo-Soprano) • CYNTHIA, their daughter (Soprano) • EROTIA, a courtesan (Coloratura-Soprano) • DR. ANTIBIOTICUS, M.D. (Tenoro-Buffo) • LUCIO, his son (Tenor)

Hermann Mohr (1830-1896)

Der Orakelspruch, Op. 50

Status: N   **Evidence:** P
Text: Salice-Contessa, Carl Wilhelm
Type: Romantische Oper   **Acts:** 2   **Language:** German
Premiere: Berlin, Germany • 1883 00 00
Play: *Winter's Tale*
Publisher: Berlin: Carl Simon 1885 [vs]
No: SCORE, LIBRETTO

Comments: Libretto and score: Frei nach C. W. Contessa.

Cast: FLORINDA, eine Fee • LUCIE, ihre Tochter • SYLVIO • MARKO, ein alter Gärtner • ROSA, ein Landmädchen • EIN GENIUS • EIN JÄGER • EIN GEIST •——•
Chorus: LANDMÄDCHEN, DER JÄGER UND GEISTER

Roderich [Elder von Mojsvár von] Mojsisovics (1877-1953)

Viel Lärm um Nichts

Status: Y   **Evidence:** S
Text: Unknown
Type: Opera   **Language:** German
Premiere: 1915 00 00
Play: *Much Ado About Nothing*
Yes: Blom, Groves V, Hartnoll, Mellen, Oxford

Comments: Groves V: composed c.1930 (Graz?). Gruber: not performed. Mellen: 1915 00 00 composed?

Kiril Vladimirovich Molchanov (1922-   )

Romeo, Dzhulyetta i t'ma [Romeo, Juliet and Darkness]

Status: ?
Text: Unknown
Type: Opera   **Language:** Russian
Premiere: 1963 00 00
Source of Premiere Information: Mellen
Play: *Romeo and Juliet*

Comments: Mellen: date is when composed.

Carlo Antonio Monza (1744-1801)

Cajo Mario

Status: ?
Text: Roccaforte, Gaetano
Type: Dramma per musica   **Acts:** 3   **Language:** Italian
Premiere: Venice, Italy: Teatro di San Benedetto • 1777 05 00
Source of Premiere Information: Schatz MS
Play: *Coriolanus*

Comments: Schatz MS: nella fiera dell'ascensione.

Melesio Morales (1838-1908)

Giulietta e Romeo

Status: Y   **Evidence:** S
Text: Romani, Felice (1788-1865)
Type: Opera   **Acts:** 4   **Language:** Spanish
Premiere: Mexico City, Mexico: Teatro National • 1863 01 27
Play: *Romeo and Juliet*
Yes: Blom, Groves V, Hartnoll, Mellen, Oxford

Comments: New Grove: began opera at age 18; Romani's libretto is based on Shakespeare.

Enrique [Enric] Morera (1865-1942)

La Fiercilla domada

Status: Y   **Evidence:** P
Text: Jordá, José e Luis de Zulueta
Type: Comedia lírica   **Acts:** 3   **Language:** Spanish
Premiere: Barcelona, Spain: Tivoli • 1913 09 00
Source of Premiere Information: Stieger
Play: *Taming of the Shrew*
Yes: LIBRETTO, Stieger

Comments: Libretto: Williams [sic] Shakespeare. Omitted from Stieger Shakespeare list but indicated in the item description.

Cast: BAUTISTA, padre de [Sr. Felipe Agulló] • CATALINA y [Sra. Maria Luisa Labal] • BLANCA [Srta. Salud Rodríguez] • PETRUCHIO (Barítono) [Sr. Josè Ortiz de Zaráte] • HORTENSIO (Tenor) [Sr. Rafel López] • GRUMIO, criado de Petrucio [Sr. Francisco Gallego] • LUCENCIO [Sr. Faustino Bretaño] • GREMIO [Sr. Jesús Navarro] • UNA VIUDA [Srta. Lola Alcántara] • JUAN, JORGE, FELIPE, NICOLAS: Criados • CONVIDADOS 1.° y 2.° • UN SASTRE •—•
Chorus: CORO GENERAL

Francesco Giuseppi Baldassare Morlacchi (1784-1841)

La Capricciosa pettita

Status: ?
Text: Romanelli, Luigi (1751-1839)
Type: Dramma giocoso   **Acts:** 2   **Language:** Italian
Premiere: Dresden, Germany: Hoftheater • 1815 00 00
Source of Premiere Information: Year and place from libretto.
Play: *Taming of the Shrew*

Comments: Libretto does not give author of text. Friedlaender: 1810. Schatz MS, Stieger: text by Romanelli; Dresden 1816 01 10, Hofth.

Cast: LINDORA, romans, destinata sposa al • BARON CASTAGNA DI VELLETRI • VALERIO, Ufficiale, servente di Lindora, e suo

compagno di viaggio • GIANNINA, locandiera, sorella di •
BERNARDO, locandiere, ma di stirpe non ignobile • SIMONE, frattore
di canpagna, al servizio del Barone • NESPOLA, Maggiordomo del
suddetto Barone •—• **Chorus:** SERVITORI, MAGHI E CONTADINI

La Gioventù di Enrico V [Das Jugendjahre Heinrich des Fünften]

Status: N   **Evidence:** S
Text: Tarducci, Filippo
Type: Dramma per musica   **Acts:** 2   **Language:** Italian
Premiere: Dresden, Germany: Königl. Sächs. Theater
• 1823 10 04
Source of Premiere Information: Place and year from libretto.
Day from Mellen.
Play: *Henry IV*
No: Groves V, Schatz MS

Comments: Groves V: an Italian version of Bouilly's libretto of *Le
Jeune Henri* set by Méhul in 1797 [score gives librettist as Saint-
Just]. Stieger, Manferrari: libretto is by Romani. Schatz MS: text nach
La Jeunesse d'Henri V des Alexandre Duval; zuerst aufgeführt in ital
Sprache u. d. Theater des Schlosses zu Pillnitz am Aug 1823.

Cast: IL PRINCIPE ENRICO • IL CONTE ROCESTER • EDUARDO •
CAPITANO COOP • BETTINA • MILEDI CLARA • WILLIAM,
Cameriere del Principe •—•
Chorus: CORTGIANI, GARZONI DI TAVERNA

Luigi Moroni

Amleto

Status: Y   **Evidence:** P
Text: Peruzzini, Giovanni (1815-1869)
Type: Tragedia lirica   **Acts:** 4   **Language:** Italian
Premiere: Rome, Italy: Teatro di Apollo • 1860 06 02
Source of Premiere Information: Place and year from libretto.
Day from Mellen.
Play: *Hamlet*
Yes: LIBRETTO, Friedlaender, Hartnoll, Mellen, Oxford, Stieger

Cast: CLAUDIO, pretendente al trono di Danimarca [Filippo Coletti] • GERTRUDE, vedova del defunto Re [Emilia Boccherini] • AMLETO, di lui figlio [Carlo Negrini] • OFELIA, figlia di Polonio [Caterina Decaroli] • NORCESTO, Cortigiano ed amico d'Amleto [Cesare Bossi] • POLONIO, confidente di Claudio, altro Cortigiano [Giuseppe Bazzoli] • LE SPETRO DEL DEFUNTO RE [N. N.] •—•
Chorus: CORI E COMPARSE

David Morton

Tempest in a Teapot

Status: Y   **Evidence:** P
Text: Composer
Type: Musical Play   **Acts:** Prolog/2/Epilogue
       Language: English
Play: *Tempest*
Yes: LIBRETTO
Cast: MICHAEL, a young boy of six • MIRANDA, a young girl of ten; later, aged 18 • MISS ARIEL, the children's governess, aged about 30; later, ARIEL, a sprite • MARY, a middle-aged servant • MR. PROSPER, the children's father, aged 35-40; later, PROSPERO, exiled King of Illyria • MASTER of a ship • BOS'N of a ship • ALONSO, King of Ardenia, aged 45 • ANTONIO, brother of Prospero, aged 35, ursurping King of Illyria • GONZALO, Counsellor in the court of Illyria, aged 60. • SEBASTIAN, brother of Alonso, aged 40 • CALIBAN, a savage, but educated monster • FERDINAND, son of Alonso and Crown Prince of Ardenia, aged 23-25 • TRINCULO, servant in the court of Ardenia, aged 30 • STEPHANO, valet to Alonso, aged 30.
Chorus: 16 SAILORS; 16 SPRITES—LATER, YOUNG LADIES

Louise Morton and others

Twelfth Night

Status: NO   **Evidence:** P
Language: English
Premiere: Northampton, Mass. (Smith College), U.S.A.: Smith
       College • 1917 06 00
Source of Premiere Information: Score

Play: *Twelfth Night*
Publisher: Boston: C.W. Thompson and Co. [1917]
No: SCORE

Comments: This is incidental music.

Giuseppe Mosca (1772-1839)

La Gioventù di Enrico V

Status: ?
Text: Romani, Felice (1788-1865)
Type: Dramma in Musica   **Acts:** 2   **Language:** Italian
Premiere: Palermo, Italy: Teatro Carolino • 1817 00 00
Source of Premiere Information: Schatz MS
Play: *Henry IV*

Comments: Mellen: Florence, Teatro Pergola, 1817 09 11.
Librettist not named in libretto. Characters seem to be the same as
those in Morlacchi's *Gioventú di Enrico V.*

Cast: IL PRINCIPE ENRICO • IL CONTE ROCESTER • MILADY
CLARA • EDUARDO, Paggio del Principe • CAPITAN COOPP •
BETTINA, di lui Nipote • WILLIAM, Cameriere •—•
Chorus: CORTIGIANI, GARSONI DI TAVERNA

Wolfgang Amadeus Mozart (1756-1791) [Music from Cosi fan tutte]

Peines d'amour perdues

Status: Y   **Evidence:** S
Text: Carré, Michel Florentin (1819-1872) and Jules Barbier
(1822-1901)
Type: Opéra comique   **Acts:** 4   **Language:** French
Premiere: Paris, France: Théâtre Lyrique, Salle de la Place du
Châtelet • 1863 03 31
Source of Premiere Information: Pitou
Play: *Love's Labour's Lost*
Yes: Mellen, Pitou, Stieger, Schatz MS

Comments: The music of this opera was that of *Cosi fan tutte.*
Pitou: Audiences welcomed Mozart's music but frowned upon the
libretto because they considered it salacious. . . . The objection to da
Ponte's libretto was its depiction of two men deceiving their fiancées
and proving thereby that all women are inconstant.

Lance Mulcahy

Shakespeare's Cabaret

Status: Y   **Evidence:** S
Text: Unknown
Type: Review   **Language:** English
Premiere: New York, U. S. A. • 1980 02 01
Play: Other
Yes: Bloom
Comments: Bloom: played 40 performances Off-Broadway and 94
on Broadway; date is for Broadway opening; text is taken from
several of Shakespeare's plays. Cast from Bloom.

Cast: [Alan Brasington] • [Catherine Cox] • [Pauletta Pearson] •
[Patti Perkins] • [Larry Riley] • [Michael Rupert]

Adolph Müller (the elder) (1801-1886)

Heinrich IV

Status: ?
Text: Schröder, Fr. (nach dem Französischen)
Type: Singspiel   **Acts:** 2   **Language:** German
Premiere: Vienna, Austria: Theater an der Wien • 1865 12 14
Source of Premiere Information: Stieger
Play: *Henry IV*

Othellerl, der Mohr von Wien [Die geheilte Eifersucht]

Status: I   **Evidence:** S
Text: Meisl, Karl (1775-1853)
Type: Parodirende Posse mit Gesang   **Acts:** 3
       Language: German
Premiere: Vienna, Austria: Theater an der Wien • 1829 06 06
Source of Premiere Information: Mellen
Play: *Othello*
Publisher: Vienna: A. Diabelli, 1830? [selections]
Yes: Friedlaender
No: A-Wn

Comments: A:Wn catalog: Parodie Der Oper *Robert der Teufel*
nach dem Franz von Carl Treumann vorgetragen von demselben.
Friedlaender: 1828.

Cast: Extracted out of score [of selections]. • CASSIO [Hrn. Scholz]
• SCHROLL • DESDEMONERL • RODRIGERL

Viel Lärm um Nichts

Status: ?
Text: Lembert, Johann Wilhelm
Type: Vaudeville   **Acts:** 1
Premiere: Vienna, Austria: Theater an der Wein • 1844 04 24
Source of Premiere Information: Stieger
Play: *Much Ado About Nothing*

Comments: Stieger: Fortsetzung von *Indienne und Zephyre*
1844 02 24.

Wenzel Müller (1767-1835)

Der Sturm oder die Zauberinsel

Status: Y   **Evidence:** P
Text: Hensler, Karl Friedrich (1759-1825)
Type: Heroisch-komische oper   **Acts:** 2
       Language: German

Premiere: Vienna, Austria: Theater in der Leopoldstadt
• 1798 11 08
Source of Premiere Information: Mellen
Play: *Tempest*
Yes: LIBRETTO, Friedlaender, Hartnoll, New Grove, Oxford, Squire,
Stieger

Comments: Baker's: full list of his operas is in 2nd supplement to
Reimann's *Opernhandbuch*. New Grove: principal sources for MSS
are A:Wgm, A:Wn, A:Wst.

Cast: ALONSO, König von Sufi • FERDINAND, dessen Sohn •
BRUNO, rechtmässiger König von Bennonien, ein Zauberer •
BIANKA, seine Tochter • ANTONIO, Bruno's Bruder, unrecthmäßiger
Besitzer von Bennonien • GONSALO, Alfonsos Gefährte • ARIEL,
ein Geist • TRINKULO, des Königs Hofnarr • KALIBAN, ein wilder,
mißgeschaffner Sklave • STEPHANO, Kellermeister • ROSINE, seine
Schwester • DER SCHIFFSPATRON **Chorus:** EDELLEUTE UND
KNECHTE IM GEFOLGE DES KÖNIGS, BOOTSLEUTE,
MATROSEN, GEISTER

Hugh Mullins

Romeo and Juliet

Status: Y   **Evidence:** S
Text: Unknown
Type: Opera   **Language:** English
Premiere: 1965 00 00
Source of Premiere Information: Mellen
Play: *Romeo and Juliet*
Yes: Mellen, Oxford

Comments: Other operas by Mullins were performed at Los
Angeles State College. Date is when composed.

Modest Petrovich Mussorgsky (1839-1881)

Hamlet

Status: Y   **Evidence:** S
Text: Unknown
Type: Opera
Premiere: 1843 00 00
Play: *Hamlet*
Yes: Neef

Comments: Neef: date is composed; work not performed.

Nikolai Nabokov (1903-1978)

Love's Labour's Lost [Verlor'ne Liebesmüh']

Status: Y   **Evidence:** P
Text: Auden, Wystan Hugh (1907-1973) and Chester Kallman
        (1921-1975)
Type: Comedy   **Acts:** 3/6 Scenes   **Language:** English
Premiere: Brussels, Belgium: Théâtre Royal de la Monnaie
        • 1973 02 07
Source of Premiere Information: Score
Play: *Love's Labour's Lost*
Publisher: Berlin: Bote & Bock, 1973 [vs]
Yes: SCORE, AMCL, New Grove, Oxford

Comments: Performed by the West-Berlin German Oper
[Deutschen Oper Berlin]. German by Claus H. Henneberg.

Cast: ROSALINE (Soprano drammatico) • KATHERINE (Soprano
lirico) • JAQUENETTA (Soprano leggiero) • MOTH (Soprano
lirico/Alto) • PRINCESS (Mezzo-Soprano) • DUMAINE (Tenore) •
BEROWNE (Baritono alto) • DON ARMADO (Baritono leggiero) •
KING (Baritono grave) • BOYET (Basso)

Éduard Frantsevich Nápravnik (1839-1916)

Der Sturm

Status: Y   **Evidence:** S
Text: Unknown
Type: Opera   **Acts:** 1   **Language:** Russian
Premiere: Prague, Czechoslovakia: Czech National Theater
• 1860 00 00
Source of Premiere Information: Stieger
Play: *Tempest*
Yes: Friedlaender, Hartnoll, Manferrari, Mellen, Oxford, Squire,
Stieger

Comments: Manferrari & MGG: died 1915 St. Petersburg. New
Grove: the work is lost. Groves V: for a detailed list of Opp. 15-72 see
Musikliterarische Blätter, 1 Feb. 1904. US:Wc catalog: died 1917.
Mellen: 1860 00 00 composed. Date: autumn.

Gouliellmo Navoigille [pseud. Guillaume Julien] (1745-1811)

L' Orage, ou Quel Guignon!

Status: ?
Text: Cuvelier de Trye, Jean Guillaume Antoine (1766-1824)
Type: Opéra comique   **Acts:** 1   **Language:** French
Premiere: Paris, France: Théâtre de la Cité • 1793 00 00
Source of Premiere Information: Mellen
Play: *Tempest*

Josef Nesvera (1842-1914)

Perdita

Status: Y   **Evidence:** S
Text: Kvapil, Jaroslav (1868-1950)
Type: Opera   **Acts:** Prologue/3   **Language:** Czech
Premiere: Prague, Czechoslovakia: Czech National Theater
• 1897 05 21

Source of Premiere Information: Loewenberg
Play: *Winter's Tale*
Publisher: MGG: Prague,\ o. j. F. A. Urbanek; New Grove: Smes
[potpourri] arr. pf (n.d.) [Prague]
Yes: Blom, Groves V, Hartnoll, Loewenberg, Mellen, MGG, New
Grove, Oxford, Stieger

Comments: Stieger, Mellen: composed in 1883.

Carl Otto Ehrenfried Nicolai (1810-1849)

Die lustigen Weiber von Windsor

Status: Y   **Evidence:** P
Text: Mosenthal, Salomon Hermann Ritter von (1821-1877)
Type: Komische-fantasche   **Acts:** 3/7 Scenes
    Language: German
Premiere: Berlin, Germany: Königl. Opernhaus • 1849 03 09
Source of Premiere Information: Libretto
Play: *Merry Wives of Windsor*
Publisher: Berlin: Bote und G. Bock, 1850 [vs]
Yes: SCORE, LIBRETTO, Baker's, Blom, Friedlaender, Groves V,
Hartnoll, Loewenberg, MGG, New Grove, Oxford, Squire,
Wilson

Comments: Mellen: recitatives added by Proch, Vienna, 1849 02
12. Given in London to Maggioni's libretto [see Balfe] and called
Falstaff.
Cast: SIR JOHN FALSTAFF [Herr Zschiesche] • HERR FLUTH,
Bürger von Windsor [Herr Krause] • HERR REICH, Bürger von
Windsor [Herr Mickler] • FENTON [Herr Pfifter] • JUNKER SPÄRLICH
[Herr Mantius] • DR. CAJUS, [Herr Lieber] • FRAU FLUTH [Fräul.
Tuczek] • FRAU REICH, [Fräul. Marr] • JUNGFER ANNA REICH [Frau
Röster] • DER KELLNER im Gasthaus zum Hofenbande [Herr Röhr] •
ERSTER BÜRGER [Herr Tägener] • ZWEITER BÜRGER [Herr Müller
II] • DRITTER BÜRGER [Herr Meinhardt] • VIERTER BÜRGER [Herr
Brandt] • WESPEN [Fräuleins Bethge, Bordowich, Koch, Ditbaner,
Starke] • ZWEI KNECHTE DES HERRN FLUTH • KELLNER •—•
Chorus: BÜRGER UND FRAUEN VON WINDSOR, KINDER,
MASKEN VON EISEN UND ANDEREN GEISTERN, MÜCKEN

Giuseppe Nicolini (1762-1842]

Coriolano

Status: N   **Evidence:** S
Text: Romanelli, Luigi
Type: Melodramma serio   **Acts:** 2   **Language:** Italian
Premiere: Milan, Italy: Teatro alla Scala • 1808 12 26
Source of Premiere Information: Year and place from libretto;
        day from Stieger.
Play: *Coriolanus*
No: Friedlaender

Comments: Libretto does not mention composer or Shakespeare.
Friedlaender: 1809.

Cast: CORIOLANO, Patrizio Romano [Il Sig. Gio. Battista Velluti] •
VOLUNNIA, Moglie di Coriolano [La Signora Isabella Colbrand] •
SICINIO, Tribuno della plebe, avversario do Coriolano [Il Sig. Girolamo
Marzocchi] • VETURIA, Madre di Coriolano [La Signora Teresa
Cesarini] • AZZIO, Capo de' Volsci, acerrimo nemico di Roma [Il Sig.
Zenobio Vitarelli] • SEMPRONIO, Console Romano, amico di
Coriolano [Il Sig. Carlo Merusì] • AQUILIO, altro Tribuno, confidente di
Sicinio [Il Sig. Gio. Beretti] • DUE FANCIULLI, figli di Coriolano •—•
Chorus: GUERRIERI VOLSCI, POPOLO ROMANO, SACERDOTI,
DONNE, PATRIZJ, ALTRI GUERRIERI, ALTRO POPOLO E DONNE
DEL SEGUITO DI VOLUNNIA, E DI VENTURIA

Manuel Nieto (1844-1915)

Otelo y Desdémona

Status: I   **Evidence:** S
Text: Navarro y Gonzalo, Calisto
Type: Juguete Cómico-Lirico   **Acts:** 1
        Language: Spanish
Premiere: Madrid, Spain: Teatro Martin • 1883 11 05
Play: *Othello*
Yes: Stieger
No: Squire

Comments: Stieger: 3 acts. Action takes place en nuestros dias y en Madrid. Libretto does not mention Shakespeare. Mellen: 3 acts, 1883 11 00.

Cast: ROSILIA [Sra. Da. Antonia García] • MONICA [Srta. Da. Rosalia del Castillo] • PEPA [Srta. Da. María Martinez] • CASTO [Sr. D. Salvador Videgain] • RAFAEL [Sr. D. Rafael Sanchez]

Édouard Marie Émile Noël (1848-1926)

Le songe d'une nuit d'été

Status: ?
Text: Unknown
Type: Opera comique   **Language:** French
Premiere: Paris, France • 1886 09 01
Play: *Midsummer Night's Dream*

Comments: The source of this listing is Friedlaender. In all likelihood Noël is the librettist and Serpette is the composer [see Serpette, *Le Songe d'une nuit d'été*]. May be another version based on Rosier and de Leuven's libretto [see Thomas, Berens, Lillo, Manusardi].

Elizabetta Oddone [Oddone Sulli-Rao] (1878-   )

Petruccio e il Cavolo Cappuccio

Status: N   **Evidence:** P
Text: Hedda (Favola di)
Type: Fabel   **Acts:** 1   **Language:** Italian
Premiere: Milan, Italy: Teatro Manzoni • 1916 02 14
Source of Premiere Information: Mellen
Play: *Taming of the Shrew*
Publisher: Milan: G. Ricordi [1925]
No: SCORE

Comments: Score: favola di Hedda; Da una leggenda siciliana.

Cast: LA MAMMA • PETRUCCIO • IL BASTONE • IL FUOCO • L'ACQUA • LA CAPRETTA • I TAFANI • I SORCI • IL GATTO

Jacques Offenbach (1819-1880)

Le Rêve d'une Nuit d'été

Status: N   **Evidence:** S
Text: Tréfeu de Fréval, Étienne Victor (1821-1903)
Type: Operetta   **Acts:** 1   **Language:** French
Premiere: Paris, France: Théâtre de Bouffes-Parisiens, Salle des Champs-Elysées • 1855 07 30
Source of Premiere Information: Mellen
Play: *Midsummer Night's Dream*
No: Squire

Comments: Manferrari: librettists are H. C. Chivot and A Duru.

John Old (1827-1892)

Herne the Hunter (A Legend of Royal Windsor)

Status: N   **Evidence:** P
Text: Oxenford, Edward
Type: Opera   **Acts:** 3   **Language:** English
Premiere: Reading, England: Town Hall • 1887 12 14
Source of Premiere Information: Hauger
Play: *Merry Wives of Windsor*
Publisher: London: Stanley Lucas, Weber & Co., 1879 [vs]
No: SCORE

Comments: Shakespeare's *Merry Wives of Windsor* is mentioned in the score's preface but it goes on to say: the conclusion is reasonable that here we have the myth treated for the first time as the basis of a lyric drama. Mellen: text by E. Oxford; 1887 12 24.

Cast: CONSTANCE, The King's Ward (Soprano) • ANNE BOLEYN, The Queen (Mezzo Soprano) • LORD L'ESTRANGE, Betrothed to Constance (Tenor) • CAPTAIN OF THE GUARDS (Tenor) • HERNE

(Baritone) • KING HENRY THE EIGHTH (Bass) •—• **Chorus:**
COURTIERS, GUARDS, USHERS, ATTENDANTS, AND HUNTERS

Carl Orff (1895-1982)

Ein Sommernachtstraum

Status: NO   **Evidence:** P
Text: Composer
Type: Incidental Music   **Acts:** 1   **Language:** German
Premiere: Darmstadt, Germany: Landestheater • 1952 00 00
Play: *Midsummer Night's Dream*
Publisher: Mainz: B. Schott's Söhne, 1962 [vs]
Yes: Hartnoll
No: SCORE, New Grove

Comments: New Grove: composed 1939-62; final version,
Stuttgart 1964; incidental music. Text arranged after the translation
by A. W. Schlegel.

Ferdinando Orlandi (1777-1848)

Rodrigo di Valencia

Status: ?
Text: Romani, Felice (1788-1865)
Type: Dramma per musica   **Acts:** 2   **Language:** Italian
Premiere: Torino, Italy: Teatro Regio • 1820 00 00
Source of Premiere Information: Year and place from libretto.
Play: *Lear*

Comments: Mellen: summer 1820. Date: Carnival. Stieger: text by
Romanelli; 1820 01 00.

Cast: RODRIGO, Duca di Valenza (Basso) [Il sig. Gaetano Crivelli] •
ALVARO, Conte di Candia, padre di (Tenore) [Il sig. Domenico
Spiaggi] • RAMIRO, amante di (Contralto) [La sig. Elisabetta Pinotti] •
ELMONDA, ultima figlia di Rodrigo (Soprano) [La sig. Emilia Bonini] •
OSVALDO, Conte di Bariana, marito di (Basso) [Il sig. Lodovico
Bonoldi] • ELVIRA, seconda figlia di Rodrigo (Soprano) [La sig.

Carolina Sivelli] • ULRICO, Conte di Mancia, marito di Rodoguna prima figlia di Rodrigo [La sig. Teresa Cantarelli] •——• **Chorus:** CAVALIERI, SOLDATI D'OSVALDO, E DI ULRICO, E DEI SEGUACI DI RAMIRO

Giovanni Pacini (1796-1867)

La Gioventù di Enrico V (also La bella tavernara; Le Aventure d'una notte)

Status: Y   **Evidence:** S
Text: Tarducci, Filippo
Type: Melo-Dramma Giocoso per musica   **Acts:** 2
        Language: Italian
Premiere: Rome, Italy: Teatro della Valle • 1820 12 26
Source of Premiere Information: Loewenberg
Play: *Henry IV*
Yes: Blom, Groves V, Loewenberg, MGG, New Grove, Oxford
No: Squire

Comments: Libretto does not name librettist. MGG: libretto by F. Tarducci or G. Ferretti; partly based on play. Schatz: Tarducci. Stieger: Romani; says textlich von Gius. Tarducci bearbeitet als *La bella tavernaia = L'avventura d'una notte.* Manferrari: F. Tarducci. Garlington: Filippo Tarducci. Mellen: Ferretti. This is not the same libretto as Romani's for Mercadante.

Cast: IL PRINCIPE ENRICO • IL CONTE ROCESTER, confidente del medesimo • EDUARDO, Paggio di Corte • MILORD CLARK, confidente della Regina • BETTINA, Nipote del • CAPITANO COOP, Tavernaro del grande Ammiraglio •——•
Chorus: CORTIGIANI, GARSONI DELLA TAVERNA

Rodrigo di Valencia

Status: ?
Text: Romani, Felice (1788-1865)
Type: Melodrama seria   **Language:** Italian
Premiere: Palermo, Italy: Teatro Carolino • 1853 00 00
Source of Premiere Information: Mellen
Play: *Lear*

Comments: Mellen: composed for Palermo but not produced.
Date: Carnival.

Carl Palliardi

Der Stein der Weisen

Status: ?
Text: Unknown
Type: Operetta
Premiere: Moravska Ostrava, Czechoslovakia • 1906 05 14
Source of Premiere Information: Stieger
Play: *Tempest*

Mdme Papavoine (ca.1720-ca.1793)

Le Vieux Coquet ou Les deux amies ou Le vieus garçon

Status: Y   **Evidence:** S
Text: Bret, Alex. [Antoine? (1717-1792)]
Type: Opéra comique   **Acts:** 3   **Language:** French
Premiere: Paris, France: Comédie Italienne • 1761 12 07
Source of Premiere Information: Stieger
Play: *Merry Wives of Windsor*
Publisher: New Grove: music unpublished and lost.
Yes: Friedlaender, Hartnoll, MGG, Mellen, Oxford, Squire

Comments: Clément: 1762 09 07. Friedlaender, Stieger, Manferrari: 1761 12 07. Manferrari: da Shakespeare, Tr. Opéra Comique. Mellen: 1762 09 07.

Nicolò Pasquali (1718-1757)

Romeo and Juliet

Status: ?
Text: Unknown
Type: Seria   **Acts:** 2
Premiere: London?, England
Play: *Romeo and Juliet*
Publisher: London: R. Bremner, 1771 [s]

Comments: Manferrari: composer's dates (1700-1757), s. 2 a., Edinburgo, Tr. Civico, 1942. The title page reads: The Solemn Dirge in Romeo and Juliet composed by Nicolo Pasquali. It is made up of five short choruses and one solo song.

Filipe Pedrell (1841-1922)

Le Roi Lear

Status: I   **Evidence:** S
Text: Baralle, Alphonse
Type: Opera   **Acts:** 5   **Language:** French
Premiere: 1876 00 00
Play: *Lear*
Yes: Stieger
No: Groves V

Comments: Stieger: Klavierauszug um 1800. Groves V: it is incidental music. Mellen: published 1876.

Edoardo Perelli (1842-1885)

Viola Pisani

Status: N   **Evidence:** P
Text: Composer
Type: Dramma Lirico-Romantico   **Acts:** 4
Language: Italian
Premiere: Milan, Italy: Teatro alla Scala • 1873 04 08

Source of Premiere Information: Year and place from libretto.
Play: *Twelfth Night*
No: LIBRETTO

Comments: Libretto: work based on Zanoni by E. Bulwer. Mellen: Brescia (t. Grande) 1860 08 00.

Cast: IL PRINCIPE [Sig. Angelo De Giuli] • MASCARI, suo bravo [Sig. Franc. Della Vedova] • NICOT, giacobino [Sig. Matteo Della Torre] • ZANONI, ultimo della confraternità dei Rosacroce [Sig. Leoni Quintili] • CLARENZO GLYNDON, giovane inglese [Sig. Italo Campanini] • MERVALE, amico suo [Sig. Pietro Zanutto] • VIOLA PISANI [Sig.a Zacchi Giovannoni] • FIDDIDE, montanara [Sig.a Filippina Von Edelsberg] • MASTRO PAOLO [Sig. Ferdinando Zanutto] • UN MESSO DEL TRIBUNALE RIVOLUZIONARIO [Sig. Giuseppe Vincenzi] • UN SERVO DEL PRINCIPE [Sig. N. N.] •——•
Chorus: SIGNORI E DAME, MONTANARI E MONTANARE, CITTADINI, PESCATORI E PESCATRICI, SOLDATI, POPOLO, CUSTODI, SERVITORI

Lorenzo Perosi (1872-1956)

Romeo and Juliet

Status: Y   **Evidence:** S
Text: Unknown
Type: Projected opera.
Play: *Romeo and Juliet*
Yes: Groves V

Mario Persico (1892-1977)

La Bisbetica Domata

Status: Y   **Evidence:** P
Text: Rossato, Arturo (1882-1942)
Type: Commedia lirica   **Acts:** 4   **Language:** Italian
Premiere: Rome, Italy: Teatro Reale dell' Opera • 1931 02 12
Source of Premiere Information: Loewenberg
Play: *Taming of the Shrew*

Publisher: Milan: G. Ricordi & C., 1930 [vs]
Yes: SCORE, Hartnoll, Loewenberg, Mellen, Oxford

Comments: Stieger: 1935.

Cast: PETRUCCIO DI VERONA (Baritono) • BATTISTA MINOLA, gentiluomo di Padova (Basso) • CATERINA, sue figlia (Soprano) • BIANCA, sue figlia (Soprano) • LUCENZIO, innamorato di Bianca (Tenore) • ORTENSIO, rivale di Lucenzio (Baritono o Basso) • LA VEDOVA (Mezzo-soprano) • GRUMIO, servo di Petruccio (Tenore) • CURTIS, servo di Petruccio (Basso) • BIONDELLO, servo di Battista (Tenore) • UN SACERDOTE (Baritono) •—•
Chorus: SERVI, ANCELLE, INVITATI, POPOLANI

Giacomo Antonio Perti (1661-1756)

Martio Coriolano

Status: N   **Evidence:** S
Text: Valsini, Frencasco [Francesco Silvani]
Type: Drama per Musica   **Acts:** 3   **Language:** Italian
Premiere: Venice, Italy: Teatro Grimano de Ss. Gio. e Paolo
    • 1683 01 20
Source of Premiere Information: Schatz MS
Play: *Coriolanus*
No: Friedlaender

Philidor [François André Danican] (1726-1795)

Herne le Chasseur

Status: Y   **Evidence:** S
Text: Douin
Type: Opéra-comique   **Language:** French
Premiere: 1773 00 00
Source of Premiere Information: Mellen
Play: *Merry Wives of Windsor*
Yes: Groves V, Hartnoll, Mellen, Oxford

Comments: Mellen: date is when published. Groves V seems to indicate that the libretto was written and published but the opera may never have been written.

Louis Alexandre Piccini [Piccinni] (1779-1850)

Macbeth

Status: Y   **Evidence:** S
Text: Ducange, Victor Henri Brahain (1783-1833) and Anicet
        Bourgeois (1806-1871)
Type: Melodrame   **Acts:** 5
Premiere: Paris, France: Théâtre de la Porte Saint Martin
        • 1829 11 09
Source of Premiere Information: Schatz MS
Play: *Macbeth*
Yes: Schatz MS

Comments: A list of his works is given in Fétis.

Niccolò Piccinni (1728-180Q)

Caio Mario

Status: ?
Text: Roccaforte, Gaetano
Type: Opera   **Acts:** 3   **Language:** Italian
Premiere: Naples, Italy: Teatro San Carlo • 1757 00 00
Source of Premiere Information: Mellen
Play: *Coriolanus*

Léon Pillaut (1833-1903)

Perdita

Status: Y   **Evidence:** P
Text: Gallet, Louis (1835-1898)
Type: Opéra-comique   **Acts:** 1   **Language:** French

Play: *Winter's Tale*
Publisher: Paris: T. Du Wast. 1907 [vs]
Yes: SCORE

Cast: AUTOLYCUS, aventurier (Baryton) • CAMILLO, Seigneur
Sicilien au service du roi de Bohême (Basse) • FLORIZEL (Ténor) •
LE ROI, son père (Basse) • LE BOUVIER (Basse) • PERDITA
(Soprano) •—• **Chorus:** JEUNES GENS, JEUNES FILLES,
SOLDATS, SEIGNEURS DE LA SUITE DU ROI

Ciro Pinsuti (1829-1888)

Il Mercante di Venezia

Status: Y   **Evidence:** P
Text: Cimino, Giorgio Tommaso (1823-1905)
Type: Melodramma   **Acts:** 4   **Language:** Italian
Premiere: Bologna, Italy: Teatro Comunale • 1873 11 08
Source of Premiere Information: Loewenberg
Play: *Merchant of Venice*
Publisher: Milan: Ricordi, 1873 [vs]
Yes: SCORE, LIBRETTO, Blom, Friedlaender, Groves V, Hartnoll,
     Loewenberg, Mellen, Oxford, Squire, Stieger, Wilson

Comments: Mellen: 1873 11 09.

Cast: PORZIA, richissima erede (Soprano) [Casanova De Cepeda] •
BASSANIO, gentiluomo (Tenore) [Bolis] • ANTONIO, suo amico,
facoltoso commerciante (Baritono) [Comm. Aldighieri] • SHYLOCK,
ebreo (1.° Basso) [Castelmary] • IL DOGE (Basso) [Buffagni] • ANNA,
cameriera di Porzia (2.° Soprano) [Simoncelli] • SACERDOTE (2.°
Basso) [Dazzi] • ARALDO (2.° Basso) [Rapini] • PRINCIPE DI
MAROCCO (non parlano) • CASTILLA, grande di Spagna (non
parlano) •—• **Chorus:** SENATORI, CAVALIERI, CITTADINI,
GIOVINETTE, RAGAZZI, MARINAI, GIULLARI, MENESTRELLI,
ALABARDIERI, EBREI E POPOLO

Hans Pless [Hans Pischinger] (1884-1966)

Macbeth

Status: ?
Text: Unknown
Play: *Macbeth*

Comments: Not performed.

Carlo Podestà (1847-1921)

Ero, ossia Molto rumore per nulla

Status: Y   **Evidence:** P
Text: Ratti, Luigi
Type: La Scena Lirica   **Acts:** 4   **Language:** Italian
Premiere: Cremona, Italy • 1900 00 00
Source of Premiere Information: Mellen
Play: *Much Ado About Nothing*
Yes: LIBRETTO, Mellen, Oxford, Squire, Wilson

Comments: Mellen: date is when composed.

Cast: DON PEDRO, principe d'Aragona (Tenore) • DON GIOVANNI, fratello spurio di Don Pedro (Basso) • CLAUDIO, favorite di Don Pedro (Tenore) • BENEDIK, favorite di Don Pedro (Baritono) • LEONATO, governatore di Messina (Baritono) • ERO, figlia di Leonato (Soprano) • BEATRICE, nipote di Leonato (Soprano) • BORACCHIO, seguace di Don Giovanni (Baritono) • PADRE ANACLETO, frate carmelitano (Basso) • DON CIRILLO, sacerdote, sagrestano e cerimoniere della Cattedrale di Messina (Baritono) • UN CAMPANARO (Baritono) • BALDASSARRE, maestro dei musicì • UN SERVO •—• **Chorus:** GENTILUOMINI, DAME, CACCIATORI, GUARDIE, MUSICI, CANTORI DI CHIESA, CHIERICI, SCACCINI, APPARATORI E SERVI

Pogodin

King Lear?

Status: Y   **Evidence:** S
Text: Unknown
Premiere: 1955 00 00
Play: *Lear*
Yes: Oxford

Carl Pohlig (1858-1928)

Der Stein der Weisen

Status: ?
Text: Bittong, Franz
Type: Weihnnachtsmärchen   **Acts:** 3
Premiere: Hamburg, Germany: Stadttheater • 1894 12 05
Source of Premiere Information: Date and city from Stieger.
Play: *Tempest*

Comments: See Gerl's opera.

Carlo Francesco Pollaroli [Pollarolo, Polaroli] (1653-1722)

Marzio Coriolano

Status: N   **Evidence:** S
Text: Noris, Matteo (-1714)
Type: Dramma per musica   **Acts:** 3   **Language:** Italian
Premiere: Venice, Italy: Teatro di San Giovanni Grisostomo
    • 1698 01 18
Source of Premiere Information: Schatz MS
Play: *Coriolanus*
No: Friedlaender

Comments: Composer not mentioned in libretto. Dedication in libretto is dated January 18, 1697. Title page of libretto reads 1698.

Cast: MARZIO CORIOLANO • VETURIA, sua Madre • VOLUNIA, sua Moglie • DOMIZIO, il più giovine frà i Consoli del Senato, e Generale dell'armi Romane • GALBA, uno de Capi de'Tribuni della Plebe • TULIO, Capitano dell'esercito de'Volsi • MILO, servo di Volunia •—•
Chorus: DUE FIGLIOLINI DI CORIOLANO E DI VOLUNIA, DONNE ROMANE CON LORO FIGLIOLI E FRATELLI, ESERCITO DE'VOLSI, ESERCITO ROMANO

Porta [Bernardo? (1758-1832)]

Roméo et Juliette

Status: Y   **Evidence:** S
Text: Moline et Cubieres-Palmezeau
Type: Tragédie Lyrique   **Acts:** Prologue/3
Premiere: Paris, France: Théâtre de Académie Impériale de
        Musique • 1806 00 00
Play: *Romeo and Juliet*
Yes: LIBRETTO, Hartnoll, Oxford, Squire, Wilson

Comments: MGG and New Grove do not list the work under Bernardo Porta's name. Oxford: 1809 00 00.

Cast: MARS • MINERVA • IRIS, ou la Renommée • CAPULET, Sénateur de Verone • LORENZO, Missionnaire attaché à la maison de Capulet • JULIETTE, fille de Capulet • ROMÉO MONTAIGU, marié scerètement avec Juliette • LE COMTE PARIS • ISAURE, suivante de Juliette • THIBALTE, parent de Capulet • BALTHAZAR •—•
Chorus: SUITE DE MINERVE ET DE MARS, TROUPE DE GUERRIERS, LES ARTS, LES TALENS, SUITE DE CAPULET, SUITE DE COMTE PARIS, LES HABITANS DE VÉRONE, PLUSIEURS MOINES

Cole Porter (1891-1964)

Kiss Me, Kate

Status: Y   **Evidence:** S
Text: Composer [lyrics] and Bella Spewack and
    Sam Spewack [book]
Type: Broadway Musical   **Acts:** 2   **Language:** English
Premiere: New York, U.S.A.: New Century Theatre • 1948 12 30
Source of Premiere Information: Bordman
Play: *Taming of the Shrew*
Publisher: New York: T.B. Harms Co., 1951 [vs]
Yes: Bordman, Green, Oxford

Comments: Score does not mention Shakespeare.

Cast: FRED GRAHAM [Bill Johnson] • HARRY TREVOR [Daniel Wherry] • LOIS LANE [Julie Wilson] • RALPH, stage manager [Ronan O'Casey] • LILLI VANESSI [Patricia Morison] • HATTIE [Adelaide Hall] • PAUL [Archie Savage] • BILL CALHOUN [Walter Long] • FIRST MAN [Danny Green] • SECOND MAN [Sidney James] • STAGE DOORMAN [Peter Bentley] • HARRISON HOWELL [Austin Trevor] • SPECIALITY DANCERS [Wallace Brothers] • TAMING OF THE SHREW PLAYERS: • BIANCA (Lois Lane) [Julie Wilson] • BAPTISTA (Harry Trevor) [Daniel Wherry] • GREMIO (First Suitor) [Bernard Davies-Rees] • HORTENSIO (Second Suitor) [Frank Lawless] • LUCENTIO (Bill Calhoun) [Walter Long] • KATHERINE (Lilli Vanessi) [Patricia Morison] • PETRUCHIO (Fred Graham) [Bill Johnson] • HABERDASHER [Michael O'Connor] •—•
Chorus: SINGING ENSEMBLE, DANCING ENSEMBLE

G. Pride [sp.?]

Otello

Status: ?
Text: Composer
Type: Parodia tragi-comico-musicale
Premiere: Genoa, Italy: Politeania Genovesa • 1888 06 00
Play: *Othello*

Comments: I am unable to decipher Schatz's handwriting for the first letter of the composer's last name.

Sergei Prokofiev (1891-1953)

Hamlet, Music to the Tragedy by Shakespeare

Status: NO   **Evidence:** P
Play: *Hamlet*
Publisher: Moscow: 1962.
No: SCORE

Comments: Incidental Music. Shakespeare is one of Prokofiev's favorite authors. He wanted to write an opera on *Hamlet*.

Paul-Charles-Marie Puget (1848-1917)

Beaucoup de bruit pour rien

Status: Y   **Evidence:** P
Text: Blau, Éduard (1836-1906)
Type: Opera comique   **Acts:** 4/5 Tableaux
          Language: French
Premiere: Paris, France: Opéra-Comique • 1899 03 24
Source of Premiere Information: Score
Play: *Much Ado About Nothing*
Publisher: Paris: Heugel & cie. [cop.1898] [vs]
Yes: SCORE, Baker's, Hartnoll, Mellen, Oxford, Squire, Stieger, Wilson

Comments: Clément gives long description of the plot in his supplement.

Cast: DON PEDRE D'ARAGON, roi de Sicile (Baryton) [M. Fugère] • LÉONATO, gouverneur de Messine (Basse) [M. Vieuille] • CLAUDIO, jeune seigneur, ami du roi (Ténor) [M. Léon Beyle] • BÉNÉDICT, jeune seigneur, ami du roi (Ténor) [M. Clément] • DON JUAN, frère bâtard de don Pèdre (Basse) [M. Isnardon] • BORACHIO, affidé de don Juan (Ténor ou Baryton) [M. Carbonne] • UN MOINE (Basse) [M. Greese] • UN OFFICIER (Basse) [M. Dangès] • HÉRO, fille de

Léonato (Soprano) [Mlle. Mastio] • BÉATRIX, nièce de Léonato
(Soprano) [Mlle. Telma] • MARGARITA, suivante d'Héro (Soprano)
[Mme. Dehelly] •—• **Chorus:** SEIGNEURS DE LA SUITE DU ROI,
SEIGNEURS ET DAMES, AMIS DE LÉONATO, JEUNES FILLES DE
LA SUITE D'HÉRO, SOLDATS, PEUPLE

Pietro Pulli

Caio Marzio Coriolano

Status: N   **Evidence:** S
Text: Seriman, Conte Zaccaria de
Type: Dramma per musica   **Acts:** 3   **Language:** Italian
Premiere: Reggio d'Emilia, Italy: Teatro del Pubblico • 1741 00 00
Source of Premiere Information: Sonneck
Play: *Coriolanus*
No: Friedlaender

Comments: Friedlaender: Naples, 1745 00 00. Mellen:
1745 00 00, Naples, Theatro San Carlo.

Cast: CAIO MARZIO CORIOLANO • VENTURIA, Madre di Coriolano
• VOLUNNIA, Moglie di Coriolano • VALERIO, Senatore Romano •
LUCIO, Capitano Volsco • FLAVIO, Capitano Volsco

Henry Purcell (c. 1659-1695)

The Fairy Queen

Status: Y   **Evidence:** P
Text: Unknown
Type: English Opera   **Acts:** Prologue/5
    Language: English
Premiere: London, England: Queen's Theatre, Dorset Gardens
    • 1692 05 02
Source of Premiere Information: White
Play: *Midsummer Night's Dream*
Publisher: London: Novello and Co. 1914 [s]
Yes: SCORE, Baker's, Blom, Friedlaender, Hartnoll, Loewenberg,
    New Grove, Mellen, Oxford, Stieger, White, Wilson

214

Comments: Schatz MS: Haymarket Theater 1692. Dent points out that Purcell did not set a single line of Shakespeare in this opera [p.162]. Dialog was taken from Shakespeare but none of his characters sings. Mellen: E. Settle, 1692 04 00. Text may be by Elkanah Settle.

Cast: THE DUKE • EGEUS, Father to Hermia • LYSANDER, in Love with Hermia • DEMETRIUS, in Love with Hermia, and Betroth'd to Helena • HERMIA, in Love with Lysander • HELENA, in Love with Demetrius • OBERON, King of the Fairies • TITANIA, the Queen • ROBIN-GOOD-FELLOW • BOTTOM, the Weaver • QUINCE, the Carpenter • SNUG, the Joyner • FLUTE, the Bellowsmenter • SNOUT, the Tinker • STARVELING, the Taylor •—•
Chorus: ATTENDANTS, SINGERS AND DANCERS

The History of Timon of Athens, the Man Hater

Status: NO   **Evidence:** P
Text: Shadwell, Thomas (1640-1692)
Type: Masque   **Acts:** 1 (Acts not mentioned)
        Language: English
Premiere: London, England: Duke of York's Theatre in Dorset Gardens • 1694 00 00
Source of Premiere Information: Year from Stieger.
Play: *Timon of Athens*
Publisher: London: Henry Herringman, 1678
Yes: Wilson
No: SCORE [Dedication by Shadwell], Groves V, Stieger

The Tempest or The Enchanted Island

Status: NO   **Evidence:** P
Text: Dryden, John (1631-1701), Sir William Davenant (1605-1668) and Thomas Shadwell (1640-1692)
Acts: 5   **Language:** English
Premiere: London, England: Duke of York's Theater in Dorset Gardens • 1695 00 00
Source of Premiere Information: Year from Stieger.
Play: *Tempest*
Publisher: London: B. Goodson 1787 [s]
Yes: Baker's, Blom, Groves V, Hartnoll, Mellen, New Grove, Oxford, Squire

No: SCORE, Preface to *The Tempest* in Vol. XIX of the Collected
    Works

Comments: New Grove gives only librettist T. Shadwell, date (c.).
Schatz MS: London (Dorset Garden) 1690. White: this is a version of
Bannister's opera published in the later 18th century and attributed
to Purcell. Mellen: masque, 1690. Score: The Music in the Comedy
of the *Tempest*.

Felice Alessandro Radicati (1778-1823)

Il Coriolano

Status: N   **Evidence:** S
Text: Romanelli, Luigi (1751-1839)
Type: Dramma per musica   **Acts:** 3   **Language:** Italian
Premiere: Amsterdam, Holland: Schonwburg in de Amstel. Straass
    • 1809 00 00
Play: *Coriolanus*
No: Friedlaender

Comments: Mellen, Stieger: t. Italiano. Friedlaender: 1810 00 00.

Aladár Radó (1882-1914)

Shylock

Status: Y   **Evidence:** S
Text: Unknown
Language: Hungarian
Premiere: 1913 00 00
Source of Premiere Information: Mellen
Play: *Merchant of Venice*
Yes: Groves V, Hartnoll, Mellen, Oxford

Comments: Mellen: date is when composed; unfinished.

Carl Friedrich Rafael

Hamlet, Prinz von Liliput

Status: ?
Text: Gieseke, Johann Georg Karl Ludwig (1770-1833)
Type: Travestie   **Acts:** 3
Premiere: Breslau [Wroclaw], Poland: Stadttheater • 1832 11 02
Play: *Hamlet*

Comments: Characters and cast from Schatz MS.

Cast: HAMLET [Herr Wohlbrück] • DER KÖNIG [Herr Paul • DIE
KÖNIGIN [Mad. Hinny] • OLDENHOLM [Herr Fischer] • LAERTES
[Herr Stotz] • OPHELIA [Mad. Mejo] • GILDENSTERN [Herr Hennes
(sp.?)] • GUSTAV [Hensel (sp.?)] • ELLRICH [Herr Reinels] •
BARNFIELD [Herr Thiel] • TROUZOW [Herr Döring] • EIN GEIST [Herr
Hausmann • TODTENGRÄBER [Herr Reder] •
SCHAUSPIELDIRECTOR [Herr Majo] • Der Herzog [Herr Majo] • DIE
HERZOGIN [Mad. Reder] • LUCIAN [Herr Peschke]

Sam Raphling (1910-   )

Prince Hamlet

Status: Y   **Evidence:** S
Text: Composer
Type: Opera   **Acts:** 1/ 3 Scenes
Premiere: 1975 00 00
Play: *Hamlet*
Publisher: Hastings, N.Y.: General Music Pub. Co. [vs]
Yes: AMCL

Comments: Date is when composed.

Edmond Rateau

Rosaline

Status: ?

Text: Chemineau
Type: Opera comique   **Acts:** 1   **Language:** French
Premiere: Nantes, France: Grand Théâtre • 1892 04 09
Source of Premiere Information: Mellen
Play: *As You Like It*

Comments: Composer might be Jules Rateau.

Édouard Raymond (1812-   )

Der Sturm

Status: Y   **Evidence:** S
Text: Unknown
Type: Opera
Premiere: 1840 00 00
Play: *Tempest*
Yes: Hartnoll, Oxford, Squire, Stieger

Comments: Date is when composed.

Johann Friedrich Reichardt (1752-1814)

Die Geisterinsel

Status: Y   **Evidence:** P
Text: Gotter, Johann Friedrich Wilhelm (1746-1797) and Friedrich
       Hildebrand von Einsiedel (1750-1828) [not mentioned
       in score]
Type: Singspiel   **Acts:** 3   **Language:** German
Premiere: Berlin, Germany: Theater am Gendarmenplatz
       [Hoftheater] • 1798 07 06
Source of Premiere Information: Loewenberg
Play: *Tempest*
Publisher: Berlin: In der neuen berlinischen Musikhandlung,
       1799 [vs]
Yes: SCORE, Blom, Friedlaender, Groves V, Hartnoll, Loewenberg,
       Mellen, New Grove, Oxford, Squire, Stieger

Comments: MGG: 1796. Mellen: 1798 06 06.

Cast: PROSPERO, gewesener Herzog von Mayland, Zauberer
(Baß) [Hr. Franz] • MIRANDA, seine Tochter (Sopran) [Mad. Schick] •
FERNANDO, Prinz v. Neapel [Hr. Beschort] • FABIO, Edelknabe
(Sopran) [Mad. Eunike, geb. Schwachh] • ORONZIO, Küchenmeister
des Prinzen (Baß) [Hr. Unzelmann] • STEFANO, Kellermeister des
Prinzen (Baß) [Hr. Kaselitz] • ARIEL, eine Sylphe (Sopran) [Mlle.
Hamel d. j.] • CALIBAN, ein Gnome, Sohn der Sykorax (Baß) [Hr.
Hübsch] • MAJA, ein Schatten [Mlle. Eigensatz] • SYKORAX, ein
Schatten [Hr. Labes] • RUPERTO, ein Bootsmann [Hr. Berger] • EIN
MATROSE [Hr. Leidel] •—•
Chorus: GEISTER UND SYLPHEN, MATROSEN

Macbeth

Status: NO   **Evidence:** P
Premiere: Berlin, Germany • 1787 12 28
Source of Premiere Information: Stieger
Play: *Macbeth*
Publisher: Berlin: Verlage der Rellstabschen Musikhandlung und
        verbesserten Musikdruckerey,1789
No: SCORE, Groves V, Stieger

Comments: Manferrari: trag. 3 a., Monaco di B., Tr. di Corte,
primavera 1795. Stieger, Groves V: incidental music. Clément
seems to indicate that it is incidental music. Riemann: it is
Hexenszene nach Bürger's uberzetzung. Score: Einige
Hexenscenen aus Schackespear's *Macbeth* nach Bügers
Verdeutschung . . . .

Aribert Reimann (1936-   )

Lear

Status: Y   **Evidence:** P
Text: Henneberg, Claus H.
Type: Opera   **Acts:** 2 (11 scenes)   **Language:** German
Premiere: Munich, Germany: Nationaltheater • 1978 07 09
Play: *Lear*
Publisher: Mainz: B. Schott, 1978 [s]
Yes: SCORE, Baker's, Mellen, Oxford

Cast: KÖNIG LEAR (Bariton) • KÖNIG VON FRANKREICH (Baßbariton) • HERZOG VON ALBANY (Bariton) • HERZOG VON CORNWALL (Tenor) • GRAF VON KENT (Tenor) • GRAF VON GLOSTER (Baßbariton) • EDGAR, Sohn Glosters (Tenor-Countertenor) • EDMUND, Bastard Glosters (Tenor) • GONERIL, Tochter König Lears (dramatischer Sopran) • REGAN, Tochter König Lears (Sopran) • CORDELIA, Tochter König Lears (Sopran) • NARR (Sprechrolle) • BEDIENTER (Tenor) • RITTER (Sprechrolle) •—•
Chorus: DIENER, WACHEN, SOLDATEN; MÄNNERCHOR—KÖNIG LEARS UND GRAF VON GLOSTERS GEFOLGE

Hermann Reutter (1900-   )

Hamlet

Status: Y   **Evidence:** P
Text: Composer
Type: Schauspiel   **Acts:** 5   **Language:** German
Premiere: Stuttgart, Germany: Wüttembergische Staatsoper
  • 1980 12 06
Source of Premiere Information: Score
Play: *Hamlet*
Publisher: Mainz: B Schott's Söhne, 1980 [vs]
Yes: SCORE

Comments: Score: frei nach Shakespeare in der Ubersetzung von A. W. Schlegel.

Cast: SÄNGER • CLAUDIUS, König von Dänemark (Bariton) • HAMLET (Bariton) [Wolfgang Schöne] • POLONIUS, Oberkämmerer (Tenor [Buffo]) • LAERTES, sein Sohn (Tenor) • HORATIO, Hamlets Freund (Tenor) • ROSENKRANZ (Tenor) • GÜLDENSTERN (Bariton) • VOLTIMAND (Bariton) • CORNELIUS (Bariton) • MARCELLUS (Bariton) • BERNARDO (Baß) • DER GEIST VON HAMLETS VATER (Tenor) • GERTRUD, Königin von Dänemark, Hamlets Mutter (Mezzosopran) • OPHELIA, Tochter des Polonius (Sopran) • TÄNZER • GONZAGO • BAPTISTA • LUCIANUS • OPHELIAS SCHATTEN • SCHAUSPIELER • OSRICK, ein Höfling • 2 TOTENGRÄBER (1. mit Baßstimme) • EIN EDELMANN • 2 MATROSEN • FORTINBRAS, Prinz von Norwegen •—• **Chorus:** MADRIGALCHOR BEI OPHELIAS BEERDIGUNG. TÄNZER: VOLK, CLOWNS, KINDER, MORISKENTÄNZER, JÜNGLINGE.

SCHAUSPIELER: RÄTE, HERREN UND DAMEN VOM HOFE, SOLDATEN, BOTEN, DIENER, DÄNEN UND ANDERES GEFOLGE

Armand Reynaud (1845-1900)

Le Roi Lear

Status: Y **Evidence:** S
Text: Lapierre, Henri
Type: Dramme lyrique **Acts:** 4 **Language:** French
Premiere: Toulouse, France: Théâtre du Capitole • 1888 06 01
Source of Premiere Information: Mellen
Play: *Lear*
Yes: Friedlaender, Hartnoll, Manferrari, Mellen, Oxford, Stieger

Comments: Manferrari: da Shakespeare dr. 3 a.

Wilhelm Rintel [W. Litner]

Was ihr Wöllt

Status: Y **Evidence:** S
Text: Unknown
Type: Komische Oper
Premiere: Berlin, Germany • 1872 03 10
Source of Premiere Information: Friedlaender
Play: *Twelfth Night*
Yes: Friedlaender, Hartnoll, Oxford
Comments: Friedlaender: Vgl. Allg. Musik-Zeitung 1872, No. 13, S. 211.

Philipp Jakob Riotte (1776-1856)

Der Orakelspruch

Status: I **Evidence:** S
Text: Unknown
Type: Schauspiel **Acts:** 5

Premiere: Vienna, Austria: Theater an der Wein • 1827 11 14
Source of Premiere Information: Stieger
Play: *Winter's Tale*
Yes: Stieger

Comments: Stieger: play in 5 acts; based on Shakespeare's *Ein Wintermärchen*. It is probably incidental music.

Der Sturm oder Die Insel des Prospero

Status: Y   **Evidence:** S
Text: Seidl, Johann Gabriel (1804-1875)
Type: Rom. Opera   **Acts:** 3   **Language:** German
Premiere: Brno [Brünn], Czechoslovakia: Kgl. Stadtisches Theater • 1833 09 20
Source of Premiere Information: Mellen
Play: *Tempest*
Yes: Blom, Groves V, Hartnoll, Mellen, MGG, Oxford, Schatz MS, Stieger

Comments: Groves V: produced at Brno, 1833 09 20.
Friedlaender: 1834.

Peter Ritter (1763-1846)

Die lustigen Weiber

Status: Y   **Evidence:** S
Text: Römer, Georg Christian (1766-1829)
Type: Singspiel   **Acts:** 4   **Language:** German
Premiere: Mannheim, Germany: Hoftheater • 1794 11 04
Source of Premiere Information: Schatz Catalog
Play: *Merry Wives of Windsor*
Yes: Blom, Friedlaender, Groves V, Hartnoll, Mellen, New Grove, Oxford, Schatz MS, Squire, Stieger

Comments: New Grove: apparently the first musical setting.
Manferrari: com. 2 a. D-brd:Mbs has a libretto dated 1792. It is also in *Deutsche Schaubühne; Singspiele/Erste Band*.

Der Sturm oder Die bezauberte Insel

Status: Y   **Evidence:** P
Text: Döring, Johann Wilhelm (1760-   )
Type: Singspiel   **Acts:** 2
Premiere: Aurich, Germany: Theater • 1799 00 00
Source of Premiere Information: Stieger
Play: *Tempest*
Publisher: Libretto [dated 1798];
Yes: LIBRETTO, Hartnoll, New Grove, Oxford, Squire, Stieger

Comments: Stieger: the Composer Index lists this work under H. Ritter.

Cast: PROSPERO, rechmäßiger Herzog von Mayland • MIRANDA, dessen Tochter • ANTONIO, dessen Bruder und unrechtmäßiger Besitzer von Mayland • FERDINAND, Sohn des Königs von Neapel • ARIEL, ein Sylphe • KALIBAN, ein wilder mißgeschaffener Sklave • TRINKULO, ein Hofnarr •——• **Chorus:** SCHIFFLEUTE, GEISTER

Richard Rogers (1902-   )

The Boys from Syracuse

Status: Y   **Evidence:** S
Text: Abbott, George and Lorenz Hart
Type: Broadway Musical   **Acts:** 2   **Language:** English
Premiere: New York, U.S.A.: Avin • 1938 11 23
Source of Premiere Information: Bordman
Play: *Comedy of Errors*
Publisher: New York: Chappell and Co. 1965 [vs]
Yes: SCORE, Bordman, Green

Comments: Bordman: employed only a single line from Shakespeare.

Cast: SINGING POLICEMAN [Bob Lawrence] • ANOTHER POLICEMAN [James Wilkinson] • ANTIPHOLUS OF EPHESUS [Ronald Graham] • DROMIO OF EPHESUS [Teddy Hart] • DANCING POLICEMAN [George Church] • TAILOR [Clifford Dunstan] • TAILOR'S APPRENTICE [Burl Ives] • ANTIPHOLUS OF SYRACUSE [Eddie Albert] • DROMIO OF SYRACUSE [Jimmy Savo] • MERCHANT OF SYRACUSE [Byron Shores] • DUKE OF EPHESUS

[Carroll Ashburn] • AEGEON [John O'Shaughnessy] • LUCE [Wynn Murray] • ADRIANNA [Muriel Angelus] • LUCIANA [Marcy Wescott] • SORCERER [Owen Martin] • COURTEZAN [Betty Bruce] • SECRETARY TO COURTEZAN [Heidi Vosseler] • ASSISTANT COURTEZAN [Dolores Anderson] • ANGELO [John Clarke] • 1ST MAID [Florine Callahan] • 2ND MAID [Claire Wolf] • 3RD MAID [Alice Craig] • MERCHANT OF EPHESUS [Clifford Dunstan] • SEERES [Florence Fair] •——• **Chorus:** SINGERS, DANCERS

Johann Heinrich Rolle (1716-1785)

Der Sturm oder Die bezauberte Insel

Status: Y   **Evidence:** S
Text: Patzke, Johann Samuel (1727-1787)
Type: Singspiel   **Acts:** 1   **Language:** German
Premiere: Berlin, Germany: Döbbelin's Oper Theater • 1782 03 28
Source of Premiere Information: Mellen
Play: *Tempest*
Yes: Friedlaender, Hartnoll, Mellen, New Grove, Oxford, Squire, Stieger

Comments: Hartnoll: 1784. Friedlaender: not published.

Léon Rosellin

Juliette et Roméo

Status: ?
Text: Composer
Type: Operetta   **Acts:** 1   **Language:** French
Premiere: Colombes, France • 1894 02 11
Source of Premiere Information: Mellen
Play: *Romeo and Juliet*

Richard Rosenberg (1894-   )

Das Liebesspiel

Status: Y   **Evidence:** S
Text: Aron, Willi
Type: Opera   **Acts:** 3
Premiere: Aachen, Germany • 1929 05 27
Play: *?*
Yes: Gruber

Lauro Rossi (1810-1885)

Biorn

Status: Y   **Evidence:** S
Text: Marshall, Frank
Type: Tragic spectacular opera   **Acts:** 5
        Language: English
Premiere: London, England: Queen's Theatre • 1877 01 17
Source of Premiere Information: Loewenberg
Play: *Macbeth*
Publisher: G: Autograph I-Nc (as Macbeth)
Yes: Blom, Hartnoll, Loewenberg, Mellen, New Grove, Oxford

Comments: MGG: composer's dates are 1812-85; title may also be Björn. Groves V: his only opera to an English libretto. Mellen: the setting is transferred to Norway.

Gioacchino Rossini (1792-1868)

Ermione

Status: N   **Evidence:** S
Text: Tottola, Andrea Leone Abbé (?-1831)
Type: Azione tragica   **Acts:** 2   **Language:** Italian
Premiere: Naples, Italy: Teatro San Carlo • 1819 03 27
Source of Premiere Information: Mellen
Play: *Winter's Tale*
Publisher: Milano: Ricordi, 1850? [vs]

No: Groves V, Riemann, Schatz MS

Comments: Groves V, Schatz MS: after Racine's *Andromaque.*

Cast: ERMIONE [Signora Colbran] • ANDROMACA [Signora Pisaroni] • ASTIANATTE [Signor N. N.] • PIRRO [Signor Nozzari] • ORESTE [Signor David] • CLEONE [Signora Manzi] • PILANDE [Signor Ciccimarra] • FENICIO [Signor Benedetti] • CEFISA [Signora De Bernardis] • ATTALO [Signor Chizzola] •—• **Chorus:** CORO

Otello, osia L'Africano di Venezia

Status: Y   **Evidence:** S
Text: Berio di Salsa, Marchese Francesco Maria
Type: Opera per musica   **Acts:** 3   **Language:** Italian
Premiere: Naples, Italy: Teatro del Fondo della Separazione dei Lucri • 1816 12 04
Source of Premiere Information: Loewenberg
Play: *Othello*
Publisher: Leipzig: Breitkopf und Härtel, 1820? [vs]
Yes: Blom, Friedlaender, Groves V, Hartnoll, Loewenberg, Mellen, New Grove, Oxford, Schatz MS, Squire, Stieger, Wilson

Comments: Based on Jean-François Ducis' adaptation of Shakespeare though not mentioned. No mention of Shakespeare in original score or libretto. Only the third act has much to do with Shakespeare's play.

Cast: OTELLO, Africano al servizio di Venezia [Sig. Nozzari] • DESDEMONA, amante, e sposa occulta di Otello, figlia di [La Sig. Colbran] • ELMIRO [Il Sig. Benedetti] • RODRIGO, figlio del Doge [Il Sig. Davide] • JAGO, amico di Rodrigo [Il Sig. Ciccimarra] • EMILIA, confidente di Desdèmona [La Sig. Manzi] • LUCIO, confidente di Otello [Il Sig. Mollo] • DOGE [Il Sig. Chizzola] •—•
Chorus: SENATORI, SEGUACI DI OTELLO, DAMIGELLE DEL SEGUITO DI DESDEMONA, POPOLO

Ernest Roters (1892-1961)

Hamlet, Op. 145

Status: Y   **Evidence:** P
Text: Composer and Therese Robinson
Type: Opera   **Acts:** 1 Vorspiel/3/8 Bilder
Premiere: Berlin, Germany • 1957 00 00
Source of Premiere Information: Libretto
Play: *Hamlet*
Yes: LIBRETTO

Comments: Gruber: Never performed.

Cast: PERSONEN DES VORSPIELS: • HAMLET, Prinz von
Dänemark (Tenor [jugendlicher Heldentenor]) • HORATIO, Freund
des Hamlet (Bariton) • ERSTER STUDENT (Tenor) • ZWEITER
STUDENT (Bariton) • DRITTER STUDENT (Tenor) • VIERTER
STUDENT (Hoher Bass) • CORNELIUS, Gesandter aus Dänemark
(Bariton) •   IN EINER PANTOMIME, DARGESTELLT VON
STUDENTEN: • EIN KÖNIG • EINE KÖNIGIN • DES KÖNIGS
BRUDER • PERSONEN DER OPER: • DER KÖNIG VON
DÄNEMARK (Bariton) • DIE KÖNIGIN (Alt [hochdramatisch]) •
HAMLET, Sohn des vorigen, Neffe des jetzigen Königs (Tenor
[jugendlicher Heldentenor]) • POLONIUS,Oberkämmerer (bass) •
LAERTES, sein Sohn (Tenor) • OPHELIA, seine Tochter (Sopran
[dramatischer Koloratur-Sopran]) • HORATIO, Freund des Hamlet
(Bariton) • GEIST VON HAMLETS VATER (Bass) • ERSTER
TOTENGRÄBER (Tenorbuffo) • ZWEITER TOTENGRÄBER
(Bassbuffo) • IN EINEM SCHAUSPIEL-BALLETT: • EIN PROLOG
(Tenor) • EIN NARR • EIN KÖNIG • EINE KÖNIGIN • DER BRUDER
DES KÖNIGS • GEFOLGE DES KÖNIGS • HOFDAMEN DER
KÖNIGIN • KRIEGER DES KÖNIGSBRUDERS •—• **Chorus:**
STUDENTEN, WIRT UND BEDIENERINNEN (Stumme Rollen),
HERREN UND DAMEN VOM HOF, PRIESTER, GEFOLGE, VOLK

Ugo Roti

Il sogno di una notte d'estate

Status: Y   **Evidence:** S
Text: Olmi, A. Mario
Type: Opera buffa   **Language:** Italian
Premiere: Turin, Italy: Palestra Ristori • 1899 11 00
Source of Premiere Information: Mellen
Play: *Midsummer Night's Dream*
Yes: Mellen, Oxford, Stieger

Paul Ruben

L' Edit royal

Status: Y   **Evidence:** S
Text: Unknown
Type: Opera comique   **Acts:** 1   **Language:** French
Premiere: Limoges, France: Théâtre municipal • 1894 04 00
Source of Premiere Information: Mellen
Play: *Love's Labours Lost*
Yes: Mellen, Stieger

Paul Alfred Rubens (1875-1917) and Frank E. Tours

The Dairymaids

Status: Y   **Evidence:** S
Text: Thompson, Alexander M. and Robert Courtneidge [Lyrics by Paul A. Rubins and Arthur Wimperis]
Type: Farcical Musical Play   **Acts:** 2/3 scenes
   Language: English
Premiere: London, England: Apollo Theatre • 1906 04 14
Source of Premiere Information: Gänzl
Play: *Measure for Measure*
Publisher: London: Chappell and Co. 1906 [vs]
Yes: Gänzl

Comments: Score does not mention Shakespeare. Characters and cast from Gänzl.

Cast: LADY BRUDENELL [Phyllis Broughton] • SAM BRUDENELL [Walter Passmore/E. Statham Staples] • FRANK BRUDENELL [Horace Lane] • CAPT. FRED LEVERTON [Frank Green (Harry Cottell)/Alec Fraser] • DR. O'BYRNE [Ambrose Manning] • JOE MIVENS [Dan Rolyat/ W. L. Rignold] • TIM CAPUS [F. W. Bowes] • LT. BRERETON [Rupert Mar] • JACK BIFFIN [Harry Cottell/Edgar Ward] • TODGERS [Carr Evans] • PEGGY [Carrie Moore/Winnie Volt/Vere Vere] • WINIFRED [Agnes Fraser/Rhoda Gordon] • HELENE [Florence Smithson/Mabel Green] • MISS PENELOPE PYECHASE [Carlotta Zerbini] • ELIZA [Gracie Leigh] • DAISY [Gertrude Kuzelle/Muriel Varna] • BETTY [Dorothy Ward] • JOAN [Alice Coleman] • JENNY [Winnie Volt] • NANCY [Louie Lochner/Olive Wade] • ROSIE [Beryl Vaudrey/Alys Read] • GERTIE [Gertie Sinclair/Bertha Russell] • BESSIE [Kittie Sparrow]

Paul Alfred Rubens (1875-1917) and Walter Rubens

Great Caesar

Status: Y **Evidence:** S
Text: Grossmith Jr., George (1874-1935), Paul A. Rubens and Harold Ellis
Type: Burlesque **Acts:** 2 **Language:** English
Premiere: London, England: Comedy Theatre • 1899 04 29
Source of Premiere Information: Gänzl
Play: *Anthony and Cleopatra*
Yes: Gänzl

Comments: Characters and cast from Gänzl.

Cast: JULIUS CAESAR [Willie Edouin] • BRUTUS [Leon Roche] • CASCA [William Cheesman] • CASSIUS [Arthur Hatherton] • TREBONIUS [Laurence R. Grossmith] • CINNA [Tim Ryley] • CICERO [Fred Emney] • NUBIAN DANCER [Edouard Espinosa] • FOURTEENTH CITIZEN [Mr. Rowe] • 1ST SOLDIER [Mr. Hill] • ONE OF THE CROWD [E. Barratt] • MARC ANTONY [George Grossmith, Jr.] • LUCIA [Decima Moore] • CALPURNIA [Nellie Christie] • NICIPPE [Jenny Owen] • ALSATIA [Lydia Flopp] • OCTAVIUS [Mary Thorne] • CLAUDIA [Looloo Halliday] • DARDANIA [Nellie Evelyn]

Sigismund Freiherr von Rumling (1739-1825)

Roméo et Juliette

Status: Y   **Evidence:** S
Text: Unknown
Type: Opera   **Language:** German
Premiere: Munich, Germany: Schloss Karlsburg • 1790 00 00
Play: *Romeo and Juliet*
Yes: Friedlaender, Hartnoll, Mellen, Oxford, Squire, Stieger, Wilson

Comments: Stieger: 1784 00 00. Mellen: Stuttgart auf der Karlsberg; Hoftheater, 1784. Friedlaender: not published.

Henrik Rung (1807-1871)

Stormen paa København [Storm over Copenhagen]

Status: Y   **Evidence:** S
Text: Overskou, Thomas (1798-1873)
Type: Opera   **Acts:** 5   **Language:** Danish
Premiere: Copenhagen, Denmark: Kongelige Theater
        • 1845 01 21
Source of Premiere Information: Schatz MS
Play: *Tempest*
Yes: Friedlaender, Hartnoll, Squire

Comments: Friedlaender: 1847.

Camille Saint-Saëns (1835-1921)

Henry VIII

Status: Y   **Evidence:** S
Text: Détroyat, Léonce and Paul Armand Silvestre (1839-1901)
Type: Opera   **Acts:** 4/6 Tableaux   **Language:** French
Premiere: Paris, France: Opéra • 1883 03 05
Source of Premiere Information: Year and place from score. Date from Mellen.

Play: *Henry VIII*
Publisher: Paris: A. Durand & Fils, 1883 [vs]
Yes: Blom

Comments: Clément gives long description of the opera. Neither score nor libretto mention Shakespeare.

Cast: HENRY VIII, roi d'Angleterre (Baryton) [M. Lassalle] • DON GOMEZ DE FÉRIA, ambassadeur d'Espagne (Ténor) [M. Sellier] • LE CARDINAL CAMPEGGIO, Légat du pape (Basse) [M. Boudouresque] • LE COMTE DE SURREY (Ténor) [M. Sapin] • LE DUC DE NORFOLK (Basse) [M. Lorrain] • CRANMER, archevéque de Cantorbéry (Basse) [M. Gaspard] • CATHERINE D'ARAGON (Soprano) [Mme. Krauss] • ANNE DE BOLEYN (Mezzo-Soprano) [Mme. Richard] • LADY CLARENCE, dame d'honneur de Catherine (Soprano) [Mme. Nastorg] • GARTER, roi d'armes (Ténor) [M. Aubry] • QUATRE SEIGNEURS (2 Ténors, 2 Basses) [MM. Piroïa, Girard, Lambert, Palianti] • UN HUISSIER DE LA COUR (Basse) [M. Boutens] • UN OFFICIER (Ténor) [M. Gesta] •—•
Chorus: SEIGNEURS, JUGES, MEMBRES DU PARLEMENT, OFFICIERS ET SOLDATS, PAGES, DAMES D'HONNEUR, HOMMES ET FEMMES DU PEUPLE, ETC.

Antonio Salieri (1750-1825)

Falstaff osia Le tre Burle

Status: Y   **Evidence:** S
Text: Franceschi, Carlo Prospero de [Defranceschi]
Type: Dramma giocoso per musica   **Acts:** 2
      Language: Italian
Premiere: Vienna, Austria: Kärntnertortheater • 1799 01 03
Source of Premiere Information: Loewenberg
Play: *Merry Wives of Windsor*
Publisher: Vienna: Nella stamperia dei teatri imperiali, 1799 [vs]
Yes: Blom, Friedlaender, Hartnoll, Loewenberg, MGG, Oxford, Squire, Stieger

Comments: Score and libretto do not mention Shakespeare.

Cast: SIR FALSTAFF, Cavalier attempato d'una grassezza deforme • MISTRESS FORD, Donna d'allegro umore, Moglie di • MASTER FORD, ricco Negoziante di Windsor, Marito geloso, e Compare di •

MASTER SLENDER, ricco Mercante, e Marito indolente • MISTRESS SLENDER, Donna d'umore piuttosto brusco • BARDOLF, Servitore di Sir Falstaff • BETTY, Cameriera di Ms. Ford •——•
Chorus: SERVI, AMICI, E AMICHE DE FORD E DEGLE SLENDER; FATE, GENJ, SPIRITI, ECC.

Franz Salmhofer (1900-1975)

King Lear

Status: I   **Evidence:** S
Text: Unknown
Play: *Lear*
Yes: Blom
No: Groves V

Comments: Groves V: composer wrote incidental music to *King Lear* and several other Shakespearean plays.

[Gervais-Bernard-] Gaston Salvayre (1847-1916)

Beaucoup de bruit pour rien

Status: ?
Text: Unknown
Play: *Much Ado About Nothing*

Riccardo III

Status: Y   **Evidence:** S
Text: Blavet, Émile Raymond (1838-   ) [Original French]
Type: Grand ópera   **Acts:** 4(6 scenes)   **Language:** Italian [Translation of the French]
Premiere: St. Petersburg, Soviet Union: Maryinsky Theater • 1883 12 21
Source of Premiere Information: Loewenberg
Play: *Richard III*
Publisher: Paris: Choudens 1883? [vs]

Yes: Friedlaender, Groves V, Hartnoll, Loewenberg, Mellen, MGG, New Grove, Oxford, Squire, Stieger

Comments: New Grove: Original French version, Nice, 29 Jan 1891. Manferrari: E. Blowet, op. 5 a. CU Catalog quotes vocal score for first performance 1883 12 09 at the Théâtre Impérial. Friedlaender: 1883 12 27.

Cast: RICARDO III (Baritono) • ENRICO DI RICHEMOND (1° Tenore) • PUCK, buffone (2° Tenore) • IL CARDINALE BOURCHIER (Basso) • STANLEY (Basso) • SURREY (Basso) • MONTAIGU (Tenore) • BLOUNT (Tenore) • UN ARALDO (Tenore) • LA REGINA, vedova di Edoardo IV (Soprano dramm.) • ELISABETTA, sua figlia (Soprano dramm.) • MARGHERITA, vedova di Enrico VI (Contralto) • LE DUE OMBRE DEI FIGLI DI EDOARDO (Soprani) • DUE ALTRE OMBRE (Mezzo-Soprani) •—• **Chorus:** LORDI E GENTILUOMINI, DAME DELLA CORTE, GIPSIE, PAGGI, GIOVINETTE, SOLDATI, CLERO, VALLETTI, SCUDIERI, ARALDI, POPOLO

Spiro Samara [Spyridon Samaras] (1863-1917)

La Furia domata

Status: Y   **Evidence:** S
Text: Butté, Enrico Annibale (1868-1912) and Gustavo Macchi
Type: Commedia musicale   **Acts:** 3   **Language:** Italian
Premiere: Milan, Italy: Teatro Lirico • 1895 11 19
Source of Premiere Information: Mellen
Play: *Taming of the Shrew*
Yes: Blom, Clément, Garlington, Groves V, Hartnoll, Mellen, Oxford, Stieger

San Severino

Romeo e Giuletta

Status: I   **Evidence:** S
Text: Unknown
Language: Italian
Premiere: Berlin, Germany • 1773 00 00

Play: *Romeo and Juliet*
Yes: Friedlaender

Comments: J. R. Sanseverino [San Severino] is a librettist, not a composer. The composer is most probably Johann Gottfried Schwanenberg (1740-1804) [Schwanberg].

Alessandro Santa Caterina

Coriolano

Status: ?
Text: Giannini, Giuseppe Sesto
Type: Tragedia lirica   **Acts:** 3   **Language:** Italian
Premiere: Padua, Italy: Teatro dei Concordi • 1846 03 14
Source of Premiere Information: Year and place from libretto.
      Day from Mellen.
Play: *Coriolanus*

Cast: CORIOLANO, duce [sig.Gaetano Pardini] • VENTURIA, sua madre [Rosalia Gariboldi] • VOLUMNIA, sua moglie [Carolina Imoda] • SICINIO, tribuno della plebe [Riccardo del Vivo] • TULLO [Antonio Bellondin] • IL CONSOLE [Luigi Centis] •—•
Chorus: SENATORI, TRIBUNI, POPOLO, E SOLDATI VOLSCI

Errico Sarria (1836-1883)

Gli Equivoci

Status: ?
Text: Golisciani, Enrico (1848-1918)
Type: Opera comica   **Acts:** 3   **Language:** Italian
Premiere: Naples, Italy: Teatro Nuovo • 1878 02 17
Source of Premiere Information: Year and place from libretto.
      Day from Mellen.
Play: *Comedy of Errors*

Comments: Libretto does not mention Shakespeare.

Cast: IL MARCHESE DI PLANTERRE, colonnello delle guardie
francesi [sig. G. Morelli] • LISETTA, fioraia [sig.a I. Giorgio] • PIERINO
[sig. V. Montanaro] • EUSTACHIO COQUENARD, vecchio finanziere
[sig. L. Manzoli] • CAVALIER RODOLFO [sig. L. Ferrajoli] • BLINVAL,
usciere del Teatro [sig. S. Sica] • VESPINA, fruttivendola [sig.a M.
Pennino] • EMMA, dama galante • DIONIGIA, dama galante •
LEONILDA, dama galante • MELANIA, dama galante • UN LACCHE
Chorus: VENDITORI, VENDITRICI, GENTILUOMINI, MASCHERE
D'AMBO I SESSI, RAGAZZI DEL POPOLO

Henri de Saussine (1859-   )

Le Marchand de Vénise

Status: Y   **Evidence:** P
Text: Composer
Type: Comédie musicale   **Acts:** 4   **Language:** French
Premiere: Paris, France: Salle Mars • 1907 01 28
Source of Premiere Information: Mellen
Play: *Merchant of Venice*
Publisher: Paris: Choudens, ca.1907 [vs]
Yes: SCORE, Mellen, Stieger

Comments: Manferrari: comd. lir. Montecarlo, Tr. Municipale,
primavera 1934.

Cast: PORTIA (Soprano) • JESSICA (Mezzo) • NERISSA (Mezzo) •
SHYLOCK (Ténor) • BASSANIO (Ténor) • ANTONIO (Baryton) •
GRATIANO (Baryton) • SALARINO (Ténor) • LE DOGE (Basse) •—•
Chorus: HUISSIERS, HÉRAUTS D'ARMES, PAGES, DAMES
D'HONNEUR, GENS DU PEUPLE

Vincenzo Savigna

Coriolano

Status: ?
Text: Unknown
Type: Opera per musica
Premiere: Turin, Italy: Teatro Regio • 1806 00 00
Play: *Coriolanus*

Comments: Date: Carnival.

Giacomo Savini

Tempeste

Status: ?
Text: Carbonetti, Amelia
Type: Opera   **Acts:** 2   **Language:** Italian
Premiere: Faenza, Italy: Teatro Comunale • 1921 05 23
Source of Premiere Information: Stieger
Play: *Tempest*

Comments: Manferrari, Mellen: 1921 04 21.

Count Friedrich Ernst von Sayn-Wittgenstein-Berleburg (1837-1915)

Antonius und Kleopatra

Status: Y   **Evidence:** S
Text: Mosenthal, Solomon Hermann
Type: Grosse Oper   **Acts:** 4/Nachspiele
         Language: German
Premiere: Graz, Austria: Landestheater • 1883 12 01
Source of Premiere Information: Mellen
Play: *Anthony and Cleopatra*
Publisher: Vienna: Albert J. Gutmann, 1885 [vs]
Yes: Friedlaender, Hartnoll, Mellen, Oxford

Cast: CAESAR OCTAVIAN, römischer Triumvir (Bariton) • MARCUS ANTONIUS, römischer Triumvir (hoher Bariton) • KLEOPATRA, Königin von Egypten (Sopran) • ARTAVAST, Prinz von Armenien (Tenor) • PLOTINUS, egyptischer Heerführer (Bariton) • ACHILLAS, egyptischer Heerführer (Bass) • HELIODOR, ein Sklave Kleopatras (Tenor) • CHARMION, eine Sklavin Kleopatras (Alt) • FLAVIUS (II. Tenor) • EIN STEUERMANN •—• **Chorus:** NYMPHEN; TRITONEN; FRAUEN IM GEFOLGE KLEOPATRAS; ARMENISCHE, EGYPTISCHE, RÖMISCHE KRIEGER; VERSCHWORENE; VOLK; VIER HEROLDE; ZWEI MOHRENSKLAVEN

Giuseppe Scarlatti (1723?-1777)

Caio Mario

Status: ?
Text: Roccaforte, Gaetano
Type: Opera   **Acts:** 3   **Language:** Italian
Premiere: Naples, Italy: Teatro San Carlo • 1755 01 20
Source of Premiere Information: Mellen
Play: *Coriolanus*

Giuseppe Domenico Scarlatti (1685-1757)

Ambleto

Status: N   **Evidence:** S
Text: Zeno, Apostolo (1668-1750) and Pietro Pariati (1665-1733)
Type: Dramma per musica   **Acts:** 3   **Language:** Italian
Premiere: Rome, Italy: Teatro Capranica, Sala dei Signori
      • 1715 00 00
Source of Premiere Information: Mellen
Play: *Hamlet*
Yes: Blom, Friedlaender, Wilson
No: Librettist

Comments: MGG: date during Carnival; Zeno's libretto, based on Saxo Grammaticus, is the same one used by Gasparini in 1705.

Louis Alexander Balthasar Schindelmeisser (1811-1864)

Malvina

Status: N   **Evidence:** S
Text: Uffer, Dr.
Type: Rom. Opera   **Acts:** 4   **Language:** German
Premiere: Pest, Hungary: Deutchestheater • 1841 12 10

Source of Premiere Information: Stieger
Play: *All's Well That Ends Well*
No: Stieger
Comments: Groves V: Malwina, 5 acts, Pest 1841. Mellen: 5 acts; 1841 12 20. Stieger: text after Tromlitz.

Alan Schmitz

Julius Caesar

Status: Y   **Evidence:** S
Text: Composer
Type: Opera   **Language:** English
Premiere: New Brunswick, N. J. (Rutgers University: Douglas
      School of Music), U.S.A.: Rutgers University: Douglas
      School of Music • 1978 04 07
Play: *Julius Caesar*
Publisher: Holograph in Rutgers Library
Yes: Mellen

Georg Abraham Schneider (1770-1839)

Der Orakelspruch

Status: ?
Text: Salice-Contessa, Carl Wilhelm
Type: Operette   **Acts:** 1   **Language:** German
Premiere: Berlin, Germany: Concordiatheater • 1813 05 13
Source of Premiere Information: Mellen
Play: *Winter's Tale*

Comments: Schatz libretto 9669 is dated 1812.

Cast: FLORINDE, eine Fee • LUCIE, ihre Tochter • MARKO, ihr Gärtner • SYLVIO • EIN GENIUS •—•
Chorus: JUNGE MÄDCHEN, BUCKLICHE

Georg Schönfeld (1855-   )

Falstaff

Status: ?
Text: Schönfeld, Alfred (1859-1916)
Type: Posse
Premiere: Berlin, Germany: Apollotheater • 1893 07 15
Source of Premiere Information: Stieger
Play: *Merry Wives of Windsor; Henry IV, Parts 1 and 2*

Comments: It is probably incidental music.

Ignaz Schuster (1770-1835)

Hamlet, Prinz vom Tandelmarkt

Status: Y   **Evidence:** S
Text: Perinet, Joachim (1763-1816)
Type: Karrikatur   **Acts:** 3   **Language:** German
Premiere: Vienna, Austria: Theater in der Leopoldstadt
    • 1807 11 05
Source of Premiere Information: Mellen
Play: *Hamlet*
Yes: Cast

Comments: Date is likely not of first performance which was probably in Italy. Stieger: 2 acts. If Maretzek's opera is based on Shakespeare, this one should be too. Schatz MS: title is *Hamlet*.

Cast: ALPHA, Herr vom Tandelmarkt • OMEGA, seine Gemahlin, Mutter des • HAMLET, Neffe des Alpha • DER SPIRITUS VON HAMLETS VATER • OLDENHOLM, Maitre des Plaisirs • OPHELIA, dessen Tochter • LAERTES, dessen Sohn • GÜLDENSTERN, Höfling • GUSTAV • BERNFIELD • ELLRICH • FRENZOW • FREYTAG, ein Theater=Prinzipal • SAMSTAG, dessen Frau • SONNTAG, Schauspieler • MONTAG, Schauspieler • DIENSTAG, Schauspieler • MITTWOCH, Schauspielerin • DONNERSTAG, Schauspielerin • EIN TODTENGRÄBER •—• **Chorus:** GEISTER, VOLK, HÖFLINGE, WACHEN, FUSSVOLK UND KAVALLERIE

Othellerl, der Mohr von Wien

Status: ?
Text: Kringsteiner, Ferdinand Josef (1776-1810)
Type: Posse   **Acts:** 1
Premiere: Vienna, Austria: Theater in der Leopoldstadt
        • 1806 05 28
Source of Premiere Information: Stieger
Play: *Othello*

Comments: G:Mds: *Othello/der Mohr in Wien/ Ein Posse mit Gesang.*

Romeo und Julie

Status: Y   **Evidence:** S
Text: Kringsteiner, Ferdinand Josef (1776-1810)
Type: Quodlibet von Karakteren mit Gesang [Travestie]   **Acts:** 2
        Language: German
Premiere: Vienna, Austria: Theater in der Leopoldstadt
        • 1808 03 18
Source of Premiere Information: Stieger
Play: *Romeo and Juliet*
Yes: Squire, Wilson

Cast: HERR VON PAMSTIG • MARTIN, ein Maurer • VEITH, Wirth • JULIE, Pamstigs Tochter • ROMEO, ihr Geliebter, ein Student, verkleidet sich als Kellner, als Apollo und Herr von Haspel • EIN TAUBER HAUSMEISTER DES PAMSTIG • WINZIWINSK, ein Schutzgeist • DOKTOR SCHNITZL • ERSTER GENIUS • MARZIBELLA, Juliens Vertraute • SUSE, Veitens Muhme • RITTER SCHRECKENSTEIN • KUNO VON LÖWENTHAL • EIN BEAMTER • CHEVALIER SCHMISS • THADDÄDL, der A B C Schütz • HERR VON KRUMPFUSS • POLDZINELLO, sein Diener • ADELHEIT, Theaterprinzipalin • FRAU WAWERL, Hausmaisterin • FRAU RÖSEL, Wäscherin • WASTEL, ein Lederer Lehrbub • BARTHEL, ein Schrankenzieher • DON PIETRO, ein Geist • RITTER BOMSEN • PURZEL, ein reisender Theaterprinzipal • SCHNAPPERL, ein Baader • DER ZWIRNHÄNDLER AUS OBERÖSTERREICH • EIN REDENDER KNECHT •—• **Chorus:** RITTER UND DAMEN, OPFERMÄDCHEN, OPFERPRIESTER, GENIEN, KNAPPEN, BANDISTEN, KNECHTE UND VOLK

Johann Gottfried Schwanenberg [Schwanberg] (1740-1804)

Romeo e Giulia

Status: Y   **Evidence:** S
Text: Sanseverino, Carlo
Type: Dramma per Musica   **Acts:** 2   **Language:** Italian
Premiere: Brunswick [Braunschweig], Germany: Fürstlich Theater
    im Schlosse • 1776 00 00
Source of Premiere Information: Sonneck
Play: *Romeo and Juliet*
Publisher: G: MMS in D-W, Wa
Yes: Blom, Friedlaender, Hartnoll, Mellen, Oxford, Squire, Stieger,
    Wilson

Comments: New Grove, MGG: libretto by J. R. Sanseverino.
Stieger, Schatz MS: Hofe im Fürstl Schlosse zu Braunschweig 1778
03 00. Sartori: *Romeo e Giulia* Drama in due alli poste in musica da
Giovani Schw. Lipsia 1776. Libretto: dedicated to II Ereditario di
Brunswick dated Berlino, Presso la Vedova di Giorgio Lodovico
Winter 1773. Friedlaender: for 2 sopranos and a tenor.

Cast: ROMEO, Amante, e sposo promesso a • GIULIA, Amante e
sposa promessa a Romeo • BENVOGLIO, Amico d'amendue

Gennaro Scognamilio

Otello ossia Catiello l'Affricano

Status: ?
Text: Petito, Davide
Type: Opera buffa   **Acts:** 3   **Language:** Italian
Premiere: Cerignola, Italy • 1894 01 00
Source of Premiere Information: Mellen
Play: *Othello*

Giuseppe Scolari (1720-1769)

Cajo Mario

Status: ?
Text: Roccaforte, Gaetano
Type: Dramma per musica   **Acts:** 3   **Language:** Italian
Premiere: Milan, Italy: Regio Ducal Teatro • 1765 01 00
Source of Premiere Information: Mellen
Play: *Coriolanus*

Comments: Schatz MS: carnevale 1765.

Humphrey Searle (1915-1982)

Hamlet, Opus 48

Status: Y   **Evidence:** P
Text: Composer
Type: Opera   **Acts:** 3(10 scenes)
       Language: German translation of English
Premiere: Hamburg, Germany: Staatsoper • 1968 03 05
Source of Premiere Information: Mellen
Play: *Hamlet*
Publisher: London: Faber Music Limited, 1971 [vs]
Yes: SCORE, New Grove, White

Comments: White: German translation by Hans Keller after A. W. von Schlegel. Mellen: in German translation by Paul Hamburger and Hans Keller.

Cast: CLAUDIUS (Tenor) • CORNELIUS (Tenor) • VOLTIMAND (Baritone) • LAERTES (Tenor) • POLONIUS (Bass-baritone) • HAMLET (Baritone) • GERTRUDE (Mezzo-soprano) • HORATIO (Baritone) • MARCELLUS (Bass) • ORPHELIA (Soprano) • GHOST [also PLAYER KING] (Bass) • ROSENCRANTZ (Tenor) • GUILDENSTERN (Baritone) • FIRST PLAYER [also PROLOGUE and LUCIANUS] (Tenor) • PLAYER QUEEN (Soprano) • FORTINBRAS (Tenor or high baritone) • CAPTAIN (Baritone) • GENTLEMAN (Baritone) • SAILOR (Baritone) • GRAVEDIGGER (Bass) • PRIEST (Bass) • OSRIC (High tenor)

M. Séméladis

Cordélia

Status: Y   **Evidence:** S
Text: Pacini, Emiliano and Émile Deschamps (1791-1871)
Type: Grand opéra   **Acts:** 1   **Language:** French
Premiere: Versailles, France • 1854 04 00
Source of Premiere Information: Mellen
Play: *Lear*
Yes: Friedlaender, Hartnoll, Mellen, Oxford

Alexander Nikolayevich Serov (1820-1871)

Merry Wives of Windsor

Status: Y   **Evidence:** S
Text: Unknown
Type: Opera sketch
Premiere: 1843 00 00
Play: *Merry Wives of Windsor*
Yes: Blom, Groves V

Comments: Groves V: did not progress beyond a sketch.

Henri Charles Antoine Gaston Serpette (1846-1904)

Shakespeare!

Status: AP   **Evidence:** P
Text: Gavaut, Paul Armand Marcel (1866-1936) and
        P. L. Flers [Fleurs]
Type: Opérette-bouffe   **Acts:** 3   **Language:** French
Premiere: Paris, France: Théâtre des Bouffes-Parisiens
        • 1899 11 23
Source of Premiere Information: Score
Play: *Shakespeare Appears*
Publisher: Paris: Heugel & Cie, 1899 [vs]
Yes: SCORE, Oxford

Comments: Stieger: 1899 11 22. Shakespeare must not be a singing role. He is not listed as a character.

Cast: BRUTUS [M. Jean Périer] • LE MAJOR [M. Régnard] • JACK [M. Maurice Lamy] • WINNING-POST [M. Vavasseur] • MIGUEL [M. Alberthal] • PÉPÉ [M. Casa] • PÉDRO [M. Roux] • EPONINE [Mme. Mariette Sully] • CONSUELO [Mme. Tariol-Baugé] • LA MAJORESSE [Mme. Laporte] • MARY [Mme. Maud D'Orby] • NELL [Mme. Eveline Janney] • UN GROOM [Mme. Muller] • ALONZO [M. Deschamps] • JOSÉ [M. Bronté] •——• **Chorus:** CONTREBANDIERS, ESPAGNOLS, SOLDATS ANGLAIS, ETC.

Le songe d'une nuit d'été

Status: N   **Evidence:** S
Text: Noël, E.
Acts: 1   **Language:** French
Premiere: Paris, France: Théâtre des Bouffes-Parisiens
    • 1886 09 01
Source of Premiere Information: Stieger
Play: *Midsummer Night's Dream*
No: Mellen

Vissarion Yakovlevich Shebalin (1902-1963)

Ukroshchenie stroptivoi [The Taming of the Shrew] Op. 46

Status: Y   **Evidence:** P
Text: Gozenpud, A.
Type: Comic opera   **Acts:** 4/5 scenes   **Language:** Russian
Premiere: Moscow, Soviet Union: Concert Version • 1955 10 01
Source of Premiere Information: Mellen
Play: *Taming of the Shrew*
Publisher: Moscow: Music State Publishers, 1969 [vs]
Yes: SCORE, Baker's, Hartnoll, Mellen, New Grove, Oxford

Comments: Stage premiere, May 25, 1957 (Kuibishev).

Cast: PETRUCHIO, a gentleman from Verona (Baritone) • BAPTISTA MINOLA, a rich merchant (Bass) • KATHERINA, Baptista's

daughter (Dramatic Soprano) • BIANCA, Baptista's daughter (Lyric Soprano) • LUCENTIO, in love with Bianca (Tenor) • HORTENSIO, in love with Bianca (Bass) • GRUMIO, Petruchio's servant (Bass) • CURTIS, Petruchio's servant (Tenor) • BIONDELLO, Baptista's servant (Tenor) • TAYLOR (Tenor) •—•
Chorus: GUESTS, SERVANTS AND COOKS

Harry Rowe Shelley (1858-1947)

Romeo and Juliet

Status: Y   **Evidence:** P
Text: Composer
Type: Lyric Dramma   **Acts:** 3/1 tableau   **Language:** English
Premiere: New York, U.S.A. • 1901 00 00
Play: *Romeo and Juliet*
Publisher: New York: Edward Schuberth & Co., 1901 [vs]
Yes: LIBRETTO, Hartnoll, Mellen, Oxford, Squire, Stieger

Comments: Mellen: composed 1875. English-German libretto is dated 1901. Vocal Score does not list anyone for the text.

Cast: JULIET (Soprano) • LADY CAPULET (Mezzo Soprano) • NURSE (Contralto) • ROMEO (Tenor) • CAPULET (Baritone) • TYBALT (Baritone) • MERCUTIO (Bass) • BENVOLIO (Baritone) • THE PRINCE (Bass) • PETER (Tenor) • PARIS (Dumb) • FRIAR LAWRENCE (Dumb)

Aleksandr Alexseivich Shenshin (1890-   )

Twelfth Night

Status: Y   **Evidence:** S
Text: Unknown
Premiere: 1940 00 00
Play: *Twelfth Night*
Yes: Oxford

Elie Siegmeister (1909-   )

Night of the Moonspell

Status: Y   **Evidence:** S
Text: Mabley, Edward
Type: Opera   **Acts:** 3/9 Scenes   **Language:** English
Premiere: Shreveport, Louisiana, U.S.A.: Shreveport Symphony
    Society • 1976 11 14
Source of Premiere Information: Slonimsky
Play: *Midsummer Night's Dream*
Publisher: New York: C. Fischer [vs, l]
Yes: AMCL

Comments: Action transfered to a mardi gras celebration in
Louisiana about 1900. It is a commissioned United States
bicentennial composition.

Charles Silver (1868-1949)

La Mégère apprivoisée

Status: Y   **Evidence:** P
Text: Cain, Henri (1859-1937) and Edouard Adenis
Type: Comédie lyrique   **Acts:** 4   **Language:** French
Premiere: Paris, France: Théâtre National de l'Opéra • 1922 01 30
Source of Premiere Information: Score
Play: *Taming of the Shrew*
Publisher: Paris: Heugel, 1922 [vs]
Yes: SCORE, Hartnoll, Loewenberg, Mellen, Oxford, Stieger

Comments: Libretto based on P. Delairs' French version, 1891.

Cast: CATHARINA (Soprano) [Mme Marthe Chenal] • BIANA
(Soprano léger) [Mme M. Monsy] • CURTIS (Mezzo ou Contralto)
[Mme Dubois-Lauger] • NICOLE (Soprano) [Mme Rex] • MARIETTA
(Mezzo) [Mme Lalande] • QUELQUES JUNES FILLES [Choryphées]
• PÉTRUCHIO (Baryton) [M. Rouard] • LORENZO (Ténor) [M.
Rambaud] • BAPTISTA (Basse chantante) [M. Huberty] •
BIONDELLO (Ténor) [M. G. Dubois] • GRÉMIO (Basse bouffe) [M.
Ernst] • LE TAILLEUR [Acte I]/NATHANIEL [Acte III] (Ténor) [M. Soria]
• TRANIO [Actes I et II]/FILIPPO [Acte III] (Baryton) [M. Bruyas] • LE

CUISINIER [Acte III] (Basse) [M. P. Combes] •——•
Chorus: QUELQUES JEUNES GENS (Choryphées ténors);
INVITÉS, DANSEURS, MUSICIENS, SERVITEURS, ETC.

Stanley Silverman

A Midsummer Night's Dream

Status: Y   **Evidence:** S
Text: Unknown
Play: *Midsummer Night's Dream*
Yes: Northouse

Julian Slade

Comedy of Errors

Status: Y   **Evidence:** S
Text: Harris, Lionel and Robert McNab
Type: Comic operetta   **Language:** English
Premiere: London, England: BBC-TV • 1954 05 16
Source of Premiere Information: Gänzl
Play: *Comedy of Errors*
Yes: Gänzl

Comments: Characters and cast from Gänzl.

Cast: DR. PINCH/SOLINUS, Duke of Ephesus [Gerald Cross] •
AEGON [Richard Vernon] • ANTIPHOLUS OF EPHESUS [David
Peel] • ANTIPHOLUS OF SYRACUSE [Paul Hansard] • DROMIO OF
EPHESUS/DROMIO OF SYRACUSE [James Cairncross] • ADRIANA
[Joan Plowright] • LUCIANA [Jane Wenham] • ANGELO [David Bird] •
ANGELO'S ASSISTANT [Roy Skelton] • COURTESAN [Christie
Humphrey] • ABBESS ÆMILIA [Lally Bowers] • OFFICER [Patrick
Horgan] • NUN [Patricia Routledge] • MERCHANT [Richard Burrell] •
LUCE [Ester Lawrence] • TOWN CRIER [Paul Garner] • HOSTESS
OF THE "PORCUPINE" [Helen Misener] • DANCER [Barbara Grimes]

Bedrich Smetana (1824-1884)

Viola

Status: Y   **Evidence:** P
Text: Krásnohorská, Eliska (1847-1926)
Type: Comic Opera   **Acts:** 4 scenes   **Language:** Czech
Premiere: Prague, Czechoslovakia: Czech National Theater
    • 1924 05 11
Play: *Twelfth Night*
Publisher: Praze: Hudebni matice Umelecké besedy, 1946 [vs]
Yes: SCORE, Blom, Groves V, Hartnoll, Mellen, New Grove, Oxford

Comments: Mellen: composed 1874-84 [unfinished]. MGG: only a
fragment of the 1st act; concert version 3/15/1900 (Prague,
Buhnenauff). Viola is bound in with *Certova Stena.* Score stops at
measure 365.

Cast: ORSINO • VIOLA • SEBASTIAN • OLIVIE • ZEMAN TOBIAS •
ZEMAN ONDREJ • MALVOLIO • MARIE • SASEK • ANTONIO •
MARKO

John Christopher Smith [Schmid, Schmidt] (1712-1793)

The Fairies

Status: Y   **Evidence:** P
Text: Composer and David Garrick (1716-1779)
Type: Drama   **Acts:** Prologue/3   **Language:** English
Premiere: London, England: Drury Lane Theatre • 1755 02 03
Source of Premiere Information: Loewenberg
Play: *Midsummer Night's Dream*
Publisher: London: I Walsh, 1755 [s]
Yes: SCORE, Baker's, Blom, Friedlaender, Groves V, Hartnoll,
    Loewenberg, Mellen, MGG, New Grove, Oxford, Squire,
    Stieger, White, Wilson

Comments: Some characters listed in Fiske. Fiske:1756 02 11.
Mellen: an early attempt to utilize recitatives in English opera; the text
is often attributed to David Garrick, who repudiated it.

Cast: HERMIA • LYSANDER • FAIRIES • GOBLIN • HYMEN? • [Mr. Beard] • [Sig.ra Passerini] • [Sig.r Guadagini] • [Miss Poitier (Potier)] • [Master Moore] • [Miss Young] • [Master Reinhold]

Rosalinda

Status: N   **Evidence:** S
Text: Lockman, John
Type: Musical drama   **Acts:** 1/5 scenes   **Language:** English
Premiere: London, England: Hickford's Great Room in Brewer Street • 1740 01 04
Source of Premiere Information: Fiske
Play: *As You Like It*
No: Squire

Comments: Sonneck, Mellen: one act, musical drama. Manferrari: London (Lincoln's Inn Fields) primavera 1739. Fiske: Rosalinda, thinking her lover Garcia has been slain in battle, retires to a 'solotude'; Garcia turns up. The libretto contains a preface titled An Enquiry into the Rise and Progress of Operas and Oratorios.

Cast: ROSALINDA, Daughter to Ferdinand, King of Castile [Mrs. Arne] • GARCIA, Generalissimo of King Ferdinand's Troups [Mr. Beard] • NUNEZ, Page to Rosalinda •—• **Chorus:** CHORUS

The Tempest

Status: Y   **Evidence:** P
Text: Composer and David Garrick (1716-1779)
Type: Opera   **Acts:** 3   **Language:** English
Premiere: London, England: Drury Lane Theatre • 1756 02 11
Source of Premiere Information: Mellen
Play: *Tempest*
Publisher: London: I. Walsh, 1756 [s]
Yes: SCORE, LIBRETTO, Baker's, Blom, Friedlaender, Groves V, Hartnoll, Mellen, MGG, New Grove, Oxford, Squire, Stieger, White, Wilson

Comments: Manferrari: librettist is E. H. Smith.

Cast: ALONZO, King of Naples • PROSPERO, The Right Duke of Milan • ANTONIO, His brother, the usurping duke of Milan •

FERDINAND, Son to the king of Naples • GONZALO, A nobleman of Naples • MIRANDA, Daughter to Prospero • CALIBAN, A savage and deformed slave • STEPHANO, Master of the Ship • VENTOSO, Mate • TRINCALO, Boatswain • MUSTACHO, Mariner • ARIEL, An airy spirit • OTHER SPIRITS ATTENDING ON PROSPERO • The Principal Characters performed by Mr. Beard, Mr. Chamness, Mr. Abington, • Mr. Rooker, Mr. G. Burton, Mr. Atkins, Signora Curioni, Mrs. Vernon, Miss Young

Friedrich Eduard de Sobolewski (1808-1872)

Imogéne

Status: Y   **Evidence:** S
Text: Composer
Type: Singspiel   **Acts:** 3   **Language:** German
Premiere: Königsberg, Germany: Stadttheater • 1832 12 06
Source of Premiere Information: Mellen
Play: *Cymbeline*
Yes: Blom, Hartnoll, Mellen, Oxford, Schatz MS, Stieger

Comments: Mellen: 1832 12 06.

Nicolai Feopemptovich Soloviev (1846-1916)

Cordélia

Status: N   **Evidence:** P
Text: Bronnikoff, P. K.
Type: Oper   **Acts:** 4   **Language:** Russian
Premiere: St. Petersburg, Soviet Union: Teatro Opera Russa • 1885 11 24
Source of Premiere Information: Mellen
Play: *Lear*
No: LIBRETTO, Groves V, Schatz MS, Squire

Comments: Libretto: Nach Victorien Sardou. Groves V, Mellen: based on Sardou's *La Haine.* Mellen: also produced as *Mest.*

Cast: JUGURTHA SARACCINI (Erster Baß) • CORDELIA, seine Schwester (Sopran [Primab.]) • UBERTA, Erzieherin derselben (Alt) • ANDREINO, Page,Sohn der Uberia (Sopran) • ORFO, Führer der Guelfen (Erster Baryton) • UGONE, Führer der Guelfen (Hoher Baß) • ERZBISCHOF (Baß) • BATTISTA, Gastwirth (Zweiter Baryton) • GIOVANNA, sein Weib (Mezzosopran) • BEPPO, Neapolitaner (Lyrischer Tenor) • EIN MÖNCH (Zweiter Tenor) • EIN AUSRUFER (Zweiter Baryton) •—• **Chorus:** TÖCHTER UND SÖHNE BEPPO'S, GUELFEN, GHIBELLINEN, MÖNCHE, NONNEN, SCHMIEDE, GASTWIRTHE, SOLDATEN UND VOLK

Charles Caroll Soule

Travesty Without a Pun.

Status: Y   **Evidence:** S
Text: Unknown
Language: English
Play: *Hamlet*
Publisher: St. Louis: Jones & Co., 1879
Yes: US-Bp

Comments: US:Bp: *Hamlet* revamped, modernized, and set to music.

Christian Joseph Franz Alexandre Stadtfeldt (1826-1853)

Hamlet

Status: Y   **Evidence:** S
Text: Guilliaume, Jules
Type: Grosse oper   **Acts:** 3   **Language:** German
Premiere: Darmstadt, Germany • 1857 00 00
Source of Premiere Information: Mellen
Play: *Hamlet*
Yes: Friedlaender, Hartnoll, Manferrari, Mellen, Oxford, Stieger, Wilson

Comments: Strongly influenced by Meyerbeer. Schatz: 1882 06 04 Weimar (Hoftheater). Stieger: 1882 06 03. Manferrari: *Amleto* (da Shakespeare) s. 2 a., postuma, Bruxelles, Tr. La Monnaie, primavera 1857. Mellen: 5 acts. MS and libretto do not mention Shakespeare.

Cast: CLAUDIUS, König von Dänemark • HAMLET, Sohn des vorigen und Neffe des gegenwärtigen Königs • GERTRUDE, Königin von Dänemark und Hamlets Mutter • OPHELIA, Tochter des Oberkämmerers Polonius • DER SCHATTEN VON HAMLETS VATER • DER HÄUPTLING DER SCHAUSPIELER •—•
Chorus: HERREN UND DAMEN VOM HOFE, ZIGEUNER UND ZIGEUNERINNEN, SOLDATEN, WÄCHTER, DIENER

Sir Charles Villiers Stanford (1852-1924)

Much Ado About Nothing, Opus 76a

Status: Y   **Evidence:** P
Text: Sturgis, Julian Russell
Type: Opera   **Acts:** 4   **Language:** English
Premiere: London, England: Covent Garden • 1901 05 30
Source of Premiere Information: Loewenberg
Play: *Much Ado About Nothing*
Publisher: MGG: Boosey and Co., 1901 [vs]
Yes: SCORE, LIBRETTO, Blom, Friedlaender, Groves V, Hartnoll, Loewenberg, Mellen, MGG, New Grove, Oxford, Squire, Stieger, White, Wilson

Comments: Wilson: 1900 05 00; has little in common with the play. Manferrari: com. 2 a. Dent: it was withdrawn after two performances.
Cast: HERO • BEATRICE • DON PEDRO • DON JOHN • CLAUDIO • BENEDIKT • LEONATO • BORACCIO • EIN VATER • HOLZAPFEL • SCHLEWEIN • SEEKOHL • MARGARETE •—•
Chorus: RITTER, DAMEN, MÄDCHEN, UND JUNGENDS VOM LANDE, WÄCHTER, MÖNCHE UND GEFOLGE

Carl David Stegmann (1751-1826)

Macbeth

Status: I   **Evidence:** S
Text: Bürger (after Shakespeare)
Type: Trauerspiel
Premiere: Hamburg, Germany: Theater beim Gänsemarkt
    • 1779 07 21
Play: *Macbeth*
Yes: Manferrari
No: New Grove, Stieger

Comments: New Grove, Stieger: incidental music. Manferrari: (da Shakespeare) com 2 a., Amburgo, Tr. di Corte, autunno 1784.

Daniel Gottlieb Steibelt (1765-1823)

Roméo et Juliette or Tout pour l'amour

Status: Y   **Evidence:** S
Text: Ségur, Alexandre Joseph Pierre vicomte de (1756-1805)
Type: Opéra   **Acts:** 3   **Language:** French
Premiere: Paris, France: Théâtre de la rue Feydeau • 1793 09 11
Source of Premiere Information: Score [vieux stile]
Play: *Romeo and Juliet*
Publisher: Paris: Chez Boyer et Nadermann, 1793 [vs].
Yes: Blom, Friedlaender, Groves V, Hartnoll, Mellen, New Grove,
    Oxford, Squire, Stieger, Wilson

Comments: Libretto, Sonneck: composer is C. Steibelt and librettist is C.J.A. Ségur. Manferrari: C.A. Ségur, 1793 10 10. Score: 10 7bre 1793 (vieux stile). Schatz MS: 1793 09 11. US:NYp: Libretto by Ségur based on Shakespeare's play. Mellen: 1793 09 10. Score and libretto do not mention Shakespeare.

Cast: CAPULET, père de Juliette • JULIETTE, fille de Capulet • ROMÉO, amant de Juliette, fils de Montaigu • CÉCILE, amie de Juliette • DON FERNAND, jeune Castillan, rival de Roméo • CÉBAS, homme de loi, ami de Capulet • ANTONIO, homme âgé, gardien de la sépulture de ses ancêtres • ALBERTI, écuyer de Roméo •——•
Chorus: SUITE ET PARENS DE DON FERNAND ET DE CAPULET

Émile Steinkühler (1824-1872)

Cäsario, oder die Verwechslung, Op. 30

Status: Y   **Evidence:** S
Text: Gollmick, Karl A. (1796-1866)
Type: Comic opera   **Acts:** 3   **Language:** German
Premiere: Düsseldorf, Germany: Stadttheater • 1848 03 00
Source of Premiere Information: Schatz MS
Play: *Twelfth Night*
Yes: Friedlaender, Hartnoll, Mellen, Oxford, Schatz MS, Stieger

Stephen Storace (1762-1796)

Gli Equivoci

Status: Y   **Evidence:** P
Text: Da Ponte, Lorenzo (1749-1838)
Type: Dramma Buffo   **Acts:** 2   **Language:** Italian
Premiere: Vienna, Austria: Burgtheater • 1786 12 27
Source of Premiere Information: Loewenberg
Play: *Comedy of Errors*
Yes: LIBRETTO, Blom, Groves V, Hartnoll, Loewenberg, Mellen,
   MGG, Oxford, White

Comments: Mellen: his *No Song, No Supper* uses some music
adapted from this work as well as works from several other
composers.

Cast: SOLINO, Duca di Efeso • EGEONE, Padre di • EUFEMIO DI
SIRAC • EUFEMIO DI EFESO • DROMIO DI SIRAC • DROMIO DI
EFESO • ANGELO, Orefice • DOCTOR PIZZICO, Ciarlatano •
SFRONIA, moglie di Sofr • SOFTRATA, sorella di Sofr • LESBIA,
moglie di Drom. Sir • UN FANCIULLO • ALCUNE PERSONE, CHE
NON PARLANO

Anton   Maria   Storch   (1813-1888)

Romeo und Julie

Status: Y   **Evidence:** S
Text: Forst, Joseph [Joseph Schall von Falkenforst] (1806-1865)
Type: Komisch-tragische Oper   **Acts:** 1
      Language: German
Premiere: Vienna, Austria: Josefstädttheater • 1862 03 02
Source of Premiere Information: Stieger
Play: *Romeo and Juliet*
Publisher: Stieger.
Yes: Friedlaender, Mellen, Oxford

Comments: Riemann, Friedlaender, Stieger: it is a burleske
Operette. Schatz MS: Vienna Theater i d Josephstadt, 1862 11 06.
Mellen: Carltheater, 1863 10 31, a parody of *Romeo and Juliet*.
Friedlaender: Vienna, 1862 11 00. Cast comes from libretto in
Schatz collection; it may not be that of first performance.

Cast: DER ALTE CAPULET [Hr. Perko] • JULIE, seine Tochter [Hr.
Rott-Lutz] • DER ALTE MONTAGUE [Hr. Oberhofer] • ROMEO, sein
Sohn [Hr. Tomaselli] • LORENZO, Emerit und Schwammerlsucher
[Hr. Jungwirth] • SCHACHTELLECKER, Apotheker [Hr. Grois] •—•
Chorus: GEFOLGE CAPULETS UND MONTAGUE

Der Stein der Weisen

Status: ?
Text: Wysber, Ludwig
Type: Zauberspiel   **Acts:** 3
Premiere: Vienna, Austria: Josefstädttheater • 1851 10 30
Source of Premiere Information: Stieger
Play: *Tempest*

Comments: See Gerl's opera.

Josef Stransky (1872-1836)

Béatrice et Bénédict

Status: I   **Evidence:** S
Text: Unknown
Type: Opera
Premiere: 1913 00 00
Play: *Much Ado About Nothing*
Yes: Blom
No: Groves V, Mellen

Comments: Groves V, Mellen: this is a new arrangement of Berlioz's *Béatrice et Bénédict.*

Nicolaus Adam Strungk [Strunck] (1640-1700)

Rosalinde

Status: N   **Evidence:** S
Text: Marchi, Antonio
Type: Oper   **Acts:** 3   **Language:** German
Premiere: Leipzig, Germany: Hoftheater • 1695 00 00
Source of Premiere Information: Mellen
Play: *As You Like It*
No: Same libretto as Ziani's opera.

Leslie Stuart [pseu. Thomas A. Barrett]

Belle of Mayfair

Status: Y   **Evidence:** S
Text: Hamilton, Cosmo Hood; Basil & Charles H. E. Brookfield
Type: Musical Comedy   **Acts:** 2   **Language:** English
Premiere: London, England: Vaudeville Theatre • 1906 04 11
Source of Premiere Information: Gänzl
Play: *Romeo and Juliet*
Publisher: London: Francis, Day & Hunter 1906 [vs]
Yes: Gänzl

Comments: Gänzl: book is by Brookfield and Basil Hood. Additional cast and characters given in Gänzl.

Cast: THE EARL OF MOUNT HIGHGATE [Mr. Sam Walsh] • HONOURABLE RAYMOND FINCHLEY, his Son [Mr. Farren Soutar] • SIR JOHN CHALDICOTT, BART., M.P. [Mr. Arthur Williams] • HUGH MEREDITH [Mr. Charles Pounds] • COMTE DE PERRIER [Mr. Charles Angelo] • DOCTOR MARMADUKE LAWRENCE, Bishop of Brighton [Mr. Charles Troode] • CAPTAIN THEOBALD, Friend of Raymond [Mr. Mervyn Dene] • CHARLIE GOODYEAR, Friend of Raymond [Mr. Philip Desborough] • BANDMASTER [Mr. Tom A. Shale] • SIMPSON, Footman to Sir John Chaldicott [Mr. W. Pringle] • GREGORY, Footman to Sir John Chaldicott [Mr. Norman Ridley] • FRANÇOIS [Mr. Murri Moncrieff] • BRAMLEY, Footman to Lord Mount Highate [Mr. C. A. Cameron] • BAGSTOCK, Gardener to Sir. John Caldicott) [Mr. John Blankley] • H.S.H. PRINCESS CARL OF EHRENBREITSTEIN [Miss Louie Pounds] • THE COUNTESS OF MOUNT HIGHGATE [Miss Irene Desmond] • LADY CHALDICOTT [Miss Maud Boyd] • LADY RODALINE ROCKESLY [Miss Ruby Ray] • LADY VIOLET GUSSOP [Miss Jane May] • THE DUTCHESS OF DUNMOW [Miss Camille Clifford] • LADY JAY [Miss Hilda Hammerton] • LADY PAQUIN [Miss Kitty Harold] • LADY LOUISE [Miss Dora Glennie] • LADY LUCILLE [Miss May Hobson] • LADY PETER ROBINSON [Miss Kitty Dale] • LADY HAYWARD [Miss Florence Randle] • LADY SWAN [Miss Ivy Desmond] • LADY EDGAR [Miss Helen Colville] • PINCOTT, Julia's Maid [Miss Lillian Digges] • SOPHIE [Miss Stella de Marney] • MISS CORRIE FAY [Miss Vivien Vowles] • JULIA CHALDICOTT [Miss Edna May] •—•
Chorus: STALL-HOLDERS, THE CHIPPY GIRLS, GUESTS

Joseph Hartmann Stuntz (1793-1859)

Heinrich IV zu Givry

Status: N   **Evidence:** S
Text: Sendtner, Joseph Ignaz (1784-1833)
Type: Opera   **Acts:** 2   **Language:** German
Premiere: Munich, Germany: Hoftheater • 1820 09 08
Source of Premiere Information: Stieger
Play: *Henry IV*
No: New Grove, Schatz MS

Comments: New Grove: libretto from Voltaire's *Charlot*. Manferrari: *Enrico IV a Ivry* (ignoto) melodr. 3 a., Monaco di B.,Tr. di Corte, primavera 1823. Mellen: 3 acts. Number of acts from libretto.

Cast: HEINRICH DER VIERTE, König von Frankreich [Hr. Staudacher] • JULIE, Gräfin von Givry [Mdme. Neumann] • LOUIS, Marquis von Givry [Mdme. Flerx] • MATHILDE, ihre Nichte [Mslle. Peßl] • CHARLOT, Milchbruder des Marquis, im Schloße erzogen [Mslle. Metzger] • BERTOU, Hausmeister [Hr. Frieß] • AUBONNE, in Diensten Heinrich des IV [Hr. Mittermaier] • GUILLOT, Sohn eines Pächters [Hr. Löhle] • BABET, Kammermädchen [Mslle. Jederl] •—•
Chorus: RICHTER, GERICHTSDIENER, WACHEN, SCHLOSSBEDIENTE, LANDLEUTE, MILITÄRISCHE PERSONEN IM GEFOLGE DES KÖNIGS

Stjepan Sulek (1914-   )

Koriolan

Status: Y   **Evidence:** S
Text: Composer
Type: Opera   **Acts:** 3   **Language:** Yugoslavian
Premiere: Zagreb, Yugoslavia: Opera • 1958 10 12
Source of Premiere Information: Mellen
Play: *Coriolanus*
Publisher: Agram: 1958.
Yes: Baker's, Hartnoll, Mellen, MGG, Oxford

Comments: Mellen: 1958 10 25.

Oluja

Status: Y   **Evidence:** S
Text: Composer
Type: Opera   **Language:** Yugoslavian
Premiere: Zagreb, Yugoslavia: Opera • 1969 11 28
Play: *Tempest*
Yes: Mellen, New Grove, Oxford

Franz von Suppé (1819-1895)

Der Sommernachtstraum

Status: Y **Evidence:** S
Text: Straube, Emanuel (1801-1872)
Type: Märchen **Acts:** 3 **Language:** German
Premiere: Vienna, Austria: Josefstädttheater • 1844 08 31
Source of Premiere Information: Mellen
Play: *Midsummer Night's Dream*
Yes: Groves V, Hartnoll, Mellen, Oxford

Heinrich Sutermeister (1910-   )

Romeo und Julia

Status: Y **Evidence:** S
Text: Sutermeister, Peter
Type: Opera **Acts:** 2(6 scenes) **Language:** German
Premiere: Dresden, Germany: Staatsoper • 1940 04 13
Source of Premiere Information: Mellen
Play: *Romeo and Juliet*
Publisher: Mainz: B. Schott's Söhne,1940 [vs]
Yes: Baker's, Blom, Groves V, Gruber, Hartnoll, Mellen, MGG, New
   Grove, Oxford

Comments: Baker's: his first and greatest success. Score does not
mention Shakespeare.

Cast: ESCALUS, Fürst von Verona (Bariton) • MONTAGUE, Haupt
eines Adelshaus (Sprechrolle) • CAPULET, Haupt eines Adelshaus
(Baß) • ROMEO, Sohn des Montague (Tenor) • BALTHASAR,
Romeos alter Diener (Bariton) • JULIA, Tochter des Capulet (Sopran)
• GRÄFIN CAPULET, ihre Mutter (Mezzosopran) • DIE AMME (Alt) •
GRAF PARIS, ein junger Edelmann (Tanzrolle [weibl.]) • DER
BEDIENTE (Tenor) • PATER LORENZO, ein Franziskaner (Baß) •
DER HIRTENKNABE (Sprechstimme) • EINE KNABENSTIMME
(Mezzosopran [Knabenstimme]) • DIE VIER VERLIEBTEN PAARE
(Madrigalchor [8 Sänger]) •—•
Chorus: VERWANDTE BEIDER HÄUSER, MÄGDE, BÜRGER UND
BÜRGERINNEN VON VERONA, FÜRSTLICHES GEFOLGE,
HEROLDE, DIENER, MASKEN, TÄNZER, TÄNZERINNEN,

STIMMEN DER NACHT, STIMMEN AUS DER TIEFE, KNECHTE DER
MONTAGUES, STIMMEN AUS DER HÖHE

Die Zauberinsel

Status: Y   **Evidence:** S
Text: Composer
Type: Opera   **Acts:** Vorspiel/2   **Language:** German
Premiere: Dresden, Germany: Staatsoper • 1942 10 31
Source of Premiere Information: Mellen
Play: *Tempest*
Publisher: Mainz: B. Schott's Söhne,1942 [vs]
Yes: Baker's, Blom, Groves V, Gruber, Hartnoll, Mellen, MGG, New
    Grove, Oxford

Comments: Manferrari: Tr. Municipale. Gruber: 1942 10 30. Score
does not mention Shakespeare.

Cast: PROSPERO, rechtmäßiger König von Neapel (Baß) •
ALONSO, unrechtmäßiger König von Neapel (Bariton) •
FERDINAND, Alonsos Sohn (Tenor) • MIRANDA, Prosperos Tochter
(Sopran) • ARIEL, ein Luftgeist (Mezzosopran) • CALIBAN, ein
Ungeheuer (Baß) • TRINCOLO, Hofkellermeister, ein Trunkenbold
(Bariton [Baß]) • STEPHANO, Hofnarr, ein Trunkenbold (Tenor) •
BOOTSMANN (Sprechrolle) •—•
Chorus: STIMMEN DES WINDES, STIMMEN DER ZEIT, STIMMEN
DER DÄMMERUNG, HÖFLINGE (8-12), MATROSEN, GENIEN,
FURIEN, NYMPHEN, KOBOLDE, KLEINE UND GROSSE GEISTER

Sándor Szokolay (1931-   )

Hamlet

Status: Y   **Evidence:** P
Text: Composer
Type: Opera   **Acts:** 3(11 scenes)   **Language:** Hungarian
Premiere: Budapest, Hungary: State Opera • 1968 10 19
Play: *Hamlet*
Publisher: Budapest: 1968 [vs]
Yes: SCORE, Baker's, Mellen, Oxford

Comments: Mellen: Janos Arany Hungarian translation of Shakespeare, 1968 10 18.

Cast: CLAUDIUS, King of Denmark • HAMLET, the former King's son, the present King's nephew (Tenor) • GERTRUD, Queen of Denmark, Hamlet's mother (Alt) • HORATIO, Hamlet's friend (Bariton) • POLONIUS, Lord Chamberlain (Bassus) • LAERTES, the Lord Chamberlain's son. (Tenor) • OPHELIA, the Lord Chamberlain's daughter (Soprán) • HAMLET ATYA SZELLEME (Bassus) • ROSENCRANTZ (Tenor) • GUILDENSTERN (Tenor) • MARCELLUS, officer (Bassus) • BERNARDO, officer (Bassbariton) • FRANCISCO (Bassus) • ELSÖ SIRASO, first grave digger (Tenor) • MASODIK SIRASO, second grave digger (Bariton) • PAP (Bassbariton) • OSRICK (Tenor) • NEMES (Tenor) • LUCIANUS, actor (Bariton) • SZINÉSZ KIRALY (Speaking part) • SZINÉSZKIRALYNÉ (Speaking part) •—• **Chorus:** Courtiers

Eug. Sztojanovics

Otello mecél

Status: ?
Text: Orban, Dezsö
Type: Operetta
Premiere: Budapest, Hungary: Kgl.Op. • 1917 05 22
Source of Premiere Information: Stieger
Play: *Othello*

Ant. Sanchez do Cunha Taboida

Dinah

Status: ?
Text: Unknown
Type: Opera
Premiere: Lisbon, Portugal: Club de Lisbonne • 1897 07 00
Play: *Cymbeline*

Ben. Tajon

The Taming of a Shrew

Status: ?
Text: Huard, Lucian
Play: *Taming of the Shrew*

Carl Gottfried Wilhelm Taubert (1811-1891)

Cesario, oder Was ihr wollt, Op. 188

Status: Y   **Evidence:** P
Text: Taubert, Emil (1844-1895)
Type: Oper   **Acts:** 3   **Language:** German
Premiere: Berlin, Germany: Königl. Opernhaus • 1874 11 13
Source of Premiere Information: Mellen
Play: *Twelfth Night*
Publisher: Berlin: E. Bote & G. Bock, 1875 [s]
Yes: SCORE, LIBRETTO, Baker's, Blom, Friedlaender, Groves V,
      Hartnoll, Mellen, Oxford, Schatz MS, Squire, Stieger, Wilson

Comments: Stieger: 4 acts; 1874 04 13; text by Eduard Taubert.

Cast: ORSINO, Herzog von Illyrien (Baryton) • SEBASTIAN VON
METELIN, ein junger Edelmann (Tenor-Baryton) • VIOLA, seine
Schwester (Sopran) • ANTONIO, Schiffhauptsmann (Baß) •
BERNARDO, Schiffhauptsmann (Baß) • GRÄFIN OLIVIA (Sopran) •
JUNKER TOBIAS, ihr Oheim (Baß) • JUNKER CHRISTOPH VON
BLEICHENWANG (Tenor) • MALVOLIO, Olivia's Haushofmeister
(Baß) • FABIO, in Olivia's Dienst (Tenor) • MARIA, Olivia's
Kammermädchen (Sopran) • EIN HAUPTMANN (Tenor) • EIN
PRIESTER • EIN WIRTH •—• **Chorus:** HERREN VOM HOFE,
MATROSEN, WACHEN, MUSIKANTEN, GAUKLER,
HOCHZEITSGÄSTE, TÄNZER, GEFOLGE, VOLK

Macbeth, Op. 133

Status: Y   **Evidence:** P
Text: Eggers, Friedrich Hartwig (1819-1872)
Type: Opera   **Acts:** 5   **Language:** German

Premiere: Berlin, Germany: Königl. Opernhaus • 1857 11 16
Source of Premiere Information: Loewenberg
Play: *Macbeth*
Publisher: Berlin: Ed. Bote & G. Bock, 1857 [vs]
Yes: SCORE, Blom, Friedlaender, Groves V, Hartnoll, Loewenberg,
    Mellen, Oxford, Squire, Stieger, Wilson

Comments: Manferrari: 3 acts, 1857 11 11.

Cast: DUNCAN, König von Schottland • MALCOLM, sein Sohn •
MACBETH, sein Feldherr • BANQUO, sein Feldherr • FLEANCE,
Banquo's Sohn • LADY MACBETH • MACDUFF, schottischer
Edelmann • EIN PFÖRTNER • EIN DIENER DER LADY MACBETH •
EIN MÖRDER • EIN ARTZ • EINE KAMMERDAME • EIN HARFNER •
ERSTE HEXE • ZWEITE HEXE • DRITTE HEXE • HEKATE •—•
Chorus: LORDS, EDELLEUTE, DAMEN, SCHOTTISCHE UND
ENGLISCHE KRIEGER, CEREMONIENMEISTER, PAGEN,
BARDEN, PFEIFER, GESINDE, LANDVOLK, ERSCHEINUNGEN,
HEXEN

Otto Taubmann (1859-1929)

Porzia

Status: Y   **Evidence:** P
Text: Wilde, Richard
Type: Opera   **Acts:** 3   **Language:** German
Premiere: Frankfurt A/M, Germany: Opernhaus • 1916 11 14
Source of Premiere Information: Mellen
Play: *Merchant of Venice*
Publisher: Berlin: Drei Masken Verlag, c.1916 [vs]
Yes: SCORE, Blom, Groves V, Hartnoll, Mellen, New Grove, Oxford

Cast: DER DOGE VON VENEDIG (Baß) • PORZIA, eine reiche Erbin
(Sopran) • BASSANIO, venezianischer Edler (Bariton) • LORENZO,
Porzias Verwandter (Tenor) • ANTONIO, reicher Kaufmann in
Venedig (Bariton) • SHYLOCK, ein Jude (Tenor) • JESSICA, seine
Tochter (Mezzosopran) • TUBAL, Shylocks Freund (Tenor) •
LANZELOT, Bassanios Diener, früher in Shylocks Diensten (Sopran)
• EIN VENEZIANISCHER STRASSENHÄNDLER (Tenor) • VIER
ANDERE HÄNDLER (1 Tenor, 3 Bäße) • EINE MÄNNLICHE MASKE
["Harlekin"] (Bariton oder Tenor) • EINE WEIBLICHE MASKE
["Colombine"] (Sopran) • EINE DAME DER PORZIA (Sopran) • EIN

DIENER DER PORZIA (Bariton oder Tenor) • EIN BOTE (Tenor oder Bariton) • EIN GERICHTSDIENER (Baß) •— **Chorus:** STRASSENHÄNDLER, MÄNNLICHE UND WEIBLICHE MASKEN, MUSIKANTEN, DAMEN, KAVALIERE, DIENER UND GESINDE DER PORTIA, EIN GEISTLICHER MIT ADJUNKTEN UND MINISTRANTEN, BLUMENSTREUENDE KINDER, SENATOREN, GERICHTSDIENER, BEWAFFNETE

Charles Louis Ambroise Thomas (1811-1896)

Hamlet

Status: Y   **Evidence:** P
Text: Carré, Michel Florentin (1819-1872) and Paul Jules Barbier (1822-1901)
Type: Opera   **Acts:** 5(7 scenes)   **Language:** French
Premiere: Paris, France: Théâtre de l'Academie Imperiale de l'Opéra • 1868 03 09
Source of Premiere Information: Libretto
Play: *Hamlet*
Publisher: Paris: Heugel et Cie,1868 [vs] (German/French)
Yes: SCORE, LIBRETTO, Baker's, Blom, Friedlaender, Groves V, Hartnoll, Loewenberg, Oxford, Stieger, Wilson

Comments: Baker's: very successful opera. Schatz MS: Paris (Théâtre de l'Academie Imperiale de l'Opéra) and (Théâtre de l'Académie imperiale de Musique, Salle provisoire de la rue Le Peletier). Score: nach Shakespeare; Auf dem Kaiserlichen-Theater der Grossen Oper in Paris. Cast and Characters out of1874 libretto. Cast listed in German/French vocal score is slightly different.

Cast: HAMLET [M. Faure] • CLAUDIUS, rio de Danemark [M. Belval] • L'OMBRE DU FEU ROI [M. David] • POLONIUS, grand chambellan [M. Ponsard] • LAERTE, fils de Polonius [M. Colin] • MARCELLUS, officier, ami d'Hamlet [M. Castelmary] • HORATIO, officier, ami d'Hamlet [M. Grisy] • PREMIER FOSSOYEUR [M. Gaspard] • DEUXIEME FOSSOYER [M. Mermant] • GERTRUDE, reine de Danemark et mère d'Hamlet [Mme. Gueymaro] • OPHELIA, fille de Polonius [Mlle. Christine Nilsson] •—
Chorus: SEIGNEURS, DAMES, SOLDATS, COMÉDIENS, SERVITEURS, PAYSANS, DANOIS

Le songe d'une nuit d'été [Shakespeare oder Der Traum einer Sommernacht]

Status: AP **Evidence:** S
Text: Rosier, Joseph Bernard [Adolphe de Ribbing] (1798-1880) and Adolph de Leuven (1800-1884)
Type: Opéra comique **Acts:** 3 **Language:** French
Premiere: Paris, France: Opéra Comique, Salle Favart • 1850 04 20
Source of Premiere Information: Loewenberg
Play: *Shakespeare Appears*
Publisher: Paris: Bureau Central de Musique, 1950 [vs]
Yes: Stieger
No: Friedlaender, Mellen, Squire

Comments: The only relation it has to Shakespeare is that Shakespeare, Queen Elizabeth, and Falstaff are brought on the stage with Queen Elizabeth I. Clément has description of the plot. Stieger: F. Rosier. Friedlaender, Loewenberg, Schatz MS: the above. Mellen: not based on the play by Shakespeare, but an original story using Queen Elizabeth I, Shakespeare and Falstaff as characters.

Cast: WILLIAM SHAKESPEARE [M. Couderc] • FALSTAFF, garde general du parc royal de Richmond [M. Battaille] • LORD LATIMER [M. Boulo] • JÉRÉMY, tavernier [M. Bellecour] • UN HUISSIER • UN ACTEUR • JARVIS, garde forestire (personnage muet) • ELISABETH [Mlle. Lefevre] • OLIVIA [Mlle. Grimm] • NELLY, nièce de Jérémy [Mlle. Marie] •—•
Chorus: ACTEURS ET ACTRICES, COURTISANS ET DAMES DE LA COUR, FORESTIERS, GARÇONS ET SERVANTES DE LA TAVERNE, CUISINIERS, SOMMELIERS, MARMITONS

François Lucien Joseph Thomé (1850-1909)

Roméo et Juliette

Status: NO **Evidence:** S
Premiere: Paris, France: Odéon • 1890 10 30
Play: *Romeo and Juliet*
No: Groves V

Comments: Groves V: incidental music to Shakespeare's *Romeo and Juliet* translated by George Lefevre.

Franz von Thul [Baron Karl Paumgartner] (1854-1911)

Hermione

Status: ?
Text: Unknown
Type: Opera
Premiere: 1892 00 00
Source of Premiere Information: Stieger
Play: *Winter's Tale*

Heinz Tiessen (1887-1971)

Cymbelin

Status: NO   **Evidence:** S
Type: Drama   **Acts:** 2
Premiere: Berlin, Germany: Deutschestheater • 1919 10 10
Source of Premiere Information: Stieger
Play: *Cymbeline*
Yes: Manferrari
No: Blom, Groves V, Stieger

Comments: Manferrari: da Shakespeare. Blom, Groves V: incidental music. Stieger: Shakespeare, German by Ludwig Berger.

Ferdinando Tommasi [Tommaso] (1826-   )

Guido e Ginevre

Status: N   **Evidence:** S
Text: Composer
Type: Melodramma   **Acts:** 4   **Language:** Italian
Premiere: Naples, Italy: Teatro di San Carlo • 1855 12 08

Source of Premiere Information: Schatz Catalog
Play: *Romeo and Juliet*
No: Characters, Plot

Comments: Mellen: 3 acts.

Cast: JACOPO SODERINI, Signor d'Arezzo, e gran Gonfaloniere di Toscana • GINEVRA, sua figlia • MANFREDI, Signor di Perugia • GUIDO, giovine dipintore • RICCIARDA, cantatrice • FORTEBRACCIO, scudiere di Manfredi e segreto confidente di Ricciarda • ANDREA, capo di avventurieri • ELEONORA, confidente di Ginevra •—• **Chorus:** CONTADINE, CONTADINI, CAVALIERI, DAME, AVVENTURIERI, FAMILIARI DI MANFREDI, COMPARSE, UN MAGGIORDOMO, SCUDIERI, PAGGI

Eugenio Torriani (1825-1873)

Romeo e Giulietta

Status: Y   **Evidence:** S
Text: Romani, Felice (1788-1865)
Type: Tragedia per musica   **Acts:** 2   **Language:** Italian
Premiere: Venice, Italy: Teatro Eretenia • 1828 07 26
Source of Premiere Information: Year and place from libretto
Play: *Romeo and Juliet*
Yes: Mellen, Oxford

Comments: Mellen: Enrico Torriani. The libretto in the Schatz collection does not give the composer's name.

Cast: CAPELLIO, Principale fra i Capelletti, e Padre di [Sig. Gian Giuseppe Giordani] • GIULIETTA, Amante di [Signora Serafina Rubini] • ROMEO, Capo dei Montecchi [Signora Teresa Belloc] • ADELE, madre di Giulietta [Signora Angiola Bussi] • TEBALDO, Partigiano dei Capelletti, destinato spose a Giulietta [Sig. Pietro Ansiglioni] • LORENZO, medico e famigliare di Capellio [Sig. Pietro Gianni] •—• **Chorus:** CAPELLETTI, MONTECCHI, DAMIGELLE, SOLDATI, ARMIGERI

Daniel Gottlieb Treu [Theofilo Tedele]

Coriolano

Status: N   **Evidence:** S
Text: Pariati, Pietro
Type: Opera   **Acts:** 3
Premiere: Breslau, Poland • 1725 12 00
Source of Premiere Information: Schatz MS
Play: *Coriolanus*
No: Friedlaender

Vincenc Tomas Vaclav [Vincenz Franz] Tuczek [Tuzeck, Tucek] (1773-1820?)

Der Travestirte Hamlet [Hamlet, Prinz von Dänemark; Hamlet, Prinz von Lilyput]

Status: ?
Text: Gieseke, Johann Georg Karl Ludwig (1770-1833)
Type: Burleske in deutchen Knittelversen   **Acts:** 3
Premiere: Vienna, Austria: Theater auf der Weiden • 1794 07 10
Source of Premiere Information: Date and city from Stieger.
Play: *Hamlet*

Comments: Stieger: Freyhaustheater.

Cast: BERNFIELD • ELLRICH • FRENZOW • HAMLET • OPHELIA • TUTTIFAR • ZORRIBEL • INKREDIBEL • OLDENHOLM •—•
Chorus: SCHLUSSCHOR

Paul H. Turok (1929-   )

Richard III

Status: Y   **Evidence:** S
Text: Composer
Type: Opera   **Acts:** 4/6 Scenes   **Language:** English

Premiere: Philadelphia, U.S.A.: Vocal Arts Academy
• 1975 00 00 ?
Play: *Richard III*
Publisher: New York: A Broude [vs]
Yes: AMCL

Unknown

Die Bezähmte Widerbellerin

Status: Y   **Evidence:** S
Text: Schink, Johann Friedrich (1755-1835)
Type: Singspiel   **Acts:** 2
Premiere: Vienna, Austria: K K prin Th auf d. Wieden. • 1794 04 08
Source of Premiere Information: Schatz MS
Play: *Taming of the Shrew*
Yes: Schatz MS, Stieger

Comments: Stieger: Freyhaustheater

Catch My Soul

Status: Y   **Evidence:** S
Text: Unknown
Language: English
Premiere: Manchester, England • 1970 00 00
Play: *Othello*
Yes: Gänzl, Green

Comments: Gänzl: A rock remake of *Othello*.

Catherine and Petruchio

Status: Y   **Evidence:** S
Text: Unknown
Type: Burletta   **Language:** English
Premiere: London, England: Covent Garden • 1791 00 00
Source of Premiere Information: Mellen
Play: *Taming of the Shrew*
Yes: Mellen

A Cure for a Scold

Status: Y   **Evidence:** P
Text: Worsdale, James
Type: Ballad farce   **Acts:** 2   **Language:** English
Premiere: London, England: Drury Lane Theatre • 1735 02 25
Source of Premiere Information: Year and place from libretto.
    Day from Sonneck.
Play: *Taming of the Shrew*
Yes: LIBRETTO, Sonneck, Squire, Fiske, White

Comments: Squire: founded on Shakespeare's play but is
considerably altered. Fiske: [p. 124] taken from John Lacy's *Sauny the Scot, or The Taming of the Shrew,* an alteration of
Shakespeare's play.

Cast: SIR WILLIAM WORTHY [Mr. Shepard] • MR. MANLY [Mr.
Mecklin] • HARTWELL [Mr. Este] • GAINLOVE [Mr. Crofs] • ARCHER
[Mr. Salway] • PHYSICIAN [Mr. Harper] • BARBER [Mr. Hallam] • PEG
[Mrs. Clive] • FLORA [Mrs. Pritchard] • LUCY [Mrs. Crofs]

The Early Reign of Oleg

Status: ?
Text: Catherine the Great (1729-1796)
Play: ?

Pulcinella rivale di Turzillo e confuso tra Capuleti e Montecchi

Status: ?
Text: Minichini, Edoardo (1845-1918)
Type: Parodie
Premiere: Naples, Italy: Teatro delle Folie Gramatici • 1880 00 00
Play: *Romeo and Juliet*

Schipbreuk

Status: ?
Text: Unknown
Type: Pantomime-Spel

Play: *Tempest*

Comments: Libretto: *De Schipbreuk* ; of Het Feest Der Engelsche Matroozen, Pantomime-Spel; versiert met zang en dans. [Dedication omitted] Op den s'Gravenhaegschen Schouwburg, Den 2den van der Sluys [songs are included].

Cast: PIET, een Arme Matroos • JAEK, een Ryke Matroos, bekend aen Piet • GRIET, Waerdin en Vrouw van • DROOGE KLAES, Waerd in de Welkomst • KNIER, Moeder van Griet • MIETJE, Nichtje van Griet • VERSCHEIDE MATROOZEN EN BUURMEISJES

Thimon le misantrope

Status: ?
Text: Isle, de l'
Type: Comédie   **Acts:** 3   **Language:** French
Premiere: Paris, France: Comédie Italienne • 1722 01 02
Source of Premiere Information: Mellen
Play: *Timon of Athens*

Timon in Love or The Innocent Theft

Status: N   **Evidence:** S
Text: Kelly, John
Type: Ballad opera   **Language:** English
Premiere: London, England: Drury Lane Theatre • 1733 12 05
Source of Premiere Information: Mellen
Play: *Timon of Athens*
No: White

Comments: White: after Delisle.

Jean [John] Urich (1849-1939)

L' Orage

Status: N   **Evidence:** S
Text: Silvestre, Paul Armand (1837-1901)
Type: Opéra comique   **Acts:** 1   **Language:** French

Premiere: Brussels, Belgium: Théâtre Royal de la Monnaie
  • 1879 05 02
Source of Premiere Information: Mellen
Play: *Tempest*
Publisher: Brussels: Schott Frères, 1880 [vs]
No: Squire

Comments: Mellen: revised in 3 acts as Le Pilote, Monte Carlo, Casino, 1890 03 29.

Cast: MARTHE (Soprano) [Mad Lonati] • MARGAITE (Contralto) [Mad. Jsmael] • JULIEN (Tenor [à défaut Bariton Martin]) [Mr. Soulacroix] • MATHURIN (Basse) [Mr. Dauphin] •—•
Chorus: FEMMES ET PÊCHEURS BRETONS

Anton Urspruch (1850-1907)

Der Sturm

Status: Y   **Evidence:** P
Text: Pirazzi, Emil (1832-1898)
Type: Oper   **Acts:** 3   **Language:** German
Premiere: Frankfurt A/M, Germany: Opernhaus • 1888 05 17
Source of Premiere Information: Mellen
Play: *Tempest*
Publisher: Hamburg: Aug. Cranz, 1888 [vs]
Yes: SCORE, LIBRETTO, Friedlaender, Hartnoll, Mellen, MGG, New
      Grove, Oxford, Squire, Stieger

Comments: Manferrari: Stadtteater. Mellen: librettist is composer.

Cast: ALONSO, König von Neapel • FERNANDO, sein Sohn • SEBASTIAN, sein Bruder • ANTONIO, Herzog von Palermo • PROSPERO, sein Bruder • MIRANDA, dessen Tochter • GONZALO, Rath des Königs • STEPHANO, Kellermeister des Königs • TRINCULO, Hofnarr des Königs • ARIEL, ein Luftgeist im Dienste Prosperos • CALIBAN, ein Waldmensch im Dienste Prosperos •—•
Chorus: EDLE UND CAVALIERE VON NEAPEL UND PALERMO IM GEFOLGE DER FÜRSTEN, TRABANTEN UND MATROSEN, JÄGERINNEN, LUFTGEISTER, GENIEN UND ERSCHEINUNGEN

Wendell Utley

Will

Status: ?
Text: Mills, John Brent
Premiere: San Francisco, U.S.A.: Bohemian Club • 1967 07 29
Play: *Other*

Comments: Sixty-second Grove Play to be presented at Bohemian Grove.

Nicola Vaccai [Vaccaj] (1790-1848)

Giulietta e Romeo

Status: Y   **Evidence:** S
Text: Romani, Felice (1788-1865)
Type: Dramma serio per musica   **Acts:** 2   **Language:** Italian
Premiere: Milan, Italy: Teatro Canobbiana • 1825 10 31
Source of Premiere Information: Loewenberg
Play: *Romeo and Juliet*
Publisher: Milan: G. Ricordi, 1825 [vs]
Yes: Baker's, Blom, Friedlaender, Groves V, Hartnoll, Loewenberg, Mellen, New Grove, Oxford, Squire, Stieger, Wilson

Comments: The last scene of this opera was frequently introduced into Bellini's *Capuleti e Montecchi*. Score and libretto do not mention Shakespeare. Friedlaender: 3 acts.

Cast: CAPPELLIO, principale fra i Capelletti, e padre di [Sig.r Gio. B.a Verger] • GIULIETTA, amante di [Sig.a Gius.a Demeric] • ROMEO, capo dei Montecchi [Sig.a Adele Cesari] • ADELE, madre di Giulietta [Sig.a N.N.] • TEBALDO, partigiano de'Capelletti, destinato sposo a Giulietta [Sig.r Raffaele Benetti] • LORENZO, medico e famigliare di Capellio [Sig.r Luigi Biondini] •—• **Chorus:** CAPELLETTI, MONTECCHI, DAME, DAMIGELLE, SOLDATI, ARMIGERI

Malvina

Status: ?
Text: Rossi, Gaetano (1774-1855)
Type: Melodrammadi sentimento   **Acts:** 2
          Language: Italian
Premiere: Venice, Italy: Teatro di San Benedetto • 1816 06 08
Source of Premiere Information: Mellen
Play: *All's Well That Ends Well*

Cast: MALVINA [Signora Rosa Morands] • EUGENIO [Signor
Domenico Saini] • CONTE D'ORMONDO [Signor Manieri Remorini] •
JACOPO [Signor Luigi Pacini] • CARLOTTA [Signora Teresa
Bartolini] • GIANNINO [Signor Franc dal Medico] •—•
Chorus: PASTORI, VILLICI, SERVI DEL CONTE

Michael Valenti (1942-   )

Oh, Brother

Status: Y   **Evidence:** S
Text: Driver, Donald (book and lyrics)
Type: Broadway Show   **Language:** English
Premiere: New York, U.S.A.: ANTA Theater • 1981 11 10
Source of Premiere Information: Simas
Play: *Comedy of Errors*
Publisher: MacMusic Co. 1982 [s]
Yes: Simas

Comments: Simas: sources are *The Menaechmi* by Plautus and
The Comedy of Errors by Shakespeare (freely adapted).

Joaquín [Quinito] Valverde y San Juan (1875-1918)

El sueño de una noche de verano

Status: N   **Evidence:** S
Text: Merino, Gabriel (1862-1903) and Celsio Lucio
Type: Fantasia Cómico-Lirica [Zarzuela]   **Acts:** 1/5 Cuadros
     Language: Spanish
Premiere: Madrid, Spain: Teatro Eldorado • 1898 08 02
Source of Premiere Information: Libretto
Play: *Midsummer Night's Dream*
No: Characters, Plot

Cast: PROLOGO: • AQUILINO, PERENCEJO [Sr. Rodríguez] •
CUADRO PRIMERO: • EL VERANO [Srta. Díaz (Coral)] • LA
PRIMAVERA [Srta. Matrás] • EL INVIERNO [Srta. Mendez] • EL
OTOÑO [Srta. Espinosa] • AQUILINO [Sr. Rodríguez] • CUADRO
SEGUNDO: • EL VERANDO [Srta. Díaz (Coral)] • EL ABANICO [Sra.
Romero] • EL ARLEQUIN [Sra. Matrás] • LA PETRA [Sra. Romero] •
AQUILINO [Sr. Rodríguez] • UNO QUE SE QUEDA [Sr. Rodríguez] •
UNO QUE SE VA [Sr. Iglesias] • EL QUITASOL [Sr. García] • UN
COCHERO [Sr. Rodríguez] • UN MAYORAL [Sr. Fuentes] •
CONDUCTOR ELÉCTRICO [Sr. Barraycoa] • CHICAS FRESCAS
[Coro de Señoras] • HORCHATERAS [Coro de Señoras] • LOS DE
LA GARRAFA [Coro de Señoras] • LOS INGLESES [Coro de
Señoras] • CUADRO TERCERO: • CLARITA [Sra. Matrás] •
ENCARNACION [Sra. Correa] • LA JUANA [Sra. Díaz (M.) • LA PEPA
[Sra. Díaz (Carmen) • NIÑA 1.° [Sra. Plana] • IDEM 2.° [Sra. Tornos] •
FELIPIN [Sr. Barraycoa] • PEREZ [Sr. Ruiloa] • JULIO [Sr. Fuentes] •
MANOLO [Sr. Soler] • EL SR. JUAN [Sr. Las Santas] • POLLO 1.° [Sr.
Iglesias] • IDEM 2.° [Sr. Martínez] • CAMARERO 1.° [Sr. Abejar] •
IDEM 2.° [Sr. Miñona] • UN FOTÓGRAFO [Sr. Candela] • QUADRO
CUARTO: • EL VERANO [Srta. Díaz (Coral)] • LA DE SAN ANTONIO
[Srta. Matrás] • LA DE SAN JUAN [Srta. Méndez] • LA DE SAN
LORENZO [Srta. Espinosa] • LA DE LA PALOMA [Srta. Romero •
CELEDONIO [Sr. Rodríguez] • AGUILINO [Sr. Rodríguez] • CRISPIN
[Sr. Fuentes] •—•
Chorus: CUADRO PRIMERO: VENDIMIADORAS, FLORES
BAÑISTAS, SEÑORITAS ABRIGADAS, ETC. CUADRO TERCERO:
PARROQUIANOS, CORO GENERAL

Jimmy Van Heusen

Swingin' the Dream

Status: Y   **Evidence:** S
Type: Broadway Show   **Language:** English
Premiere: New York, U.S.A.: Center Theater • 1939 11 29
Source of Premiere Information: Bordman
Play: *Midsummer Night's Dream*
Yes: Bordman

Comments: Bordman: reset in 1890 Louisiana.

Cast: BOTTOM [Louis Armstrong] • PUCK [Butterfly McQueen] • QUINCE [Jackie "Moms" Mabley]

Ralph Vaughan Williams (1872-1958)

Sir John in Love

Status: Y   **Evidence:** P
Text: Composer
Type: Opera   **Acts:** 4 (7 scenes)   **Language:** English
Premiere: London, England: Royal College of Music • 1929 03 21
Source of Premiere Information: Loewenberg
Play: *Merry Wives of Windsor*
Publisher: London: Oxford University Press, 1930 [vs]
Yes: SCORE, Baker's, Blom, Groves V, Hartnoll, Loewenberg,
        Mellen, MGG, New Grove, Oxford, White

Cast: SHALLOW, a country Justice (Tenor or Baritone) • SIR HUGH EVANS, a Welsh parson (High Baritone) • SLENDER, a foolish young gentleman, Shallow's cousin (Tenor) • PETER SIMPLE, his servant (Tenor or Baritone) • PAGE, a citizen of Windsor (Baritone) • SIR JOHN FALSTAFF (Baritone) • BARDOLPH, sharper attending on Falstaff (Tenor) • NYM, sharper attending on Falstaff (Baritone) • PISTOL, sharper attending on Falstaff (Bass) • ANNE PAGE, Page's daughter (Soprano) • MRS. PAGE, Page's wife (Soprano) • MRS. FORD, Ford's wife (Mezzo Soprano) • FENTON, a young gentleman of the Court at Windsor (Tenor) • DR. CAIUS, a French physician (High Baritone) • RUGBY, his servant (Bass) • MRS. QUICKLY, his housekeeper (Mezzo Soprano or Contralto) • THE HOST OF THE

"GARTER INN" (Baritone) • ROBIN, Falstaff's page (Non-singing) • FORD, a citizen of Windsor (Bass) • JOHN, servant to Ford (Baritone) • ROBERT, servant to Ford (Baritone) • WILLIAM, Mrs. Page's son (Non-singing) • ALICE SHORTCAKE, Bardolph's sweetheart (Non-singing) • JENNY PLUCKPEARS, Nym's sweetheart (Non-singing) • BOY FRIENDS OF WILLIAM PAGE (Non-singing) • DANCERS [Act IV] • FLUTE PLAYER [Act IV] •— **Chorus:** GIRL FRIENDS OF ANNE PAGE, WOMEN SERVANTS OF FORD, CITIZENS OF WINDSOR, SERVANTS OF FORD AND PAGE

Francesco Maria Veracini (1690-1750)

Rosalinda

Status: Y   **Evidence:** P
Text: Rolli, Paolo Antonio (1687-1765)
Type: Melodrama   **Acts:** 3   **Language:** Italian
Premiere: London, England: King's Theatre in the Haymarket
    • 1744 01 31
Source of Premiere Information: Fiske
Play: *As You Like It*
Publisher: London: I. Walsh, 1744 [arias]
Yes: LIBRETTO: Blom, Fiske, Hartnoll, Mellen, New Grove, Oxford, Wilson

Comments: Groves V: title is *Roselinda.* Manferrari: Haymarket, autunno 1744. Fiske: distantly based on *As You Like It.* Characters and cast from Sartori.

Cast: ROSALINDA [Signora Visconti] • CELIA [Signora Nancini] • COSTANTE [Sig. Monticelli] • ERNESTO [Signora Frasi] • MARTANO [Signora Caselli] • SALVAGGIO [Sig. Fratesanti]

Giuseppe Verdi (1813-1901)

Falstaff

Status: Y   **Evidence:** P
Text: Boito, Arrigo (1842-1918)
Type: Commedia lirica   **Acts:** 3 (6 scenes)

Language: Italian
Premiere: Milan, Italy: Teatro alla Scala • 1893 02 09
Source of Premiere Information: Year and place from libretto.
Date from Loewenberg
Play: *Merry Wives of Windsor; Henry IV, Parts 1 and 2*
Publisher: Milan: G. Recordi, 1893 [vs]
Yes: LIBRETTO, Baker's, Blom, Friedlaender, Groves V, Hartnoll,
Loewenberg, New Grove, Oxford, Squire, Stieger, Wilson

Comments: Score does not mention Shakespeare.

Cast: SIR JOHN FALSTAFF (baritono) [Vittorio Maurel] • FORD,
marito d'Alice (baritono) [Antonio Pini-Corsi] • FENTON (Tenore)
[Edoardo Garbin] • DR. CAJUS (Tenore) [Giovanni Paroli] •
BARDOLFO (Tenore) [Paolo Pelagalli-Rossetti] • PISTOLA (Basso)
[Vittorio Arimondi] • MRS. ALICE FORD (Soprano) [Emma Zilli] •
NANNETTA [Anne], figlia d'Alice (Soprano) [Adelina Stehle] • MRS.
QUICKLY (Mezzosoprano) [Giuseppina Pasqua] • MRS. MEG PAGE
(Mezzosoprano) [Virginia Guerrini] • L'OSTE DELLA GIARRETTIERA
[Attilio Pulcini] • ROBIN, paggio di Falstaff • UN PAGGETTO DI FORD
Chorus: BORGHESI E POPOLANI, SERVI DI FORD

Lear

Status: Y   **Evidence:** S
Text: Unknown
Type: Sketched opera
Play: *Lear*
Yes: Blom, Groves V

Comments: Wilson: In the Athenaeum of June 8, 1912, occurs the
following passage: According to Le Ménestrel, a complete libretto of
King Lear in Verdi's handwriting has been discovered among his
papers, this confirms the report that he intended to write an opera on
the subject.

Macbeth

Status: Y   **Evidence:** P
Text: Piave, Francesco Maria (1810-1876) and Andrea Maffei
Type: Melodramma   **Acts:** 4 (10 scenes)   **Language:** Italian
Premiere: Florence, Italy: Teatro di via della Pergola • 1847 03 14
Source of Premiere Information: Loewenberg

Play: *Macbeth*
Publisher: Milan: G. Recordi, 1847 [vs]
Yes: SCORE, LIBRETTO, Baker's, Blom, Friedlaender, Groves V,
   Hartnoll, Loewenberg, New Grove, Oxford, Squire, Stieger,
   Wilson

Comments: French libretto by C. Nuitter and A. Beaumont. New
Grove: after Shakespeare's play and Shiller's German version.
Schatz MS does not mention Maffei. Cast from Osborne.

Cast: DUNCANO, Re di Scozia • MACBETH, Generale dell'escrito
del Re Duncano (Baritono) [Felice Varesi] • BANCO, Generale
dell'escrito del Re Duncano (Basso profondo) [Michele Benedetti] •
LADY MACBETH, moglie di Macbeth (Prima donna Soprano)
[Marianna Barbieri-Nini] • DAMA, di Lady Macbeth (Seconda Donna) •
MACDUFF, nobile Scozzese, Signore di Fiff (Primo Tenore)
[Brunacci] • MALCOLM, figlio di Duncano (Secondo Tenore) •
FLEANZIO, figlio di Banco • DOMESTICO, di Macbeth (Corifeo
Basso) • MEDICO (Secondo Basso) • SICARIO (Corifeo Basso) • LE
APPARIZIONI • L'OMBRA DI BANCO •—•
Chorus: STREGHE, MESSAGGERI DEL RE, NOBILI E PROFUGHI
SCOZZESI, SICARII, SOLDATI INGLESI, SPIRITI AEREI

Otello

Status: Y   **Evidence:** S
Text: Boito, Arrigo (1824-1918)
Type: Dramma lirico   **Acts:** 4   **Language:** Italian
Premiere: Milan, Italy: Teatro alla Scala • 1887 02 05
Source of Premiere Information: Year and place from libretto.
   Date from Loewenberg.
Play: *Othello*
Publisher: Milan: G. Recordi, 1887 [vs]
Yes: Baker's, Blom, Friedlaender, Groves V, Hartnoll, Loewenberg,
   New Grove, Oxford, Schatz MS, Squire, Stieger, Wilson

Comments: Score and libretto do not mention Shakespeare.

Cast: OTELLO, moro, generale dell'Armata Veneta (Tenore)
[Francesco Tamagno] • JAGO, alfiere (Baritono) [Vittorio Maurel] •
CASSIO, capo di squadra (Tenore) [Giovanni Paroli] • RODERIGO,
gentiluomo Veneziano (Tenore) [Vincenzo Fornari] • LODOVICO,
ambasciatore della Repubblica Veneta (Basso) [Francesco Navarrini]
• MONTANO, predecessore d'Otello nel governo dell'isola di Cipro

(Tenore) [Napoleone Limonta] • UN ARALDO (Tenore) [Angelo Lagomarsino] • DESDEMONA, moglie d'Otello (Soprano) [Romilda Pantaleoni] • EMILIA, moglie di Jago (Mezzosoprano) [Ginevra Petrovich] •——•
Chorus: SOLDATI E MARINAI DELLA REPUBBLICA VENETA; GENTILDONNE E GENTILNOMINI VENEZIANI; POPOLANI CIPRIOTTI D'AMBO I SESSI; UOMINI D'ARME GRECI, DALMATI, ALBANESI; FANCIULLI DELL'ISOLA; UN TAVERNIERE; QUATTRO SERVI DI TAVERNA; BASSA CIURMA

Paul Antonin Vidal (1863-1931)

Comme il vous Plaire

Status: ?
Text: Shakespeare
Type: Pastorale
Premiere: Paris, France: Théâtre Shakespeare • 1912 03 21
Play: *As You Like It*

Peines d'amour perdues

Status: Y   **Evidence:** S
Text: Unknown
Type: Comédie   **Acts:** 4
Premiere: Paris, France: Fémina • 1911 03 03
Play: *Love's Labour's Lost*
Yes: Stieger

Giuseppe Vignali [Act I], Carlo Baglioni [Act II], and Giacomo Cozzi [Act III]

Ambleto

Status: N   **Evidence:** S
Text: Zeno, Apostolo (1668-1750) and Pietro Pariati (1665-1733)
Type: Dramma per musica   **Acts:** 3   **Language:** Italian
Premiere: Milan, Italy: Regio Ducal Teatro • 1719 08 27
Source of Premiere Information: Mellen

Play: *Hamlet*
No: Schatz MS

Comments: New Groves: 1719 08 28. Manferrari: 1719 08 27.

Piere Jean de Volder (1767-1841)

La Jeunesse de Henri Cinq

Status: ?
Text: Unknown
Type: Opera   **Acts:** 3   **Language:** French
Premiere: Gent, Belgium • 1810 00 00
Source of Premiere Information: Mellen
Play: *Henry V*

Comments: Stieger: *Henri IV*.

Pavel Vranicky [Paul Wranitzky (Wraniczky)] (1756-1808)

Oberon, König der Elfen

Status: N   **Evidence:** P
Text: Seyler, Friederike Sophie (1738-1789)
Type: Romantisches Singspiel   **Acts:** 3
          Language: German
Premiere: Frankfurt A/M, Germany: Nationaltheater • 1790 10 15
Source of Premiere Information: Sonneck
Play: *Midsummer Night's Dream*
Publisher: Worms: J. M. Goetz, 1795? [vs]
No: LIBRETTO

Comments: Libretto: nach Wieland *[Oberon]*. Vocal score and libretto do not mention Shakespeare. Mellen: libretto by K. L. Gieseke.

Cast: OBERON, König der Elfen • TITANIA, Königen der Feen, seine Gattin • HÜON, ein deutscher Ritter • SCHERASMIN, sein Schildknappe • DER SULTAN VON BAGDAD • AMANDE, seine

Tochter • BABEKAN, Fürst der Drusen, ihr Bräutigam • JATINE, ihre Vertraute • ALMANSOR, Bassa von Tunis • ALMANSARIS, seine erste Sultanin • OSMIN, ein Verschnittener • EIN KADI • BALFIS, ein Sklavin • DAS ORAKEL • ZWEI GENIEN •—• **Chorus:** FEEN, DERVISCHE, HOCHZEITGÄSTE, JANITSCHAREN UND MOHREN

Rudolf von Felseck (Die Schwarzthaler) oder La Tempestà

Status: I   **Evidence:** S
Text: Korompay, J.
Type: Singspiel
Premiere: Vienna, Austria: Burgtheater • 1792 10 06
Source of Premiere Information: MGG
Play: *Tempest*
Yes: Squire
No: Stieger

Comments: Stieger: it is incidental music; Schauspiel, Linz 1794 09 09.

Victor Vreuls (1876-1944)

Un songe d'une nuit d'été

Status: Y   **Evidence:** P
Text: Spaak, Paul
Type: Comédie féerique   **Acts:** 3/4 tableaux
     Language: French
Premiere: Brussels, Belgium: Théâtre Royal de la Monnaie • 1925 12 17
Source of Premiere Information: Score
Play: *Midsummer Night's Dream*
Publisher: Brussels: A. Cranz, 1934 [vs]
Yes: SCORE, Baker's, Blom, Hartnoll, Loewenberg, Mellen, Oxford, Stieger

Comments: Manferrari: com. 1 a.

Cast: THÉSÉE, duc d'Athènes (Baryton) [M. L. Richard] • HIPPOLYTE, reine des amazones (Soprano) [Mme R. Laudy] •

LYSANDRE (Ténor) [M. E. Gallins] • DÉMÉTRIUS (Baryton) [M. E.
Colonne] • HERMIA (Mezzo-soprano) [Mme Y. Andry] • HÉLÈNE
(Soprano) [Mme Lina Bianchini] • ÉGÉE, père d'Hermia (Basse) [M.
M. Demoulin] • TITANIA, reine des fées (Soprano) [Mme Cl. Clairbert]
• PUCK OU ROBIN BON ENFANT (Soprano) [Melle L. Mertens] •
OBÉRON, roi des Elfes (Ténor) [M. M. Claudel] • FLEUR DES POIS
(Soprano) [Melle L Mertens] • GRAIN DE MOUTARDE (Soprano)
[Melle Dupont] • TOILE D'ARAIGNÉE (Mezzo-soprano) [Melle Perret]
• PHALÈNE (Contralto) [Melle Duquesne] • CULASSE, tisserand
(Baryton) [M. A. Boyer] • GROIN, chaudronnier (Ténor) [M. L.
Maudier] • COING, charpentier (Ténor) [M. H. Dognies] • JOINT,
menuisier (Ténor) [M. J. Salès] • FLUTE, raccommodeur de soufflets
Basse [M. H. Raidich] • L'AFFAMÉ, tailleur (Baryton) [M. F. Deckers]
Chorus: SERVITEURS DE THÉSÉE ET D'HIPPOLYTE,
CHASSEURS ET CHASSERESSES, GARDES ET GENS DE
PEUPLE, FÉES, LUTINS ET SYLPHES DE LA SUITE D'OBÉRON
ET DE TITANIA.

Wilhelm Richard Wagner (1813-1883)

Das Liebesverbot oder Die Novize von Palermo

Status: Y   **Evidence:** S
Text: Composer
Type: Gross Komische Oper   **Acts:** 2   **Language:** German
Premiere: Magdeburg, Germany: Stadttheater • 1836 03 29
Source of Premiere Information: Loewenberg
Play: *Measure for Measure*
Publisher: Leipzig: Breitkoph & Härtel, 1922 [vs]
Yes: Baker's, Blom, Friedlaender, Groves V, Hartnoll, Loewenberg,
    Mellen, MGG, New Grove, Oxford, Schatz MS, Stieger,
    Wilson

Comments: Characters from score. Cast from Culshaw. Sources
disagree on which roles some of the cast performed [see WWV,
p.131].

Cast: FRIEDRICH, ein Deutscher, in Abwesenheit des Königs
Statthalter von Sizilien (Baß) [Hr. Gräfe] • LUZIO, ein junger
Edelmann (Tenor) [Hr. Freimuller] • CLAUDIO, ein junger Edelmann
(Tenor) [Hr. Schreiber] • ANTONIO, Freund von Luzio und Claudio
(Tenor) [unknown] • ANGELO, Freunde von Luzio und Claudio (Baß)
[Friedrich Krug] • ISABELLA, Claudios Schwester, Novize im Kloster

der Elisabethinerinnen (Sopran) [Caroline Pollert] • MARIANA, Novize im Kloster der Elisabethinerinnen (Sopran) [Fr. Limbach (or Schindler)] • BRIGHELLA, Chef der Sbirren (Baß buffo) [Wilhelm Kneisel] • DANIELI, Wirt eines Weinhauses (Baß) [unknown] • DORELLA, früher Isabellas Kammermädchen, in Danielis Diensten (Sopran) [Fr. Schindler (or Limbach)] • PONTIO PILATO, in Danielis Diensten (Tenor buffo) [unknown] •—• **Chorus:** GERICHTSHERREN, SBIRREN, EINWOHNER JEDES STANDES VON PALERMO, VOLK, MASKEN, EIN MUSIKKORPS

Sir William Walton (1902-1983)

Troilus and Cressida

Status: N   **Evidence:** S
Text: Hassell, Christopher Vernon (1912-)
Type: Opera   **Acts:** 3   **Language:** English
Premiere: London, England: Covent Garden • 1954 12 03
Source of Premiere Information: Mellen
Play: *Troilus and Cressida*
Publisher: London: Oxford University Press, 1956 [vs]
No: New Grove

Comments: New Grove: based on Chaucer, not Shakespeare. White: originally commissioned by the B.B.C.

Cast: CALKAS, High Priest of Pallas (Bass) • ANTENOR, Captain of Trojan Spears (Baritone) • TROILUS, Prince of Troy (Tenor) • PANDARUS, Brother of Calkas (Tenor buffo) • CRESSIDA, Daughter of Calkas, a widow (Soprano) • EVADNE, Servant of Cressida (Mezzo-soprano) • HORASTE, A friend of Pandarus (Baritone) • DIOMEDE, Prince of Argos (Baritone) • A PRIEST (Bass) • FIRST SOLDIER (Tenor) • SECOND SOLDIER (Bass) • LADIES IN ATTENDANCE ON CRESSIDA (2 Sopranos, 2 Contraltos) •—• **Chorus:** PRIESTS AND PRIESTESSES OF PALLAS, TROJANS, GREEKS

William Henry Ware

Cymbeline

Status: NO   **Evidence:** S
Premiere: London, England • 1808 00 00
Play: *Cymbeline*
No: Stieger

Comments: Stieger: it is incidental music. The British Library: The much admired Overture to *Cymbeline* pub by W. Hodsoll of London where may be had by the same Author, the Act Symphonies to the above, The Overture and Act Symphonies to *Macbeth* and *Coriolanus* and the Overture & Airs to *Mother Goose.*

Macbeth

Status: NO   **Evidence:** P
Premiere: London, England • 1806 00 00
Source of Premiere Information: Stieger
Play: *Macbeth*
No: SCORE

Comments: Score: The music in *Macbeth* [incidental music]. Vocal part by Locke.

Carl Maria von Weber (1786-1826)

Euryanthe

Status: N   **Evidence:** S
Text: Chézy, Helmina von (1783-1856)
Type: Grose romantische Oper   **Acts:** 3 (6 scenes)
        Language: German
Premiere: Vienna, Austria: Kärntnertortheater • 1823 10 25
Source of Premiere Information: Loewenberg
Play: *Cymbeline*
Publisher: Vienna: S. A. Steiner und Comp., 1824 [vs]
No: Schatz MS

Comments: See sources of the libretto in Groves V. Schatz MS: taken from *La Violette* or *Histoire de Gérard de Nevers et de la belle et virtueuse Euryanthe de Savoye, sa vie* by Gilbert or Gybers [sp?] de Montreuil [sp?] Dichtung von Helmine von Chezy, geborne Freyin von Klencke. Mellen: produced as *Die seiben Raben,* with text revised by H. J. Moser, Darmstadt, Landestheater, 1922 02 02.

Cast: KÖNIG LUDWIG DER VI (Baß) [Hr. Seipelt] • ADOLAR, Graf zu Nevers und Rethel (Tenor) [Hr. Haizinger] • EURYANTHE VON SAVOYEN, seine Braut (Sopran) [Dlle. Sonntag] • LYSIART, Graf von Forest und Beaujolois (Bariton) [Hr. Forti] • EGLANTINE VON TUISET, die gefangene Tochter eines Empörers (Mezzosopran) [Mad. Grünbaum] • RUDOLPH (Tenor) [Hr. Rauscher] • BERTHA (Sopran) [Dell. Teimer] •—• **Chorus:** HERZOGE, FÜRSTEN, GRAFEN, EDLE, DAMEN, EDELKNABEN, RITTER, GEWAPPNETE UND BURGBEWOHNER ZU NEVERS, LANDLEUTE

Oberon [or the Elf-King's Oath]

Status: N   **Evidence:** P
Text: Planché, James Robinson (1796-1880)
Type: Romantische Feenoper   **Acts:** 3 (10 scenes)
        Language: English
Premiere: London, England: Covent Garden • 1826 04 12
Source of Premiere Information: Mellen
Play: *Midsummer Night's Dream*
Publisher: Berlin: A. M. Schlesinger's Buch-und-Musikhandlung, 1826 [vs]
Yes: Groves V
No: LIBRETTO, Schatz MS

Comments: Has no closer link with Shakespeare than a quarrel between Oberon and Titania. Libretto: based on William Sotheby's translation of Wieland's *Oberon* and farther back, on the French romance of *Huon de Bordeaux.* Clément gives information about the opera.

Cast: CHARLEMAGNE, Emperor of the Franks (Speaking Part) [Mr. Franks] • SIR HUON OF BORDEAUX, Duke of Guienne (Tenor) [Mr. Braham] • SHERASMIN, his squire (Baritone) [Mr. Fawcett] • HAROUN ALRASHID, Caliph (Speaking Part) [Mr. Chapman] • BABEKAN, a Saracen Prince (Speaking Part) [Mr. Baker]FATIMA, her attendant (Mezzo-Soprano) [Mme. Vestris] • ALMANZOR, Emir of Tunis (Speaking Part) [Mr. Cooper] • FIRST SARACEN [Mr. Evans]A

SEA NYMPH (Soprano) • SECOND SARACEN [Mr. Atkins] • THIRD
SARACEN [Mr. Ryals] • FOURTH SARACEN [Mr. Tinney] •
ABDULLAH, a Corsair (Speaking Part) [Mr. Horrebow] • OBERON,
King of the Faries (Tenor) [Mr. C. Bland] • PUCK (Soprano) [Miss H.
Cawse] • FAIRY [Mr. Henry] • NEGRO SLAVE [Mr. Griffiths] •
CAPTAIN OF A VESSEL [Mr. Issacs] • SEA NYMPH [Miss Goward] •
TITANIA, Queen of the Fairies (Speaking Part) [Miss Smith] • REIZA
[Rezia in German versions], daughter of Haroun el Rashid (Soprano)
[Miss Paton] • ROSHANA, wife of Almanzor (Speaking Part) [Miss
Lacy] • NAMOUNA, Fatima's grandmother (Speaking Part) [Mrs.
Davenport] • NADINA, a female of Almanzor's harem (Speaking Part)
[Mrs. Wilson] •—• **Chorus:** FAIRIES, MERMAIDS, SLAVES,
FOLLOWERS OF THE CALIPH, DANCING GIRLS, ETC.

Jean Baptiste Théodore Weckerlin

Tout est bien qui finit bien

Status: ?
Text: Malherbe, Jules
Type: Opera comique   **Acts:** 1   **Language:** French
Premiere: Paris, France: Théâtre au Palais des Tuileries
          • 1856 02 28
Source of Premiere Information: Schatz MS
Play: *All's Well That Ends Well*

Comments: Stieger: Palais Tailbout, 1856 02 18.

Joseph Weigl [Giuseppe Veigl] (1766-1846)

Amleto

Status: Y   **Evidence:** S
Text: Unknown
Type: Melodrama
Premiere: Vienna, Austria: Theater im Palais der Fürstin
          Lubonsirsky [Sp?] • 1794 00 00
Play: *Hamlet*

Yes: Blom, Friedlaender

Comments: Friedlaender: Vienna, about 1810.

Karél Weis [Weiss] (1862-1944)

Comme il vous Plaira

Status: ?
Text: Unknown
Type: Commedia   **Acts:** 2
Premiere: Prague, Czechoslovakia: Czech National Theater
    • 1892 00 00
Play: *As You Like It*

Viola [Die Zwillinge, Blizenci]

Status: Y   **Evidence:** P
Text: Adler, B. (with R. Schubert and V. Novohradsky)
Type: Comic Opera   **Acts:** 3   **Language:** Czech
Premiere: Prague, Czechoslovakia: Czech National Theater
    • 1892 01 17
Source of Premiere Information: Loewenberg
Play: *Twelfth Night*
Publisher: Prag: Em. Stary, c.1890 [vs]
Yes: SCORE, LIBRETTO, Baker's, Blom, Friedlaender, Groves V,
    Hartnoll, Loewenberg, New Grove, Oxford, Stieger

Comments: Clément lists it as *Was ihr Wöllt.* Manferrari: autunno 1897. Groves V: this is his first opera; Later titles *Die Zwillinge* in German and *Blizenci [The Twins]* in Czech.

Cast: SEBASTIAN, ein junger Edelmann (Tenor) • VIOLA, seine Schwester (Jugendl. dramat. Sopran) • OLIVIA, eine reiche Gräfin (Jugendl. dramat. Sopran) • ORSINO, Herzog von Illyrien (Bariton) • ANDREAS VON BLEICHWANG (Spieltenor) • MALVOLIO, Olivias Haushofmeister (I. Bass-Buffo) • TOBIAS VON RÜLP, Olivias Oheim (Bariton) • MARIA, Kammermädchen, im Dienste Olivias (Soubrette) • NARR, im Dienste Olivias (II. Bass-Buffo) • ANTONIO, ein Seemann (Bass oder Bariton) • LORENZO, ein Schiffshauptmann (Bass oder Bariton) • EIN HAUPTMANN DER WACHE (Tenor) •—
Chorus: WACHE, DIENERSCHAFT DER OLIVIA, FISCHER,

ALLERLEI VOLK, STADTLEUTE, MATROSEN, VERKÄUFER UND VERKÄUFERINNEN

Hugo Weisgall (1912-   )

The Gardens of Adonis

Status: Y   **Evidence:** S
Text: Olon-Scrymgeour, John
Type: Opera   **Acts:** Prologue/2 Scenes
    Language: English
Premiere: 1974 00 00
Play: *Venus and Adonis* [Poem]
Publisher: New York: American Music Center [vs, l]
Yes: AMCL

Henry IV

Status: ?
Text: Unknown
Type: Opera   **Language:** English
Play: *Henry IV*

Comments: Mellen: based on Pirandello.

Niccolò van Westerhout [Van Westerhout] (1857-1898)

Il Cimbelino

Status: Y   **Evidence:** S
Text: Golisciani, Enrico (1848-1918)
Type: Dramma lirico   **Acts:** 4   **Language:** Italian
Premiere: Rome, Italy: Teatro Argentino • 1892 04 07
Source of Premiere Information: Libretto
Play: *Cymbeline*
Yes: Oxford, Schatz MS

Comments: See Baker's. *Oxford Dictionary* gives incorrect composer. Manferrari: dr. lir. 4 a. Stieger, Mellen: a private performance was given in Naples in Dec. 1887. Schatz MS: Representato la prima volta in Sala [sp?] particolare in Napoli il ... XI 1887. Libretto does not mention Shakespeare.

Cast: CIMBELINO, re di Britannia [Giuseppe Rapp] • LA REGINA [Giulia Sporeni] • IMOGENE, figlio in primo letto del re [Elvira Colonnese] • CLOTENO, figlio in primo letto della regina [Vittorina Fabbri] • LEONATO POSTUMO, duce britanno [Benedetto Lucignani] • JACHIMO, duce romano [Leone Fumagalli] • CAJO LUCIO, legato romano [Costantino Caldani] • PISANIO, vecchio confidente di Leonato [Francesco Niccoletti] • L'ARCHIDRUIDO [Costantino Caldani] • UN'ANCELLA D'IMOGENE •—•
Chorus: DUCI, GUERRIERI, BARDI, DRUIDE E DONNE BRITANNE, CENTURIONI, LEGIONARI E NOCCHIERI ROMANI, ANCELLE, PASTORI

Christoph Ernst Friedrich Weyse (1774-1842)

Macbeth

Status: NO **Evidence:** S
Premiere: Copenhagen, Denmark • 1817 00 00
Source of Premiere Information: Stieger
Play: *Macbeth*
Publisher: Copenhagen: C. C. Lose, 1829 [vs]
No: CU Catalog, Stieger

Comments: Title: Musik zu dem Trauerspiele *Macbeth.* It is incidental music.

John Whitaker (1776-1847)

The Weird Sisters or The Thane and the Throne

Status: Y **Evidence:** S
Text: Unknown
Type: Pantomime **Language:** English
Premiere: London, England: Sadler's Wells Theatre • 1819 04 12

Play: *Macbeth*
Yes: Groves V

Comments: Groves V: In it occurred the famous clown's song "Hot Codlins," written for Grimaldi.

Adolf Wiedeke

Die lustigen Weiber von Hamburg

Status: ?
Text: Shafer, Fritz
Acts: 5
Premiere: Hamburg, Germany: Ernst Druker Theater • 1898 10 15
Source of Premiere Information: Schatz MS
Play: *Merry Wives of Windsor*

James Wilson

Twelfth Night

Status: Y   **Evidence:** S
Text: Unknown
Language: English
Premiere: Wexford, England • 1969 11 01
Source of Premiere Information: Mellen
Play: *Twelfth Night*
Yes: Mellen, Northouse

Peter von Winter (1754-1825)

Der Sturm

Status: Y   **Evidence:** S
Text: Caspar, Franz Xaver von (1772-1833)
Type: Komishe Oper   **Acts:** 2   **Language:** German
Premiere: Munich, Germany: National Schau. in alt. Opernhaus)
      • 1798 10 19

Source of Premiere Information: Date from Friedlaender.
   Place from Stieger.
Play: *Tempest*
Publisher: G: DS
Yes: LIBRETTO, Friedlaender, Hartnoll, Mellen, MGG, New Grove,
   Oxford, Schatz MS, Squire, Stieger

Comments: New Grove, MGG., Mellen, Stieger: 1798. Manferrari:
(Caspar) com. 3 a. Monaco di B., Tr. Reale, anno 1793. Schatz MS:
1793 10 00; indicates the libretto is based on Doring's libretto. D-
brd:Mbs catalog: Nach Shakespeare bearbitet von Anton Bergh.
LIBRETTO GB:Lbm: bearbeitet von J. W. D.

Cast: PROSPERO, rechmäsiger Herzog von Mayland • MIRANDA,
dessen Tochter • ANTONIO, dessen Bruder und unrechtmäßiger
Besitzer von Mayland • FERDINAND, Sohn des Königs von Neapel •
ARIEL, eine Sylphe • KALABAN, ein wilder mißgeschaffener Sklave
• TRINKULO, ein Hofnarr •—• **Chorus:** SCHIFFLEUTE, GEISTER

Franz Wödl (1899-   )

Komödie der Irrungen

Status: Y   **Evidence:** S
Text: Gugg, Roland
Type: Opera   **Acts:** 5   **Language:** German
Premiere: Beuthen • 1941 03 21
Play: *Comedy of Errors*
Yes: Gruber

Ernst Wilhelm Wolf (1735-1792)

Die Zauberirrungen [Die Irrtümer der Zauberei]

Status: Y   **Evidence:** S
Text: Einsiedel, Friedrich Hildebrand von (1750-1828)
Type: Schauspiel   **Acts:** 2   **Language:** German
Premiere: Weimar, Germany: Comödienhaus • 1785 10 24
Play: *Midsummer Night's Dream*
Yes: Blom, Hartnoll, Mellen, Oxford, Schatz MS

Ermanno Wolf-Ferrari (1876-1948)

Sly, ovvero La leggenda del dormiente risvegliato

Status: Y **Evidence:** S
Text: Forzano, Giovacchino (1883-1970)
Type: Dramma Lirico **Acts:** 3 **Language:** Italian
Premiere: Milan, Italy: Teatro alla Scala • 1927 12 29
Source of Premiere Information: Mellen
Play: *Taming of the Shrew*
Publisher: Milan: Casa Musicale Sonzogno, 1928 [vs]
Yes: Blom, Groves V, Mellen, New Grove, Oxford

Comments: Oxford: based on the introduction to the play only.
Stieger: Gioacchino Forzano. Score does not mention
Shakespeare.

Cast: SLY • DOLLY • IL CONTE DI WESTMORELAND • GLI AMICI
DEL CONTE • JOHN PLAKE, attore del Teatro Blakfriars • SNARE,
agente dello sceriffo • L'OSTESSA • IL GIUDICE CAMPESTRE •
ROSALINA • UN SOLDATO • UN VETTURALE • IL CUOCO • IL
GARZONE •—• **Chorus:** PAGGI, BEONI, AVVENTORI DELLA
TAVERNA, SERVI DEL CONTE

Kurt von Wolfurt (1880-1957)

Porzia

Status: ?
Text: Unknown
Play: *Merchant of Venice*

Comments: Gruber: not performed.

Mario Zafred (1922-   )

Amleto

Status: Y   **Evidence:** P
Text: Composer and Lilyan E. M. Zafred
Type: Opera   **Acts:** 3 (9 scenes)   **Language:** Italian
Premiere: Rome, Italy: Teatro dell'Opera • 1961 01 07
Source of Premiere Information: Libretto
Play: *Hamlet*
Publisher: Milan: G. Ricordi 1960 [vs]
Yes: SCORE, LIBRETTO, Hartnoll, Mellen, MGG, New Grove

Comments: Mellen: 1961 01 09.

Cast: AMLETO (Baritono) [Antonio Boyer] • RE (Tenore) [Luigi
Infantino] • REGINA (Contralto) [Anna Maria Rota] • OFELIA
(Soprano) [Maria di Giovanna] • LAERTE (Tenore) [Gastone Limarilli] •
ORAZIO (Tenore) [Agostino Lazzari] • SPETTRO (Basso) [Paolo Dari]
• POLONIO, BECCHINO (Basso) [Carlo Cava] • ATTRICE: RE
(Contralto) [Adelio Zagonara] • ATTRICE: REGINA (Soprano) [Valeria
Mariconda] • ATTORE: PROLOGO (Tenore) [Sergio Tedesco] •
ATTORE: LUCIANO (Tenore) [Enzo Tei] • OSRIC (Tenore) [Sergio
Tedesco] • MARCELLO (Tenore) [Sergio Tedesco] • PRETE
(Tenore) [Enzo Tei] • ROSENCRANTZ (Tenore) [Ero Schiano] •
GUILDENSTERN (Basso) [Roberto Sommer] • BERNARDO (Basso)
[Alfredo Colella]

Ivan Zajc (1832-1914)

Cordelia

Status: ?
Text: Unknown
Type: com.   **Acts:** 1
Premiere: Zagreb, Yugoslavia: Tr. d'Opera • 1901 00 00
Play: *Lear*

Benedict Emanuel Zák [Cziak, Schak, Schak, Schack] (1758-1826)

Dem Stein der Weisen oder Die Zauber Insel

Status: ?
Text: Schikaneder, Emanuel [originally Johann Schikeneder]
 (1751-1812)
Type: Heroisch-komische oper   **Acts:** 2
  Language: German
Premiere: Vienna, Austria: Theater auf der Wieden • 1790 09 11
Source of Premiere Information: Mellen
Play: *Tempest*

Cast: ASTROMONTE, Halbgott • EUTIFRONTE • GENIUS • SADIF,
Oberpriester • NADIR, sein Ziehsohn • NADINE, seine Tochter •
LUBANO, Aufseher der Wälder • LUBANARA, dessen Weib •—•
Chorus: SCHÄFER, SCHÄFERINNEN, JÄGER, UNTERIRDISCHE
GEISTER, KLAGEWEIBER

Angelo Zanardini (1820-1893)

Amleto

Status: Y   **Evidence:** S
Text: Composer
Type: Tragedia lirica   **Acts:** 4   **Language:** Italian
Premiere: Venice, Italy: Teatro Gallo a San Benedetto • 1854 05 30
Source of Premiere Information: Year and place from libretto.
  Day from Mellen.
Play: *Hamlet*
Yes: Mellen, Oxford, Stieger

Comments: Libretto does not mention Shakespeare.

Cast: ALSTANO, Conte di Elsinoro [Filippo Coletti] • ADELIA, sua
moglie e madre di [Marietta Spezia] • AMLETO [Giovanni Landi] •
OFELIA, amante d'Amleto [Luigia Morselli] • ORAZIO, amico d'Amleto
[Antonio Galetti] • LO SPETTRO DEL CONTE AMLETO, padre di
Amleto [N. N.] •—•
Chorus: UOMINI D'ARMI, CORTIGIANI E DAMIGELLE

Riccardo Zandonai (1883-1944)

Giulietta e Romeo

Status: Y   **Evidence:** S
Text: Rossato, Arturo (1882-1942)
Type: Tragedia   **Acts:** 3   **Language:** Italian
Premiere: Rome, Italy: Teatro Costanzi • 1922 02 14
Source of Premiere Information: Loewenberg
Play: *Romeo and Juliet*
Publisher: Milan: G. Ricordi, 1922 [vs]
Yes: Blom, Groves V, Hartnoll, Loewenberg, Mellen, MGG, New
        Grove, Oxford, Stieger

Comments: Libretto after da Porta and Shakespeare. Score and
libretto do not mention Shakespeare.

Cast: GIULIETTA CAPULETO • ROMEO MONTECCHIO •
ISABELLA, fante di Giulietta • TEBALDO, il Capuleto • IL
CANTATORE • GREGORIO, uomo dei Capuleti • SANSONE, uomo
dei Capuleti • BERNABO • UN MONTECCHIO • UN FAMIGLIO DI
ROMEO • UNA DONNA • UN BANDITORE •——•
Chorus: MONTECCHI, CAPULETI, FANTI, MASCHERE

Antonio Zanettini [Gianettini, Zanetti] (1648-1721)

Érmione [Die wiedergefundene Hermione]

Status: N   **Evidence:** S
Text: Aureli, Aurelio
Type: Dramma per musica   **Acts:** 3/Prologue
        Language: German
Premiere: Wolfenbüttel, Germany: Fürstlich Theater im Schlosse
        • 1686 02 11
Source of Premiere Information: Schatz MS
Play: *Winter's Tale*
No: Riemann

Comments: Riemann: Ermonie is the daughter of Menalaus and
Helen just as in Bernabei's Érmione. Manferrari: Ermoine
Riacquistato (V. Terzago) dr. 3 a., Amburgo, Tr. di Corte, anno 1695.

Antonio B. Zanon

La Leggenda di Giulietta

Status: Y   **Evidence:** S
Text: Spiritini, Massimo
Type: Opera   **Acts:** 1   **Language:** Italian
Premiere: Bergamo, Italy: Teatro Donizetti • 1969 10 22
Source of Premiere Information: Mellen
Play: *Romeo and Juliet*
Yes: Mellen, Oxford

Felix Zavodsky

Othello

Status: Y   **Evidence:** S
Text: Composer and Friedrich Langer
Type: Opera   **Acts:** 3   **Language:** German
Premiere: Vienna, Austria: Studio der Hochschulen • 1945 06 14
Source of Premiere Information: Mellen
Play: *Othello*
Yes: Mellen, Oxford

Jan Evangelista Zelinka (1893-1969)

Spring With Shakespeare

Status: AP   **Evidence:** S
Text: Kosta, P.
Type: Opera
Premiere: 1955 00 00
Play: *Other*
Yes: Oxford

Comments: New Grove: *Jaro u Shakespeara (Spring in Shakespeare).*

Marc Antonio Ziani (c.1653-1715)

La Rosalinda or Erginia mascherata

Status: N   **Evidence:** S
Text: Marchi, Antonio
Type: Dramma per Musica   **Acts:** 3   **Language:** Italian
Premiere: Venice, Italy: Theatro di San Angiolo • 1692 11 11
Source of Premiere Information: Year and place from libretto.
    Day from Mellen.
Play: *As You Like It*
No: Squire

Comments: Author's dedication in libretto is dated 1692 11 11.
Manferrari, Schatz MS: 1692 11 11. Libretto does not mention
Shakespeare.

Cast: ROSALINDA, Amante di Lealdo • LEALDO, Amante di
Rosalinda • AMET, Rè di Tunisi • LAURINDO, suo Figlio • FLORI, figlia
di Amurat, Bassà di Rodi, Amante di Laurindo • ZELISSA, Incantatrice
• GUSMANO, Corsaro • AMURAT, Bassà di Rodi • GRINO, Servo

Winfried Zillig (1905-1963)

Troilus und Cressida

Status: Y   **Evidence:** P
Text: Composer
Type: Oper   **Acts:** 6 Choruses/6 Scenes
    Language: German
Premiere: Düsseldorf, Germany: Stadttheater • 1951 02 03
Source of Premiere Information: Mellen
Play: *Troilus and Cressida*
Publisher: Wiesbaden: Brucknerverlag, 1950 [vs]
Yes: SCORE, Hartnoll, Mellen, MGG, New Grove, Oxford

Comments: New Grove: opera revised 1963. Gruber: 3 acts.

Cast: TROILUS (Bariton) • ACHILLES (Tenor) • PANDARUS (Tenor)
• TERSITES (Baß-Bariton) • EIN HEROLD (Baß) • CRESSIDA
(Sopran) • KASSANDRA (Alt) • HELENA (Sopran) •——•
Chorus: AENEAS, PARIS, HEKTOR UND TROJANISCHE

KRIEGER; MÄDCHEN AUS DEM GEFOLGE HELENAS;
KÄMPFENDE GRIECHEN UND TROJANER; MYRMIDONEN AUS
DEM GEFOLGE DES ACHILLES

Balduin Zimmermann (1867-1948)

Ein Wintermärchen

Status: Y **Evidence:** P
Text: Composer
Type: Musikalisches Schauspiel **Acts:** 4
Language: German
Premiere: Erfurt, Germany: Stadttheater • 1900 03 11
Source of Premiere Information: Mellen
Play: *Winter's Tale*
Publisher: Erfurt: 1900.
Yes: LIBRETTO, Gruber, Mellen, Oxford, Stieger

Comments: Stieger: 3 acts, *Das Wintermärchen*. Manferrari: 2 acts.

Cast: LEONTES, König von Sizilien (Tenor) • MAMILIUS, kleiner
Prinz von Sizilien (Sopran) • CAMILLO (Baß) Edelmann von Sizilien •
ANTIGINUS (Bariton) Edelmann von Sizilien • POLYRENES, König
von Böhmen (Bariton) • FLORIZEL, Prinz von Böhmen (Tenor) •
HERMIONE, des Leontes Gemahlin (Sopran) • PERDITA, ihre
Tochter (Sopran) • PAULINA, Frau des Antigonus (Mezzo-Sopran) •
VIER ORAKELBEWAHRER (2 Tenöre und 2 Bäße) • EIN
GERICHTSBEAMTER (Bariton) • EIN ALTER SCHÄFER,
vermeinlicher Vater Perdita's (Baß) • AUTOLYCUS, ein Spitzbube
(Tenor) • MOPSA, Schäferin • DORCAS, Schäferin • EIN DIENER •
EIN EDELMANN •——• **Chorus:** EDELLEUTE, KAMMERFRAUEN,
VOLK, SOLDATEN, SCHÄFER, SCHÄFERINNEN

Niccolò Antonio Zingarelli (1752-1837)

Giulietta e Romeo

Status: Y **Evidence:** P
Text: Foppa, Giuseppe Maria (1760-1845)
Type: Dramma tragico per musica **Acts:** 3

Language: Italian
Premiere: Milan, Italy: Teatro alla Scala • 1796 01 30
Source of Premiere Information: Year and place from libretto.
Date from Loewenberg.
Play: *Romeo and Juliet*
Publisher: Bonna: N. Simrock, 1814 [vs] (Overture and Arie)
Yes: LIBRETTO, Baker's, Blom, Friedlaender, Groves V, Hartnoll,
Loewenberg, Mellen, New Grove, Oxford, Squire, Stieger,
Wilson

Comments: Libretto: carnevale dell'anno 1796; dedication is dated
1796 01 30.

Cast: EVERARDO CAPPELLIO [Sig. Adamo Bianchi] • GIULIETTA,
sua figlia [Signora Giuseppa Grassini] • ROMEO MONTECCHIO [Sig.
Girolamo Crescentini] • GILBERTO, amico delle due Frazioni [Sig.
Angelo Monani] • MATILDE, confidente di Giulietta [Signora Carolina
Dianand] • TEOBALDO, della fazione de'Cappelli promesso Sposo a
Giulietta [Sig. Gaetano De Paoli] •——•
Chorus: CAPPELLI, MONTECCHI

Alexandru Zirra (1883-1946)

Furtuna [TheTempest]

Status: N   **Evidence:** S
Text: Composer
Type: Opera   **Language:** Romanian
Premiere: 1941 00 00
Source of Premiere Information: Mellen
Play: *Tempest*
No: Mellen

Comments: Mellen: date is when composed; based on G. Ureche.

Johann Rudolf Zumsteeg (1760-1802)

Die Geisterinsel

Status: Y   **Evidence:** S
Text: Gotter, Johann Friedrich Wilhelm (1746-1797) and Friedrich
    Hildebrand von Einsiedel (1750-1828)
Type: Singspiel   **Acts:** 3   **Language:** German
Premiere: Stuttgart, Germany: Herzogl. Hoftheater • 1798 11 07
Source of Premiere Information: Loewenberg
Play: *Tempest*
Publisher: Leipzig: Breitkopf & Härtel, 1799 [vs]
Yes: Baker's, Blom, Friedlaender, Groves V, Hartnoll, Loewenberg,
    Mellen, MGG, New Grove, Oxford, Schatz MS, Squire,
    Stieger

Comments: Manferrari: Berlino, Kgl. Nationaltheater, 6 luglio 1798;
all' Hoftheater di Stoccarda, settember stesso anno. Score does not
give place or date. Autograph was lost in a fire which destroyed the
Kleines Komödienhaus at Stuttgart.

Cast: PROSPERO, gewesener Herzog von Mailand, Zauberer •
MIRANDA, seine Tochter • FERNANDO, Prinz von Neapel • FABIO,
Edelknabe • DRONZIO, Küchenmeister • STEFANO, Kellermeister •
ARIEL, ein Sylphe • CALIBAN, ein Gnome • MAJA, ein Schatten •
SYCORAX, ein Schatten • RUPERTO, ein Bootsmann •—•
Chorus: GEISTER UND SYLPHEN, MATROSEN

SORTINGS

Title

City

Date of Premiere

Text

Play

Status

Library of Corgress

British Library

SORTING BY TITLE

TITLE	COMPOSER
Admeto, Re di Tessaglia	Guglielmi, Pietro Alessandro
Admeto, Re di Tessaglia	Händel, Georg Friederich
Admeto, Rè di Tessaglia	Magni, Giuseppe Paolo
Againcourt	Boughton, Rutland
Amantes de Verona, Los	Campo y Zabaleta, Conrado del
Amantes de Vérone, Les	Gaujac, Edmond Germain
Amantes de Vérone, Les	Ivry, Paul Xaver Désiré Richard, Marquis d'
Ambleto	Carcani, Giuseppe
Ambleto	Gasperini, Carlo Francesco
Ambleto	Scarlatti, Giuseppe Domenico
Ambleto	Vignali, Giuseppe [Act I]; Carlo Baglioni [Act II] and Giacomo Cozzi [Act III]
Amleto	Andreozzi, Gaetano
Amleto	Buzzolla, Antonio
Amleto	Caruso, Lodovico Luigi
Amleto	Faccio, Franco
Amleto	Fontmichel, Hippolyte Honoré Joseph Court de
Amleto	Gallenberg, Wenzel Robert Count von
Amleto	Grandi, Alfredo
Amleto	Marescotti
Amleto	Mercadante, Giuseppe Saverio Raffele
Amleto	Moroni, Luigi
Amleto	Weigl, Joseph [Veigl, Giuseppe]
Amleto	Zafred, Mario
Amleto	Zanardini, Angelo
Anthony and Cleopatra	Durme, Jef Van
Antonine et Cléopatre	Bondeville, Emmanuel de
Antonio e Cleopatra	Malipiero, Gian Francesco
Antonius und Cleopatra	Kaffka [Kafka], Johann Christian
Antonius und Kleopatra	Sayn-Wittgenstein-Berleburg, Count Friedrich Ernst von
Antony and Cleopatra	Ardin, Leon
Antony and Cleopatra	Bishop, Sir Henry Rowley
Antony and Cleopatra, Op. 40	Barber, Samuel
As You Like It	Balamos, John

TITLE	COMPOSER
As You Like It	Bishop, Sir Henry Rowley
As You Like It	Debussy, Claude
As You Like It	Lueder, Florence Pauline
At the Boar's Head, Opus 42	Holst, Gustav
At the Sign of the Angel or A Little Touch of Harry in the Night	Brawn, Geoffrey
Babes in the Wood, or Who Killed Cock Robin	Besoyan, Rick
Béatrice et Bénédict	Berlioz, Hector
Béatrice et Bénédict	Stransky, Josef
Beaucoup de bruit pour rien	Hahn, Reynaldo
Beaucoup de bruit pour rien	Puget, Paul-Charles-Marie
Beaucoup de bruit pour rien	Salvayre, Gaston
Belle of Bohemia, The	Engländer, Ludwig
Belle of Mayfair	Stuart, Leslie
Bezähmte Widerbellerin, Die	Unknown
Biorn	Rossi, Lauro
Bisbetica Domata, La	Bottacio, Pietro
Bisbetica Domata, La	Persico, Mario
Boure, Opus 40 [Der Sturm]	Fibich, Zdenko
Boys from Syracuse, The	Rogers, Richard
Brati [Brothers]	Khrennikov, Tikhon Nikolaevich
Caesario	Brandauer, Hermann
Caio Mario	Piccinni, Niccolò
Caio Mario	Scarlatti, Giuseppe
Caio Mario [Cajo Mario]	Jommelli, Nicolo
Caio Marzio Coriolano	Pulli, Pietro
Cajo Mario	Anfossi, Pasquale
Cajo Mario	Bertoni, Ferdinando Giuseppe
Cajo Mario	Bianchi, Francesco
Cajo Mario	Cimarosa, Domenico Nicola [Cimmarosa]
Cajo Mario	Galuppi, Baldassarre [called Buranello]
Cajo Mario	Monza, Carlo Antonio
Cajo Mario	Scolari, Giuseppe
Cajo Marzio Coriolano	Caldara, Antonio
Cajo Marzio Coriolano	Cattani, Lorenzo
Cajo Marzio Coriolano	Maggioni, Francesco
Cajo Marzio Coriolano [Marzio Coriolano]	Conti, Nicolò

TITLE	COMPOSER
Caliban by the Yellow Sands, Opus 47	Farwell, Arthur George
Capricciosa corretta, La [So bessert sie sich]	Martín y Soler, Vicente
Capricciosa pentita, La	Fioravanti, Valentino
Capricciosa pettita, La	Morlacchi, Francesco Giuseppi Baldassare
Capuleti e i Montecchi, I	Bellini, Vincenzo
Cäsario, oder die Verwechslung, Op. 30	Steinkühler, Émile
Catch My Soul	Unknown
Catherine and Petruchio	Unknown
Cesario, oder Was ihr wollt, Op. 188	Taubert, Carl Gottfried Wilhelm
Christopher Sly	Argento, Dominick
Christopher Sly	Eastwood, Thomas Hugh
Cimbelino, Il	Westerhout, Niccolò van
Comedy of Errors	Slade, Julian
Comedy of Errors, The	Bishop, Sir Henry Rowley
Comme il vous Plaira	Weis, Karél
Comme il vous Plaire	Vidal, Paul Antonin
Cordelia	Gobatti, Stefano
Cordélia	Séméladis, M.
Cordélia	Soloviev, Nicolai Feopemptovich
Cordelia	Zajc, Ivan
Cordelia (Floretta ou La Folle de Glaris)[First named Adele von Budoy]	Kreutzer, Conradin
Cordelia (Re Lear)	Cottrau, Giulio
Coriolano	Cavalli, Pietro Francesco
Coriolano	Graun, Karl Heinrich
Coriolano	Nicolini, Giuseppe
Coriolano	Santa Caterina, Alessandro
Coriolano	Savigna, Vincenzo
Coriolano	Treu, Daniel Gottlieb
Coriolano, Il	Ariosti, Attilio
Coriolano, Il	Lavina, Vincenzo
Coriolano, Il	Radicati, Felice Alessandro
Coriolanus	Baeyens, August Louis
Coriolanus	Cikker, Ján
Cressida	MacDermot, Galt
Cure for a Scold, A	Unknown
Cymbelin	Tiessen, Heinz

TITLE	COMPOSER
Cymbeline	Choudens, Antony
Cymbeline	Ware, William Henry
Cymbelyn	Eggen, Arne
Dairymaids, The	Rubens, Paul Alfred and Frank E. Tours
Dick Deterred	Field, Graham
Dinah	Missa, Edmond Jean Louis
Dinah	Taboida, Ant. Sanchez do Cunha
Dodisesima Notte, La	Farina, Guido
Double Trouble [Zwillingskomödie]	Mohaupt, Richard
Dreamstuff	Malamet, Marsha
Early Reign of Oleg, The	Unknown
Edit royal, L'	Ruben, Paul
Enchanted Isle, The [Scenes from Shakespeare's 'Tempest']	Jenkins, David
Ende gut, alles gut	Lichtenstein, Carl August Freiherr von
Ende gut, alles gut oder Der Fürst und sein Volk	Antoine, Ferdinand d'
Enrico	Galuppi, Baldassarre
Enrico IV al passo della Marna	Balfe, Michael William
Enrico IV al passo della Marna	Fioravanti, Valentino
Enrico IV al passo della Marna	Maganini, Giovanni
Equivoci d'amore e d'innocenza, Gl'	Gasperini, Carlo Francesco
Equivoci d'Amore, Gli	Bernabei, Vincenzo
Equivoci, Gli	Gazzaniga, Giuseppe
Equivoci, Gli	Sarria, Errico
Equivoci, Gli	Storace, Stephen
Erminie	Jakobowski, Edward
Érmione	Bernabei, Giuseppe Antonio
Ermione	Rossini, Gioacchino
Érmione [Die wiedergefundene Hermione]	Zanettini, Antonio
Ermordung Cäsars, Die Op. 32	Klebe, Giselher Wolfgang
Ero, ossia Molto rumore per nulla	Podestà, Carlo
Euryanthe	Weber, Carl Maria von
Fair Fugitives	Busby, Thomas

TITLE	COMPOSER
Fairies, The	Smith, John Christopher
Fairy Prince, The	Arne, Thomas Augustine
Fairy Queen, The	Purcell, Henry
Fairy Tale	Arne, Michael and C. Dibdin, J. Battishill, C. Burney, Hook, J. C. Smith
Falstaff	Adam, Adolphe-Charles
Falstaff	Balfe, Michael William
Falstaff	Kaun, Hugo
Falstaff	Schönfeld, Georg
Falstaff	Verdi, Giuseppe
Falstaff osia Le tre Burle	Salieri, Antonio
Fiercilla domada, La	Morera, Enrique
Fire Angel	Haines, Roger
Florizel and Perdita	Boyce, William
Four Scenes from Shakespeare	Logar, Mihovil
Furia domata, La	Samara, Spiro
Furtuna [TheTempest]	Zirra, Alexandru
Gardens of Adonis, The	Weisgall, Hugo
Gay Venetians, The	Chatburn, Tom
Geisterinsel, Die	Fleischmann, Friedrich
Geisterinsel, Die	Haack, Friedrich
Geisterinsel, Die	Hensel, Johann Daniel
Geisterinsel, Die	Reichardt, Johann Friedrich
Geisterinsel, Die	Zumsteeg, Johann Rudolf
Georget et Georgette	Alexandre, Charles Guillaume
Gillette de Narbonne	Campenhout, François van
Gillette de Narbonne	Hanssens, J. F. J.
Gillette de Narbonne	Mélésville, Honoré Marie Joseph, Baron Duveyrier]
Gillette de Narbonne [Gillette, or Count and Countess; Gilda di Guascogna]	Audran, Edmond
Gioventù di Enrico V, La	Aspa, Mario
Gioventù di Enrico V, La	Carlini, Luigi
Gioventù di Enrico V, La	Garcia, Manuel Vincente del Popolo
Gioventù di Enrico V, La	Mercadante, Giuseppe Saverio Raffele
Gioventù di Enrico V, La	Mosca, Giuseppe

TITLE	COMPOSER
Gioventù di Enrico V, La (also La bella tavernara; Le Aventure d'una notte)	Pacini, Giovanni
Gioventù di Enrico V, La [Das Jugendjahre Heinrich des Fünften]	Morlacchi, Francesco Giuseppi Baldassare
Gioventù di Enrico V, La [La Jeunesse d'Henry V]	Hérold, Louis Joseph Ferdinand
Giuletta e Romeo	Marescalchi, Luigi
Giulietta e Romeo	Garcia, Manuel Vincente del Popolo
Giulietta e Romeo	Mercadal y Pons, Antonio
Giulietta e Romeo	Morales, Melesio
Giulietta e Romeo	Vaccai, Nicola
Giulietta e Romeo	Zandonai, Riccardo
Giulietta e Romeo	Zingarelli, Niccolò Antonio
Giulio Cesare	Malipiero, Gian Francesco
Good Time Johnny	Gilbert, James
Great Caesar	Rubens, Paul Alfred and Walter Rubens
Guglielmo Shakespeare	Benvenuti, Tommaso
Guido e Ginevre	Tommasi, Ferdinando [Tommaso]
Guido et Ginevre ou La Peste de Florence	Halévy, Jacques François Fromental Elie
Hamlet	Berlioz, Hector
Hamlet	Bizet, Georges
Hamlet	Forest, Jean Kurt
Hamlet	Glinka, Mikhail Ivanovitch
Hamlet	Heward, Leslie Hays
Hamlet	Hignard, Aristide
Hamlet	Hignett, J. L. A.
Hamlet	Kagen, Sergius
Hamlet	Keurvels, Edward H. J.
Hamlet	MacFarren, George Alexander
Hamlet	Machavariani, Alexei
Hamlet	Maretzek, Maximilian
Hamlet	Mussorgsky, Modest Petrovich
Hamlet	Reutter, Hermann
Hamlet	Stadtfeldt, Christian Joseph Franz Alexandre
Hamlet	Szokolay, Sándor
Hamlet	Thomas, Charles Louis Ambroise

TITLE	COMPOSER
Hamlet, Music to the Tragedy by Shakespeare	Prokofiev, Sergei
Hamlet, Op. 145	Roters, Ernest
Hamlet, Op. 18	Bentoiu, Pascal
Hamlet, Opus 48	Searle, Humphrey
Hamlet, Pantomime zu	Holland, Jan David
Hamlet, Prince of Denmark or The Sport, the Spook and the Spinster	Atherton, Percy Lee and Ernest Hamlin Abbott
Hamlet, Prinz vom Tandelmarkt	Kleinheinz, Carl Franz Xaver
Hamlet, Prinz vom Tandelmarkt	Schuster, Ignaz
Hamlet, Prinz von Liliput	Rafael, Carl Friedrich
Hamlets	Kalnins, Janis
Hammlet	Hopp, Julius
Heinrich IV	Müller (the elder), Adolph
Heinrich IV zu Givry	Stuntz, Joseph Hartmann
Henri IV, ou La Bataille d'Ivry	Martini, Giovanni
Henri Quatre [Paris in the Olden Times]	Bishop, Sir Henry Rowley
Henrik den Fjerde	Küster, Johann Heinrich
Henry IV	Francastel, A.
Henry IV	Weisgall, Hugo
Henry VIII	Saint-Saëns, Camille
Hermione	Thul, Franz von
Hermione, oder Der kleine Vicomte	Hohmann, Gustav
Hermione, Op. 40	Bruch, Max
Hermione, or Valour's Triumph	Attwood, Thomas
Herne le Chasseur	Philidor
Herne the Hunter (A Legend of Royal Windsor)	Old, John
Herne's Oak, or The Rose of Windsor [also Herne the Hunter]	Andrews, John Charles Bond-
History of Timon of Athens, the Man Hater, The	Purcell, Henry
Holger Danske oder Oberon [Holgar the Dane]	Kunzen, Friedrich Ludwig Æmilius
Hylas et Sylvie	Gossec, François Joseph
Imogéne	Sobolewski, Friedrich Eduard de

TITLE	COMPOSER
Imogène, ou La Gageure indiscrète	Kreutzer, Rodolphe
In Town	Carr, Frank Osmond
Jed z Elsinoru [The Poison from Elsinore]	Horky, Karel
Jessica	Deffès, Louis Pierre
Jessika, Opus 60	Foerster, Joseph Brohuslav
Jeune Henri, Le [Gabrielle d'Estrées où les Amours d'Henri IV]	Méhul, Étienne Nicolas
Jeunesse de Henri Cinq, La	Volder, Piere Jean de
Julia i Romeo	Matuszczak, Bernadetta
Julia und Romeo	Didam, Otto
Julietta, Op. 15	Erbse, Heimo
Juliette et Roméo	Rosellin, Léon
Julius Caesar	Carl, M.
Julius Caesar	Schmitz, Alan
King Lear	Durme, Jef Van
King Lear	Salmhofer, Franz
King Lear ?	Pogodin
King's Bride, The [Violette]	Ansell, John
Kiss Me, Kate	Porter, Cole
Kleopatra	Freudenberg, Wilhelm
Komödie der Irrungen	Wödl, Franz
Komödie der Irrungen, Die	Lorenz, Carl Adolf
König Lear	André, Johann
König Lear	Beck, Curt
König Lear	Borodcicz, Hans von
König Lear	Horner
König Lear	Litolff, Henry Charles
Koriolan	Sulek, Stjepan
Lásky hra osudná [The Fateful Game of Love], Opus 3	Folprecht, Zdenek
Lear	Reimann, Aribert
Lear	Verdi, Giuseppe
Leben und Tod des Königs Macbeth	Asplmayr, Franz
Leggenda di Giulietta, La	Zanon, Antonio B.
Liebesspiel, Das	Rosenberg, Richard
Liebesverbot, Das oder Die Novize von Palermo	Wagner, Wilhelm Richard
Love and Let Love	Gelber, Stanley Jay

TITLE	COMPOSER
Love Scene from Shakespeare's Romeo and Juliet for Contralto and Baritone	Bedford, Herbert
Love's Labour's Lost [Peines d'Amour Perdues]	Beecham, Adrian Wells
Love's Labour's Lost [Verlor'ne Liebesmüh']	Nabokov, Nikolai
Lustigen Weiber von Berlin, Die	Michaelis, Gustave
lustigen Weiber von Hamburg, Die	Wiedeke, Adolf
lustigen Weiber von Windsor und der dicke Hans, Die	Dittersdorf, Carl Ditters von
lustigen Weiber von Windsor, Die	Nicolai, Carl Otto Ehrenfried
lustigen Weiber, Die	Ritter, Peter
Macbeth	André, Johann
Macbeth	Bizet, Georges
Macbeth	Bloch, Ernest
Macbeth	Chélard, Hippolyte-André-Jean-Baptiste
Macbeth	Collingwood, Lawrance Arthur
Macbeth	Daffner, Hugo
Macbeth	Fisher, John Abraham
Macbeth	Gatty, Nicholas Comyn
Macbeth	Goedicke, Alexander
Macbeth	Goldman, Edward M.
Macbeth	Halpern, Sidney
Macbeth	Leverage, Richard
Macbeth	Locke, Matthew and Robert Johnson
Macbeth	Piccini, Louis Alexandre
Macbeth	Pless, Hans
Macbeth	Reichardt, Johann Friedrich
Macbeth	Stegmann, Carl David
Macbeth	Verdi, Giuseppe
Macbeth	Ware, William Henry
Macbeth	Weyse, Christoph Ernst Friedrich
Macbeth, Op. 133	Taubert, Wilhelm
Macbeth, Op. 79	Koppel, Herman David
Malvina	Cooke, Thomas Simpson
Malvina	Costa, Michael Andrew Angus

313

TITLE	COMPOSER
Malvina	Hahn, Reynaldo
Malvina	Hamel, Eduard
Malvina	Schindelmeisser, Louis Alexander Balthasar
Malvina	Vaccai, Nicola
Malvina [Die Wolfsjagd]	Danzi, Franz
Malvina, oder Putzerls Abenteuer	Kanne, Friedrich August
Malvine I re [The first]	Hulemann, Th
Malvolio	De Filippi, Amadeo
Malvolio, Opus 14	Hart, Fritz Bennicke
Marchand de Venise, Le	Brumagne, Fernand
Marchand de Vénise, Le	Hahn, Reynaldo
Marchand de Vénise, Le	Saussine, Henri de
marchand de Venise, Le [Koopman van Smyrna]	Just, Johann August
Marjolaine	Lecocq, Charles Alexandre
Martio Coriolano	Perti, Giacomo Antonio
Marzio Coriolano	Pollaroli, Carlo Francesco
Maß für Maß	Gulda, Friedrich
Mégère apprivoisée, La	Le Rey, Frédéric
Mégère apprivoisée, La	Silver, Charles
Mercante di Venezia, Il	Pinsuti, Ciro
Mercante di Venezia, Il, Op. 181	Castelnuovo-Tedesco, Mario
Merchant of Venice	Carlson, Charles Frederick
Merchant of Venice	Clarke, James Siree Hamilton
Merchant of Venice, The	Beecham, Adrian Wells
Merry Wives of Windsor	Horn, Charles Edward, and Samuel Webbe Jr.
Merry Wives of Windsor	Serov, Alexander Nikolayevich
Merry Wives of Windsor, The	Bishop, Sir Henry Rowley
Merry-Go-Round	Lutz, William Meyer
Midsummer Night's Dream, A	Arundell, Dennis Drew
Midsummer Night's Dream, A	Aylward, Theodore
Midsummer Night's Dream, A	Bishop, Sir Henry Rowley
Midsummer Night's Dream, A	Silverman, Stanley
Midsummer Night's Dream, A, Op. 64	Britten, Lord Edward Benjamin
Miranda	Alfano, Franco
Miranda	Canonica, Pietro
Miranda (Poliedniaia bor'ba) [Der Letzte Kampf]	Kasanli, Nikolai Ivanovich [Kazanli, Kazanly]

TITLE	COMPOSER
Miranda oder Das Schwert der Rache	Kanne, Friedrich August
Mnogo shuma iz nichego [Viel Lärm aus Leidenschaft, Much Ado About Hearts]	Khrennikov, Tikhon Nikolaevich
Montano et Stéphanie	Berton, Henri-Montan
Much Ado About Nothing, Opus 76a	Stanford, Sir Charles Villiers
Music Is	Adler, Richard
Musik Til William Shakspeare [sic], Op. 74	Kuhlau, Friedrich Daniel Rudolph
Night of the Moonspell	Siegmeister, Elie
Oberon [or the Elf-King's Oath]	Weber, Carl Maria von
Oberon, König der Elfen	Vranicky, Pavel
Oberon, or The Charmed Horn	Cooke, Thomas Simpson
Oberon, the Fairy Prince	Ferraboso II, Alfonso and Robert Johnson
Oh, Brother	Valenti, Michael
Oluja	Sulek, Stjepan
Ophelia, Op. 36	Engelmann, Hans Ulrich
Orage, L'	David, Adolphe Isaac
Orage, L'	Foignet, Jacques
Orage, L'	Urich, Jean
Orage, L' ou Quel Guignon!	Navoigille, Gouliellmo
Orakelspruch, Der	Herx, Werner
Orakelspruch, Der	Lauer, Adolph L. [Freiherr von Münchofen]
Orakelspruch, Der	Riotte, Philipp Jakob
Orakelspruch, Der	Schneider, Georg Abraham
Orakelspruch, Der Op. 50	Mohr, Hermann
Otello	La Rosa, Arturo
Otello	Pride [sp?], G.
Otello	Verdi, Giuseppe
Otello mecél	Sztojanovics, Eug.
Otello ossia Catiello l'Affricano	Scognamilio, Gennaro
Otello Tamburo	Macarig, Hector and Alfonso Deperis
Otello, osia L'Africano di Venezia	Rossini, Gioacchino
Otelo y Desdémona	Nieto, Manuel
Othellerl, der Mohr von Wien	Schuster, Ignaz

315

TITLE	COMPOSER
Othellerl, der Mohr von Wien [Die geheilte Eifersucht]	Müller (the elder), Adolph
Othello	Hirschbach, Hermann
Othello	Machavariani, Alexei
Othello	Zavodsky, Felix
Othello in Kyritz	Michaelis, Gustave
Othello Story	Claudric, Jean
Othello, Un	Legouix, Isidore Édouard
Peines d'amour perdues	Mozart, Wolfgang Amadeus
Peines d'amour perdues	Vidal, Paul Antonin
Perdita	Kovarovic, Karel
Perdita	Nesvera, Josef
Perdita	Pillaut, Léon
Perdita oder Das Rosenfest	Kipper, Herman
Perdita oder Ein Wintermärchen	Barbieri, Carlo Emanuele di
Pericle re di Tiro	Cottrau, Giulio
Petruccio	Maclean, Alick
Petruccio e il Cavolo Cappuccio	Oddone, Elizabetta
Petruchio	Groth, Howard
Pop	Cribari, Donna
Porzia	Taubmann, Otto
Porzia	Wolfurt, Kurt von
Pozdvizení v Efesu [The Upheaval in Ephesus]	Krejcí, Isa
Prince Hamlet	Raphling, Sam
Puck	Delannoy, Marcel
Pulcinella rivale di Turzillo e confuso tra Capuleti e Montecchi	Unknown
Pyramus and Thisbe	Bruce, Neely
Pyramus and Thisbe	Lampe, John Frederich
Pyramus and Thisbe, The Comic Masque of	Leverage, Richard
R Loves J	Faris, Alexander
Re Lear	Frazzi, Vito
Re Lear	Ghislanzoni, Alberto
Re Lear, Il	Cagnoni, Antonio
Rêve d'une Nuit d'été, Le	Offenbach, Jacques
Rhum et eau en juillet	Déjazet, Eugène

TITLE	COMPOSER
Ricardus Impius, Angliae Rex, ab Henrico Richmondæ Comite vita simul et regno excitus	Eberlin, Johann Ernst
Riccardo	Berens, Johann Hermann
Riccardo III	Canepá, Luigi
Riccardo III	Meiners, Giambattista
Riccardo III	Salvayre, Gaston
Richard III	Durme, Jef Van
Richard III	Turok, Paul H.
Rinaldo und Camilla oder Die Zauberinsel	Gevel, Franz Xaver
Ritter Hans von Dampf	Hofmann, Johann
Robin Goodfellow or the Frolics of Puck	Loder, Edward James
Rockabye Hamlet	Jones, Cliff
Rodrigo di Valencia	Generali, Pietro Mercandetti
Rodrigo di Valencia	Orlandi, Ferdinando
Rodrigo di Valencia	Pacini, Giovanni
Roi Lear, Le	Pedrell, Filipe
Roi Lear, Le	Reynaud, Armand
Romeo and Julia auf dem Lande	Kurzbach, Paul
Romeo and Juliet	Barkworth, John Edmond
Romeo and Juliet	Chignell, Robert
Romeo and Juliet	Ferroni, Vencenzo Emidio Carmine
Romeo and Juliet	Fribec, Kresimir
Romeo and Juliet	Liota, A.
Romeo and Juliet	Marshall-Hall, George William Louis
Romeo and Juliet	Mullins, Hugh
Romeo and Juliet	Pasquali, Nicolò
Romeo and Juliet	Perosi, Lorenzo
Romeo and Juliet	Shelley, Harry Rowe
Romeo and Juliet Up to Larks	Douglas, Hugh A.
Romeo e Giuletta	San Severino
Romeo e Giulia	Schwanenberg, Johann Gottfried
Romeo e Giulietta	Marchetti, Filippo
Romeo e Giulietta	Torriani, Eugenio
Romeo e Giulietta [I Capuletti ed i Montecchi]	Guglielmi, Pietro Carlo

317

TITLE	COMPOSER
Romeo e Guilietta (scene 5 of Monde celesti e infernali)	Malipiero, Gian Francesco
Romeo en Marielle [Tout pour l'amour]	Acker, Jean Van den
Roméo et Juliette	Crescentini, Girolamo
Roméo et Juliette	Gerber, René
Roméo et Juliette	Gounod, Charles François
Roméo et Juliette	Membrée, Edmond
Roméo et Juliette	Porta, [Bernardo ?]
Roméo et Juliette	Rumling, Sigismund Freiherr von
Roméo et Juliette	Thomé, François Lucien Joseph
Roméo et Juliette or Tout pour l'amour	Steibelt, Daniel Gottlieb
Romeo und Julia	Blacher, Boris
Romeo und Julia	Damrosch, Leopold
Romeo und Julia	Sutermeister, Heinrich
Romeo und Julie	Benda, George Anton
Romeo und Julie	Eberwein, Max Carl
Romeo und Julie	Ludwig, Otto
Romeo und Julie	Schuster, Ignaz
Romeo und Julie	Storch, Anton Maria
Romeo und Juliet auf dem Dorfe [A Village Romeo and Juliet]	Delius, Frederick
Romeo, Dzhulyetta i t'ma [Romeo, Juliet and Darkness]	Molchanov, Kiril Vladimirovich
Romeo, Julie a tma (Romeo, Juliet and Darkness)	Fischer, Jan F.
Romeo, the Radical or Obstruction and Effect	Emery, Charles P.
Rosalind	Lueder, Florence Pauline
Rosalinda	Freschi, Giovanni Domenico
Rosalinda	Smith, John Christopher
Rosalinda	Veracini, Francesco Maria
Rosalinda [Erginia Mascherata]	Capelli, Giovanni Maria
Rosalinda, La or Erginia mascherata	Ziani, Marc Antonio
Rosalinde	Duyse, Florimond Van
Rosalinde	Strungk, Nicolaus Adam
Rosalinde, oder Die Macht der Feen	Hoffmeister, Franz Anton
Rosaline	Rateau, Edmond

TITLE	COMPOSER
Rudolf von Felseck (Die Schwarzthaler) oder La Tempestà	Vranicky, Pavel
Saphir, Le or Tout est bien, qui finit bien	David, Félicien César
Schiffbruch, Der	Hoffmeister, Franz Anton
Schipbreuk	Unknown
Sen noci svatojanske	Doubrava, Jaroslav
Sensations	Harper, Wally
Shakespeare!	Serpette, Henri Charles Antoine Gaston
Shakespeare's Cabaret	Mulcahy, Lance
Shakespeare, the Playmaker	Conte, Paolo
Sheep-Shearing, The or Florizel and Perdita	Arne, Thomas Augustine, Samuel Arnold and others
Shylock	Alpaerts, Florent
Shylock	Laufer, B.
Shylock	LaViolette, Wesley
Shylock	Radó, Aladár
Shylock or The Venus of Venice	Barry, H. C.
Shylock [Fire Angel]	Haines, Roger
Sir John in Love	Vaughan Williams, Ralph
Sly, ovvero La leggenda del dormiente risvegliato	Wolf-Ferrari, Ermanno
Sogno d'una Notte estiva, Il or La Gioventù di Shakespeare	Lillo, Giuseppe
sogno di Primavera, Un [Un rêve de printemps]	Manusardi, Giuseppe
Sogno di una notte d'estate, Il	Mancinelli, Luigi
Sogno di una notte d'estate, Il	Roti, Ugo
Sogno di una Notte, Il	Allegra, Giuseppe
Sommarnattsdröm, En	Berens, Johann Hermann
Sommernachtstraum, Der	Suppé, Franz von
Sommernachtstraum, Ein	Orff, Carl
songe d'une nuit d'été, Le	Noël, Édouard Marie Émile
Songe d'une nuit d'été, Le	Serpette, Henri Charles Antoine Gaston
Songe d'une nuit d'été, Le [Shakespeare oder Der Traum einer Sommernacht]	Thomas, Charles Louis Ambroise
Songe d'une nuit d'été, Un	Leoncavallo, Ruggiero
Songe d'une nuit d'été, Un	Vreuls, Victor

TITLE	COMPOSER
Sourwood Mountain	Kreutz, Arthur
Spring With Shakespeare	Zelinka, Jan Evangelista
Stein der Weisen, Dem oder Die Zauber Insel	Zák, Benedict Emanuel
Stein der Weisen, Der	Feigerl, R.
Stein der Weisen, Der	Palliardi, Carl
Stein der Weisen, Der	Pohlig, Carl
Stein der Weisen, Der	Storch, Anton Maria
Stein der Weisen, Der oder Die Zauberinsel	Gerl, Thaddäus; Henneberg and Benedikt Schack
Storm, The	Aliabiev, Alexander
Storm, The [Groza]	Kashperov, Vladimir Nikititch
Stormen	Kunzen, Friedrich Ludwig Æmilius
Stormen paa København [Storm over Copenhagen]	Rung, Henrik
Stormen, Op. 49	Atterberg, Kurt
Sturm oder Die bezauberte Insel, Der	Rolle, Johann Heinrich
Sturm oder die Zauberinsel, Der	Müller, Wenzel
Sturm, Der	Asplmayr [Aspelmayr], Franz
Sturm, Der	Beer-Walbrunn, Anton
Sturm, Der	Emmert, Adam Joseph
Sturm, Der	Frank, Ernst
Sturm, Der	Martin, Frank
Sturm, Der	Nápravnik, Éduard Frantsevich
Sturm, Der	Raymond, Édouard
Sturm, Der	Urspruch, Anton
Sturm, Der	Winter, Peter von
Sturm, Der oder Die bezauberte Insel	Ritter, Peter
Sturm, Der oder Die Insel des Prospero	Riotte, Philipp Jakob
sueño de una noche de verano, El	Gaztambide y Garbayo, Joaquin Romualdo
sueño de una noche de verano, El	Valverde y San Juan, Joaquín
Swingin' the Dream	Van Heusen, Jimmy
Taming of a Shrew, The	Tajon, Ben.
Taming of the Shrew, The	Clapp, Philip Greeley
Taming of the Shrew, The	Cooke, Thomas Simpson and Braham, John and Others

TITLE	COMPOSER
Taming of the Shrew, The	Giannini, Vittorio
Tempest	Hába, Alois
Tempest in a Teapot	Morton, David
Tempest or Enchanted Island, The	Purcell, Henry
Tempest, The	Angyal, Lázló
Tempest, The	Arne, Thomas Augustine
Tempest, The	Bishop, Sir Henry Rowley
Tempest, The	Gatty, Nicholas Comyn
Tempest, The	Hale, Alfred Matthew
Tempest, The	Johnson, Robert
Tempest, The	Kunz, [Konrad Max ?]
Tempest, The	Leichtling, Alan
Tempest, The	Smith, John Christopher
Tempest, The or The Enchanted Island	Linley II, Thomas
Tempest, The [The Enchanted Island]	Banister, John; Giovanni Battista Draghi; Matthew Locke; Pelham Humfrey; and Pietro Reggio
Tempestà ossia Da un disordine ne nasce un ordine, La	Fabrizi, Vincenzo
Tempesta, La	Angelis, Arturo de
Tempesta, La	Caruso, Lodovico Luigi
Tempesta, La	Del Fante, Raffaele
Tempesta, La	Halévy, Jacques Franoçis Fromental Élie
Tempesta, La	Lattuada, Felice
Tempestad, La	Chapí y Lorente, Ruperto
Tempeste	Savini, Giacomo
Tempète, La	Duvernoy, Victor-Alphonse
Tempête, La	Honegger, Arturo
Thimon le misantrope	Unknown
Three Caskets, The or Venice Re-served	Greenwall, Peter
Timon	Frank, Johann Wolfgang
Timon in Love or The Innocent Theft	Unknown
Timone misantropo	Draghi, Antonio
Timòne, Misantropo	Leopold I, Holy Roman Emperor
Titania	Hüe, George
Titania, oder Liebe durch Zauberei	Grosheim, Georg Christoph

TITLE	COMPOSER
Titus Andronicus	Clarke, Jeremiah
Tout est bien qui finit bien	Weckerlin, Jean Baptiste Théodore
Tout pour l'amour ou Roméo et Juliette	Dalayrac, Nicolas
Travestirte Hamlet, Der [Hamlet, Prinz von Dänemark; Hamlet, Prinz von Lilyput]	Tuczek, Vincenc Tomas Vaclav
Travesty Without a Pun.	Soule, Charles Caroll
Troilus and Cressida	Walton, Sir William
Troilus und Cressida	Zillig, Winfried
Tutto e bène quello che finisce bène, Op. 182	Castelnuovo-Tedesco, Mario
Twelfth Night	Morton, Louise, and others
Twelfth Night	Amram, David
Twelfth Night	Bishop, Sir Henry Rowley
Twelfth Night	Shenshin, Aleksandr Alexseivich
Twelfth Night	Wilson, James
Twelfth Night, Opus 115	Gibbs, Cecil Armstrong
Twelfth Night, Scenes from	Hughes, Gervase
Twelfth Night, The [Vecer Trikralovy]	Jirko, Ivan
Two Gentlemen of Verona	MacDermot, Galt
Two Gentlemen of Verona, The	Bishop, Sir Henry Rowley
Ukroshchenie stroptivoi [The Taming of the Shrew] Op. 46	Shebalin, Vissarion Yakovlevich
V buriu [Im Sturm, Into the Storm]	Khrennikov, Tikhon Nikolaevich
Viel Lärm um Lichts	Doppler, Arpád
Viel Lärm um Nichts	Heinrich, Hermann
Viel Lärm um Nichts	Mojsisovics, Roderich
Viel Lärm um Nichts	Müller (the elder), Adolph
Vieux Coquet, Le; ou Les deux amies ou Le vieus garçon	Papavoine, Mdme
Viola	Arensen, Adolf
Viola	Heuberger, Richard Franz Joseph
Viola	Kirchner, Hermann

TITLE	COMPOSER
Viola	Smetana, Bedrich
Viola Pisani	Perelli, Edoardo
Viola [Die Zwillinge, Blizenci]	Weis, Karél
Viola, Opus 21 [Was Ihr wollt]	Holenia, Hans
Violetas, As	Freitas Gazul, Francisco de
Violetta	Berens, Johann Hermann
Violetta	Mercadante, Giuseppe Saverio Raffele
Violette, La ou Gérard de Nevers	Carafa di Colobrano, Michele Enrico and Aimé Ambroise Simon Leborne
Volpino il Calderaio, Op. 32	Bossi, Renzo
Volshebnaya noch	Aliabiev, Alexander
Was ihr Wollt	Falk, Richard
Was ihr Wollt	Hess, Ludwig
Was ihr Wollt	Krohn, Max
Was ihr Wollt	Kusterer, Arthur
Was ihr Wöllt	Rintel, Wilhelm
Weird Sisters, The or The Thane and the Throne	Whitaker, John
West Side Story	Bernstein, Leonard
Widerspänstigen Zähmung, Der [La Megère apprivoisée; Caterina e Petruccio]	Goetz, Herman
Will	Utley, Wendell
Winter's Tale, The	Harbison, John
Wintermärchen, Das	Berény, Henri
Wintermärchen, Das	Leukauf, Robert
Wintermärchen, Ein	Flotow, Friedrich von
Wintermärchen, Ein	Goldmark, Carl
Wintermärchen, Ein	Zimmermann, Balduin
Winternachtsdroom, Een	De Boeck, Auguste de
Your Own Thing	Hester, Hal and Danny Apolinar
Zauberinsel, Die	Sutermeister, Heinrich
Zauberirrungen, Die [Die Irrtümer der Zauberei]	Wolf, Ernst Wilhelm
Zkroceni zlé zeny [The Taming of the Shrew]	Karel, Rudolf
Zwillinge	Genée, Franz Friedrich Richard and Louis Roth

SORTING BY CITY

PLACE	DATE	COMPOSITION
Aachen, Germany	1929 05 27	Rosenberg, Richard • Liebesspiel, Das
Aldeburgh, England • Jubilee Hall	1960 06 11	Britten, Lord Edward Benjamin • Midsummer Night's Dream, A, Op. 64
Amsterdam, Holland	1787 00 00	Just, Johann August • marchand de Venise, Le [Koopman van Smyrna]
Amsterdam, Holland • Schonwburg in de Amstel. Straass	1809 00 00	Radicati, Felice Alessandro • Coriolano, Il
Antwerp, Belgium • National Tooneel	1859 10 26	Acker, Jean Van den • Romeo en Marielle [Tout pour l'amour]
Antwerp, Belgium • National Tooneel	1864 01 17	Duyse, Florimond Van • Rosalinde
Antwerp, Belgium • Royal Flemish Opera	1891 00 00	Keurvels, Edward H. J. • Hamlet
Antwerp, Belgium • Nederlandsch Lyrisch Tooneel	1902 12 20	De Boeck, Auguste de • Winternachtsdroom, Een
Antwerp, Belgium • Royal Flemish Opera	1913 11 22	Alpaerts, Florent • Shylock
Antwerp, Belgium • Royal Flemish Opera	1941 11 27	Baeyens, August Louis • Coriolanus
Aurich, Germany • Theater	1799 00 00	Ritter, Peter • Sturm, Der oder Die bezauberte Insel
Baden-Baden, Germany • Nouveau théâtre	1862 08 09	Berlioz, Hector • Béatrice et Bénédict
Baltimore, U.S.A. • Peabody Conservatory of Music	1962 11 09	Kagen, Sergius • Hamlet
Barcelona, Spain • Tivoli	1913 09 00	Morera, Enrique • Fiercilla domada, La
Bautzen, Germany • Stadttheater	1922 01 00	Feigerl, R. • Stein der Weisen, Der
Bergamo, Italy • Teatro Donizetti	1969 10 22	Zanon, Antonio B. • Leggenda di Giulietta, La

PLACE	DATE	COMPOSITION
Berlin, Germany • Hoftheater	1749 12 03	Graun, Karl Heinrich • Coriolano
Berlin, Germany	1773 00 00	San Severino • Romeo e Giuletta
Berlin, Germany • Dobbinschestheater	1779 11 15	Kaffka [Kafka], Johann Christian • Antonius und Cleopatra
Berlin, Germany • Döbbelin's Oper Theater	1780 00 00 ?	André, Johann • König Lear
Berlin, Germany • Döbbelin's Oper Theater	1780 10 03	André, Johann • Macbeth
Berlin, Germany • Döbbelin's Oper Theater	1782 03 28	Rolle, Johann Heinrich • Sturm oder Die bezauberte Insel, Der
Berlin, Germany	1787 12 28	Reichardt, Johann Friedrich • Macbeth
Berlin, Germany • Theater am Gendarmenplatz [Hoftheater]	1798 07 06	Reichardt, Johann Friedrich • Geisterinsel, Die
Berlin, Germany • Concordiatheater	1813 05 13	Schneider, Georg Abraham • Orakelspruch, Der
Berlin, Germany • Königl. Opernhaus	1832 01 08	Lauer, Adolph L. [Freiherr von Münchofen] • Orakelspruch, Der
Berlin, Germany • Königl. Opernhaus	1849 03 09	Nicolai, Carl Otto Ehrenfried • lustigen Weiber von Windsor, Die
Berlin, Germany • Königl. Opernhaus	1857 11 16	Taubert, Wilhelm • Macbeth, Op. 133
Berlin, Germany • Callenbach's Vaudeville Theater	1862 05 00	Michaelis, Gustave • Lustigen Weiber von Berlin, Die
Berlin, Germany	1872 03 10	Rintel, Wilhelm • Was ihr Wöllt
Berlin, Germany • Staatsoper	1872 03 21	Bruch, Max • Hermione, Op. 40
Berlin, Germany • Königl. Opernhaus	1874 11 13	Taubert, Carl Gottfried Wilhelm • Cesario, oder Was ihr wollt, Op. 188

PLACE	DATE	COMPOSITION
Berlin, Germany	1883 00 00	Mohr, Hermann • Orakelspruch, Der Op. 50
Berlin, Germany • Apollotheater	1893 07 15	Schönfeld, Georg • Falstaff
Berlin, Germany • Komische Oper	1907 02 21	Delius, Frederick • Romeo und Juliet auf dem Dorfe [A Village Romeo and Juliet]
Berlin, Germany • Deutschestheater	1919 10 10	Tiessen, Heinz • Cymbelin
Berlin, Germany • Radio	1947 00 00	Blacher, Boris • Romeo und Julia
Berlin, Germany	1957 00 00	Roters, Ernest • Hamlet, Op. 145
Berlin, Germany • Berlin/DDR (concert)	1973 10 15	Forest, Jean Kurt • Hamlet
Beuthen	1941 03 21	Wödl, Franz • Komödie der Irrungen
Birmingham, England • Grand Theatre	1885 10 26	Jakobowski, Edward • Erminie
Birmingham, England • Repertory Theatre	1971 12 16	Gilbert, James • Good Time Johnny
Bologna, Italy • Teatro Comunale	1873 11 08	Pinsuti, Ciro • Mercante di Venezia, Il
Bologna, Italy • Teatro Comunale	1881 12 06	Gobatti, Stefano • Cordelia
Bologna, Italy • Teatro Brunetti	1898 03 27	Grandi, Alfredo • Amleto
Bonn, Germany • Hoftheater	1792 05 09	Antoine, Ferdinand d' • Ende gut, alles gut oder Der Fürst und sein Volk
Bratislava, Czechoslovakia	1926 11 13	Folprecht, Zdenek • Lásky hra osudná [The Fateful Game of Love], Opus 3
Breslau, Poland	1725 12 00	Treu, Daniel Gottlieb • Coriolano
Breslau [Wroclaw], Poland • Stadttheater	1832 11 02	Rafael, Carl Friedrich • Hamlet, Prinz von Liliput
Brno, Czechoslovakia • Stadttheater	1840 11 05	Maretzek, Maximilian • Hamlet

PLACE	DATE	COMPOSITION
Brno [Brünn], Czechoslovakia • Kgl. Stadtisches Theater	1833 09 20	Riotte, Philipp Jakob • Sturm, Der oder Die Insel des Prospero
Brno [Brünn], Czechoslovakia • Státní Divádlo	1962 09 14	Fischer, Jan F. • Romeo, Julie a tma (Romeo, Juliet and Darkness)
Brno [Brünn], Czechoslovakia • Státní Divádlo	1969 11 11	Horky, Karel • Jed z Elsinoru [The Poison from Elsinore]
Brunn • Stadtheater		Borodcicz, Hans von • König Lear
Brunswick [Braunschweig], Germany • Fürstlich Theater im Schlosse	1776 00 00	Schwanenberg, Johann Gottfried • Romeo e Giulia
Brunswick [Oels], Germany • Braunschweig-Oelsische Hoftheater	1796 06 25	Dittersdorf, Carl Ditters von • lustigen Weiber von Windsor und der dicke Hans, Die
Brussels, Belgium • Théâtre Royal de la Monnaie	1879 05 02	Urich, Jean • Orage, L'
Brussels, Belgium • Théâtre Royal de la Monnaie	1925 12 17	Vreuls, Victor • Songe d'une nuit d'été, Un
Brussels, Belgium • Théâtre Royal de la Monnaie	1933 01 30	Brumagne, Fernand • Marchand de Venise, Le
Brussels, Belgium • Théâtre Royal de la Monnaie	1973 02 07	Nabokov, Nikolai • Love's Labour's Lost [Verlor'ne Liebesmüh']
Bucharest, Rumania	1971 11 19	Bentoiu, Pascal • Hamlet, Op. 18
Budapest, Hungary • K Stadt Theater	1826 02 13	Kleinheinz, Carl Franz Xaver • Hamlet, Prinz vom Tandelmarkt
Budapest, Hungary • Kgl.Op.	1917 05 22	Sztojanovics, Eug. • Otello mecél
Budapest, Hungary • State Opera	1968 10 19	Szokolay, Sándor • Hamlet

PLACE	DATE	COMPOSITION
Cassel, Germany • Hof-Operntheater	1792 00 00	Grosheim, Georg Christoph • Titania, oder Liebe durch Zauberei
Cerignola, Italy	1894 01 00	Scognamilio, Gennaro • Otello ossia Catiello l'Affricano
Chichester, England • Chichester Festival	1973 07 11	Faris, Alexander • R Loves J
Cincinnati, U.S.A. • Music Hall [in concert form]	1953 01 31	Giannini, Vittorio • Taming of the Shrew, The
Colombes, France	1894 02 11	Rosellin, Léon • Juliette et Roméo
Conway, Arkansas, U.S.A. • Arkansas State College: Ida Waldron Memorial Auditorium	1954 03 29	Groth, Howard • Petruchio
Copenhagen, Denmark • Konglige Theater	1789 03 31	Kunzen, Friedrich Ludwig Æmilius • Holger Danske oder Oberon [Holgar the Dane]
Copenhagen, Denmark	1817 00 00	Weyse, Christoph Ernst Friedrich • Macbeth
Copenhagen, Denmark	1818 00 00	Kunzen, Friedrich Ludwig Æmilius • Stormen
Copenhagen, Denmark • Konglige Theater	1826 03 28	Kuhlau, Friedrich Daniel Rudolph • Musik Til William Shakspeare [sic], Op. 74
Copenhagen, Denmark • Kongelige Theater	1845 01 21	Rung, Henrik • Stormen paa København [Storm over Copenhagen]
Copenhagen, Denmark • Konglige Theater	1970 05 22	Koppel, Herman David • Macbeth, Op. 79
Cormons, Italy	1892 05 00	Macarig, Hector and Alfonso Deperis • Otello Tamburo
Cremona, Italy	1900 00 00	Podestà, Carlo • Ero, ossia Molto rumore per nulla

PLACE	DATE	COMPOSITION
Darmstadt, Germany	1857 00 00	Stadtfeldt, Christian Joseph Franz Alexandre • Hamlet
Darmstadt, Germany • Landestheater	1952 00 00	Orff, Carl • Sommernachtstraum, Ein
Derby, England • Hippodrome	1955 04 04	Chatburn, Tom • Gay Venetians, The
Dessau, Germany • Hoftheater	1800 10 26	Lichtenstein, Carl August Freiherr von • Ende gut, alles gut
Donaueschingen, Germany • Hoftheater	1819 00 00	Kreutzer, Conradin • Cordelia (Floretta ou La Folle de Glaris)[First named Adele von Budoy]
Dresden, Germany • Hoftheater	1815 00 00	Morlacchi, Francesco Giuseppi Baldassare • Capricciosa pettita, La
Dresden, Germany • Königl. Sächs. Theater	1823 10 04	Morlacchi, Francesco Giuseppi Baldassare • Gioventù di Enrico V, La [Das Jugendjahre Heinrich des Fünften]
Dresden, Germany	1932 12 16	Kusterer, Arthur • Was ihr Wollt
Dresden, Germany	1938 00 00	Lueder, Florence Pauline • Rosalind
Dresden, Germany • Staatsoper	1940 04 13	Sutermeister, Heinrich • Romeo und Julia
Dresden, Germany • Staatsoper	1942 10 31	Sutermeister, Heinrich • Zauberinsel, Die
Düsseldorf, Germany • Stadtheater	1848 03 00	Steinkühler, Émile • Cäsario, oder die Verwechslung, Op. 30
Düsseldorf, Germany • Stadttheater	1951 02 03	Zillig, Winfried • Troilus und Cressida
Edinburgh, Scotland • St Columbia-by-the-Castle	1974 08 16	Haines, Roger • Shylock [Fire Angel]
Erfurt, Germany • Stadttheater	1900 03 11	Zimmermann, Balduin • Wintermärchen, Ein
Essen, Germany • Städtische Bühnen	1959 09 20	Klebe, Giselher Wolfgang • Ermordung Cäsars, Die Op. 32

PLACE	DATE	COMPOSITION
Faenza, Italy • Teatro Comunale	1921 05 23	Savini, Giacomo • Tempeste
Florence, Italy • Accademia di Casino	1686 00 00	Cattani, Lorenzo • Cajo Marzio Coriolano
Florence, Italy • Teatro degl' Immobili in via della Pergola	1789 12 27	Caruso, Lodovico Luigi • Amleto
Florence, Italy • Teatro di via della Pergola	1847 03 14	Verdi, Giuseppe • Macbeth
Florence, Italy • Teatro Alfieri	1931 03 00	Allegra, Giuseppe • Sogno di una Notte, Il
Florence, Italy • R. teatro Vitorio Emanuele II	1938 05 04	Malipiero, Gian Francesco • Antonio e Cleopatra
Florence, Italy • Teatro Comunale	1939 04 29	Frazzi, Vito • Re Lear
Florence, Italy • Maggio Musicale	1961 05 25	Castelnuovo-Tedesco, Mario • Mercante di Venezia, Il, Op. 181
Frankfurt A/M, Germany • Nationaltheater	1790 10 15	Vranicky, Pavel • Oberon, König der Elfen
Frankfurt A/M, Germany • Opernhaus	1888 05 17	Urspruch, Anton • Sturm, Der
Frankfurt A/M, Germany • Opernhaus	1916 11 14	Taubmann, Otto • Porzia
Frankfurt/Oder, Germany	1956 08 18	Heinrich, Hermann • Viel Lärm um Nichts
Gastonbury, England • Festival	1924 08 26	Boughton, Rutland • Againcourt
Genoa, Italy • Teatro Carlo Felice	1865 05 30	Faccio, Franco • Amleto
Genoa, Italy • Politeania Genovesa	1888 06 00	Pride [sp?], G. • Otello
Genoa, Italy • Politeania Genovesa	1897 02 00	La Rosa, Arturo • Otello
Genoa, Italy • Teatro Carlo Felice	1936 02 08	Malipiero, Gian Francesco • Giulio Cesare
Gent, Belgium	1810 00 00	Volder, Piere Jean de • Jeunesse de Henri Cinq, La

PLACE	DATE	COMPOSITION
Glens Falls, NY, U.S.A. • Lake George Opera Company	1968 00 00	Amram, David • Twelfth Night
Gotha, Germany • Herzogl. Hoftheater	1776 09 25	Benda, George Anton • Romeo und Julie
Graz, Austria • Landestheater	1883 12 01	Sayn-Wittgenstein-Berleburg, Count Friedrich Ernst von • Antonius und Kleopatra
Graz, Austria • Opernhaus	1934 11 17	Holenia, Hans • Viola, Opus 21 [Was Ihr wollt]
Hamburg, Germany • Theater beim Gänsemarkt	1779 07 21	Stegmann, Carl David • Macbeth
Hamburg, Germany	1786 00 00	Holland, Jan David • Hamlet, Pantomime zu
Hamburg, Germany • Stadttheater	1857 03 16	Hamel, Eduard • Malvina
Hamburg, Germany • Stadttheater	1893 03 16	Arensen, Adolf • Viola
Hamburg, Germany • Stadttheater	1894 12 05	Pohlig, Carl • Stein der Weisen, Der
Hamburg, Germany • Ernst Druker Theater	1898 10 15	Wiedeke, Adolf • lustigen Weiber von Hamburg, Die
Hamburg, Germany • Staatsoper	1968 03 05	Searle, Humphrey • Hamlet, Opus 48
Hannover, Germany • Stadttheatre	1887 10 15	Frank, Ernst • Sturm, Der
Hannover, Germany • Radio	1969 02 01	Engelmann, Hans Ulrich • Ophelia, Op. 36
Hermannstadt, Germany • Stadttheater	1904 02 05	Kirchner, Hermann • Viola
Hirschberg, Germany	1799 01 00	Hensel, Johann Daniel • Geisterinsel, Die
Karlsruhe, Germany • Hoftheater	1814 12 26	Danzi, Franz • Malvina [Die Wolfsjagd]
Königsberg, Germany • Stadttheater	1832 12 06	Sobolewski, Friedrich Eduard de • Imogéne
Leipzig, Germany • Hoftheater	1695 00 00	Strungk, Nicolaus Adam • Rosalinde

PLACE	DATE	COMPOSITION
Leipzig, Germany	1815 00 00	Kanne, Friedrich August • Malvina, oder Putzerls Abenteuer
Leipzig, Germany • Stadttheater	1896 00 00	Alfano, Franco • Miranda
Leipzig, Germany • Neues Stadttheater auf d. Augustusplatz	1896 03 13	Doppler, Arpád • Viel Lärm um Lichts
Liberec, Czechoslovakia	1967 02 25	Jirko, Ivan • Twelfth Night, The [Vecer Trikralovy]
Limoges, France • Théâtre municipal	1894 04 00	Ruben, Paul • Edit royal, L'
Lincoln, England • Theatre Royal	1892 08 01	Barry, H. C. • Shylock or The Venus of Venice
Lisbon, Portugal • Stadttheater	1887 03 27	Hohmann, Gustav • Hermione, oder Der kleine Vicomte
Lisbon, Portugal • Théâtre Trinidade	1892 00 00	Freitas Gazul, Francisco de • Violetas, As
Lisbon, Portugal • Club de Lisbonne	1897 07 00	Taboida, Ant. Sanchez do Cunha • Dinah
Liverpool, England • Prince of Wales Theatre	1887 10 24	Andrews, John Charles Bond- • Herne's Oak, or The Rose of Windsor [also Herne the Hunter]
Livorno, Italy • Teatro di San Sebastiano	1744 00 00	Maggioni, Francesco • Cajo Marzio Coriolano
Livorno, Italy • Teatro Politeama	1900 08 14	Del Fante, Raffaele • Tempesta, La
London, England • Whitehall, Banqueting House	1611 01 01	Ferraboso II, Alfonso and Robert Johnson • Oberon, the Fairy Prince
London, England	1612 00 00	Johnson, Robert • Tempest, The
London, England • Duke of York's Theatre in Dorset Gardens	1673 02 18	Locke, Matthew and Robert Johnson • Macbeth

PLACE	DATE	COMPOSITION
London, England • Duke of York's Theater in Dorset Gardens	1674 04 30	Banister, John; Giovanni Battista Draghi; Matthew Locke; Pelham Humfrey; and Pietro Reggio • Tempest, The [The Enchanted Island]
London, England • Queen's Theatre, Dorset Gardens	1692 05 02	Purcell, Henry • Fairy Queen, The
London, England • Duke of York's Theatre in Dorset Gardens	1694 00 00	Purcell, Henry • History of Timon of Athens, the Man Hater, The
London, England • Duke of York's Theater in Dorset Gardens	1695 00 00	Purcell, Henry • Tempest or Enchanted Island, The
London, England	1702 11 21	Leverage, Richard • Macbeth
London, England • Theatre in Lincoln's Inn Fields	1716 04 11	Leverage, Richard • Pyramus and Thisbe, The Comic Masque of
London, England • King's Theater in the Haymarket	1723 02 19	Ariosti, Attilio • Coriolano, II
London, England • King's Theatre in the Haymarket	1727 01 31	Händel, Georg Friederich • Admeto, Re di Tessaglia
London, England • Drury Lane Theatre	1733 12 05	Unknown • Timon in Love or The Innocent Theft
London, England • Drury Lane Theatre	1735 02 25	Unknown • Cure for a Scold, A
London, England • Hickford's Great Room in Brewer Street	1740 01 04	Smith, John Christopher • Rosalinda
London, England • King's Theater in the Haymarket	1743 01 01	Galuppi, Baldassarre • Enrico
London, England • King's Theatre in the Haymarket	1744 01 31	Veracini, Francesco Maria • Rosalinda

PLACE	DATE	COMPOSITION
London, England • Covent Garden	1745 01 25	Lampe, John Frederich • Pyramus and Thisbe
London, England • Drury Lane	1746 00 00	Arne, Thomas Augustine • Tempest, The
London, England • Covent Garden	1754 03 25	Arne, Thomas Augustine, Samuel Arnold and others • Sheep-Shearing, The or Florizel and Perdita
London, England • Drury Lane Theatre	1755 02 03	Smith, John Christopher • Fairies, The
London, England • Drury Lane?	1756 01 21	Boyce, William • Florizel and Perdita
London, England • Drury Lane Theatre	1756 02 11	Smith, John Christopher • Tempest, The
London, England • Drury Lane Theatre	1763 11 26	Arne, Michael and C. Dibdin, J. Battishill, C. Burney, Hook, J. C. Smith • Fairy Tale
London, England • Covent Garden	1771 11 12	Arne, Thomas Augustine • Fairy Prince, The
London, England	1777 00 00 ?	Fisher, John Abraham • Macbeth
London, England • Drury Lane Theatre	1777 01 04	Linley II, Thomas • Tempest, The or The Enchanted Island
London, England • Covent Garden	1791 00 00	Unknown • Catherine and Petruchio
London, England • Haymarket	1794 05 17	Martín y Soler, Vicente • Capricciosa corretta, La [So bessert sie sich]
London, England	179? 00 00	Aylward, Theodore • Midsummer Night's Dream, A
London, England • Covent Garden	1800 04 05	Attwood, Thomas • Hermione, or Valour's Triumph
London, England • Covent Garden	1803 05 12	Busby, Thomas • Fair Fugitives
London, England	1806 00 00	Ware, William Henry • Macbeth
London, England	1808 00 00	Ware, William Henry • Cymbeline

PLACE	DATE	COMPOSITION
London, England • King's Theater in the Haymarket	1810 02 20	Guglielmi, Pietro Carlo • Romeo e Giulietta [I Capuletti ed i Montecchi]
London, England • Covent Garden	1816 00 00	Bishop, Sir Henry Rowley • As You Like It
London, England • Covent Garden	1816 01 17	Bishop, Sir Henry Rowley • Midsummer Night's Dream, A
London, England • Sadler's Wells Theatre	1819 04 12	Whitaker, John • Weird Sisters, The or The Thane and the Throne
London, England • Covent Garden	1819 12 11	Bishop, Sir Henry Rowley • Comedy of Errors, The
London, England • Covent Garden	1820 04 22	Bishop, Sir Henry Rowley • Henri Quatre [Paris in the Olden Times]
London, England • Drury Lane Theatre	1820 11 08	Bishop, Sir Henry Rowley • Twelfth Night
London, England • Covent Garden	1821 05 15	Bishop, Sir Henry Rowley • Tempest, The
London, England • Covent Garden	1821 11 29	Bishop, Sir Henry Rowley • Two Gentlemen of Verona, The
London, England • Drury Lane Theatre	1823 00 00	Horn, Charles Edward, and Samuel Webbe Jr. • Merry Wives of Windsor
London, England • Drury Lane Theatre	1824 02 20	Bishop, Sir Henry Rowley • Merry Wives of Windsor, The
London, England • Drury Lane Theatre	1826 00 00	Cooke, Thomas Simpson • Oberon, or The Charmed Horn
London, England • Drury Lane Theatre	1826 01 28	Cooke, Thomas Simpson • Malvina
London, England • Covent Garden	1826 04 12	Weber, Carl Maria von • Oberon [or the Elf-King's Oath]
London, England • Drury Lane Theatre	1828 05 14	Cooke, Thomas Simpson and Braham, John and Others • Taming of the Shrew, The

PLACE	DATE	COMPOSITION
London, England • Her Majesty's Theatre in the Haymarket	1838 07 19	Balfe, Michael William • Falstaff
London, England • Princess's Theater, Oxford Street	1848 12 06	Loder, Edward James • Robin Goodfellow or the Frolics of Puck
London, England • Her Majesty's Theatre in the Haymarket	1850 06 08	Halévy, Jacques Franoçis Fromental Élie • Tempesta, La
London, England • Queen's Theatre	1861 00 00	MacFarren, George Alexander • Hamlet
London, England • Queen's Theatre	1877 01 17	Rossi, Lauro • Biorn
London, England • Lyceum Theatre	1879 11 01	Clarke, James Siree Hamilton • Merchant of Venice
London, England	1890 00 00 ?	Douglas, Hugh A. • Romeo and Juliet Up to Larks
London, England • Prince of Wales Theatre	1892 10 15	Carr, Frank Osmond • In Town
London, England • Covent Garden	1895 07 29	Maclean, Alick • Petruccio
London, England • Coronet Theatre	1899 04 24	Lutz, William Meyer • Merry-Go-Round
London, England • Comedy Theatre	1899 04 29	Rubens, Paul Alfred and Walter Rubens • Great Caesar
London, England • Covent Garden	1901 05 30	Stanford, Sir Charles Villiers • Much Ado About Nothing, Opus 76a
London, England • Vaudeville Theatre	1906 04 11	Stuart, Leslie • Belle of Mayfair
London, England • Apollo Theatre	1906 04 14	Rubens, Paul Alfred and Frank E. Tours • Dairymaids, The
London, England • Queen's Hall [Only parts performed]	1912 02 28	Hale, Alfred Matthew • Tempest, The
London, England • Lyric Theater	1918 05 11	Ansell, John • King's Bride, The [Violette]
London, England • Surrey Theatre	1920 00 00 c.	Gatty, Nicholas Comyn • Macbeth

PLACE	DATE	COMPOSITION
London, England • Surrey Theatre	1920 04 17	Gatty, Nicholas Comyn • Tempest, The
London, England • Duke of York's Theatre	1920 11 20	Beecham, Adrian Wells • Merchant of Venice, The
London, England • Royal College of Music	1929 03 21	Vaughan Williams, Ralph • Sir John in Love
London, England • Sadler's Wells Theatre	1934 04 12	Collingwood, Lawrance Arthur • Macbeth
London, England • BBC-TV	1954 05 16	Slade, Julian • Comedy of Errors
London, England • Covent Garden	1954 12 03	Walton, Sir William • Troilus and Cressida
London, England • Players' Theatre	1956 11 05	Greenwall, Peter • Three Caskets, The or Venice Re-served
London, England • Royal Court Theatre	1960 01 24	Eastwood, Thomas Hugh • Christopher Sly
London, England • Bush Theatre	1974 02 25	Field, Graham • Dick Deterred
London, England • Players' Theatre	1975 09 24	Brawn, Geoffrey • At the Sign of the Angel or A Little Touch of Harry in the Night
London, England • Wimbledon Theatre	1977 02 25	Haines, Roger • Fire Angel
London?, England		Pasquali, Nicolò • Romeo and Juliet
Louisville, Kentucky, U.S.A. • Kentucky Opera Association	1954 12 04	Mohaupt, Richard • Double Trouble [Zwillingskomödie]
Madrid, Spain • Teatro del Circo	1852 02 21	Gaztambide y Garbayo, Joaquin Romualdo • sueño de una noche de verano, El
Madrid, Spain • Teatro de la Jovellanos	1882 03 11	Chapí y Lorente, Ruperto • Tempestad, La
Madrid, Spain • Teatro Martin	1883 11 05	Nieto, Manuel • Otelo y Desdémona

338

PLACE	DATE	COMPOSITION
Madrid, Spain • Teatro Eldorado	1898 08 02	Valverde y San Juan, Joaquín • sueño de una noche de verano, El
Madrid?, Spain	1909 00 00	Campo y Zabaleta, Conrado del • Amantes de Verona, Los
Magdeburg, Germany • Stadttheater	1836 03 29	Wagner, Wilhelm Richard • Liebesverbot, Das oder Die Novize von Palermo
Magdeburg, Germany • Stadttheater	1882 01 12	Freudenberg, Wilhelm • Kleopatra
Manchester, England • British National Opera Company	1925 04 03	Holst, Gustav • At the Boar's Head, Opus 42
Manchester, England	1970 00 00	Unknown • Catch My Soul
Mannheim, Germany • Hoftheater	1794 11 04	Ritter, Peter • lustigen Weiber, Die
Mannheim, Germany • Nationaltheater	1874 10 11	Goetz, Herman • Widerspänstigen Zähmung, Der [La Megère apprivoisée; Caterina e Petruccio]
Melbourne, Australia • By Conservatory Students	1918 12 05	Hart, Fritz Bennicke • Malvolio, Opus 14
Mexico City, Mexico • Teatro National	1863 01 27	Morales, Melesio • Giulietta e Romeo
Middlesborough, England • Harrison-Frewin Company	1916 01 07	Barkworth, John Edmond • Romeo and Juliet
Milan, Italy • Regio Ducal Teatro	1702 00 00	Magni, Giuseppe Paolo • Admeto, Rè di Tessaglia
Milan, Italy • Regio Ducal Teatro	1719 08 27	Vignali, Giuseppe [Act I]; Carlo Baglioni [Act II] and Giacomo Cozzi [Act III] • Ambleto
Milan, Italy • Regio Ducal Teatro	1765 01 00	Scolari, Giuseppe • Cajo Mario
Milan, Italy • Teatro alla Scala	1796 01 30	Zingarelli, Niccolò Antonio • Giulietta e Romeo
Milan, Italy • Teatro alla Scala	1802 10 02	Fioravanti, Valentino • Capricciosa pentita, La

PLACE	DATE	COMPOSITION
Milan, Italy • Teatro alla Scala	1808 12 26	Nicolini, Giuseppe • Coriolano
Milan, Italy • Teatro alla Scala	1817 03 08	Generali, Pietro Mercandetti • Rodrigo di Valencia
Milan, Italy • Teatro alla Scala	1822 12 26	Mercadante, Giuseppe Saverio Raffele • Amleto
Milan, Italy • Teatro Canobbiana	1825 10 31	Vaccai, Nicola • Giulietta e Romeo
Milan, Italy • Teatro Carcano	1833 02 19	Balfe, Michael William • Enrico IV al passo della Marna
Milan, Italy • Teatro alla Scala	1834 11 25	Mercadante, Giuseppe Saverio Raffele • Gioventù di Enrico V, La
Milan, Italy • Teatro Re in San Salvatore	1842 12 00	Manusardi, Giuseppe • sogno di Primavera, Un [Un rêve de printemps]
Milan, Italy • Teatro alla Scala	1859 11 12	Meiners, Giambattista • Riccardo III
Milan, Italy • Teatro alla Scala	1873 04 08	Perelli, Edoardo • Viola Pisani
Milan, Italy • Teatro Carcano	1879 11 10	Canepá, Luigi • Riccardo III
Milan, Italy • Teatro alla Scala	1887 02 05	Verdi, Giuseppe • Otello
Milan, Italy • Teatro alla Scala	1893 02 09	Verdi, Giuseppe • Falstaff
Milan, Italy • Teatro Lirico	1895 11 19	Samara, Spiro • Furia domata, La
Milan, Italy • Teatro Manzoni	1916 02 14	Oddone, Elizabetta • Petruccio e il Cavolo Cappuccio
Milan, Italy • Teatro dal Verme	1922 11 23	Lattuada, Felice • Tempesta, La
Milan, Italy • Teatro Carcano	1925 11 13	Bossi, Renzo • Volpino il Calderaio, Op. 32
Milan, Italy • Teatro alla Scala	1927 12 29	Wolf-Ferrari, Ermanno • Sly, ovvero La leggenda del dormiente risvegliato
Milan, Italy • Teatro Filodrammatici	1929 05 11	Farina, Guido • Dodisesima Notte, La

PLACE	DATE	COMPOSITION
Minneapolis, U.S.A. • University of Minnesota	1963 05 31	Argento, Dominick • Christopher Sly
Moravska Ostrava, Czechoslovakia	1906 05 14	Palliardi, Carl • Stein der Weisen, Der
Moscow, U.S.S.R. • Musikalisches Theater W. I. Nemirowitsch-Dantschenko	1939 05 31	Khrennikov, Tikhon Nikolaevich • Brati [Brothers]
Moscow, U.S.S.R. • V. I. Nemirovi	1939 10 10	Khrennikov, Tikhon Nikolaevich • V buriu [Im Sturm, Into the Storm]
Moscow, Soviet Union • Concert Version	1955 10 01	Shebalin, Vissarion Yakovlevich • Ukroshchenie stroptivoi [The Taming of the Shrew] Op. 46
Moscow, Soviet Union • Chamber Music Theater	1972 03 29	Khrennikov, Tikhon Nikolaevich • Mnogo shuma iz nichego [Viel Lärm aus Leidenschaft, Much Ado About Hearts]
Munich, Germany • Teatro di Corte	1680 07 11	Bernabei, Giuseppe Antonio • Érmione
Munich, Germany • Schloss Karlsburg	1790 00 00	Rumling, Sigismund Freiherr von • Roméo et Juliette
Munich, Germany • National Schau. in alt. Opernhaus)	1798 10 19	Winter, Peter von • Sturm, Der
Munich, Germany • Hoftheater	1820 09 08	Stuntz, Joseph Hartmann • Heinrich IV zu Givry
Munich, Germany	1914 07 00	Beer-Walbrunn, Anton • Sturm, Der
Munich, Germany • Nationaltheater	1978 07 09	Reimann, Aribert • Lear
Nantes, France • Grand Théâtre	1888 04 21	Hignard, Aristide • Hamlet
Nantes, France • Grand Théâtre	1892 04 09	Rateau, Edmond • Rosaline

PLACE	DATE	COMPOSITION
Napels, Italy • Teatro s. Bartolomeo	1734 00 00	Conti, Nicolò • Cajo Marzio Coriolano [Marzio Coriolano]
Naples, Italy • Teatro San Carlo	1755 01 20	Scarlatti, Giuseppe • Caio Mario
Naples, Italy • Teatro San Carlo	1757 00 00	Piccinni, Niccolò • Caio Mario
Naples, Italy • Real Teatro di San Carlo	1784 05 30	Bianchi, Francesco • Cajo Mario
Naples, Italy • Teatro del Fondo della Separazione dei Lucri	1794 10 05	Guglielmi, Pietro Alessandro • Admeto, Re di Tessaglia
Naples, Italy • Teatro Nuovo	1799 00 00	Caruso, Lodovico Luigi • Tempesta, La
Naples, Italy • Teatro del Fondo	1815 01 05	Hérold, Louis Joseph Ferdinand • Gioventù di Enrico V, La [La Jeunesse d'Henry V]
Naples, Italy • Teatro del Fondo della Separazione dei Lucri	1816 12 04	Rossini, Gioacchino • Otello, osia L'Africano di Venezia
Naples, Italy • Teatro Nuovo	1819 00 00	Carlini, Luigi • Gioventù di Enrico V, La
Naples, Italy • Teatro San Carlo	1819 03 27	Rossini, Gioacchino • Ermione
Naples, Italy • Teatro di San Carlo	1829 02 07	Costa, Michael Andrew Angus • Malvina
Naples, Italy • Teatro Nuovo	1851 12 29	Lillo, Giuseppe • Sogno d'una Notte estiva, Il or La Gioventù di Shakespeare
Naples, Italy • Teatro Nuovo	1853 10 01	Mercadante, Giuseppe Saverio Raffele • Violetta
Naples, Italy • Teatro di San Carlo	1855 12 08	Tommasi, Ferdinando [Tommaso] • Guido e Ginevre
Naples, Italy • Teatro Nuovo	1878 02 17	Sarria, Errico • Equivoci, Gli
Naples, Italy • Teatro delle Folie Gramatici	1880 00 00	Unknown • Pulcinella rivale di Turzillo e confuso tra Capuleti e Montecchi

PLACE	DATE	COMPOSITION
New Brunswick, N. J. (Rutgers University: Douglas School of Music), U.S.A. • Rutgers University: Douglas School of Music	1978 04 07	Schmitz, Alan • Julius Caesar
New York, U.S.A. • Park Theater	1826 00 00	Garcia, Manuel Vincente del Popolo • Giulietta e Romeo
New York, U.S.A. • Park Theater	1827 00 00	Garcia, Manuel Vincente del Popolo • Gioventù di Enrico V, La
New York, U.S.A. • Casino Theatre	1900 09 24	Engländer, Ludwig • Belle of Bohemia, The
New York, U.S.A.	1901 00 00	Shelley, Harry Rowe • Romeo and Juliet
New York, U.S.A.	1916 05 00	Farwell, Arthur George • Caliban by the Yellow Sands, Opus 47
New York, U.S.A. • Tr. d. Opera	1916 06 00	Conte, Paolo • Shakespeare, the Playmaker
New York, U.S.A. • Avin	1938 11 23	Rogers, Richard • Boys from Syracuse, The
New York, U.S.A. • Center Theater	1939 11 29	Van Heusen, Jimmy • Swingin' the Dream
New York, U.S.A. • New Century Theatre	1948 12 30	Porter, Cole • Kiss Me, Kate
New York, U.S.A. • Winter Garden	1957 09 26	Bernstein, Leonard • West Side Story
New York, U.S.A. • Theater de Lys	1964 10 27	Balamos, John • As You Like It
New York, U.S.A. • Orpheum Theatre	1964 12 28	Besoyan, Rick • Babes in the Wood, or Who Killed Cock Robin
New York, U.S.A. • Off-Broadway Opera Company	1965 04 04	Halpern, Sidney • Macbeth
New York, U.S.A. • Metropolitan Opera	1966 09 16	Barber, Samuel • Antony and Cleopatra, Op. 40

PLACE	DATE	COMPOSITION
New York, U.S.A. • Sheridan Square Playhouse	1968 01 03	Gelber, Stanley Jay • Love and Let Love
New York, U.S.A. • Off-Broadway	1968 01 13	Hester, Hal and Danny Apolinar • Your Own Thing
New York, U.S.A.	1969 01 07	Liota, A. • Romeo and Juliet
New York, U.S.A. • Theatre Four	1970 10 25	Harper, Wally • Sensations
New York, U.S.A. • St. James Theatre	1971 12 01	MacDermot, Galt • Two Gentlemen of Verona
New York, U.S.A. • Players Theater	1974 04 03	Cribari, Donna • Pop
New York, U.S.A. • Minskoff Theatre	1976 02 17	Jones, Cliff • Rockabye Hamlet
New York, U.S.A. • WPA Theatre	1976 04 02	Malamet, Marsha • Dreamstuff
New York, U.S.A. • St. James Theatre	1976 12 20	Adler, Richard • Music Is
New York, U. S. A.	1980 02 01	Mulcahy, Lance • Shakespeare's Cabaret
New York, U.S.A. • ANTA Theater	1981 11 10	Valenti, Michael • Oh, Brother
New York, Boston, and Cambridge, U.S.A.	1893 04 00	Atherton, Percy Lee and Ernest Hamlin Abbott • Hamlet, Prince of Denmark or The Sport, the Spook and the Spinster
Northampton, Mass. (Smith College), U.S.A. • Smith College	1917 06 00	Morton, Louise, and others • Twelfth Night
Norwich, England • Festival	1902 00 00	Bedford, Herbert • Love Scene from Shakespeare's Romeo and Juliet for Contralto and Baritone
Opava, Czechoslovakia	1969 12 21	Doubrava, Jaroslav • Sen noci svatojanske
Oslo, Norway	1951 12 07	Eggen, Arne • Cymbelyn
Padua, Italy • Teatro Nuovo	1792 06 13	Andreozzi, Gaetano • Amleto

344

PLACE	DATE	COMPOSITION
Padua, Italy • Teatro dei Concordi	1846 03 14	Santa Caterina, Alessandro • Coriolano
Padua, Italy • Teatro del Corso	1913 08 24	Cottrau, Giulio • Cordelia (Re Lear)
Palermo, Italy • Teatro Carolino	1817 00 00	Mosca, Giuseppe • Gioventù di Enrico V, La
Palermo, Italy • Teatro Carolino	1853 00 00	Pacini, Giovanni • Rodrigo di Valencia
Paris, France • Comédie Italienne	1722 01 02	Unknown • Thimon le misantrope
Paris, France • Théâtre de l'Opéra comique a la foire St. Laurent	1761 07 28	Alexandre, Charles Guillaume • Georget et Georgette
Paris, France • Comédie Italienne	1761 12 07	Papavoine, Mdme • Vieux Coquet, Le; ou Les deux amies ou Le vieus garçon
Paris, France • Comédie-Française	1768 12 10	Gossec, François Joseph • Hylas et Sylvie
Paris, France • Comédiens italiens ordinaires du Roy	1774 11 14	Martini, Giovanni • Henri IV, ou La Bataille d'Ivry
Paris, France • Opéra Comique, rue Favart	1792 07 06	Dalayrac, Nicolas • Tout pour l'amour ou Roméo et Juliette
Paris, France • Théâtre de la Cité	1793 00 00	Navoigille, Gouliellmo • Orage, L' ou Quel Guignon!
Paris, France • Théâtre de la rue Feydeau	1793 09 11	Steibelt, Daniel Gottlieb • Roméo et Juliette or Tout pour l'amour
Paris, France • Théâtre de l'Opéra Comique National, rue Favart	1796 04 27	Kreutzer, Rodolphe • Imogène, ou La Gageure indiscrète
Paris, France • Opéra Comique, rue Favart	1797 05 01	Méhul, Étienne Nicolas • Jeune Henri, Le [Gabrielle d'Estrées où les Amours d'Henri IV]
Paris, France • Théâtre des Variétés [Montansier]	1798 06 09	Foignet, Jacques • Orage, L'
Paris, France • Opéra Comique	1799 04 15	Berton, Henri-Montan • Montano et Stéphanie

PLACE	DATE	COMPOSITION
Paris, France • Théâtre de Académie Impériale de Musique	1806 00 00	Porta, [Bernardo ?] • Roméo et Juliette
Paris, France	1816 00 00	Gallenberg, Wenzel Robert Count von • Amleto
Paris, France • Théâtre de l'Academie royale de musique, Salle provisoire de la rue Le Peletier	1827 06 29	Chélard, Hippolyte-André-Jean-Baptiste • Macbeth
Paris, France • Opéra Comique	1828 10 07	Carafa di Colobrano, Michele Enrico and Aimé Ambroise Simon Leborne • Violette, La ou Gérard de Nevers
Paris, France • Theatre Nouveauté	1829 00 00	Mélésville, Honoré Marie Joseph, Baron Duveyrier] • Gillette de Narbonne
Paris, France • Théâtre de la Porte Saint Martin	1829 11 09	Piccini, Louis Alexandre • Macbeth
Paris, France • Théâtre del Académie royale de Musique, Salle provisoire de la rue Le Peletier	1838 03 05	Halévy, Jacques François Fromental Elie • Guido et Ginevre ou La Peste de Florence
Paris, France • Théâtre National du Cirque-Olympiade	1846 10 17	Francastel, A. • Henry IV
Paris, France • Vaudeville Théâtre	1849 00 00	Herx, Werner • Orakelspruch, Der
Paris, France • Opéra Comique, Salle Favart	1850 04 20	Thomas, Charles Louis Ambroise • Songe d'une nuit d'été, Le [Shakespeare oder Der Traum einer Sommernacht]
Paris, France • Théâtre de Bouffes-Parisiens, Salle des Champs-Elysées	1855 07 30	Offenbach, Jacques • Rêve d'une Nuit d'été, Le

PLACE	DATE	COMPOSITION
Paris, France • Théâtre Lyrique, Salle du Théâtre-Ristorique	1856 01 18	Adam, Adolphe-Charles • Falstaff
Paris, France • Théâtre au Palais des Tuileries	1856 02 28	Weckerlin, Jean Baptiste Théodore • Tout est bien qui finit bien
Paris, France • Théâtre Lyrique, Salle de la Place du Châtelet	1863 03 31	Mozart, Wolfgang Amadeus • Peines d'amour perdues
Paris, France • Théâtre des Champs-Élysées	1863 06 19	Legouix, Isidore Édouard • Othello, Un
Paris, France • Théâtre de l'Opéra Comique	1865 03 08	David, Félicien César • Saphir, Le or Tout est bien, qui finit bien
Paris, France • Théâtre Lyrique	1867 04 27	Gounod, Charles François • Roméo et Juliette
Paris, France • Théâtre Déjazet	1867 07 00	Déjazet, Eugène • Rhum et eau en juillet
Paris, France • Théâtre de l'Academie Imperiale de l'Opéra	1868 03 09	Thomas, Charles Louis Ambroise • Hamlet
Paris, France • Théâtre de La Renaissance	1877 02 03	Lecocq, Charles Alexandre • Marjolaine
Paris, France • Théâtre Ventadour	1878 10 12	Ivry, Paul Xaver Désiré Richard, Marquis d' • Amantes de Vérone, Les
Paris, France • Théâtre du Châtelet	1880 11 18	Duvernoy, Victor-Alphonse • Tempète, La
Paris, France • Bouffes-Parisiens	1882 11 11	Audran, Edmond • Gillette de Narbonne [Gillette, or Count and Countess; Gilda di Guascogna]
Paris, France • Opéra	1883 03 05	Saint-Saëns, Camille • Henry VIII
Paris, France • Théâtre Lyrique	1884 00 00	Choudens, Antony • Cymbeline
Paris, France	1886 09 01	Noël, Édouard Marie Émile • songe d'une nuit d'été, Le
Paris, France • Théâtre des Bouffes-Parisiens	1886 09 01	Serpette, Henri Charles Antoine Gaston • Songe d'une nuit d'été, Le

PLACE	DATE	COMPOSITION
Paris, France • Private performance	1889 11 00	Leoncavallo, Ruggiero • Songe d'une nuit d'été, Un
Paris, France • Odéon	1890 10 30	Thomé, François Lucien Joseph • Roméo et Juliette
Paris, France • Bodinière	1893 11 29	David, Adolphe Isaac • Orage, L'
Paris, France • Théâtre de la Comédie Parisienne	1894 06 25	Missa, Edmond Jean Louis • Dinah
Paris, France • Opéra-Comique	1899 03 24	Puget, Paul-Charles-Marie • Beaucoup de bruit pour rien
Paris, France • Théâtre des Bouffes-Parisiens	1899 11 23	Serpette, Henri Charles Antoine Gaston • Shakespeare!
Paris, France • Théâtre des Folies Dramatiques	1900 06 23	Hulemann, Th • Malvine I re [The first]
Paris, France • Opéra Comique	1903 01 20	Hüe, George • Titania
Paris, France • Salle Mars	1907 01 28	Saussine, Henri de • Marchand de Vénise, Le
Paris, France • Opéra Comique	1910 11 30	Bloch, Ernest • Macbeth
Paris, France • Fémina	1911 03 03	Vidal, Paul Antonin • Peines d'amour perdues
Paris, France • Théâtre Shakespeare	1912 03 21	Vidal, Paul Antonin • Comme il vous Plaire
Paris, France • Théâtre National de l'Opéra	1922 01 30	Silver, Charles • Mégère apprivoisée, La
Paris, France • Théâtre Municipal de la Gaité-Lyrique	1935 03 23	Hahn, Reynaldo • Malvina
Paris, France • Théâtre National de l'Opéra	1935 03 25	Hahn, Reynaldo • Marchand de Vénise, Le
Paris, France • Théâtre de la Madeleine	1936 03 00	Hahn, Reynaldo • Beaucoup de bruit pour rien
Parma, Italy • Regio Teatro	1861 02 14	Benvenuti, Tommaso • Guglielmo Shakespeare

PLACE	DATE	COMPOSITION
Perugia, Italy • Teatro Morlacchi	1905 05 07	Angelis, Arturo de • Tempesta, La
Pest, Hungary • Deutchestheater	1841 12 10	Schindelmeisser, Louis Alexander Balthasar • Malvina
Philadelphia, U.S.A. • Vocal Arts Academy	1975 00 00 ?	Turok, Paul H. • Richard III
Piacenza, Italy • Teatro Ducale	1669 00 00	Cavalli, Pietro Francesco • Coriolano
Pisa, Italy • Teatro de' Ravrivati [sp?]	1825 00 00	Maganini, Giovanni • Enrico IV al passo della Marna
Port-Mahon [Minorca], Spain • Teatro dell'Opera	1873 03 00	Mercadal y Pons, Antonio • Giulietta e Romeo
Prague		Horner • König Lear
Prague, Czechoslovakia • Kgl. bohemian Landes- Nationaltheatre		Kovarovic, Karel • Perdita
Prague, Czechoslovakia • Czech National Theater	1860 00 00	Nápravnik, Éduard Frantsevich • Sturm, Der
Prague, Czechoslovakia • Deutsches Landestheater	1865 01 11	Barbieri, Carlo Emanuele di • Perdita oder Ein Wintermärchen
Prague, Czechoslovakia • Czech National Theater	1892 00 00	Weis, Karél • Comme il vous Plaira
Prague, Czechoslovakia • Czech National Theater	1892 01 17	Weis, Karél • Viola [Die Zwillinge, Blizenci]
Prague, Czechoslovakia • Narodni Divádlo	1895 03 01	Fibich, Zdenko • Boure, Opus 40 [Der Sturm]
Prague, Czechoslovakia • Czech National Theater	1897 05 21	Nesvera, Josef • Perdita

PLACE	DATE	COMPOSITION
Prague, Czechoslovakia • Czech National Theater	1905 04 16	Foerster, Joseph Brohuslav • Jessika, Opus 60
Prague, Czechoslovakia • Czech National Theater	1924 05 11	Smetana, Bedrich • Viola
Prague, Czechoslovakia • Narodni Divádlo	1946 09 08	Krejcí, Isa • Pozdvizení v Efesu [The Upheaval in Ephesus]
Prague, Czechoslovakia • Narodni Divádlo	1974 03 21	Cikker, Ján • Coriolanus
Reading, England • Town Hall	1887 12 14	Old, John • Herne the Hunter (A Legend of Royal Windsor)
Reggio Calabria, Italy • Teatro Borbonio	1822 00 00	Aspa, Mario • Gioventù di Enrico V, La
Reggio d'Emilia, Italy • Teatro del Pubblico	1741 00 00	Pulli, Pietro • Caio Marzio Coriolano
Riga, Soviet Union • Latvijas Nacionata Opera	1936 02 17	Kalnins, Janis • Hamlets
Rome, Italy • Teatro Capranica, Sala dei Signori	1715 00 00	Scarlatti, Giuseppe Domenico • Ambleto
Rome, Italy • Teatro di Torre Argentina	1746 02 06	Jommelli, Nicolo • Caio Mario [Cajo Mario]
Rome, Italy • Teatro Dame	1780 01 00	Cimarosa, Domenico Nicola [Cimmarosa] • Cajo Mario
Rome, Italy • Teatro Capranica	1788 01 00	Fabrizi, Vincenzo • Tempestà ossia Da un disordine ne nasce un ordine, La
Rome, Italy • Teatro di Torre Argentina	1789 00 00	Marescalchi, Luigi • Giuletta e Romeo
Rome, Italy • Teatro della Valle	1818 09 09	Fioravanti, Valentino • Enrico IV al passo della Marna

PLACE	DATE	COMPOSITION
Rome, Italy • Teatro della Valle	1820 12 26	Pacini, Giovanni • Gioventù di Enrico V, La (also La bella tavernara; Le Aventure d'una notte)
Rome, Italy • Teatro di Apollo	1860 06 02	Moroni, Luigi • Amleto
Rome, Italy • Teatro Argentino	1892 04 07	Westerhout, Niccolò van • Cimbelino, Il
Rome, Italy	1917 00 00	Mancinelli, Luigi • Sogno di una notte d'estate, Il
Rome, Italy • Teatro Costanzi	1922 02 14	Zandonai, Riccardo • Giulietta e Romeo
Rome, Italy • Teatro Reale dell' Opera	1931 02 12	Persico, Mario • Bisbetica Domata, La
Rome, Italy • Teatro Reale dell'Opera	1937 04 24	Ghislanzoni, Alberto • Re Lear
Rome, Italy • Teatro dell'Opera	1961 01 07	Zafred, Mario • Amleto
Rouen, France • Théâtre des Arts	1895 12 00	Le Rey, Frédéric • Mégère apprivoisée, La
Rouen, France • Théâtre des Arts	1974 03 08	Bondeville, Emmanuel de • Antonine et Cléopatre
Salzburg, Austria • Benedictine Convent	1750 09 04	Eberlin, Johann Ernst • Ricardus Impius, Angliae Rex, ab Henrico Richmondæ Comite vita simul et regno excitus
Salzburg, Austria • Hoftheater	1806 00 00	Emmert, Adam Joseph • Sturm, Der
Salzburg, Austria • Salzburger Festspiele	1959 08 17	Erbse, Heimo • Julietta, Op. 15
San Francisco, U.S.A. • Bohemian Club	1967 07 29	Utley, Wendell • Will
San Francisco, U.S.A. • Opera	1979 08 20	Harbison, John • Winter's Tale, The
San Remo, Italy • Teatro Casino Municipale	1937 03 05	Canonica, Pietro • Miranda
Saratoga, N.Y., U.S.A.	1895 00 00	Kaun, Hugo • Falstaff
Shreveport, LA, U.S.A. • Shreveport Symphony Society	1976 11 14	Siegmeister, Elie • Night of the Moonspell

PLACE	DATE	COMPOSITION
Siena, Italy	1894 00 00	Marescotti • Amleto
St. Petersburg, Russia	1867 11 11	Kashperov, Vladimir Nikititch • Storm, The [Groza]
St. Petersburg, Soviet Union • Maryinsky Theater	1883 12 21	Salvayre, Gaston • Riccardo III
St. Petersburg, Soviet Union • Teatro Opera Russa	1885 11 24	Soloviev, Nicolai Feopemptovich • Cordélia
St. Petersburg, Soviet Union • Maria Theater	1910 03 00	Kasanli, Nikolai Ivanovich [Kazanli, Kazanly] • Miranda (Poliedniaia bor'ba) [Der Letzte Kampf]
Stettin, Poland • Neues Theater	1794 00 00	Haack, Friedrich • Geisterinsel, Die
Stettin, Poland	1939 03 11	Lorenz, Carl Adolf • Komödie der Irrungen, Die
Stettin, Poland	1941 03 30	Hess, Ludwig • Was ihr Wollt
Stockholm, Sweden • Kongl Operalmset	1810 12 19	Küster, Johann Heinrich • Henrik den Fjerde
Stockholm, Sweden • Kgl.Th.	1855 02 00	Berens, Johann Hermann • Violetta
Stockholm, Sweden • Mindre Theater	1856 10 27	Berens, Johann Hermann • Sommarnattsdröm, En
Stockholm, Sweden	1869 03 00	Berens, Johann Hermann • Riccardo
Stockholm, Sweden • Royal Theater	1948 09 19	Atterberg, Kurt • Stormen, Op. 49
Strasbourg, France • Théâtre Municipal	1949 01 29	Delannoy, Marcel • Puck
Stuttgart, Germany • Herzogl. Hoftheater	1798 11 07	Zumsteeg, Johann Rudolf • Geisterinsel, Die
Stuttgart, Germany • Wüttembergische Staatsoper	1980 12 06	Reutter, Hermann • Hamlet
Tbilisi, Soviet Union	1963 00 00	Machavariani, Alexei • Othello
Tbilisi, Soviet Union	1964 00 00	Machavariani, Alexei • Hamlet

PLACE	DATE	COMPOSITION
Torino, Italy • Teatro Regio	1806 00 00	Lavina, Vincenzo • Coriolano, II
Torino, Italy • Teatro Regio	1820 00 00	Orlandi, Ferdinando • Rodrigo di Valencia
Toulouse, France • Théâtre du Capitole	1888 06 01	Reynaud, Armand • Roi Lear, Le
Toulouse, France • Théâtre du Capitole	1898 03 25	Deffès, Louis Pierre • Jessica
Toulouse, France	1950 00 00	Gaujac, Edmond Germain • Amantes de Vérone, Les
Trieste, Italy • Teatro Comunale	1865 10 24	Marchetti, Filippo • Romeo e Giulietta
Turin, Italy • Teatro Regio	1806 00 00	Savigna, Vincenzo • Coriolano
Turin, Italy • Palestra Ristori	1899 11 00	Roti, Ugo • Sogno di una notte d'estate, II
University, Alabama, U.S.A. • University of Alabama	1967 11 14	Bruce, Neely • Pyramus and Thisbe
University, Miss., U.S.A. • University of Mississippi Music Department	1959 01 08	Kreutz, Arthur • Sourwood Mountain
Venice, Italy • Teatro Grimano de Ss. Gio. e Paolo	1683 01 20	Perti, Giacomo Antonio • Martio Coriolano
Venice, Italy • Teatro di San Angelo	1692 00 00	Capelli, Giovanni Maria • Rosalinda [Erginia Mascherata]
Venice, Italy • Theatro di San Angiolo	1692 11 11	Ziani, Marc Antonio • Rosalinda, La or Erginia mascherata
Venice, Italy • Teatro di Piazza o delle Grazie	1694 00 00	Freschi, Giovanni Domenico • Rosalinda
Venice, Italy • Teatro di San Giovanni Grisostomo	1698 01 18	Pollaroli, Carlo Francesco • Marzio Coriolano
Venice, Italy • Teatro Tron di San Cassano	1705 12 26	Gasperini, Carlo Francesco • Ambleto
Venice, Italy • Teatro Grimani San Giovanni Grisostomo	1723 11 23	Gasperini, Carlo Francesco • Equivoci d'amore e d'innocenza, Gl'

PLACE	DATE	COMPOSITION
Venice, Italy • Theatro di Sant' Angelo	1741 12 26	Carcani, Giuseppe • Ambleto
Venice, Italy • Teatro San Giovanni Grisostomo	1764 05 31	Galuppi, Baldassarre [called Buranello] • Cajo Mario
Venice, Italy • Teatro di San Benedetto	1770 11 00	Anfossi, Pasquale • Cajo Mario
Venice, Italy • Teatro di San Benedetto	1777 05 00	Monza, Carlo Antonio • Cajo Mario
Venice, Italy • Teatro di La Benedetto	1781 05 04	Bertoni, Ferdinando Giuseppe • Cajo Mario
Venice, Italy • Teatro di San Benedetto	1816 06 08	Vaccai, Nicola • Malvina
Venice, Italy • Teatro Eretenia	1828 07 26	Torriani, Eugenio • Romeo e Giulietta
Venice, Italy • Gran Teatro La Fenice	1830 03 11	Bellini, Vincenzo • Capuleti e i Montecchi, I
Venice, Italy • Teatro La Fenice	1848 02 24	Buzzolla, Antonio • Amleto
Venice, Italy • Teatro Gallo a San Benedetto	1854 05 30	Zanardini, Angelo • Amleto
Venice, Italy • Teatro la Fenice	1961 02 02	Malipiero, Gian Francesco • Romeo e Guilietta (scene 5 of Monde celesti e infernali)
Verona , Italy • Teatre Filharmonica	1928 03 00	Bottacio, Pietro • Bisbetica Domata, La
Versailles, France	1854 04 00	Séméladis, M. • Cordélia
Vienna, Austria • Hoftheater	1689 00 00	Bernabei, Vincenzo • Equivoci d'Amore, Gli
Vienna, Austria	1696 00 00	Leopold I, Holy Roman Emperor • Timòne, Misantropo
Vienna, Austria • Hoftheater	1696 00 00	Draghi, Antonio • Timone misantropo
Vienna, Austria • Theater der Favorita	1717 08 28	Caldara, Antonio • Cajo Marzio Coriolano
Vienna, Austria	1777 00 00	Asplmayr, Franz • Leben und Tod des Königs Macbeth
Vienna, Austria	1781 00 00	Asplmayr [Aspelmayr], Franz • Sturm, Der

Shakespeare and the Musical Stage

PLACE	DATE	COMPOSITION
Vienna, Austria • Burgtheater	1786 12 27	Storace, Stephen • Equivoci, Gli
Vienna, Austria • Theater auf der Wieden	1790 09 11	Zák, Benedict Emanuel • Stein der Weisen, Dem oder Die Zauber Insel
Vienna, Austria • Theater auf der Weiden	1790 09 11	Gerl, Thaddäus; Henneberg and Benedikt Schack • Stein der Weisen, Der oder Die Zauberinsel
Vienna, Austria • Theater auf der Landstrasse	1792 07 22	Hoffmeister, Franz Anton • Schiffbruch, Der
Vienna, Austria • Burgtheater	1792 10 06	Vranicky, Pavel • Rudolf von Felseck (Die Schwarzthaler) oder La Tempestà
Vienna, Austria • Theater im Palais der Fürstin Lubonsirsky [Sp?]	1794 00 00	Weigl, Joseph [Veigl, Giuseppe] • Amleto
Vienna, Austria • K K prin Th auf d. Wieden.	1794 04 08	Unknown • Bezähmte Widerbellerin, Die
Vienna, Austria • Theater auf der Weiden	1794 07 10	Tuczek, Vincenc Tomas Vaclav • Travestirte Hamlet, Der [Hamlet, Prinz von Dänemark; Hamlet, Prinz von Lilyput]
Vienna, Austria • Theater auf der Weiden	1796 04 23	Hoffmeister, Franz Anton • Rosalinde, oder Die Macht der Feen
Vienna, Austria • Theater in der Leopoldstadt	1798 11 08	Müller, Wenzel • Sturm oder die Zauberinsel, Der
Vienna, Austria • Kärntnertortheater	1799 01 03	Salieri, Antonio • Falstaff osia Le tre Burle
Vienna, Austria • Theater in der Leopoldstadt	1800 11 06	Hofmann, Johann • Ritter Hans von Dampf
Vienna, Austria • Theater in der Leopoldstadt	1806 05 28	Schuster, Ignaz • Othellerl, der Mohr von Wien

PLACE	DATE	COMPOSITION
Vienna, Austria • Theater in der Leopoldstadt	1807 11 05	Schuster, Ignaz • Hamlet, Prinz vom Tandelmarkt
Vienna, Austria • Theater in der Leopoldstadt	1808 03 18	Schuster, Ignaz • Romeo und Julie
Vienna, Austria • Theater an der Wien	1811 09 14	Kanne, Friedrich August • Miranda oder Das Schwert der Rache
Vienna, Austria • Theater in der Leopoldstadt	1812 01 22	Gevel, Franz Xaver • Rinaldo und Camilla oder Die Zauberinsel
Vienna, Austria • Kärntnertortheater	1823 10 25	Weber, Carl Maria von • Euryanthe
Vienna, Austria • Theater an der Wein	1827 11 14	Riotte, Philipp Jakob • Orakelspruch, Der
Vienna, Austria • Theater an der Wien	1829 06 06	Müller (the elder), Adolph • Othellerl, der Mohr von Wien [Die geheilte Eifersucht]
Vienna, Austria • Theater an der Wein	1844 04 24	Müller (the elder), Adolph • Viel Lärm um Nichts
Vienna, Austria • Josefstädttheater	1844 08 31	Suppé, Franz von • Sommernachtstraum, Der
Vienna, Austria • Josefstädttheater	1851 10 30	Storch, Anton Maria • Stein der Weisen, Der
Vienna, Austria • Josefstädttheater	1862 03 02	Storch, Anton Maria • Romeo und Julie
Vienna, Austria • Theater an der Wien	1865 12 14	Müller (the elder), Adolph • Heinrich IV
Vienna, Austria • Strampfer Theater	1874 01 29	Hopp, Julius • Hammlet
Vienna, Austria • Theater an d. Wien	1885 02 14	Genée, Franz Friedrich Richard and Louis Roth • Zwillinge
Vienna, Austria • Opernhaus	1908 01 02	Goldmark, Carl • Wintermärchen, Ein
Vienna, Austria • Studio der Hochschulen	1945 06 14	Zavodsky, Felix • Othello
Vienna, Austria • Staatsoper	1956 06 17	Martin, Frank • Sturm, Der

PLACE	DATE	COMPOSITION
Walsall, England • Alexandra Theatre	1882 08 14	Emery, Charles P. • Romeo, the Radical or Obstruction and Effect
Warsaw, Poland • Wielki t.	1970 11 19	Matuszczak, Bernadetta • Julia i Romeo
Weimar, Germany • Comödienhaus	1785 10 24	Wolf, Ernst Wilhelm • Zauberirrungen, Die [Die Irrtümer der Zauberei]
Weimar, Germany • Herzogl. Gostfuirtur [Sp?]	1798 05 19	Fleischmann, Friedrich • Geisterinsel, Die
Weimar, Germany • Hoftheater	1859 10 23	Flotow, Friedrich von • Wintermärchen, Ein
Wexford, England	1969 11 01	Wilson, James • Twelfth Night
Wolfenbüttel, Germany • Fürstlich Theater im Schlosse	1686 02 11	Zanettini, Antonio • Érmione [Die wiedergefundene Hermione]
Wroclaw [Breslau], Poland	1862 00 00	Damrosch, Leopold • Romeo und Julia
Zagreb, Yugoslavia • Tr. d'Opera	1901 00 00	Zajc, Ivan • Cordelia
Zagreb, Yugoslavia	1955 06 21	Fribec, Kresimir • Romeo and Juliet
Zagreb, Yugoslavia • Opera	1958 10 12	Sulek, Stjepan • Koriolan
Zagreb, Yugoslavia • Opera	1969 11 28	Sulek, Stjepan • Oluja

SORTING BY DATE OF PREMIERE

DATE	PLACE	COMPOSITION
1611 01 01	London, England	Ferraboso II, Alfonso and Robert Johnson • Oberon, the Fairy Prince
1612 00 00	London, England	Johnson, Robert • Tempest, The
1669 00 00	Piacenza, Italy	Cavalli, Pietro Francesco • Coriolano
1673 02 18	London, England	Locke, Matthew and Robert Johnson • Macbeth
1674 04 30	London, England	Banister, John; Giovanni Battista Draghi; Matthew Locke; Pelham Humfrey; and Pietro Reggio • Tempest, The [The Enchanted Island]
1680 07 11	Munich, Germany	Bernabei, Giuseppe Antonio • Érmione
1683 01 20	Venice, Italy	Perti, Giacomo Antonio • Martio Coriolano
1686 00 00	Florence, Italy	Cattani, Lorenzo • Cajo Marzio Coriolano
1686 02 11	Wolfenbüttel, Germany	Zanettini, Antonio • Érmione [Die wiedergefundene Hermione]
1687 00 00		Clarke, Jeremiah • Titus Andronicus
1689 00 00	Vienna, Austria	Bernabei, Vincenzo • Equivoci d'Amore, Gli
1692 00 00	Venice, Italy	Capelli, Giovanni Maria • Rosalinda [Erginia Mascherata]
1692 05 02	London, England	Purcell, Henry • Fairy Queen, The
1692 11 11	Venice, Italy	Ziani, Marc Antonio • Rosalinda, La or Erginia mascherata
1694 00 00	London, England	Purcell, Henry • History of Timon of Athens, the Man Hater, The
1694 00 00	Venice, Italy	Freschi, Giovanni Domenico • Rosalinda
1695 00 00	Leipzig, Germany	Strungk, Nicolaus Adam • Rosalinde
1695 00 00	London, England	Purcell, Henry • Tempest or Enchanted Island, The

359

DATE	PLACE	COMPOSITION
1696 00 00	Vienna, Austria	Leopold I, Holy Roman Emperor • Timòne, Misantropo
1696 00 00	Vienna, Austria	Draghi, Antonio • Timone misantropo
1698 01 18	Venice, Italy	Pollaroli, Carlo Francesco • Marzio Coriolano
1702 00 00	Milan, Italy	Magni, Giuseppe Paolo • Admeto, Rè di Tessaglia
1702 11 21	London, England	Leverage, Richard • Macbeth
1705 12 26	Venice, Italy	Gasperini, Carlo Francesco • Ambleto
1715 00 00	Rome, Italy	Scarlatti, Giuseppe Domenico • Ambleto
1716 04 11	London, England	Leverage, Richard • Pyramus and Thisbe, The Comic Masque of
1717 08 28	Vienna, Austria	Caldara, Antonio • Cajo Marzio Coriolano
1719 08 27	Milan, Italy	Vignali, Giuseppe [Act I]; Carlo Baglioni [Act II] and Giacomo Cozzi [Act III] • Ambleto
1722 01 02	Paris, France	Unknown • Thimon le misantrope
1723 02 19	London, England	Ariosti, Attilio • Coriolano, II
1723 11 23	Venice, Italy	Gasperini, Carlo Francesco • Equivoci d'amore e d'innocenza, Gl'
1725 12 00	Breslau, Poland	Treu, Daniel Gottlieb • Coriolano
1727 01 31	London, England	Händel, Georg Friederich • Admeto, Re di Tessaglia
1733 12 05	London, England	Unknown • Timon in Love or The Innocent Theft
1734 00 00	Napels, Italy	Conti, Nicolò • Cajo Marzio Coriolano [Marzio Coriolano]
1735 02 25	London, England	Unknown • Cure for a Scold, A
1740 01 04	London, England	Smith, John Christopher • Rosalinda
1741 00 00	Reggio d'Emilia, Italy	Pulli, Pietro • Caio Marzio Coriolano
1741 12 26	Venice, Italy	Carcani, Giuseppe • Ambleto
1743 01 01	London, England	Galuppi, Baldassarre • Enrico

360

DATE	PLACE	COMPOSITION
1744 00 00	Livorno, Italy	Maggioni, Francesco • Cajo Marzio Coriolano
1744 01 31	London, England	Veracini, Francesco Maria • Rosalinda
1745 01 25	London, England	Lampe, John Frederich • Pyramus and Thisbe
1746 00 00	London, England	Arne, Thomas Augustine • Tempest, The
1746 02 06	Rome, Italy	Jommelli, Nicolo • Caio Mario [Cajo Mario]
1749 12 03	Berlin, Germany	Graun, Karl Heinrich • Coriolano
1750 09 04	Salzburg, Austria	Eberlin, Johann Ernst • Ricardus Impius, Angliae Rex, ab Henrico Richmondæ Comite vita simul et regno excitus
1754 03 25	London, England	Arne, Thomas Augustine, Samuel Arnold and others • Sheep-Shearing, The or Florizel and Perdita
1755 01 20	Naples, Italy	Scarlatti, Giuseppe • Caio Mario
1755 02 03	London, England	Smith, John Christopher • Fairies, The
1756 01 21	London, England	Boyce, William • Florizel and Perdita
1756 02 11	London, England	Smith, John Christopher • Tempest, The
1757 00 00	Naples, Italy	Piccinni, Niccolò • Caio Mario
1761 07 28	Paris, France	Alexandre, Charles Guillaume • Georget et Georgette
1761 12 07	Paris, France	Papavoine, Mdme • Vieux Coquet, Le; ou Les deux amies ou Le vieus garçon
1763 11 26	London, England	Arne, Michael and C. Dibdin, J. Battishill, C. Burney, Hook, J. C. Smith • Fairy Tale
1764 05 31	Venice, Italy	Galuppi, Baldassarre [called Buranello] • Cajo Mario
1765 01 00	Milan, Italy	Scolari, Giuseppe • Cajo Mario
1768 12 10	Paris, France	Gossec, François Joseph • Hylas et Sylvie
1770 11 00	Venice, Italy	Anfossi, Pasquale • Cajo Mario
1771 11 12	London, England	Arne, Thomas Augustine • Fairy Prince, The

DATE	PLACE	COMPOSITION
1773 00 00		Philidor • Herne le Chasseur
1773 00 00	Berlin, Germany	San Severino • Romeo e Giuletta
1774 11 14	Paris, France	Martini, Giovanni • Henri IV, ou La Bataille d'Ivry
1776 00 00	Brunswick [Braun-schweig], Germany	Schwanenberg, Johann Gottfried • Romeo e Giulia
1776 09 25	Gotha, Germany	Benda, George Anton • Romeo und Julie
1777 00 00	Vienna, Austria	Asplmayr, Franz • Leben und Tod des Königs Macbeth
1777 00 00 ?	London, England	Fisher, John Abraham • Macbeth
1777 01 04	London, England	Linley II, Thomas • Tempest, The or The Enchanted Island
1777 05 00	Venice, Italy	Monza, Carlo Antonio • Cajo Mario
1779 07 21	Hamburg, Germany	Stegmann, Carl David • Macbeth
1779 11 15	Berlin, Germany	Kaffka [Kafka], Johann Christian • Antonius und Cleopatra
1780 00 00 ?	Berlin, Germany	André, Johann • König Lear
1780 01 00	Rome, Italy	Cimarosa, Domenico Nicola [Cimmarosa] • Cajo Mario
1780 10 03	Berlin, Germany	André, Johann • Macbeth
1781 00 00	Vienna, Austria	Asplmayr [Aspelmayr], Franz • Sturm, Der
1781 05 04	Venice, Italy	Bertoni, Ferdinando Giuseppe • Cajo Mario
1782 03 28	Berlin, Germany	Rolle, Johann Heinrich • Sturm oder Die bezauberte Insel, Der
1784 05 30	Naples, Italy	Bianchi, Francesco • Cajo Mario
1785 10 24	Weimar, Germany	Wolf, Ernst Wilhelm • Zauberirrungen, Die [Die Irrtümer der Zauberei]
1786 00 00	Hamburg, Germany	Holland, Jan David • Hamlet, Pantomime zu
1786 12 27	Vienna, Austria	Storace, Stephen • Equivoci, Gli
1787 00 00	Amsterdam, Holland	Just, Johann August • marchand de Venise, Le [Koopman van Smyrna]

DATE	PLACE	COMPOSITION
1787 12 28	Berlin, Germany	Reichardt, Johann Friedrich • Macbeth
1788 01 00	Rome, Italy	Fabrizi, Vincenzo • Tempestà ossia Da un disordine ne nasce un ordine, La
1789 00 00	Rome, Italy	Marescalchi, Luigi • Giuletta e Romeo
1789 03 31	Copenhagen, Denmark	Kunzen, Friedrich Ludwig Æmilius • Holger Danske oder Oberon [Holgar the Dane]
1789 12 27	Florence, Italy	Caruso, Lodovico Luigi • Amleto
1790 00 00	Munich, Germany	Rumling, Sigismund Freiherr von • Roméo et Juliette
1790 09 11	Vienna, Austria	Zák, Benedict Emanuel • Stein der Weisen, Dem oder Die Zauber Insel
1790 09 11	Vienna, Austria	Gerl, Thaddäus; Henneberg and Benedikt Schack • Stein der Weisen, Der oder Die Zauberinsel
1790 10 15	Frankfurt A/M, Germany	Vranicky, Pavel • Oberon, König der Elfen
1791 00 00	London, England	Unknown • Catherine and Petruchio
1792 00 00	Cassel, Germany	Grosheim, Georg Christoph • Titania, oder Liebe durch Zauberei
1792 05 09	Bonn, Germany	Antoine, Ferdinand d' • Ende gut, alles gut oder Der Fürst und sein Volk
1792 06 13	Padua, Italy	Andreozzi, Gaetano • Amleto
1792 07 06	Paris, France	Dalayrac, Nicolas • Tout pour l'amour ou Roméo et Juliette
1792 07 22	Vienna, Austria	Hoffmeister, Franz Anton • Schiffbruch, Der
1792 10 06	Vienna, Austria	Vranicky, Pavel • Rudolf von Felseck (Die Schwarzthaler) oder La Tempestà
1793 00 00	Paris, France	Navoigille, Gouliellmo • Orage, L' ou Quel Guignon!
1793 09 11	Paris, France	Steibelt, Daniel Gottlieb • Roméo et Juliette or Tout pour l'amour
1794 00 00	Stettin, Poland	Haack, Friedrich • Geisterinsel, Die

DATE	PLACE	COMPOSITION
1794 00 00	Vienna, Austria	Weigl, Joseph [Veigl, Giuseppe] • Amleto
1794 04 08	Vienna, Austria	Unknown • Bezähmte Widerbellerin, Die
1794 05 17	London, England	Martín y Soler, Vicente • Capricciosa corretta, La [So bessert sie sich]
1794 07 10	Vienna, Austria	Tuczek, Vincenc Tomas Vaclav • Travestirte Hamlet, Der [Hamlet, Prinz von Dänemark; Hamlet, Prinz von Lilyput]
1794 10 05	Naples, Italy	Guglielmi, Pietro Alessandro • Admeto, Re di Tessaglia
1794 11 04	Mannheim, Germany	Ritter, Peter • lustigen Weiber, Die
1796 01 30	Milan, Italy	Zingarelli, Niccolò Antonio • Giulietta e Romeo
1796 04 23	Vienna, Austria	Hoffmeister, Franz Anton • Rosalinde, oder Die Macht der Feen
1796 04 27	Paris, France	Kreutzer, Rodolphe • Imogène, ou La Gageure indiscrète
1796 06 25	Brunswick [Oels], Germany	Dittersdorf, Carl Ditters von • lustigen Weiber von Windsor und der dicke Hans, Die
1797 05 01	Paris, France	Méhul, Étienne Nicolas • Jeune Henri, Le [Gabrielle d'Estrées où les Amours d'Henri IV]
1798 05 19	Weimar, Germany	Fleischmann, Friedrich • Geisterinsel, Die
1798 06 09	Paris, France	Foignet, Jacques • Orage, L'
1798 07 06	Berlin, Germany	Reichardt, Johann Friedrich • Geisterinsel, Die
1798 10 19	Munich, Germany	Winter, Peter von • Sturm, Der
1798 11 07	Stuttgart, Germany	Zumsteeg, Johann Rudolf • Geisterinsel, Die
1798 11 08	Vienna, Austria	Müller, Wenzel • Sturm oder die Zauberinsel, Der
1799 00 00	Aurich, Germany	Ritter, Peter • Sturm, Der oder Die bezauberte Insel
1799 00 00	Naples, Italy	Caruso, Lodovico Luigi • Tempesta, La

DATE	PLACE	COMPOSITION
1799 01 00	Hirschberg, Germany	Hensel, Johann Daniel • Geisterinsel, Die
1799 01 03	Vienna, Austria	Salieri, Antonio • Falstaff osia Le tre Burle
1799 04 15	Paris, France	Berton, Henri-Montan • Montano et Stéphanie
179? 00 00	London, England	Aylward, Theodore • Midsummer Night's Dream, A
1800 04 05	London, England	Attwood, Thomas • Hermione, or Valour's Triumph
1800 10 26	Dessau, Germany	Lichtenstein, Carl August Freiherr von • Ende gut, alles gut
1800 11 06	Vienna, Austria	Hofmann, Johann • Ritter Hans von Dampf
1802 10 02	Milan, Italy	Fioravanti, Valentino • Capricciosa pentita, La
1803 05 12	London, England	Busby, Thomas • Fair Fugitives
1806 00 00	London, England	Ware, William Henry • Macbeth
1806 00 00	Paris, France	Porta, [Bernardo ?] • Roméo et Juliette
1806 00 00	Salzburg, Austria	Emmert, Adam Joseph • Sturm, Der
1806 00 00	Torino, Italy	Lavina, Vincenzo • Coriolano, Il
1806 00 00	Turin, Italy	Savigna, Vincenzo • Coriolano
1806 05 28	Vienna, Austria	Schuster, Ignaz • Othellerl, der Mohr von Wien
1807 11 05	Vienna, Austria	Schuster, Ignaz • Hamlet, Prinz vom Tandelmarkt
1808 00 00	London, England	Ware, William Henry • Cymbeline
1808 03 18	Vienna, Austria	Schuster, Ignaz • Romeo und Julie
1808 12 26	Milan, Italy	Nicolini, Giuseppe • Coriolano
1809 00 00	Amsterdam, Holland	Radicati, Felice Alessandro • Coriolano, Il
1810 00 00	Gent, Belgium	Volder, Piere Jean de • Jeunesse de Henri Cinq, La
1810 02 20	London, England	Guglielmi, Pietro Carlo • Romeo e Giulietta [I Capuletti ed i Montecchi]
1810 12 19	Stockholm, Sweden	Küster, Johann Heinrich • Henrik den Fjerde

DATE	PLACE	COMPOSITION
1811 09 14	Vienna, Austria	Kanne, Friedrich August • Miranda oder Das Schwert der Rache
1812 01 22	Vienna, Austria	Gevel, Franz Xaver • Rinaldo und Camilla oder Die Zauberinsel
1813 00 00	England	Bishop, Sir Henry Rowley • Antony and Cleopatra
1813 05 13	Berlin, Germany	Schneider, Georg Abraham • Orakelspruch, Der
1814 12 26	Karlsruhe, Germany	Danzi, Franz • Malvina [Die Wolfsjagd]
1815 00 00	Dresden, Germany	Morlacchi, Francesco Giuseppi Baldassare • Capricciosa pettita, La
1815 00 00	Leipzig, Germany	Kanne, Friedrich August • Malvina, oder Putzerls Abenteuer
1815 01 05	Naples, Italy	Hérold, Louis Joseph Ferdinand • Gioventù di Enrico V, La [La Jeunesse d'Henry V]
1816 00 00	London, England	Bishop, Sir Henry Rowley • As You Like It
1816 00 00	Paris, France	Gallenberg, Wenzel Robert Count von • Amleto
1816 01 17	London, England	Bishop, Sir Henry Rowley • Midsummer Night's Dream, A
1816 06 08	Venice, Italy	Vaccai, Nicola • Malvina
1816 12 04	Naples, Italy	Rossini, Gioacchino • Otello, osia L'Africano di Venezia
1817 00 00	Copenhagen, Denmark	Weyse, Christoph Ernst Friedrich • Macbeth
1817 00 00	Palermo, Italy	Mosca, Giuseppe • Gioventù di Enrico V, La
1817 03 08	Milan, Italy	Generali, Pietro Mercandetti • Rodrigo di Valencia
1818 00 00	Copenhagen, Denmark	Kunzen, Friedrich Ludwig Æmilius • Stormen
1818 09 09	Rome, Italy	Fioravanti, Valentino • Enrico IV al passo della Marna
1819 00 00	Donaueschingen, Germany	Kreutzer, Conradin • Cordelia (Floretta ou La Folle de Glaris)[First named Adele von Budoy]
1819 00 00	Naples, Italy	Carlini, Luigi • Gioventù di Enrico V, La

DATE	PLACE	COMPOSITION
1819 03 27	Naples, Italy	Rossini, Gioacchino • Ermione
1819 04 12	London, England	Whitaker, John • Weird Sisters, The or The Thane and the Throne
1819 12 11	London, England	Bishop, Sir Henry Rowley • Comedy of Errors, The
1820 00 00	Torino, Italy	Orlandi, Ferdinando • Rodrigo di Valencia
1820 04 22	London, England	Bishop, Sir Henry Rowley • Henri Quatre [Paris in the Olden Times]
1820 09 08	Munich, Germany	Stuntz, Joseph Hartmann • Heinrich IV zu Givry
1820 11 08	London, England	Bishop, Sir Henry Rowley • Twelfth Night
1820 12 26	Rome, Italy	Pacini, Giovanni • Gioventù di Enrico V, La (also La bella tavernara; Le Aventure d'una notte)
1821 05 15	London, England	Bishop, Sir Henry Rowley • Tempest, The
1821 11 29	London, England	Bishop, Sir Henry Rowley • Two Gentlemen of Verona, The
1822 00 00	Reggio Calabria, Italy	Aspa, Mario • Gioventù di Enrico V, La
1822 12 26	Milan, Italy	Mercadante, Giuseppe Saverio Raffele • Amleto
1823 00 00	London, England	Horn, Charles Edward, and Samuel Webbe Jr. • Merry Wives of Windsor
1823 10 04	Dresden, Germany	Morlacchi, Francesco Giuseppi Baldassare • Gioventù di Enrico V, La [Das Jugendjahre Heinrich des Fünften]
1823 10 25	Vienna, Austria	Weber, Carl Maria von • Euryanthe
1824 02 20	London, England	Bishop, Sir Henry Rowley • Merry Wives of Windsor, The
1825 00 00	Pisa, Italy	Maganini, Giovanni • Enrico IV al passo della Marna
1825 10 31	Milan, Italy	Vaccai, Nicola • Giulietta e Romeo
1826 00 00	London, England	Cooke, Thomas Simpson • Oberon, or The Charmed Horn

DATE	PLACE	COMPOSITION
1826 00 00	New York, U.S.A.	Garcia, Manuel Vincente del Popolo • Giulietta e Romeo
1826 01 28	London, England	Cooke, Thomas Simpson • Malvina
1826 02 13	Budapest, Hungary	Kleinheinz, Carl Franz Xaver • Hamlet, Prinz vom Tandelmarkt
1826 03 28	Copenhagen, Denmark	Kuhlau, Friedrich Daniel Rudolph • Musik Til William Shakspeare [sic], Op. 74
1826 04 12	London, England	Weber, Carl Maria von • Oberon [or the Elf-King's Oath]
1827 00 00	New York, U.S.A.	Garcia, Manuel Vincente del Popolo • Gioventù di Enrico V, La
1827 06 29	Paris, France	Chélard, Hippolyte-André-Jean-Baptiste • Macbeth
1827 11 14	Vienna, Austria	Riotte, Philipp Jakob • Orakelspruch, Der
1828 05 14	London, England	Cooke, Thomas Simpson and Braham, John and Others • Taming of the Shrew, The
1828 07 26	Venice, Italy	Torriani, Eugenio • Romeo e Giulietta
1828 10 07	Paris, France	Carafa di Colobrano, Michele Enrico and Aimé Ambroise Simon Leborne • Violette, La ou Gérard de Nevers
1829 00 00	Paris, France	Mélésville, Honoré Marie Joseph, Baron Duveyrier] • Gillette de Narbonne
1829 02 07	Naples, Italy	Costa, Michael Andrew Angus • Malvina
1829 06 06	Vienna, Austria	Müller (the elder), Adolph • Othellerl, der Mohr von Wien [Die geheilte Eifersucht]
1829 11 09	Paris, France	Piccini, Louis Alexandre • Macbeth
1830 00 00 ?		Hanssens, J. F. J. • Gillette de Narbonne
1830 03 11	Venice, Italy	Bellini, Vincenzo • Capuleti e i Montecchi, I
1832 01 08	Berlin, Germany	Lauer, Adolph L. [Freiherr von Münchofen] • Orakelspruch, Der

DATE	PLACE	COMPOSITION
1832 11 02	Breslau [Wroclaw], Poland	Rafael, Carl Friedrich • Hamlet, Prinz von Liliput
1832 12 06	Königsberg, Germany	Sobolewski, Friedrich Eduard de • Imogéne
1833 02 19	Milan, Italy	Balfe, Michael William • Enrico IV al passo della Marna
1833 09 20	Brno [Brünn], Czechoslovakia	Riotte, Philipp Jakob • Sturm, Der oder Die Insel des Prospero
1834 11 25	Milan, Italy	Mercadante, Giuseppe Saverio Raffele • Gioventù di Enrico V, La
1835 00 00 c.		Aliabiev, Alexander • Storm, The
1836 03 29	Magdeburg, Germany	Wagner, Wilhelm Richard • Liebesverbot, Das oder Die Novize von Palermo
1837 00 00 ?		Fontmichel, Hippolyte Honoré Joseph Court de (1799-?) • Amleto
1838 03 05	Paris, France	Halévy, Jacques François Fromental Elie • Guido et Ginevre ou La Peste de Florence
1838 07 19	London, England	Balfe, Michael William • Falstaff
1839 00 00		Aliabiev, Alexander • Volshebnaya noch
1840 00 00		Raymond, Édouard • Sturm, Der
1840 11 05	Brno, Czechoslovakia	Maretzek, Maximilian • Hamlet
1841 12 10	Pest, Hungary	Schindelmeisser, Louis Alexander Balthasar • Malvina
1842 12 00	Milan, Italy	Manusardi, Giuseppe • sogno di Primavera, Un [Un rêve de printemps]
1843 00 00	U.S.S.R.	Glinka, Mikhail Ivanovitch • Hamlet
1843 00 00		Serov, Alexander Nikolayevich • Merry Wives of Windsor
1843 00 00		Mussorgsky, Modest Petrovich • Hamlet

DATE	PLACE	COMPOSITION
1844 04 24	Vienna, Austria	Müller (the elder), Adolph • Viel Lärm um Nichts
1844 08 31	Vienna, Austria	Suppé, Franz von • Sommernachtstraum, Der
1845 01 21	Copenhagen, Denmark	Rung, Henrik • Stormen paa København [Storm over Copenhagen]
1846 03 14	Padua, Italy	Santa Caterina, Alessandro • Coriolano
1846 10 17	Paris, France	Francastel, A. • Henry IV
1847 00 00		Kunz, [Konrad Max ?] • Tempest, The
1847 03 14	Florence, Italy	Verdi, Giuseppe • Macbeth
1848 02 24	Venice, Italy	Buzzolla, Antonio • Amleto
1848 03 00	Düsseldorf, Germany	Steinkühler, Émile • Cäsario, oder die Verwechslung, Op. 30
1848 12 06	London, England	Loder, Edward James • Robin Goodfellow or the Frolics of Puck
1849 00 00	Paris, France	Herx, Werner • Orakelspruch, Der
1849 03 09	Berlin, Germany	Nicolai, Carl Otto Ehrenfried • lustigen Weiber von Windsor, Die
1850 04 20	Paris, France	Thomas, Charles Louis Ambroise • Songe d'une nuit d'été, Le [Shakespeare oder Der Traum einer Sommernacht]
1850 06 08	London, England	Halévy, Jacques Franoçis Fromental Élie • Tempesta, La
1851 10 30	Vienna, Austria	Storch, Anton Maria • Stein der Weisen, Der
1851 12 29	Naples, Italy	Lillo, Giuseppe • Sogno d'una Notte estiva, Il or La Gioventù di Shakespeare
1852 02 21	Madrid, Spain	Gaztambide y Garbayo, Joaquin Romualdo • sueño de una noche de verano, El
1853 00 00	Palermo, Italy	Pacini, Giovanni • Rodrigo di Valencia
1853 10 01	Naples, Italy	Mercadante, Giuseppe Saverio Raffele • Violetta
1854 04 00	Versailles, France	Séméladis, M. • Cordélia

DATE	PLACE	COMPOSITION
1854 05 30	Venice, Italy	Zanardini, Angelo • Amleto
1855 02 00	Stockholm, Sweden	Berens, Johann Hermann • Violetta
1855 07 30	Paris, France	Offenbach, Jacques • Rêve d'une Nuit d'été, Le
1855 12 08	Naples, Italy	Tommasi, Ferdinando [Tommaso] • Guido e Ginevre
1856 01 18	Paris, France	Adam, Adolphe-Charles • Falstaff
1856 02 28	Paris, France	Weckerlin, Jean Baptiste Théodore • Tout est bien qui finit bien
1856 10 27	Stockholm, Sweden	Berens, Johann Hermann • Sommarnattsdröm, En
1857 00 00	Darmstadt, Germany	Stadtfeldt, Christian Joseph Franz Alexandre • Hamlet
1857 03 16	Hamburg, Germany	Hamel, Eduard • Malvina
1857 11 16	Berlin, Germany	Taubert, Wilhelm • Macbeth, Op. 133
1858 00 00 ?		Eberwein, Max Carl • Romeo und Julie
1859 10 23	Weimar, Germany	Flotow, Friedrich von • Wintermärchen, Ein
1859 10 26	Antwerp, Belgium	Acker, Jean Van den • Romeo en Marielle [Tout pour l'amour]
1859 11 12	Milan, Italy	Meiners, Giambattista • Riccardo III
1860 00 00	Prague, Czechoslovakia	Nápravnik, Éduard Frantsevich • Sturm, Der
1860 06 02	Rome, Italy	Moroni, Luigi • Amleto
1861 00 00	London, England	MacFarren, George Alexander • Hamlet
1861 02 14	Parma, Italy	Benvenuti, Tommaso • Guglielmo Shakespeare
1862 00 00	Wroclaw [Breslau], Poland	Damrosch, Leopold • Romeo und Julia
1862 03 02	Vienna, Austria	Storch, Anton Maria • Romeo und Julie
1862 05 00	Berlin, Germany	Michaelis, Gustave • Lustigen Weiber von Berlin, Die
1862 08 09	Baden-Baden, Germany	Berlioz, Hector • Béatrice et Bénédict

DATE	PLACE	COMPOSITION
1863 01 27	Mexico City, Mexico	Morales, Melesio • Giulietta e Romeo
1863 03 31	Paris, France	Mozart, Wolfgang Amadeus • Peines d'amour perdues
1863 06 19	Paris, France	Legouix, Isidore Édouard • Othello, Un
1864 01 17	Antwerp, Belgium	Duyse, Florimond Van • Rosalinde
1865 01 11	Prague, Czechoslova-kia	Barbieri, Carlo Emanuele di • Perdita oder Ein Wintermärchen
1865 03 08	Paris, France	David, Félicien César • Saphir, Le or Tout est bien, qui finit bien
1865 05 30	Genoa, Italy	Faccio, Franco • Amleto
1865 10 24	Trieste, Italy	Marchetti, Filippo • Romeo e Giulietta
1865 12 14	Vienna, Austria	Müller (the elder), Adolph • Heinrich IV
1867 04 27	Paris, France	Gounod, Charles François • Roméo et Juliette
1867 07 00	Paris, France	Déjazet, Eugène • Rhum et eau en juillet
1867 11 11	St. Petersburg, Russia	Kashperov, Vladimir Nikititch • Storm, The [Groza]
1868 03 09	Paris, France	Thomas, Charles Louis Ambroise • Hamlet
1869 03 00	Stockholm, Sweden	Berens, Johann Hermann • Riccardo
1870 00 00 c.		Carl, M. • Julius Caesar
1872 03 10	Berlin, Germany	Rintel, Wilhelm • Was ihr Wöllt
1872 03 21	Berlin, Germany	Bruch, Max • Hermione, Op. 40
1873 03 00	Port-Mahon [Minorca], Spain	Mercadal y Pons, Antonio • Giulietta e Romeo
1873 04 08	Milan, Italy	Perelli, Edoardo • Viola Pisani
1873 11 08	Bologna, Italy	Pinsuti, Ciro • Mercante di Venezia, Il
1874 01 29	Vienna, Austria	Hopp, Julius • Hammlet
1874 10 11	Mannheim, Germany	Goetz, Herman • Widerspänstigen Zähmung, Der [La Megère apprivoisée; Caterina e Petruccio]

DATE	PLACE	COMPOSITION
1874 11 13	Berlin, Germany	Taubert, Carl Gottfried Wilhelm • Cesario, oder Was ihr wollt, Op. 188
1876 00 00		Pedrell, Filipe • Roi Lear, Le
1877 01 17	London, England	Rossi, Lauro • Biorn
1877 02 03	Paris, France	Lecocq, Charles Alexandre • Marjolaine
1878 02 17	Naples, Italy	Sarria, Errico • Equivoci, Gli
1878 10 12	Paris, France	Ivry, Paul Xaver Désiré Richard, Marquis d' • Amantes de Vérone, Les
1879 05 02	Brussels, Belgium	Urich, Jean • Orage, L'
1879 11 01	London, England	Clarke, James Siree Hamilton • Merchant of Venice
1879 11 10	Milan, Italy	Canepá, Luigi • Riccardo III
1880 00 00		Jenkins, David • Enchanted Isle, The [Scenes from Shakespeare's 'Tempest']
1880 00 00	Naples, Italy	Unknown • Pulcinella rivale di Turzillo e confuso tra Capuleti e Montecchi
1880 11 18	Paris, France	Duvernoy, Victor-Alphonse • Tempète, La
1881 12 06	Bologna, Italy	Gobatti, Stefano • Cordelia
1882 01 12	Magdeburg, Germany	Freudenberg, Wilhelm • Kleopatra
1882 03 11	Madrid, Spain	Chapí y Lorente, Ruperto • Tempestad, La
1882 08 14	Walsall, England	Emery, Charles P. • Romeo, the Radical or Obstruction and Effect
1882 11 11	Paris, France	Audran, Edmond • Gillette de Narbonne [Gillette, or Count and Countess; Gilda di Guascogna]
1883 00 00	Berlin, Germany	Mohr, Hermann • Orakelspruch, Der Op. 50
1883 03 05	Paris, France	Saint-Saëns, Camille • Henry VIII
1883 11 05	Madrid, Spain	Nieto, Manuel • Otelo y Desdémona

DATE	PLACE	COMPOSITION
1883 12 01	Graz, Austria	Sayn-Wittgenstein-Berleburg, Count Friedrich Ernst von • Antonius und Kleopatra
1883 12 21	St. Petersburg, Soviet Union	Salvayre, Gaston • Riccardo III
1884 00 00	Paris, France	Choudens, Antony • Cymbeline
1885 02 14	Vienna, Austria	Genée, Franz Friedrich Richard and Louis Roth • Zwillinge
1885 10 26	Birmingham, England	Jakobowski, Edward • Erminie
1885 11 24	St. Petersburg, Soviet Union	Soloviev, Nicolai Feopemptovich • Cordélia
1886 09 01	Paris, France	Noël, Édouard Marie Émile • songe d'une nuit d'été, Le
1886 09 01	Paris, France	Serpette, Henri Charles Antoine Gaston • Songe d'une nuit d'été, Le
1887 02 05	Milan, Italy	Verdi, Giuseppe • Otello
1887 03 27	Lisbon, Portugal	Hohmann, Gustav • Hermione, oder Der kleine Vicomte
1887 10 15	Hannover, Germany	Frank, Ernst • Sturm, Der
1887 10 24	Liverpool, England	Andrews, John Charles Bond- • Herne's Oak, or The Rose of Windsor [also Herne the Hunter]
1887 12 14	Reading, England	Old, John • Herne the Hunter (A Legend of Royal Windsor)
1888 04 21	Nantes, France	Hignard, Aristide • Hamlet
1888 05 17	Frankfurt A/M, Germany	Urspruch, Anton • Sturm, Der
1888 06 00	Genoa, Italy	Pride [sp?], G. • Otello
1888 06 01	Toulouse, France	Reynaud, Armand • Roi Lear, Le
1889 11 00	Paris, France	Leoncavallo, Ruggiero • Songe d'une nuit d'été, Un
1890 00 00 ?	London, England	Douglas, Hugh A. • Romeo and Juliet Up to Larks
1890 10 30	Paris, France	Thomé, François Lucien Joseph • Roméo et Juliette
1891 00 00	Antwerp, Belgium	Keurvels, Edward H. J. • Hamlet
1892 00 00		Thul, Franz von • Hermione

DATE	PLACE	COMPOSITION
1892 00 00	Lisbon, Portugal	Freitas Gazul, Francisco de • Violetas, As
1892 00 00	Prague, Czechoslova-kia	Weis, Karél • Comme il vous Plaira
1892 01 17	Prague, Czechoslova-kia	Weis, Karél • Viola [Die Zwillinge, Blizenci]
1892 04 07	Rome, Italy	Westerhout, Niccolò van • Cimbelino, Il
1892 04 09	Nantes, France	Rateau, Edmond • Rosaline
1892 05 00	Cormons, Italy	Macarig, Hector and Alfonso Deperis • Otello Tamburo
1892 08 01	Lincoln, England	Barry, H. C. • Shylock or The Venus of Venice
1892 10 15	London, England	Carr, Frank Osmond • In Town
1893 00 00		Cagnoni, Antonio • Re Lear, Il
1893 02 09	Milan, Italy	Verdi, Giuseppe • Falstaff
1893 03 16	Hamburg, Germany	Arensen, Adolf • Viola
1893 04 00	New York, Boston, and Cambridge, U.S.A.	Atherton, Percy Lee and Ernest Hamlin Abbott • Hamlet, Prince of Denmark or The Sport, the Spook and the Spinster
1893 07 15	Berlin, Germany	Schönfeld, Georg • Falstaff
1893 11 29	Paris, France	David, Adolphe Isaac • Orage, L'
1894 00 00	Siena, Italy	Marescotti • Amleto
1894 01 00	Cerignola, Italy	Scognamilio, Gennaro • Otello ossia Catiello l'Affricano
1894 02 11	Colombes, France	Rosellin, Léon • Juliette et Roméo
1894 04 00	Limoges, France	Ruben, Paul • Edit royal, L'
1894 06 25	Paris, France	Missa, Edmond Jean Louis • Dinah
1894 12 05	Hamburg, Germany	Pohlig, Carl • Stein der Weisen, Der
1895 00 00	Saratoga, N.Y., U.S.A.	Kaun, Hugo • Falstaff
1895 03 01	Prague, Czechoslova-kia	Fibich, Zdenko • Boure, Opus 40 [Der Sturm]
1895 07 29	London, England	Maclean, Alick • Petruccio

DATE	PLACE	COMPOSITION
1895 11 19	Milan, Italy	Samara, Spiro • Furia domata, La
1895 12 00	Rouen, France	Le Rey, Frédéric • Mégère apprivoisée, La
1896 00 00	Leipzig, Germany	Alfano, Franco • Miranda
1896 03 13	Leipzig, Germany	Doppler, Arpád • Viel Lärm um Lichts
1897 02 00	Genoa, Italy	La Rosa, Arturo • Otello
1897 05 21	Prague, Czechoslovakia	Nesvera, Josef • Perdita
1897 07 00	Lisbon, Portugal	Taboida, Ant. Sanchez do Cunha • Dinah
1898 00 00		Berény, Henri • Wintermärchen, Das
1898 03 25	Toulouse, France	Deffès, Louis Pierre • Jessica
1898 03 27	Bologna, Italy	Grandi, Alfredo • Amleto
1898 08 02	Madrid, Spain	Valverde y San Juan, Joaquín • sueño de una noche de verano, El
1898 10 15	Hamburg, Germany	Wiedeke, Adolf • lustigen Weiber von Hamburg, Die
1899 03 24	Paris, France	Puget, Paul-Charles-Marie • Beaucoup de bruit pour rien
1899 04 24	London, England	Lutz, William Meyer • Merry-Go-Round
1899 04 29	London, England	Rubens, Paul Alfred and Walter Rubens • Great Caesar
1899 11 00	Turin, Italy	Roti, Ugo • Sogno di una notte d'estate, Il
1899 11 23	Paris, France	Serpette, Henri Charles Antoine Gaston • Shakespeare!
1900 00 00	Cremona, Italy	Podestà, Carlo • Ero, ossia Molto rumore per nulla
1900 00 00 c.		Angyal, Lázló • Tempest, The
1900 00 00 c.		Ferroni, Vencenzo Emidio Carmine • Romeo and Juliet
1900 03 11	Erfurt, Germany	Zimmermann, Balduin • Wintermärchen, Ein
1900 06 23	Paris, France	Hulemann, Th • Malvine I re [The first]

DATE	PLACE	COMPOSITION
1900 08 14	Livorno, Italy	Del Fante, Raffaele • Tempesta, La
1900 09 24	New York, U.S.A.	Engländer, Ludwig • Belle of Bohemia, The
1901 00 00	New York, U.S.A.	Shelley, Harry Rowe • Romeo and Juliet
1901 00 00	Zagreb, Yugoslavia	Zajc, Ivan • Cordelia
1901 05 30	London, England	Stanford, Sir Charles Villiers • Much Ado About Nothing, Opus 76a
1902 00 00	Norwich, England	Bedford, Herbert • Love Scene from Shakespeare's Romeo and Juliet for Contralto and Baritone
1902 12 20	Antwerp, Belgium	De Boeck, Auguste de • Winternachtsdroom, Een
1903 01 20	Paris, France	Hüe, George • Titania
1904 02 05	Hermannstadt, Germany	Kirchner, Hermann • Viola
1905 04 16	Prague, Czechoslovakia	Foerster, Joseph Brohuslav • Jessika, Opus 60
1905 05 07	Perugia, Italy	Angelis, Arturo de • Tempesta, La
1906 04 11	London, England	Stuart, Leslie • Belle of Mayfair
1906 04 14	London, England	Rubens, Paul Alfred and Frank E. Tours • Dairymaids, The
1906 05 14	Moravska Ostrava, Czechoslovakia	Palliardi, Carl • Stein der Weisen, Der
1907 01 28	Paris, France	Saussine, Henri de • Marchand de Vénise, Le
1907 02 21	Berlin, Germany	Delius, Frederick • Romeo und Juliet auf dem Dorfe [A Village Romeo and Juliet]
1908 01 02	Vienna, Austria	Goldmark, Carl • Wintermärchen, Ein
1909 00 00	Madrid?, Spain	Campo y Zabaleta, Conrado del • Amantes de Verona, Los
1910 03 00	St. Petersburg, Soviet Union	Kasanli, Nikolai Ivanovich [Kazanli, Kazanly] • Miranda (Poliedniaia bor'ba) [Der Letzte Kampf]
1910 11 30	Paris, France	Bloch, Ernest • Macbeth

DATE	PLACE	COMPOSITION
1911 03 03	Paris, France	Vidal, Paul Antonin • Peines d'amour perdues
1912 02 28	London, England	Hale, Alfred Matthew • Tempest, The
1912 03 21	Paris, France	Vidal, Paul Antonin • Comme il vous Plaire
1913 00 00		Stransky, Josef • Béatrice et Bénédict
1913 00 00		Radó, Aladár • Shylock
1913 08 24	Padua, Italy	Cottrau, Giulio • Cordelia (Re Lear)
1913 09 00	Barcelona, Spain	Morera, Enrique • Fiercilla domada, La
1913 11 22	Antwerp, Belgium	Alpaerts, Florent • Shylock
1914 00 00 ?		Marshall-Hall, George William Louis • Romeo and Juliet
1914 07 00	Munich, Germany	Beer-Walbrunn, Anton • Sturm, Der
1915 00 00		Cottrau, Giulio • Pericle re di Tiro
1915 00 00		Mojsisovics, Roderich • Viel Lärm um Nichts
1916 00 00		Heward, Leslie Hays • Hamlet
1916 01 07	Middlesborough, England	Barkworth, John Edmond • Romeo and Juliet
1916 02 14	Milan, Italy	Oddone, Elizabetta • Petruccio e il Cavolo Cappuccio
1916 05 00	New York, U.S.A.	Farwell, Arthur George • Caliban by the Yellow Sands, Opus 47
1916 06 00	New York, U.S.A.	Conte, Paolo • Shakespeare, the Playmaker
1916 11 14	Frankfurt A/M, Germany	Taubmann, Otto • Porzia
1917 00 00	Rome, Italy	Mancinelli, Luigi • Sogno di una notte d'estate, Il
1917 05 22	Budapest, Hungary	Sztojanovics, Eug. • Otello mecél
1917 06 00	Northampton, Mass. (Smith College), U.S.A.	Morton, Louise, and others • Twelfth Night
1918 05 11	London, England	Ansell, John • King's Bride, The [Violette]

DATE	PLACE	COMPOSITION
1918 12 05	Melbourne, Australia	Hart, Fritz Bennicke • Malvolio, Opus 14
1919 00 00		Ardin, Leon • Antony and Cleopatra
1919 10 10	Berlin, Germany	Tiessen, Heinz • Cymbelin
191? 00 00		Chignell, Robert • Romeo and Juliet
1920 00 00		Carlson, Charles Frederick • Merchant of Venice
1920 00 00 c.	London, England	Gatty, Nicholas Comyn • Macbeth
1920 04 17	London, England	Gatty, Nicholas Comyn • Tempest, The
1920 11 20	London, England	Beecham, Adrian Wells • Merchant of Venice, The
1921 05 23	Faenza, Italy	Savini, Giacomo • Tempeste
1922 01 00	Bautzen, Germany	Feigerl, R. • Stein der Weisen, Der
1922 01 30	Paris, France	Silver, Charles • Mégère apprivoisée, La
1922 02 14	Rome, Italy	Zandonai, Riccardo • Giulietta e Romeo
1922 11 23	Milan, Italy	Lattuada, Felice • Tempesta, La
1923 00 00		Honegger, Arturo • Tempête, La
1924 05 11	Prague, Czechoslovakia	Smetana, Bedrich • Viola
1924 08 26	Gastonbury, England	Boughton, Rutland • Againcourt
1925 04 03	Manchester, England	Holst, Gustav • At the Boar's Head, Opus 42
1925 11 13	Milan, Italy	Bossi, Renzo • Volpino il Calderaio, Op. 32
1925 12 17	Brussels, Belgium	Vreuls, Victor • Songe d'une nuit d'été, Un
1926 11 13	Bratislava, Czechoslovakia	Folprecht, Zdenek • Lásky hra osudná [The Fateful Game of Love], Opus 3
1927 12 29	Milan, Italy	Wolf-Ferrari, Ermanno • Sly, ovvero La leggenda del dormiente risvegliato
1928 03 00	Verona , Italy	Bottacio, Pietro • Bisbetica Domata, La

DATE	PLACE	COMPOSITION
1929 00 00		Laufer, B. • Shylock
1929 00 00		LaViolette, Wesley • Shylock
1929 03 21	London, England	Vaughan Williams, Ralph • Sir John in Love
1929 05 11	Milan, Italy	Farina, Guido • Dodisesima Notte, La
1929 05 27	Aachen, Germany	Rosenberg, Richard • Liebesspiel, Das
1930 00 00		Daffner, Hugo • Macbeth
1930 00 00		Arundell, Dennis Drew • Midsummer Night's Dream, A
1931 02 12	Rome, Italy	Persico, Mario • Bisbetica Domata, La
1931 03 00	Florence, Italy	Allegra, Giuseppe • Sogno di una Notte, Il
1932 12 16	Dresden, Germany	Kusterer, Arthur • Was ihr Wollt
1933 01 30	Brussels, Belgium	Brumagne, Fernand • Marchand de Venise, Le
1934 04 12	London, England	Collingwood, Lawrance Arthur • Macbeth
1934 11 17	Graz, Austria	Holenia, Hans • Viola, Opus 21 [Was Ihr wollt]
1935 03 23	Paris, France	Hahn, Reynaldo • Malvina
1935 03 25	Paris, France	Hahn, Reynaldo • Marchand de Vénise, Le
1936 00 00		Beecham, Adrian Wells • Love's Labour's Lost [Peines d'Amour Perdues]
1936 02 08	Genoa, Italy	Malipiero, Gian Francesco • Giulio Cesare
1936 02 17	Riga, Soviet Union	Kalnins, Janis • Hamlets
1936 03 00	Paris, France	Hahn, Reynaldo • Beaucoup de bruit pour rien
1937 00 00		De Filippi, Amadeo • Malvolio
1937 03 05	San Remo, Italy	Canonica, Pietro • Miranda
1937 04 24	Rome, Italy	Ghislanzoni, Alberto • Re Lear
1938 00 00	Dresden, Germany	Lueder, Florence Pauline • Rosalind
1938 05 04	Florence, Italy	Malipiero, Gian Francesco • Antonio e Cleopatra

DATE	PLACE	COMPOSITION
1938 11 23	New York, U.S.A.	Rogers, Richard • Boys from Syracuse, The
1939 03 11	Stettin, Poland	Lorenz, Carl Adolf • Komödie der Irrungen, Die
1939 04 29	Florence, Italy	Frazzi, Vito • Re Lear
1939 05 31	Moscow, U.S.S.R.	Khrennikov, Tikhon Nikolaevich • Brati [Brothers]
1939 10 10	Moscow, U.S.S.R.	Khrennikov, Tikhon Nikolaevich • V buriu [Im Sturm, Into the Storm]
1939 11 29	New York, U.S.A.	Van Heusen, Jimmy • Swingin' the Dream
1940 00 00		Shenshin, Aleksandr Alexseivich • Twelfth Night
1940 04 13	Dresden, Germany	Sutermeister, Heinrich • Romeo und Julia
1941 00 00		Zirra, Alexandru • Furtuna [TheTempest]
1941 03 21	Beuthen,	Wödl, Franz • Komödie der Irrungen
1941 03 30	Stettin, Poland	Hess, Ludwig • Was ihr Wollt
1941 11 27	Antwerp, Belgium	Baeyens, August Louis • Coriolanus
1942 10 31	Dresden, Germany	Sutermeister, Heinrich • Zauberinsel, Die
1943 00 00		Karel, Rudolf • Zkroceni zlé zeny [The Taming of the Shrew]
1944 00 00		Goedicke, Alexander • Macbeth
1945 06 14	Vienna, Austria	Zavodsky, Felix • Othello
1946 09 08	Prague, Czechoslovakia	Krejcí, Isa • Pozdvizení v Efesu [The Upheaval in Ephesus]
1947 00 00		Gibbs, Cecil Armstrong • Twelfth Night, Opus 115
1947 00 00	Berlin, Germany	Blacher, Boris • Romeo und Julia
1948 00 00		Clapp, Philip Greeley • Taming of the Shrew, The
1948 09 19	Stockholm, Sweden	Atterberg, Kurt • Stormen, Op. 49
1948 12 30	New York, U.S.A.	Porter, Cole • Kiss Me, Kate
1949 01 29	Strasbourg, France	Delannoy, Marcel • Puck

381

DATE	PLACE	COMPOSITION
1950 00 00	Toulouse, France	Gaujac, Edmond Germain • Amantes de Vérone, Les
1951 02 03	Düsseldorf, Germany	Zillig, Winfried • Troilus und Cressida
1951 12 07	Oslo, Norway	Eggen, Arne • Cymbelyn
1952 00 00	Darmstadt, Germany	Orff, Carl • Sommernachtstraum, Ein
1953 01 31	Cincinnati, U.S.A.	Giannini, Vittorio • Taming of the Shrew, The
1954 03 29	Conway, Arkansas, U.S.A.	Groth, Howard • Petruchio
1954 05 16	London, England	Slade, Julian • Comedy of Errors
1954 12 03	London, England	Walton, Sir William • Troilus and Cressida
1954 12 04	Louisville, Kentucky, U.S.A.	Mohaupt, Richard • Double Trouble [Zwillingskomödie]
1955 00 00		Pogodin • King Lear?
1955 00 00		Zelinka, Jan Evangelista • Spring With Shakespeare
1955 04 04	Derby, England	Chatburn, Tom • Gay Venetians, The
1955 06 21	Zagreb, Yugoslavia	Fribec, Kresimir • Romeo and Juliet
1955 10 01	Moscow, Soviet Union	Shebalin, Vissarion Yakovlevich • Ukroshchenie stroptivoi [The Taming of the Shrew] Op. 46
1956 00 00 ?		Logar, Mihovil • Four Scenes from Shakespeare
1956 06 17	Vienna, Austria	Martin, Frank • Sturm, Der
1956 08 18	Frankfurt/Oder, Germany	Heinrich, Hermann • Viel Lärm um Nichts
1956 11 05	London, England	Greenwall, Peter • Three Caskets, The or Venice Re-served
1957 00 00	Berlin, Germany	Roters, Ernest • Hamlet, Op. 145
1957 00 00 c.		Durme, Jef Van • King Lear
1957 09 26	New York, U.S.A.	Bernstein, Leonard • West Side Story

DATE	PLACE	COMPOSITION
1958 00 00		Castelnuovo-Tedesco, Mario • Tutto e bène quello che finisce bène, Op. 182
1958 10 12	Zagreb, Yugoslavia	Sulek, Stjepan • Koriolan
1959 00 00 c.		Durme, Jef Van • Anthony and Cleopatra
1959 01 08	University, Miss., U.S.A.	Kreutz, Arthur • Sourwood Mountain
1959 08 17	Salzburg, Austria	Erbse, Heimo • Julietta, Op. 15
1959 09 20	Essen, Germany	Klebe, Giselher Wolfgang • Ermordung Cäsars, Die Op. 32
1960 01 24	London, England	Eastwood, Thomas Hugh • Christopher Sly
1960 06 11	Aldeburgh, England	Britten, Lord Edward Benjamin • Midsummer Night's Dream, A, Op. 64
1961 00 00		Goldman, Edward M. • Macbeth
1961 00 00 c.		Durme, Jef Van • Richard III
1961 01 07	Rome, Italy	Zafred, Mario • Amleto
1961 02 02	Venice, Italy	Malipiero, Gian Francesco • Romeo e Guilietta (scene 5 of Monde celesti e infernali)
1961 05 25	Florence, Italy	Castelnuovo-Tedesco, Mario • Mercante di Venezia, Il, Op. 181
1962 09 14	Brno [Brünn], Czechoslova-kia	Fischer, Jan F. • Romeo, Julie a tma (Romeo, Juliet and Darkness)
1962 11 09	Baltimore, U.S.A.	Kagen, Sergius • Hamlet
1963 00 00		Molchanov, Kiril Vladimirovich • Romeo, Dzhulyetta i t'ma [Romeo, Juliet and Darkness]
1963 00 00	Tbilisi, Soviet Union	Machavariani, Alexei • Othello
1963 05 31	Minneapolis, U.S.A.	Argento, Dominick • Christopher Sly
1964 00 00	Tbilisi, Soviet Union	Machavariani, Alexei • Hamlet
1964 10 27	New York, U.S.A.	Balamos, John • As You Like It
1964 12 28	New York, U.S.A.	Besoyan, Rick • Babes in the Wood, or Who Killed Cock Robin
1965 00 00		Mullins, Hugh • Romeo and Juliet

DATE	PLACE	COMPOSITION
1965 04 04	New York, U.S.A.	Halpern, Sidney • Macbeth
1966 09 16	New York, U.S.A.	Barber, Samuel • Antony and Cleopatra, Op. 40
1967 02 25	Liberec, Czechoslovakia	Jirko, Ivan • Twelfth Night, The [Vecer Trikralovy]
1967 07 29	San Francisco, U.S.A.	Utley, Wendell • Will
1967 11 14	University, Alabama, U.S.A.	Bruce, Neely • Pyramus and Thisbe
1968 00 00	Glens Falls, NY, U.S.A.	Amram, David • Twelfth Night
1968 01 03	New York, U.S.A.	Gelber, Stanley Jay • Love and Let Love
1968 01 13	New York, U.S.A.	Hester, Hal and Danny Apolinar • Your Own Thing
1968 03 05	Hamburg, Germany	Searle, Humphrey • Hamlet, Opus 48
1968 10 19	Budapest, Hungary	Szokolay, Sándor • Hamlet
1969 01 07	New York, U.S.A.	Liota, A. • Romeo and Juliet
1969 02 01	Hannover, Germany	Engelmann, Hans Ulrich • Ophelia, Op. 36
1969 10 22	Bergamo, Italy	Zanon, Antonio B. • Leggenda di Giulietta, La
1969 11 01	Wexford, England	Wilson, James • Twelfth Night
1969 11 11	Brno [Brünn], Czechoslovakia	Horky, Karel • Jed z Elsinoru [The Poison from Elsinore]
1969 11 28	Zagreb, Yugoslavia	Sulek, Stjepan • Oluja
1969 12 21	Opava, Czechoslovakia	Doubrava, Jaroslav • Sen noci svatojanske
1970 00 00	Manchester, England	Unknown • Catch My Soul
1970 05 22	Copenhagen, Denmark	Koppel, Herman David • Macbeth, Op. 79
1970 10 25	New York, U.S.A.	Harper, Wally • Sensations
1970 11 19	Warsaw, Poland	Matuszczak, Bernadetta • Julia i Romeo

DATE	PLACE	COMPOSITION
1971 11 19	Bucharest, Rumania	Bentoiu, Pascal • Hamlet, Op. 18
1971 12 01	New York, U.S.A.	MacDermot, Galt • Two Gentlemen of Verona
1971 12 16	Birmingham, England	Gilbert, James • Good Time Johnny
1972 00 00		Claudric, Jean • Othello Story
1972 03 29	Moscow, Soviet Union	Khrennikov, Tikhon Nikolaevich • Mnogo shuma iz nichego [Viel Lärm aus Leidenschaft, Much Ado About Hearts]
1973 02 07	Brussels, Belgium	Nabokov, Nikolai • Love's Labour's Lost [Verlor'ne Liebesmüh']
1973 07 11	Chichester, England	Faris, Alexander • R Loves J
1973 10 15	Berlin, Germany	Forest, Jean Kurt • Hamlet
1974 00 00		Weisgall, Hugo • Gardens of Adonis, The
1974 02 25	London, England	Field, Graham • Dick Deterred
1974 03 08	Rouen, France	Bondeville, Emmanuel de • Antonine et Cléopatre
1974 03 21	Prague, Czechoslovakia	Cikker, Ján • Coriolanus
1974 04 03	New York, U.S.A.	Cribari, Donna • Pop
1974 08 16	Edinburgh, Scotland	Haines, Roger • Shylock [Fire Angel]
1975 00 00		Raphling, Sam • Prince Hamlet
1975 00 00 ?	Philadelphia, U.S.A.	Turok, Paul H. • Richard III
1975 09 24	London, England	Brawn, Geoffrey • At the Sign of the Angel or A Little Touch of Harry in the Night
1976 02 17	New York, U.S.A.	Jones, Cliff • Rockabye Hamlet
1976 04 02	New York, U.S.A.	Malamet, Marsha • Dreamstuff
1976 11 14	Shreveport, LA, U.S.A.	Siegmeister, Elie • Night of the Moonspell
1976 12 20	New York, U.S.A.	Adler, Richard • Music Is
1977 02 25	London, England	Haines, Roger • Fire Angel

1978 04 07	New Brunswick, N. J. (Rutgers University: Douglas School of Music), U.S.A.	Schmitz, Alan • Julius Caesar
1978 07 09	Munich, Germany	Reimann, Aribert • Lear
1979 08 20	San Francisco, U.S.A.	Harbison, John • Winter's Tale, The
1980 02 01	New York, U. S. A.	Mulcahy, Lance • Shakespeare's Cabaret
1980 12 06	Stuttgart, Germany	Reutter, Hermann • Hamlet
1981 11 10	New York, U.S.A.	Valenti, Michael • Oh, Brother

SORTING BY TEXT

TEXT	COMPOSITION
Abbott, George (book) and Will Holt (lyrics)	Adler, Richard • Music Is
Abbott, George and Lorenz Hart	Rogers, Richard • Boys from Syracuse, The
Adenis, Jules and Eugène Adenis	Litolff, Henry Charles • König Lear
Adenis, Jules and Henri Boisseaux	Deffès, Louis Pierre • Jessica
Adler, B. (with R. Schubert and V. Novohradsky)	Weis, Karél • Viola [Die Zwillinge, Blizenci]
Ahlgren, Johan Samuel	Küster, Johann Heinrich • Henrik den Fjerde
Arien, Bernhard Christian d'	Kaffka [Kafka], Johann Christian • Antonius und Cleopatra
Arienzo, Marco d'	Mercadante, Giuseppe Saverio Raffele • Violetta
Arlberg, Fritz	Berens, Johann Hermann • Riccardo
Aron, Willi	Rosenberg, Richard • Liebesspiel, Das
Ashman, Howard (book) and Dennis Green (lyrics)	Malamet, Marsha • Dreamstuff
Auden, Wystan Hugh and Chester Kallman	Nabokov, Nikolai • Love's Labour's Lost [Verlor'ne Liebesmüh']
Auerara, Abbé Pietro d'	Magni, Giuseppe Paolo • Admeto, Rè di Tessaglia
Aureli, Aurelio	Zanettini, Antonio • Érmione [Die wiedergefundene Hermione]
Bachtík, Josef	Krejcí, Isa • Pozdvizení v Efesu [The Upheaval in Ephesus]
Baggesen, Jens Emanuel	Kunzen, Friedrich Ludwig Æmilius • Holger Danske oder Oberon [Holgar the Dane]
Baralle, Alphonse	Pedrell, Filipe • Roi Lear, Le
Barbier, Jules and Michel Florentin Carré	Gounod, Charles François • Roméo et Juliette
Bellamy, Claxson and Harry Paulton	Jakobowski, Edward • Erminie
Bentley, Paul	Haines, Roger • Fire Angel

TEXT	COMPOSITION
Bentley, Paul	Haines, Roger • Shylock [Fire Angel]
Berio di Salsa, Marchese Francesco Maria	Rossini, Gioacchino • Otello, osia L'Africano di Venezia
Bernardi, Carlo	Canonica, Pietro • Miranda
Bertossi, A. and Alfonso Deperis	Macarig, Hector and Alfonso Deperis • Otello Tamburo
Besoyan, Rick (book and lyrics)	Besoyan, Rick • Babes in the Wood, or Who Killed Cock Robin
Bittong, Franz	Pohlig, Carl • Stein der Weisen, Der
Blake, G. B., J. A. Wilder, and Samuel Francis Batchelder	Atherton, Percy Lee and Ernest Hamlin Abbott • Hamlet, Prince of Denmark or The Sport, the Spook and the Spinster
Blau, Éduard	Puget, Paul-Charles-Marie • Beaucoup de bruit pour rien
Blavet, Émile Raymond	Salvayre, Gaston • Riccardo III
Blum, Carl Ludwig	Hohmann, Gustav • Hermione, oder Der kleine Vicomte
Boito, Arrigo	Faccio, Franco • Amleto
Boito, Arrigo	Verdi, Giuseppe • Falstaff
Boito, Arrigo	Verdi, Giuseppe • Otello
Boll, André	Delannoy, Marcel • Puck
Boutet de Monvel, Jaques Marie	Dalayrac, Nicolas • Tout pour l'amour ou Roméo et Juliette
Boye, Caspar Johannes	Kuhlau, Friedrich Daniel Rudolph • Musik Til William Shakspeare [sic], Op. 74
Bret, Alex. [Antoine ?]	Papavoine, Mdme • Vieux Coquet, Le; ou Les deux amies ou Le vieus garçon
Bronnikoff, P. K.	Soloviev, Nicolai Feopemptovich • Cordélia
Buonaiuti, Serafino	Guglielmi, Pietro Carlo • Romeo e Giulietta [I Capuletti ed i Montecchi]
Bürger	Stegmann, Carl David • Macbeth
Burgerdijk, A. T.	Baeyens, August Louis • Coriolanus
Butté, Enrico Annibale and Gustavo Macchi	Samara, Spiro • Furia domata, La

TEXT	COMPOSITION
Cain, Henri and Edouard Adenis	Silver, Charles • Mégère apprivoisée, La
Cane, Claude and M. B. Lucas	Douglas, Hugh A. • Romeo and Juliet Up to Larks
Capek, Josef and Karel Capek	Folprecht, Zdenek • Lásky hra osudná [The Fateful Game of Love], Opus 3
Carbonetti, Amelia	Savini, Giacomo • Tempeste
Carré, Michel Antoine and Paul de Choudens	Missa, Edmond Jean Louis • Dinah
Carré, Michel Florentin and Jules Barbier	Mozart, Wolfgang Amadeus • Peines d'amour perdues
Carré, Michel Florentin and Paul Jules Barbier	Thomas, Charles Louis Ambroise • Hamlet
Caspar, Franz Xaver von	Winter, Peter von • Sturm, Der
Catherine the Great	Unknown • Early Reign of Oleg, The
Chekhov, Michael	Kalnins, Janis • Hamlets
Chemineau	Rateau, Edmond • Rosaline
Chézy, Helmina von	Weber, Carl Maria von • Euryanthe
Chivot, Henri Charles and Henri Alfred Duru	Audran, Edmond • Gillette de Narbonne [Gillette, or Count and Countess; Gilda di Guascogna]
Cimino, Giorgio Tommaso	Pinsuti, Ciro • Mercante di Venezia, Il
Codebò, Andrea	Meiners, Giambattista • Riccardo III
Colman (Sr.), George	Arne, Michael and C. Dibdin, J. Battishill, C. Burney, Hook, J. C. Smith • Fairy Tale
Colman (Sr.), George	Arne, Thomas Augustine • Fairy Prince, The
Composer	Ardin, Leon • Antony and Cleopatra
Composer	Atterberg, Kurt • Stormen, Op. 49
Composer	Barkworth, John Edmond • Romeo and Juliet
Composer	Bentoiu, Pascal • Hamlet, Op. 18
Composer	Berlioz, Hector • Béatrice et Bénédict
Composer	Blacher, Boris • Romeo und Julia
Composer	Bondeville, Emmanuel de • Antonine et Cléopatre
Composer	Borodcicz, Hans von • König Lear

TEXT	COMPOSITION
Composer	Boughton, Rutland • Againcourt
Composer	Carlson, Charles Frederick • Merchant of Venice
Composer	Castelnuovo-Tedesco, Mario • Mercante di Venezia, Il, Op. 181
Composer	Castelnuovo-Tedesco, Mario • Tutto e bène quello che finisce bène, Op. 182
Composer	Chatburn, Tom • Gay Venetians, The
Composer	Cikker, Ján • Coriolanus
Composer	Collingwood, Lawrance Arthur • Macbeth
Composer	Cottrau, Giulio • Cordelia (Re Lear)
Composer	Cottrau, Giulio • Pericle re di Tiro
Composer	Emery, Charles P. • Romeo, the Radical or Obstruction and Effect
Composer	Erbse, Heimo • Julietta, Op. 15
Composer	Fischer, Jan F. • Romeo, Julie a tma (Romeo, Juliet and Darkness)
Composer	Forest, Jean Kurt • Hamlet
Composer	Ghislanzoni, Alberto • Re Lear
Composer	Goedicke, Alexander • Macbeth
Composer	Goldman, Edward M. • Macbeth
Composer	Groth, Howard • Petruchio
Composer	Halpern, Sidney • Macbeth
Composer	Harbison, John • Winter's Tale, The
Composer	Hart, Fritz Bennicke • Malvolio, Opus 14
Composer	Heinrich, Hermann • Viel Lärm um Nichts
Composer	Hensel, Johann Daniel • Geisterinsel, Die
Composer	Hérold, Louis Joseph Ferdinand • Gioventù di Enrico V, La [La Jeunesse d'Henry V]
Composer	Hess, Ludwig • Was ihr Wollt
Composer	Holst, Gustav • At the Boar's Head, Opus 42
Composer	Hopp, Julius • Hammlet

TEXT	COMPOSITION
Composer	Horner • König Lear
Composer	Ivry, Paul Xaver Désiré Richard, Marquis d' • Amantes de Vérone, Les
Composer	Jirko, Ivan • Twelfth Night, The [Vecer Trikralovy]
Composer	Kagen, Sergius • Hamlet
Composer	Kanne, Friedrich August • Miranda oder Das Schwert der Rache
Composer	Kashperov, Vladimir Nikititch • Storm, The [Groza]
Composer	Kirchner, Hermann • Viola
Composer	Klebe, Giselher Wolfgang • Ermordung Cäsars, Die Op. 32
Composer	Kusterer, Arthur • Was ihr Wollt
Composer	La Rosa, Arturo • Otello
Composer	Leverage, Richard • Pyramus and Thisbe, The Comic Masque of
Composer	Loder, Edward James • Robin Goodfellow or the Frolics of Puck
Composer	Lorenz, Carl Adolf • Komödie der Irrungen, Die
Composer	Lueder, Florence Pauline • Rosalind
Composer	Malipiero, Gian Francesco • Antonio e Cleopatra
Composer	Malipiero, Gian Francesco • Giulio Cesare
Composer	Malipiero, Gian Francesco • Romeo e Guilietta (scene 5 of Monde celesti e infernali)
Composer	Martin, Frank • Sturm, Der
Composer	Morton, David • Tempest in a Teapot
Composer	Orff, Carl • Sommernachtstraum, Ein
Composer	Perelli, Edoardo • Viola Pisani
Composer	Pride [sp?], G. • Otello
Composer	Raphling, Sam • Prince Hamlet
Composer	Reutter, Hermann • Hamlet
Composer	Rosellin, Léon • Juliette et Roméo

TEXT	COMPOSITION
Composer	Saussine, Henri de • Marchand de Vénise, Le
Composer	Schmitz, Alan • Julius Caesar
Composer	Searle, Humphrey • Hamlet, Opus 48
Composer	Shelley, Harry Rowe • Romeo and Juliet
Composer	Sobolewski, Friedrich Eduard de • Imogéne
Composer	Sulek, Stjepan • Koriolan
Composer	Sulek, Stjepan • Oluja
Composer	Sutermeister, Heinrich • Zauberinsel, Die
Composer	Szokolay, Sándor • Hamlet
Composer	Tommasi, Ferdinando [Tommaso] • Guido e Ginevre
Composer	Turok, Paul H. • Richard III
Composer	Vaughan Williams, Ralph • Sir John in Love
Composer	Wagner, Wilhelm Richard • Liebesverbot, Das oder Die Novize von Palermo
Composer	Zanardini, Angelo • Amleto
Composer	Zillig, Winfried • Troilus und Cressida
Composer	Zimmermann, Balduin • Wintermärchen, Ein
Composer	Zirra, Alexandru • Furtuna [TheTempest]
Composer after Shakespeare	Beecham, Adrian Wells • Love's Labour's Lost [Peines d'Amour Perdues]
Composer after Shakespeare	Beecham, Adrian Wells • Merchant of Venice, The
Composer and David Garrick	Smith, John Christopher • Fairies, The
Composer and David Garrick	Smith, John Christopher • Tempest, The
Composer and Dorothy Fee	Giannini, Vittorio • Taming of the Shrew, The
Composer and Friedrich Langer	Zavodsky, Felix • Othello

TEXT	COMPOSITION
Composer and Lilyan E. M. Zafred	Zafred, Mario • Amleto
Composer and Peter Pears	Britten, Lord Edward Benjamin • Midsummer Night's Dream, A, Op. 64
Composer and Rudolf Vonásek	Doubrava, Jaroslav • Sen noci svatojanske
Composer and Scribe	Mélésville, Honoré Marie Joseph, Baron Duveyrier] • Gillette de Narbonne
Composer and Therese Robinson	Roters, Ernest • Hamlet, Op. 145
Composer [lyrics] and Bella Spewack and Sam Spewack [book]	Porter, Cole • Kiss Me, Kate
Composer?	Hale, Alfred Matthew • Tempest, The
Composer?	Marshall-Hall, George William Louis • Romeo and Juliet
Cooksey, Curtis	Lueder, Florence Pauline • As You Like It
Currie	Gibbs, Cecil Armstrong • Twelfth Night, Opus 115
Cuvelier de Trye, Jean Guillaume Antoine	Navoigille, Gouliellmo • Orage, L' ou Quel Guignon!
Da Ponte, Lorenzo	Storace, Stephen • Equivoci, Gli
Davenant, Charles	Leverage, Richard • Macbeth
Davenant, Sir William	Locke, Matthew and Robert Johnson • Macbeth
Dejaure	Berton, Henri-Montan • Montano et Stéphanie
Dejaure	Kreutzer, Rodolphe • Imogène, ou La Gageure indiscrète
Delius, Jelka	Delius, Frederick • Romeo und Juliet auf dem Dorfe [A Village Romeo and Juliet]
Deshays, Émile	Le Rey, Frédéric • Mégère apprivoisée, La
Détroyat, Léonce and Paul Armand Silvestre	Saint-Saëns, Camille • Henry VIII
Dibdin, Thomas John	Attwood, Thomas • Hermione, or Valour's Triumph

TEXT	COMPOSITION
Donnay, Maurice and Henri Duvernois [Henri Simon Schwabacher]	Hahn, Reynaldo • Malvina
Döring, Johann Wilhelm	Ritter, Peter • Sturm, Der oder Die bezauberte Insel
Douin	Philidor • Herne le Chasseur
Driver, Donald (book and lyrics)	Valenti, Michael • Oh, Brother
Driver, Donald (book) Hal Hester and Danny Apolinar (lyrics)	Hester, Hal and Danny Apolinar • Your Own Thing
Dryden, John, Sir William Davenant and Thomas Shadwell	Purcell, Henry • Tempest or Enchanted Island, The
Du Catillon, Léonce	De Boeck, Auguste de • Winternachtsdroom, Een
Ducange, Victor Henri Brahain and Anicet Bourgeois	Piccini, Louis Alexandre • Macbeth
Duncan, Ronald Frederic Henry	Eastwood, Thomas Hugh • Christopher Sly
Edgar, David	Field, Graham • Dick Deterred
Eggers, Friedrich Hartwig	Taubert, Wilhelm • Macbeth, Op. 133
Einsiedel, Friedrich Hildebrand von	Wolf, Ernst Wilhelm • Zauberirrungen, Die [Die Irrtümer der Zauberei]
Escosura, Patricio de la	Gaztambide y Garbayo, Joaquin Romualdo • sueño de una noche de verano, El
Faiko, Alexei and Nicolai Bitry	Khrennikov, Tikhon Nikolaevich • V buriu [Im Sturm, Into the Storm]
Fajko, Alexej	Khrennikov, Tikhon Nikolaevich • Brati [Brothers]
Fleg, Edmond	Bloch, Ernest • Macbeth
Fleres, Ugo	Del Fante, Raffaele • Tempesta, La
Fogazzaro, Antonio	Alfano, Franco • Miranda
Folchi, Fr.	Freschi, Giovanni Domenico • Rosalinda
Foppa, Giuseppe Maria	Andreozzi, Gaetano • Amleto
Foppa, Giuseppe Maria	Caruso, Lodovico Luigi • Amleto
Foppa, Giuseppe Maria	Marescalchi, Luigi • Giuletta e Romeo

TEXT	COMPOSITION
Foppa, Giuseppe Maria	Zingarelli, Niccolò Antonio • Giulietta e Romeo
Forst, Joseph	Storch, Anton Maria • Romeo und Julie
Forzano, Giovacchino	Wolf-Ferrari, Ermanno • Sly, ovvero La leggenda del dormiente risvegliato
Franceschi, Carlo Prospero de	Salieri, Antonio • Falstaff osia Le tre Burle
Fulgonio, Fulvio	Canepá, Luigi • Riccardo III
Gallet, Louis	Pillaut, Léon • Perdita
Gallet, Louis and André Corneau	Hüe, George • Titania
Garal, Pierre de	Hignard, Aristide • Hamlet
Gargano, Aristide	Grandi, Alfredo • Amleto
Garrick, David	Boyce, William • Florizel and Perdita
Garrick, David and new lyrics by Frederic Reynolds	Bishop, Sir Henry Rowley • Midsummer Night's Dream, A
Gatty, Reginald M.	Gatty, Nicholas Comyn • Tempest, The
Gavaut, Paul Armand Marcel and P. L. Flers	Serpette, Henri Charles Antoine Gaston • Shakespeare!
Genée, Franz Friedrich Richard	Arensen, Adolf • Viola
Ghislanzoni, Antonio	Cagnoni, Antonio • Re Lear, Il
Giannini, Giuseppe Sesto	Lillo, Giuseppe • Sogno d'una Notte estiva, Il or La Gioventù di Shakespeare
Giannini, Giuseppe Sesto	Santa Caterina, Alessandro • Coriolano
Gieseke, Johann Georg Carl Ludwig	Rafael, Carl Friedrich • Hamlet, Prinz von Liliput
Gieseke, Johann Georg Carl Ludwig	Tuczek, Vincenc Tomas Vaclav • Travestirte Hamlet, Der [Hamlet, Prinz von Dänemark; Hamlet, Prinz von Lilyput]
Goldschmidt, Miriam	Engelmann, Hans Ulrich • Ophelia, Op. 36
Golisciani, Enrico	Sarria, Errico • Equivoci, Gli
Golisciani, Enrico	Westerhout, Niccolò van • Cimbelino, Il
Gollmick, Karl A.	Steinkühler, Émile • Cäsario, oder die Verwechslung, Op. 30

TEXT	COMPOSITION
Gotter, Friedrich Wilhelm	Benda, George Anton • Romeo und Julie
Gotter, Johann Friedrich Wilhelm and Friedrich Hildebrand von Einsiedel	Fleischmann, Friedrich • Geisterinsel, Die
Gotter, Johann Friedrich Wilhelm and Friedrich Hildebrand von Einsiedel	Haack, Friedrich • Geisterinsel, Die
Gotter, Johann Friedrich Wilhelm and Friedrich Hildebrand von Einsiedel	Reichardt, Johann Friedrich • Geisterinsel, Die
Gotter, Johann Friedrich Wilhelm and Friedrich Hildebrand von Einsiedel	Zumsteeg, Johann Rudolf • Geisterinsel, Die
Gozenpud, A.	Shebalin, Vissarion Yakovlevich • Ukroshchenie stroptivoi [The Taming of the Shrew] Op. 46
Granberg, J. L.	Berens, Johann Hermann • Violetta
Gross, Karl	Barbieri, Carlo Emanuele di • Perdita oder Ein Wintermärchen
Grossmith Jr., George, Paul A. Rubens and Harold Ellis	Rubens, Paul Alfred and Walter Rubens • Great Caesar
Guare, John and Mell Shapiro [lyrics by John Guare]	MacDermot, Galt • Two Gentlemen of Verona
Guerville, Harny de	Alexandre, Charles Guillaume • Georget et Georgette
Gugg, Roland	Wödl, Franz • Komödie der Irrungen
Guilliaume, Jules	Stadtfeldt, Christian Joseph Franz Alexandre • Hamlet
Hamilton, Cosmo Hood; Basil & Charles H. E. Brookfield	Stuart, Leslie • Belle of Mayfair
Harlacher, August	Doppler, Arpád • Viel Lärm um Lichts
Harris, Lionel and Robert McNab	Slade, Julian • Comedy of Errors
Hassell, Christopher Vernon	Walton, Sir William • Troilus and Cressida
Haym, Nicola Francesco	Ariosti, Attilio • Coriolano, II
Hedda (Favola di)	Oddone, Elizabetta • Petruccio e il Cavolo Cappuccio
Henneberg, Claus H.	Reimann, Aribert • Lear

TEXT	COMPOSITION
Henry, L.	Gallenberg, Wenzel Robert Count von • Amleto
Hensler, Karl Friedrich	Müller, Wenzel • Sturm oder die Zauberinsel, Der
Hicks, Seymour	Lutz, William Meyer • Merry-Go-Round
Hille	Gevel, Franz Xaver • Rinaldo und Camilla oder Die Zauberinsel
Hopffer, Karl Emil Heinrich	Bruch, Max • Hermione, Op. 40
Huard, Lucian	Tajon, Ben. • Taming of a Shrew, The
Huber, Franz Xaver	Lichtenstein, Carl August Freiherr von • Ende gut, alles gut
Isle, de l'	Unknown • Thimon le misantrope
Islwyn	Jenkins, David • Enchanted Isle, The [Scenes from Shakespeare's 'Tempest']
Ivanovich, Christoforo	Cavalli, Pietro Francesco • Coriolano
Iwaszkiewicza, Jaroslav	Matuszczak, Bernadetta • Julia i Romeo
Jallais, Amedée de	Déjazet, Eugène • Rhum et eau en juillet
Jones, Cliff (book and lyrics)	Jones, Cliff • Rockabye Hamlet
Jonson, Ben	Ferraboso II, Alfonso and Robert Johnson • Oberon, the Fairy Prince
Jordá, José e Luis de Zulueta	Morera, Enrique • Fiercilla domada, La
Kelly, John	Unknown • Timon in Love or The Innocent Theft
Kemble, John Philip adaptation from Shakespeare-Dryden	Linley II, Thomas • Tempest, The or The Enchanted Island
Kokmüller, Aug	Eberwein, Max Carl • Romeo und Julie
Korndorfer, Georg	Hoffmeister, Franz Anton • Schiffbruch, Der
Korompay, J.	Vranicky, Pavel • Rudolf von Felseck (Die Schwarzthaler) oder La Tempestà
Kosta, P.	Zelinka, Jan Evangelista • Spring With Shakespeare
Krásnohorská, Eliska	Smetana, Bedrich • Viola

TEXT	COMPOSITION
Kreutz, Zoë Lund Schiller	Kreutz, Arthur • Sourwood Mountain
Kringsteiner, Ferdinand Josef	Schuster, Ignaz • Othellerl, der Mohr von Wien
Kringsteiner, Ferdinand Josef	Schuster, Ignaz • Romeo und Julie
Kvapil, Jaroslav	Nesvera, Josef • Perdita
Lapierre, Henri	Reynaud, Armand • Roi Lear, Le
Lembert, Johann Wilhelm	Müller (the elder), Adolph • Viel Lärm um Nichts
Leuven, Adolphe de Michel Florentin Carré, and T. Hadot	David, Félicien César • Saphir, Le or Tout est bien, qui finit bien
Leveridge, Richard	Lampe, John Frederich • Pyramus and Thisbe
Linberer, Robert	Michaelis, Gustave • Othello in Kyritz
Lockman, John	Smith, John Christopher • Rosalinda
Lollos, John (book); John Lollos and Don Christopher (lyrics)	Gelber, Stanley Jay • Love and Let Love
Mabley, Edward	Siegmeister, Elie • Night of the Moonspell
Macfarren, George, Sr.	Cooke, Thomas Simpson • Malvina
Mackaye, Percy Wallace	Farwell, Arthur George • Caliban by the Yellow Sands, Opus 47
MacNab and P. Manoury	Hulemann, Th • Malvine I re [The first]
Maggioni, S. Manfredo	Balfe, Michael William • Falstaff
Malherbe, Jules	Weckerlin, Jean Baptiste Théodore • Tout est bien qui finit bien
Mallio, Michele	Fabrizi, Vincenzo • Tempestà ossia Da un disordine ne nasce un ordine, La
Manlove, John	Argento, Dominick • Christopher Sly
Marcello, Marco Marcelliano	Marchetti, Filippo • Romeo e Giulietta
Marchi, Antonio	Capelli, Giovanni Maria • Rosalinda [Erginia Mascherata]
Marchi, Antonio	Strungk, Nicolaus Adam • Rosalinde

TEXT	COMPOSITION
Marchi, Antonio	Ziani, Marc Antonio • Rosalinda, La or Erginia mascherata
Maren, Roger	Mohaupt, Richard • Double Trouble [Zwillingskomödie]
Marshall, Frank	Rossi, Lauro • Biorn
Meilhac, Henri	Choudens, Antony • Cymbeline
Meisl, Karl	Müller (the elder), Adolph • Othellerl, der Mohr von Wien [Die geheilte Eifersucht]
Mélis, Hubert	Alpaerts, Florent • Shylock
Merino, Gabriel and Celsio Lucio	Valverde y San Juan, Joaquín • sueño de una noche de verano, El
Meyer, Felix	Michaelis, Gustave • Lustigen Weiber von Berlin, Die
Millanvoye, Bertrand Casimir and Paul Eudel	David, Adolphe Isaac • Orage, L'
Mills, John Brent	Utley, Wendell • Will
Minato, Niccolò	Draghi, Antonio • Timone misantropo
Minichini, Edoardo	Unknown • Pulcinella rivale di Turzillo e confuso tra Capuleti e Montecchi
Moline et Cubieres-Palmezeau	Porta, [Bernardo ?] • Roméo et Juliette
Moll, [Franz?]	Asplmayr, Franz • Leben und Tod des Königs Macbeth
Moniglia, Giovanni Andrea	Cattani, Lorenzo • Cajo Marzio Coriolano
Monnet	Foignet, Jacques • Orage, L'
More, Julian [Lyrics by Julian More and James Gilbert]	Gilbert, James • Good Time Johnny
Morgan, Mac Namara	Arne, Thomas Augustine, Samuel Arnold and others • Sheep-Shearing, The or Florizel and Perdita
Morton, Thomas	Bishop, Sir Henry Rowley • Henri Quatre [Paris in the Olden Times]
Mosenthal, Salomon Hermann Ritter von	Nicolai, Carl Otto Ehrenfried • lustigen Weiber von Windsor, Die

TEXT	COMPOSITION
Mosenthal, Solomon Hermann	Sayn-Wittgenstein-Berleburg, Count Friedrich Ernst von • Antonius und Kleopatra
Navarro y Gonzalo, Calisto	Nieto, Manuel • Otelo y Desdémona
Noël, E.	Serpette, Henri Charles Antoine Gaston • Songe d'une nuit d'été, Le
Noris, Matteo	Pollaroli, Carlo Francesco • Marzio Coriolano
Novelli, Auguste	Allegra, Giuseppe • Sogno di una Notte, Il
Nuitter, Charles and A. de Beaumont	Legouix, Isidore Édouard • Othello, Un
Olmi, A. Mario	Roti, Ugo • Sogno di una notte d'estate, Il
Olon-Scrymgeour, John	Weisgall, Hugo • Gardens of Adonis, The
Orban, Dezsö	Sztojanovics, Eug. • Otello mecél
Ormeville, Carlo d'	Gobatti, Stefano • Cordelia
Orsini, Luigi	Bossi, Renzo • Volpino il Calderaio, Op. 32
Overskou, Thomas	Rung, Henrik • Stormen paa København [Storm over Copenhagen]
Oxenford, Edward	Old, John • Herne the Hunter (A Legend of Royal Windsor)
Pacini, Emiliano and Émile Deschamps	Séméladis, M. • Cordélia
Palomba, Giuseppe	Guglielmi, Pietro Alessandro • Admeto, Re di Tessaglia
Papini, Giovanni	Frazzi, Vito • Re Lear
Papp, Joseph	MacDermot, Galt • Cressida
Papp, Joseph and Composer	Amram, David • Twelfth Night
Pariati, Pietro	Caldara, Antonio • Cajo Marzio Coriolano
Pariati, Pietro	Conti, Nicolò • Cajo Marzio Coriolano [Marzio Coriolano]
Pariati, Pietro	Maggioni, Francesco • Cajo Marzio Coriolano
Pariati, Pietro	Treu, Daniel Gottlieb • Coriolano

TEXT   COMPOSITION

Parke, Walter   Andrews, John Charles Bond- •
                                       Herne's Oak, or The Rose of
                                       Windsor [also Herne the Hunter]
Pasqué, Ernst Heinrich Anton   Freudenberg, Wilhelm • Kleopatra
Patzke, Johann Samuel   Rolle, Johann Heinrich • Sturm
                                       oder Die bezauberte Insel, Der
Perinet, Joachim   Kleinheinz, Carl Franz Xaver •
                                       Hamlet, Prinz vom Tandelmarkt
Perinet, Joachim   Maretzek, Maximilian • Hamlet
Perinet, Joachim   Schuster, Ignaz • Hamlet, Prinz
                                       vom Tandelmarkt
Peruzzini, Giovanni   Buzzolla, Antonio • Amleto
Peruzzini, Giovanni   Moroni, Luigi • Amleto
Petito, Davide   Scognamilio, Gennaro • Otello
                                       ossia Catiello l'Affricano
Pfahler, Adalbert   Kanne, Friedrich August • Malvina,
                                       oder Putzerls Abenteuer
Piave, Francesco Maria   Benvenuti, Tommaso • Guglielmo
                                       Shakespeare
Piave, Francesco Maria and   Verdi, Giuseppe • Macbeth
   Andrea Maffei
Pirazzi, Emil   Urspruch, Anton • Sturm, Der
Planard, François Antoine   Carafa di Colobrano, Michele
   Eugène de   Enrico and Aimé Ambroise
                                       Simon Leborne • Violette, La ou
                                       Gérard de Nevers
Planché, James Robinson   Weber, Carl Maria von • Oberon [or
                                       the Elf-King's Oath]
Polilova, N.   Kasanli, Nikolai Ivanovich [Kazanli,
                                       Kazanly] • Miranda (Poliedniaia
                                       bor'ba) [Der Letzte Kampf]
Ponte, Lorenzo da   Martín y Soler, Vicente •
                                       Capricciosa corretta, La [So
                                       bessert sie sich]
Porter, Anna Maria   Busby, Thomas • Fair Fugitives
Possenti, A.   Farina, Guido • Dodisesima
                                       Notte, La
Prasch   Berény, Henri • Wintermärchen,
                                       Das
Principessa in Campagna, La   Manusardi, Giuseppe • sogno di
                                       Primavera, Un [Un rêve de
                                       printemps]

401

TEXT	COMPOSITION
Ramos Carrión, Miguel	Chapí y Lorente, Ruperto • Tempestad, La
Ratti, Luigi	Podestà, Carlo • Ero, ossia Molto rumore per nulla
Ravenscroft, E.	Clarke, Jeremiah • Titus Andronicus
Renc, Václav	Horky, Karel • Jed z Elsinoru [The Poison from Elsinore]
Reynolds, F.	Bishop, Sir Henry Rowley • Merry Wives of Windsor, The
Reynolds, F.	Bishop, Sir Henry Rowley • Twelfth Night
Reynolds, Frederic	Bishop, Sir Henry Rowley • Comedy of Errors, The
Reynolds, Frederic	Bishop, Sir Henry Rowley • Tempest, The
Roccaforte, Gaetano	Anfossi, Pasquale • Cajo Mario
Roccaforte, Gaetano	Bertoni, Ferdinando Giuseppe • Cajo Mario
Roccaforte, Gaetano	Bianchi, Francesco • Cajo Mario
Roccaforte, Gaetano	Cimarosa, Domenico Nicola [Cimmarosa] • Cajo Mario
Roccaforte, Gaetano	Galuppi, Baldassarre [called Buranello] • Cajo Mario
Roccaforte, Gaetano	Jommelli, Nicolo • Caio Mario [Cajo Mario]
Roccaforte, Gaetano	Monza, Carlo Antonio • Cajo Mario
Roccaforte, Gaetano	Piccinni, Niccolò • Caio Mario
Roccaforte, Gaetano	Scarlatti, Giuseppe • Caio Mario
Roccaforte, Gaetano	Scolari, Giuseppe • Cajo Mario
Rochon de Chabannes, Marc-Antoine-Jacques	Gossec, François Joseph • Hylas et Sylvie
Roepke, Gabriella	Leichtling, Alan • Tempest, The
Rolli, Paolo Antonio	Händel, Georg Friederich • Admeto, Re di Tessaglia
Rolli, Paolo Antonio	Veracini, Francesco Maria • Rosalinda
Romanelli, Luigi	Fioravanti, Valentino • Capricciosa pentita, La
Romanelli, Luigi	Lavina, Vincenzo • Coriolano, Il
Romanelli, Luigi	Morlacchi, Francesco Giuseppi Baldassare • Capricciosa pettita, La

TEXT	COMPOSITION
Romanelli, Luigi	Nicolini, Giuseppe • Coriolano
Romanelli, Luigi	Radicati, Felice Alessandro • Coriolano, II
Romani, Felice	Bellini, Vincenzo • Capuleti e i Montecchi, I
Romani, Felice	Carlini, Luigi • Gioventù di Enrico V, La
Romani, Felice	Generali, Pietro Mercandetti • Rodrigo di Valencia
Romani, Felice	Mercadante, Giuseppe Saverio Raffele • Amleto
Romani, Felice	Mercadante, Giuseppe Saverio Raffele • Gioventù di Enrico V, La
Romani, Felice	Morales, Melesio • Giulietta e Romeo
Romani, Felice	Mosca, Giuseppe • Gioventù di Enrico V, La
Romani, Felice	Orlandi, Ferdinando • Rodrigo di Valencia
Romani, Felice	Pacini, Giovanni • Rodrigo di Valencia
Romani, Felice	Torriani, Eugenio • Romeo e Giulietta
Romani, Felice	Vaccai, Nicola • Giulietta e Romeo
Romani, Felice?	Garcia, Manuel Vincente del Popolo • Gioventù di Enrico V, La
Römer	Danzi, Franz • Malvina [Die Wolfsjagd]
Römer, Georg Christian	Dittersdorf, Carl Ditters von • lustigen Weiber von Windsor und der dicke Hans, Die
Römer, Georg Christian	Ritter, Peter • lustigen Weiber, Die
Rosier, Joseph Bernard and Adolph de Leuven	Thomas, Charles Louis Ambroise • Songe d'une nuit d'été, Le [Shakespeare oder Der Traum einer Sommernacht]
Rosoi, Barnabé Farmian de	Martini, Giovanni • Henri IV, ou La Bataille d'Ivry
Ross, Adrian and James Leader	Carr, Frank Osmond • In Town
Ross, Sheridan	Maclean, Alick • Petruccio

TEXT	COMPOSITION
Rossato, Arturo	Lattuada, Felice • Tempesta, La
Rossato, Arturo	Persico, Mario • Bisbetica Domata, La
Rossato, Arturo	Zandonai, Riccardo • Giulietta e Romeo
Rosseels, E.	Duyse, Florimond Van • Rosalinde
Rossi, Gaetano	Vaccai, Nicola • Malvina
Rougêt de Lisle, Claude Joseph and Augustin Hix	Chélard, Hippolyte-André-Jean-Baptiste • Macbeth
Rytter, Henrik	Eggen, Arne • Cymbelyn
Saint-Hilaire V. de and Michel Delaporte	Francastel, A. • Henry IV
Saint-Just, Claude Godard d'Aucour de	Méhul, Étienne Nicolas • Jeune Henri, Le [Gabrielle d'Estrées où les Amours d'Henri IV]
Salice-Contessa, Carl Wilhelm	Lauer, Adolph L. [Freiherr von Münchofen] • Orakelspruch, Der
Salice-Contessa, Carl Wilhelm	Mohr, Hermann • Orakelspruch, Der Op. 50
Salice-Contessa, Carl Wilhelm	Schneider, Georg Abraham • Orakelspruch, Der
Salice-Contessa, Carl Wilhelm and Christoph Ernest von Houwald	Herx, Werner • Orakelspruch, Der
Salvatori, Fausto	Mancinelli, Luigi • Sogno di una notte d'estate, Il
Salvi, Antonio	Gasperini, Carlo Francesco • Equivoci d'amore e d'innocenza, Gl'
Sander, Levin Christian	Kunzen, Friedrich Ludwig Æmilius • Stormen
Sanseverino, Carlo	Schwanenberg, Johann Gottfried • Romeo e Giulia
Sarment, Jean	Hahn, Reynaldo • Beaucoup de bruit pour rien
Schiff, Larry and Chuck Knull (book and lyrics)	Cribari, Donna • Pop
Schikaneder, Emanuel	Gerl, Thaddäus; Henneberg and Benedikt Schack • Stein der Weisen, Der oder Die Zauberinsel

TEXT	COMPOSITION
Schikaneder, Emanuel	Hoffmeister, Franz Anton • Rosalinde, oder Die Macht der Feen
Schikaneder, Emanuel	Zák, Benedict Emanuel • Stein der Weisen, Dem oder Die Zauber Insel
Schink, Johann Friedrich	Asplmayr [Aspelmayr], Franz • Sturm, Der
Schink, Johann Friedrich	Unknown • Bezähmte Widerbellerin, Die
Schmidt, Giovanni	Costa, Michael Andrew Angus • Malvina
Schönfeld, Alfred	Schönfeld, Georg • Falstaff
Schröder, Fr.	Müller (the elder), Adolph • Heinrich IV
Scribe, Augustin Eugène	Halévy, Jacques François Fromental Elie • Guido et Ginevre ou La Peste de Florence
Scribe, Augustin Eugène	Halévy, Jacques Franoçis Fromental Élie • Tempesta, La
Ségur, Alexandre Joseph Pierre vicomte de	Steibelt, Daniel Gottlieb • Roméo et Juliette or Tout pour l'amour
Seidl, Johann Gabriel	Riotte, Philipp Jakob • Sturm, Der oder Die Insel des Prospero
Seitz, Dran and Tani [book and lyrics]	Balamos, John • As You Like It
Sendtner, Joseph Ignaz	Stuntz, Joseph Hartmann • Heinrich IV zu Givry
Seriman, Conte Zaccaria de	Pulli, Pietro • Caio Marzio Coriolano
Seyler, Friederike Sophie	Vranicky, Pavel • Oberon, König der Elfen
Shadwell, Thomas	Banister, John; Giovanni Battista Draghi; Matthew Locke; Pelham Humfrey; and Pietro Reggio • Tempest, The [The Enchanted Island]
Shadwell, Thomas	Purcell, Henry • History of Timon of Athens, the Man Hater, The
Shafer, Fritz	Wiedeke, Adolf • lustigen Weiber von Hamburg, Die

TEXT	COMPOSITION
Shakespeare	Vidal, Paul Antonin • Comme il vous Plaire
Silvestre, Paul Armand	Urich, Jean • Orage, L'
Silvestre, Paul Armand and Pierre Berton	Duvernoy, Victor-Alphonse • Tempète, La
Slee, Norman D.	Ansell, John • King's Bride, The [Violette]
Smith, Harry Bache	Engländer, Ludwig • Belle of Bohemia, The
Snell, Gordon	Greenwall, Peter • Three Caskets, The or Venice Re-served
Sodini, Angelo	Angelis, Arturo de • Tempesta, La
Sondheim, Stephen and Arthur Laurents	Bernstein, Leonard • West Side Story
Spaak, Paul	Brumagne, Fernand • Marchand de Venise, Le
Spaak, Paul	Vreuls, Victor • Songe d'une nuit d'été, Un
Spiritini, Massimo	Bottacio, Pietro • Bisbetica Domata, La
Spiritini, Massimo	Zanon, Antonio B. • Leggenda di Giulietta, La
Steppes, Dr. Adolph	Hamel, Eduard • Malvina
Stevens, Dudley	Brawn, Geoffrey • At the Sign of the Angel or A Little Touch of Harry in the Night
Stjernström, J.	Berens, Johann Hermann • Sommarnattsdröm, En
Straube, Emanuel	Suppé, Franz von • Sommernachtstraum, Der
Sturgis, Julian Russell	Stanford, Sir Charles Villiers • Much Ado About Nothing, Opus 76a
Sutermeister, Peter	Sutermeister, Heinrich • Romeo und Julia
Tarducci, Filippo	Morlacchi, Francesco Giuseppi Baldassare • Gioventù di Enrico V, La [Das Jugendjahre Heinrich des Fünften]
Tarducci, Filippo	Pacini, Giovanni • Gioventù di Enrico V, La (also La bella tavernara; Le Aventure d'una notte)

TEXT	COMPOSITION
Taubert, Emil	Taubert, Carl Gottfried Wilhelm • Cesario, oder Was ihr wollt, Op. 188
Teofilo, Giovanni	Bernabei, Vincenzo • Equivoci d'Amore, Gli
Terzago, Ventura	Bernabei, Giuseppe Antonio • Érmione
Thompson, Alexander M. and Robert Courtneidge [Lyrics by Paul A. Rubins and Arthur Wimperis]	Rubens, Paul Alfred and Frank E. Tours • Dairymaids, The
Torelli, Serafino	Fioravanti, Valentino • Enrico IV al passo della Marna
Torelli, Serafino	Maganini, Giovanni • Enrico IV al passo della Marna
Tottola, Andrea Leone Abbé	Rossini, Gioacchino • Ermione
Tréfeu de Fréval, Étienne Victor	Offenbach, Jacques • Rêve d'une Nuit d'été, Le
Turner, Montague	Barry, H. C. • Shylock or The Venus of Venice
Uffer, Dr.	Schindelmeisser, Louis Alexander Balthasar • Malvina
Ustinov, Peter [Lyrics by Julian More]	Faris, Alexander • R Loves J
Valsini, Frencasco	Perti, Giacomo Antonio • Martio Coriolano
Vanloo, Abert and Eugène Leterrier	Lecocq, Charles Alexandre • Marjolaine
Vanneschi, Francesco	Galuppi, Baldassarre • Enrico
Vernoy de Saint-Georges, Jules, and Adolphe de Leuven	Adam, Adolphe-Charles • Falstaff
Vidalin, Maurice	Claudric, Jean • Othello Story
Villati, Leopoldo de	Graun, Karl Heinrich • Coriolano
Vrchlicky, Jaroslav	Fibich, Zdenko • Boure, Opus 40 [Der Sturm]
Vrchlicky, Jaroslav	Foerster, Joseph Brohuslav • Jessika, Opus 60
Weber, Oberst von	Grosheim, Georg Christoph • Titania, oder Liebe durch Zauberei

TEXT	COMPOSITION
Widmann, Joseph Victor	Goetz, Herman • Widerspänstigen Zähmung, Der [La Megère apprivoisée; Caterina e Petruccio]
Widowitz, Oskar	Holenia, Hans • Viola, Opus 21 [Was Ihr wollt]
Wilde, Richard	Taubmann, Otto • Porzia
Wildmann, Joseph Victor	Frank, Ernst • Sturm, Der
Willner, Alfred Maria	Goldmark, Carl • Wintermärchen, Ein
Wolff, Pius Alexander	Kreutzer, Conradin • Cordelia (Floretta ou La Folle de Glaris)[First named Adele von Budoy]
Worsdale, James	Unknown • Cure for a Scold, A
Wysber, Ludwig	Storch, Anton Maria • Stein der Weisen, Der
Zakrzewski, Paul (book and lyrics)	Harper, Wally • Sensations
Zamaçois, Miguel	Hahn, Reynaldo • Marchand de Vénise, Le
Zeffirelli, Franco	Barber, Samuel • Antony and Cleopatra, Op. 40
Zell, F. and Composer	Genée, Franz Friedrich Richard and Louis Roth • Zwillinge
Zeno, Apostolo and Pietro Pariati	Carcani, Giuseppe • Ambleto
Zeno, Apostolo and Pietro Pariati	Gasperini, Carlo Francesco • Ambleto
Zeno, Apostolo and Pietro Pariati	Scarlatti, Giuseppe Domenico • Ambleto
Zeno, Apostolo and Pietro Pariati	Vignali, Giuseppe [Act I]; Carlo Baglioni [Act II] and Giacomo Cozzi [Act III] • Ambleto

SORTING BY PLAY

PLAY	COMPOSITION	S	E
?	Rosenberg, Richard • Liebesspiel, Das	Y	S
?	Unknown • Early Reign of Oleg, The	?	
All's Well That Ends Well	Antoine, Ferdinand d' • Ende gut, alles gut oder Der Fürst und sein Volk	?	
All's Well That Ends Well	Audran, Edmond • Gillette de Narbonne [Gillette, or Count and Countess; Gilda di Guascogna]	Y	S
All's Well That Ends Well	Campenhout, François van • Gillette de Narbonne	?	
All's Well That Ends Well	Castelnuovo-Tedesco, Mario • Tutto e bène quello che finisce bène, Op. 182	Y	S
All's Well That Ends Well	Cooke, Thomas Simpson • Malvina	?	
All's Well That Ends Well	Costa, Michael Andrew Angus • Malvina	?	
All's Well That Ends Well	Danzi, Franz • Malvina [Die Wolfsjagd]	?	
All's Well That Ends Well	David, Félicien César • Saphir, Le or Tout est bien, qui finit bien	Y	S
All's Well That Ends Well	Hahn, Reynaldo • Malvina	?	
All's Well That Ends Well	Hamel, Eduard • Malvina	Y	S
All's Well That Ends Well	Hanssens, J. F. J. • Gillette de Narbonne	?	
All's Well That Ends Well	Hulemann, Th • Malvine I re [The first]	?	
All's Well That Ends Well	Kanne, Friedrich August • Malvina, oder Putzerls Abenteuer	?	
All's Well That Ends Well	Lichtenstein, Carl August Freiherr von • Ende gut, alles gut	?	

PLAY	COMPOSITION	S	E
All's Well That Ends Well	Mélésville, Honoré Marie Joseph, Baron Duveyrier] • Gillette de Narbonne	?	
All's Well That Ends Well	Schindelmeisser, Louis Alexander Balthasar • Malvina	N	S
All's Well That Ends Well	Vaccai, Nicola • Malvina	?	
All's Well That Ends Well	Weckerlin, Jean Baptiste Théodore • Tout est bien qui finit bien	?	
Anthony and Cleopatra	Ardin, Leon • Antony and Cleopatra	Y	P
Anthony and Cleopatra	Durme, Jef Van • Anthony and Cleopatra	Y	S
Anthony and Cleopatra	Rubens, Paul Alfred and Walter Rubens • Great Caesar	Y	S
Anthony and Cleopatra	Sayn-Wittgenstein-Berleburg, Count Friedrich Ernst von • Antonius und Kleopatra	Y	S
Antony and Cleopatra	Barber, Samuel • Antony and Cleopatra, Op. 40	Y	P
Antony and Cleopatra	Bishop, Sir Henry Rowley • Antony and Cleopatra	N O	S
Antony and Cleopatra	Bondeville, Emmanuel de • Antonine et Cléopatre	Y	P
Antony and Cleopatra	Freudenberg, Wilhelm • Kleopatra	Y	S
Antony and Cleopatra	Kaffka [Kafka], Johann Christian • Antonius und Cleopatra	Y	S
Antony and Cleopatra	Malipiero, Gian Francesco • Antonio e Cleopatra	Y	P
As You Like It	Balamos, John • As You Like It	Y	S
As You Like It	Bishop, Sir Henry Rowley • As You Like It	N O	P
As You Like It	Capelli, Giovanni Maria • Rosalinda [Erginia Mascherata]	N	S
As You Like It	Debussy, Claude • As You Like It	Y	S
As You Like It	Duyse, Florimond Van • Rosalinde	?	
As You Like It	Freschi, Giovanni Domenico • Rosalinda	?	

PLAY	COMPOSITION	S	E
As You Like It	Hoffmeister, Franz Anton • Rosalinde, oder Die Macht der Feen	?	
As You Like It	Lueder, Florence Pauline • As You Like It	Y	P
As You Like It	Lueder, Florence Pauline • Rosalind	Y	P
As You Like It	Rateau, Edmond • Rosaline	?	
As You Like It	Smith, John Christopher • Rosalinda	N	S
As You Like It	Strungk, Nicolaus Adam • Rosalinde	N	S
As You Like It	Veracini, Francesco Maria • Rosalinda	Y	P
As You Like It	Vidal, Paul Antonin • Comme il vous Plaire	?	
As You Like It	Weis, Karél • Comme il vous Plaira	?	
As You Like It	Ziani, Marc Antonio • Rosalinda, La or Erginia mascherata	N	S
Comedy of Errors	Bishop, Sir Henry Rowley • Comedy of Errors, The	N O	P
Comedy of Errors	Engländer, Ludwig • Belle of Bohemia, The	Y	S
Comedy of Errors	Gazzaniga, Giuseppe • Equivoci, Gli	?	
Comedy of Errors	Genée, Franz Friedrich Richard and Louis Roth • Zwillinge	?	
Comedy of Errors	Krejcí, Isa • Pozdvizení v Efesu [The Upheaval in Ephesus]	Y	P
Comedy of Errors	Lorenz, Carl Adolf • Komödie der Irrungen, Die	Y	S
Comedy of Errors	Mohaupt, Richard • Double Trouble [Zwillingskomödie]	N	P
Comedy of Errors	Rogers, Richard • Boys from Syracuse, The	Y	S
Comedy of Errors	Sarria, Errico • Equivoci, Gli	?	
Comedy of Errors	Slade, Julian • Comedy of Errors	Y	S
Comedy of Errors	Storace, Stephen • Equivoci, Gli	Y	P
Comedy of Errors	Valenti, Michael • Oh, Brother	Y	S
Comedy of Errors	Wödl, Franz • Komödie der Irrungen	Y	S
Coriolanus	Anfossi, Pasquale • Cajo Mario	?	

411

PLAY	COMPOSITION	S	E
Coriolanus	Ariosti, Attilio • Coriolano, II	N	S
Coriolanus	Baeyens, August Louis • Coriolanus	Y	S
Coriolanus	Bertoni, Ferdinando Giuseppe • Cajo Mario	?	
Coriolanus	Bianchi, Francesco • Cajo Mario	?	
Coriolanus	Caldara, Antonio • Cajo Marzio Coriolano	N	S
Coriolanus	Cattani, Lorenzo • Cajo Marzio Coriolano	N	S
Coriolanus	Cavalli, Pietro Francesco • Coriolano	N	S
Coriolanus	Cikker, Ján • Coriolanus	Y	P
Coriolanus	Cimarosa, Domenico Nicola [Cimmarosa] • Cajo Mario	?	
Coriolanus	Conti, Nicolò • Cajo Marzio Coriolano [Marzio Coriolano]	?	
Coriolanus	Galuppi, Baldassarre [called Buranello] • Cajo Mario	?	
Coriolanus	Graun, Karl Heinrich • Coriolano	N	S
Coriolanus	Jommelli, Nicolo • Caio Mario [Cajo Mario]	N	S
Coriolanus	Lavina, Vincenzo • Coriolano, II	N	S
Coriolanus	Maggioni, Francesco • Cajo Marzio Coriolano	?	
Coriolanus	Monza, Carlo Antonio • Cajo Mario	?	
Coriolanus	Nicolini, Giuseppe • Coriolano	N	S
Coriolanus	Perti, Giacomo Antonio • Martio Coriolano	N	S
Coriolanus	Piccinni, Niccolò • Caio Mario	?	
Coriolanus	Pollaroli, Carlo Francesco • Marzio Coriolano	N	S
Coriolanus	Pulli, Pietro • Caio Marzio Coriolano	N	S
Coriolanus	Radicati, Felice Alessandro • Coriolano, II	N	S
Coriolanus	Santa Caterina, Alessandro • Coriolano	?	
Coriolanus	Savigna, Vincenzo • Coriolano	?	
Coriolanus	Scarlatti, Giuseppe • Caio Mario	?	
Coriolanus	Scolari, Giuseppe • Cajo Mario	?	
Coriolanus	Sulek, Stjepan • Koriolan	Y	S

PLAY	COMPOSITION	S	E
Coriolanus	Treu, Daniel Gottlieb • Coriolano	N	S
Cymbeline	Choudens, Antony • Cymbeline	?	
Cymbeline	Eggen, Arne • Cymbelyn	Y	S
Cymbeline	Kreutzer, Rodolphe • Imogène, ou La Gageure indiscrète	Y	S
Cymbeline	Lecocq, Charles Alexandre • Marjolaine	Y	S
Cymbeline	Missa, Edmond Jean Louis • Dinah	Y	P
Cymbeline	Sobolewski, Friedrich Eduard de • Imogéne	Y	S
Cymbeline	Taboida, Ant. Sanchez do Cunha • Dinah	?	
Cymbeline	Tiessen, Heinz • Cymbelin	NO	S
Cymbeline	Ware, William Henry • Cymbeline	NO	S
Cymbeline	Weber, Carl Maria von • Euryanthe	N	S
Cymbeline	Westerhout, Niccolò van • Cimbelino, Il	Y	S
Hamlet	Andreozzi, Gaetano • Amleto	Y	P
Hamlet	Atherton, Percy Lee and Ernest Hamlin Abbott • Hamlet, Prince of Denmark or The Sport, the Spook and the Spinster	Y	S
Hamlet	Bentoiu, Pascal • Hamlet, Op. 18	Y	P
Hamlet	Berlioz, Hector • Hamlet	Y	S
Hamlet	Bizet, Georges • Hamlet	Y	S
Hamlet	Buzzolla, Antonio • Amleto	Y	P
Hamlet	Carcani, Giuseppe • Ambleto	N	P
Hamlet	Caruso, Lodovico Luigi • Amleto	Y	S
Hamlet	Engelmann, Hans Ulrich • Ophelia, Op. 36	Y	S
Hamlet	Faccio, Franco • Amleto	Y	S
Hamlet	Fontmichel, Hippolyte Honoré Joseph Court de (1799-?) • Amleto	Y	S
Hamlet	Forest, Jean Kurt • Hamlet	N	S
Hamlet	Gallenberg, Wenzel Robert Count von • Amleto	I	S
Hamlet	Gasperini, Carlo Francesco • Ambleto	N	S

413

PLAY	COMPOSITION	S	E
Hamlet	Glinka, Mikhail Ivanovitch • Hamlet	Y	S
Hamlet	Grandi, Alfredo • Amleto	Y	S
Hamlet	Guglielmi, Pietro Alessandro • Admeto, Re di Tessaglia	N	S
Hamlet	Händel, Georg Friederich • Admeto, Re di Tessaglia	N	S
Hamlet	Heward, Leslie Hays • Hamlet	Y	S
Hamlet	Hignard, Aristide • Hamlet	Y	P
Hamlet	Hignett, J. L. A. • Hamlet	N	S
Hamlet	Holland, Jan David • Hamlet, Pantomime zu	N O	P
Hamlet	Hopp, Julius • Hammlet	Y	P
Hamlet	Horky, Karel • Jed z Elsinoru [The Poison from Elsinore]	Y	P
Hamlet	Jones, Cliff • Rockabye Hamlet	Y	S
Hamlet	Kagen, Sergius • Hamlet	Y	P
Hamlet	Kalnins, Janis • Hamlets	Y	P
Hamlet	Keurvels, Edward H. J. • Hamlet	Y	S
Hamlet	Kleinheinz, Carl Franz Xaver • Hamlet, Prinz vom Tandelmarkt	?	
Hamlet	MacFarren, George Alexander • Hamlet	?	
Hamlet	Machavariani, Alexei • Hamlet	Y	S
Hamlet	Magni, Giuseppe Paolo • Admeto, Rè di Tessaglia	?	
Hamlet	Marescotti • Amleto	Y	S
Hamlet	Maretzek, Maximilian • Hamlet	Y	S
Hamlet	Mercadante, Giuseppe Saverio Raffele • Amleto	Y	P
Hamlet	Moroni, Luigi • Amleto	Y	P
Hamlet	Mussorgsky, Modest Petrovich • Hamlet	Y	S
Hamlet	Prokofiev, Sergei • Hamlet, Music to the Tragedy by Shakespeare	N O	P
Hamlet	Rafael, Carl Friedrich • Hamlet, Prinz von Liliput	?	
Hamlet	Raphling, Sam • Prince Hamlet	Y	S
Hamlet	Reutter, Hermann • Hamlet	Y	P
Hamlet	Roters, Ernest • Hamlet, Op. 145	Y	P

PLAY	COMPOSITION	S	E
Hamlet	Scarlatti, Giuseppe Domenico • Ambleto	N	S
Hamlet	Schuster, Ignaz • Hamlet, Prinz vom Tandelmarkt	Y	S
Hamlet	Searle, Humphrey • Hamlet, Opus 48	Y	P
Hamlet	Soule, Charles Caroll • Travesty Without a Pun.	Y	S
Hamlet	Stadtfeldt, Christian Joseph Franz Alexandre • Hamlet	Y	S
Hamlet	Szokolay, Sándor • Hamlet	Y	P
Hamlet	Thomas, Charles Louis Ambroise • Hamlet	Y	P
Hamlet	Tuczek, Vincenc Tomas Vaclav • Travestirte Hamlet, Der [Hamlet, Prinz von Dänemark; Hamlet, Prinz von Lilyput]	?	
Hamlet	Vignali, Giuseppe [Act I]; Carlo Baglioni [Act II] and Giacomo Cozzi [Act III] • Ambleto	N	S
Hamlet	Weigl, Joseph [Veigl, Giuseppe] • Amleto	Y	S
Hamlet	Zafred, Mario • Amleto	Y	P
Hamlet	Zanardini, Angelo • Amleto	Y	S
Henry IV	Aspa, Mario • Gioventù di Enrico V, La	?	
Henry IV	Balfe, Michael William • Enrico IV al passo della Marna	?	
Henry IV	Bishop, Sir Henry Rowley • Henri Quatre [Paris in the Olden Times]	N	P
Henry IV	Carlini, Luigi • Gioventù di Enrico V, La	?	
Henry IV	Fioravanti, Valentino • Enrico IV al passo della Marna	?	
Henry IV	Francastel, A. • Henry IV	?	
Henry IV	Galuppi, Baldassarre • Enrico	N	P
Henry IV	Garcia, Manuel Vincente del Popolo • Gioventù di Enrico V, La	Y	S
Henry IV	Hérold, Louis Joseph Ferdinand • Gioventù di Enrico V, La [La Jeunesse d'Henry V]	N	P

PLAY	COMPOSITION	S	E
Henry IV	Küster, Johann Heinrich • Henrik den Fjerde	?	
Henry IV	Maganini, Giovanni • Enrico IV al passo della Marna	N	P
Henry IV	Martini, Giovanni • Henri IV, ou La Bataille d'Ivry	N	S
Henry IV	Méhul, Étienne Nicolas • Jeune Henri, Le [Gabrielle d'Estrées où les Amours d'Henri IV]	?	
Henry IV	Morlacchi, Francesco Giuseppi Baldassare • Gioventù di Enrico V, La [Das Jugendjahre Heinrich des Fünften]	N	S
Henry IV	Mosca, Giuseppe • Gioventù di Enrico V, La	?	
Henry IV	Müller (the elder), Adolph • Heinrich IV	?	
Henry IV	Pacini, Giovanni • Gioventù di Enrico V, La (also La bella tavernara; Le Aventure d'una notte)	Y	S
Henry IV	Stuntz, Joseph Hartmann • Heinrich IV zu Givry	N	S
Henry IV	Weisgall, Hugo • Henry IV	?	
Henry IV Parts I and II	Brawn, Geoffrey • At the Sign of the Angel or A Little Touch of Harry in the Night	Y	S
Henry IV, Parts 1 and 2	Holst, Gustav • At the Boar's Head, Opus 42	Y	P
Henry IV, Parts 1 and 2	Mercadante, Giuseppe Saverio Raffele • Gioventù di Enrico V, La	Y	S
Henry V	Boughton, Rutland • Againcourt	NO	P
Henry V	Volder, Piere Jean de • Jeunesse de Henri Cinq, La	?	
Henry VIII	Saint-Saëns, Camille • Henry VIII	Y	S
Julius Caesar	Carl, M. • Julius Caesar	Y	S
Julius Caesar	Klebe, Giselher Wolfgang • Ermordung Cäsars, Die Op. 32	Y	P
Julius Caesar	Malipiero, Gian Francesco • Giulio Cesare	Y	P

PLAY	COMPOSITION	S	E
Julius Caesar	Schmitz, Alan • Julius Caesar	Y	S
Lear	André, Johann • König Lear	Y	S
Lear	Beck, Curt • König Lear	?	
Lear	Borodcicz, Hans von • König Lear	?	
Lear	Cagnoni, Antonio • Re Lear, Il	Y	P
Lear	Cottrau, Giulio • Cordelia (Re Lear)	Y	P
Lear	Cribari, Donna • Pop	Y	S
Lear	Durme, Jef Van • King Lear	Y	S
Lear	Frazzi, Vito • Re Lear	Y	P
Lear	Generali, Pietro Mercandetti • Rodrigo di Valencia	Y	S
Lear	Ghislanzoni, Alberto • Re Lear	Y	S
Lear	Gobatti, Stefano • Cordelia	Y	S
Lear	Horner • König Lear	?	
Lear	Kreutzer, Conradin • Cordelia (Floretta ou La Folle de Glaris)[First named Adele von Budoy]	N	P
Lear	Litolff, Henry Charles • König Lear	Y	P
Lear	Orlandi, Ferdinando • Rodrigo di Valencia	?	
Lear	Pacini, Giovanni • Rodrigo di Valencia	?	
Lear	Pedrell, Filipe • Roi Lear, Le	I	S
Lear	Pogodin • King Lear?	Y	S
Lear	Reimann, Aribert • Lear	Y	P
Lear	Reynaud, Armand • Roi Lear, Le	Y	S
Lear	Salmhofer, Franz • King Lear	I	S
Lear	Séméladis, M. • Cordélia	Y	S
Lear	Soloviev, Nicolai Feopemptovich • Cordélia	N	P
Lear	Verdi, Giuseppe • Lear	Y	S
Lear	Zajc, Ivan • Cordelia	?	
Love's Labour's Lost	Beecham, Adrian Wells • Love's Labour's Lost [Peines d'Amour Perdues]	Y	P
Love's Labour's Lost	Folprecht, Zdenek • Lásky hra osudná [The Fateful Game of Love], Opus 3	Y	S

417

PLAY	COMPOSITION	S	E
Love's Labour's Lost	Mozart, Wolfgang Amadeus • Peines d'amour perdues	Y	S
Love's Labour's Lost	Nabokov, Nikolai • Love's Labour's Lost [Verlor'ne Liebesmüh']	Y	P
Love's Labour's Lost	Vidal, Paul Antonin • Peines d'amour perdues	Y	S
Love's Labours Lost	Ruben, Paul • Edit royal, L'	Y	S
Macbeth	André, Johann • Macbeth	NO	S
Macbeth	Asplmayr, Franz • Leben und Tod des Königs Macbeth	I	S
Macbeth	Bizet, Georges • Macbeth	?	
Macbeth	Bloch, Ernest • Macbeth	Y	P
Macbeth	Chélard, Hippolyte-André-Jean-Baptiste • Macbeth	Y	P
Macbeth	Collingwood, Lawrance Arthur • Macbeth	Y	S
Macbeth	Daffner, Hugo • Macbeth	Y	S
Macbeth	Fisher, John Abraham • Macbeth	NO	S
Macbeth	Gatty, Nicholas Comyn • Macbeth	Y	S
Macbeth	Goedicke, Alexander • Macbeth	Y	S
Macbeth	Goldman, Edward M. • Macbeth	Y	S
Macbeth	Halpern, Sidney • Macbeth	Y	S
Macbeth	Koppel, Herman David • Macbeth, Op. 79	Y	S
Macbeth	Leverage, Richard • Macbeth	NO	S
Macbeth	Locke, Matthew and Robert Johnson • Macbeth	NO	P
Macbeth	Piccini, Louis Alexandre • Macbeth	Y	S
Macbeth	Pless, Hans • Macbeth	?	
Macbeth	Reichardt, Johann Friedrich • Macbeth	NO	P
Macbeth	Rossi, Lauro • Biorn	Y	S
Macbeth	Stegmann, Carl David • Macbeth	I	S
Macbeth	Taubert, Wilhelm • Macbeth, Op. 133	Y	P
Macbeth	Verdi, Giuseppe • Macbeth	Y	P

PLAY	COMPOSITION	S	E
Macbeth	Ware, William Henry • Macbeth	NO	P
Macbeth	Weyse, Christoph Ernst Friedrich • Macbeth	NO	S
Macbeth	Whitaker, John • Weird Sisters, The or The Thane and the Throne	Y	S
Measure for Measure	Gulda, Friedrich • Maß für Maß	?	
Measure for Measure	Rubens, Paul Alfred and Frank E. Tours • Dairymaids, The	Y	S
Measure for Measure	Wagner, Wilhelm Richard • Liebesverbot, Das oder Die Novize von Palermo	Y	S
Merchant of Venice	Alpaerts, Florent • Shylock	Y	S
Merchant of Venice	Barry, H. C. • Shylock or The Venus of Venice	Y	S
Merchant of Venice	Beecham, Adrian Wells • Merchant of Venice, The	Y	P
Merchant of Venice	Brumagne, Fernand • Marchand de Venise, Le	Y	S
Merchant of Venice	Carlson, Charles Frederick • Merchant of Venice	Y	S
Merchant of Venice	Castelnuovo-Tedesco, Mario • Mercante di Venezia, Il, Op. 181	Y	S
Merchant of Venice	Chatburn, Tom • Gay Venetians, The	Y	S
Merchant of Venice	Clarke, James Siree Hamilton • Merchant of Venice	NO	P
Merchant of Venice	Deffès, Louis Pierre • Jessica	Y	S
Merchant of Venice	Foerster, Joseph Brohuslav • Jessika, Opus 60	Y	P
Merchant of Venice	Greenwall, Peter • Three Caskets, The or Venice Re-served	Y	S
Merchant of Venice	Hahn, Reynaldo • Marchand de Vénise, Le	Y	P
Merchant of Venice	Haines, Roger • Fire Angel	Y	S
Merchant of Venice	Haines, Roger • Shylock [Fire Angel]	Y	S
Merchant of Venice	Just, Johann August • marchand de Venise, Le [Koopman van Smyrna]	I	S

419

PLAY	COMPOSITION	S	E
Merchant of Venice	Laufer, B. • Shylock	Y	S
Merchant of Venice	LaViolette, Wesley • Shylock	Y	S
Merchant of Venice	Pinsuti, Ciro • Mercante di Venezia, Il	Y	P
Merchant of Venice	Radó, Aladár • Shylock	Y	S
Merchant of Venice	Saussine, Henri de • Marchand de Vénise, Le	Y	P
Merchant of Venice	Taubmann, Otto • Porzia	Y	P
Merchant of Venice	Wolfurt, Kurt von • Porzia	?	
Merry Wives of Windsor	Adam, Adolphe-Charles • Falstaff	Y	S
Merry Wives of Windsor	Andrews, John Charles Bond- • Herne's Oak, or The Rose of Windsor [also Herne the Hunter]	Y	S
Merry Wives of Windsor	Balfe, Michael William • Falstaff	Y	P
Merry Wives of Windsor	Bishop, Sir Henry Rowley • Merry Wives of Windsor, The	I	S
Merry Wives of Windsor	Dittersdorf, Carl Ditters von • lustigen Weiber von Windsor und der dicke Hans, Die	Y	S
Merry Wives of Windsor	Gilbert, James • Good Time Johnny	Y	S
Merry Wives of Windsor	Hofmann, Johann • Ritter Hans von Dampf	Y	S
Merry Wives of Windsor	Horn, Charles Edward, and Samuel Webbe Jr. • Merry Wives of Windsor	I	S
Merry Wives of Windsor	Kaun, Hugo • Falstaff	I	S
Merry Wives of Windsor	Michaelis, Gustave • Lustigen Weiber von Berlin, Die	?	
Merry Wives of Windsor	Nicolai, Carl Otto Ehrenfried • lustigen Weiber von Windsor, Die	Y	P
Merry Wives of Windsor	Old, John • Herne the Hunter (A Legend of Royal Windsor)	N	P
Merry Wives of Windsor	Papavoine, Mdme • Vieux Coquet, Le; ou Les deux amies ou Le vieus garçon	Y	S
Merry Wives of Windsor	Philidor • Herne le Chasseur	Y	S
Merry Wives of Windsor	Ritter, Peter • lustigen Weiber, Die	Y	S

PLAY	COMPOSITION	S	E
Merry Wives of Windsor	Salieri, Antonio • Falstaff osia Le tre Burle	Y	S
Merry Wives of Windsor	Serov, Alexander Nikolayevich • Merry Wives of Windsor	Y	S
Merry Wives of Windsor	Vaughan Williams, Ralph • Sir John in Love	Y	P
Merry Wives of Windsor	Wiedeke, Adolf • lustigen Weiber von Hamburg, Die	?	
Merry Wives of Windsor; Henry IV, Parts 1 and 2	Schönfeld, Georg • Falstaff	?	
Merry Wives of Windsor; Henry IV, Parts 1 and 2	Verdi, Giuseppe • Falstaff	Y	P
Midsummer Night's Dream	Aliabiev, Alexander • Volshebnaya noch	Y	S
Midsummer Night's Dream	Allegra, Giuseppe • Sogno di una Notte, Il	?	
Midsummer Night's Dream	Arne, Michael and C. Dibdin, J. Battishill, C. Burney, Hook, J. C. Smith • Fairy Tale	Y	P
Midsummer Night's Dream	Arne, Thomas Augustine • Fairy Prince, The	Y	P
Midsummer Night's Dream	Arundell, Dennis Drew • Midsummer Night's Dream, A	Y	S
Midsummer Night's Dream	Aylward, Theodore • Midsummer Night's Dream, A	NO	S
Midsummer Night's Dream	Berens, Johann Hermann • Sommarnattsdröm, En	AP	S
Midsummer Night's Dream	Bernabei, Vincenzo • Equivoci d'Amore, Gli	?	
Midsummer Night's Dream	Besoyan, Rick • Babes in the Wood, or Who Killed Cock Robin	Y	S
Midsummer Night's Dream	Bishop, Sir Henry Rowley • Midsummer Night's Dream, A	I	S
Midsummer Night's Dream	Britten, Lord Edward Benjamin • Midsummer Night's Dream, A, Op. 64	Y	P
Midsummer Night's Dream	Bruce, Neely • Pyramus and Thisbe	?	
Midsummer Night's Dream	Busby, Thomas • Fair Fugitives	N	S

PLAY	COMPOSITION	S	E
Midsummer Night's Dream	Cooke, Thomas Simpson • Oberon, or The Charmed Horn	?	
Midsummer Night's Dream	De Boeck, Auguste de • Winternachtsdroom, Een	Y	S
Midsummer Night's Dream	Delannoy, Marcel • Puck	Y	P
Midsummer Night's Dream	Doubrava, Jaroslav • Sen noci svatojanske	Y	S
Midsummer Night's Dream	Ferraboso II, Alfonso and Robert Johnson • Oberon, the Fairy Prince	?	
Midsummer Night's Dream	Gasperini, Carlo Francesco • Equivoci d'amore e d'innocenza, Gl'	?	
Midsummer Night's Dream	Gaztambide y Garbayo, Joaquin Romualdo • sueño de una noche de verano, El	?	
Midsummer Night's Dream	Grosheim, Georg Christoph • Titania, oder Liebe durch Zauberei	Y	S
Midsummer Night's Dream	Hüe, George • Titania	I	S
Midsummer Night's Dream	Kunzen, Friedrich Ludwig Æmilius • Holger Danske oder Oberon [Holgar the Dane]	N	P
Midsummer Night's Dream	Lampe, John Frederich • Pyramus and Thisbe	Y	P
Midsummer Night's Dream	Leoncavallo, Ruggiero • Songe d'une nuit d'été, Un	Y	S
Midsummer Night's Dream	Leverage, Richard • Pyramus and Thisbe, The Comic Masque of	Y	S
Midsummer Night's Dream	Loder, Edward James • Robin Goodfellow or the Frolics of Puck	?	
Midsummer Night's Dream	Mancinelli, Luigi • Sogno di una notte d'estate, Il	Y	P
Midsummer Night's Dream	Manusardi, Giuseppe • sogno di Primavera, Un [Un rêve de printemps]	Y	S
Midsummer Night's Dream	Noël, Édouard Marie Émile • songe d'une nuit d'été, Le	?	

PLAY	COMPOSITION	S	E
Midsummer Night's Dream	Offenbach, Jacques • Rêve d'une Nuit d'été, Le	N	S
Midsummer Night's Dream	Orff, Carl • Sommernachtstraum, Ein	N O	P
Midsummer Night's Dream	Purcell, Henry • Fairy Queen, The	Y	P
Midsummer Night's Dream	Roti, Ugo • Sogno di una notte d'estate, Il	Y	S
Midsummer Night's Dream	Serpette, Henri Charles Antoine Gaston • Songe d'une nuit d'été, Le	N	S
Midsummer Night's Dream	Siegmeister, Elie • Night of the Moonspell	Y	S
Midsummer Night's Dream	Silverman, Stanley • Midsummer Night's Dream, A	Y	S
Midsummer Night's Dream	Smith, John Christopher • Fairies, The	Y	P
Midsummer Night's Dream	Suppé, Franz von • Sommernachtstraum, Der	Y	S
Midsummer Night's Dream	Valverde y San Juan, Joaquín • sueño de una noche de verano, El	N	S
Midsummer Night's Dream	Van Heusen, Jimmy • Swingin' the Dream	Y	S
Midsummer Night's Dream	Vranicky, Pavel • Oberon, König der Elfen	N	P
Midsummer Night's Dream	Vreuls, Victor • Songe d'une nuit d'été, Un	Y	P
Midsummer Night's Dream	Weber, Carl Maria von • Oberon [or the Elf-King's Oath]	N	P
Midsummer Night's Dream	Wolf, Ernst Wilhelm • Zauberirrungen, Die [Die Irrtümer der Zauberei]	Y	S
Much Ado About Nothing	Berlioz, Hector • Béatrice et Bénédict	Y	P
Much Ado About Nothing	Berton, Henri-Montan • Montano et Stéphanie	N	S
Much Ado About Nothing	Doppler, Arpád • Viel Lärm um Lichts	Y	P
Much Ado About Nothing	Hahn, Reynaldo • Beaucoup de bruit pour rien	Y	S
Much Ado About Nothing	Heinrich, Hermann • Viel Lärm um Nichts	Y	S

PLAY	COMPOSITION	S	E
Much Ado About Nothing	Khrennikov, Tikhon Nikolaevich • Mnogo shuma iz nichego [Viel Lärm aus Leidenschaft, Much Ado About Hearts]	Y	S
Much Ado About Nothing	Mojsisovics, Roderich • Viel Lärm um Nichts	Y	S
Much Ado About Nothing	Müller (the elder), Adolph • Viel Lärm um Nichts	?	
Much Ado About Nothing	Podestà, Carlo • Ero, ossia Molto rumore per nulla	Y	P
Much Ado About Nothing	Puget, Paul-Charles-Marie • Beaucoup de bruit pour rien	Y	P
Much Ado About Nothing	Salvayre, Gaston • Beaucoup de bruit pour rien	?	
Much Ado About Nothing	Stanford, Sir Charles Villiers • Much Ado About Nothing, Opus 76a	Y	P
Much Ado About Nothing	Stransky, Josef • Béatrice et Bénédict	I	S
Othello	Claudric, Jean • Othello Story	?	
Othello	Hirschbach, Hermann • Othello	Y	S
Othello	La Rosa, Arturo • Otello	?	
Othello	Legouix, Isidore Édouard • Othello, Un	N	S
Othello	Macarig, Hector and Alfonso Deperis • Otello Tamburo	?	
Othello	Machavariani, Alexei • Othello	NO	P
Othello	Michaelis, Gustave • Othello in Kyritz	?	
Othello	Müller (the elder), Adolph • Othellerl, der Mohr von Wien [Die geheilte Eifersucht]	I	S
Othello	Nieto, Manuel • Otelo y Desdémona	I	S
Othello	Pride [sp?], G. • Otello	?	
Othello	Rossini, Gioacchino • Otello, osia L'Africano di Venezia	Y	S
Othello	Schuster, Ignaz • Othellerl, der Mohr von Wien	?	
Othello	Scognamilio, Gennaro • Otello ossia Catiello l'Affricano	?	

PLAY	COMPOSITION	S	E
Othello	Sztojanovics, Eug. • Otello mecél	?	
Othello	Unknown • Catch My Soul	Y	S
Othello	Verdi, Giuseppe • Otello	Y	S
Othello	Zavodsky, Felix • Othello	Y	S
Other	Conte, Paolo • Shakespeare, the Playmaker	AP	
Other	Kuhlau, Friedrich Daniel Rudolph • Musik Til William Shakspeare [sic], Op. 74	NO	P
Other	Logar, Mihovil • Four Scenes from Shakespeare	I	S
Other	Lutz, William Meyer • Merry-Go-Round	AP	S
Other	Mulcahy, Lance • Shakespeare's Cabaret	Y	S
Other	Utley, Wendell • Will	?	
Other	Zelinka, Jan Evangelista • Spring With Shakespeare	AP	S
Pericles, Prince of Tyre	Cottrau, Giulio • Pericle re di Tiro	Y	P
Richard III	Berens, Johann Hermann • Riccardo	?	
Richard III	Canepá, Luigi • Riccardo III	N	P
Richard III	Durme, Jef Van • Richard III	Y	S
Richard III	Eberlin, Johann Ernst • Ricardus Impius, Angliae Rex, ab Henrico Richmondæ Comite vita simul et regno excitus	NO	S
Richard III	Field, Graham • Dick Deterred	Y	S
Richard III	Meiners, Giambattista • Riccardo III	Y	S
Richard III	Salvayre, Gaston • Riccardo III	Y	S
Richard III	Turok, Paul H. • Richard III	Y	S
Romeo and Juliet	Acker, Jean Van den • Romeo en Marielle [Tout pour l'amour]	?	
Romeo and Juliet	Barkworth, John Edmond • Romeo and Juliet	Y	P
Romeo and Juliet	Bedford, Herbert • Love Scene from Shakespeare's Romeo and Juliet for Contralto and Baritone	NO	P
Romeo and Juliet	Bellini, Vincenzo • Capuleti e i Montecchi, I	Y	S

425

PLAY	COMPOSITION	S	E
Romeo and Juliet	Benda, George Anton • Romeo und Julie	Y	P
Romeo and Juliet	Bernstein, Leonard • West Side Story	Y	S
Romeo and Juliet	Blacher, Boris • Romeo und Julia	Y	P
Romeo and Juliet	Campo y Zabaleta, Conrado del • Amantes de Verona, Los	Y	S
Romeo and Juliet	Carr, Frank Osmond • In Town	Y	S
Romeo and Juliet	Chignell, Robert • Romeo and Juliet	Y	S
Romeo and Juliet	Crescentini, Girolamo • Roméo et Juliette	?	
Romeo and Juliet	Dalayrac, Nicolas • Tout pour l'amour ou Roméo et Juliette	Y	S
Romeo and Juliet	Damrosch, Leopold • Romeo und Julia	Y	S
Romeo and Juliet	Déjazet, Eugène • Rhum et eau en juillet	Y	S
Romeo and Juliet	Delius, Frederick • Romeo und Juliet auf dem Dorfe [A Village Romeo and Juliet]	N	P
Romeo and Juliet	Didam, Otto • Julia und Romeo	?	
Romeo and Juliet	Douglas, Hugh A. • Romeo and Juliet Up to Larks	Y	S
Romeo and Juliet	Eberwein, Max Carl • Romeo und Julie	?	
Romeo and Juliet	Emery, Charles P. • Romeo, the Radical or Obstruction and Effect	Y	S
Romeo and Juliet	Erbse, Heimo • Julietta, Op. 15	N	P
Romeo and Juliet	Faris, Alexander • R Loves J	Y	S
Romeo and Juliet	Ferroni, Vencenzo Emidio Carmine • Romeo and Juliet	Y	S
Romeo and Juliet	Fischer, Jan F. • Romeo, Julie a tma (Romeo, Juliet and Darkness)	N	P
Romeo and Juliet	Fribec, Kresimir • Romeo and Juliet	Y	S
Romeo and Juliet	Garcia, Manuel Vincente del Popolo • Giulietta e Romeo	Y	S
Romeo and Juliet	Gaujac, Edmond Germain • Amantes de Vérone, Les	Y	S

PLAY	COMPOSITION	S	E
Romeo and Juliet	Gerber, René • Roméo et Juliette	?	
Romeo and Juliet	Gounod, Charles François • Roméo et Juliette	Y	P
Romeo and Juliet	Guglielmi, Pietro Carlo • Romeo e Giulietta [I Capuletti ed i Montecchi]	Y	P
Romeo and Juliet	Halévy, Jacques François Fromental Elie • Guido et Ginevre ou La Peste de Florence	I	S
Romeo and Juliet	Harper, Wally • Sensations	Y	S
Romeo and Juliet	Ivry, Paul Xaver Désiré Richard, Marquis d' • Amantes de Vérone, Les	Y	P
Romeo and Juliet	Kreutz, Arthur • Sourwood Mountain	Y	S
Romeo and Juliet	Kurzbach, Paul • Romeo and Julia auf dem Lande	?	
Romeo and Juliet	Liota, A. • Romeo and Juliet	Y	S
Romeo and Juliet	Ludwig, Otto • Romeo und Julie	Y	S
Romeo and Juliet	Malipiero, Gian Francesco • Romeo e Guilietta (scene 5 of Monde celesti e infernali)	Y	P
Romeo and Juliet	Marchetti, Filippo • Romeo e Giulietta	Y	P
Romeo and Juliet	Marescalchi, Luigi • Giuletta e Romeo	Y	S
Romeo and Juliet	Marshall-Hall, George William Louis • Romeo and Juliet	Y	P
Romeo and Juliet	Matuszczak, Bernadetta • Julia i Romeo	Y	P
Romeo and Juliet	Membrée, Edmond • Roméo et Juliette	?	
Romeo and Juliet	Mercadal y Pons, Antonio • Giulietta e Romeo	Y	S
Romeo and Juliet	Molchanov, Kiril Vladimirovich • Romeo, Dzhulyetta i t'ma [Romeo, Juliet and Darkness]	?	
Romeo and Juliet	Morales, Melesio • Giulietta e Romeo	Y	S
Romeo and Juliet	Mullins, Hugh • Romeo and Juliet	Y	S

427

PLAY	COMPOSITION	S	E
Romeo and Juliet	Pasquali, Nicolò • Romeo and Juliet	?	
Romeo and Juliet	Perosi, Lorenzo • Romeo and Juliet	Y	S
Romeo and Juliet	Porta, [Bernardo ?] • Roméo et Juliette	Y	S
Romeo and Juliet	Rosellin, Léon • Juliette et Roméo	?	
Romeo and Juliet	Rumling, Sigismund Freiherr von • Roméo et Juliette	Y	S
Romeo and Juliet	San Severino • Romeo e Giuletta	I	S
Romeo and Juliet	Schuster, Ignaz • Romeo und Julie	Y	S
Romeo and Juliet	Schwanenberg, Johann Gottfried • Romeo e Giulia	Y	S
Romeo and Juliet	Shelley, Harry Rowe • Romeo and Juliet	Y	P
Romeo and Juliet	Steibelt, Daniel Gottlieb • Roméo et Juliette or Tout pour l'amour	Y	S
Romeo and Juliet	Storch, Anton Maria • Romeo und Julie	Y	S
Romeo and Juliet	Stuart, Leslie • Belle of Mayfair	Y	S
Romeo and Juliet	Sutermeister, Heinrich • Romeo und Julia	Y	S
Romeo and Juliet	Thomé, François Lucien Joseph • Roméo et Juliette	NO	S
Romeo and Juliet	Tommasi, Ferdinando [Tommaso] • Guido e Ginevre	N	S
Romeo and Juliet	Torriani, Eugenio • Romeo e Giulietta	Y	S
Romeo and Juliet	Unknown • Pulcinella rivale di Turzillo e confuso tra Capuleti e Montecchi	?	
Romeo and Juliet	Vaccai, Nicola • Giulietta e Romeo	Y	S
Romeo and Juliet	Zandonai, Riccardo • Giulietta e Romeo	Y	S
Romeo and Juliet	Zanon, Antonio B. • Leggenda di Giulietta, La	Y	S
Romeo and Juliet	Zingarelli, Niccolò Antonio • Giulietta e Romeo	Y	P

PLAY	COMPOSITION	S	E
Shakespeare Appears	Benvenuti, Tommaso • Guglielmo Shakespeare	A P	P
Shakespeare Appears	Lillo, Giuseppe • Sogno d'una Notte estiva, Il or La Gioventù di Shakespeare	A P	P
Shakespeare Appears	Serpette, Henri Charles Antoine Gaston • Shakespeare!	A P	P
Shakespeare Appears	Thomas, Charles Louis Ambroise • Songe d'une nuit d'été, Le [Shakespeare oder Der Traum einer Sommernacht]	A P	S
Taming of the Shrew	Argento, Dominick • Christopher Sly	Y	P
Taming of the Shrew	Bossi, Renzo • Volpino il Calderaio, Op. 32	Y	S
Taming of the Shrew	Bottacio, Pietro • Bisbetica Domata, La	?	
Taming of the Shrew	Clapp, Philip Greeley • Taming of the Shrew, The	Y	S
Taming of the Shrew	Cooke, Thomas Simpson and Braham, John and Others • Taming of the Shrew, The	I	S
Taming of the Shrew	Eastwood, Thomas Hugh • Christopher Sly	Y	S
Taming of the Shrew	Fioravanti, Valentino • Capricciosa pentita, La	?	
Taming of the Shrew	Giannini, Vittorio • Taming of the Shrew, The	Y	P
Taming of the Shrew	Goetz, Herman • Widerspänstigen Zähmung, Der [La Megère apprivoisée; Caterina e Petruccio]	Y	P
Taming of the Shrew	Groth, Howard • Petruchio	Y	S
Taming of the Shrew	Karel, Rudolf • Zkroceni zlé zeny [The Taming of the Shrew]	Y	S
Taming of the Shrew	Le Rey, Frédéric • Mégère apprivoisée, La	Y	P
Taming of the Shrew	Maclean, Alick • Petruccio	I	S
Taming of the Shrew	Martín y Soler, Vicente • Capricciosa corretta, La [So bessert sie sich]	N	S

PLAY	COMPOSITION	S	E
Taming of the Shrew	Morera, Enrique • Fiercilla domada, La	Y	P
Taming of the Shrew	Morlacchi, Francesco Giuseppi Baldassare • Capricciosa pettita, La	?	
Taming of the Shrew	Oddone, Elizabetta • Petruccio e il Cavolo Cappuccio	N	P
Taming of the Shrew	Persico, Mario • Bisbetica Domata, La	Y	P
Taming of the Shrew	Porter, Cole • Kiss Me, Kate	Y	S
Taming of the Shrew	Samara, Spiro • Furia domata, La	Y	S
Taming of the Shrew	Shebalin, Vissarion Yakovlevich • Ukroshchenie stroptivoi [The Taming of the Shrew] Op. 46	Y	P
Taming of the Shrew	Silver, Charles • Mégère apprivoisée, La	Y	P
Taming of the Shrew	Tajon, Ben. • Taming of a Shrew, The	?	
Taming of the Shrew	Unknown • Bezähmte Widerbellerin, Die	Y	S
Taming of the Shrew	Unknown • Catherine and Petruchio	Y	S
Taming of the Shrew	Unknown • Cure for a Scold, A	Y	P
Taming of the Shrew	Wolf-Ferrari, Ermanno • Sly, ovvero La leggenda del dormiente risvegliato	Y	S
Tempest	Alexandre, Charles Guillaume • Georget et Georgette	Y	S
Tempest	Alfano, Franco • Miranda	?	
Tempest	Aliabiev, Alexander • Storm, The	NO	P
Tempest	Angelis, Arturo de • Tempesta, La	Y	S
Tempest	Angyal, Lázló • Tempest, The	Y	S
Tempest	Arne, Thomas Augustine • Tempest, The	NO	P
Tempest	Asplmayr [Aspelmayr], Franz • Sturm, Der	I	S
Tempest	Atterberg, Kurt • Stormen, Op. 49	Y	S

PLAY	COMPOSITION	S	E
Tempest	Banister, John; Giovanni Battista Draghi; Matthew Locke; Pelham Humfrey; and Pietro Reggio • Tempest, The [The Enchanted Island]	Y	P
Tempest	Beer-Walbrunn, Anton • Sturm, Der	Y	S
Tempest	Bishop, Sir Henry Rowley • Tempest, The	I	S
Tempest	Canonica, Pietro • Miranda	Y	P
Tempest	Caruso, Lodovico Luigi • Tempesta, La	Y	S
Tempest	Chapí y Lorente, Ruperto • Tempestad, La	N	P
Tempest	David, Adolphe Isaac • Orage, L'	?	
Tempest	Del Fante, Raffaele • Tempesta, La	Y	S
Tempest	Duvernoy, Victor-Alphonse • Tempête, La	N O	P
Tempest	Emmert, Adam Joseph • Sturm, Der	Y	S
Tempest	Fabrizi, Vincenzo • Tempestà ossia Da un disordine ne nasce un ordine, La	Y	S
Tempest	Farwell, Arthur George • Caliban by the Yellow Sands, Opus 47	Y	S
Tempest	Feigerl, R. • Stein der Weisen, Der	?	
Tempest	Fibich, Zdenko • Boure, Opus 40 [Der Sturm]	Y	P
Tempest	Fleischmann, Friedrich • Geisterinsel, Die	Y	S
Tempest	Foignet, Jacques • Orage, L'	?	
Tempest	Frank, Ernst • Sturm, Der	Y	S
Tempest	Gatty, Nicholas Comyn • Tempest, The	Y	P
Tempest	Gerl, Thaddäus; Henneberg and Benedikt Schack • Stein der Weisen, Der oder Die Zauberinsel	?	
Tempest	Gevel, Franz Xaver • Rinaldo und Camilla oder Die Zauberinsel	?	

431

PLAY	COMPOSITION	S	E
Tempest	Gossec, François Joseph • Hylas et Sylvie	I	S
Tempest	Haack, Friedrich • Geisterinsel, Die	Y	S
Tempest	Hába, Alois • Tempest	I	S
Tempest	Hale, Alfred Matthew • Tempest, The	Y	S
Tempest	Halévy, Jacques Franoçis Fromental Élie • Tempesta, La	Y	P
Tempest	Hensel, Johann Daniel • Geisterinsel, Die	Y	P
Tempest	Hoffmeister, Franz Anton • Schiffbruch, Der	Y	S
Tempest	Honegger, Arturo • Tempête, La	NO	P
Tempest	Jenkins, David • Enchanted Isle, The [Scenes from Shakespeare's 'Tempest']	NO	P
Tempest	Johnson, Robert • Tempest, The	NO	S
Tempest	Kanne, Friedrich August • Miranda oder Das Schwert der Rache	I	S
Tempest	Kasanli, Nikolai Ivanovich [Kazanli, Kazanly] • Miranda (Poliedniaia bor'ba) [Der Letzte Kampf]	I	S
Tempest	Kashperov, Vladimir Nikititch • Storm, The [Groza]	I	S
Tempest	Khrennikov, Tikhon Nikolaevich • Brati [Brothers]	N	S
Tempest	Khrennikov, Tikhon Nikolaevich • V buriu [Im Sturm, Into the Storm]	N	S
Tempest	Kunz, [Konrad Max ?] • Tempest, The	Y	S
Tempest	Kunzen, Friedrich Ludwig Æmilius • Stormen	Y	P
Tempest	Lattuada, Felice • Tempesta, La	Y	P
Tempest	Leichtling, Alan • Tempest, The	?	
Tempest	Linley II, Thomas • Tempest, The or The Enchanted Island	NO	S
Tempest	Malamet, Marsha • Dreamstuff	Y	S

PLAY	COMPOSITION	S	E
Tempest	Martin, Frank • Sturm, Der	Y	P
Tempest	Morton, David • Tempest in a Teapot	Y	P
Tempest	Müller, Wenzel • Sturm oder die Zauberinsel, Der	Y	P
Tempest	Nápravnik, Éduard Frantsevich • Sturm, Der	Y	S
Tempest	Navoigille, Gouliellmo • Orage, L' ou Quel Guignon!	?	
Tempest	Palliardi, Carl • Stein der Weisen, Der	?	
Tempest	Pohlig, Carl • Stein der Weisen, Der	?	
Tempest	Purcell, Henry • Tempest or Enchanted Island, The	NO	P
Tempest	Raymond, Édouard • Sturm, Der	Y	S
Tempest	Reichardt, Johann Friedrich • Geisterinsel, Die	Y	P
Tempest	Riotte, Philipp Jakob • Sturm, Der oder Die Insel des Prospero	Y	S
Tempest	Ritter, Peter • Sturm, Der oder Die bezauberte Insel	Y	P
Tempest	Rolle, Johann Heinrich • Sturm oder Die bezauberte Insel, Der	Y	S
Tempest	Rung, Henrik • Stormen paa København [Storm over Copenhagen]	Y	S
Tempest	Savini, Giacomo • Tempeste	?	
Tempest	Smith, John Christopher • Tempest, The	Y	P
Tempest	Storch, Anton Maria • Stein der Weisen, Der	?	
Tempest	Sulek, Stjepan • Oluja	Y	S
Tempest	Sutermeister, Heinrich • Zauberinsel, Die	Y	S
Tempest	Unknown • Schipbreuk	?	
Tempest	Urich, Jean • Orage, L'	N	S
Tempest	Urspruch, Anton • Sturm, Der	Y	P
Tempest	Vranicky, Pavel • Rudolf von Felseck (Die Schwarzthaler) oder La Tempestà	I	S
Tempest	Winter, Peter von • Sturm, Der	Y	S

PLAY	COMPOSITION	S	E
Tempest	Zák, Benedict Emanuel • Stein der Weisen, Dem oder Die Zauber Insel	?	
Tempest	Zirra, Alexandru • Furtuna [TheTempest]	N	S
Tempest	Zumsteeg, Johann Rudolf • Geisterinsel, Die	Y	S
Timon of Athens	Draghi, Antonio • Timone misantropo	?	
Timon of Athens	Frank, Johann Wolfgang • Timon	Y	S
Timon of Athens	Leopold I, Holy Roman Emperor • Timòne, Misantropo	Y	S
Timon of Athens	Purcell, Henry • History of Timon of Athens, the Man Hater, The	N O	P
Timon of Athens	Unknown • Thimon le misantrope	?	
Timon of Athens	Unknown • Timon in Love or The Innocent Theft	N	S
Titus Andronicus	Clarke, Jeremiah • Titus Andronicus	I	S
Troilus and Cressida	MacDermot, Galt • Cressida	Y	S
Troilus and Cressida	Walton, Sir William • Troilus and Cressida	N	S
Troilus and Cressida	Zillig, Winfried • Troilus und Cressida	Y	P
Twelfth Night	Adler, Richard • Music Is	Y	S
Twelfth Night	Amram, David • Twelfth Night	Y	P
Twelfth Night	Ansell, John • King's Bride, The [Violette]	?	
Twelfth Night	Arensen, Adolf • Viola	Y	P
Twelfth Night	Berens, Johann Hermann • Violetta	N	S
Twelfth Night	Bishop, Sir Henry Rowley • Twelfth Night	N O	P
Twelfth Night	Brandauer, Hermann • Caesario	?	
Twelfth Night	Carafa di Colobrano, Michele Enrico and Aimé Ambroise Simon Leborne • Violette, La ou Gérard de Nevers	N	P
Twelfth Night	De Filippi, Amadeo • Malvolio	Y	S
Twelfth Night	Falk, Richard • Was ihr Wollt	?	
Twelfth Night	Farina, Guido • Dodisesima Notte, La	Y	S

PLAY	COMPOSITION	S	E
Twelfth Night	Freitas Gazul, Francisco de • Violetas, As	?	
Twelfth Night	Gelber, Stanley Jay • Love and Let Love	Y	P
Twelfth Night	Gibbs, Cecil Armstrong • Twelfth Night, Opus 115	Y	S
Twelfth Night	Hart, Fritz Bennicke • Malvolio, Opus 14	Y	S
Twelfth Night	Hess, Ludwig • Was ihr Wollt	Y	S
Twelfth Night	Hester, Hal and Danny Apolinar • Your Own Thing	Y	P
Twelfth Night	Heuberger, Richard Franz Joseph • Viola	?	
Twelfth Night	Holenia, Hans • Viola, Opus 21 [Was Ihr wollt]	Y	S
Twelfth Night	Hughes, Gervase • Twelfth Night, Scenes from	Y	S
Twelfth Night	Jirko, Ivan • Twelfth Night, The [Vecer Trikralovy]	Y	S
Twelfth Night	Kirchner, Hermann • Viola	Y	S
Twelfth Night	Krohn, Max • Was ihr Wollt	?	
Twelfth Night	Kusterer, Arthur • Was ihr Wollt	Y	P
Twelfth Night	Mercadante, Giuseppe Saverio Raffele • Violetta	?	
Twelfth Night	Morton, Louise, and others • Twelfth Night	NO	P
Twelfth Night	Perelli, Edoardo • Viola Pisani	N	P
Twelfth Night	Rintel, Wilhelm • Was ihr Wöllt	Y	S
Twelfth Night	Shenshin, Aleksandr Alexseivich • Twelfth Night	Y	S
Twelfth Night	Smetana, Bedrich • Viola	Y	P
Twelfth Night	Steinkühler, Émile • Cäsario, oder die Verwechslung, Op. 30	Y	S
Twelfth Night	Taubert, Carl Gottfried Wilhelm • Cesario, oder Was ihr wollt, Op. 188	Y	P
Twelfth Night	Weis, Karél • Viola [Die Zwillinge, Blizenci]	Y	P
Twelfth Night	Wilson, James • Twelfth Night	Y	S
Two Gentlemen of Verona	Bishop, Sir Henry Rowley • Two Gentlemen of Verona, The	NO	S

435

PLAY	COMPOSITION	S	E
Two Gentlemen of Verona	MacDermot, Galt • Two Gentlemen of Verona	Y	P
Venus and Adonis [Poem]	Weisgall, Hugo • Gardens of Adonis, The	Y	S
Winter's Tale	Arne, Thomas Augustine, Samuel Arnold and others • Sheep-Shearing, The or Florizel and Perdita	Y	P
Winter's Tale	Attwood, Thomas • Hermione, or Valour's Triumph	?	
Winter's Tale	Barbieri, Carlo Emanuele di • Perdita oder Ein Wintermärchen	Y	P
Winter's Tale	Berény, Henri • Wintermärchen, Das	Y	S
Winter's Tale	Bernabei, Giuseppe Antonio • Érmione	N	P
Winter's Tale	Boyce, William • Florizel and Perdita	N O	S
Winter's Tale	Bruch, Max • Hermione, Op. 40	Y	P
Winter's Tale	Flotow, Friedrich von • Wintermärchen, Ein	I	S
Winter's Tale	Goldmark, Carl • Wintermärchen, Ein	Y	P
Winter's Tale	Harbison, John • Winter's Tale, The	Y	S
Winter's Tale	Herx, Werner • Orakelspruch, Der	?	
Winter's Tale	Hohmann, Gustav • Hermione, oder Der kleine Vicomte	N	S
Winter's Tale	Jakobowski, Edward • Erminie	N	S
Winter's Tale	Kipper, Herman • Perdita oder Das Rosenfest	?	
Winter's Tale	Kovarovic, Karel • Perdita	?	
Winter's Tale	Lauer, Adolph L. [Freiherr von Münchofen] • Orakelspruch, Der	?	
Winter's Tale	Leukauf, Robert • Wintermärchen, Das	?	
Winter's Tale	Mohr, Hermann • Orakelspruch, Der Op. 50	N	P
Winter's Tale	Nesvera, Josef • Perdita	Y	S
Winter's Tale	Pillaut, Léon • Perdita	Y	P

PLAY	COMPOSITION	S	E
Winter's Tale	Riotte, Philipp Jakob • Orakelspruch, Der	I	S
Winter's Tale	Rossini, Gioacchino • Ermione	N	S
Winter's Tale	Schneider, Georg Abraham • Orakelspruch, Der	?	
Winter's Tale	Thul, Franz von • Hermione	?	
Winter's Tale	Zanettini, Antonio • Érmione [Die wiedergefundene Hermione]	N	S
Winter's Tale	Zimmermann, Balduin • Wintermärchen, Ein	Y	P

SORTING BY STATUS

STATUS   EVIDENCE   COMPOSITION

?	Acker, Jean Van den • Romeo en Marielle [Tout pour l'amour]
?	Alfano, Franco • Miranda
?	Allegra, Giuseppe • Sogno di una Notte, Il
?	Anfossi, Pasquale • Cajo Mario
?	Ansell, John • King's Bride, The [Violette]
?	Antoine, Ferdinand d' • Ende gut, alles gut oder Der Fürst und sein Volk
?	Aspa, Mario • Gioventù di Enrico V, La
?	Attwood, Thomas • Hermione, or Valour's Triumph
?	Balfe, Michael William • Enrico IV al passo della Marna
?	Beck, Curt • König Lear
?	Berens, Johann Hermann • Riccardo
?	Bernabei, Vincenzo • Equivoci d'Amore, Gli
?	Bertoni, Ferdinando Giuseppe • Cajo Mario
?	Bianchi, Francesco • Cajo Mario
?	Bizet, Georges • Macbeth
?	Borodcicz, Hans von • König Lear
?	Bottacio, Pietro • Bisbetica Domata, La
?	Brandauer, Hermann • Caesario
?	Bruce, Neely • Pyramus and Thisbe
?	Campenhout, François van • Gillette de Narbonne
?	Carlini, Luigi • Gioventù di Enrico V, La
?	Choudens, Antony • Cymbeline
?	Cimarosa, Domenico Nicola [Cimmarosa] • Cajo Mario
?	Claudric, Jean • Othello Story

439

STATUS EVIDENCE COMPOSITION

?	Conti, Nicolò • Cajo Marzio Coriolano [Marzio Coriolano]
?	Cooke, Thomas Simpson • Malvina
?	Cooke, Thomas Simpson • Oberon, or The Charmed Horn
?	Costa, Michael Andrew Angus • Malvina
?	Crescentini, Girolamo • Roméo et Juliette
?	Danzi, Franz • Malvina [Die Wolfsjagd]
?	David, Adolphe Isaac • Orage, L'
?	Didam, Otto • Julia und Romeo
?	Draghi, Antonio • Timone misantropo
?	Duyse, Florimond Van • Rosalinde
?	Eberwein, Max Carl • Romeo und Julie
?	Falk, Richard • Was ihr Wollt
?	Feigerl, R. • Stein der Weisen, Der
?	Ferraboso II, Alfonso and Robert Johnson • Oberon, the Fairy Prince
?	Fioravanti, Valentino • Capricciosa pentita, La
?	Fioravanti, Valentino • Enrico IV al passo della Marna
?	Foignet, Jacques • Orage, L'
?	Francastel, A. • Henry IV
?	Freitas Gazul, Francisco de • Violetas, As
?	Freschi, Giovanni Domenico • Rosalinda
?	Galuppi, Baldassarre [called Buranello] • Cajo Mario
?	Gasperini, Carlo Francesco • Equivoci d'amore e d'innocenza, Gl'
?	Gaztambide y Garbayo, Joaquin Romualdo • sueño de una noche de verano, El

STATUS EVIDENCE COMPOSITION

STATUS	EVIDENCE	COMPOSITION
	?	Gazzaniga, Giuseppe • Equivoci, Gli
	?	Genée, Franz Friedrich Richard and Louis Roth • Zwillinge
	?	Gerber, René • Roméo et Juliette
	?	Gerl, Thaddäus; Henneberg and Benedikt Schack • Stein der Weisen, Der oder Die Zauberinsel
	?	Gevel, Franz Xaver • Rinaldo und Camilla oder Die Zauberinsel
	?	Gulda, Friedrich • Maß für Maß
	?	Hahn, Reynaldo • Malvina
	?	Hanssens, J. F. J. • Gillette de Narbonne
	?	Herx, Werner • Orakelspruch, Der
	?	Heuberger, Richard Franz Joseph • Viola
	?	Hoffmeister, Franz Anton • Rosalinde, oder Die Macht der Feen
	?	Horner • König Lear
	?	Hulemann, Th • Malvine I re [The first]
	?	Kanne, Friedrich August • Malvina, oder Putzerls Abenteuer
	?	Kipper, Herman • Perdita oder Das Rosenfest
	?	Kleinheinz, Carl Franz Xaver • Hamlet, Prinz vom Tandelmarkt
	?	Kovarovic, Karel • Perdita
	?	Krohn, Max • Was ihr Wollt
	?	Kurzbach, Paul • Romeo and Julia auf dem Lande
	?	Küster, Johann Heinrich • Henrik den Fjerde
	?	La Rosa, Arturo • Otello
	?	Lauer, Adolph L. [Freiherr von Münchofen] • Orakelspruch, Der
	?	Leichtling, Alan • Tempest, The
	?	Leukauf, Robert • Wintermärchen, Das

441

STATUS	EVIDENCE	COMPOSITION
?		Lichtenstein, Carl August Freiherr von • Ende gut, alles gut
?		Loder, Edward James • Robin Goodfellow or the Frolics of Puck
?		Macarig, Hector and Alfonso Deperis • Otello Tamburo
?		MacFarren, George Alexander • Hamlet
?		Maggioni, Francesco • Cajo Marzio Coriolano
?		Magni, Giuseppe Paolo • Admeto, Rè di Tessaglia
?		Méhul, Étienne Nicolas • Jeune Henri, Le [Gabrielle d'Estrées où les Amours d'Henri IV]
?		Mélésville, Honoré Marie Joseph, Baron Duveyrier] • Gillette de Narbonne
?		Membrée, Edmond • Roméo et Juliette
?		Mercadante, Giuseppe Saverio Raffele • Violetta
?		Michaelis, Gustave • Lustigen Weiber von Berlin, Die
?		Michaelis, Gustave • Othello in Kyritz
?		Molchanov, Kiril Vladimirovich • Romeo, Dzhulyetta i t'ma [Romeo, Juliet and Darkness]
?		Monza, Carlo Antonio • Cajo Mario
?		Morlacchi, Francesco Giuseppi Baldassare • Capricciosa pettita, La
?		Mosca, Giuseppe • Gioventù di Enrico V, La
?		Müller (the elder), Adolph • Heinrich IV
?		Müller (the elder), Adolph • Viel Lärm um Nichts
?		Navoigille, Gouliellmo • Orage, L' ou Quel Guignon!

442

STATUS EVIDENCE COMPOSITION

STATUS	EVIDENCE COMPOSITION
?	Noël, Édouard Marie Émile • songe d'une nuit d'été, Le
?	Orlandi, Ferdinando • Rodrigo di Valencia
?	Pacini, Giovanni • Rodrigo di Valencia
?	Palliardi, Carl • Stein der Weisen, Der
?	Pasquali, Nicolò • Romeo and Juliet
?	Piccinni, Niccolò • Caio Mario
?	Pless, Hans • Macbeth
?	Pohlig, Carl • Stein der Weisen, Der
?	Pride [sp?], G. • Otello
?	Rafael, Carl Friedrich • Hamlet, Prinz von Liliput
?	Rateau, Edmond • Rosaline
?	Rosellin, Léon • Juliette et Roméo
?	Salvayre, Gaston • Beaucoup de bruit pour rien
?	Santa Caterina, Alessandro • Coriolano
?	Sarria, Errico • Equivoci, Gli
?	Savigna, Vincenzo • Coriolano
?	Savini, Giacomo • Tempeste
?	Scarlatti, Giuseppe • Caio Mario
?	Schneider, Georg Abraham • Orakelspruch, Der
?	Schönfeld, Georg • Falstaff
?	Schuster, Ignaz • Othellerl, der Mohr von Wien
?	Scognamilio, Gennaro • Otello ossia Catiello l'Affricano
?	Scolari, Giuseppe • Cajo Mario
?	Storch, Anton Maria • Stein der Weisen, Der
?	Sztojanovics, Eug. • Otello mecél
?	Taboida, Ant. Sanchez do Cunha • Dinah
?	Tajon, Ben. • Taming of a Shrew, The

STATUS   EVIDENCE   COMPOSITION

STATUS	EVIDENCE	COMPOSITION
?		Thul, Franz von • Hermione
?		Tuczek, Vincenc Tomas Vaclav • Travestirte Hamlet, Der [Hamlet, Prinz von Dänemark; Hamlet, Prinz von Lilyput]
?		Unknown • Early Reign of Oleg, The
?		Unknown • Pulcinella rivale di Turzillo e confuso tra Capuleti e Montecchi
?		Unknown • Schipbreuk
?		Unknown • Thimon le misantrope
?		Utley, Wendell • Will
?		Vaccai, Nicola • Malvina
?		Vidal, Paul Antonin • Comme il vous Plaire
?		Volder, Piere Jean de • Jeunesse de Henri Cinq, La
?		Weckerlin, Jean Baptiste Théodore • Tout est bien qui finit bien
?		Weis, Karél • Comme il vous Plaira
?		Weisgall, Hugo • Henry IV
?		Wiedeke, Adolf • lustigen Weiber von Hamburg, Die
?		Wolfurt, Kurt von • Porzia
?		Zajc, Ivan • Cordelia
?		Zák, Benedict Emanuel • Stein der Weisen, Dem oder Die Zauber Insel
AP		Conte, Paolo • Shakespeare, the Playmaker
AP	P	Benvenuti, Tommaso • Guglielmo Shakespeare
AP	P	Lillo, Giuseppe • Sogno d'una Notte estiva, Il or La Gioventù di Shakespeare
AP	P	Serpette, Henri Charles Antoine Gaston • Shakespeare!
AP	S	Berens, Johann Hermann • Sommarnattsdröm, En

STATUS EVIDENCE COMPOSITION

STATUS	EVIDENCE	COMPOSITION
AP	S	Lutz, William Meyer • Merry-Go-Round
AP	S	Thomas, Charles Louis Ambroise • Songe d'une nuit d'été, Le [Shakespeare oder Der Traum einer Sommernacht]
AP	S	Zelinka, Jan Evangelista • Spring With Shakespeare
I	S	Asplmayr [Aspelmayr], Franz • Sturm, Der
I	S	Asplmayr, Franz • Leben und Tod des Königs Macbeth
I	S	Bishop, Sir Henry Rowley • Merry Wives of Windsor, The
I	S	Bishop, Sir Henry Rowley • Midsummer Night's Dream, A
I	S	Bishop, Sir Henry Rowley • Tempest, The
I	S	Clarke, Jeremiah • Titus Andronicus
I	S	Cooke, Thomas Simpson and Braham, John and Others • Taming of the Shrew, The
I	S	Flotow, Friedrich von • Wintermärchen, Ein
I	S	Gallenberg, Wenzel Robert Count von • Amleto
I	S	Gossec, François Joseph • Hylas et Sylvie
I	S	Hába, Alois • Tempest
I	S	Halévy, Jacques François Fromental Elie • Guido et Ginevre ou La Peste de Florence
I	S	Horn, Charles Edward, and Samuel Webbe Jr. • Merry Wives of Windsor
I	S	Hüe, George • Titania
I	S	Just, Johann August • marchand de Venise, Le [Koopman van Smyrna]
I	S	Kanne, Friedrich August • Miranda oder Das Schwert der Rache

STATUS EVIDENCE COMPOSITION

STATUS	EVIDENCE	COMPOSITION
I	S	Kasanli, Nikolai Ivanovich [Kazanli, Kazanly] • Miranda (Poliedniaia bor'ba) [Der Letzte Kampf]
I	S	Kashperov, Vladimir Nikititch • Storm, The [Groza]
I	S	Kaun, Hugo • Falstaff
I	S	Logar, Mihovil • Four Scenes from Shakespeare
I	S	Maclean, Alick • Petruccio
I	S	Müller (the elder), Adolph • Othellerl, der Mohr von Wien [Die geheilte Eifersucht]
I	S	Nieto, Manuel • Otelo y Desdémona
I	S	Pedrell, Filipe • Roi Lear, Le
I	S	Riotte, Philipp Jakob • Orakelspruch, Der
I	S	Salmhofer, Franz • King Lear
I	S	San Severino • Romeo e Giuletta
I	S	Stegmann, Carl David • Macbeth
I	S	Stransky, Josef • Béatrice et Bénédict
I	S	Vranicky, Pavel • Rudolf von Felseck (Die Schwarzthaler) oder La Tempestà
N	P	Bernabei, Giuseppe Antonio • Érmione
N	P	Bishop, Sir Henry Rowley • Henri Quatre [Paris in the Olden Times]
N	P	Canepá, Luigi • Riccardo III
N	P	Carafa di Colobrano, Michele Enrico and Aimé Ambroise Simon Leborne • Violette, La ou Gérard de Nevers
N	P	Carcani, Giuseppe • Ambleto
N	P	Chapí y Lorente, Ruperto • Tempestad, La
N	P	Delius, Frederick • Romeo und Juliet auf dem Dorfe [A Village Romeo and Juliet]
N	P	Erbse, Heimo • Julietta, Op. 15

STATUS EVIDENCE COMPOSITION

STATUS	EVIDENCE	COMPOSITION
N	P	Fischer, Jan F. • Romeo, Julie a tma (Romeo, Juliet and Darkness)
N	P	Galuppi, Baldassarre • Enrico
N	P	Hérold, Louis Joseph Ferdinand • Gioventù di Enrico V, La [La Jeunesse d'Henry V]
N	P	Kreutzer, Conradin • Cordelia (Floretta ou La Folle de Glaris)[First named Adele von Budoy]
N	P	Kunzen, Friedrich Ludwig Æmilius • Holger Danske oder Oberon [Holgar the Dane]
N	P	Maganini, Giovanni • Enrico IV al passo della Marna
N	P	Mohaupt, Richard • Double Trouble [Zwillingskomödie]
N	P	Mohr, Hermann • Orakelspruch, Der Op. 50
N	P	Oddone, Elizabetta • Petruccio e il Cavolo Cappuccio
N	P	Old, John • Herne the Hunter (A Legend of Royal Windsor)
N	P	Perelli, Edoardo • Viola Pisani
N	P	Soloviev, Nicolai Feopemptovich • Cordélia
N	P	Vranicky, Pavel • Oberon, König der Elfen
N	P	Weber, Carl Maria von • Oberon [or the Elf-King's Oath]
N	S	Ariosti, Attilio • Coriolano, II
N	S	Berens, Johann Hermann • Violetta
N	S	Berton, Henri-Montan • Montano et Stéphanie
N	S	Busby, Thomas • Fair Fugitives
N	S	Caldara, Antonio • Cajo Marzio Coriolano
N	S	Capelli, Giovanni Maria • Rosalinda [Erginia Mascherata]
N	S	Cattani, Lorenzo • Cajo Marzio Coriolano

STATUS EVIDENCE COMPOSITION

STATUS	EVIDENCE	COMPOSITION
N	S	Cavalli, Pietro Francesco • Coriolano
N	S	Forest, Jean Kurt • Hamlet
N	S	Gasperini, Carlo Francesco • Ambleto
N	S	Graun, Karl Heinrich • Coriolano
N	S	Guglielmi, Pietro Alessandro • Admeto, Re di Tessaglia
N	S	Händel, Georg Friederich • Admeto, Re di Tessaglia
N	S	Hignett, J. L. A. • Hamlet
N	S	Hohmann, Gustav • Hermione, oder Der kleine Vicomte
N	S	Jakobowski, Edward • Erminie
N	S	Jommelli, Nicolo • Caio Mario [Cajo Mario]
N	S	Khrennikov, Tikhon Nikolaevich • Brati [Brothers]
N	S	Khrennikov, Tikhon Nikolaevich • V buriu [Im Sturm, Into the Storm]
N	S	Lavina, Vincenzo • Coriolano, Il
N	S	Legouix, Isidore Édouard • Othello, Un
N	S	Martín y Soler, Vicente • Capricciosa corretta, La [So bessert sie sich]
N	S	Martini, Giovanni • Henri IV, ou La Bataille d'Ivry
N	S	Morlacchi, Francesco Giuseppi Baldassare • Gioventù di Enrico V, La [Das Jugendjahre Heinrich des Fünften]
N	S	Nicolini, Giuseppe • Coriolano
N	S	Offenbach, Jacques • Rêve d'une Nuit d'été, Le
N	S	Perti, Giacomo Antonio • Martio Coriolano
N	S	Pollaroli, Carlo Francesco • Marzio Coriolano
N	S	Pulli, Pietro • Caio Marzio Coriolano

STATUS EVIDENCE COMPOSITION

STATUS	EVIDENCE	COMPOSITION
N	S	Radicati, Felice Alessandro • Coriolano, II
N	S	Rossini, Gioacchino • Ermione
N	S	Scarlatti, Giuseppe Domenico • Ambleto
N	S	Schindelmeisser, Louis Alexander Balthasar • Malvina
N	S	Serpette, Henri Charles Antoine Gaston • Songe d'une nuit d'été, Le
N	S	Smith, John Christopher • Rosalinda
N	S	Strungk, Nicolaus Adam • Rosalinde
N	S	Stuntz, Joseph Hartmann • Heinrich IV zu Givry
N	S	Tommasi, Ferdinando [Tommaso] • Guido e Ginevre
N	S	Treu, Daniel Gottlieb • Coriolano
N	S	Unknown • Timon in Love or The Innocent Theft
N	S	Urich, Jean • Orage, L'
N	S	Valverde y San Juan, Joaquín • sueño de una noche de verano, El
N	S	Vignali, Giuseppe [Act I]; Carlo Baglioni [Act II] and Giacomo Cozzi [Act III] • Ambleto
N	S	Walton, Sir William • Troilus and Cressida
N	S	Weber, Carl Maria von • Euryanthe
N	S	Zanettini, Antonio • Érmione [Die wiedergefundene Hermione]
N	S	Ziani, Marc Antonio • Rosalinda, La or Erginia mascherata
N	S	Zirra, Alexandru • Furtuna [TheTempest]
NO	P	Aliabiev, Alexander • Storm, The
NO	P	Arne, Thomas Augustine • Tempest, The
NO	P	Bedford, Herbert • Love Scene from Shakespeare's Romeo and Juliet for Contralto and Baritone

STATUS   EVIDENCE   COMPOSITION

STATUS	EVIDENCE	COMPOSITION
NO	P	Bishop, Sir Henry Rowley • As You Like It
NO	P	Bishop, Sir Henry Rowley • Comedy of Errors, The
NO	P	Bishop, Sir Henry Rowley • Twelfth Night
NO	P	Boughton, Rutland • Againcourt
NO	P	Clarke, James Siree Hamilton • Merchant of Venice
NO	P	Duvernoy, Victor-Alphonse • Tempête, La
NO	P	Holland, Jan David • Hamlet, Pantomime zu
NO	P	Honegger, Arturo • Tempête, La
NO	P	Jenkins, David • Enchanted Isle, The [Scenes from Shakespeare's 'Tempest']
NO	P	Kuhlau, Friedrich Daniel Rudolph • Musik Til William Shakspeare [sic], Op. 74
NO	P	Locke, Matthew and Robert Johnson • Macbeth
NO	P	Machavariani, Alexei • Othello
NO	P	Morton, Louise, and others • Twelfth Night
NO	P	Orff, Carl • Sommernachtstraum, Ein
NO	P	Prokofiev, Sergei • Hamlet, Music to the Tragedy by Shakespeare
NO	P	Purcell, Henry • History of Timon of Athens, the Man Hater, The
NO	P	Purcell, Henry • Tempest or Enchanted Island, The
NO	P	Reichardt, Johann Friedrich • Macbeth
NO	P	Ware, William Henry • Macbeth
NO	S	André, Johann • Macbeth
NO	S	Aylward, Theodore • Midsummer Night's Dream, A
NO	S	Bishop, Sir Henry Rowley • Antony and Cleopatra
NO	S	Bishop, Sir Henry Rowley • Two Gentlemen of Verona, The

STATUS EVIDENCE COMPOSITION

STATUS	EVIDENCE	COMPOSITION
NO	S	Boyce, William • Florizel and Perdita
NO	S	Eberlin, Johann Ernst • Ricardus Impius, Angliae Rex, ab Henrico Richmondæ Comite vita simul et regno excitus
NO	S	Fisher, John Abraham • Macbeth
NO	S	Johnson, Robert • Tempest, The
NO	S	Leverage, Richard • Macbeth
NO	S	Linley II, Thomas • Tempest, The or The Enchanted Island
NO	S	Thomé, François Lucien Joseph • Roméo et Juliette
NO	S	Tiessen, Heinz • Cymbelin
NO	S	Ware, William Henry • Cymbeline
NO	S	Weyse, Christoph Ernst Friedrich • Macbeth
Y	P	Amram, David • Twelfth Night
Y	P	Andreozzi, Gaetano • Amleto
Y	P	Ardin, Leon • Antony and Cleopatra
Y	P	Arensen, Adolf • Viola
Y	P	Argento, Dominick • Christopher Sly
Y	P	Arne, Michael and C. Dibdin, J. Battishill, C. Burney, Hook, J. C. Smith • Fairy Tale
Y	P	Arne, Thomas Augustine • Fairy Prince, The
Y	P	Arne, Thomas Augustine, Samuel Arnold and others • Sheep-Shearing, The or Florizel and Perdita
Y	P	Balfe, Michael William • Falstaff
Y	P	Banister, John; Giovanni Battista Draghi; Matthew Locke; Pelham Humfrey; and Pietro Reggio • Tempest, The [The Enchanted Island]
Y	P	Barber, Samuel • Antony and Cleopatra, Op. 40
Y	P	Barbieri, Carlo Emanuele di • Perdita oder Ein Wintermärchen

STATUS EVIDENCE COMPOSITION

STATUS	EVIDENCE	COMPOSITION
Y	P	Barkworth, John Edmond • Romeo and Juliet
Y	P	Beecham, Adrian Wells • Love's Labour's Lost [Peines d'Amour Perdues]
Y	P	Beecham, Adrian Wells • Merchant of Venice, The
Y	P	Benda, George Anton • Romeo und Julie
Y	P	Bentoiu, Pascal • Hamlet, Op. 18
Y	P	Berlioz, Hector • Béatrice et Bénédict
Y	P	Blacher, Boris • Romeo und Julia
Y	P	Bloch, Ernest • Macbeth
Y	P	Bondeville, Emmanuel de • Antonine et Cléopatre
Y	P	Britten, Lord Edward Benjamin • Midsummer Night's Dream, A, Op. 64
Y	P	Bruch, Max • Hermione, Op. 40
Y	P	Buzzolla, Antonio • Amleto
Y	P	Cagnoni, Antonio • Re Lear, II
Y	P	Canonica, Pietro • Miranda
Y	P	Chélard, Hippolyte-André-Jean-Baptiste • Macbeth
Y	P	Cikker, Ján • Coriolanus
Y	P	Cottrau, Giulio • Cordelia (Re Lear)
Y	P	Cottrau, Giulio • Pericle re di Tiro
Y	P	Delannoy, Marcel • Puck
Y	P	Doppler, Arpád • Viel Lärm um Lichts
Y	P	Fibich, Zdenko • Boure, Opus 40 [Der Sturm]
Y	P	Foerster, Joseph Brohuslav • Jessika, Opus 60
Y	P	Frazzi, Vito • Re Lear
Y	P	Gatty, Nicholas Comyn • Tempest, The
Y	P	Gelber, Stanley Jay • Love and Let Love
Y	P	Giannini, Vittorio • Taming of the Shrew, The

STATUS EVIDENCE COMPOSITION

STATUS	EVIDENCE	COMPOSITION
Y	P	Goetz, Herman • Widerspänstigen Zähmung, Der [La Megère apprivoisée; Caterina e Petruccio]
Y	P	Goldmark, Carl • Wintermärchen, Ein
Y	P	Gounod, Charles François • Roméo et Juliette
Y	P	Guglielmi, Pietro Carlo • Romeo e Giulietta [I Capuletti ed i Montecchi]
Y	P	Hahn, Reynaldo • Marchand de Vénise, Le
Y	P	Halévy, Jacques Franoçis Fromental Élie • Tempesta, La
Y	P	Hensel, Johann Daniel • Geisterinsel, Die
Y	P	Hester, Hal and Danny Apolinar • Your Own Thing
Y	P	Hignard, Aristide • Hamlet
Y	P	Holst, Gustav • At the Boar's Head, Opus 42
Y	P	Hopp, Julius • Hammlet
Y	P	Horky, Karel • Jed z Elsinoru [The Poison from Elsinore]
Y	P	Ivry, Paul Xaver Désiré Richard, Marquis d' • Amantes de Vérone, Les
Y	P	Kagen, Sergius • Hamlet
Y	P	Kalnins, Janis • Hamlets
Y	P	Klebe, Giselher Wolfgang • Ermordung Cäsars, Die Op. 32
Y	P	Krejcí, Isa • Pozdvizení v Efesu [The Upheaval in Ephesus]
Y	P	Kunzen, Friedrich Ludwig Æmilius • Stormen
Y	P	Kusterer, Arthur • Was ihr Wollt
Y	P	Lampe, John Frederich • Pyramus and Thisbe
Y	P	Lattuada, Felice • Tempesta, La
Y	P	Le Rey, Frédéric • Mégère apprivoisée, La
Y	P	Litolff, Henry Charles • König Lear

STATUS   EVIDENCE   COMPOSITION

STATUS	EVIDENCE	COMPOSITION
Y	P	Lueder, Florence Pauline • As You Like It
Y	P	Lueder, Florence Pauline • Rosalind
Y	P	MacDermot, Galt • Two Gentlemen of Verona
Y	P	Malipiero, Gian Francesco • Antonio e Cleopatra
Y	P	Malipiero, Gian Francesco • Giulio Cesare
Y	P	Malipiero, Gian Francesco • Romeo e Guilietta (scene 5 of Monde celesti e infernali)
Y	P	Mancinelli, Luigi • Sogno di una notte d'estate, Il
Y	P	Marchetti, Filippo • Romeo e Giulietta
Y	P	Marshall-Hall, George William Louis • Romeo and Juliet
Y	P	Martin, Frank • Sturm, Der
Y	P	Matuszczak, Bernadetta • Julia i Romeo
Y	P	Mercadante, Giuseppe Saverio Raffele • Amleto
Y	P	Missa, Edmond Jean Louis • Dinah
Y	P	Morera, Enrique • Fiercilla domada, La
Y	P	Moroni, Luigi • Amleto
Y	P	Morton, David • Tempest in a Teapot
Y	P	Müller, Wenzel • Sturm oder die Zauberinsel, Der
Y	P	Nabokov, Nikolai • Love's Labour's Lost [Verlor'ne Liebesmüh']
Y	P	Nicolai, Carl Otto Ehrenfried • lustigen Weiber von Windsor, Die
Y	P	Persico, Mario • Bisbetica Domata, La
Y	P	Pillaut, Léon • Perdita
Y	P	Pinsuti, Ciro • Mercante di Venezia, Il

STATUS   EVIDENCE   COMPOSITION

STATUS	EVIDENCE	COMPOSITION
Y	P	Podestà, Carlo • Ero, ossia Molto rumore per nulla
Y	P	Puget, Paul-Charles-Marie • Beaucoup de bruit pour rien
Y	P	Purcell, Henry • Fairy Queen, The
Y	P	Reichardt, Johann Friedrich • Geisterinsel, Die
Y	P	Reimann, Aribert • Lear
Y	P	Reutter, Hermann • Hamlet
Y	P	Ritter, Peter • Sturm, Der oder Die bezauberte Insel
Y	P	Roters, Ernest • Hamlet, Op. 145
Y	P	Saussine, Henri de • Marchand de Vénise, Le
Y	P	Searle, Humphrey • Hamlet, Opus 48
Y	P	Shebalin, Vissarion Yakovlevich • Ukroshchenie stroptivoi [The Taming of the Shrew] Op. 46
Y	P	Shelley, Harry Rowe • Romeo and Juliet
Y	P	Silver, Charles • Mégère apprivoisée, La
Y	P	Smetana, Bedrich • Viola
Y	P	Smith, John Christopher • Fairies, The
Y	P	Smith, John Christopher • Tempest, The
Y	P	Stanford, Sir Charles Villiers • Much Ado About Nothing, Opus 76a
Y	P	Storace, Stephen • Equivoci, Gli
Y	P	Szokolay, Sándor • Hamlet
Y	P	Taubert, Carl Gottfried Wilhelm • Cesario, oder Was ihr wollt, Op. 188
Y	P	Taubert, Wilhelm • Macbeth, Op. 133
Y	P	Taubmann, Otto • Porzia
Y	P	Thomas, Charles Louis Ambroise • Hamlet
Y	P	Unknown • Cure for a Scold, A
Y	P	Urspruch, Anton • Sturm, Der

STATUS EVIDENCE COMPOSITION

STATUS	EVIDENCE	COMPOSITION
Y	P	Vaughan Williams, Ralph • Sir John in Love
Y	P	Veracini, Francesco Maria • Rosalinda
Y	P	Verdi, Giuseppe • Falstaff
Y	P	Verdi, Giuseppe • Macbeth
Y	P	Vreuls, Victor • Songe d'une nuit d'été, Un
Y	P	Weis, Karél • Viola [Die Zwillinge, Blizenci]
Y	P	Zafred, Mario • Amleto
Y	P	Zillig, Winfried • Troilus und Cressida
Y	P	Zimmermann, Balduin • Wintermärchen, Ein
Y	P	Zingarelli, Niccolò Antonio • Giulietta e Romeo
Y	S	Adam, Adolphe-Charles • Falstaff
Y	S	Adler, Richard • Music Is
Y	S	Alexandre, Charles Guillaume • Georget et Georgette
Y	S	Aliabiev, Alexander • Volshebnaya noch
Y	S	Alpaerts, Florent • Shylock
Y	S	André, Johann • König Lear
Y	S	Andrews, John Charles Bond- • Herne's Oak, or The Rose of Windsor [also Herne the Hunter]
Y	S	Angelis, Arturo de • Tempesta, La
Y	S	Angyal, Lázló • Tempest, The
Y	S	Arundell, Dennis Drew • Midsummer Night's Dream, A
Y	S	Atherton, Percy Lee and Ernest Hamlin Abbott • Hamlet, Prince of Denmark or The Sport, the Spook and the Spinster
Y	S	Atterberg, Kurt • Stormen, Op. 49
Y	S	Audran, Edmond • Gillette de Narbonne [Gillette, or Count and Countess; Gilda di Guascogna]
Y	S	Baeyens, August Louis • Coriolanus
Y	S	Balamos, John • As You Like It

STATUS EVIDENCE COMPOSITION

STATUS	EVIDENCE	COMPOSITION
Y	S	Barry, H. C. • Shylock or The Venus of Venice
Y	S	Beer-Walbrunn, Anton • Sturm, Der
Y	S	Bellini, Vincenzo • Capuleti e i Montecchi, I
Y	S	Berény, Henri • Wintermärchen, Das
Y	S	Berlioz, Hector • Hamlet
Y	S	Bernstein, Leonard • West Side Story
Y	S	Besoyan, Rick • Babes in the Wood, or Who Killed Cock Robin
Y	S	Bizet, Georges • Hamlet
Y	S	Bossi, Renzo • Volpino il Calderaio, Op. 32
Y	S	Brawn, Geoffrey • At the Sign of the Angel or A Little Touch of Harry in the Night
Y	S	Brumagne, Fernand • Marchand de Venise, Le
Y	S	Campo y Zabaleta, Conrado del • Amantes de Verona, Los
Y	S	Carl, M. • Julius Caesar
Y	S	Carlson, Charles Frederick • Merchant of Venice
Y	S	Carr, Frank Osmond • In Town
Y	S	Caruso, Lodovico Luigi • Amleto
Y	S	Caruso, Lodovico Luigi • Tempesta, La
Y	S	Castelnuovo-Tedesco, Mario • Mercante di Venezia, Il, Op. 181
Y	S	Castelnuovo-Tedesco, Mario • Tutto e bène quello che finisce bène, Op. 182
Y	S	Chatburn, Tom • Gay Venetians, The
Y	S	Chignell, Robert • Romeo and Juliet
Y	S	Clapp, Philip Greeley • Taming of the Shrew, The
Y	S	Collingwood, Lawrance Arthur • Macbeth

457

STATUS EVIDENCE COMPOSITION

STATUS	EVIDENCE	COMPOSITION
Y	S	Cribari, Donna • Pop
Y	S	Daffner, Hugo • Macbeth
Y	S	Dalayrac, Nicolas • Tout pour l'amour ou Roméo et Juliette
Y	S	Damrosch, Leopold • Romeo und Julia
Y	S	David, Félicien César • Saphir, Le or Tout est bien, qui finit bien
Y	S	De Boeck, Auguste de • Winternachtsdroom, Een
Y	S	De Filippi, Amadeo • Malvolio
Y	S	Debussy, Claude • As You Like It
Y	S	Deffès, Louis Pierre • Jessica
Y	S	Déjazet, Eugène • Rhum et eau en juillet
Y	S	Del Fante, Raffaele • Tempesta, La
Y	S	Dittersdorf, Carl Ditters von • lustigen Weiber von Windsor und der dicke Hans, Die
Y	S	Doubrava, Jaroslav • Sen noci svatojanske
Y	S	Douglas, Hugh A. • Romeo and Juliet Up to Larks
Y	S	Durme, Jef Van • Anthony and Cleopatra
Y	S	Durme, Jef Van • King Lear
Y	S	Durme, Jef Van • Richard III
Y	S	Eastwood, Thomas Hugh • Christopher Sly
Y	S	Eggen, Arne • Cymbelyn
Y	S	Emery, Charles P. • Romeo, the Radical or Obstruction and Effect
Y	S	Emmert, Adam Joseph • Sturm, Der
Y	S	Engelmann, Hans Ulrich • Ophelia, Op. 36
Y	S	Engländer, Ludwig • Belle of Bohemia, The
Y	S	Fabrizi, Vincenzo • Tempestà ossia Da un disordine ne nasce un ordine, La
Y	S	Faccio, Franco • Amleto

STATUS EVIDENCE COMPOSITION

STATUS	EVIDENCE	COMPOSITION
Y	S	Farina, Guido • Dodisesima Notte, La
Y	S	Faris, Alexander • R Loves J
Y	S	Farwell, Arthur George • Caliban by the Yellow Sands, Opus 47
Y	S	Ferroni, Vencenzo Emidio Carmine • Romeo and Juliet
Y	S	Field, Graham • Dick Deterred
Y	S	Fleischmann, Friedrich • Geisterinsel, Die
Y	S	Folprecht, Zdenek • Lásky hra osudná [The Fateful Game of Love], Opus 3
Y	S	Fontmichel, Hippolyte Honoré Joseph Court de (1799-?) • Amleto
Y	S	Frank, Ernst • Sturm, Der
Y	S	Frank, Johann Wolfgang • Timon
Y	S	Freudenberg, Wilhelm • Kleopatra
Y	S	Fribec, Kresimir • Romeo and Juliet
Y	S	Garcia, Manuel Vincente del Popolo • Gioventù di Enrico V, La
Y	S	Garcia, Manuel Vincente del Popolo • Giulietta e Romeo
Y	S	Gatty, Nicholas Comyn • Macbeth
Y	S	Gaujac, Edmond Germain • Amantes de Vérone, Les
Y	S	Generali, Pietro Mercandetti • Rodrigo di Valencia
Y	S	Ghislanzoni, Alberto • Re Lear
Y	S	Gibbs, Cecil Armstrong • Twelfth Night, Opus 115
Y	S	Gilbert, James • Good Time Johnny
Y	S	Glinka, Mikhail Ivanovitch • Hamlet
Y	S	Gobatti, Stefano • Cordelia
Y	S	Goedicke, Alexander • Macbeth
Y	S	Goldman, Edward M. • Macbeth
Y	S	Grandi, Alfredo • Amleto
Y	S	Greenwall, Peter • Three Caskets, The or Venice Re-served

STATUS EVIDENCE COMPOSITION

STATUS	EVIDENCE	COMPOSITION
Y	S	Grosheim, Georg Christoph • Titania, oder Liebe durch Zauberei
Y	S	Groth, Howard • Petruchio
Y	S	Haack, Friedrich • Geisterinsel, Die
Y	S	Hahn, Reynaldo • Beaucoup de bruit pour rien
Y	S	Haines, Roger • Fire Angel
Y	S	Haines, Roger • Shylock [Fire Angel]
Y	S	Hale, Alfred Matthew • Tempest, The
Y	S	Halpern, Sidney • Macbeth
Y	S	Hamel, Eduard • Malvina
Y	S	Harbison, John • Winter's Tale, The
Y	S	Harper, Wally • Sensations
Y	S	Hart, Fritz Bennicke • Malvolio, Opus 14
Y	S	Heinrich, Hermann • Viel Lärm um Nichts
Y	S	Hess, Ludwig • Was ihr Wollt
Y	S	Heward, Leslie Hays • Hamlet
Y	S	Hirschbach, Hermann • Othello
Y	S	Hoffmeister, Franz Anton • Schiffbruch, Der
Y	S	Hofmann, Johann • Ritter Hans von Dampf
Y	S	Holenia, Hans • Viola, Opus 21 [Was Ihr wollt]
Y	S	Hughes, Gervase • Twelfth Night, Scenes from
Y	S	Jirko, Ivan • Twelfth Night, The [Vecer Trikralovy]
Y	S	Jones, Cliff • Rockabye Hamlet
Y	S	Kaffka [Kafka], Johann Christian • Antonius und Cleopatra
Y	S	Karel, Rudolf • Zkroceni zlé zeny [The Taming of the Shrew]
Y	S	Keurvels, Edward H. J. • Hamlet

STATUS EVIDENCE COMPOSITION

STATUS	EVIDENCE	COMPOSITION
Y	S	Khrennikov, Tikhon Nikolaevich • Mnogo shuma iz nichego [Viel Lärm aus Leidenschaft, Much Ado About Hearts]
Y	S	Kirchner, Hermann • Viola
Y	S	Koppel, Herman David • Macbeth, Op. 79
Y	S	Kreutz, Arthur • Sourwood Mountain
Y	S	Kreutzer, Rodolphe • Imogène, ou La Gageure indiscrète
Y	S	Kunz, [Konrad Max ?] • Tempest, The
Y	S	Laufer, B. • Shylock
Y	S	LaViolette, Wesley • Shylock
Y	S	Lecocq, Charles Alexandre • Marjolaine
Y	S	Leoncavallo, Ruggiero • Songe d'une nuit d'été, Un
Y	S	Leopold I, Holy Roman Emperor • Timòne, Misantropo
Y	S	Leverage, Richard • Pyramus and Thisbe, The Comic Masque of
Y	S	Liota, A. • Romeo and Juliet
Y	S	Lorenz, Carl Adolf • Komödie der Irrungen, Die
Y	S	Ludwig, Otto • Romeo und Julie
Y	S	MacDermot, Galt • Cressida
Y	S	Machavariani, Alexei • Hamlet
Y	S	Malamet, Marsha • Dreamstuff
Y	S	Manusardi, Giuseppe • sogno di Primavera, Un [Un rêve de printemps]
Y	S	Marescalchi, Luigi • Giuletta e Romeo
Y	S	Marescotti • Amleto
Y	S	Maretzek, Maximilian • Hamlet
Y	S	Meiners, Giambattista • Riccardo III
Y	S	Mercadal y Pons, Antonio • Giulietta e Romeo
Y	S	Mercadante, Giuseppe Saverio Raffele • Gioventù di Enrico V, La

STATUS EVIDENCE COMPOSITION

STATUS	EVIDENCE	COMPOSITION
Y	S	Mojsisovics, Roderich • Viel Lärm um Nichts
Y	S	Morales, Melesio • Giulietta e Romeo
Y	S	Mozart, Wolfgang Amadeus • Peines d'amour perdues
Y	S	Mulcahy, Lance • Shakespeare's Cabaret
Y	S	Mullins, Hugh • Romeo and Juliet
Y	S	Mussorgsky, Modest Petrovich • Hamlet
Y	S	Nápravnik, Éduard Frantsevich • Sturm, Der
Y	S	Nesvera, Josef • Perdita
Y	S	Pacini, Giovanni • Gioventù di Enrico V, La (also La bella tavernara; Le Aventure d'una notte)
Y	S	Papavoine, Mdme • Vieux Coquet, Le; ou Les deux amies ou Le vieus garçon
Y	S	Perosi, Lorenzo • Romeo and Juliet
Y	S	Philidor • Herne le Chasseur
Y	S	Piccini, Louis Alexandre • Macbeth
Y	S	Pogodin • King Lear?
Y	S	Porta, [Bernardo ?] • Roméo et Juliette
Y	S	Porter, Cole • Kiss Me, Kate
Y	S	Radó, Aladár • Shylock
Y	S	Raphling, Sam • Prince Hamlet
Y	S	Raymond, Édouard • Sturm, Der
Y	S	Reynaud, Armand • Roi Lear, Le
Y	S	Rintel, Wilhelm • Was ihr Wöllt
Y	S	Riotte, Philipp Jakob • Sturm, Der oder Die Insel des Prospero
Y	S	Ritter, Peter • lustigen Weiber, Die
Y	S	Rogers, Richard • Boys from Syracuse, The
Y	S	Rolle, Johann Heinrich • Sturm oder Die bezauberte Insel, Der
Y	S	Rosenberg, Richard • Liebesspiel, Das

STATUS EVIDENCE COMPOSITION

STATUS	EVIDENCE	COMPOSITION
Y	S	Rossi, Lauro • Biorn
Y	S	Rossini, Gioacchino • Otello, osia L'Africano di Venezia
Y	S	Roti, Ugo • Sogno di una notte d'estate, Il
Y	S	Ruben, Paul • Edit royal, L'
Y	S	Rubens, Paul Alfred and Frank E. Tours • Dairymaids, The
Y	S	Rubens, Paul Alfred and Walter Rubens • Great Caesar
Y	S	Rumling, Sigismund Freiherr von • Roméo et Juliette
Y	S	Rung, Henrik • Stormen paa København [Storm over Copenhagen]
Y	S	Saint-Saëns, Camille • Henry VIII
Y	S	Salieri, Antonio • Falstaff osia Le tre Burle
Y	S	Salvayre, Gaston • Riccardo III
Y	S	Samara, Spiro • Furia domata, La
Y	S	Sayn-Wittgenstein-Berleburg, Count Friedrich Ernst von • Antonius und Kleopatra
Y	S	Schmitz, Alan • Julius Caesar
Y	S	Schuster, Ignaz • Hamlet, Prinz vom Tandelmarkt
Y	S	Schuster, Ignaz • Romeo und Julie
Y	S	Schwanenberg, Johann Gottfried • Romeo e Giulia
Y	S	Séméladis, M. • Cordélia
Y	S	Serov, Alexander Nikolayevich • Merry Wives of Windsor
Y	S	Shenshin, Aleksandr Alexseivich • Twelfth Night
Y	S	Siegmeister, Elie • Night of the Moonspell
Y	S	Silverman, Stanley • Midsummer Night's Dream, A
Y	S	Slade, Julian • Comedy of Errors
Y	S	Sobolewski, Friedrich Eduard de • Imogéne
Y	S	Soule, Charles Caroll • Travesty Without a Pun.

STATUS EVIDENCE COMPOSITION

STATUS	EVIDENCE	COMPOSITION
Y	S	Stadtfeldt, Christian Joseph Franz Alexandre • Hamlet
Y	S	Steibelt, Daniel Gottlieb • Roméo et Juliette or Tout pour l'amour
Y	S	Steinkühler, Émile • Cäsario, oder die Verwechslung, Op. 30
Y	S	Storch, Anton Maria • Romeo und Julie
Y	S	Stuart, Leslie • Belle of Mayfair
Y	S	Sulek, Stjepan • Koriolan
Y	S	Sulek, Stjepan • Oluja
Y	S	Suppé, Franz von • Sommernachtstraum, Der
Y	S	Sutermeister, Heinrich • Romeo und Julia
Y	S	Sutermeister, Heinrich • Zauberinsel, Die
Y	S	Torriani, Eugenio • Romeo e Giulietta
Y	S	Turok, Paul H. • Richard III
Y	S	Unknown • Bezähmte Widerbellerin, Die
Y	S	Unknown • Catch My Soul
Y	S	Unknown • Catherine and Petruchio
Y	S	Vaccai, Nicola • Giulietta e Romeo
Y	S	Valenti, Michael • Oh, Brother
Y	S	Van Heusen, Jimmy • Swingin' the Dream
Y	S	Verdi, Giuseppe • Lear
Y	S	Verdi, Giuseppe • Otello
Y	S	Vidal, Paul Antonin • Peines d'amour perdues
Y	S	Wagner, Wilhelm Richard • Liebesverbot, Das oder Die Novize von Palermo
Y	S	Weigl, Joseph [Veigl, Giuseppe] • Amleto
Y	S	Weisgall, Hugo • Gardens of Adonis, The
Y	S	Westerhout, Niccolò van • Cimbelino, Il

STATUS	EVIDENCE	COMPOSITION
Y	S	Whitaker, John • Weird Sisters, The or The Thane and the Throne
Y	S	Wilson, James • Twelfth Night
Y	S	Winter, Peter von • Sturm, Der
Y	S	Wödl, Franz • Komödie der Irrungen
Y	S	Wolf, Ernst Wilhelm • Zauberirrungen, Die [Die Irrtümer der Zauberei]
Y	S	Wolf-Ferrari, Ermanno • Sly, ovvero La leggenda del dormiente risvegliato
Y	S	Zanardini, Angelo • Amleto
Y	S	Zandonai, Riccardo • Giulietta e Romeo
Y	S	Zanon, Antonio B. • Leggenda di Giulietta, La
Y	S	Zavodsky, Felix • Othello
Y	S	Zumsteeg, Johann Rudolf • Geisterinsel, Die

COMPOSITION	US: Wc	Schatz
Acker, Jean Van den • Romeo en Marielle [Tout pour l'amour]	N	N
Adam, Adolphe-Charles • Falstaff	M1503.A193F17	N
Adler, Richard • Music Is	M1508	N
Alexandre, Charles Guillaume • Georget et Georgette	MUSIC 3197 Reel 3 Item 12	N
Alfano, Franco • Miranda	N	N
Aliabiev, Alexander • Storm, The	M1505.A4M58	N
Aliabiev, Alexander • Volshebnaya noch	N	N
Allegra, Giuseppe • Sogno di una Notte, Il	N	N
Alpaerts, Florent • Shylock	N	N
Amram, David • Twelfth Night	M1503.A476T9 1972	N
André, Johann • König Lear	N	N
André, Johann • Macbeth	N	N
Andreozzi, Gaetano • Amleto	N	212(R5)
Andrews, John Charles Bond- • Herne's Oak, or The Rose of Windsor [also Herne the Hunter]	N	N
Anfossi, Pasquale • Cajo Mario		
Angelis, Arturo de • Tempesta, La	N	N
Angyal, Lázló • Tempest, The	N	N
Ansell, John • King's Bride, The [Violette]	N	N
Antoine, Ferdinand d' • Ende gut, alles gut oder Der Fürst und sein Volk	N	N
Ardin, Leon • Antony and Cleopatra	MUSIC 3197 Reel 3 Item 11	N
Arensen, Adolf • Viola	N	311(R7)
Argento, Dominick • Christopher Sly	N	N
Ariosti, Attilio • Coriolano, Il	MUSIC 3166 Item 2	N

COMPOSITION	US: Wc	Schatz
Arne, Michael and C. Dibdin, J. Battishill, C. Burney, Hook, J. C. Smith • Fairy Tale	M1508 Case/PR1241. L6 Vol. 243	N
Arne, Thomas Augustine • Fairy Prince, The	PR 1241.L6 Vol. 52	N
Arne, Thomas Augustine • Tempest, The	N	N
Arne, Thomas Augustine, Samuel Arnold and others • Sheep-Shearing, The or Florizel and Perdita	PR 1241.L6 Vol. 201	11753A (R238)
Arundell, Dennis Drew • Midsummer Night's Dream, A	N	N
Aspa, Mario • Gioventù di Enrico V, La	N	N
Asplmayr [Aspelmayr], Franz • Sturm, Der	N	N
Asplmayr, Franz • Leben und Tod des Königs Macbeth	N	N
Atherton, Percy Lee and Ernest Hamlin Abbott • Hamlet, Prince of Denmark or The Sport, the Spook and the Spinster	M1504.A83H2	N
Atterberg, Kurt • Stormen, Op. 49	N	N
Attwood, Thomas • Hermione, or Valour's Triumph	N	N
Audran, Edmond • Gillette de Narbonne [Gillette, or Count and Countess; Gilda di Guascogna]	M1503.A915G44/ ML50.A918G52 Case	491(R11) [German]
Aylward, Theodore • Midsummer Night's Dream, A	N	N
Baeyens, August Louis • Coriolanus	N	N
Balamos, John • As You Like It	N	N
Balfe, Michael William • Enrico IV al passo della Marna	N	589(R14)
Balfe, Michael William • Falstaff	M1503.B185F3	575(R13)

COMPOSITION	US: Wc	Schatz
Banister, John; Giovanni Battista Draghi; Matthew Locke; Pelham Humfrey; and Pietro Reggio • Tempest, The [The Enchanted Island]	N	N
Barber, Samuel • Antony and Cleopatra, Op. 40	M1503.B226A6 1966/ML50. B234A5 1966	N
Barbieri, Carlo Emanuele di • Perdita oder Ein Wintermärchen	M1500.B3P4 Case	603(R14)
Barkworth, John Edmond • Romeo and Juliet	M1503.B248R5	N
Barry, H. C. • Shylock or The Venus of Venice	N	N
Beck, Curt • König Lear	N	N
Bedford, Herbert • Love Scene from Shakespeare's Romeo and Juliet for Contralto and Baritone	N	N
Beecham, Adrian Wells • Love's Labour's Lost [Peines d'Amour Perdues]	M1503.B412P3	N
Beecham, Adrian Wells • Merchant of Venice, The	M1503.B412M3	N
Beer-Walbrunn, Anton • Sturm, Der	N	N
Bellini, Vincenzo • Capuleti e i Montecchi, I	MUSIC 2075 etc.	718-29(R16)
Benda, George Anton • Romeo und Julie	M1500.B46R5	776-7(R17)
Bentoiu, Pascal • Hamlet, Op. 18	N	N
Benvenuti, Tommaso • Guglielmo Shakespeare	N	802(R18)
Berens, Johann Hermann • Riccardo	N	N
Berens, Johann Hermann • Sommarnattsdröm, En	N	N
Berens, Johann Hermann • Violetta	N	N
Berény, Henri • Wintermärchen, Das	N	N

COMPOSITION	US: Wc	Schatz
Berlioz, Hector • Béatrice et Bénédict	M1503.B514B34	814(R18)
Berlioz, Hector • Hamlet	N	N
Bernabei, Giuseppe Antonio • Érmione	N	826(R18)
Bernabei, Vincenzo • Equivoci d'Amore, Gli	N	N
Bernstein, Leonard • West Side Story	M1503.B53W4	N
Berton, Henri-Montan • Montano et Stéphanie	M1500.B54M5	895(R20)
Bertoni, Ferdinando Giuseppe • Cajo Mario		
Besoyan, Rick • Babes in the Wood, or Who Killed Cock Robin	M1508	N
Bianchi, Francesco • Cajo Mario		
Bishop, Sir Henry Rowley • Antony and Cleopatra	N	N
Bishop, Sir Henry Rowley • As You Like It	M1513.B59A7	N
Bishop, Sir Henry Rowley • Comedy of Errors, The	M1513.B59C6/ 11824.g.2.	N
Bishop, Sir Henry Rowley • Henri Quatre [Paris in the Olden Times]	N	N
Bishop, Sir Henry Rowley • Merry Wives of Windsor, The	N	N
Bishop, Sir Henry Rowley • Midsummer Night's Dream, A	N	N
Bishop, Sir Henry Rowley • Tempest, The	N	N
Bishop, Sir Henry Rowley • Twelfth Night	M1513.B59T6	N
Bishop, Sir Henry Rowley • Two Gentlemen of Verona, The	M1513.B59T8	N
Bizet, Georges • Hamlet	N	N
Bizet, Georges • Macbeth	N	N
Blacher, Boris • Romeo und Julia	M1503.B632R6 1950/ML50. B63R6	N
Bloch, Ernest • Macbeth	M1503.B649M3	N

COMPOSITION	US: Wc	Schatz
Bondeville, Emmanuel de • Antonine et Cléopatre	N	N
Borodcicz, Hans von • König Lear		
Bossi, Renzo • Volpino il Calderaio, Op. 32	N	N
Bottacio, Pietro • Bisbetica Domata, La	N	N
Boughton, Rutland • Againcourt	M1540.B79A4	N
Boyce, William • Florizel and Perdita	N	N
Brandauer, Hermann • Caesario	N	N
Brawn, Geoffrey • At the Sign of the Angel or A Little Touch of Harry in the Night	N	N
Britten, Lord Edward Benjamin • Midsummer Night's Dream, A, Op. 64	M1503.B8608M5 /ML50.B8685 M5 1960 Case	N
Bruce, Neely • Pyramus and Thisbe	N	N
Bruch, Max • Hermione, Op. 40	M1503.B886H3	1343(R29)
Brumagne, Fernand • Marchand de Venise, Le	N	N
Busby, Thomas • Fair Fugitives	N	N
Buzzolla, Antonio • Amleto	N	1440(R31)
Cagnoni, Antonio • Re Lear, Il	M1503.C131R3	N
Caldara, Antonio • Cajo Marzio Coriolano	N	N
Campenhout, François van • Gillette de Narbonne	N	N
Campo y Zabaleta, Conrado del • Amantes de Verona, Los	N	N
Canepá, Luigi • Riccardo III	M1503.C2624R5 1880	1568(R33)
Canonica, Pietro • Miranda	M1503.C228M5 1938/ML50. C226M5 1938	N
Capelli, Giovanni Maria • Rosalinda [Erginia Mascherata]	N	N

COMPOSITION	US: Wc	Schatz
Carafa di Colobrano, Michele Enrico and Aimé Ambroise Simon Leborne • Violette, La ou Gérard de Nevers	M1500.C17V5	1617(R34)
Carcani, Giuseppe • Ambleto	N	1620(R34)
Carl, M. • Julius Caesar	N	N
Carlini, Luigi • Gioventù di Enrico V, La	M48.A54 Vol.13	1629(R34)
Carlson, Charles Frederick • Merchant of Venice	N	N
Carr, Frank Osmond • In Town	M1503.C311 I5	N
Caruso, Lodovico Luigi • Amleto	N	N
Caruso, Lodovico Luigi • Tempesta, La	N	N
Castelnuovo-Tedesco, Mario • Mercante di Venezia, Il, Op. 181	M1500.C38M52/ M1503.C354M 52/ML50. C34M5 1966 Case	N
Castelnuovo-Tedesco, Mario • Tutto e bène quello che finisce bène, Op. 182	N	N
Cattani, Lorenzo • Cajo Marzio Coriolano	N	N
Cavalli, Pietro Francesco • Coriolano	N	N
Chapí y Lorente, Ruperto • Tempestad, La	M1503.C463T3	N
Chatburn, Tom • Gay Venetians, The	N	N
Chélard, Hippolyte-André- Jean-Baptiste • Macbeth	M1503.C514M2	1804-5(R38)
Chignell, Robert • Romeo and Juliet	N	N
Choudens, Antony • Cymbeline	N	N
Cikker, Ján • Coriolanus	M1503.C695C74	N
Cimarosa, Domenico Nicola [Cimmarosa] • Cajo Mario		
Clapp, Philip Greeley • Taming of the Shrew, The	N	N

COMPOSITION	US: Wc	Schatz
Clarke, James Siree Hamilton • Merchant of Venice	M1513.C59M4	N
Clarke, Jeremiah • Titus Andronicus	N	N
Claudric, Jean • Othello Story	M1508	N
Collingwood, Lawrance Arthur • Macbeth	N	N
Conte, Paolo • Shakespeare, the Playmaker	N	N
Conti, Nicolò • Cajo Marzio Coriolano [Marzio Coriolano]	N	N
Cooke, Thomas Simpson • Malvina	M1503.C773M2	2209(R45)
Cooke, Thomas Simpson • Oberon, or The Charmed Horn	N	N
Cooke, Thomas Simpson and Braham, John and Others • Taming of the Shrew, The	N	N
Costa, Michael Andrew Angus • Malvina		
Cottrau, Giulio • Cordelia (Re Lear)	N	N
Cottrau, Giulio • Pericle re di Tiro	N	N
Crescentini, Girolamo • Roméo et Juliette	N	N
Cribari, Donna • Pop	N	N
Daffner, Hugo • Macbeth	N	N
Dalayrac, Nicolas • Tout pour l'amour ou Roméo et Juliette	N	N
Damrosch, Leopold • Romeo und Julia	N	N
Danzi, Franz • Malvina [Die Wolfsjagd]		
David, Adolphe Isaac • Orage, L'	N	N
David, Félicien César • Saphir, Le or Tout est bien, qui finit bien	M1503.D249S3	N
De Boeck, Auguste de • Winternachtsdroom, Een	N	N
De Filippi, Amadeo • Malvolio	N	N

COMPOSITION	US: Wc	Schatz
Debussy, Claude • As You Like It	N	N
Deffès, Louis Pierre • Jessica	N	N
Déjazet, Eugène • Rhum et eau en juillet	N	N
Del Fante, Raffaele • Tempesta, La	N	N
Delannoy, Marcel • Puck	M1503.D337P8	N
Delius, Frederick • Romeo und Juliet auf dem Dorfe [A Village Romeo and Juliet]	M1503.D358R6/ ML50.D37R62	N
Didam, Otto • Julia und Romeo	N	N
Dittersdorf, Carl Ditters von • lustigen Weiber von Windsor und der dicke Hans, Die	MUSIC 3299 Item 9	N
Doppler, Arpád • Viel Lärm um Lichts	N	2773(R56)
Doubrava, Jaroslav • Sen noci svatojanske	N	N
Douglas, Hugh A. • Romeo and Juliet Up to Larks	M1503.D736R6	N
Draghi, Antonio • Timone misantropo	N	N
Durme, Jef Van • Anthony and Cleopatra	N	N
Durme, Jef Van • King Lear	N	N
Durme, Jef Van • Richard III	N	N
Duvernoy, Victor-Alphonse • Tempète, La	M1533.D875T3	N
Duyse, Florimond Van • Rosalinde	N	N
Eastwood, Thomas Hugh • Christopher Sly	N	N
Eberlin, Johann Ernst • Ricardus Impius, Angliae Rex, ab Henrico Richmondæ Comite vita simul et regno excitus	N	N
Eberwein, Max Carl • Romeo und Julie	N	N
Eggen, Arne • Cymbelyn	N	N

COMPOSITION	US: Wc	Schatz
Emery, Charles P. • Romeo, the Radical or Obstruction and Effect	N	N
Emmert, Adam Joseph • Sturm, Der	N	N
Engelmann, Hans Ulrich • Ophelia, Op. 36	N	N
Engländer, Ludwig • Belle of Bohemia, The	M1508 [Selections]	N
Erbse, Heimo • Julietta, Op. 15	M1503.E663J8 1958	N
Fabrizi, Vincenzo • Tempestà ossia Da un disordine ne nasce un ordine, La	N	N
Faccio, Franco • Amleto	N	2977(R59)
Falk, Richard • Was ihr Wollt	N	N
Farina, Guido • Dodisesima Notte, La	N	N
Faris, Alexander • R Loves J	N	N
Farwell, Arthur George • Caliban by the Yellow Sands, Opus 47	M1523.F27C2 (Choruses from)	N
Feigerl, R. • Stein der Weisen, Der	N	N
Ferraboso II, Alfonso and Robert Johnson • Oberon, the Fairy Prince	N	N
Ferroni, Vencenzo Emidio Carmine • Romeo and Juliet	N	N
Fibich, Zdenko • Boure, Opus 40 [Der Sturm]	M1503.F443B7	N
Field, Graham • Dick Deterred	N	N
Fioravanti, Valentino • Capricciosa pentita, La	N	3126(R62)
Fioravanti, Valentino • Enrico IV al passo della Marna	N	N
Fischer, Jan F. • Romeo, Julie a tma (Romeo, Juliet and Darkness)	M1503.F528R7 1964	N
Fisher, John Abraham • Macbeth	N	N
Fleischmann, Friedrich • Geisterinsel, Die	N	N

COMPOSITION	US: Wc	Schatz
Flotow, Friedrich von • Wintermärchen, Ein	M1510.F64W4	N
Foerster, Joseph Brohuslav • Jessika, Opus 60	M1503.F66J3	N
Foignet, Jacques • Orage, L'	N	N
Folprecht, Zdenek • Lásky hra osudná [The Fateful Game of Love], Opus 3	N	N
Fontmichel, Hippolyte Honoré Joseph Court de (1799-?) • Amleto	N	N
Forest, Jean Kurt • Hamlet	N	N
Francastel, A. • Henry IV	N	N
Frank, Ernst • Sturm, Der	N	N
Frank, Johann Wolfgang • Timon	N	N
Frazzi, Vito • Re Lear	M1500.F86R4 (Case)	N
Freitas Gazul, Francisco de • Violetas, As	N	N
Freschi, Giovanni Domenico • Rosalinda	N	N
Freudenberg, Wilhelm • Kleopatra	N	3361(R66)
Fribec, Kresimir • Romeo and Juliet	N	N
Gallenberg, Wenzel Robert Count von • Amleto	N	N
Galuppi, Baldassarre • Enrico	M1500.G2E5	N
Galuppi, Baldassarre [called Buranello] • Cajo Mario		
Garcia, Manuel Vincente del Popolo • Gioventù di Enrico V, La	N	N
Garcia, Manuel Vincente del Popolo • Giulietta e Romeo	N	N
Gasperini, Carlo Francesco • Ambleto	N	3556(R70)
Gasperini, Carlo Francesco • Equivoci d'amore e d'innocenza, Gl'	N	3565(R70)
Gatty, Nicholas Comyn • Macbeth	N	N

COMPOSITION	US: Wc	Schatz
Gatty, Nicholas Comyn • Tempest, The	M1503.G266T4	N
Gaujac, Edmond Germain • Amantes de Vérone, Les	N	N
Gaztambide y Garbayo, Joaquin Romualdo • sueño de una noche de verano, El	N	N
Gazzaniga, Giuseppe • Equivoci, Gli	N	N
Gelber, Stanley Jay • Love and Let Love	M1503. G3155L72 1969	N
Genée, Franz Friedrich Richard and Louis Roth • Zwillinge		3722(R74)
Generali, Pietro Mercandetti • Rodrigo di Valencia	N	3761(R74)
Gerber, René • Roméo et Juliette	N	N
Gerl, Thaddäus; Henneberg and Benedikt Schack • Stein der Weisen, Der oder Die Zauberinsel	N	N
Gevel, Franz Xaver • Rinaldo und Camilla oder Die Zauberinsel	N	N
Ghislanzoni, Alberto • Re Lear	M1503.G452R3	N
Giannini, Vittorio • Taming of the Shrew, The	M 1503.G43T3 1954	N
Gibbs, Cecil Armstrong • Twelfth Night, Opus 115	N	N
Gilbert, James • Good Time Johnny	N	N
Glinka, Mikhail Ivanovitch • Hamlet	N	N
Gobatti, Stefano • Cordelia	N	3973(R79)
Goedicke, Alexander • Macbeth	N	N
Goetz, Herman • Widerspänstigen Zähmung, Der [La Megère apprivoisée; Caterina e Petruccio]	M1500.G61W5, etc.	3979(R79)
Goldman, Edward M. • Macbeth	N	N

COMPOSITION	US: Wc	Schatz
Goldmark, Carl • Wintermärchen, Ein	M1503.G621W5	N
Gossec, François Joseph • Hylas et Sylvie	N	N
Gounod, Charles François • Roméo et Juliette	M1500.G71R6, etc.	4049-51,56(R81)
Grandi, Alfredo • Amleto	N	N
Graun, Karl Heinrich • Coriolano	M1500.G76C65 Case	4093(R82)
Greenwall, Peter • Three Caskets, The or Venice Re-served	N	N
Grosheim, Georg Christoph • Titania, oder Liebe durch Zauberei	N	4215(R85)
Groth, Howard • Petruchio	N	N
Guglielmi, Pietro Alessandro • Admeto, Re di Tessaglia	N	4286(R87)
Guglielmi, Pietro Carlo • Romeo e Giulietta [I Capuletti ed i Montecchi]	N	N
Gulda, Friedrich • Maß für Maß	N	N
Haack, Friedrich • Geisterinsel, Die	N	N
Hába, Alois • Tempest	M1513.W45S6	N
Hahn, Reynaldo • Beaucoup de bruit pour rien	N	N
Hahn, Reynaldo • Malvina	M1503.H147M2	N
Hahn, Reynaldo • Marchand de Vénise, Le	M1503.H147M3/ ML50.HI48M2 1935	N
Haines, Roger • Fire Angel	N	N
Haines, Roger • Shylock [Fire Angel]	N	N
Hale, Alfred Matthew • Tempest, The	N	N
Halévy, Jacques François Fromental Elie • Guido et Ginevre ou La Peste de Florence	M1503.H168G7	N
Halévy, Jacques Franoçis Fromental Élie • Tempesta, La	M1503.H168T32	N

COMPOSITION	US: Wc	Schatz
Halpern, Sidney • Macbeth	N	N
Hamel, Eduard • Malvina	N	4450(R91)
Händel, Georg Friederich • Admeto, Re di Tessaglia	MUSIC 3558, Item Ia/b, etc.	N
Hanssens, J. F. J. • Gillette de Narbonne	N	N
Harbison, John • Winter's Tale, The	N	N
Harper, Wally • Sensations	N	N
Hart, Fritz Bennicke • Malvolio, Opus 14	N	N
Heinrich, Hermann • Viel Lärm um Nichts	N	N
Hensel, Johann Daniel • Geisterinsel, Die	N	4637(R96)
Hérold, Louis Joseph Ferdinand • Gioventù di Enrico V, La [La Jeunesse d'Henry V]	M1503.H564G5	N
Herx, Werner • Orakelspruch, Der	N	4691(R97)
Hess, Ludwig • Was ihr Wollt	N	N
Hester, Hal and Danny Apolinar • Your Own Thing	M1503.H594Y72 1968	N
Heuberger, Richard Franz Joseph • Viola	N	N
Heward, Leslie Hays • Hamlet	N	N
Hignard, Aristide • Hamlet	M1503.H638H2	N
Hignett, J. L. A. • Hamlet	N	N
Hirschbach, Hermann • Othello	N	N
Hoffmeister, Franz Anton • Rosalinde, oder Die Macht der Feen	M1503.H696R6 (Case)	N
Hoffmeister, Franz Anton • Schiffbruch, Der	N	N
Hofmann, Johann • Ritter Hans von Dampf	N	N
Hohmann, Gustav • Hermione, oder Der kleine Vicomte	N	N
Holenia, Hans • Viola, Opus 21 [Was Ihr wollt]	N	N
Holland, Jan David • Hamlet, Pantomime zu	N	N

COMPOSITION	US: Wc	Schatz
Holst, Gustav • At the Boar's Head, Opus 42	M1503.H751A6	N
Honegger, Arturo • Tempête, La	N	N
Hopp, Julius • Hammlet	N	4798(R99)
Horky, Karel • Jed z Elsinoru [The Poison from Elsinore]	N	N
Horn, Charles Edward, and Samuel Webbe Jr. • Merry Wives of Windsor	M1513.H77M3	N
Horner • König Lear		
Hüe, George • Titania	M1503.H887T5	N
Hughes, Gervase • Twelfth Night, Scenes from	N	N
Hulemann, Th • Malvine I re [The first]	N	N
Ivry, Paul Xaver Désiré Richard, Marquis d' • Amantes de Vérone, Les	M1503.I96A4	4946(R102)
Jakobowski, Edward • Erminie	M1503.J26E7	N
Jenkins, David • Enchanted Isle, The [Scenes from Shakespeare's 'Tempest']	M1533.J52S8	N
Jirko, Ivan • Twelfth Night, The [Vecer Trikralovy]	N	N
Johnson, Robert • Tempest, The	M1620.J72S6	N
Jommelli, Nicolo • Caio Mario [Cajo Mario]	M1500.J72C3	4896(R101)
Jones, Cliff • Rockabye Hamlet	N	N
Just, Johann August • marchand de Venise, Le [Koopman van Smyrna]	N	N
Kaffka [Kafka], Johann Christian • Antonius und Cleopatra	N	4772(R99) & 4981(R103)
Kagen, Sergius • Hamlet	M1503.K122H3 1962	N
Kalnins, Janis • Hamlets	N	N
Kanne, Friedrich August • Malvina, oder Putzerls Abenteuer		

COMPOSITION	US: Wc	Schatz
Kanne, Friedrich August • Miranda oder Das Schwert der Rache	Has overture	5002(R103)
Karel, Rudolf • Zkroceni zlé zeny [The Taming of the Shrew]	N	N
Kasanli, Nikolai Ivanovich [Kazanli, Kazanly] • Miranda (Poliedniaia bor'ba) [Der Letzte Kampf]	Mi503.K188M64 1908	N
Kashperov, Vladimir Nikititch • Storm, The [Groza]	N	N
Kaun, Hugo • Falstaff	N	N
Keurvels, Edward H. J. • Hamlet	N	N
Khrennikov, Tikhon Nikolaevich • Brati [Brothers]	M1503.K46V5 1954	N
Khrennikov, Tikhon Nikolaevich • Mnogo shuma iz nichego [Viel Lärm aus Leidenschaft, Much Ado About Hearts]	N	N
Khrennikov, Tikhon Nikolaevich • V buriu [Im Sturm, Into the Storm]		
Kipper, Herman • Perdita oder Das Rosenfest	N	N
Kirchner, Hermann • Viola	N	N
Klebe, Giselher Wolfgang • Ermordung Cäsars, Die Op. 32	M1503.K629E7	N
Kleinheinz, Carl Franz Xaver • Hamlet, Prinz vom Tandelmarkt	N	N
Koppel, Herman David • Macbeth, Op. 79	N	N
Kovarovic, Karel • Perdita	N	N
Krejcí, Isa • Pozdvizení v Efesu [The Upheaval in Ephesus]	M1503.K9187U6	N
Kreutz, Arthur • Sourwood Mountain	M1503.K926S72 1963	N

481

COMPOSITION	US: Wc	Schatz
Kreutzer, Conradin • Cordelia (Floretta ou La Folle de Glaris)[First named Adele von Budoy]	N	5250(R108)
Kreutzer, Rodolphe • Imogène, ou La Gageure indiscrète	N	N
Krohn, Max • Was ihr Wollt	N	N
Kuhlau, Friedrich Daniel Rudolph • Musik Til William Shakspeare [sic], Op. 74	M1004.K968	N
Kunz, [Konrad Max ?] • Tempest, The	N	N
Kunzen, Friedrich Ludwig Æmilius • Holger Danske oder Oberon [Holgar the Dane]	M1503.K966H6 (Case)	5321(R110)
Kunzen, Friedrich Ludwig Æmilius • Stormen	N	5330(R110)
Kurzbach, Paul • Romeo and Julia auf dem Lande	N	N
Küster, Johann Heinrich • Henrik den Fjerde	N	N
Kusterer, Arthur • Was ihr Wollt	ML50.K978W3 1932	N
La Rosa, Arturo • Otello	N	N
Lampe, John Frederick • Pyramus and Thisbe	M1500.L23P7 (Case)	N
Lattuada, Felice • Tempesta, La	M1503.L366T3	N
Lauer, Adolph L. [Freiherr von Münchofen] • Orakelspruch, Der	N	N
Laufer, B. • Shylock	N	N
Lavina, Vincenzo • Coriolano, Il	N	N
LaViolette, Wesley • Shylock	N	N
Le Rey, Frédéric • Mégère apprivoisée, La	M1503.L618M3	N
Lecocq, Charles Alexandre • Marjolaine	M1503.L464M2	5526(R114)
Legouix, Isidore Édouard • Othello, Un	M1503.L49907	N
Leichtling, Alan • Tempest, The	N	N
Leoncavallo, Ruggiero • Songe d'une nuit d'été, Un	N	N

COMPOSITION	US: Wc	Schatz
Leopold I, Holy Roman Emperor • Timòne, Misantropo	M2.A23 Band II (Excerpt)	N
Leukauf, Robert • Wintermärchen, Das	N	N
Leverage, Richard • Macbeth	N	N [but see Longe 271]
Leverage, Richard • Pyramus and Thisbe, The Comic Masque of	N	N [but see Longe 50]
Lichtenstein, Carl August Freiherr von • Ende gut, alles gut	N	N
Lillo, Giuseppe • Sogno d'una Notte estiva, Il or La Gioventù di Shakespeare	ML50.L693G5 1851 Case	N
Linley II, Thomas • Tempest, The or The Enchanted Island	M1513.D26T4	N
Liota, A. • Romeo and Juliet	N	N
Litolff, Henry Charles • König Lear	M1004.L78K5	N
Locke, Matthew and Robert Johnson • Macbeth	M1510.L82M42	N
Loder, Edward James • Robin Goodfellow or the Frolics of Puck	N	N
Logar, Mihovil • Four Scenes from Shakespeare	N	N
Lorenz, Carl Adolf • Komödie der Irrungen, Die	N	N
Ludwig, Otto • Romeo und Julie	N	N
Lueder, Florence Pauline • As You Like It	ML50.L945A7 1933	N
Lueder, Florence Pauline • Rosalind	N	N
Lutz, William Meyer • Merry-Go-Round	N	N
Macarig, Hector and Alfonso Deperis • Otello Tamburo	N	N
MacDermot, Galt • Cressida	N	N

COMPOSITION	US: Wc	Schatz
MacDermot, Galt • Two Gentlemen of Verona	M1503. M1344T932 1973	N
MacFarren, George Alexander • Hamlet	N	N
Machavariani, Alexei • Hamlet	N	N
Machavariani, Alexei • Othello	M1523.M198O8	N
Maclean, Alick • Petruccio	M1503.M163P3	N
Maganini, Giovanni • Enrico IV al passo della Marna	M1507.C73A6 [Excerpt]	5825(R120)
Maggioni, Francesco • Cajo Marzio Coriolano	N	N
Magni, Giuseppe Paolo • Admeto, Rè di Tessaglia	N	5839(R121)
Malamet, Marsha • Dreamstuff	N	N
Malipiero, Gian Francesco • Antonio e Cleopatra	M1503.M228A4	N
Malipiero, Gian Francesco • Giulio Cesare	M1503.M228G4	N
Malipiero, Gian Francesco • Romeo e Guilietta (scene 5 of Monde celesti e infernali)	M1503.M228M7	N
Mancinelli, Luigi • Sogno di una notte d'estate, Il	N	N
Manusardi, Giuseppe • sogno di Primavera, Un [Un rêve de printemps]	N	N
Marchetti, Filippo • Romeo e Giulietta	M1503.M317R6	5931(R122)
Marescalchi, Luigi • Giuletta e Romeo	N	N
Marescotti • Amleto	N	N
Maretzek, Maximilian • Hamlet	N	N
Marshall-Hall, George William Louis • Romeo and Juliet	M1503.H18R6	N
Martín y Soler, Vicente • Capricciosa corretta, La [So bessert sie sich]	M1503.M38C3 Case	6008(R124)
Martin, Frank • Sturm, Der	M1503.M376S8	N
Martini, Giovanni • Henri IV, ou La Bataille d'Ivry	M1500.M36H4	6039(R125)
Matuszczak, Bernadetta • Julia i Romeo	N	N

COMPOSITION	US: Wc	Schatz
Méhul, Étienne Nicolas • Jeune Henri, Le [Gabrielle d'Estrées où les Amours d'Henri IV]	M1500.M49G3	N
Meiners, Giambattista • Riccardo III	N	N
Mélésville, Honoré Marie Joseph, Baron Duveyrier] • Gillette de Narbonne	N	N
Membrée, Edmond • Roméo et Juliette	N	N
Mercadal y Pons, Antonio • Giulietta e Romeo	N	N
Mercadante, Giuseppe Saverio Raffele • Amleto	N	6312(R130)
Mercadante, Giuseppe Saverio Raffele • Gioventù di Enrico V, La	N	6337(R131)
Mercadante, Giuseppe Saverio Raffele • Violetta	N	6369(R131)
Michaelis, Gustave • Lustigen Weiber von Berlin, Die	N	6477(R134)
Michaelis, Gustave • Othello in Kyritz	N	N
Missa, Edmond Jean Louis • Dinah	M1503.M688D5	N
Mohaupt, Richard • Double Trouble [Zwillingskomödie]	M1503.M7D7	N
Mohr, Hermann • Orakelspruch, Der Op. 50	M1503.M71507	6546(R135)
Mojsisovics, Roderich • Viel Lärm um Nichts	N	N
Molchanov, Kiril Vladimirovich • Romeo, Dzhulyetta i t'ma [Romeo, Juliet and Darkness]		N
Monza, Carlo Antonio • Cajo Mario		
Morales, Melesio • Giulietta e Romeo	N	N
Morera, Enrique • Fiercilla domada, La	N	N
Morlacchi, Francesco Giuseppi Baldassare • Capricciosa pettita, La	N	6644(R137)

COMPOSITION	US: Wc	Schatz
Morlacchi, Francesco Giuseppi Baldassare • Gioventù di Enrico V, La [Das Jugendjahre Heinrich des Fünften]	N	6655(R137)
Moroni, Luigi • Amleto	N	6677(R137)
Morton, David • Tempest in a Teapot	ML50.M8767T4 Case	N
Morton, Louise, and others • Twelfth Night	M1513.M86T8	N
Mosca, Giuseppe • Gioventù di Enrico V, La	N	6699(R138)
Mozart, Wolfgang Amadeus • Peines d'amour perdues	N	N
Mulcahy, Lance • Shakespeare's Cabaret	N	N
Müller (the elder), Adolph • Heinrich IV	N	N
Müller (the elder), Adolph • Othellerl, der Mohr von Wien [Die geheilte Eifersucht]	M1508 (Selections)	N
Müller (the elder), Adolph • Viel Lärm um Nichts	N	N
Müller, Wenzel • Sturm oder die Zauberinsel, Der	N	6967(R144)
Mullins, Hugh • Romeo and Juliet	N	N
Mussorgsky, Modest Petrovich • Hamlet	N	N
Nabokov, Nikolai • Love's Labour's Lost [Verlor'ne Liebesmüh']	N	N
Nápravnik, Éduard Frantsevich • Sturm, Der	N	N
Navoigille, Gouliellmo • Orage, L' ou Quel Guignon!	N	N
Nesvera, Josef • Perdita	N	N
Nicolai, Carl Otto Ehrenfried • lustigen Weiber von Windsor, Die	M1503.N637L84	7106-7(R147)
Nicolini, Giuseppe • Coriolano	N	7125(R147)
Nieto, Manuel • Otelo y Desdémona	N	N

COMPOSITION	US: Wc	Schatz
Noël, Édouard Marie Émile • songe d'une nuit d'été, Le	N	N
Oddone, Elizabetta • Petruccio e il Cavolo Cappuccio	M1503.O19P3	N
Offenbach, Jacques • Rêve d'une Nuit d'été, Le	N	N
Old, John • Herne the Hunter (A Legend of Royal Windsor)	M1503.O45H3	N
Orff, Carl • Sommernachtstraum, Ein	M1510.O	N
Orlandi, Ferdinando • Rodrigo di Valencia	N	7313(R151)
Pacini, Giovanni • Gioventù di Enrico V, La (also La bella tavernara; Le Aventure d'una notte)	M1500.P13G6 (Case)	7418(R153)
Pacini, Giovanni • Rodrigo di Valencia	N	N
Palliardi, Carl • Stein der Weisen, Der	N	N
Papavoine, Mdme • Vieux Coquet, Le; ou Les deux amies ou Le vieus garçon	N	N
Pasquali, Nicolò • Romeo and Juliet	N	N
Pedrell, Filipe • Roi Lear, Le	N	N
Perelli, Edoardo • Viola Pisani	N	N
Perosi, Lorenzo • Romeo and Juliet	N	N
Persico, Mario • Bisbetica Domata, La	M1503.P472B4/ M50.D4685B6 1929	N
Perti, Giacomo Antonio • Martio Coriolano	N	7957(R164)
Philidor • Herne le Chasseur	N	N
Piccini, Louis Alexandre • Macbeth	N	N
Piccinni, Niccolò • Caio Mario		
Pillaut, Léon • Perdita	M1503.P642P4	N
Pinsuti, Ciro • Mercante di Venezia, Il	M1503.P658M4	8184(R169)
Pless, Hans • Macbeth	N	N

COMPOSITION	US: Wc	Schatz
Podestà, Carlo • Ero, ossia Molto rumore per nulla	N	N
Pogodin • King Lear?	N	N
Pohlig, Carl • Stein der Weisen, Der	N	N
Pollaroli, Carlo Francesco • Marzio Coriolano	N	8303(R171)
Porta, [Bernardo ?] • Roméo et Juliette	N	N
Porter, Cole • Kiss Me, Kate	M1503. P846K5 1951a	N
Pride [sp?], G. • Otello	N	N
Prokofiev, Sergei • Hamlet, Music to the Tragedy by Shakespeare	M1513.P9H32	N
Puget, Paul-Charles-Marie • Beaucoup de bruit pour rien	N [NUC says yes.]	N
Pulli, Pietro • Caio Marzio Coriolano	N	8513(R175)
Purcell, Henry • Fairy Queen, The	See Collected Works	N
Purcell, Henry • History of Timon of Athens, the Man Hater, The	See Collected Works	N
Purcell, Henry • Tempest or Enchanted Island, The	M1510.P98T3 Case	N
Radicati, Felice Alessandro • Coriolano, II	N	N
Radó, Aladár • Shylock	N	N
Rafael, Carl Friedrich • Hamlet, Prinz von Liliput	N	N
Raphling, Sam • Prince Hamlet	N	N
Rateau, Edmond • Rosaline	N	N
Raymond, Édouard • Sturm, Der	N	N
Reichardt, Johann Friedrich • Geisterinsel, Die	M1503.R58G3 Case	8641(R178)
Reichardt, Johann Friedrich • Macbeth	M1513.R32M3 Case	N
Reimann, Aribert • Lear	M1503.R365L4 (Case)	N
Reutter, Hermann • Hamlet	M1500.R447H3	N

COMPOSITION	US: Wc	Schatz
Reynaud, Armand • Roi Lear, Le	N	N
Rintel, Wilhelm • Was ihr Wöllt	N	N
Riotte, Philipp Jakob • Orakelspruch, Der	N	N
Riotte, Philipp Jakob • Sturm, Der oder Die Insel des Prospero	N	N
Ritter, Peter • lustigen Weiber, Die	ML96.R5A7	8825(R181)
Ritter, Peter • Sturm, Der oder Die bezauberte Insel	N	8831(R181)
Rogers, Richard • Boys from Syracuse, The	M1503.684B72 1965	N
Rolle, Johann Heinrich • Sturm oder Die bezauberte Insel, Der	N	N
Rosellin, Léon • Juliette et Roméo	N	N
Rosenberg, Richard • Liebesspiel, Das	N	N
Rossi, Lauro • Biorn	N	N
Rossini, Gioacchino • Ermione	N	N
Rossini, Gioacchino • Otello, osia L'Africano di Venezia	M1500.R86O74	9016-7 (R184); 18-23(R185)
Roters, Ernest • Hamlet, Op. 145	ML50.R844H3 1957 Case	N
Roti, Ugo • Sogno di una notte d'estate, Il	N	N
Ruben, Paul • Edit royal, L'	N	N
Rubens, Paul Alfred and Frank E. Tours • Dairymaids, The	M1508.R	N
Rubens, Paul Alfred and Walter Rubens • Great Caesar	N	N
Rumling, Sigismund Freiherr von • Roméo et Juliette	N	N
Rung, Henrik • Stormen paa København [Storm over Copenhagen]	N	N
Saint-Saëns, Camille • Henry VIII	M1503.S155H5	N

COMPOSITION	US: Wc	Schatz
Salieri, Antonio • Falstaff osia Le tre Burle	M1503.S15F3	9289-90 (R190)
Salmhofer, Franz • King Lear	N	N
Salvayre, Gaston • Beaucoup de bruit pour rien	N	N
Salvayre, Gaston • Riccardo III	M1503.S18R5	9345(R191)
Samara, Spiro • Furia domata, La	N	N
San Severino • Romeo e Giuletta	N	N
Santa Caterina, Alessandro • Coriolano	N	9392 (R192)
Sarria, Errico • Equivoci, Gli	N	N
Saussine, Henri de • Marchand de Vénise, Le	M1503.S258M3	N
Savigna, Vincenzo • Coriolano	N	N
Savini, Giacomo • Tempeste	N	N
Sayn-Wittgenstein-Berleburg, Count Friedrich Ernst von • Antonius und Kleopatra	M1503.S275A5	9510(R194)
Scarlatti, Giuseppe • Caio Mario		
Scarlatti, Giuseppe Domenico • Ambleto	N	N
Schindelmeisser, Louis Alexander Balthasar • Malvina	N	N
Schmitz, Alan • Julius Caesar	N	N
Schneider, Georg Abraham • Orakelspruch, Der	N	9669(197)
Schönfeld, Georg • Falstaff	N	N
Schuster, Ignaz • Hamlet, Prinz vom Tandelmarkt	N	9737(R199)
Schuster, Ignaz • Othellerl, der Mohr von Wien	N	N
Schuster, Ignaz • Romeo und Julie	N	9740(R199)
Schwanenberg, Johann Gottfried • Romeo e Giulia	ML50.2.R67	9766(R199)
Scognamilio, Gennaro • Otello ossia Catiello l'Affricano	N	N
Scolari, Giuseppe • Cajo Mario		
Searle, Humphrey • Hamlet, Opus 48	M1503.S44H32	N
Séméladis, M. • Cordélia	N	N

COMPOSITION	US: Wc	Schatz
Serov, Alexander Nikolayevich • Merry Wives of Windsor		N
Serpette, Henri Charles Antoine Gaston • Shakespeare!	M1503.S486S4	N
Serpette, Henri Charles Antoine Gaston • Songe d'une nuit d'été, Le		
Shebalin, Vissarion Yakovlevich • Ukroshchenie stroptivoi [The Taming of the Shrew] Op. 46	M1500.S55U47 Case/ M1503. S542U47	N
Shelley, Harry Rowe • Romeo and Juliet	M1503.S545R6	N
Shenshin, Aleksandr Alexseivich • Twelfth Night	N	N
Siegmeister, Elie • Night of the Moonspell	N	N
Silver, Charles • Mégère apprivoisée, La	M1503.S57M3	N
Silverman, Stanley • Midsummer Night's Dream, A	N	N
Slade, Julian • Comedy of Errors	N	N
Smetana, Bedrich • Viola	M1503.S626C32	N
Smith, John Christopher • Fairies, The	MUSIC 3195	N
Smith, John Christopher • Rosalinda	N	N[but see ML 50.2.R72] (Couldn't Find)
Smith, John Christopher • Tempest, The	MUSIC 3195	N[but see Longe 198]
Sobolewski, Friedrich Eduard de • Imogéne	N	N
Soloviev, Nicolai Feopemptovich • Cordélia	N	9954(R203)
Soule, Charles Caroll • Travesty Without a Pun.	N	N
Stadtfeldt, Christian Joseph Franz Alexandre • Hamlet	N	10020(R204)

COMPOSITION	US: Wc	Schatz
Stanford, Sir Charles Villiers • Much Ado About Nothing, Opus 76a	M1503.S79M8	10028(R204)
Stegmann, Carl David • Macbeth	N	N
Steibelt, Daniel Gottlieb • Roméo et Juliette or Tout pour l'amour	MUSIC 3704	N[but see ML 50.2R68 S8 and ML50.2. 2R68S82]
Steinkühler, Émile • Cäsario, oder die Verwechslung, Op. 30	N	N
Storace, Stephen • Equivoci, Gli	MUSIC 3708	10079-80 (R205)
Storch, Anton Maria • Romeo und Julie	N	10088(R205)
Storch, Anton Maria • Stein der Weisen, Der	N	N
Stransky, Josef • Béatrice et Bénédict	N	N
Strungk, Nicolaus Adam • Rosalinde	N	N
Stuart, Leslie • Belle of Mayfair	M1503.S934B3	N
Stuntz, Joseph Hartmann • Heinrich IV zu Givry	N	10130(R206)
Sulek, Stjepan • Koriolan	N	N
Sulek, Stjepan • Oluja	N	N
Suppé, Franz von • Sommernachtstraum, Der	M1060.S P [Orchestra parts]	N
Sutermeister, Heinrich • Romeo und Julia	M1503.S975R6	N
Sutermeister, Heinrich • Zauberinsel, Die	M1503.S975Z3	N
Szokolay, Sándor • Hamlet	M1503. S9936H35	N
Sztojanovics, Eug. • Otello mecél	N	N
Taboida, Ant. Sanchez do Cunha • Dinah	N	N
Tajon, Ben. • Taming of a Shrew, The	N	N

COMPOSITION	US: Wc	Schatz
Taubert, Carl Gottfried Wilhelm • Cesario, oder Was ihr wollt, Op. 188	M1503.T22C4	10242(R208)
Taubert, Wilhelm • Macbeth, Op. 133	M1503.T22M2	10245(R208)
Taubmann, Otto • Porzia	M1503.T226P6	N
Thomas, Charles Louis Ambroise • Hamlet	M1503.T453H2/ ML50.T453H2 1869	10321-3 (R209)
Thomas, Charles Louis Ambroise • Songe d'une nuit d'été, Le [Shakespeare oder Der Traum einer Sommernacht]	M1503.T453S6/ 2296.B.27.	10335-6 (R210)
Thomé, François Lucien Joseph • Roméo et Juliette	N	N
Thul, Franz von • Hermione	N	N
Tiessen, Heinz • Cymbelin	Song out of ML5.M18	N
Tommasi, Ferdinando [Tommaso] • Guido e Ginevre	N	10361(R210)
Torriani, Eugenio • Romeo e Giulietta	N	10369(R210)
Treu, Daniel Gottlieb • Coriolano	N	N
Tuczek, Vincenc Tomas Vaclav • Travestirte Hamlet, Der [Hamlet, Prinz von Dänemark; Hamlet, Prinz von Lilyput]	N	10506(R213)
Turok, Paul H. • Richard III	N	N
Unknown • Bezähmte Widerbellerin, Die	N	N
Unknown • Catch My Soul	N	N
Unknown • Catherine and Petruchio	N	N
Unknown • Cure for a Scold, A	PR1241.L6 Vol. 275, No. 4	N
Unknown • Early Reign of Oleg, The	N	N
Unknown • Pulcinella rivale di Turzillo e confuso tra Capuleti e Montecchi	N	N
Unknown • Schipbreuk	N	N

COMPOSITION	US: Wc	Schatz
Unknown • Thimon le misantrope	N	N
Unknown • Timon in Love or The Innocent Theft	N	N
Urich, Jean • Orage, L'	M1503.U76O7	N
Urspruch, Anton • Sturm, Der	M1503.U82S7	10543(R213)
Utley, Wendell • Will	N	N
Vaccai, Nicola • Giulietta e Romeo	MUSIC 3735/M1503.V 117G5	10555(R214)
Vaccai, Nicola • Malvina	Music 3735 Vol. I, Item 1	10556(R214)
Valenti, Michael • Oh, Brother	M1503.V16204	N
Valverde y San Juan, Joaquín • sueño de una noche de verano, El	N	N
Van Heusen, Jimmy • Swingin' the Dream		NA
Vaughan Williams, Ralph • Sir John in Love	M1503.W725S5	N
Veracini, Francesco Maria • Rosalinda	MUSIC 3738	N
Verdi, Giuseppe • Falstaff	M1503.V484F26	10645-7 (R215)
Verdi, Giuseppe • Lear	N	N
Verdi, Giuseppe • Macbeth	M1503.V484M2	10661(R215)-10662 (R216)
Verdi, Giuseppe • Otello	M1503.V484O7	10670-1 (R216)
Vidal, Paul Antonin • Comme il vous Plaire	N	N
Vidal, Paul Antonin • Peines d'amour perdues	N	N
Vignali, Giuseppe [Act I]; Carlo Baglioni [Act II] and Giacomo Cozzi [Act III] • Ambleto	N	N
Volder, Piere Jean de • Jeunesse de Henri Cinq, La	N	N
Vranicky, Pavel • Oberon, König der Elfen	N	11112(225)

COMPOSITION	US: Wc	Schatz
Vranicky, Pavel • Rudolf von Felseck (Die Schwarzthaler) oder La Tempestà	N	N
Vreuls, Victor • Songe d'une nuit d'été, Un	M1004.V93S6	N
Wagner, Wilhelm Richard • Liebesverbot, Das oder Die Novize von Palermo	M3.W13	N
Walton, Sir William • Troilus and Cressida	M1503.W238T7	N
Ware, William Henry • Cymbeline	N	N
Ware, William Henry • Macbeth	1513.L82M24	N
Weber, Carl Maria von • Euryanthe	M1503.W363E8	10888(R220)
Weber, Carl Maria von • Oberon [or the Elf-King's Oath]	M1503.W363O22	10899-904 (R220)
Weckerlin, Jean Baptiste Théodore • Tout est bien qui finit bien	N	N
Weigl, Joseph [Veigl, Giuseppe] • Amleto	N	N
Weis, Karél • Comme il vous Plaira	N	N
Weis, Karél • Viola [Die Zwillinge, Blizenci]	N	10981(R222)
Weisgall, Hugo • Gardens of Adonis, The	N	N
Weisgall, Hugo • Henry IV		NA
Westerhout, Niccolò van • Cimbelino, II	N	N
Weyse, Christoph Ernst Friedrich • Macbeth	N	N
Whitaker, John • Weird Sisters, The or The Thane and the Throne	N	N
Wiedeke, Adolf • lustigen Weiber von Hamburg, Die		
Wilson, James • Twelfth Night	N	N
Winter, Peter von • Sturm, Der	N	N
Wödl, Franz • Komödie der Irrungen	N	N

COMPOSITION	US: Wc	Schatz
Wolf, Ernst Wilhelm • Zauberirrungen, Die [Die Irrtümer der Zauberei]	N	N
Wolf-Ferrari, Ermanno • Sly, ovvero La leggenda del dormiente risvegliato	M1503.W865S5	N
Wolfurt, Kurt von • Porzia	N	N
Zafred, Mario • Amleto	N	N
Zajc, Ivan • Cordelia	N	N
Zák, Benedict Emanuel • Stein der Weisen, Dem oder Die Zauber Insel	N	9570(R196)
Zanardini, Angelo • Amleto	N	N
Zandonai, Riccardo • Giulietta e Romeo	M1503.Z28G4/ ML50.Z28G4 1927	N
Zanettini, Antonio • Érmione [Die wiedergefundene Hermione]	N	N
Zanon, Antonio B. • Leggenda di Giulietta, La	N	N
Zavodsky, Felix • Othello	N	N
Zelinka, Jan Evangelista • Spring With Shakespeare	N	N
Ziani, Marc Antonio • Rosalinda, La or Erginia mascherata	N	11210(R227)
Zillig, Winfried • Troilus und Cressida	N	N
Zimmermann, Balduin • Wintermärchen, Ein	N	11235(R227)
Zingarelli, Niccolò Antonio • Giulietta e Romeo	M1500.Z77G4	11247-9,71 (R228)
Zirra, Alexandru • Furtuna [TheTempest]		
Zumsteeg, Johann Rudolf • Geisterinsel, Die	M1503.Z95G3 (Case)	11294(R229)

SORTING BY BRITISH LIBRARY

COMPOSITION	GB:Lbm
Acker, Jean Van den • Romeo en Marielle [Tout pour l'amour]	N
Adam, Adolphe-Charles • Falstaff	N
Adler, Richard • Music Is	N
Alexandre, Charles Guillaume • Georget et Georgette	H.509./11735.d.2.
Alfano, Franco • Miranda	N
Aliabiev, Alexander • Storm, The	N
Aliabiev, Alexander • Volshebnaya noch	N
Allegra, Giuseppe • Sogno di una Notte, Il	N
Alpaerts, Florent • Shylock	N
Amram, David • Twelfth Night	N
André, Johann • König Lear	N
André, Johann • Macbeth	N
Andreozzi, Gaetano • Amleto	N
Andrews, John Charles Bond- • Herne's Oak, or The Rose of Windsor [also Herne the Hunter]	N
Anfossi, Pasquale • Cajo Mario	
Angelis, Arturo de • Tempesta, La	N
Angyal, Lázló • Tempest, The	N
Ansell, John • King's Bride, The [Violette]	F.688.I.(1.)/ 11779.ee.6.
Antoine, Ferdinand d' • Ende gut, alles gut oder Der Fürst und sein Volk	
Ardin, Leon • Antony and Cleopatra	N
Arensen, Adolf • Viola	N
Argento, Dominick • Christopher Sly	G.1273.t.(2.)
Ariosti, Attilio • Coriolano, II	N/ 162.g.36.
Arne, Michael and C. Dibdin, J. Battishill, C. Burney, Hook, J. C. Smith • Fairy Tale	D.268.(3.)
Arne, Thomas Augustine • Fairy Prince, The	D.263.(3.)/ 841.c.13.(2.)
Arne, Thomas Augustine • Tempest, The	G.1243.
Arne, Thomas Augustine, Samuel Arnold and others • Sheep-Shearing, The or Florizel and Perdita	N
Arundell, Dennis Drew • Midsummer Night's Dream, A	N
Aspa, Mario • Gioventù di Enrico V, La	N
Asplmayr [Aspelmayr], Franz • Sturm, Der	N

497

COMPOSITION	GB:Lbm
Asplmayr, Franz • Leben und Tod des Königs Macbeth	N
Atherton, Percy Lee and Ernest Hamlin Abbott • Hamlet, Prince of Denmark or The Sport, the Spook and the Spinster	N
Atterberg, Kurt • Stormen, Op. 49	N
Attwood, Thomas • Hermione, or Valour's Triumph	
Audran, Edmond • Gillette de Narbonne [Gillette, or Count and Countess; Gilda di Guascogna]	F.711.e./ 11740.e.15.(7.)
Aylward, Theodore • Midsummer Night's Dream, A	N
Baeyens, August Louis • Coriolanus	N
Balamos, John • As You Like It	N
Balfe, Michael William • Enrico IV al passo della Marna	N
Balfe, Michael William • Falstaff	G.252.
Banister, John; Giovanni Battista Draghi; Matthew Locke; Pelham Humfrey; and Pietro Reggio • Tempest, The [The Enchanted Island]	N/ 11762.e.14
Barber, Samuel • Antony and Cleopatra, Op. 40	G. 1404.b.
Barbieri, Carlo Emanuele di • Perdita oder Ein Wintermärchen	N/ 11765.aa.9.(1.)
Barkworth, John Edmond • Romeo and Juliet	G.1093.a.
Barry, H. C. • Shylock or The Venus of Venice	N
Beck, Curt • König Lear	N
Bedford, Herbert • Love Scene from Shakespeare's Romeo and Juliet for Contralto and Baritone	N
Beecham, Adrian Wells • Love's Labour's Lost [Peines d'Amour Perdues]	G.1043.b.
Beecham, Adrian Wells • Merchant of Venice, The	G.1043.
Beer-Walbrunn, Anton • Sturm, Der	N
Bellini, Vincenzo • Capuleti e i Montecchi, I	E.143.o./ 11714.aa.38.(4.)
Benda, George Anton • Romeo und Julie	F.98.g./ 11746.bbb.29.
Bentoiu, Pascal • Hamlet, Op. 18	N

COMPOSITION	GB:Lbm
Benvenuti, Tommaso • Guglielmo Shakespeare	N
Berens, Johann Hermann • Riccardo	N
Berens, Johann Hermann • Sommarnattsdröm, En	N
Berens, Johann Hermann • Violetta	N
Berény, Henri • Wintermärchen, Das	N
Berlioz, Hector • Béatrice et Bénédict	E.175./ 11736.h.25.
Berlioz, Hector • Hamlet	N
Bernabei, Giuseppe Antonio • Érmione	N
Bernabei, Vincenzo • Equivoci d'Amore, Gli	N
Bernstein, Leonard • West Side Story	G.760.oo.(2.)
Berton, Henri-Montan • Montano et Stéphanie	H.625./ 11738.dd.20. (10.)
Bertoni, Ferdinando Giuseppe • Cajo Mario	
Besoyan, Rick • Babes in the Wood, or Who Killed Cock Robin	N
Bianchi, Francesco • Cajo Mario	
Bishop, Sir Henry Rowley • Antony and Cleopatra	
Bishop, Sir Henry Rowley • As You Like It	H.159.j.(1.)
Bishop, Sir Henry Rowley • Comedy of Errors, The	
Bishop, Sir Henry Rowley • Henri Quatre [Paris in the Olden Times]	H.159.c.(3.)/ 11779.c.68.
Bishop, Sir Henry Rowley • Merry Wives of Windsor, The	
Bishop, Sir Henry Rowley • Midsummer Night's Dream, A	H.160.b.
Bishop, Sir Henry Rowley • Tempest, The	
Bishop, Sir Henry Rowley • Twelfth Night	H.159.e.(3.)
Bishop, Sir Henry Rowley • Two Gentlemen of Verona, The	H.159.g.(2.)
Bizet, Georges • Hamlet	N
Bizet, Georges • Macbeth	N
Blacher, Boris • Romeo und Julia	G.1286.a.(1.)
Bloch, Ernest • Macbeth	G.1049/ 11764.P.13
Bondeville, Emmanuel de • Antonine et Cléopatre	N
Borodcicz, Hans von • König Lear	

COMPOSITION	GB:Lbm
Bossi, Renzo • Volpino il Calderaio, Op. 32	N
Bottacio, Pietro • Bisbetica Domata, La	N
Boughton, Rutland • Againcourt	E.1510.c.(2.)
Boyce, William • Florizel and Perdita	N
Brandauer, Hermann • Caesario	N
Brawn, Geoffrey • At the Sign of the Angel or A Little Touch of Harry in the Night	N
Britten, Lord Edward Benjamin • Midsummer Night's Dream, A, Op. 64	H.2472.z.
Bruce, Neely • Pyramus and Thisbe	N
Bruch, Max • Hermione, Op. 40	H.641.a./ 11765.aa.43.(5.)
Brumagne, Fernand • Marchand de Venise, Le	N
Busby, Thomas • Fair Fugitives	N
Buzzolla, Antonio • Amleto	E.28./11765.ee.9. (2.)
Cagnoni, Antonio • Re Lear, Il	F.507.b.
Caldara, Antonio • Cajo Marzio Coriolano	N
Campenhout, François van • Gillette de Narbonne	N
Campo y Zabaleta, Conrado del • Amantes de Verona, Los	N
Canepá, Luigi • Riccardo III	N
Canonica, Pietro • Miranda	N
Capelli, Giovanni Maria • Rosalinda [Erginia Mascherata]	N
Carafa di Colobrano, Michele Enrico and Aimé Ambroise Simon Leborne • Violette, La ou Gérard de Nevers	H.571.b.
Carcani, Giuseppe • Ambleto	N
Carl, M. • Julius Caesar	
Carlini, Luigi • Gioventù di Enrico V, La	N
Carlson, Charles Frederick • Merchant of Venice	N
Carr, Frank Osmond • In Town	F. 128.b.(3.)
Caruso, Lodovico Luigi • Amleto	N
Caruso, Lodovico Luigi • Tempesta, La	N
Castelnuovo-Tedesco, Mario • Mercante di Venezia, Il, Op. 181	H.2433.
Castelnuovo-Tedesco, Mario • Tutto e bène quello che finisce bène, Op. 182	N
Cattani, Lorenzo • Cajo Marzio Coriolano	N/905.k.3.(4.)

COMPOSITION	GB:Lbm
Cavalli, Pietro Francesco • Coriolano	N
Chapí y Lorente, Ruperto • Tempestad, La	H.780.h.(2.)
Chatburn, Tom • Gay Venetians, The	N
Chélard, Hippolyte-André-Jean-Baptiste • Macbeth	E.959./ 11740.g.30.(4.)
Chignell, Robert • Romeo and Juliet	N
Choudens, Antony • Cymbeline	N
Cikker, Ján • Coriolanus	G.1274.I.
Cimarosa, Domenico Nicola [Cimmarosa] • Cajo Mario	
Clapp, Philip Greeley • Taming of the Shrew, The	N
Clarke, James Siree Hamilton • Merchant of Venice	F.1208.a.(1.)
Clarke, Jeremiah • Titus Andronicus	N
Claudric, Jean • Othello Story	N
Collingwood, Lawrance Arthur • Macbeth	N
Conte, Paolo • Shakespeare, the Playmaker	N
Conti, Nicolò • Cajo Marzio Coriolano [Marzio Coriolano]	N
Cooke, Thomas Simpson • Malvina	H.84.(1.)/642.a.18
Cooke, Thomas Simpson • Oberon, or The Charmed Horn	N
Cooke, Thomas Simpson and Braham, John and Others • Taming of the Shrew, The	N
Costa, Michael Andrew Angus • Malvina	
Cottrau, Giulio • Cordelia (Re Lear)	G.691.d.(3.)
Cottrau, Giulio • Pericle re di Tiro	H.1614.c.
Crescentini, Girolamo • Roméo et Juliette	N
Cribari, Donna • Pop	N
Daffner, Hugo • Macbeth	N
Dalayrac, Nicolas • Tout pour l'amour ou Roméo et Juliette	N
Damrosch, Leopold • Romeo und Julia	N
Danzi, Franz • Malvina [Die Wolfsjagd]	
David, Adolphe Isaac • Orage, L'	N
David, Félicien César • Saphir, Le or Tout est bien, qui finit bien	F.111.g./11739. bb.11.(7.)
De Boeck, Auguste de • Winternachtsdroom, Een	N
De Filippi, Amadeo • Malvolio	N
Debussy, Claude • As You Like It	N
Deffès, Louis Pierre • Jessica	N

COMPOSITION	GB:Lbm
Déjazet, Eugène • Rhum et eau en juillet	N
Del Fante, Raffaele • Tempesta, La	N
Delannoy, Marcel • Puck	N
Delius, Frederick • Romeo und Juliet auf dem Dorfe [A Village Romeo and Juliet]	H.600.d.
Didam, Otto • Julia und Romeo	N
Dittersdorf, Carl Ditters von • lustigen Weiber von Windsor und der dicke Hans, Die	N
Doppler, Arpád • Viel Lärm um Lichts	N
Doubrava, Jaroslav • Sen noci svatojanske	N
Douglas, Hugh A. • Romeo and Juliet Up to Larks	F.1257.y.(1.)
Draghi, Antonio • Timone misantropo	N
Durme, Jef Van • Anthony and Cleopatra	N
Durme, Jef Van • King Lear	N
Durme, Jef Van • Richard III	N
Duvernoy, Victor-Alphonse • Tempète, La	F.1220./11763. df.6.(4.)
Duyse, Florimond Van • Rosalinde	N
Eastwood, Thomas Hugh • Christopher Sly	N
Eberlin, Johann Ernst • Ricardus Impius, Angliae Rex, ab Henrico Richmondæ Comite vita simul et regno excitus	N
Eberwein, Max Carl • Romeo und Julie	N
Eggen, Arne • Cymbelyn	N
Emery, Charles P. • Romeo, the Radical or Obstruction and Effect	N
Emmert, Adam Joseph • Sturm, Der	N
Engelmann, Hans Ulrich • Ophelia, Op. 36	N
Engländer, Ludwig • Belle of Bohemia, The	
Erbse, Heimo • Julietta, Op. 15	
Fabrizi, Vincenzo • Tempestà ossia Da un disordine ne nasce un ordine, La	N
Faccio, Franco • Amleto	H.426.a. [selections]
Falk, Richard • Was ihr Wollt	N
Farina, Guido • Dodisesima Notte, La	N
Faris, Alexander • R Loves J	N
Farwell, Arthur George • Caliban by the Yellow Sands, Opus 47	N
Feigerl, R. • Stein der Weisen, Der	N
Ferraboso II, Alfonso and Robert Johnson • Oberon, the Fairy Prince	N

COMPOSITION	GB:Lbm
Ferroni, Vencenzo Emidio Carmine • Romeo and Juliet	N
Fibich, Zdenko • Boure, Opus 40 [Der Sturm]	H.747.c.
Field, Graham • Dick Deterred	N
Fioravanti, Valentino • Capricciosa pentita, La	
Fioravanti, Valentino • Enrico IV al passo della Marna	N
Fischer, Jan F. • Romeo, Julie a tma (Romeo, Juliet and Darkness)	G.1268.kk.
Fisher, John Abraham • Macbeth	N
Fleischmann, Friedrich • Geisterinsel, Die	N
Flotow, Friedrich von • Wintermärchen, Ein	N
Foerster, Joseph Brohuslav • Jessika, Opus 60	G.1273.aa.
Foignet, Jacques • Orage, L'	N
Folprecht, Zdenek • Lásky hra osudná [The Fateful Game of Love], Opus 3	N
Fontmichel, Hippolyte Honoré Joseph Court de (1799-?) • Amleto	N
Forest, Jean Kurt • Hamlet	N
Francastel, A. • Henry IV	N
Frank, Ernst • Sturm, Der	N
Frank, Johann Wolfgang • Timon	N
Frazzi, Vito • Re Lear	D.324.
Freitas Gazul, Francisco de • Violetas, As	N
Freschi, Giovanni Domenico • Rosalinda	N
Freudenberg, Wilhelm • Kleopatra	N
Fribec, Kresimir • Romeo and Juliet	N
Gallenberg, Wenzel Robert Count von • Amleto	N
Galuppi, Baldassarre • Enrico	G.190.(2.)/ 904.i.4.(3.)
Galuppi, Baldassarre [called Buranello] • Cajo Mario	
Garcia, Manuel Vincente del Popolo • Gioventù di Enrico V, La	N
Garcia, Manuel Vincente del Popolo • Giulietta e Romeo	N
Gasperini, Carlo Francesco • Ambleto	H.114.(1.)[songs]/ 11764.bb.47.
Gasperini, Carlo Francesco • Equivoci d'amore e d'innocenza, Gl'	N
Gatty, Nicholas Comyn • Macbeth	N

COMPOSITION	GB:Lbm
Gatty, Nicholas Comyn • Tempest, The	F.943.h.(1.)
Gaujac, Edmond Germain • Amantes de Vérone, Les	N
Gaztambide y Garbayo, Joaquin Romualdo • sueño de una noche de verano, El	N
Gazzaniga, Giuseppe • Equivoci, Gli	N
Gelber, Stanley Jay • Love and Let Love	N
Genée, Franz Friedrich Richard and Louis Roth • Zwillinge	11746.bb.15.(5.)
Generali, Pietro Mercandetti • Rodrigo di Valencia	N
Gerber, René • Roméo et Juliette	N
Gerl, Thaddäus; Henneberg and Benedikt Schack • Stein der Weisen, Der oder Die Zauberinsel	N
Gevel, Franz Xaver • Rinaldo und Camilla oder Die Zauberinsel	N
Ghislanzoni, Alberto • Re Lear	H.230.ss.
Giannini, Vittorio • Taming of the Shrew, The	F.1267.hh.(1.)
Gibbs, Cecil Armstrong • Twelfth Night, Opus 115	N
Gilbert, James • Good Time Johnny	N
Glinka, Mikhail Ivanovitch • Hamlet	
Gobatti, Stefano • Cordelia	N
Goedicke, Alexander • Macbeth	N
Goetz, Herman • Widerspänstigen Zähmung, Der [La Megère apprivoisée; Caterina e Petruccio]	E.35./11745. de.11.(10.)
Goldman, Edward M. • Macbeth	N
Goldmark, Carl • Wintermärchen, Ein	G719.c.
Gossec, François Joseph • Hylas et Sylvie	N
Gounod, Charles François • Roméo et Juliette	F.126.dd./11765. aaa.30.(6.)
Grandi, Alfredo • Amleto	N
Graun, Karl Heinrich • Coriolano	N
Greenwall, Peter • Three Caskets, The or Venice Re-served	N
Grosheim, Georg Christoph • Titania, oder Liebe durch Zauberei	N
Groth, Howard • Petruchio	N
Guglielmi, Pietro Alessandro • Admeto, Re di Tessaglia	N

COMPOSITION	GB:Lbm
Guglielmi, Pietro Carlo • Romeo e Giulietta [I Capuletti ed i Montecchi]	N/907.K.7.(9.)
Gulda, Friedrich • Maß für Maß	N
Haack, Friedrich • Geisterinsel, Die	N
Hába, Alois • Tempest	G.770.dd.(2.)
Hahn, Reynaldo • Beaucoup de bruit pour rien	N
Hahn, Reynaldo • Malvina	G.999.d.
Hahn, Reynaldo • Marchand de Vénise, Le	F.1410.f.
Haines, Roger • Fire Angel	N
Haines, Roger • Shylock [Fire Angel]	N
Hale, Alfred Matthew • Tempest, The	N/ 11712.aaa.20.(4.)
Halévy, Jacques François Fromental Elie • Guido et Ginevre ou La Peste de Florence	H.546.e.
Halévy, Jacques Franoçis Fromental Élie • Tempesta, La	F.85.k.
Halpern, Sidney • Macbeth	N
Hamel, Eduard • Malvina	N
Händel, Georg Friederich • Admeto, Re di Tessaglia	F.90/639.d.19.(3.)
Hanssens, J. F. J. • Gillette de Narbonne	N
Harbison, John • Winter's Tale, The	N
Harper, Wally • Sensations	N
Hart, Fritz Bennicke • Malvolio, Opus 14	N
Heinrich, Hermann • Viel Lärm um Nichts	N
Hensel, Johann Daniel • Geisterinsel, Die	N
Hérold, Louis Joseph Ferdinand • Gioventù di Enrico V, La [La Jeunesse d'Henry V]	F.783.b.
Herx, Werner • Orakelspruch, Der	N
Hess, Ludwig • Was ihr Wollt	N
Hester, Hal and Danny Apolinar • Your Own Thing	N
Heuberger, Richard Franz Joseph • Viola	N
Heward, Leslie Hays • Hamlet	N
Hignard, Aristide • Hamlet	F.1268.oo./ 11763.h.8.
Hignett, J. L. A. • Hamlet	N
Hirschbach, Hermann • Othello	N
Hoffmeister, Franz Anton • Rosalinde, oder Die Macht der Feen	N
Hoffmeister, Franz Anton • Schiffbruch, Der	N
Hofmann, Johann • Ritter Hans von Dampf	N

COMPOSITION	GB:Lbm
Hohmann, Gustav • Hermione, oder Der kleine Vicomte	N
Holenia, Hans • Viola, Opus 21 [Was Ihr wollt]	N
Holland, Jan David • Hamlet, Pantomime zu	Hirsch iv 1348.a.
Holst, Gustav • At the Boar's Head, Opus 42	F.1412.(2.)
Honegger, Arturo • Tempête, La	N
Hopp, Julius • Hammlet	N
Horky, Karel • Jed z Elsinoru [The Poison from Elsinore]	N
Horn, Charles Edward, and Samuel Webbe Jr. • Merry Wives of Windsor	N
Horner • König Lear	
Hüe, George • Titania	F.794.e.
Hughes, Gervase • Twelfth Night, Scenes from	N
Hulemann, Th • Malvine I re [The first]	N
Ivry, Paul Xaver Désiré Richard, Marquis d' • Amantes de Vérone, Les	F.388./ 11740.b.13.(9.)
Jakobowski, Edward • Erminie	F.796./906.i.8.(6.)
Jenkins, David • Enchanted Isle, The [Scenes from Shakespeare's 'Tempest']	F.123.e.
Jirko, Ivan • Twelfth Night, The [Vecer Trikralovy]	N
Johnson, Robert • Tempest, The	A.1170 [2 songs]
Jommelli, Nicolo • Caio Mario [Cajo Mario]	Add.16030/32 etc.
Jones, Cliff • Rockabye Hamlet	N
Just, Johann August • marchand de Venise, Le [Koopman van Smyrna]	N
Kaffka [Kafka], Johann Christian • Antonius und Cleopatra	N
Kagen, Sergius • Hamlet	N
Kalnins, Janis • Hamlets	N
Kanne, Friedrich August • Malvina, oder Putzerls Abenteuer	
Kanne, Friedrich August • Miranda oder Das Schwert der Rache	N
Karel, Rudolf • Zkroceni zlé zeny [The Taming of the Shrew]	N
Kasanli, Nikolai Ivanovich [Kazanli, Kazanly] • Miranda (Poliedniaia bor'ba) [Der Letzte Kampf]	G.1278.l.
Kashperov, Vladimir Nikititch • Storm, The [Groza]	N

COMPOSITION	GB:Lbm
Kaun, Hugo • Falstaff	N
Keurvels, Edward H. J. • Hamlet	N
Khrennikov, Tikhon Nikolaevich • Brati [Brothers]	
Khrennikov, Tikhon Nikolaevich • Mnogo shuma iz nichego [Viel Lärm aus Leidenschaft, Much Ado About Hearts]	
Khrennikov, Tikhon Nikolaevich • V buriu [Im Sturm, Into the Storm]	
Kipper, Herman • Perdita oder Das Rosenfest	N
Kirchner, Hermann • Viola	N
Klebe, Giselher Wolfgang • Ermordung Cäsars, Die Op. 32	G.1269.gg.(1.)
Kleinheinz, Carl Franz Xaver • Hamlet, Prinz vom Tandelmarkt	N
Koppel, Herman David • Macbeth, Op. 79	N
Kovarovic, Karel • Perdita	N
Krejcí, Isa • Pozdvizení v Efesu [The Upheaval in Ephesus]	E.1598.pp.(1.)
Kreutz, Arthur • Sourwood Mountain	N
Kreutzer, Conradin • Cordelia (Floretta ou La Folle de Glaris)[First named Adele von Budoy]	N
Kreutzer, Rodolphe • Imogène, ou La Gageure indiscrète	N
Krohn, Max • Was ihr Wollt	N
Kuhlau, Friedrich Daniel Rudolph • Musik Til William Shakspeare [sic], Op. 74	G.728
Kunz, [Konrad Max ?] • Tempest, The	N
Kunzen, Friedrich Ludwig Æmilius • Holger Danske oder Oberon [Holgar the Dane]	E.517./ 11766.b.23.(2.)
Kunzen, Friedrich Ludwig Æmilius • Stormen	N/11766.b.23.(2.)
Kurzbach, Paul • Romeo and Julia auf dem Lande	N
Küster, Johann Heinrich • Henrik den Fjerde	N
Kusterer, Arthur • Was ihr Wollt	N
La Rosa, Arturo • Otello	N
Lampe, John Frederich • Pyramus and Thisbe	G.193.(5.)
Lattuada, Felice • Tempesta, La	N
Lauer, Adolph L. [Freiherr von Münchofen] • Orakelspruch, Der	N

COMPOSITION	GB:Lbm
Laufer, B. • Shylock	N
Lavina, Vincenzo • Coriolano, Il	
LaViolette, Wesley • Shylock	N
Le Rey, Frédéric • Mégère apprivoisée, La	F.1454
Lecocq, Charles Alexandre • Marjolaine	
Legouix, Isidore Édouard • Othello, Un	N
Leichtling, Alan • Tempest, The	N
Leoncavallo, Ruggiero • Songe d'une nuit d'été, Un	N
Leopold I, Holy Roman Emperor • Timòne, Misantropo	N
Leukauf, Robert • Wintermärchen, Das	N
Leverage, Richard • Macbeth	E.105
Leverage, Richard • Pyramus and Thisbe, The Comic Masque of	N
Lichtenstein, Carl August Freiherr von • Ende gut, alles gut	
Lillo, Giuseppe • Sogno d'una Notte estiva, Il or La Gioventù di Shakespeare	N
Linley II, Thomas • Tempest, The or The Enchanted Island	N
Liota, A. • Romeo and Juliet	N
Litolff, Henry Charles • König Lear	N
Locke, Matthew and Robert Johnson • Macbeth	G.242.(2.)
Loder, Edward James • Robin Goodfellow or the Frolics of Puck	H.173.e.
Logar, Mihovil • Four Scenes from Shakespeare	N
Lorenz, Carl Adolf • Komödie der Irrungen, Die	N
Ludwig, Otto • Romeo und Julie	N
Lueder, Florence Pauline • As You Like It	
Lueder, Florence Pauline • Rosalind	N
Lutz, William Meyer • Merry-Go-Round	
Macarig, Hector and Alfonso Deperis • Otello Tamburo	N
MacDermot, Galt • Cressida	N
MacDermot, Galt • Two Gentlemen of Verona	
MacFarren, George Alexander • Hamlet	N
Machavariani, Alexei • Hamlet	N
Machavariani, Alexei • Othello	N
Maclean, Alick • Petruccio	N/1906.i.10.(6.)

COMPOSITION	GB:Lbm
Maganini, Giovanni • Enrico IV al passo della Marna	N
Maggioni, Francesco • Cajo Marzio Coriolano	N
Magni, Giuseppe Paolo • Admeto, Rè di Tessaglia	N
Malamet, Marsha • Dreamstuff	N
Malipiero, Gian Francesco • Antonio e Cleopatra	I.485.f.
Malipiero, Gian Francesco • Giulio Cesare	I.599.
Malipiero, Gian Francesco • Romeo e Guilietta (scene 5 of Monde celesti e infernali)	I.485.c.
Mancinelli, Luigi • Sogno di una notte d'estate, Il	H.1043.b.
Manusardi, Giuseppe • sogno di Primavera, Un [Un rêve de printemps]	N
Marchetti, Filippo • Romeo e Giulietta	H.2643.b./ 011765.ee.9.(5.)
Marescalchi, Luigi • Giuletta e Romeo	N
Marescotti • Amleto	N
Maretzek, Maximilian • Hamlet	N
Marshall-Hall, George William Louis • Romeo and Juliet	N
Martín y Soler, Vicente • Capricciosa corretta, La [So bessert sie sich]	N
Martin, Frank • Sturm, Der	H.2109.9.
Martini, Giovanni • Henri IV, ou La Bataille d'Ivry	G.226.c./ 11738.cc.40.(4.)
Matuszczak, Bernadetta • Julia i Romeo	I.343.d.
Méhul, Étienne Nicolas • Jeune Henri, Le [Gabrielle d'Estrées où les Amours d'Henri IV]	N
Meiners, Giambattista • Riccardo III	N/11761.aaa.8.(1.)
Mélésville, Honoré Marie Joseph, Baron Duveyrier] • Gillette de Narbonne	N
Membrée, Edmond • Roméo et Juliette	N
Mercadal y Pons, Antonio • Giulietta e Romeo	N
Mercadante, Giuseppe Saverio Raffele • Amleto	N/11762.a.1.(1.)
Mercadante, Giuseppe Saverio Raffele • Gioventù di Enrico V, La	N/906.g.5.(5.)
Mercadante, Giuseppe Saverio Raffele • Violetta	E.123.q.

COMPOSITION	GB:Lbm
Michaelis, Gustave • Lustigen Weiber von Berlin, Die	
Michaelis, Gustave • Othello in Kyritz	N
Missa, Edmond Jean Louis • Dinah	F.831.a.
Mohaupt, Richard • Double Trouble [Zwillingskomödie]	N
Mohr, Hermann • Orakelspruch, Der Op. 50	N
Mojsisovics, Roderich • Viel Lärm um Nichts	N
Molchanov, Kiril Vladimirovich • Romeo, Dzhulyetta i t'ma [Romeo, Juliet and Darkness]	
Monza, Carlo Antonio • Cajo Mario	
Morales, Melesio • Giulietta e Romeo	N
Morera, Enrique • Fiercilla domada, La	N
Morlacchi, Francesco Giuseppi Baldassare • Capricciosa pettita, La	
Morlacchi, Francesco Giuseppi Baldassare • Gioventù di Enrico V, La [Das Jugendjahre Heinrich des Fünften]	N
Moroni, Luigi • Amleto	N
Morton, David • Tempest in a Teapot	
Morton, Louise, and others • Twelfth Night	N
Mosca, Giuseppe • Gioventù di Enrico V, La	N
Mozart, Wolfgang Amadeus • Peines d'amour perdues	N
Mulcahy, Lance • Shakespeare's Cabaret	
Müller (the elder), Adolph • Heinrich IV	N
Müller (the elder), Adolph • Othellerl, der Mohr von Wien [Die geheilte Eifersucht]	E.38.(4.)
Müller (the elder), Adolph • Viel Lärm um Nichts	N
Müller, Wenzel • Sturm oder die Zauberinsel, Der	N/ 11746.aaa.68.(4.)
Mullins, Hugh • Romeo and Juliet	N
Mussorgsky, Modest Petrovich • Hamlet	
Nabokov, Nikolai • Love's Labour's Lost [Verlor'ne Liebesmüh']	G.190.p.
Nápravnik, Éduard Frantsevich • Sturm, Der	N
Navoigille, Gouliellmo • Orage, L' ou Quel Guignon!	N
Nesvera, Josef • Perdita	N
Nicolai, Carl Otto Ehrenfried • lustigen Weiber von Windsor, Die	H.640./ 11761.f.3.(1.)

COMPOSITION	GB:Lbm
Nicolini, Giuseppe • Coriolano	E.601.rr.(5.)
Nieto, Manuel • Otelo y Desdémona	N/11728. bbb.12.(5.)
Noël, Édouard Marie Émile • songe d'une nuit d'été, Le	N
Oddone, Elizabetta • Petruccio e il Cavolo Cappuccio	N
Offenbach, Jacques • Rêve d'une Nuit d'été, Le	N
Old, John • Herne the Hunter (A Legend of Royal Windsor)	F.843.
Orff, Carl • Sommernachtstraum, Ein	G.1201.1.(1.)
Orlandi, Ferdinando • Rodrigo di Valencia	N
Pacini, Giovanni • Gioventù di Enrico V, La (also La bella tavernara; Le Aventure d'una notte)	N/906.d.6.(2.)
Pacini, Giovanni • Rodrigo di Valencia	N
Palliardi, Carl • Stein der Weisen, Der	N
Papavoine, Mdme • Vieux Coquet, Le; ou Les deux amies ou Le vieus garçon	N
Pasquali, Nicolò • Romeo and Juliet	G.806.i.(12.)
Pedrell, Filipe • Roi Lear, Le	N
Perelli, Edoardo • Viola Pisani	N/906.h.11.(5.)
Perosi, Lorenzo • Romeo and Juliet	N
Persico, Mario • Bisbetica Domata, La	N
Perti, Giacomo Antonio • Martio Coriolano	
Philidor • Herne le Chasseur	N
Piccini, Louis Alexandre • Macbeth	N
Piccinni, Niccolò • Caio Mario	
Pillaut, Léon • Perdita	N
Pinsuti, Ciro • Mercante di Venezia, Il	F.852./ 11715.e.54.(7.)
Pless, Hans • Macbeth	N
Podestà, Carlo • Ero, ossia Molto rumore per nulla	N/11765.K.13.
Pogodin • King Lear?	N
Pohlig, Carl • Stein der Weisen, Der	N
Pollaroli, Carlo Francesco • Marzio Coriolano	
Porta, [Bernardo ?] • Roméo et Juliette	N/11738.c.31.(4.)
Porter, Cole • Kiss Me, Kate	F.943.aa.(3.)
Pride [sp?], G. • Otello	N
Prokofiev, Sergei • Hamlet, Music to the Tragedy by Shakespeare	G.1095.j.(4.)

511

COMPOSITION	GB:Lbm
Puget, Paul-Charles-Marie • Beaucoup de bruit pour rien	F.1584.a./ 11765.gg.30.(2.)
Pulli, Pietro • Caio Marzio Coriolano	N
Purcell, Henry • Fairy Queen, The	F.659.d.(2.)/ 643.d.52.
Purcell, Henry • History of Timon of Athens, the Man Hater, The	I.466. [Vol. II]
Purcell, Henry • Tempest or Enchanted Island, The	H.130.(6.)
Radicati, Felice Alessandro • Coriolano, Il	N
Radó, Aladár • Shylock	N
Rafael, Carl Friedrich • Hamlet, Prinz von Liliput	N
Raphling, Sam • Prince Hamlet	N
Rateau, Edmond • Rosaline	N
Raymond, Édouard • Sturm, Der	N
Reichardt, Johann Friedrich • Geisterinsel, Die	G.434.d.
Reichardt, Johann Friedrich • Macbeth	N
Reimann, Aribert • Lear	I.340.zz.
Reutter, Hermann • Hamlet	
Reynaud, Armand • Roi Lear, Le	N
Rintel, Wilhelm • Was ihr Wöllt	N
Riotte, Philipp Jakob • Orakelspruch, Der	N
Riotte, Philipp Jakob • Sturm, Der oder Die Insel des Prospero	N
Ritter, Peter • lustigen Weiber, Die	N
Ritter, Peter • Sturm, Der oder Die bezauberte Insel	N
Rogers, Richard • Boys from Syracuse, The	G.1282.d.(1.)
Rolle, Johann Heinrich • Sturm oder Die bezauberte Insel, Der	N
Rosellin, Léon • Juliette et Roméo	N
Rosenberg, Richard • Liebesspiel, Das	N
Rossi, Lauro • Biorn	N
Rossini, Gioacchino • Ermione	F.69.m.
Rossini, Gioacchino • Otello, osia L'Africano di Venezia	G.927./1342.c.47.
Roters, Ernest • Hamlet, Op. 145	N
Roti, Ugo • Sogno di una notte d'estate, Il	L
Ruben, Paul • Edit royal, L'	N
Rubens, Paul Alfred and Frank E. Tours • Dairymaids, The	F.1486.b.(1.)

COMPOSITION	GB:Lbm
Rubens, Paul Alfred and Walter Rubens • Great Caesar	N
Rumling, Sigismund Freiherr von • Roméo et Juliette	N
Rung, Henrik • Stormen paa København [Storm over Copenhagen]	N
Saint-Saëns, Camille • Henry VIII	F.877.e./ 11746.ee.5.(5.)
Salieri, Antonio • Falstaff osia Le tre Burle	Hirsch IV.1276./ 11765.ad.6.
Salmhofer, Franz • King Lear	N
Salvayre, Gaston • Beaucoup de bruit pour rien	N
Salvayre, Gaston • Riccardo III	F.875.
Samara, Spiro • Furia domata, La	N
San Severino • Romeo e Giuletta	
Santa Caterina, Alessandro • Coriolano	N
Sarria, Errico • Equivoci, Gli	N
Saussine, Henri de • Marchand de Vénise, Le	N
Savigna, Vincenzo • Coriolano	N
Savini, Giacomo • Tempeste	N
Sayn-Wittgenstein-Berleburg, Count Friedrich Ernst von • Antonius und Kleopatra	N
Scarlatti, Giuseppe • Caio Mario	
Scarlatti, Giuseppe Domenico • Ambleto	N/905.I.8.(5.)
Schindelmeisser, Louis Alexander Balthasar • Malvina	N
Schmitz, Alan • Julius Caesar	N
Schneider, Georg Abraham • Orakelspruch, Der	N
Schönfeld, Georg • Falstaff	N
Schuster, Ignaz • Hamlet, Prinz vom Tandelmarkt	N
Schuster, Ignaz • Othellerl, der Mohr von Wien	N
Schuster, Ignaz • Romeo und Julie	N/11747.c.9.(6.)
Schwanenberg, Johann Gottfried • Romeo e Giulia	N/11715.bb.14.
Scognamilio, Gennaro • Otello ossia Catiello l'Affricano	N
Scolari, Giuseppe • Cajo Mario	
Searle, Humphrey • Hamlet, Opus 48	I.340.dd.

COMPOSITION	GB:Lbm
Séméladis, M. • Cordélia	N
Serov, Alexander Nikolayevich • Merry Wives of Windsor	N
Serpette, Henri Charles Antoine Gaston • Shakespeare!	F.883.o.
Serpette, Henri Charles Antoine Gaston • Songe d'une nuit d'été, Le	
Shebalin, Vissarion Yakovlevich • Ukroshchenie stroptivoi [The Taming of the Shrew] Op. 46	P.P.1933.c.(2.)
Shelley, Harry Rowe • Romeo and Juliet	N/11762. bbb.21.(3.)
Shenshin, Aleksandr Alexseivich • Twelfth Night	N
Siegmeister, Elie • Night of the Moonspell	N
Silver, Charles • Mégère apprivoisée, La	F.1496.
Silverman, Stanley • Midsummer Night's Dream, A	N
Slade, Julian • Comedy of Errors	N
Smetana, Bedrich • Viola	F.918.e.
Smith, John Christopher • Fairies, The	G.240.a.
Smith, John Christopher • Rosalinda	N/T.655.(15.)
Smith, John Christopher • Tempest, The	G.240./643.i.3.(7.)
Sobolewski, Friedrich Eduard de • Imogéne	N
Soloviev, Nicolai Feopemptovich • Cordélia	N
Soule, Charles Caroll • Travesty Without a Pun.	N
Stadtfeldt, Christian Joseph Franz Alexandre • Hamlet	N/11766.i.9.(6.)
Stanford, Sir Charles Villiers • Much Ado About Nothing, Opus 76a	F.890.h./ 11762.d.14.(2.)
Stegmann, Carl David • Macbeth	N
Steibelt, Daniel Gottlieb • Roméo et Juliette or Tout pour l'amour	H.535/ 11738.n.16.(7.)
Steinkühler, Émile • Cäsario, oder die Verwechslung, Op. 30	N
Storace, Stephen • Equivoci, Gli	N
Storch, Anton Maria • Romeo und Julie	N
Storch, Anton Maria • Stein der Weisen, Der	N
Stransky, Josef • Béatrice et Bénédict	N
Strungk, Nicolaus Adam • Rosalinde	N
Stuart, Leslie • Belle of Mayfair	F.1501.e.(1.)

COMPOSITION	GB:Lbm
Stuntz, Joseph Hartmann • Heinrich IV zu Givry	N
Sulek, Stjepan • Koriolan	N
Sulek, Stjepan • Oluja	N
Suppé, Franz von • Sommernachtstraum, Der	N
Sutermeister, Heinrich • Romeo und Julia	H.653.c.(1.)
Sutermeister, Heinrich • Zauberinsel, Die	H.653.a.
Szokolay, Sándor • Hamlet	F.1257.nn.
Sztojanovics, Eug. • Otello mecél	N
Taboida, Ant. Sanchez do Cunha • Dinah	N
Tajon, Ben. • Taming of a Shrew, The	N
Taubert, Carl Gottfried Wilhelm • Cesario, oder Was ihr wollt, Op. 188	H.181.a./ 11764.aa.2.
Taubert, Wilhelm • Macbeth, Op. 133	H.181.d.
Taubmann, Otto • Porzia	N
Thomas, Charles Louis Ambroise • Hamlet	F.138.n./ 11739.b.15.
Thomas, Charles Louis Ambroise • Songe d'une nuit d'été, Le [Shakespeare oder Der Traum einer Sommernacht]	R.M.10.d.5.
Thomé, François Lucien Joseph • Roméo et Juliette	N
Thul, Franz von • Hermione	N
Tiessen, Heinz • Cymbelin	N
Tommasi, Ferdinando [Tommaso] • Guido e Ginevre	N
Torriani, Eugenio • Romeo e Giulietta	N
Treu, Daniel Gottlieb • Coriolano	
Tuczek, Vincenc Tomas Vaclav • Travestirte Hamlet, Der [Hamlet, Prinz von Dänemark; Hamlet, Prinz von Lilyput]	N
Turok, Paul H. • Richard III	N
Unknown • Bezähmte Widerbellerin, Die	
Unknown • Catch My Soul	
Unknown • Catherine and Petruchio	N
Unknown • Cure for a Scold, A	N/163.i.7.
Unknown • Early Reign of Oleg, The	
Unknown • Pulcinella rivale di Turzillo e confuso tra Capuleti e Montecchi	
Unknown • Schipbreuk	N/636.c.20.(8.)
Unknown • Thimon le misantrope	N
Unknown • Timon in Love or The Innocent Theft	N

COMPOSITION	GB:Lbm
Urich, Jean • Orage, L'	F.919.
Urspruch, Anton • Sturm, Der	G.1092.
Utley, Wendell • Will	N
Vaccai, Nicola • Giulietta e Romeo	E.189./ 11764.dd.4.(4.)
Vaccai, Nicola • Malvina	N
Valenti, Michael • Oh, Brother	N
Valverde y San Juan, Joaquín • sueño de una noche de verano, El	N
Van Heusen, Jimmy • Swingin' the Dream	
Vaughan Williams, Ralph • Sir John in Love	H.3951.b.
Veracini, Francesco Maria • Rosalinda	N/907.i.4.(8.)
Verdi, Giuseppe • Falstaff	F.125.s./ 11764.e.15
Verdi, Giuseppe • Lear	N
Verdi, Giuseppe • Macbeth	E.190.mm/ 11763.bbb.15.
Verdi, Giuseppe • Otello	F.125.k./ 11714.b.29.
Vidal, Paul Antonin • Comme il vous Plaire	N
Vidal, Paul Antonin • Peines d'amour perdues	N
Vignali, Giuseppe [Act I]; Carlo Baglioni [Act II] and Giacomo Cozzi [Act III] • Ambleto	N
Volder, Piere Jean de • Jeunesse de Henri Cinq, La	N
Vranicky, Pavel • Oberon, König der Elfen	D.308./11748.f.74.
Vranicky, Pavel • Rudolf von Felseck (Die Schwarzthaler) oder La Tempestà	
Vreuls, Victor • Songe d'une nuit d'été, Un	F.244.y.(8.)
Wagner, Wilhelm Richard • Liebesverbot, Das oder Die Novize von Palermo	F.530.ff.
Walton, Sir William • Troilus and Cressida	G.1451.a.
Ware, William Henry • Cymbeline	N
Ware, William Henry • Macbeth	N
Weber, Carl Maria von • Euryanthe	E.164.
Weber, Carl Maria von • Oberon [or the Elf-King's Oath]	Hirsch iv. 1298./ 11781.aa.43.(1.)
Weckerlin, Jean Baptiste Théodore • Tout est bien qui finit bien	
Weigl, Joseph [Veigl, Giuseppe] • Amleto	N
Weis, Karél • Comme il vous Plaira	N
Weis, Karél • Viola [Die Zwillinge, Blizenci]	G.662.a.

COMPOSITION	GB:Lbm
Weisgall, Hugo • Gardens of Adonis, The	N
Weisgall, Hugo • Henry IV	
Westerhout, Niccolò van • Cimbelino, Il	N/11763. bbb.15.(5.5)
Weyse, Christoph Ernst Friedrich • Macbeth	E.1305.d.
Whitaker, John • Weird Sisters, The or The Thane and the Throne	N
Wiedeke, Adolf • lustigen Weiber von Hamburg, Die	
Wilson, James • Twelfth Night	N
Winter, Peter von • Sturm, Der	N/11766. aaa.25.(1.)
Wödl, Franz • Komödie der Irrungen	N
Wolf, Ernst Wilhelm • Zauberirrungen, Die [Die Irrtümer der Zauberei]	N
Wolf-Ferrari, Ermanno • Sly, ovvero La leggenda del dormiente risvegliato	G.1103.e.
Wolfurt, Kurt von • Porzia	N
Zafred, Mario • Amleto	H.232.kk.
Zajc, Ivan • Cordelia	N
Zák, Benedict Emanuel • Stein der Weisen, Dem oder Die Zauber Insel	
Zanardini, Angelo • Amleto	N
Zandonai, Riccardo • Giulietta e Romeo	G.1109.c.
Zanettini, Antonio • Érmione [Die wiedergefundene Hermione]	N
Zanon, Antonio B. • Leggenda di Giulietta, La	N
Zavodsky, Felix • Othello	N
Zelinka, Jan Evangelista • Spring With Shakespeare	N
Ziani, Marc Antonio • Rosalinda, La or Erginia mascherata	N/905.I.10.(3.)
Zillig, Winfried • Troilus und Cressida	H.4020.
Zimmermann, Balduin • Wintermärchen, Ein	N
Zingarelli, Niccolò Antonio • Giulietta e Romeo	E. 1598. k. (2.)/ 11764.aaa.19.(1.)
Zirra, Alexandru • Furtuna [TheTempest]	
Zumsteeg, Johann Rudolf • Geisterinsel, Die	Hirsch iv. 1311.